Padres in No Man's Land

Padres in No Man's Land is the compelling story of brave and deeply committed army chaplains who brought faith and courage to Canada's troops during one of history's most devastating wars.

Tracing the growth of the Canadian Chaplain Service from its chaotic and controversy-ridden early days to its maturation as an efficient field force, Duff Crerar highlights both the role of the Service on the battlefield and the personal experiences of the chaplains. Refuting the widely held view that chaplains serving overseas were cloistered from front-line realities, Crerar describes the padres' experiences in camps, hospitals, and on the battlefield. He examines how they maintained their faith in the face of death and destruction, and explores the bonds forged between chaplains and troops.

Padres in No Man's Land concludes in the post-war era with the decline of the chaplains' hopes for spiritual renewal on their return to Canada – their dreams dashed not by the war, but by the subsequent peace.

DUFF CRERAR is instructor of history, Department of Humanities and Social Sciences, Grande Prairie Regional College.

MCGILL-QUEEN'S STUDIES IN THE HISTORY OF RELIGION
Volumes in this series have been supported by the Jackman Foundation of Toronto.

SERIES ONE: G.A. RAWLYK, EDITOR

1 Small Differences
Irish Catholics and Irish Protestants, 1815–1922
An International Perspective
Donald Harman Akenson

2 Two Worlds
The Protestant Culture of Nineteenth-Century Ontario
William Westfall

3 An Evangelical Mind
Nathanael Burwash and the Methodist Tradition in Canada, 1839–1918
Marguerite Van Die

4 The Dévotes
Women and Church in Seventeenth-Century France
Elizabeth Rapley

5 The Evangelical Century
College and Creed in English Canada from the Great Revival to the Great Depression
Michael Gauvreau

6 The German Peasants' War and Anabaptist Community of Goods
James M. Stayer

7 A World Mission
Canadian Protestantism and the Quest for a New International Order, 1918–1939
Robert Wright

8 Serving the Present Age
Revivalism, Progressivism, and the Methodist Tradition in Canada
Phyllis D. Airhart

9 A Sensitive Independence
Canadian Methodist Women Missionaries in Canada and the Orient, 1881–1925
Rosemary R. Gagan

10 God's Peoples
Covenant and Land in South Africa, Israel, and Ulster
Donald Harman Akenson

11 Creed and Culture
The Place of English-Speaking Catholics in Canadian Society, 1750–1930
Edited by Terrence Murphy and Gerald Stortz

12 Piety and Nationalism
Lay Voluntary Associations and the Creation of an Irish-Catholic Community in Toronto, 1850–1895
Brian P. Clarke

13 Amazing Grace
Studies in Evangelicalism in Australia, Britain, Canada, and the United States
Edited by George Rawlyk and Mark A. Noll

14 Children of Peace
W. John McIntyre

15 A Solitary Pillar
Montreal's Anglican Church and the Quiet Revolution
Joan Marshall

16 Padres in No Man's Land
Canadian Chaplains and the Great War (second edition)
Duff Crerar

Padres in No Man's Land

Canadian Chaplains and the Great War

DUFF CRERAR

Second Edition

McGill-Queen's University Press
Montreal & Kingston • London • Ithaca

ISBN 978-0-7735-4441-3 (paper)
ISBN 978-0-7735-8168-5 (ePDF)

Legal deposit third quarter 2014
Bibliothèque nationale du Québec

First edition 1995

Printed in Canada on acid-free paper that is 100% ancient forest free (100% post-consumer recycled), processed chlorine free

This book was first published with the help of a grant from the Canadian Federation for the Humanities, using funds provided by the Social Sciences and Humanities Research Council of Canada.

McGill-Queen's University Press acknowledges the support of the Canada Council for the Arts for our publishing program. We also acknowledge the financial support of the Government of Canada through the Canada Book Fund for our publishing activities.

Library and Archives Canada Cataloguing in Publication

Crerar, Duff W. (Duff Willis), 1955–, author
Padres in no man's land: Canadian chaplains and the Great War / Duff Crerar. – Second edition.

(McGill-Queen's studies in the history of religion; 16)
Includes bibliographical references and index.
Issued in print and electronic formats.
ISBN 978-0-7735-4441-3 (pbk.). – ISBN 978-0-7735-8168-5 (ePDF)

1. World War, 1914–1918 – Chaplains – Canada – Biography. 2. Canada. Canadian Army. Royal Canadian Army Chaplain Corps – Biography. 3. Military chaplains – Canada – Biography. 4. Canada. Canadian Army. Royal Canadian Army Chaplain Corps – History. 5. World War, 1914–1918 – Personal narratives, Canadian. I. Title. II Series: McGill-Queen's studies in the history of religion; 16.

D639.C38C74 2014 940.4'78092271 C2014-904224-8
C2014-904225-6

This book was typeset by Interscript in 10/12 New Baskerville.

For G. Duff Crerar
145854, Private
77th, 73rd, and 13th Battalions, CEF
1898–1953
and Rev. Edward Ernest Graham, MC, DSO
Methodist and United Churches of Canada
1881–1934
– his chaplain.

Contents

Acknowledgments

This study could never have been completed in solitude. From its inception, members of the academy, ecclesia, and the Canadian Armed Forces have generously offered advice and encouragement, while the Department of History at Queen's University provided the academic and financial base for the graduate research presented here. In particular, the late Ernest Foote, OBE, and the Rev. Waldo Smith, MC, gave helpful interviews, while Dr A.M.J. Hyatt of the University of Western Ontario and Miss Barbara Wilson of the National Archives of Canada gave generously of their extensive knowledge of the Canadian Great War. In addition, Drs Don Schurman, the late Catherine Brown, Marguerite Van Die, James Stayer, Jane Errington, Ian Germani, Douglas Dodds, and Marina Robinson all greatly assisted me through their interest, sharp questions, and sublime long-suffering. To my first supervisor, the late Roger Graham, however, I owe a special debt of gratitude for his wise guidance.

Over the years, a "great cloud of witnesses" have kept vigil while I wrestled with the padres and their war. Jake Heinrichs, Dale Edmonds-Mutcher, and especially Rob James-Sadouski have given freely of their computing expertise, while the Department of Humanities and Social Sciences at Grande Prairie Regional College provided both the equipment and software to edit the manuscript. The Chaplain-General (Protestant) David Estey, Gerry Peddle and Bill Fairlie, Al Fowler, and the chaplains of the Canadian Armed Forces have consistently given their support, while colleagues at Grande Prairie Regional College, especially Jerry Petryshyn, Scott McAlpine, Campbell Ross, Vince

Salvo, and Louise Saldanha, have read portions of the manuscript and offered their own critical comments.

Since 1981 the librarians and archivists of the Royal Military College, Queen's University, the University of Western Ontario, the United Church of Canada, and the University of Saskatchewan, as well as those of the Ottawa Diocese and General Synod of the Anglican Church of Canada, McMaster University Baptist Divinity College, and the Province of Alberta have tirelessly rooted out sources, answered silly questions, and copied innumerable documents. I especially thank the Photographic Records staff of the National Archives of Canada, particularly Sheila Mendonca, who speedily converted cryptic messages from northern Alberta into high-quality prints.

First the thesis, and now this book would never have seen the light of day without the constant interest, wide knowledge, and searching criticism of George Rawlyk. For his faithful shepherding I give great thanks and credit for whatever this study contributes to the intellectual enterprise. To the cheerful and worldly wise staff of McGill-Queen's University Press, especially Don Akenson and his staff, I owe special thanks for guiding me through the publication maze. Special thanks to Susan Kent Davidson, most conscientious and judicious of copy editors. I give thanks for my parents, Ian and Bette, and my brothers and sisters, who gave me the name and the character of a Crerar. Finally, to my wife, Carol, and daughters Heather and Alison, who have waited longer than any padre's family to get their husband and father back from the war, I offer my thanks and love.

Burial of a Canadian officer, October 1916, at the battle of the Somme. Reverend Webster Harris was mortally wounded while performing a service such as this. NA PA-652

Setting out: Congregationalist Harold Horsey blesses the colours of his unit, the Thirty-eighth Battalion, on Parliament Hill, August 1915. NA C-79763

Camp work: John Almond visits his Shoreham Camp staff. Back row, left to right: Capt. McGillivray, Capt. Cooke, Capt. Laws, Capt. Suckling; centre row: Capt. McLeod, Capt. Buckland, Capt. Spencer, Capt. Anderson; front: Col. J.M. Almond. NA PA-22672

Bellicose priests: Bishop Fallon meets with Canadian Catholic chaplains, Corps Headquarters, France, 1918. NA PA-8209

Formal worship: Padres' perspective, Brigade service, 1 July 1917. NA PA-1369

"Is it a Hun?" Brigade service, 1 July 1917. Rear ranks follow air activity, not the order of service. NA PA-1447

Heroes: Three of Canada's most decorated First World War chaplains. Left to right: Alex Gordon, MC, DSO; F.G. Scott, CMG, DSO; Ernest Graham, MC, DSO. NA PA-7601

Planting a harvest: Burials at Doullens, May 1918. NA PA-4352

PREFACE TO THE SECOND EDITION

The Return of the Padre: Chaplain Studies since *Padres in No Man's Land*

When *Padres in No Man's Land* was published in 1995, scholarship centring on the Great War padres was thin. Yet in hindsight, it is clear that in World War I studies, the era of the chaplain had already begun. In Canada, Jonathan Vance, David Marshall, Michel Gauvreau, and Mark McGowan had already reconsidered Canadian religious and cultural history at least partially through the prism of the padre. Marshall's influential study of secularization, Gauvreau's revisionist study of Protestant thought, McGowan's examination of Irish-Canadian Catholics, and Vance's study of the construction of post-war memory and metanarrative all drew on the utterances and writings of Canadian Great War chaplains.[1] Scholars of Canadian religious history, theology, and social discourse would never again think about the Great War, or Canada, in quite the same way.

Since the 1990s, Canadian scholars have deepened and enriched our knowledge of Canadian churches and chaplaincy. The Great War built on a tradition of militant idealism and church-led social Christianity – a national gospel metanarrative that had its roots before Confederation – eventually proving to bear the grief and suffering while still mobilizing for a powerful public role in total war. Gordon Heath illustrated how the script followed by church leaders, their presses, and most chaplains of 1914–18 had been written by the optimistic theodicy of the South African War, a "war with a silver lining."[2] His study of the Canadian South African War chaplains put vital flesh on the bones laid out in *Padres*, just as his subsequent book draws together a new generation of Canadian scholars assessing the impact of the Great War on churches and chaplains of Canada.[3] *Padres* suggested that the twenty-odd years of peacetime struggle and disappointments in the 1920s and '30s generally swallowed up chaplain idealism and energy. It seems clearer now that the chaplains were dismissed by the government, shut out of the Permanent Force, and suppressed by their own church hierarchies within two or three years of their return. Denominational leaders, fearing that time spent overseas had ruined their clergy for peacetime work and suspicious of any calls for radical reforms, ignored and dismissed their own chaplains' views.[4]

Canadian religious scholars have been hard at work examining religion and military chaplaincy in both Canada's Second World War and the contemporary chaplaincy of the Canadian Forces, with more publications pending.[5] The contemporary researcher can now locate scholarly research on padres through almost the entire national period, including the early days of the Afghanistan deployment. Among historians, though, acceptance of *Padres* has been restrained. Since the 1960s, scholars of Canada's armed forces have tended to snort and sniff at padres, though recent military writers have acknowledged that the chaplains worked hard, took risks, and offered practical support to the troops. *Padres* provided the chaplaincy research that confirmed Desmond Morton's thesis that Canadian political and military leaders overcame their amateurish and uneven record by facing up to challenges at the professional, operational, and tactical levels.[6] Tim Cook has probed soldiers' metaphysical world, and credits padres for having the guts to try and help, but is skeptical about claims that morale hinged on conventional religion or its military representatives. To him, soldiers blended fatalism, superstition, numerology, amulets, lucky objects, obscure biblical prophecies, and a wide variety of irrational psychological mechanisms to get through their tours of duty. Like many other historians, he observes that soldiers could be profanely sarcastic about cheap theologizing and simplistic portrayals of a loving God and a benevolent Christianized world to come. Their Christianity, if any, was expressed in the rule of doing good for one's pals and not being hypocrites.[7]

Where the military and morale-building accomplishments of Canadian padres first found sympathy and support was in studies on Australian chaplains by Michael McKernan,[8] and more recent

British chaplain studies by Edward Madigan, Michael Snape, and Linda Parker. Madigan's book about the Church of England's chaplains at the front demolished the persistent myth of the "disillusionment school" of soldier-writers (and most historians) that padres were cowards, class-bound hypocrites, and the laughingstock of the British Expeditionary Force.[9] Parker re-examined the Church of England chaplains, arguing that their relevance, idealism, militancy, and service under fire, despite their many divisions and internal bickering, has been misrepresented.[10] Snape's two studies of religion in the British army brought to light the wider religious world of the army during the world wars, one inhabited by devout senior officers, ubiquitous padres, and soldiers robustly religious, if at times theologically inarticulate. His account of the British army's Chaplains' Department found parallels to the Canadians' disorganization, plucky operational service, and crusading message (at a magnitude which dwarfed Canada's).[11] Snape corrects some claims made in *Padres* about Canadian trend-setters, pointing out that, like Julian Byng and Arthur Currie, senior officers in the British army removed the ban on chaplains in trenches, increased their numbers, and supported the religious work in the trenches as a vital aspect of fighting spirit.[12] He argues that never before had the British chaplaincy been positioned (and exploited) by leaders of the army to boost morale, and that the chaplaincy drew from the influence of a "diffusive Christianity" (based on Christian social ethics), in the ranks and in wider British prewar society. Madigan, Snape, and Parker, with a growing cohort of British scholars, have created what amounts to a new school of research in the United Kingdom, as seen in annual symposiums held by the British Armed Forces Chaplain School at Amport House.[13]

Scholars in France and the United States have also reassessed their own Great War chaplaincies. Jonathan Ebel's and Richard Schweitzer's studies of chaplains, crusading US churches, and religious faith in the army reassert the powerful role of personal faith and the chaplains who promoted it.[14] Xavier Boniface has explored the French army's chaplains and their post-war emergence from the social and political margins where state secularization had positioned them after 1905.[15] New studies include a recent chronicling of the rabbis who served in the German Imperial Army, bringing to light the similar experiences and nationalist statements as their Christian chaplain counterparts on both sides of the trenches. The field rabbis proved their dedication and loyalty to Germany and its

Jewish soldiers, but sadly were unable to escape from Nazi anti-Semitism. Those who did not die before 1939 met their end in the Holocaust.[16]

In November 2012, almost fifty scholars gathered in the vault of the old Abbey of Verdun for a scholarly conference on religion during the First World War. The papers overwhelmingly documented the power of wartime crusading nationalism in all the religious groups of the belligerents and military representatives, strong enough in Catholic circles to confound Vatican mediation. Raberh Achi presented a new perspective on Muslims in various imperial contingents, laying the basis for comparative chaplaincy studies with Muslim religious workers of the war.[17] Though no consensus will be achieved on whether or not the churches and padres should have so enthusiastically endorsed the war, the chaplains have emerged with more credit for their efforts, sacrifices, and influence at the front.

By the time this essay reaches the public, the centenary of the beginning of the First World War will have come. The soldiers, the captains, and the kings have departed, and our questions will never again be answered by living voices. Today the roar of heavy traffic mars the peace of the cemeteries in Flanders, Artois, and the Somme. From time to time a new breed of archaeologist uncovers souvenirs of war, including devotional artefacts, religious trench art, and sodden scraps of sacred writings. The war haunts us, and when we view the sepia-toned faces of the men and women in digital archives and family albums, and gather at the memorials, we honour their hope that they and their sacrifices will not be forgotten. In spring, larks will be heard, in summer, poppies will blow, and in the autumn and winter the iron harvest will rise through the soil, wan sunlight breaking through the mist and gloom, bringing out in stark relief the world we have almost, but not quite lost. In times like theirs, and places like these, they needed all the hope they could get. Perhaps so do we, and *Padres*, accompanied now by a family of new scholarship, will reconnect us with the missing men who were Great War chaplains – and hope.

NOTES

1 Jonathan Vance, *Death So Noble: Memory, Meaning, and the First World War* (Vancouver: UBC Press, 1997); David Marshall, *Secularizing the Faith:*

Canadian Protestant Ministers and the Crisis of Belief, 1850–1940 (Toronto: University of Toronto Press, 1992); Michel Gauvreau, *The Evangelical Century: College and Creed in English Canada from the Great Revival to the Great Depression* (Montreal and Kingston: McGill-Queen's University Press, 1993); Mark G. McGowan, *The Waning of the Green: Catholics, the Irish, and Identity in Toronto, 1887–1922* (Montreal and Kingston: McGill-Queen's University Press, 1999).

2 Gordon L. Heath, *A War with a Silver Lining: Canadian Protestant Churches and the South African War, 1899–1902* (Montreal and Kingston: McGill-Queen's University Press, 2009).

3 Gordon L. Heath, ed., *Canadian Churches and the First World War* (Eugene, OR: Pickwick Publications, 2014).

4 Duff Crerar, "Dismissed: Military Chaplains and Canadian Great War History," in Gordon Heath, ed. *Canadian Churches and the First World War.* See also Crerar, "Perpetually on the Verge: Canadian Great War Chaplains and Their Experience of the Liminal," *British Defence Academy Yearbook, 2013*, 11–18 and "Sacrifice and Regeneration on the Weary Road: Canadian Chaplains, Canadian Historians, and the Great War, 1914–1919," unpublished paper given at Verdun, 8 November 2012, at Foi, Religions et sacré dans la Grande Guerre, a conference held at Centre Mondial de la Paix, Verdun, 7–9 November 2012.

5 Thomas J. Hamilton, "Padres under Fire: A Study of the Canadian Chaplain Service (Protestant and Roman Catholic) during the Second World War," PhD dissertation, University of Toronto, 2003; Yves Yvon J. Pelletier, "Fighting for the Chaplains: Bishop Charles Leo Nelligan and the Creation of the Canadian Chaplain Service (Roman Catholic), 1939–1945," *Canadian Catholic Historical Studies* 72 (2006), 95–123; Yves Yvon J. Pelletier, "Faith on the Battlefield: Canada's Catholic Chaplaincy Service during the Second World War," *Canadian Catholic Historical Studies* 69 (2003), 64–84; and Joanne Benham Rennick, *Religion in the Ranks: Belief and Religious Experience in the Canadian Forces* (Toronto: University of Toronto Press, 2011).

6 Desmond Morton, *A Peculiar Kind of Politics: Canada's Overseas Ministry in the First World War* (Toronto: University of Toronto Press, 1982).

7 Tim Cook, "Anti-heroes of the Canadian Expeditionary Force," *Journal of the Canadian Historical Association* 19, 1 (2008), 171–93; see also *At the Sharp End: Canadians Fighting the Great War, 1914–1916* (Toronto: Viking, 2007) and *Shock Troops: Canadians Fighting the Great War, 1917–1918* (Toronto: Viking, 2008).

8 For Australia, see Michael McKernan, "Clergy in Khaki: The Chaplain in [the] Australian Imperial Force," *Journal of the Royal Australian Historical*

Society 64, 3 (1978), 145–66; Michael McKernan, *Padre: Australian Chaplains in Gallipoli and France* (Sydney: George Allen and Unwin, 1986); Patrick Porter, "The Sacred Service: Australian Chaplains and the Great War," *War and Society* 20, 2 (2002), 23–52; and also J. Bryant Haigh, *Men of Faith and Courage: The Official History of New Zealand's Army Chaplains* (Auckland: Word Publishers, 1983).

9 Edward Madigan, *Faith under Fire: Anglican Army Chaplains and the Great War* (Basingstoke: Palgrave Macmillan, 2011).

10 Linda Parker, *The Whole Armour of God: Anglican Army Chaplains in the Great War* (London: Helion and Company, 2009).

11 Michael Snape, *The Royal Army Chaplains' Department: Clergy under Fire* (Woodbridge: Boydell, 2008).

12 Snape, *God and the British Soldier: Religion and the British Army in the First and Second World Wars* (London: Routledge, 2005).

13 Edward Madigan and Michael Snape, eds, *Clergy in Khaki: New Perspectives on British Army Chaplaincy in the First World War* (Farnham, Surrey: Ashgate, 2013).

14 Jonathan Ebel, *Faith in the Fight: Religion and the American Soldier the First World War* (Princeton: Princeton University Press, 2010); and also Richard Schweitzer, *The Cross and the Trenches: Religious Faith and Doubt among British and American Great War Soldiers* (Westport: Praeger, 2003).

15 Xavier Boniface, *L'armée, l'Église et la République (1879–1914)* (Paris: Nouveau Monde éditions et Ministère de la Défense DPMA, 2012); and also Boniface, *L'aumônerie militaire française (1914–1962)* (Paris: Éditions du Cerf, 2001).

16 Peter Appelbaum, *Loyalty Betrayed: Jewish Chaplains in the German Army During the First World War* (London: Valentine Mitchell, 2014).

17 Raberh Achi, "L'islam dans l'armée française: entre pratique religieuse et l'identité collective (1914–1918)," unpublished paper given at Foi, religions et sacré dans la Grande Guerre, Centre Mondial de la Paix, Verdun, 7–9 November, 2012. See also Gordon Corrigan, *Sepoys in the Trenches: The Indian Corps on the Western Front, 1914–1915* (Stroud: Spellmount, 2006) and Mustafa Akaskal, "Holy War Made in Germany?: Ottoman Origins of the 1914 Jihad," *War in History* 18, 2 (2001), 184–99.

Padres in No Man's Land

Introduction

In the early hours of 1 June 1866 word of the Fenian capture of Fort Erie reached Hamilton, Canada West. The next day the city's militia unit was shipped off by train to meet the enemy. A few hours later two Evangelical ministers, David Inglis, a Presbyterian, and Nathanael Burwash, a Wesleyan Methodist – unofficial chaplains hastily appointed by the local ministerial association – went off in search of their men. After a night of perching on railway cars and hiking the back roads of the Niagara peninsula, they caught up with the men just in time to witness the battle of Ridgeway. Nearby, in a dark little cabin, stifled by the sweltering heat, they tended the wounded and prayed with the dying. Slipping out during a lull, Inglis witnessed the disastrous confusion in the Canadian ranks that led to their panic and defeat. A few minutes later, with rifle bullets slapping into the fence rails behind them, he and Burwash hoisted the casualties into wagons and began their retreat. Defeat at Ridgeway was followed by victory a few days later, however, and when the Fenian emergency ended, the erstwhile chaplains returned to their parishes, reassured anxious relatives, and related their experiences to admiring audiences and, perhaps, envious colleagues. Burwash and Inglis learned then that several other clergymen in the Canadas had also followed their local regiments into the field as voluntary chaplains, a clear indication of both their eagerness to participate in military endeavour and the perceived gravity of the Fenian situation.[1]

The Ridgeway escapade made an indelible impression on Burwash and Inglis, linking together vital aspects of their personal piety with the public dimensions of their Evangelical creed. Young Burwash, whose paternal ancestors had served under the Union Jack since the American Revolution, had been stirred into a holy rage by the news of the Fenian invasion. To him, every young and active Christian man was duty-bound to resist the intruders. A telegraph operator in Hamilton was startled when he encountered the twenty-six-year-old minister that day: "I question if he had ever entertained as strong and bitter feeling at any time; it reminded one of some other man rather than the quiet, unassuming Methodist preacher I had known." The next day, at Ridgeway, his work with the casualties confirmed theological training and personal religious experience. The dying words of a Wesleyan ensign from the Queen's Own Rifles movingly illuminated for Burwash the Methodist doctrine of salvation, fixing in his own mind "the necessity of such assurance in a vital religious experience.[2]"

Inglis, for his part, testified that the campaign had also stirred his public conscience. A few months later he told his congregation that God used wars to teach nations invaluable spiritual lessons. At Ridgeway he had discovered the secret of national greatness. Honest citizens, rallying in defence of a righteous cause, would inevitably prevail over anarchy and evil. To him the campaign of 1866 summoned all Canadians to thanksgiving, repentance, and the pledging of a solemn covenant with God to make Canada a righteous nation. World events, he pointed out, supported his message, for in that same year Lutheran Prussia had been victorious over Roman Catholic Austria, assuring Germany's continued transformation from a collection of separate political entities into one confederated nation.[3] Ironically, these sentiments still coloured the preaching of Canadian military chaplains half a century later, though by then Canadian padres had swung from commendation of the North German Confederation to condemnation of the German Empire. For in 1917 the great northern nations confederated in 1867 were at war with each other.

Although it might not have seemed so at the time, Burwash and Inglis's experiences were more than a vignette in the historical albums of Canadian churchmen. In fact the improvised nature of their appointment, their active participation in battle, and the consolidating effect of their experiences on personal faith and public ideals were archetypical of the Canadian military chaplaincy from 1867 to the First World War. While Ridgeway initiated in the national period the tradition of clergymen accompanying Canadians to battle, the federal government was reluctant to create an official military chaplaincy. As a result, from 1896 until the outbreak of the First World War, the government sponsored an honorary militia chaplaincy, seemingly as an outlet for extroverted and hyperpatriotic clerics.

During the First World War this parochial system became, not without difficulty, an efficient field force. As a result, between 1914 and 1921 at least 524 Canadian clergymen, representing each of the major denominations, donned the uniform of the new Canadian Chaplain Service (CCS). Of this number at least 447 served overseas, in France and Flanders, Siberia, and the Mediterranean. Nevertheless, the history of the institution and the significance of its contribution to Canadian life have not yet been told, nor have the experiences and beliefs of Canadian chaplains been examined thoroughly. Though Canadian historians occasionally refer to them in their traditional role of consolation, the Great War padres have usually been of secondary interest. Similarly, historians have paid little attention to the post-war careers of the padres in Canadian religious and social life. Yet chaplains have been literate and articulate participants in some of the most tumultuous years of our history. In fact, their military archives contain significant documents bearing upon our knowledge of religious and social history, while the archives of Canadian religious denominations contain valuable material previously overlooked by military and social historians. The history of the Canadian military chaplaincy in the Great War (as the chaplains themselves called it), therefore invites closer examination.

The only official history of the Chaplain Service in the Great War ever attempted was deemed unsuitable by government editors and remains unpublished.[4] Except for Canon Frederick George Scott's and Father Benedict Joseph Murdoch's personal accounts, a brief chapter on the padre's typical war experiences published in a popular history, and an occasional mention by one or another regimental chronicle, the first decade after the war generated very little literature on the chaplaincy indeed.[5] Although later years saw a handful of impressionistic personal accounts by individuals, they added little new information to the story of the CCS.[6] The 1930s and 1940s saw two brief accounts of the Roman Catholic Great War chaplaincy, written for fellow priests by Father John R. O'Gorman, while in 1948 the introduction to Walter Steven's official history of the Protestant service in the Second World War only sketched the Protestant side of the Great War chaplaincy. These accounts, however, were compiled by ex-chaplains to commemorate and illuminate, not to assess their forebears in chaplaincy.[7]

Since 1948 a handful of Canadian studies have focused on the institutional growth of our armed forces chaplaincies, though their authors, graduate students and chaplains both, have usually based their work on the earlier narratives.[8] Even the official account of the Canadian Expeditionary Force (CEF), which appeared in 1962, devoted more attention to the veterinary and dental branches than to the Chaplain Service.[9] Desmond Morton, however, significantly advanced our understanding of the internal administration of the service while examining the command and control of the CEF in the First World War. Since the 1940s knowledgeable Roman Catholics had hinted that their priests overseas suffered from command and reinforcement problems created by the Canadian government's establishment of the Chaplain Service as an ecumenical organization under an Anglican director.[10] Historians have noted former Prime Minister Borden's private indictment of CCS administration under its first director.[11] Morton's 1982 study revealed that the Canadian military chaplaincy suffered initially from maladministration and, for the first two years of the Great War, was judged infuriatingly inefficient by officer and politician alike. Yet subsequent historians have neither explored nor explained this situation because the Chaplain Service record remains a footnote to their discussions of the military unpreparedness of Canada, the byzantine evolution of Canadian command and control administration overseas, or the ludicrous results of giving military rank and privileges to political appointees.[12]

A similar situation exists among contemporary historians of religion in Canada, who debate the war's impact upon social reform, Canadian ecumenicalism, and religious thought. Most have been struck by the impact of the 1914–18 conflict on heightened militant idealism at home, especially among Protestants, whose war became a crusade where ultimate moral values clashed.[13] Apparently Canadian reformers achieved their greatest successes because they proclaimed the war a crucible of national regeneration.[14] Even among English-speaking Catholics 1914 seems to have appeared a providential opportunity to demonstrate their own nationalist vision (conflicting sharply with that of their French-speaking counterparts) by playing a leading part in the Canadian war effort.[15] In these studies, however, padres have been regarded simply as further examples from overseas of the same idealism expressed by churchmen and women back in Canada. The chaplains themselves still linger in the historiographic background, relegated to the role of consoling soldiers and their kin or endorsing calls for reform made by home church leaders.

Recently this portrait has been challenged by two historians who link the Protestant chaplains' experiences with a profound and deep church disillusionment with older views of providence, salvation, the mission of the church and religious authority. A study of Methodists and

Presbyterians by David Marshall has proposed that the war drove chaplains, clerics, and students overseas away from the facile idealism proclaimed by the home clergy, even from orthodox Christianity itself, contributing to secularization, the shaking of church credibility, and, among the clergy, to bifurcation into hostile conservative and liberal religious camps.[16] This thesis has been qualified by an interpreter of theological trends in Presbyterian and Methodist churches, who emphasizes the "new religious temper" created overseas among chaplains who encountered the spirit of bitterness and revolt bred in the trenches. Thus, to Michael Gauvreau, the forces of "Christian Realism" rather than declension matured during the war into their distinctive Canadian forms.[17] Both studies, however, fail to reconstruct fully either the institutional or the personal worlds of service, sacrament, and sacrifice that all Canadian padres inhabited overseas. The chaplains' world has been sieved for statements that illustrate other themes, but neither surveyed nor assayed for its own intrinsic wealth. Thus, among Canadian scholars, the figures of our Great War chaplains, their experience overseas, and their response to the war remain very shadowy indeed.

In most other countries that participated in the First World War, the historical literature on military chaplains is equally meagre and uneven. Most German and American accounts (written by chaplains and ex-chaplains) deal more with institutional structure than with the war's impact on the chaplains' beliefs or their influence upon soldiers and society. Chaplaincy history has often been treated as an antiquarian pursuit for retired or neophyte padres writing to indoctrinate new chaplains and commemorate past heroes.[18] Concerning the First World War, American religious sociologists have shown the most interest in chaplain mentality and beliefs, although their best-known work is coloured by a fierce indictment of crusading theology and chaplain preaching.[19] Over the last three decades a handful of studies have been done by American sociologists probing for tensions between Christianity and militarism within the role of military chaplain, but these usually reflect the ongoing debate between pacifists and others reading history for answers to contemporary military, theological, and moral dilemmas.[20]

A somewhat richer literature exists for the British chaplaincy of the First World War. During the interwar decades memoirs by disillusioned veterans created an indelible portrait of the British Army chaplaincy that has been perpetuated in most Commonwealth war literature to this day. To Robert Graves and Guy Chapman, Anglican chaplains were afraid to share the dangers of the trenches with the troops, while Roman Catholic padres were continually found in the front line, visiting with and offering prayers for their men. They categorically and authoritatively state that Anglican chaplains were held in widespread contempt by officers and men while Roman Catholic chaplains were highly regarded.[21] It was partly to counter this critical tradition as well as to chronicle the history of the Royal Army Chaplains' Department that new institutional studies of the English and Scottish chaplaincies appeared during and after the Second World War.[22] Although such accounts attempted to balance the picture, the stereotypical portrait of the cowardly Anglican curate with inadequate theology, outflanked and outranked, as it were, by the compassionate and courageous Roman Catholic padre, remains embedded firmly in contemporary historical accounts and popular perceptions of life in the trenches of the British Expeditionary Force (BEF).[23]

The most recent British scholarship, however, focuses attention on the English national church and examines its chaplaincy in the context of Anglican theological and institutional responses to the conflict. According to Albert Marrin, Church of England leaders viewed the war as a purifying furnace, destroying the dross of the church and renewing its hold on a rapidly secularizing nation. The war quickly became a crusade in which an early or negotiated peace became anathema until Germany had been defeated and England purged of materialism, class warfare, and social injustice. The army was portrayed as a school of character and its chaplains as agents in a religious revival in the trenches, where the manhood of England had rediscovered the faith and fellowship of the primitive church. As a result, the church came to expect too much from the padres and the veterans while giving them little meaningful assistance or prominence in the councils of the church. While their churches were seduced by nationalism, the padres, overworked and hamstrung by limitations imposed on their work by bishops and senior army officers, were unable to achieve the high expectations of the church. Marrin accordingly accepts the criticisms of the chaplains by ex-soldiers such as Graves and Chapman, pronouncing the Church of England chaplaincy a failure, even damaging to the post-war reputation and influence of the church.[24] Alan Wilkinson, by contrast, views the Anglican padre more charitably, arguing that too many historians have unquestioningly accepted the disillusioned soldier's view, and he offers an insightful assessment of the experience and thought of some chaplains who not only served under fire but had great sympathy for their men. Nevertheless, he too generally accepts the critique of chaplains made by British authors, adding that the leaders of the Army Chaplains' Department and the Army Council, sunk in ecclesiastical factionalism, gave inadequate supervision to the army's spiritual needs.[25]

Perhaps the scholarship most relevant to Canadians, however, comes from Australia. Michael McKernan has examined the relationship among the different Australian churches as well as their chaplains in the Great War. He shows that all Australian denominations had been challenged by the secularism and anticlericalism of Australian society and welcomed the war as an opportunity to establish some hold on the nation. As a result, churchmen at home quickly adopted a crusading mentality, anticipated national regeneration, and even wished that the iron of sacrifice would strike deeper when the looked-for revival seemed too long in coming. In their crusading preaching, support for conscription, and competitive feuding, McKernan argues, the churches discredited themselves and actually lost ground with Australian soldiers and citizens, especially with the non-arrival of the Kingdom of God in Australia by 1918.[26] McKernan pays special attention to the organization, work, and experiences of Australian chaplains overseas, comparing the work of all denominations among the troops. Chaplain preaching, their assessment of the religion of the Australian soldier, and their prophetic messages to the homeland all come under his scrutiny, including the unsympathetic response of the churches to the padres' calls for social reform and ecumenicism. McKernan concludes that, in neglecting their chaplains, the Australian churches lost one of their greatest opportunities.[27] Considering their own experiences, Canada's Great War chaplains might have agreed.

This study examines primarily the chaplains who served overseas in the Canadian Expeditionary Force between September 1914 and June 1921, when the last CCS chaplain was demobilized and the service placed on the Non-Permanent Active Militia list. It is not a study of every Canadian cleric who served as a Great War chaplain, as several served in other armies (including Episcopalian Bishop Charles Brent, who served at the headquarters of the American Expeditionary Force under General John J. Pershing). Nor does this study explore any ministry to the infant Canadian naval and air forces in the Great War, for our government did not create separate chaplaincies for them. Readers familiar with Canada's war record may wonder why more coverage has not been allotted to Canon F.G. Scott, perhaps the most famous chaplain in Canadian military history. My purpose was rather to set his legendary work and writings (probably the most powerful historiographic lodestone of the field) in the context of the similar work and words of all the padres and senior chaplains of the CEF. Scott's lifelong career as a national figure, including his pilgrimage as a chaplain from glory-filled crusader to priest and fellow sufferer with the common soldier, deserves fuller treatment than this effort can give. Neither can my study render an authoritative representation of how every Canadian soldier viewed the padre, or the entire army viewed the military chaplaincy. Although some insightful assessments of war, padres, and religion by some of Canada's thousands of veterans have been cited, this book is primarily about the war as the padres experienced and represented it. Until historians produce a comprehensive portrait of the universal Canadian soldier of the Great War, there can be no universal padre, and no authoritative pronouncement upon his worth.

After tracing the lessons learned by Canadians from the active-service escapades of the early national period and the hectic Valcartier days of 1914, this survey will sketch and assess the growth of the Canadian Chaplain Service as an institution, emphasizing the administrative controversies that marked the maturing of a professional chaplaincy in the Canadian forces overseas. Subsequent chapters discuss the service's work on the battlefield, evaluating just how cloistered Canadian chaplains were from front-line realities. From battlefield service I turn to the personal world of the Canadian padres as they progressed by stages towards the front and developed strong psychological bonds with their men. When we link the preaching and writing of the chaplains with their pre-war education, it becomes apparent that most were not disillusioned with their cause during war service. Their pre-war formation evidently equipped them well with the language and convictions to fight without disillusionment or despair a sacrificial war of personal and national regeneration. What emerges most strikingly from this study, contrary to Marshall's, is the continuity, not the decline, of padre faith and preaching from pre-1914 days to their return from overseas. This book proposes that it was, rather, during the years when chaplains returned to civilian life that the anger and bitterness deferred in wartime became manifest, as the chaplains saw their highest hopes dashed by 1939, and many again enlisted for yet another foreign war.

The Great War experiences of Canadians overseas have always fascinated us. Yet, curiously, our uniformed clergy have never been given much attention or credit. Perhaps both our popular and scholarly memories have been uneasy with their legacy. The post-millennial world they prophesied did not come to pass. The transformation they claimed the war worked in the men at the front seemed to have so little impact on the nation when they got back. Tracing the contours of the padres' war along bureaucratic, theological, and psychological lines, one finds them, after they had conquered No Man's Land, seemingly defeated in the years that followed. With the men they had served and sacrificed alongside, the padres were baffled when the transformation that the war had wrought seemed so impotent in the changing circumstances of the peace. How could the clerics who had touched the face of battle have been so defeated by the peace? Perhaps this book may help to explain their journey.

1 Adventurers: Days of Preparation

Reports that Louis Riel's Métis followers had clashed with the Mounted Police at Duck Lake reached Toronto on the evening of 27 March 1885. The eastern churches quickly rallied to the government's side, condemning the rebels and praising the militia, prophesying that the war would be a turning-point on the road to national unity.[1] Two weeks later, however, the Anglican editor of Toronto's *Canadian Churchman* waxed indignant over the chaplaincy arrangements made, or rather not made, for the troops:

As strange a question as we ever heard arise, and as complete a stripping of religious prejudices usually called "principles" as ever took place, has come to light in the demand for chaplains for the troops in the Northwest. Chaplains indeed! Here again we see the advantages of the Romanists, they have sent priests with their troops, and the Government of Canada will pay for these chaplains, and most properly so ... But what sort of chaplains are the non-denominationalists going to send? The lovely theory of an invisible church, made of an heterogeneous assortment of denominations goes off into space like an airy nothing, when faced by a practical test of its existence. The Roman Church asks no questions in the press, but as a matter of course sends the chaplains. What is called [the Protestant Church] is sending its members by the thousands to dangers most grave ... but this amazing organization must be either stone blind, or deaf, or dead, or callous, for it is sending no clergy, no chaplains ... Here is a problem for the ministerial association! Men are asking for chaplains to be sent to the Northwest, who, in ordinary time are bitterly antagonistic to a government recognizing or aiding any Church. Let these men now leave their talk and their theories and act by meeting the demand for chaplains for the brave fellows ... Surely the "Protestant church" is at least as anxious for its children as the Romanist Church?[2]

THE CANADIAN MILITARY CHAPLAINCY drew its inspiration from the British. By 1867 the British Army chaplaincy had largely completed the process of professionalization that began during the French Revolutionary wars. In 1796 the Crown had abolished the purchase of regimental chaplaincies and created its own Chaplains' Department under a chaplain-general. This checked the rampant venality and absenteeism that had seen many regimental chaplains refuse to accompany their units on foreign expeditions or even to send deputy clerics in their place, and most of the units serving in North America dependent on the occasional services of civilian clergymen. Even after 1796 the War Office found that few British clergymen were eager to leave their civilian parishes for the low-paying and far-flung chaplaincies to the regiments and garrisons serving in the colonies. Consequently, between 1796 and the 1870s, when the last British regiment was withdrawn from Canada, the War Office favoured local colonials ministering to army units. Such garrison chaplains were paid a stipend and their parishes received pew rents, while at several stations the War Office undertook to provide Anglican chapels for the use of the troops and local residents.[3]

Although the post-Waterloo British chaplaincy slipped into decline, the Crimean War led to reforms and the extension of the Army Chaplains' Department, which grew from seven Anglican chaplains in 1854 to twenty-one Anglicans and thirty-five non-Anglicans in 1856. By 1859 both Presbyterian and Roman Catholic chaplains had been given commissions and status equivalent to that of the Anglicans. Somewhere along the line British regiments with service in India began using the generic term "padre," formerly given to any Christian cleric on the subcontinent, to their chaplains. The practice spread to the rest of the British Army. Rank based upon seniority was conferred on full-time chaplains in 1858, and two years later a uniform for active service was approved. Canada thus began wrestling with the problem of providing religious ministry to her militia defenders just as the office of military chaplain acquired the acknowledged status of a profession in the British Empire.[4] In spite of the precedent of the Fenian Raids and the growing practice of individual clergymen attaching themselves to various militia units in the 1860s, however, the Canadian government was unwilling to consider creating an official military chaplaincy. George-Étienne Cartier's 1868 Militia Bill established a skeletal military staff with no place for parsons. Clergymen were exempt from all military service, along with judges, professors, the infirm, only sons, and keepers of prisons and asylums.[5] Nevertheless, by 1914 a few Canadian clergymen had acquired some experience of the chaplain's work on active-service. In fact, over twenty Canadian clergymen, representing four denominations, served in one of the active-service contingents to the Red River and North-West Rebellions or the fighting in South Africa. Recruiting these first active-service chaplains resulted in considerable denominational tension, as might be expected given the competitive spirit animating so much of Canadian church life at the time and which continued unabated in the feverish opening days of the Great War.

The government of John A. Macdonald first learned how politically volatile the military chaplaincy could be when it authorized an expedition to quell the Red River Rebellion. Difficulties arose almost immediately, first with the British commander, then with the Protestant churches and the Toronto press. Colonel Garnet Wolseley objected to taking along any extra baggage, much less the Anglican parson and Oblate priest whom the minister of Militia, Georges Cartier, had attached to his headquarters.[6] Then the Wesleyan Methodist church entered the fray. To the delight of the Liberal press, its 1870 General Conference officially censured Cartier for blatant religious discrimination. Morley Punshon and an aging Egerton Ryerson denounced the insult to Methodism when Cartier ignored its offer of a chaplain.[7] Cartier's attempt to refute the charges led to a lively skirmish in the House of Commons, where Opposition Leader Alexander Mackenzie, a committed Baptist, argued that chaplaincy selection was an important indicator of the government's view of the relations between church and state, a perennially divisive issue in Canada. After a heated exchange the chaplaincy controversy was quickly overtaken by a bitter row over Manitoba land reserves. Eventually laughter erupted when Cartier admitted that the soldiers, for all his troubles, had not wanted the chaplains anyway. After authorizing a sessional report publishing all correspondence on the matter, the House turned to other matters.[8]

Despite the humorous outcome, the ecclesiastical outcry proved that Canadian church-state relations were as explosive as in previous decades. Ryerson thundered against the dangers that Anglo-Catholic chaplains held for young Methodist volunteers and the influence popish priestcraft had on Cartier's choice of chaplains, warning that voluntarist principles were in danger so long as governments, not denominations, controlled chaplaincy appointments.[9] The rueful Macdonald government, too, learned its lesson from the Red River episode. Even if British officers, at least, found padres a nuisance, the Tories knew that any active-service force with Catholics in the ranks would have to have its priest. Unfortunately for the government, there seemed to be no easy way of providing parsons for Protestants. The option of recruiting from a flock of prospective padres representing several quarrelsome denominations was politically unthinkable. The onus of chaplain selection, they realized, must be shifted from the government's shoulders. Militia regulations allowed church parades (led by civilian clergymen at no expense to the public) only when troops were in camp and on exercises.[10] But under no circumstances would the government allow a peacetime chaplaincy.

There the matter rested until 1884, when the Anglican rector at St John (later St Jean, Quebec) tried to strengthen his hand as unofficial padre to the little band of Protestants at the infantry school located there. In response to his request for formal appointment, commandant Lt-Col. G.O. D'Orsonnens informed the adjutant-general: "I do not see why he should apply to be a RECOGNIZED chaplain. If he were appointed as such, I would be obliged to have a Catholic chaplain appointed for the majority of the men. As I do not wish to have the two in 'official' contact in a camp compound of different nationalities or religion and proselytism made here I think it my duty to recommend that such an appointment be not made. Besides I think it would simply lead to claims for services rendered which I believe is not provided for by our regulations."[11]

IRONICALLY, A FEW MONTHS LATER, events in the Canadian northwest required another hasty chaplaincy expedient, though this time with a more satisfying outcome. This time it was Canadian militia officers, not the minister, who touched off the explosion. Regimental officers of the French Canadian units independently recruited two Roman Catholic priests as soon as mobilization orders were received.[12] The commanders of the French Canadian contingent urged Minister of Militia Adolphe Caron to sanction these "absolutely necessary" appointments.[13] Caron complied, on condition that each priest be acceptable to his men and obey militia regulations.[14] Caron did not know, however, that the commander of Toronto's Queen's Own Rifles had surreptitiously offered two places in the ranks to Anglican divinity students of the cadet company; or that General Thomas Strange, commander of the Alberta force, had signed on three armed Protestant missionaries, W.P. Mackenzie, a Presbyterian, W.R. Mackay, an Anglican, and John McDougall, a Methodist, to serve as scouts and interpreters as well as padres.[15]

By then Protestants demanded that every mobilized unit have its own chaplain.[16] News of the Catholic head start spurred Presbyterians in Ottawa to extract a promise from Caron that he would grant chaplaincies to their ministers on the same basis as the Catholics. He would pay and transport a Protestant chaplain, selected by the unit concerned, to each remaining battalion in the field. Thus Caron adroitly side-stepped the pitfall encountered by Cartier, for no opposition critic would dare object to a chaplain selected by the very men who were doing the fighting.[17] Caron's political instincts did not fail him. The Presbyterians endorsed the procedure, and the other Protestant communions followed suit.[18] In the excitement and urgency of the crisis, no one complained that it would have been better to send the chaplains out with their men in the first place.[19]

Campaign news soon overshadowed denominational rivalry as churchmen hustled clergymen off to the field. Toronto Anglicans, after some procedural skirmishing with the Militia Ministry and still grumbling about sectarian divisions, bundled a minister on to the Winnipeg train, bound for Middleton's column.[20] By this time the Presbyterians already had their first padre at the front, someone who had befriended the regiment in its early days, Daniel Miner Gordon. Relatives of the men of the Ninetieth Winnipeg Rifles, alarmed by reports from Fish Creek, had urged their men to summon a chaplain. Laden with their letters and a brand new revolver, Gordon arrived at the Fish Creek camp a week after the battle, destined to be the only chaplain present at the taking of Batoche. The Methodists, for their part, were strangely passive. Two days after the Presbyterians had bearded Caron in his office, the editor of the *Christian Guardian* was patiently explaining to readers the delicacy of striking an agreeable denominational balance.[21] Methodist ministers were evidently not popular enough with any local militia units to be called on to the field.[22]

Over the following weeks eleven regimental chaplains – five Anglicans, four Presbyterians, and two Roman Catholics – eventually caught up to their militia congregations.[23] They found their ministry determined by geography, as most units broke up into scattered groups along the lines of communication.[24] There they learned that military service was largely composed of long stretches of inactivity and boredom. Many would eagerly have exchanged places with Daniel Gordon at Batoche or Father Philemon Prévost at Frenchman's Butte. Gordon's coolness under fire made him popular with Middleton's men. By naïvely remaining on his feet while volunteers dove for cover from Métis sharpshooters, visiting with the Gatling gun crew in the firing line, dismissing a service interrupted by enemy fire with a curt benediction, and loping along behind the ambulance wagon during the final charge, he created an enviable reputation (as "Fighting Dan Gordon") in both militia and church circles.[25] He learned, as did his successors in South Africa and the Great War, that a padre's popularity with the men rose the more visible he became in the actual firing line. At Frenchman's Butte, Father Prévost's pronouncement of general absolution over the bowed heads of Montreal's Sixty-fifth Regiment before it attacked Big Bear's position, as well as his daring in helping the commander to recover a wounded Quebec soldier under "sharp fire," immortalized him in French Canadian regimental circles.[26]

But most of the 1885 campaign was spent in idleness as the columns converged on Fort Pitt and waited for the Indian bands to surrender. In these long weeks the patience and ingenuity of all the chaplains were challenged by the growing restlessness of the bored troops.[27] They learned that there was more to a good chaplain's qualifications than physical bravery. He had to have a sense of humour, broad sympathies with the common man, and a flair for social or recreational organization.[28] Required also was the ability to get along with other denominations, though the mild ecclesiastical skirmishing between Anglicans and dissenters in Middleton's column never reached the heights of emotion being scaled back in Toronto.[29] At last the troops at Fort Pitt were ordered home. As they returned to the acclamation of a grateful public, the chaplains felt, like Burwash and Inglis in 1866, that they had just passed a high point in their careers.[30] Fellow churchmen basked in the reflected glory won by the chaplains in the field.[31] Although Ontario and Quebec church and statesmen had already begun the bickering that blighted their victory, the chaplaincy, at least, remained one of the 1885 campaign's success stories.

THE CHAPLAINS' POPULARITY with the troops and favourable press coverage almost fostered a peacetime chaplaincy. Militia units maintained cordial ties with their chaplains and invited local clergymen to minister in camp and barracks.[32] The Conservative government did not waver from its original policy, however, and requests from both clergymen and unit commanders to make official chaplaincy appointments were therefore denied.[33] The wisdom of this policy became evident in 1886, after a priest who had voluntarily taken responsibility for the Catholic soldiers at the St John infantry school requested recognition and payment (or at least, he hinted, a free CPR excursion) for two years of faithful service. When Caron refused, Father Aubry turned to the French Canadian press. While editors raged about the government's neglect of the poor boys prepared to offer their lives in the country's defence, the minister of Militia maintained that any voluntary ministry performed for soldiers would be welcomed, but without official appointment or public expense.[34]

While Ottawa held the line against bellicose priests, by the 1890s most of the better-organized urban militia regiments had unofficial chaplains and "garrison churches", where they assembled on ceremonial occasions.[35] The practice of keeping civilian clerics on regimental paylists began as unit commanders realized that their presence aided recruiting. In 1894, when scrupulous militia authorities ordered such practices in Quebec City's Ninth Regiment to cease, the commander insisted that Father Faguy (of Riel Rebellion fame) remain on the paylist as honourary chaplain: "Should he be removed, the confidence of officers and men will be disturbed, and it will be necessarily more difficult to keep them in the ranks." Headquarters obligingly turned a blind eye to the practice, though it reiterated the ban on official appointments.[36]

By this time the practice had spread to several other regiments, whose "unofficial chaplains" repeatedly suggested that it was time for militia policy to change.[37] In 1895 W. Witten (just elected chaplain by the Forty-third Regiment) suggested that Ottawa grant honorary commissions to clergymen elected padres by their regiments, with ranks ranging from captain to lieutenant-colonel, based on their militia seniority. Such chaplains would be unpaid except when on active duty, provide their own uniforms modelled on their British counterparts, and consent to serve when and wherever duty called. Since these chaplains were elected by the men, there would be no denominational complaint. Thus the only expense to the government would be the price of their commission parchment, and "patriotic clergymen … filled with military zeal and enthusiasm and … the desire to do their *Duty*, and to assist in maintaining the integrity of our glorious British Empire" would be standing by ready for immediate service.[38]

Initially, militia authorities laid aside Witten's suggestions with the routine comment that chaplains were not permitted by regulations, but the new – Liberal – Militia minister, Frederick Borden, had a different outlook. Militia headquarters granted honorary appointments to the Anglican priest of Toronto's Royal Grenadiers and, in 1896, to the Catholic padre of Montreal's Sixty-fifth, "as a special case."[39] That October, Ottawa authorized honorary peacetime chaplains for all units "on the condition that no expense to the public is incurred." Ottawa-approved clergymen would wear, on parade or in camp, the uniform of a British chaplain, third class.[40] Ottawa made it plain, however, that no chaplaincies would be created for the small standing army of soldiers, cavalry troopers, and gunners stationed across the country – the "permanent force."[41]

Before many of the new militia chaplains took office, war rumours from South Africa stirred the nation. Patriotic offers of service flowed into political, militia, and denominational headquarters. The government initially replied that chaplains would not be needed, but English Canadian imperial sentiment and untimely press leaks concerning tentative contingent proposals forced Wilfrid Laurier's hand.[42] On 14 October 1899 Militia General Orders announced the recruitment, at the expense of the British government, of an infantry regiment for service in South Africa.[43]

This time Methodist leaders were eager to seize such an opportunity, ignoring the call by some of the rural clergy to remain aloof from the war. W.G. Lane, a Nova Scotia minister, wrote Methodist General Secretary Albert Carman, "We must range up not only alongside, but ahead of other Churches in our duty to God and our Country." Carman immediately offered him to Borden.[44] The Presbyterians were not far behind in recommending Charlottetown's Thomas Fullerton.[45] Even the YMCA, on the strength of its experience running canteens at the summer camps, offered Dr H.G. Barrie as its representative. After initial inquiries as to whether or not the British would accept the services of Canadian chaplains to the contingent, Borden authorized one Protestant and one Roman Catholic chaplaincy.[46] The day before the troop-ship sailed he appointed Fullerton and Father Peter O'Leary of Quebec to the coveted posts, with Barrie thrown in as a special welfare officer.[47] The general officer commanding (GOC) the Militia, Edward Hutton, recommended that the padres be gazetted militia captains, though all three sailed on one condition: if British authorities did not accept them, they would return to Canada.[48] Colonel William Otter, contingent commander, was told to find room on the crowded transport and fit them into the regiment as comfortably as possible. No one at the time was sure that the British would not send them all back to Canada as soon as they reached Capetown, but the opportunity was too good to be missed.[49]

The same day that the O'Leary, Barrie, and Fullerton appointments were made, Anglicans discovered that not one priest of their church had been included. The Presbyterians, Catholics, even the sectarian YMCA had stolen a march on them. The bishop of Ottawa and leading Quebec notables protested in vain. Finally the bishop of Quebec was driven by fast coach twenty miles to catch a midnight train to meet with Laurier himself. On the word of the prime minister, one hour before sailing Anglican authorities hustled John Almond, a young missionary priest from Montreal, up the gangplank. The next day Capetown was notified that not one but four religious representatives were on their way.[50] Borden now faced the music in the Anglican press and the House of Commons. The editor of the *Canadian Churchman* raged about the favours granted Catholics and dissenters, and Laurier's Catholicity was denounced in the same terms as Cartier's had been in 1870. In the House of Commons, Opposition members, led by Ontario Orangeman Clarke Wallace, demanded an explanation from the Militia minister.[51] One angry churchman fumed:

> There is no doubt the Minister of Militia would have lent as willing an ear to the authorities of our church as he did to the spokesman of the Church of Rome ... An officer of the contingent told me that if the Roman Catholics had only had one man there his church would have provided him with a chaplain. The YMCA, an undenominational organization founded by the late Lord Shaftsbury, and a most excellent institution for disturbing and unsettling the mind of churchmen, had its agent appointed and its equipment ready. Where was the Church of England all this time? Just where she is in every other enterprise for her protection and extension. "Nowhere".[52]

The government was embarrassed further when a denominational census established the justice of the Anglican case: the Royal Canadian Regiment's Anglican cadre dwarfed the combined number of Presbyterians and Catholics.[53]

As the smoke cleared from ecclesiastical skirmishes, the government organized a mounted force of cavalry and field artillery. This time Borden paid stricter attention to the matter of chaplains. An Anglican and a Catholic chaplain were carefully selected. So was another YMCA welfare officer.[54] Further, after some jostling among eager candidates boasting of their "manly" natures or muscular frames, Methodist minister W.G. Lane was added to the list.[55] Thus all major denominations (except the Baptists) were satisfied with their chaplain representation, though Lane stirred up the Methodist Maritime Conference with charges that the troops were being marched to worship exclusively at the Anglican and Catholic cathedrals.[56] To him it was a battle against "the eddy and scum of churchism ... It is time Methodism became a factor in Church and State and not permit so much to go by default."[57] His victory was hailed by other Protestant onlookers, especially the Presbyterians, who were unhappy about the appointment of another ritualistic Anglican to the second contingent.[58]

Lane, J.W. Cox, the Anglican, and Father J.C. Sinnett, the Catholic priest, each sailed with one of the transport ships. Upon arrival in Capetown the six chaplains and two YMCA workers learned that their work would have many frustrations. Remaining physically close to their men, much less maintaining good relations with them, proved difficult. This especially was the case for the Royal Canadian Regiment. The hasty addition of three parsons to his headquarters staff, along with Dr Barrie, newspaper correspondents, nurses, instructional officers, and Sam Hughes, an opinionated militia booster and Conservative member of Parliament, did little to impress Colonel Otter, who was trying to make his unit conform in every way to British standards.[59] British officials also refused to pay for such Canadian frills as padres and nurses. Otter had to tide the insolvent chaplains over with regimental funds until the Canadian High Commissioner in London visited the War Office to sort out the matter.[60]

Further, the regiment was an amalgamation of several tightly knit cliques, as each recruitment area had formed its company cadre out of old militia comrades and school chums eager for imperial adventure.[61] Chaplain Fullerton, written off by Otter as a "sour Presbyterian minister", soon wore out his welcome, even among Maritimers, with his explicitly prohibitionist Evangelicalism.[62] Meanwhile, John Almond, completely unknown to the men, seemed unable to make a good impression on them.[63] The two padres were left on the margins of regimental life: when the unit, unhappy with its commander's hard-driving discipline, split over Otter's plan to extend their tour of duty, Almond allied himself with the colonel's faction, while Fullerton supported the "rebels" desiring early repatriation.[64] Almond's choice may have been an attempt to redeem himself with the commander after being caught while intoxicated with hospital wines during the long unhappy summer of 1900.[65] The regiment generally had little good to say about its Protestant padres when it returned to Canada.[66]

The opposite was the case with Father O'Leary and Dr Barrie. Otter and his entire command were won over by O'Leary's good humour and willingness to join in the difficult marches, in spite of his forty-nine years.[67] This respect grew after the regiment's first battle at Paardeberg. Almond, Fullerton, and Barrie had been left behind tending stragglers on the march, but O'Leary remained with the men during their reckless charge and its disastrous aftermath, when enemy sharpshooters pinned the Canadians down in the open.[68] Here, moving about openly despite Boer sniping, giving first aid, encouragement, or last rites, O'Leary won a prominent place in the limelight. Back home, enthusiasts inflated his exploits to epic proportions.[69] With many others of the regiment, however, he collapsed from enteric fever a few days after Paardeberg and was evacuated from the theatre for recuperation in Britain.[70] The regiment had found and lost its favourite chaplain in a few short days, but not before his exploits put the other chaplains' reputations in the shade.

Barrie, while he never had the support of Colonel Otter, quickly won the soldiers' trust. Otter had little respect for the Evangelical welfare worker, whose melodeon and hymn-books, as well as his prohibitionist fervour, jarred Otter's sense of military efficiency.[71] He often contrived to leave Barrie and his impedimenta behind, but the men wanted his medical advice and appreciated his ability to supply the staples and treats not provided by quartermaster's stores.[72] By the end of the RCR's African sojourn almost every soldier had benefited from Barrie's friendly and practical assistance, if not his religious enthusiasm.[73]

Similar experiences characterized the religious work with the Canadian mounted contingents. Although chaplains had been with British troops in the early fighting, the burgeoning numbers of sick led senior chaplains to post them from the front to the hospitals. As the Boers adopted mounted guerrilla tactics and the British deployed far-flung cavalry and horse-artillery columns to check them, chaplains could not keep up with the troops. The British senior chaplain in Capetown detached Cox from his unit for base and hospital work in the rear, limiting his contact with Canadian troops in the field to occasional visits.[74] Lane and Sinnet equipped themselves with horses, but the Canadians usually saw more of the British chaplains than their own.[75] Often the YMCA's Thomas Best performed the everyday work of a chaplain, holding prayers and burying Protestant dead after an ambush or skirmish. As a result, the mounted contingent, too, had nothing but praise for the YMCA.[76]

The South African adventure confirmed that a chaplain's influence was directly proportional to the amount of danger and hardship he shared with the men. Almost any administrative or personal shortcoming in a padre would be forgiven if he showed the right blend of courage and sympathy when it counted most. Patriotic writers embroidered to the point of parody the religious attitudes of the Canadians in South Africa, and O'Leary's reputation remained untarnished. Veterans' tales of his reading prayers over dead Orangemen and dodging Boer bullets, taking last messages, and burying by candle or moonlight set a high public standard for subsequent clergymen taking the war path.[77] The other record – of wooden, hidebound religiosity and even moral failure – was redeemed by the memory of O'Leary, Barrie, and Best. Soldiers and troopers respected the dedication and good sense shown by Catholics and the manly, pony-mounted nonconformists who rode up, gave a short sermon on a pressing subject, then with a cheery wave rode on, rather than the stiff, learned, and fully robed Anglicans who meandered behind the columns in ox-carts.[78] It was the former sort that trooper George Wells, a subsequent Great War chaplain, and, more importantly, Sam Hughes, as minister of Militia, remembered during the early days of the Great War.

The early escapades confirmed the tendency of church leaders to guard their rights jealously, not merely for reasons of denominational pride but because of the high value placed on the moral and spiritual character of the new nation's great enterprises. The churches could not abide being left out of the forging of a nation in the smithy of war. Denominational truculence over appointments thus indicated a growing awareness of the opportunities offered in militia service as the Protestant churches developed their conceptions of mission and denominational agenda. Nevertheless, the churches could not yet overcome the competitive nature of ecclesiastical life in the Dominion, nor offer a united front to the government.

Politicians perhaps learned the most from the early adventures. Militia ministers stopped taking the churches for granted. Chaplaincies became necessary fixtures to establish the militia as a respectable national institution. Far from the indifferent days of the 1870s, officers and men now desired chaplains – of the right sort. Nevertheless, the best recruitment method seemed to be to allow each regiment to find one for itself. In fact, a shrewd Militia minister could turn such controversial issues to political advantage by playing on ecclesiastical patriotism. Whatever the original argument against it, by 1900 the padre's office was here to stay.

THE SOUTH AFRICAN WAR was followed by almost a decade and a half of peacetime militia ministry. By 1914 over 150 clergymen wore the militia uniform, and at least 275 active Canadian ministers had been initiated, albeit in a rudimentary fashion, into unit life and lore. Militia service became an attractive home mission field where the clergy of Canada could demonstrate as well as preach to Canadian men their vision of the nation's essentially Christian character and destiny. Under Frederick Borden defence expenditures rose, and the militia created new regiments and organized the auxiliary services considered indispensable to a modern army. After 1911 this process was accelerated by Sam Hughes, who was dedicated to enlarging the militia and increasing its popularity.[79]

All this encouraged churchmen to play a greater role in the fashionable national institution. The first nineteen chaplains appointed in 1897 were joined annually by dozens more until, by 1911, nearly every militia unit had a padre. Yet unlike the engineers and medical officers, the chaplains remained regimental officers without separate departmental status or command structure. In 1903, after another denominational row between W.G. Lane and the Anglicans at Aldershot camp, Ottawa granted honorary rank based on militia seniority.[80] Junior chaplains were placed exclusively under the authority of senior chaplains of their own denomination. As in the British Army, chaplains were permitted to write directly to the heads of their communions, who would intercede with the Militia minister or Militia Council. In 1905 Ottawa decreed that the chaplains would wear the khaki drill service dress (with a large Maltese Cross, rank badges, and the fashionable Sam Browne belt) when in the field. Padres now looked and perhaps felt more at home when in camp and leading church parades.[81]

The selection of a padre depended on the internal politics of each unit. In order not to harm recruiting or blight the social life of the regiment, the chaplain had to be acceptable to most of his unit. As the regiments were social clubs as well as military units, over time many identified themselves with a particular church and denomination. Judging from pre-war militia and church clergy lists, the chaplaincy, like the militia, remained largely English-speaking and Protestant. In fact the denominational proportions of the militia chaplaincy were in inverse proportion to those of the country. Although Anglicans were outnumbered by Roman Catholics, Presbyterians, and Methodists in the 1911 Dominion census, the old maxim that the official militia religion was Church of England was strongly evident, especially among the older units of the Maritimes and central Canada.[82] The cavalry, the most expensive and prestigious militia arm, employed Anglican chaplains almost exclusively, followed at a distance by the Presbyterians, with a few Methodists bringing up the rear. Significantly, not one cavalry regiment employed a Roman Catholic chaplain.[83] The same proportions characterized the rest of the militia. Nearly half of the infantry units were considered Anglican.[84] English-speaking regiments in Quebec and central Ontario were monopolized by the Anglicans, while in Montreal and rural areas largely settled by Scots the Presbyterians dominated.[85] More junior units, however, often departed from those traditions, even in areas where the Anglican proportion of the population was increasing in strength or dominated by recent British immigrants. This was especially true of those in the west, where a noticeably non-conformist component of the militia arose.[86]

Sincc many French Canadians regarded the militia as an agency of English-Protestant assimilation, the number of Roman Catholic priests in uniform was predictably low.[87] Nevertheless, sixteen of the older

Quebec regiments attracted French Canadian priests. After 1911, however, feuds between Quebec units and Sam Hughes over participation in religious processions, and the continued neglect of the French language by militia officers, discouraged widespread French Canadian support.[88] At the other end of the scale stood the Methodists and the Baptists, who fielded only a handful of padres (drawn mostly from the Maritimes) between them.[89] The very small number of Methodist chaplains remains, in the light of their earlier controversies, a curious anomaly. Evidently some Methodists were still repelled by militia training and wary of the rhetoric of Empire and flag underpinning its philosophy.[90] Furthermore, militia service used up time and money on the part of the volunteer and may have appealed, especially in the city battalions, more to Anglican white-collar immigrants than to Canadian-born Methodists bred to a tradition of peace and limited preparedness. Such recruiting considerations were inevitably reflected in the selection of chaplains. Finally, given the "wet canteen" and boisterous summer camps of the militia, few Methodist ministers and fewer Methodist mothers would have encouraged their young men to join such a notorious school of iniquity.[91]

Such a negative view of military life evidently did not deter many other clergymen, however, from donning khaki and following the regiments into camp and drill hall. In fact, judging by their published activities and attitudes, militia padres were a distinct and recognizable type among the nation's clergymen.[92] Though many of Canada's clergymen were immigrants, most chaplains were born and educated in Canada.[93] Nor were they all young. In the eyes of the regiment a chaplain had to be mature enough to guide and influence men of widely varying backgrounds and ages.[94] While obscure priests and ministers served, so did the Anglican primate of Canada, Archbishop S.P. Matheson, as chaplain to the Ninetieth Winnipeg Rifles.[95] The chaplains were a diverse group: Conservatives, Liberals, imperialists, reformers, idealists, and pragmatists all came to the colours, along with clergymen in favour of "church union" and those opposed to it. Some scorned prohibition, while others were crusaders for purity and probity.[96] Yet most shared some common characteristics and concerns. Effective chaplains were leaders of men, respected for their manly nature and prowess in sports. A number were noted athletes and outdoorsmen.[97] Others, drawn to military life as young men, kept up their connections after ordination.[98] By 1914 many chaplains had forged strong links with their regiments through long association. Few, though, went as far back as A.C. Hill, chaplain to the Twenty-fifth Regiment from 1897 to 1915. In 1866, Hill had served in the University Company of the Queen's Own Rifles at Ridgeway.[99]

Like most clerics of the day, chaplains belonged to a host of public, private, and patriotic bodies. The same sense of mission that fired imperialists and social reformers also drew energetic clergymen to military service. Chaplains sponsored cadet corps and joined athletic clubs, school boards, and the governing bodies of colleges and universities. Many belonged to men's societies, Masonic Lodges, and in some cases the Orange Lodge. But many also joined religious and social-reforming bodies such as the Lord's Day Alliance and the Moral and Social Reform Council of Canada, as well as temperance societies. Though not as outspoken as Thurlow Fraser, chaplain to the Ninety-ninth Regiment, many would have endorsed his views, echoing his own "social passion." In 1912 he denounced political corruption as the crying sin of national life. While he hoped that Canadian ethnic and religious factions could be drawn together into one nation, he considered that nationalism must be linked to a closer political connection with Great Britain. Without the British connection Canada "would be but the fag of her none too conscientious neighbour to the south." Canada must share in the support of British armies and fleets and give trade preference in return for closer ties with the Mother Country. Fraser too favoured Christian unity in Canada, urging denominations to accentuate the points of agreement over the points of difference.[100] Clearly he saw militia work as part of the churches' mission to Christianize every aspect of national life.

Regimental lore insisted that good padres were certainly more than preachers. They had to win "the esteem of officers and men, and exercise an influence which makes for a high conception of a citizen soldier's duty."[101] This meant shedding some of the gravity of the Canadian clerical stereotype:

> The padre, as he is generally called by the boys, does all he can to impress upon them the nobility of their calling, not only as soldiers of the King ... He goes with them into camp, and shares their innocent joys and pleasures. Around the camp fire no one is more willing to tell a pawky Scotch story or sing one of his country's many ballads, of which he has a large repertoire. During his tenure of the chaplaincy there have been an average of three church parades a year, and these have been always well attended. The chaplain is somewhat Bohemian in his ways, but in spite of that, he has managed to gain some influence for good in the Regiment.[102]

But the ideal chaplain was also expected by both Militia ministers and parents to ensure that the recreational pleasures of the camp, while manly, were indeed innocent. The antics of rowdy militiamen had filled summer columns of the Canadian press for years, suggesting that the army was an ideal instrument for the moral corruption of husbands, sons, and brothers. Traditionally, evenings were spent at the canteen, the recreational heart of each camp, where vendors (sometimes sponsored by the officers) did a roaring trade. Militia Headquarters routinely banned strong drink and just as routinely was disobeyed or ignored.[103] Many Protestants welcomed the YMCA into the camps to run dry canteens and recreational programs. By the turn of the century these ministries, which included Bible studies and evangelistic services in the evenings, were a routine feature of camp life.[104]

For Borden first, but especially for Hughes, who conceived of the militia as a citizen army and school for national character, good padres improved the militia's public reputation. He therefore gave chaplains a more prominent role in the annual camps. The padre (with the YMCA representative) was expected to substitute wholesome entertainment and sports for liquor, beer, cards, and dice. The chaplains received some help from Hughes when he banned alcohol in the camps. While angering militiamen, this won the congratulations of the Protestant churches and temperance organizations.[105] The minister also gathered around himself a number of notable clergymen as consultants on cadet training and recruiting: Hughes even amended regulations so that he could appoint such chaplains to the rank of lieutenant-colonel "if in the opinion of the Minister ... this is ... likely to promote the efficiency of the Militia."[106] Special appointees, from Nathanael Burwash to Daniel Gordon, proudly sat on Militia committees. While often making profane and outrageous statements to clergymen and press, Hughes thus cultivated a relationship with both churchmen and chaplains that was a curious blend of bemusement and loyalty – one of Hughes's greatest assets in 1914.

Hughes also wanted padres to preach the correct blend of Christianity and patriotism, especially at the church parades held semi-annually in city and better-organized rural units. There the whole community watched while the regiments, in their best uniforms, performed solemn ceremonial roles in chapels decorated with stacked arms and banners. It was the militia chaplain's most widely attended sermon of the service year. While the church parade was as much a social as religious or military ceremony (a splendid occasion, one officer recalled, on which to show off one's uniform), press correspondents, admiring relatives, and spectators also closely monitored the sermon.[107] Most often the parade sermon was a rousing call to Christian service. As the chaplain of Toronto's Forty-eighth Highlanders told the men in the 1890s:

You have come to the house of God to join for the first time as a regiment in the worship of God, to seek his blessing and to listen to his word ... I speak to you as one of yourselves, and desiring to be fully identified with you in your work, and to be of such service to you as I may as a minister of Jesus Christ, which, I take it, is the duty of a chaplain of a regiment. What does your coming here today mean? It means that you acknowledge God as your God, and the God of your country. It means that you desire that his blessing may rest upon you as volunteers in whatever duty may be assigned you. It means that you believe that God cares for this land, that he has to do with the defence of Canada, against whatever enemies that may threaten it, and that in serving your country you are doing the will of God.[108]

The same was true in French Canada: at a joint parade of the Sixty-fifth and the Eighty-fourth regiments in 1903, the padre, a former French Army officer (now a Dominican), preached "to members of both regiments a sermon ringing with patriotism, reminding them of their duties both as soldiers of the State and as soldiers of Christ."[109]

In blending the symbols of cross and sword with the principles of duty and service, both English- and French-speaking chaplains affirmed the concept of imperial mission. During the North-West Rebellion, Quebec chaplains reminded their men of the imperilled state of Catholic missions to the Indians. Canadien troops defended French Canada's vocation to spread the Catholic faith in North America.[110] Father Prévost brought this point forcefully home in a Pentecost Day sermon to the Sixty-fifth at Frog Lake after burying the remains of the murdered Oblate missionaries under a memorial cross. He told them that they should be proud of their action, for they carried on the tradition of their ancestors, who raised the cross in each new land they discovered, to show that "barbarity must submit to the faith and the Cross."[111] For English speakers the South African War heightened their Christian imperialism. Guarding the British Empire from "degenerate" Boers or pagan savages was one kind of social service on behalf of Christian civilization, for it furthered the march of the gospel and civilized liberty.[112] So preached the Catholic bishop of London, Ontario, Michael Francis Fallon, to the Seventh Fusiliers. Hughes was so delighted with Fallon's warning to the Empire of the dangers of Germany and Japan that he had copies of the message printed and circulated to other militia officers.[113] To him Fallon had the right ideals, even if he was a Catholic.

But while the padres preached, neither church nor state authorities moved towards greater chaplaincy professionalism. The Methodists were the only denomination to discuss forming a denominational military service board before the war. Members of the Nova Scotia

Conference, where the constant presence of British and Canadian servicemen was felt in Halifax, created their own chaplaincy committee, but elsewhere the denomination showed little official interest.[114] The government too left the chaplains as a disparate band of regimental padres, fixing a per capita rate for "officiating clergymen" or tinkering with individual unit chaplaincies in Militia Council meetings.[115] Denominational outcries against the pro-Anglican bias of Canadian military life in Halifax were, however, occasionally heard, such as the protests over the monopoly of the Halifax garrison chapel by Anglican chaplains (Frederick Borden favoured giving all denominations a turn as garrison chaplains, since Canada had no established church).[116] In 1913 a Halifax protest that the band of the Royal Canadian Regiment escorted only Anglicans, Catholics, and Presbyterians to their respective churches prompted Ottawa to order that all denominations without exception would have the band. On Sunday, 27 April, this led to what is known in regimental lore as "the march of the Lone Baptist." Only three Baptists belonged to the unit, and two were away, but orders were orders. The Baptist was paraded to his church, escorted by an officer, the regimental sergeant-major, two provosts, and the forty-piece band. By the next week the Baptist had seen the commander and changed his denomination.[117] Military religion had evidently made little ecumenical progress since Cartier's day.

ON 28 JULY 1914 Prime Minister R.L. Borden's Muskoka holiday was interrupted by warnings from Ottawa that Great Britain would almost certainly intervene if Germany attacked France. As Borden returned to the capital, Hughes met with the Militia Council, telling reporters he would send twenty thousand men overseas.[118] Canon Frederick Scott, scanning the news bulletins, remarked, "that means that I have to go to the war … I am a chaplain of the 8th Royal Rifles. I must volunteer." On Sunday he telephoned his offer to militia headquarters and broke the news to his "surprised and disconcerted" churchwardens, who had not expected their fifty-three-year-old priest to go chasing after soldier souls in Europe. His only knowledge of war came "from books I had read." Scott also had secret doubts about his nerves. Years later he described these thoughts in terms taught overseas: "I knew that an ordinary officer on running away under fire would get the sympathy of a large number of people, who would say, 'the poor fellow has got shell shock' … But if a chaplain ran away, about six hundred men would say at once, 'we have no more use for religion.'" The worship service he led that night left him "with a queer feeling that some mysterious power was dragging me into a whirlpool, and the ordinary life around me and the things that were so dear to me had already begun to shift away." By 23 August, clad in a borrowed private's uniform, Scott was at Valcartier, where the First Canadian Contingent was being assembled.[119]

George Wells of the Minnedosa Anglican parish also heard the call. Chaplain to the thirty-fourth Fort Garry Horse, he restlessly watched the Twelfth Manitoba Dragoons detachment leave for Valcartier. The next Sunday he could not keep his mind on the service. As a South African War veteran, he told the congregation that he "was speaking from experience when I said I knew the seriousness of war, and that for me there was no choice but to join the regiment immediately." In a few days he had notified his bishop that he was leaving, arranged with his unit commander to take him to Valcartier as padre, and, wearing his camp uniform and a Union Jack wrapped around his neck, boarded the eastbound train.[120] Without hesitation most Canadian Christians supported his decision, as they praised the decisions of all the volunteers. Reporters extensively covered the farewell sermons preached by militia chaplains as they and their detachments set out for Valcartier.[121] An Anglican chaplain told the Winnipeg Canadian Club: "There may have been wars in the history of the British Empire that have not been justified but this is a war into which everyone can go with a clear conscience."[122] The justice of Britain's cause seemed never in doubt: it was "a Holy War." Even the Methodists proclaimed a crusade: "Our war is to destroy war ... Go to the front bravely, as one who hears the call of God."[123] Surprisingly, Monsignor Bruchési issued a similar call, and so did editors of the French and Irish Catholic press.[124]

This time both the churches and the minister of Militia were already lining up chaplains for the troops, although a rumour circulated at Valcartier that Hughes "did not believe in chaplains."[125] Hughes asked Methodist General Secretaries Albert Carman and T.A. Moore to nominate candidates for the first contingent.[126] One of the first volunteers was W.G. Lane, though he admitted that he was nearly seventy years old. If Lane was the oldest Methodist volunteer, Louis Moffit of the Toronto Conference was one of the youngest; a student probationer at Victoria College, he was not yet ordained when he sailed with the contingent.[127] Some Methodists worried that the clergy drain would hinder church extension work, especially in the west, but Frank Bushfield, a South African War veteran, brushed them aside: "I think a year at the outside will finish it and there is a great possibility of getting back before June."[128] While Methodist authorities negotiated with Militia Headquarters, Roman Catholics requested permission to enlist from their bishops. Anglicans too needed their bishop's consent, as well as one-year leaves of absence from their parishes. Even in the patriotic surge of war, however, bishops of missionary dioceses were reluctant to jeopardize home work for a brief military adventure. Anglican Bishop Pinkham of Calgary told his priests that, patriotism or no, he would not let the work in his diocese suffer.[129]

As clergymen with militia connections packed, they wondered in vain when headquarters would call them up. Hughes ignored the militia mobilization plans and attempted to organize the contingent single-handedly. Militia officers seethed with rage, but their anger had to be restrained as Hughes moved from Ottawa to Valcartier, there holding court on horseback and dispensing promotions and demotions at will.[130] Accordingly, few militia chaplains came to Valcartier with their old units and fewer still got into the contingent.[131] William Beattie, a Presbyterian militia chaplain, found that civilian parsons flocked into Valcartier, jostling and competing with each other for the minister's attention.[132] In the end only six of the thirty-three chaplains who sailed had come to Valcartier with their militia units. Of the six, only four went to battalions containing men from their old regiments.[133]

Such random tactics generated considerable friction between rival communions closely monitoring Valcartier. Ontario Anglicans complained that the government had given out only two Anglican chaplaincies and six to clergymen of other denominations – including the Salvation Army – although 75 per cent of the contingent was supposed to be Church of England.[134] This may have precipitated the angry visit to Valcartier from the Anglican bishop of Montreal. Hughes had him ejected from his quarters.[135] T.A. Moore contacted Hughes, demanding to know why no Methodist appointments had been made. His suspicions that Anglicans were getting more than their share seemed justified when Richard Steacy, one of Hughes's Ottawa cronies and an Anglican priest, writing as the senior chaplain of the contingent, blandly informed him that the minister had not made any chaplain appointments yet.[136]

The chaos at Valcartier probably had more to do with the minister's erratic recruiting policy and bad staff work than with religious prejudice. Evidently, the least important information solicited from the thousands of men milling about the camp was their religious denomination. Wells remembered the widespread surprise when it became evident that the number of British immigrants enlisting had indeed forced up the Anglican proportion of the force to around 75 per cent.[137] When, inevitably, the Methodists challenged this figure, it became known that the attestation papers had been drafted in such complete dependence upon British models that the only designation for Methodism was Wesleyan. A glance at the almanac would have told even the most indifferent staff officer that the Wesleyan church had not existed in Canada since 1874.[138] Outraged Methodists claimed that most adherents to Canadian Methodism would rather be attested as Anglicans than Wesleyan. Hughes brushed them off, quietly inquiring of London: "What are the regulations having regard to chaplains STOP Will there be one for each regiment." Trying to be helpful, the minister added: "In Canada use made of them in many other ways such as supervision of sanitary arrangements entertainments kitchens etc. etc."[139]

In the meantime, the silence from headquarters about who would go kept the Valcartier chaplains in a state of confused suspense. Hughes took advantage of this to help weed out the half hearted. Wells recalled the minister's first meeting with the candidates: "He looked us over and then said sharply, 'Do you fellows all expect to go with the First Division?' With one accord we answered, 'Yes sir.' 'Then,' he said, 'some of you are going to be greatly disappointed. Ten of you will go, and not another damn one!'"[140] Perhaps he hoped that some of their congregations would call them back rather than carry on with an empty pulpit throughout the fall. Those who stayed threw themselves into their camp work, trying to forget the rumours about Hughes and his contempt for padres.[141]

During the hectic weeks at Valcartier a number of conflicting conceptions emerged concerning what a chaplain was supposed to be and do. The *Canadian Churchman* shocked some when it stated that his duty would be "to open service with a pot of coffee, to clean rifles while giving benediction." Equally important, to civilians, was his role of preserving souls from the brutalizing effect of war: "The battle-hardened soul needs our prayers more than some of us imagine ... To kill if possible has its undeniable effect on any man. Anything in uniform is fair game. It is hard, it is impossible to repress the exultation which carries off one's feelings as the shots 'go home' ... The hardening effect of destroying those who would destroy you is not to be denied."[142] Most of the Valcartier padres also thought they had a pretty clear idea of what they were about. The militia lore of Dan Gordon and Father O'Leary was revived in contemporary conceptions of the ideal chaplain. Those with Boer War experience believed that the methods used fifteen years before would still be appropriate for the fighting in Europe. In mid-September Senior Chaplain Steacy called for reports from his chaplains, and B. Whitaker, an Anglican chaplain from Manitoba, presented his ideas:

> In the first place I tried to get into personal touch with every man in my Battalion, by taking them in companies ... I had a quiet conversation, pointing

out to them that it was not a chaplain's duty to make 'molly coddles' of them, nor yet to make a company of Psalm singing saints, but that it was a chaplain's work to induce every man to remember always that his first idea must be, that he is a British soldier, and as such must act always and speak always as a gentleman; also that while occasionally words may be used by them in a fit of passion, still in no way would I allow the taking of God's name in vain, nor would I ever listen to blasphemy. I think … many of the men now realize that the bridling of the tongue is a necessary part of a soldier's training … The hospital … is the main point, more especially in the field, where I consider my work lies; as one gets into touch more closely with a sick soldier than with one in perfect health … In South Africa I found that the hospital was about the only place the chaplain could work satisfactorily, first, by assisting the doctor … and also by taking the list of casualties and writing to the parents of those killed or wounded … One thing more … there has been a great deal of coarseness shown by the men [when women visited the camp], this I have tried to counter act, and though perhaps in this particular results are not what they might have been, there certainly has been a marked difference in the men's language.[143]

Other chaplains with less experience but impeccable militia ancestry followed the same routine.[144] As well as the weekly chaplains' meetings, daily visits to the military hospital in the city and the two field hospitals in camp were part of their routine. Some chaplains held early morning communion and evening song services, while others took part in the YMCA meetings. Chaplains ran errands, assisted hard-pressed staff drawing up unit rosters, wired unit recreation funds to England, located missing soldiers for relatives, and helped those with dependents to make financial arrangements. The challenge to the chaplains was to become the individual soldier's "friend and counsellor." Padres pursued their men into tent lines as well as the hospitals, and also on to training fields and rifle ranges.[145] The evening was a favourite time for visits, and chaplains felt an urgency in their work. John Almond (whose South African weaknesses had been forgiven or forgotten) wrote, "I consider Valcartier camp the chaplains' opportunity. The spirit of the camp in the lines is splendid, but, at the same time, there is a grim earnestness suggestive of the seriousness of the mission."[146]

Preaching and private talks became the keynote of Canon Scott's approach. In the evening he began what he called "parish visiting," going around among the tents, sometimes after lights out, talking to the troops about their problems. But to Scott the preacher, the chaplain's supreme moment was the church parade. By September parade and voluntary services had swollen to huge proportions. Scott once preached to an audience he estimated at fifteen thousand men, assisted by a signaller who notified the bands by semaphore which hymn to play. Probably no better than a tenth heard a word he shouted, yet Scott was thrilled by the experience: "Here was Canada quickening into national life and girding on the sword to take her place among the independent nations of the world. It had been my privilege, fifteen years before to preach at the farewell service in Quebec Cathedral to the Canadian contingent ... It seemed to me then that never again would I have such an experience ... Here were fifteen times that number, ... on that occasion I used the second personal pronoun 'you,' now I was privileged to use the first personal pronoun 'we.'"[147]

At last the day came in October when Hughes announced his choices: thirty-three chaplains in all.[148] His neglect of the militia chaplaincy was immediately apparent. Clerics claiming South African War experience, even in the British Army or as combatants, stood a better chance of being chosen than experienced militia chaplains.[149] Famous home missionaries, such as Presbyterian John Pringle (known to the Yukon Field Force and to gold miners as "Pringle of the Yukon"), received appointments.[150] The same criteria, along with Conservative politics, could be applied to the son of "Fighting Dan" Gordon of Batoche. Alexander Gordon reminded his father: "You know it was parentage that got me the appointment, for you recall the Minister's characteristic comment when I mentioned that the Moderator was writing about me. It was – 'Damn the Moderator, I know your father'. That was the form his promise took and that was about all the commission I ever got."[151] Especially erratic was the selection of Richard Steacy as senior chaplain. A forty-five-year-old Ottawa cleric, Steacy had only one claim to militia experience: his membership on the Militia Department's Cadet Committee since 1913. Hughes, blatantly passing over clergymen with more militia seniority, gazetted him a major and made him senior chaplain. Steacy's friend William Emsley was sixty-four years old and seems to have been appointed on the strength of the senior chaplain's personal recommendation as well as the Methodism he shared with Hughes.[152]

In fact the First Contingent chaplaincy reflected all the strengths and weaknesses of the 1914 whirlwind mobilization. Virtually ignoring the militia chaplains and selecting padres on the basis of zeal alone led to the recruitment of unproven and sometimes unsuitable padres: the first Canadian Great War chaplains left an uneven record of spectacular leadership and embarrassing failure. While future leaders of the Chaplain Service came from this original group, five were subsequently discharged quietly from the service as unfit, including the senior chaplain. At least one was on bishop's probation for moral indiscretion.[153] Somehow during one of his whirlwind visits to Valcartier, Hughes found time to give his padres a soldierly talk. C.F. Winter, an aide, recorded Hughes's conception of the chaplaincy:

> He wished them to be the friends and guides of "the boys," but told them too much "soft stuff" was not needed. They were all going on a real man's job, and they must act as men. Long and windy sermons were a mistake, and he hoped they would do everything possible in their own particular sphere to add to the efficacy of the troops ... After a short interval of silence, for the clergymen looked generally as if his address had left them somewhat befogged and puzzled as to what was expected of them, a retiring looking little parson at the end of the line spoke up and said "Do you think, sir, we should carry revolvers?" For a moment the minister looked at the timid little man, and then rapped out in his most scornful accents: "revolvers nothing! Much better take a bottle of castor oil!"

Hughes suggested that the padres make friends of the men and cheer them on their way. It was the only good advice he ever gave them.[154] Arrogant and bombastic, delighting in outraging clergymen, Hughes left his mark on the Chaplain Service as well as on the rest of the Canadian Expeditionary Force over the next two years. Even at his worst, however, most Protestant chaplains and churches hesitated to criticize his excesses because of the way the minister ably played on Protestant prejudices. Hughes outraged French Canadian Catholics, although he seems to have believed that his Huguenot ancestry gave him special insight into Quebec attitudes.[155] Yet he had, after all, enforced prohibition in militia camps, and proclaimed the church, along with the school and the militia, a cornerstone of national morality.[156]

In the meantime, the excitement, the enthusiasm of the volunteers, Hughes's energy and the Valcartier "miracle" covered up the weaknesses of the minister and those of some of his padres. Hughes's faith in the amateur soldier, his scorn for red tape, and his ability to keep all around him engaged in frantic activity intimidated churchmen and politicians alike. Hughes had to be in charge of everything; he made ruthless political appointments and he continually fell back on improvisation, favouritism, and patronage to deal with problems of his own creation.[157] The chaplains discovered that his chosen senior chaplain was not above some of the same methods. Even as the chaplains sailed for England, Hughes had the last word on the composition of their contingent: "Just as the gangway was being raised away from the side of the ship an officer was observed to run up to it and though the end was between two and three feet from the rail he jumped across the intervening space and landed safely on the deck. He was Honorary Lieutenant Leonard Dunne, a Baptist chaplain, who had been ordered at the last moment to report to the Officer Commanding Number One General Hospital by the Minister of Militia and Defence."[158]

2 Beginners: Turmoil in the Service

Arthur Currie was never very patient with inefficiency. Within a week of taking command of the First Division on the Flanders front, he sent an exasperated plea to the director of the Canadian Chaplain Service to send the replacements he needed. Currie could not understand why Steacy took longer to give him the parsons he needed than Headquarters took with a battalion officer.[1] General Alderson, the Corps commander, and Richard Turner, Currie's Second Division counterpart, were also irritated by the dribble of experienced chaplains back from the front because their one-year pulpit leaves had expired and congregations or bishops demanded that they come home. Alderson knew that the morale of his other officers suffered when padres got out of their overseas commitments so easily. He refused their resignations and requests for return to Canada and demanded that Steacy do something about it. There was a war on, after all.[2]

Over the next few months the generals' opinion of Steacy sank even lower. In 1916 Currie and Corps commander Lt-Gen. Sir Julian Byng were confronted by Roman Catholic priests revolting against Steacy and Alfred E. Burke, the eccentric monsignor claiming to be their chief. Currie's estimation of John Almond, the efficient assistant chaplain director at Corps HQ, rose steadily as his opinion of the erratic and quarrelsome Steacy fell. Almond himself had fallen out with the DCS, and Currie knew of his difficulties getting Steacy to understand the needs of front-line padres. So did Richard Turner, now in charge of Canadian Headquarters in London: in early 1917 he quietly began to document Steacy's inadequacies. He asked Almond, "Has Steacy played the game?"[3] Almond's answer was a firm negative. Within weeks Turner and George Perley, the new Overseas Forces minister, replaced Steacy with Almond and set him to work on a major house cleaning of the Chaplain Service. For its own sake, the service muddles had to be stopped.

AFTER THE FLURRY of Valcartier, chaplains and soldiers settled down to the Atlantic crossing, dissenters getting used to the Anglican forms of worship, Roman Catholics on many of the thirty-three ships doing without priests altogether. Protestants usually concluded evening devotions with the national anthem and an evangelistic appeal, for they were getting closer to the battlefield. Chaplains organized recreation events and tried to fraternize with the more or less captive shipboard congregation.[4] The work forced new padres to drop their ingrained sabbatarianism, though a few silently wished that boxing matches would be scheduled for weekdays or envied the priest with no scruples about a little deck shuffleboard on Sunday afternoons. Not all chaplains were able to do this: their censorious attitude indicated real incompatibility with military ministry. For these and other reasons, some of Hughes's impulsive appointments did not make a very good impression.[5]

After three weeks at sea the Canadians reached England, conducted an epic carouse in Plymouth, and settled into more quotidian training on Salisbury Plain. By the end of October life there had become the muddy misery that later became so familiar at the front. Only the foulest weather prevented parade services, however, and in better weather chaplains tried to lighten the dreary days and sodden nights spent under canvas by organizing evening concerts.[6] During the sojourn on the plain, chaplains also encountered tensions between their roles as officers and as priests. Soldiers scorned Sam Hughes's prohibitionism, drinking up the potent brew of the local pubs, until contingent commander General Alderson adopted the British practice of "wet canteens" (where light beer was sold under supervision). Notified by some of the padres, Canadian prohibitionists demanded an explanation. By sticking to his ban on drinking in Canadian camps, Hughes rode out the controversy, but the chaplains found themselves on the horns of a dilemma. Presbyterian and Methodist padres resentfully but obediently muted their criticism when the "wet canteen" policy was settled beyond appeal by military authorities on both sides of the Atlantic. As pastors, most subscribed to the views of the outraged and powerful temperance lobby at home,[7] but as officers they put up with it, and most, including Canon Scott, later admitted that the canteens toned down disorderly conduct.[8]

There were other difficulties. Some padres doubted that they had any influence on the soldiers, thanks to the indifference of many officers to church parades. Chaplains naturally wanted to hold as many as possible, and on Sundays expected them to take precedence over almost every military exigency. Officers, however, sometimes saw the parade service as little more than a handy way to assemble units for lectures on preventing typhus or purifying water, or for inoculations.[9] What brightened the picture for all was the coming Christmas.[10] Chaplains tried to re-create something of the atmosphere and cheer of the season, joining Christmas masses and Eucharists with sports, parties, and banquets. Protestants were granted the use of local churches, but Roman Catholics were not so fortunate and had to be paraded to mass in plain camp huts.[11] As a result, quiet complaints about the lack of Catholic facilities of their own emanated from the contingent. After all, a senior British Jewish chaplain had visited the Jewish troops, and even the Salvation Army, at Hughes's fiat, was promised its own chaplain.[12] And then New Year's festivities were dampened by an outbreak of spinal meningitis. In a hospital rather than on the front line the first chaplain fatality occurred. G.L. Ingles of Toronto, an Anglican, contracted the disease during ward visits and died on New Year's Day. He had been ordained for less than a year. The chaplains laid him to rest as their first official act of the new year.[13]

Soon after, the impending move of the Canadian division to the front stirred up bad blood between Steacy and the War Office. British officers at the brigade and regimental level seemed anything but hospitable to chaplains. Their view that padres were a particularly useless military fixture, with little influence on the men and certainly best kept out of the way, tacitly dominated army policy during the first months of the war. As a result, while sixty British chaplains had gone with the BEF to Flanders in 1914, their organization was still primitive indeed. In infantry divisions an Anglican cleric had been attached to each field ambulance unit, with responsibility for the adjacent brigade's Sunday worship. At the base each general or stationary hospital (as well as each casualty clearing station closer to the front) also rated one Anglican chaplain. A smaller assortment of "other denominations" were scattered through the medical units. A mere five padres were allotted to an infantry division, therefore serving an average congregation of about twenty thousand men. Lord Kitchener was most annoyed when informed that he had been given thirty-three Canadian parsons from Valcartier, and Hughes was advised to use more restraint in future.[14]

The Canadians in England resented such limitations, especially when Steacy's request that they all cross the Channel was simply ignored by the War Office. In January 1915 he grudgingly reduced his request to twenty-five. The War Office bluntly replied that, as only five chaplains were allotted to a British division, the Canadians would have the same. The Canadian chaplains were furious. Steacy sent Canon Scott and a Catholic padre up to the War Office. The British chaplain-general pointed out that the Canadians had defied Kitchener's recommendations. Scott retorted that, since the Canadian government was paying for them, the country could have as many as it wanted at the front. The chaplain-general pointed out that the flock of chaplains already with the contingent had not moderated the wild behaviour of the Canadian troops. Scott countered that they would be even more unruly at the front with only five padres. The chaplain-general agreed to intercede with Kitchener, and on 2 February 1915 the War Office sanctioned eleven chaplaincies for the Canadian division.[15] Because the British subsequently raised their own divisional establishment from five to eleven, the Canadians took credit for increasing divisional chaplaincy complements throughout the army. Actually, the chaplains merely asserted the quasi-independent status Hughes claimed for the whole contingent. In a small show of nationalism, the chaplains, with Hughes's backing, had demonstrated their independence.[16]

On the matter of where they would serve, however, Steacy meekly took the advice of those with experience of the trenches. Six of his eleven chaplains went to field ambulances and hospital units. Only three were left for the infantry brigades, while Steacy took charge of the Headquarters staff as divisional senior chaplain, and John Almond (of South African fame), his assistant director, was posted with the artillery.[17] An Anglican ex-militia chaplain, Major Frederick Piper, was put in charge of the nineteen padres unwillingly left behind at Shorncliffe Camp. Steacy and Piper each had complete autonomy over their commands on the understanding that reinforcements could be transferred to each other's cadre as needed. This resulted in three quick transfers to Steacy's thinly spread force as Anglican, Roman Catholic, and Baptist chaplains (the latter using "strong influence" to get at least one representative to the front) were detached for units in France or Flanders.[18]

As a result, the first clouds of denominational tension appeared, perhaps because some communions seemed to be privileged by Steacy and Piper. Invoking the British tradition permitting padres to communicate directly with their denominational heads, Canadian Methodist Harold Frost immediately complained to S.D. Chown, "I sincerely hope that with the second and third contingents, the Senior Chaplains are not Anglican ... I do want to express to you, as Secretary of General Conference that the unmistakable attitude of the Anglicans is as near that of a state church as they dare to go. They would gladly make us feel that we are here by their courtesy if they could. This would receive a decided check if other contingents had senior chaplains from other branches of the Christian church. You will readily see my point." His was the first of several Methodist alarms sent home.[19] Catholics, too, were frustrated in their last-minute attempt to get more than two priests to go with the division. An appeal to Catholics at the War Office and even Cardinal Bourne of Westminster (senior Catholic ecclesiastic of the British forces) had no effect on the situation, the first of many attempts to overcome serious clergy shortages. Like Frost's, soon a Catholic letter reached the home church, protesting that their priests were not receiving fair treatment from the Anglican heads of the Canadian chaplaincy.[20] With such small murmurs began the dissent that ended in a dramatic show-down in France a year later.

Not much help could be expected from Canada, however, as both bureaucrats and churchmen paid scant heed to chaplain concerns. Ottawa allowed district and camp commanders to recognize civilian clergymen as "camp chaplains," authorized to lead services and visit the men. When Hughes permitted them to wear military uniform and hold honorary commissions, however, each camp soon attracted a flock of chaplains jostling with one another over seniority.[21] As usual, all appointments and questions of seniority were left to the discretion of the minister and the exasperation of the camp commanders. Only in Toronto (Military District 2) was a district command chaplain appointed, G.H. Williams, Methodist minister and district chief recruiting officer, to manage the work of Exhibition and Niagara camps. By the end of the year Williams commanded a dozen full and part-time chaplains (some, especially Anglicans, resenting their subordination to a Methodist).[22] Elsewhere Hughes refused to relinquish any chaplaincy control to the churches. He preferred to work with leading clergymen of each denomination separately, thus ensuring that their political influence with the government remained safely muted.

In the meantime, the religious leaders and editors of English Canada who had proclaimed a holy war in 1914 were joined by dozens more. In 1915 the sinking of the *Lusitania*, the Bryce Report on alleged German atrocities in Belgium and France, and especially the poison gas attack on Canadian troops at Ypres transformed the dominant themes of their sermons and editorials into those of a crusade against the forces of darkness. From Ottawa, W.T. Herridge, militia chaplain and Presbyterian moderator, preached that Christ's "supreme passion at whatever cost is to sweep the earth clean of the evils which defile it ... It will be our fault, then, if we do not make this war a holy war ... A war which has no meaner purpose than the establishment of Christian principles among the nations of the world." John McCaskill, a Presbyterian destined for chaplaincy, quoted Ruskin's famous maxim that war founded, united, and ennobled nations, while peace sapped their moral fibre. This war would make Canada holier and stronger if she entered in with idealism and high resolve.[23] Even churches historically sympathetic to pacifism or non-resistance found, by the war's first Easter, their objections to such crusading weakening. The Baptist press decried war and militarism yet encouraged its readers with the hope of a new social order appearing in a chastened world: "Out of war shall we fight our way to peace; out of hate shall we think our way to love. The heart of man believes it."[24]

Preoccupied with mobilizing the spiritual resources of the nation for total war, churches paid surprisingly little attention to the overseas ministry. The 1915 Presbyterian General Assembly simply passed a fraternal resolution praising its overseas padres and turned all chaplains' matters over to Herridge's office. Anglicans followed suit, sending padres a fraternal greeting from their General Synod meetings in Toronto but leaving their interests entirely up to individual bishops – who seemed mostly concerned with the dangers to their local work resulting from sending too many priests on military service.[25] Eventually the primate designated Bishop J.C. Roper of Ottawa, a former militia chaplain, as Anglican representative to the government. In 1915 his prime function, however, was relaying priestly offers of service to Militia Headquarters. Individual bishops did little battling for padres' rights, though the bishop of New Westminster, Adam De Pencier, volunteered as chaplain to an overseas battalion.[26]

If these denominations were complacent, Roman Catholics were not. Yet as complaints flowed back from overseas, the hierarchy, divided by language and culture, seemed paralysed by war matters. While C.J. Doherty of Montreal, Borden's minister of Justice and the leading Catholic in the Cabinet, had secured the Quebec hierarchy's support, they were unable to give much attention to overseas work because of domestic conflicts over language, education, and conscription.[27] In French Canada nationalist laymen denounced their prelate's endorsement of the war, strengthening the sullen resistance to the recruiting effort among many lower clergy, already alienated by their bishops' refusal to intervene in the Ontario educational-language controversy.[28] The result was an open breach between Henri Bourassa and Archbishop Bruchési in Quebec and angry criticism from the

English-speaking hierarchy, led by Bishop Michael Fallon of London (resented by French Canadians for his support of the Ontario government's position in the schools question), Archbishop Neil McNeil of Toronto, and Archbishop Gauthier of Ottawa (French in name but Irish in attitude).[29] This state of affairs, combined with the lower number of Quebec enlistments before the advent of conscription, led to desultory chaplaincy recruitment there and little active supervision of the work of French Canadian padres.

The English-speaking hierarchy, by contrast, spurred on churchmen to demonstrate their loyalty to Canada as a mature Dominion in the British Empire.[30] Supported by Bishop Morrison of Antigonish, Archbishop Casey of Vancouver, and Bishop Sinnot in the west, Gauthier, McNeil, and Fallon joined with Cardinal Bourne of Westminster in supporting the British cause. McNeil and Fallon assisted volunteers for the chaplaincy, while Fallon, in March 1915, even called for conscription. The Irish Catholic communities in cities such as Montreal and Toronto, far from shunning the war effort, contributed men to the overseas contingents and patriotic gifts of money, and even voted for Union government and conscription in 1917. Gauthier stood behind the most outspoken of his Ottawa priests, John J. O'Gorman, who proclaimed it the sacred duty of Canadian Catholics to enlist.[31] Thus, by war's end, two-thirds of the Canadian Catholic chaplains, including O'Gorman, had come from the English-speaking church.[32]

Leading the English Catholic press was Toronto's *Catholic Register*, the periodical of the Church Extension Society edited by Monsignor Alfred E. Burke. His outrage over the German annexation of Belgium and praise of the French Canadian hierarchy's "patriotic" pastoral letter did nothing to heal the internal breaches in the church but made him a favourite of English-speaking patriots and Tories. At the same time, his editorials decrying the shortage of Catholic priests overseas and his close monitoring of the British chaplaincy situation were making some Canadian government officials uneasy. His publication, in April 1915, of complaints from Wolston Workman, a Franciscan ministering with the First Canadian Division, that Anglican padres were granted unwarranted privileges, and of complaints from wounded Catholics that they were dying without the sacraments, warned Ottawa of the tactics he was capable of using.[33] No one, except perhaps his opponent Archbishop McNeil, however, foresaw his next attempt to claim responsibility for the Catholic chaplaincy. That summer Burke managed to have himself appointed a chaplain by the acting minister of Militia, Senator James Lougheed, and set out for England and France to see things for himself.

The Methodists, too, oscillated between complacency and outrage over the treatment of their chaplains. Fraternal greetings from T.A. Moore, secretary of the Committee on Evangelism and Moral Reform, and S.D. Chown, secretary of the General Conference, to fellow Methodists overseas were accompanied in 1915 by calls for recruits to come forward. These became more urgent when the first religious census of recruits was released by the government. Anglicans were gratified and Methodists appalled to read that Church of England recruits outnumbered Methodists (numerically the largest of the Protestant denominations) by a ratio of approximately six to one.[34] Anglicans soon charged that Methodism was not doing its fair share. Chown and Moore repudiated the government's figures but, behind the scenes, began a hasty count of recruits known to have enlisted from each conference or circuit.[35] Eventually they asked Methodist chaplains to confirm or deny the published figures. It was during this sensitive episode of the war that more alarming reports of denominational skulduggery among the chaplains overseas stung the general secretaries into confronting General Hughes himself.

While the First Division covered itself with glory and home churchmen proclaimed a crusade, the chaplains languishing in England yearned for action. After Ypres many of the Canadian troops at Shorncliffe had been sent to France as reinforcements. Again their chaplains were left behind, and while some were posted to the new hospitals going to the Mediterranean or training units being organized in England, those lingering behind requested that no further appointments be made in Canada until those already in England were situated in France.[36] For the Valcartier originals the Shorncliffe chaplains' pool was a backwater. Even when Piper posted nine to the Canadian Mediterranean Force hospitals, it turned out that the available chaplains were not always of the required denomination. He had to take a Roman Catholic and a Presbyterian from recently arrived Second Division units to complete his MEF roster.[37] He was still short one Roman Catholic when they left. Piper understandably had added his own name to the Mediterranean list; after his departure W.H. Bayley, an Anglican priest from Ottawa, appeared in the Shorncliffe commandant's office claiming that he had been sent by General Hughes to take over. Bayley's first official act was to send an unsatisfactory chaplain home in civilian clothes. He told Carson, "I hope that you will not have any more trouble with the Chaplains Department."[38]

It was a vain hope. Shorncliffe's chaplains were fed up with Steacy's management of the front-line chaplaincy, as Anglican chaplaincies increased while other denominations cooled their heels in England.[39] Steacy's aloof and non-committal attitude at a joint meeting on the subject only increased their suspicion. Continuing rumours about Steacy's pro-Anglican scheming prompted Frost to write both T.A. Moore and General Hughes. To Moore he reported Steacy's transparent ambition to win promotion over Piper, his senior on the Militia list, and permanent appointment as chief chaplain of the Canadians:

> Major Steacy is at present in London and he has been ill advised enough to state his future plans … he is writing General Hughes to be made Chaplain General … or at least obtain an advancement in rank in order that he may have more power … Confidentially I may say that Major Steacy is very much of a political trickster, who through pull has already succeeded in getting position far beyond his due. His name never appeared in the Militia lists until last year. His work over here has been marked by inefficiency and favouritism … I feel very strongly about this whole matter … because of the future of the chaplain's status in the Canadian Army. If there ever is a Chaplain General in our army, he should be a man, who will command the respect of all persons independent of church distinction or other differences. Major Steacy is not the man.[40]

This letter sparked explosions in both Toronto and Ottawa when S.D. Chown confronted Hughes with the letter. J.W. Carson, one of Hughes's operatives in England, received a menacing telegram from Hughes demanding to know why Steacy did not send any Methodists to the front.[41] As Frost explained, Hughes's telegram was a most effective stimulus for Steacy:

> I think my letter to General Hughes, followed as it was by Dr. Chown's has brought about much improvement in the general situation … General MacDougall threatened to send me home for breach of discipline but that didn't amount to anything … I was afraid you might form the impression that I was an overzealous agitator, but you shall be glad to learn that as a result of our conjoined efforts that, today Methodism is being more fairly recognized in this work than ever before … Major Piper has asked for two more Canadian Methodist chaplains. They haven't come. Anglicans turn up everywhere. The Presbyterians and Methodists and other Protestants hold joint parades, can't cover our work otherwise. But we are short of chaplains.[42]

The Army and Navy Board of the Methodist Church, already uneasy about the rights of Methodist soldiers and chaplains, had learned that non-Anglicans had to begin fighting for their rights.[43]

Padre alarums continued. Steacy, undaunted, proposed that the formation of a Canadian Corps made it necessary to meet with Carson and "our friend Sam" to arrange the "re-formation of the Chaplains Department."[44] Steacy met Hughes at Alderson's headquarters in Flanders. On 19 August 1915 the Canadian Chaplain Service was born. Ottawa announced Steacy's appointment as Director Chaplain Service (DCS), with Almond as his assistant director (ADCS) at Corps Headquarters. Steacy became a full colonel, with the services of John MacDonald, a Baptist chaplain, as his staff captain. He would command all Canadian chaplains sent over by Hughes and provide chaplain services to all Canadian troops. Almond would be promoted to lieutenant-colonel and be placed in command of the four divisional senior chaplains. Each senior chaplain, in turn, would command ten or eleven chaplains (with captain's rank), representing (in descending order) the Anglican, non-Anglican Protestant, and Roman Catholic churches.

Knowledgeable officers at the Corps had their doubts about Steacy's capacity for the new post. Already he had alienated most of his divisional padres. Alderson remarked that the divisional chaplains would be happier under Almond's rather than Steacy's supervision. Base chaplains who lobbied for Piper were disappointed; he was in the eastern Mediterranean, unable to contest Steacy's appointment. On 28 August 1915 Canada's first DCS left Canadian Headquarters in Flanders to set up his own office in London.[45] On the surface – but only on the surface – it appeared that the first year of the war had ended successfully for the chaplains. From its beginning as a nondescript clerical grafting on to the expeditionary force the chaplaincy now enjoyed the autonomy and status of a distinct branch of the Canadian Army overseas. Optimists hoped that Steacy's appointment would help to eliminate the inconsistency and awkwardness shown in the chaplaincy and stop the denominational bickering that had begun during its first year of the war. They were wrong. The Chaplain Service had only begun to grapple with the challenges it was encountering in 1915.

THE DIRECTOR OF CHAPLAIN SERVICES began his official duties with a simple mandate, though fulfilling it proved anything but simple. From the outset Steacy ran into personnel problems for which the minister of Militia was largely responsible and that Steacy was unable to solve. It soon became clear to senior officers and overseas chaplains that the DCS was unprepared by his brief army experience to manage the staff he was given. By the end of his first year in office Steacy's methods had created widespread resentment throughout the service and an insurrection among its Roman Catholic members. From the beginning he either did not have enough chaplains or they were of the wrong denominations – or both. His initial staff of fifty-four chaplains (twenty-eight Anglicans, eleven Roman Catholics, nine Presbyterians, four Methodists, and two Baptists) was far too small to serve a contingent already nearing ninety-five thousand men.[46] Steacy needed at least forty-one more padres immediately. From the front came the generals' complaints, while the Shorncliffe staff chafed under Bayley, an unpopular Hughes appointee who had less army experience than they did. Meanwhile, the Salvation Army was furious with the War Office, demanding that its workers receive official recognition as chaplains and employment at the front.

Steacy appeased the generals by arranging for the most valuable Corps chaplains to take a brief Canadian leave, arrange pulpit supply in their old parishes, and then return to duty.[47] Next came the Salvation Army. The War Office refused to recognize Canadian Salvation Army officers as chaplains, defining Salvationism as a sect, not a religious denomination. Hughes had already sent three Salvationists overseas as CEF chaplains. An irate Salvation Army commissioner descended upon Canadian Headquarters. Steacy and Carson shrewdly informed the minister that British officialdom kept them from carrying out his will, and, as expected, the enraged minister took up matters directly with the War Office.[48] The British allowed the Canadians to post one Salvationist to the LeHavre base, but only as a "special officer" for social work.[49] Steacy, backed by Hughes, defiantly employed the officer as a "Non-Conformist chaplain." In retaliation the War Office vowed that Canadians would never have another Salvationist chaplain in France, but Hughes was appeased, and Steacy had strengthened his credibility with the minister. Steacy (who had little love for the Salvation Army) now felt secure enough to keep the other Salvationists in England waiting.[50]

Next Steacy turned to the Shorncliffe senior chaplaincy problem. Bayley's evident contempt for Salvationists, Baptists, and Methodists outraged the padres, who complained to Hughes. He selected another favourite, Charles W. Gordon (a Presbyterian better known as the novelist Ralph Connor), but Bayley refused to step down gracefully. Reassuring Hughes that his will was being done, Steacy turned a deaf ear to Bayley and his allies, posting him abruptly to a field ambulance in France. After a few weeks of such treatment, Bayley returned to Ottawa.[51] By then Gordon had alienated Shorncliffe officers with his impulsive methods, but the situation was saved by his desire to go with his old battalion to Flanders. George Wells (an Anglican Valcartier original) was recalled from hospital duty in France to restore harmony, and the new Canadian camp at Bramshott received a non-Anglican senior chaplain in order to appease Hughes.[52]

In resolving such problems, Steacy clearly indicated the principle he brought to matters of greater administrative import: fulfilling the will of the minister of Militia was paramount. While rector of Westboro Steacy had come to Hughes's attention as a genial fellow Orangeman and Conservative who had the right sort of loyalties to be useful to him. Steacy's chaplains, however, found him a stubborn and stuffy churchman who could not take advice or criticism well. Like many other CEF service heads overseas, including Carson, Steacy knew that his continuation in office depended on keeping on Hughes's good side. Whatever necessities arose, the director was unwilling to bear bad news, much less criticize Hughes's policies. With no political links to the non-Anglican Canadian churches (in fact, because of his Anglicanism and Orange connections, Steacy was virtually identified as an enemy by Methodist or Roman Catholic churchmen), the DCS had no political base from which to negotiate with his military chief. These were serious liabilities in a young and increasingly politicized branch of the CEF, with an inexperienced director trying to appease jealous denominations and bellicose churchmen at the same time.

Steacy soon discovered he had virtually no control over manpower, thanks to Hughes's recruitment and reinforcement methods. Since the winter of 1915 Hughes had authorized the creation of nearly 250 infantry battalions for overseas service. These units supplied their own officers and sailed to England believing that they would join the Canadian Corps as a complete unit. Hughes and Canadian officials, however, created the Second, Third, and Fourth divisions from the first units to get overseas, which were then reinforced by breaking up the remaining battalions as they arrived in England. It was from the chaplains to the latter that Hughes expected Steacy to get his reinforcements. To make sure that the non-Anglican denominations were satisfied, Hughes granted extra chaplaincies to units with large Methodist, Presbyterian, or Baptist elements. The unit commanders instead of the politicians thus bore the brunt of the work and the odium of padre recruitment, selecting the patriotic cleric most popular or representing the largest denomination in the unit.[53]

As overseas battalions arrived with at least one padre (and some with three or four), such a plan might have worked if Hughes's view that all denominations were the same – except for Roman Catholics, of course – had been correct. To the War Office, though, chaplains were anything but interchangeable. British quotas granted two Church of England chaplains for every non-conformist or Roman Catholic. Hughes, and Canadian churchmen, however, knowing that the largest Canadian denominations were, in descending order, Roman Catholic, Methodist, Presbyterian, and Church of England, expected his army to employ more non-conformists and far fewer Anglicans than did the British. Steacy, however, quickly discovered that the Canadian contingent was 47 per cent Church of England, 24 per cent Presbyterian, 12 per cent Roman Catholic, and only 7 per cent Methodist.[54] The British system would work out rather well for the Canadians after all, as long as those on the other side of the Atlantic did not cry foul.

Such was too much to expect. Throughout the fall of 1915 unit commanders complained of Anglican and Roman Catholic chaplain shortages, while, to Steacy's dismay, most chaplains arriving in England were Presbyterian or Methodist.[55] When he requested permission to appoint English temporary Anglican chaplains, Hughes insisted that only Canadians minister to Canadian troops. Besides, the minister demanded, "Why must they be Church of England? Would not chaplains of other denominations do?" Steacy requested an emergency shipment of ten Anglican parsons from Canada. Hughes grumbled, "It strikes me you will soon be able to form a brigade of these gentlemen." Two months later, at the end of January 1916, he hastily appointed nine Church of England chaplains and shipped them overseas in one batch. Well aware of how the other Canadian denominations would react if they learned of this, he ordered the newly minted padres to travel in mufti until they reached England.[56]

Knowing Hughes, Steacy delayed making a similar request for Roman Catholics. Yet their chaplaincy situation had been unsatisfactory throughout 1915, both in England and at the front.[57] After press complaints, the British doubled their allotment to two priests for every thousand Catholics. In practice this increased the divisional ratio of priests from two to three and added several additional priests to training camps. Steacy, however, could barely come up with two for each Canadian division. The situation was even more critical in the Second Division's Fifth Brigade, where Canadian regional, ethnic, and language divisions complicated matters. There the presence of Nova Scotia's Twenty-fifth Battalion (with a high proportion of Cape Breton recruits), as well as the French Canadian Twenty-second Battalion created an unusually high number that gave Constant Doyon, the brigade's French-speaking priest, a combined flock of about eighteen hundred men – in short, the work of a normal division. In vain he pointed out to Steacy that English speakers (as well as Gaelic-speaking Maritime or Glengarry soldiers) shunned French Canadian padres.[58] Making matters worse, the remaining priests in the Second Division were, indeed, French Canadians. Major William Beattie, the Second's senior chaplain, asked Steacy for at least one English-speaking priest for the Fifth Brigade.[59] None, however, was forthcoming from London or Ottawa, even after more soldier complaints appeared in Toronto's *Catholic Register*:

> I must say that it is simply rotten the way the English-speaking Catholics are treated here. We are in danger of losing our lives, yet the officials are indifferent to our appeal for at least a chance to make our Easter duty ... Other creeds have their ministers here with them, who preach to their following at every opportunity. Now what do these think of us Catholic boys who never see a priest at all? I don't know if this letter will pass the censor, but if it does I and all the Catholic boys here on the firing line would like you to ask the question, 'Why are we not supplied with a priest?'[60]

Almond warned Steacy that the Catholic padres were growing increasingly bitter at the unfilled vacancies, and more of Father Doyon's complaints appeared in Canada's English Catholic press.[61] Finally, Corps officers and the British command chaplains stationed an English-speaking priest intended for another post to the Fifth Brigade, but Steacy angrily vetoed any interference in his command by British officials. Rather than provoke a quarrel over the matter of Dominion autonomy, the British command chaplains acquiesced. A chagrined Almond asked the Second Division's other Catholic chaplains to help out Doyon in their spare time. It was the best he could do.

At last, in January 1916 six hastily appointed priests arrived in England. Steacy dispatched an urgent request for five more at the end of the month. Hughes sent him only two, who arrived in May.[62] In spite of his critics Steacy then came up with a solution: he proposed that the Chaplain Service have its own branch at Militia Headquarters in Ottawa. A "chaplain-general" appointed to supervise chaplaincy work in Canada would link chaplains with their denominations and, most importantly, dispatch qualified reinforcements overseas. Carson quashed the plan: he coldly informed the DCS that Hughes did not appreciate getting advice on how to manage affairs in his own territory.[63] Steacy took the hint.

Clearly, Steacy was in an impossible situation: a growing nonconformist surplus, units at the front or training in England going without padres, and Steacy unable to order home his surplus non-Anglicans. Ottawa would not tolerate taking orders from England, nor would the surplus chaplains, after making the pilgrimage to England, consent to being sent back home without seeing the front. While commanders complained, Steacy was reduced to hoping that the next padres reporting to his office would be Anglican or Catholic, shipping towards the front whatever staff he could pry loose from England, and praying that the minister would stop sending so many non-conformists overseas. Steacy eventually initiated a policy by which the CEF would promote from the ranks and transfer to the Chaplain Service qualified clergymen (especially Anglicans) serving in the ranks as combatants or stretcher-bearers.[64]

While Steacy tinkered with his overseas personnel, impatient Roman Catholics grew increasingly resentful of their subordination to Anglicans and non-conformists. While other Protestants were promoted to honorary major and appointed senior chaplains of front-line divisions, not one Roman Catholic received such an appointment, leaving them subordinate to chaplains of other communions. Yet while Steacy pondered the stream of chaplains – usually of the wrong denomination – arriving unannounced from Canada, he vetoed Workman's petition for a Catholic senior chaplain at Corps HQ. With one eye on Ottawa, Steacy argued that there was no British Army regulation or precedent for an independent Catholic senior chaplaincy. Only if that faith predominated in an entire Canadian division would it rate a Catholic senior chaplain.

Because Steacy refused to make any concessions to Catholicism that might anger Hughes, the DCS needed a Roman Catholic ally with enough military and ecclesiastical seniority to cow the rebellious field padres. Thus the arrival in England of Alfred Burke, an ecclesiastic with, apparently, the prestige and credibility to ease Steacy's Catholic burdens, seemed providential. Burke had acquired national stature and some notoriety in Ottawa as a Tory booster of settlement and development ventures, while Pope Pius X, in 1910, confirmed his appointment as head of the Catholic Church Extension Society and editor of the *Catholic Register.* Before the war, however, he had become embroiled in the Ontario French-language schools question, where his public and private statements angered both French- and English-speaking Catholics, including Archbishop Gauthier and Bishop Fallon, as well as his own superior, McNeil.[65] Burke had made some powerful enemies within the church by the time he set out for the war, making him a most unlikely candidate for success at the task Steacy wished him to perform.

Burke proved incapable of bringing peace to the Chaplain Service, becoming instead the storm-centre of Catholic chaplain discontent. From the moment he arrived in England his actions raised doubts about his status and credibility: he demanded a promotion and told the press that Canadian political and church officials had appointed him supervisor of Catholic chaplains.[66] Though Hughes initially refused these demands, Burke travelled to Rome and met with the pope. To the dismay of British and Canadian Catholic officials, he returned from the Vatican vested with sufficient prestige to intimidate military authorities.[67] Canadian Catholics and the apostolic delegate to Canada, Monsignor Stagni, warned chaplains overseas that Burke had no extraordinary authority. Stagni directly ordered him to stop the charade, but he and Steacy ignored him. Steacy found Burke quite handy at disarming angry critics, Hughes, and even the Canadian high commissioner, who was inquiring about the charges of deficiencies at the front. Burke publicly dismissed accusations that the troops were being neglected.[68]

If it was highly unlikely that Catholic chaplains would ever have accepted Burke's leadership, after such statements it became impossible. To them Burke had betrayed every Canadian Catholic overseas.[69] Yet in spite of his periodic rages over the situation, Hughes still refused to discipline or recall Burke (though he refused to pay his growing expense account or sanction his acquisition of a Cuban secretary in a lieutenant's uniform). If the Canadian political situation had been more secure, perhaps Hughes would have curbed Burke's antics, but by mid-1916 so many embarrassing questions were being asked in Ottawa that he could not risk provoking Burke or the many friends he claimed to have. Besides, Burke still had his uses. After another florid press statement prompted demands that the publicity seeking monsignor be disciplined, Carson reassured Steacy that such indiscretion was "one of the things we are apt to wink at."[70]

By then it was getting harder for Canadian denominational leaders to wink at the reports of maladministration coming from their padres overseas. Methodist, Anglican, and Presbyterian officials successively abandoned their complacency and demanded a voice in the chaplaincy decisions previously made for them in Ottawa. In late 1915 Methodists and Presbyterians had formed their own military-service committees, though Hughes continued to brush off their most vehement complaints. Were the Catholic bishops as powerless in these matters, Anglicans pointedly asked?[71] They would have been surprised to know that the answer to their rhetorical question was affirmative. Roman Catholics as yet had not seen the need to organize a coordinated watch on the government. Nor did the hierarchy care to air publicly for the amusement of other denominations the details surrounding Burke's self-appointment. For as long as communions regarded each other as rivals, the minister of Militia continued to divide and rule.

Hughes's power to ignore church inquiries also remained potent as long as Burke and Steacy reassured Canadians that the overseas complaints came from ill-informed malcontents. In March 1916 Bishop Morrison protested to Prime Minister Borden that Steacy and Burke had posted away the Gaelic-speaking priests he had hand-picked for the Nova Scotians of the Twenty-fifth Battalion. Morrison blamed Burke for abandoning the Maritimers to padre Doyon's left-over ministrations and threatened to warn his flocks at home of "what to expect" if they enlisted.[72] This threat to recruiting prompted Cabinet reaction.. Again Perley approached Steacy, who retorted that he was giving Canadian Catholics "just and generous treatment." Steacy assured Morrison that "not a single Catholic soldier has suffered for spiritual supply, and every single one, whether here or in France, who wants the priest can have him." Burke reassured Steacy that the number of Catholics in the Fifth Brigade was not excessive and that its single padre was well able to manage the work, despite the language differences between units.[73] Sneering at Morrison's parochialism, he reassured Prime Minister Borden, "We have done wonders, I think, since I came over here ... in this regard. You know me well enough to believe me when I tell you that I would not tolerate for a moment any neglect ... not a single soldier's soul has suffered for want of spiritual assistance."[74]

After further questions from Liberals in the House of Commons, Hughes used Burke's and Steacy's denials to fend off critics. Clearly, in early 1916, initiating remedial action was still impossible for the Catholic as well as the Protestant churches. Without corroboration of the rumours from overseas, Bishops Morrison and Fallon had no basis for their demands to the government. Equally helpless was the apostolic delegate, a visiting ecclesiastical diplomat who, despite his disgust with Burke, tried to avoid charges of interfering in Canadian politics. Naturally, Hughes protected Steacy and Burke from critics. While there was little love lost between the minister and his chief chaplains, political expediency required solidarity against churchmen and politicians. Workman, Sylvestre, the Canadian hierarchy – none was able to make any headway as long as Steacy, Burke, and Hughes stood by each other.

Nevertheless, during the summer of 1916 Workman and his colleagues unrelentingly campaigned against the DCS and Burke, writing directly to higher military authorities and preparing a direct and deafening blast of the trumpet to wake up the home church. Workman lobbied Carson to have Steacy and Hughes keep a long-dormant promise to appoint a Catholic to the senior chaplaincy of the new Fourth Division. A few weeks later the post went to a Presbyterian. By then Corps priests were on the road to mutiny. Workman contacted the British Army's Catholic principal chaplain in France, A.P. Rawlinson, who challenged through British channels the Canadians' subordination of Catholic chaplains to Protestants. Steacy responded to War Office queries with another lecture on British interference in Canadian affairs. He stated to both British and Canadian authorities that he would never grant concessions that might in Canada be seen as favours to Catholics.[75]

Now the Corps Roman Catholic chaplains took matters into their own hands. John O'Gorman, recently transferred to the Third Brigade, led a padres' revolt. The thirty-year-old Ottawa priest was the most likely chaplain to do so, given his connections with the English-speaking hierarchy at home. A graduate of Bishop Fallon's alma mater, the University of Ottawa, he had undertaken several years' post-graduate study in Paris, Bonn, Munich, and Rome before returning to Ottawa's Blessed Sacrament Church in 1913. Boyish in appearance but with the combativeness of a terrier, his outspoken sympathies with Irish agitation for Dominion status and the cause of English-only separate schools in Ontario attracted the attention of Archbishop Gauthier and Bishop Fallon, who regarded him as an exceptionally promising cleric. O'Gorman called on Burke to act on the front-line shortages: "This is not a favour we ask but a right we demand ... Are you with us or against us?"[76] After looking over Almond's correspondence with the DCS on Catholic grievances, Workman and O'Gorman presented Steacy with an ultimatum: he had until the end of June to provide the Corps priests with their own senior chaplain and the extra padres that were required. O'Gorman warned Steacy that there were other ways for chaplains, when frustrated by military superiors, to obtain redress: "I have, as is my right as a chaplain, kept my ecclesiastical superiors informed on matters concerning the Catholic chaplains ... If, however, you fear that Bishop Fallon has been misinformed by me, I will send him a copy of our entire correspondence, and he will be able to judge for himself."[77]

O'Gorman's point-blank refusal to take any orders from the Protestant senior chaplain of his division forced a hasty conference with senior officers at Corps Headquarters. As a result, Workman was made Corps Catholic senior chaplain: Protestants now had only nominal authority over Catholics. Almond and the British then transferred Workman to Corps Headquarters, but Steacy protested on the grounds of breach of establishment. Only in August 1916, despite Steacy's protests, was Workman confirmed by the British in his new post. By then Almond too had identified himself with the Catholics. He warned Steacy that they openly accused him of rank Orange bigotry and were going over his head directly to Hughes. Steacy rebuked Almond for co-operating with the rebels and brushed aside his warnings.[78] He also vaguely threatened Workman not to try anything as "unmilitary" as a direct appeal to the minister. Workman was outraged:

> I regard it as a very serious thing to be cautioned in this matter, principally because … I am not allowed to forget that the caution falls on my office of Senior Chaplain … Until now I thought that the one fault of my relations with your office was that of over-frankness. As persistently and forcibly as I respectfully could I have brought to your attention every question that was legitimately yours to deal with. The King's Regulations and Orders provide a perfectly discreet and military manner of communicating with the Higher Powers when the subordinate personnel fails and that manner alone is used by me when I deem fit to communicate with the Honourable the Minister of Militia.[79]

There is no evidence that the director heeded such warnings.

Workman and O'Gorman now shifted their appeal to Bishop Morrison, blaming Catholic troubles on Steacy's "ultra-Protestant view." Steacy's careless remark to Workman that "the Roman Catholic Church in Canada had an unenviable reputation for getting from the Government anything that it wanted and that he would not be a partner to our obtaining favours over here" had completely discredited him.[80] Then, on 31 July, the twelve Corps priests delivered to Almond a lengthy and vehement petition. They denied Steacy's claim that Catholic troops had received just and generous treatment and described his attitude towards Catholic affairs at the Corps as "simply scandalous." They repudiated Burke, noting how his misleading statements sabotaged their claims.[81] A copy of the petition was sent directly to General Carson, who naturally demanded an explanation from Steacy. Then word reached England that both the Canadian hierarchy and Prime Minister Borden had received copies of the petition from Workman. While Steacy fumed in London, charging O'Gorman and Workman with insubordination and dishonour, Bishop Morrison demanded a complete investigation of the padres' charges by the prime minister.

Workman had also appealed to Hughes, who curtly ordered him to address his complaints to Steacy, his military superior. It was Hughes's last letter to Workman before the minister of Militia was dismissed by Robert Borden. Three weeks later Workman contacted George Perley, the new Overseas Forces minister. He did not mince words: "What I would especially draw your attention to is the summary and contemptuous answer of Colonel Steacy. Our patience with this man's bigotry and inefficiency is exhausted, and I would welcome an investigation into the record of his dealings with us. As Roman Catholics we do not care who may be our Administrative head so long as he intends to do us justice ... We are ... in duty bound to see that the members of our church belonging to the Expeditionary Force get that fair treatment which was promised them by the Government."[82]

In spite of the tremendous pressure on him Steacy refused to give ground until the battle over chaplaincies reached a climax in November, when Steacy, in an attempt to stop his non-conformist numbers from sky-rocketing, asked Ottawa to cease dispatching chaplains of any denomination. The Canadian hierarchy entered the fray. An outraged Fallon wrote to Edward Kemp, the new minister of Militia and Defence, reminding him that the bishop himself had stopped the Corps chaplains' petition from appearing in the Canadian Catholic press.[83] Providentially for the church, a German shell had delivered the required evidence – in the form of John O'Gorman himself – virtually into the laps of the bishops and Borden's Cabinet. The shrapnel that crippled O'Gorman on the Somme forced a long recuperation leave in Ottawa. Thus was Steacy and Burke's nemesis placed within arm's length of the Borden government – a government that no longer sported Sam Hughes as its Militia minister.

BY THEN, NON-CATHOLICS of the service had also had enough of Steacy's maladministration. Chaplain shortages, especially of Anglicans, continued. Many of Hughes's appointments, thanks to poor health, age, or congregational or compassionate recalls, continued to trickle back to Canada. Through the winter of 1916 and at the onset of the autumn rains a few months later, these chaplains, complaining of bronchitis, arthritis, or other chronic ailments, were barred from further duty by medical officers. Between November 1915 and January 1917 Steacy relieved at least twenty-nine chaplains because of age or failing health. On average, a padre a month was also recalled for home service by bishop or congregation, in spite of Steacy's appeals and War Office disapproval.[84] While some padres refused such peremptory recalls, the loss of so many chaplains (replaced haphazardly by chaplains trickling in with the new overseas battalions) was a vexation.[85]

Canadian commanders and Steacy's own staff were disgusted with the situation. Every one of these premature vacancies had to be filled by detaching a padre from his current unit in England and rushing him into the breach. The vacancies thus created in England could only be filled as battalions from Canada brought padres of the correct denomination. Usually the denominations of those arriving were not the same as the existing vacancies, so Steacy juggled his existing staff, plucking up chaplains from anywhere, shuttling them back and forth across England. He often hustled a newly arrived chaplain right across the channel, over the heads of clerics of other denominations who had been waiting for their turn at the front. Such methods destabilized the relationships between unit commanders and chaplains. When commanders protested or requested a favoured chaplain's return, Steacy often replied with a lecture on the autonomy of the Chaplain Service.[86]

By mid-1916 denominational imbalances had spread to Baptists and Presbyterians. Steacy tried sending a Methodist to the Forty-second Highlanders (fighting with the Third Division), but BEF command chaplains sent him back, reminding him that it was a Presbyterian vacancy he was filling. Steacy grudgingly accepted a Scottish chaplain, though his heated lectures on contemporary Canadian undenominationalism caused considerable bad feeling between the British and Canadian chaplaincy commands. The British were unimpressed by Steacy's claim that Canadian Presbyterians and Methodists were on the verge of organic union.[87] A flock of Presbyterian ministers arrived with the next flight of battalions. Six of them angrily resigned their commissions and returned to Canada when Steacy eventually admitted that there was little chance all would get to the front.[88] Baptist officials were incensed when the Nova Scotia Highland Brigade reached England with seven (instead of the usual four) chaplains, over one thousand Baptists in its ranks, but not one of their ministers. Steacy soon received from Canada four ministers for his two vacancies. Like the Presbyterians, the surplus Baptists had to be persuaded to resign and return to Canada.[89] By the end of 1916 the roller-coaster imbalance had again swung heavily towards an unnecessary surplus, especially at Shorncliffe. Senior Chaplain Wells reported in November that he had thirty-nine chaplains on staff for only thirty-four thousand Canadian troops. By January 1917, however, so many soldiers had moved on to France as new padres arrived that he now commanded forty-three padres for only twenty-four thousand troops.[90] By then the bizarre non-conformist surpluses and continuing Catholic shortages had drawn the criticism of senior Canadian officers.

So had Steacy's methods, or lack thereof, for effectively handling disciplinary issues that came his way. Hughes's penchant for last-minute, politically motivated appointments contributed greatly to Steacy's discipline problems, which were made worse by Steacy's tendency to personal favouritism.[91] This was especially true when the Orange Lodge connections of Hughes's many choices became known.[92] The most spectacular of these incidents occurred in the Mediterranean, at No. 4 Canadian General Hospital. The staff were already disgusted with its drunken Roman Catholic padre, and their opinion of Chaplain Service judgment dropped even lower thanks to the Ulster Presbyterian whom Steacy posted to the unit. His boycott of a funeral conducted by the popular Anglican padre, on the grounds that the deceased was a Presbyterian and by rights belonged to him, completely soured the relationship with hospital officers. Even after getting rid of both offenders, No. 4 General remained convinced that Steacy, was using the Mediterranean as a dumping ground for cast-offs.[93] By the end of 1915 two more Canadian padres from the MEF had been sent home, one for alcoholism, the other for rumoured immorality.

Church leaders too complained that Hughes allowed some unqualified or unsuitable clergymen into the chaplaincy. At least a dozen times denominational heads either apologized to Steacy for the dud Hughes had appointed without their knowledge or demanded that Steacy return chaplains they considered unfit to represent their denomination overseas. Yet Steacy was reluctant to part with any padre, no matter how unpopular with his church.[94] A few disgusted unit commanders also demanded the removal or discipline of padres he had inflicted on their commands.[95] Desperately short-handed, Steacy tended to reply to such communications with much heat and little humour, especially if there was the slightest hope of salvaging a defaulter. Thus, by the end of 1916 other chaplains (several of them Anglican) reported to be drinking to excess had been reassigned to camp duties in England, where they could make a fresh start.[96] Although he was well aware that, even after an official court of inquiry had cleared a chaplain's service record, army gossip inevitably ended such a man's usefulness as a chaplain, the director continued to dally over repatriation orders and to stave off the dismissal as long as possible. As a result, a disgruntled George Wells, senior chaplain at Shorncliffe, soon accumulated under his command half a dozen chaplains with stained reputations. His advice to Steacy was to send them packing, for the honour of the service.[97] The director paid no attention to this recommendation.

Steacy's inability to get along with senior CEF officers became clear when he picked a fight with General David Watson, the first commander of the Fourth Canadian Division, over Watson's choice of Alexander Gordon, a Presbyterian, as his senior chaplain. Steacy insisted that an Anglican deserved the appointment. He warned Carson: "The church in Canada will not take kindly to the usurpation of her rights ... since General Watson has demanded, not requested Gordon's appointment ... the matter becomes one of principle, not of favour." Carson bluntly ordered Steacy to appease Watson: he was supposed to assist, not impede the work of the high command.[98] Steacy also could not get along with the British. The BEF chaplain authorities in France (Deputy Chaplain-General L. Gwynne for Anglicans, Principal Chaplain J. Simms for non-conformists, and Assistant Principal Chaplain A.P. Rawlinson for Roman Catholics) found Steacy's consistent refusal to work through them most annoying. Although Canadian units drew on their own manpower reserve in England, chaplains were transferred from there to the continent or back through the BEF Chaplain Headquarters at St Omer, which was also directly responsible for chaplains to Canadian units operating outside the Corps. As far as the British were concerned, Steacy had no authority to supervise or interfere with the postings of any Canadian chaplain in Flanders or France. Such were to be left up to them or, in Corps matters, settled in concert with Almond.[99] This the DCS consistently denied, constantly quarrelling with Gwynne, Simms, or Rawlinson about who in fact commanded these clerics.[100] The result was a firm impression at Boulogne and St Omer that the Canadian Chaplain Service was poorly managed.

Steacy also quarrelled with Almond, who found too many of the reinforcements sent him from England old, sick, aloof, or otherwise incompetent. To him Steacy was preoccupied with trivialities in England and needed to see the opportunities at the front for himself.[101] Steacy was unresponsive, especially after Almond's comments at Corps HQ about Steacy's incompetence were relayed back to him by a scheming Anglican chaplain.[102] Even more annoying, on the eve of the Somme offensive, was Steacy's lobbying for more padres on establishment in England when the work at the Corps was so understaffed.[103] Convinced that a revival among those facing death in the field was imminent, Almond became progressively more impatient: "The men here have caught hold on religion ... Don't leave me short of the right sort of chaplains, and there will be a work accomplished that will regenerate the world."[104] Almond grew increasingly blunt with his superior, especially after the DCS tried to transfer some of his friends in Almond's command to less taxing posts behind the line without his permission.[105]

Steacy's solution to the deterioration of his authority was to acquire more power. On 3 August 1916 he petitioned Hughes for an increase in the size of the Chaplain Service and promotions for some of its members. Falling back on the tried and true method of having his way with the minister, Steacy portrayed his new scheme as an infallible way for Hughes to increase his stature at home:

> We have the honour and pleasure to transmit for your high sanction, the attached form of Establishment, elaborated ... with a due regard for economy and efficiency, for Canada and overseas ... The dignity, importance, and

> magnitude of the chaplaincy of the Canadian Army demand that its Head should be of a rank equal at least to the Head of the Medical Service, to whom you have given the rank of Major General. The intimate relations always existing between you and the churches of Canada, and the hearty and loyal support which they have ever given to your patriotic efforts in the praiseworthy work of applying an efficient and commensurate Canadian Army, leads us to believe that you will further every effort to make the chaplains of your Army as self-respecting and dignified as the circumstances and times permit ... Such being the case, we feel we can confidently appeal to you, Honourable Sir, to approve it and put it into effect with your accustomed despatch and farsightedness. This action will remove all suspicions that the Chaplain Service is being inferiorated to any other Branch of the Service; and, we are sure, meet with approval of the people of Canada who as a Unit are behind our chaplains and desirous of their just and generous treatment ... The other Dominions, on our initiative are also taking steps in the direction of these proposals and we feel that Canada should lead, not follow ... We can confidently trust in you, Honourable Sir, judging from your past treatment of this Service, to meet our wishes in this matter of adequate Establishment, and dignifying our Department and its Head, pay a just and delicate compliment to the loyal Canadian Churches, as well as bringing increased spiritual comfort to the dear boys in the trenches, fighting the battles of the Empire.[106]

Politics at home made it impossible for Major-General J.W. Carson, Hughes's man in England, to act on the petition. Hughes's administration was beginning to rock on its foundations. So, evidently, was his chaplains' administration.

After the conclusion of the bloody Somme offensive, Almond renewed his pressure on Steacy, for the spring would bring new offensives and greater needs at Corps, but Steacy refused to increase the number of chaplains per division, even though the British Army Council approved.[107] Finally Almond threatened to go personally to British GHQ and call for direct action on the request.[108] The Canadian Adjutant-General's Branch agreed, bluntly advising Steacy, for his own good, to visit the Corps to see the need for himself.[109] As Steacy dithered and delayed, however, Almond agitated for Steacy's removal. When General Turner, now commanding the Canadian contingent overseas, asked for a confidential report on the first DCS, Almond and his Roman Catholic counterparts overseas brought the matter of Steacy's fitness for command to a crisis.

AS STEACY WRESTLED with Chaplain Service problems in London, Methodist, Anglican, and Presbyterian officials successively abandoned their initial complacency about chaplaincy matters. But owing to the continuing rivalry between denominations, little interdenominational co-operation was initiated or even discussed. Consequently, the churches had only separately begun to marshal their forces by the autumn of 1916, when it had become apparent not only that something had gone seriously wrong within the Steacy regime but that only one denomination, the Roman Catholic church, might have the political leverage to do anything about it.

Despite their small contribution in military manpower during the opening months of the war, the Methodists led the way in the shift from complacency to concern. On 23 November 1915 the General Conference had created the Army and Navy Board. The new board took over chaplaincy and other wartime church concerns (including the campaign against the wet canteen and rum ration overseas) from the church's Department of Social Service and Evangelism.[110] On 26 November, Army and Navy Board Chairman Chown and Secretary T.A. Moore presented their demands in Ottawa to Sam Hughes, who promised that all Methodists receiving chaplain appointments would require board endorsement.[111] Back in Toronto the board set about mobilizing their denomination for total war, screening offers of service from ministers eager to go overseas and passing on the top-ranked to General Hughes. Probationers would no longer be considered for chaplaincies: only the church's most experienced and capable clergymen, with the higher education and zeal to influence the cream of Canada's manhood, should receive chaplaincies. Probationers were advised to enlist as stretcher-bearers or combatants.[112]

Chaplains overseas were told to report to the board twice monthly.[113] Soon T.A. Moore received a number of disgruntled reports of Chaplain Service inefficiency, the large numbers of Anglicans getting to the front while Methodists were declared surplus, and the break-up of their battalions.[114] The board, however, seemed more concerned about Anglican sneers at low Methodist enlistments, especially since the number of chaplaincies as well as denominational honour rested upon such statistics.[115] When the government refused to review its statistics on denominational enlistments, the board tried to make its own count, calling on chaplains overseas to do their own census. This effort also proved inconclusive, as many of the chaplains resented such additional demands on their time. A few flatly stated that, in their experience, Methodists had not volunteered in proportion to their size as a Canadian denomination.[116]

The tension between Methodists and Anglicans flared into open recrimination during the summer and fall of 1916. But while the Anglican bishop of Huron, and "Spectator," from his column in the *Canadian Churchman*, suggested that the real recruitment failure in

Canada lay not in Quebec but in Methodism, other leading Anglicans felt a growing suspicion that their own denomination needed to shake off its complacency.[117] The *Churchman* complained that bishops were ignored by military authorities; Headquarters picked its non-conformist chaplains (it was accurately alleged) because of political considerations.[118] In August 1916 "Spectator" and the editor of the *Churchman* called on the bishops to intervene with Militia Headquarters for more Anglican overseas chaplaincies.[119] While Anglicans vainly called for a General Synod military board and a Canadian branch of the service in Canada (under an Anglican chaplain-general), the Army and Navy Board prepared to present such a proposal to Militia Headquarters (except that, naturally, their candidate for the head of such a branch was a Methodist).[120] Ironically, the government was able to ignore such initiatives because the churchmen had not co-ordinated their proposals. Evidently it would take chaplains overseas, not clerics at home, to forge an ecumenical coalition with which to confront the government.[121]

While Anglicans continued their internal debate, the Presbyterians, at the request of their overseas chaplains, had taken more decisive action. During the 1916 General Assembly the church created a Military Service Board and began the same processes as the Methodists.[122] While co-operation with the Anglicans was out of the question at this stage of the war, Methodists and Presbyterians were drawn into joint consultation and protests against Hughes's neglect of chaplaincies in Canadian camps (especially Camp Hughes). But little else was achieved immediately.[123] The churches, despite their immature war organizations' energy and dedication, were not strong enough to earn Hughes's respect for the ecclesiastical point of view. Despite the increasing vehemence of their rhetoric, the minister of Militia enjoyed the freedom to divide and rule. If any further reform of the Chaplain Service overseas or the situation at home was to take place, pressure had to come from a more influential quarter.

In the first weeks of 1917 Catholics opened up a two-front offensive against Steacy and Burke. Workman called on Perley to dismiss the DCS and his self-appointed assistant. P.M.H. Casgrain, a prominent Canadian priest working at the War Office, added his voice. Back in Ottawa, O'Gorman visited C.J. Doherty, who eagerly relayed his memoranda to Perley, Kemp, and the prime minister.[124] Borden and Kemp (advised by O'Gorman and the Ontario hierarchy) directed Perley to recall Steacy and Burke. Though somewhat intimidated by Burke's ecclesiastical rank and threats of powerful friends at home, Perley reluctantly obeyed, especially as Gauthier and Morrison kept up the pressure on the Cabinet.[125] Getting rid of Burke was not easy while he played on Perley's fear of political repercussions and claimed that

Workman, a British-born monk, was unfit to take his place.[126] But Burke proved to have far more enemies than friends back home, from the apostolic delegate to the archbishops of Toronto and Ottawa, and even Senator Lougheed. "Don't let Burke butt in or spend his time between Picadilly and the Strand," O'Gorman reassured Workman; "the Bishops are sick of Burke."[127] Borden, arriving in England, heard Burke's appeal but backed Almond and Turner, who ordered him home. The long Catholic fight was won.[128]

At this juncture the Roman Catholics again found a worthy ally in John Almond and his Protestant senior chaplains. Almond persuaded General Turner to audit Steacy and Burke's administration. As a result he too recommended the dismissal of the DCS and his self-appointed Catholic director. Turner advised appointing replacements who had experience of the front: Almond, Wolstan Workman, William Beattie (Almond's senior Presbyterian lieutenant), and Alfred McGreer (a dependable Anglican padre from the First Division).[129] Perley duly notified Steacy that his services were no longer needed as DCS. He offered a senior position in the reorganized Chaplain Service, but Steacy checked into a British hospital and remained on sick leave. Perley decided that he would be shipped home, though Kemp, back in Ottawa, vetoed a face-saving supervisory chaplaincy in Canada:

> As I understand it you desire to create a position in Canada in order that this officer may be returned – Have no objection to assist you in deposing an officer but am bound to object to Steacy's being appointed to such a position as you suggest – appointments of chaplains in this country have nearly distracted me – this owing to fact that we have so many different sects – if this officer is appointed every sect with which he is not connected will be up in arms and it will result in my opinion in serious political disadvantage to Government – Hope you appreciate my argument.[130]

Kemp's veto sealed Steacy's fate: Almond was given Steacy's post and the mandate to reform the Chaplain Service. He immediately insisted on Workman's transfer back to headquarters and promotion to assistant director for Roman Catholics.[131] A few days later Almond requested seven Roman Catholic priests from Ottawa. By March he had both his requests for Catholic reinforcements and Workman's promotion granted.[132] As Workman unpacked his bags in London, Almond had already begun the extensive house-cleaning that the service had needed for so very long.

3 Officers: The Almond Reforms

On a foul December day John Almond was in an even fouler mood. The bishop of New Westminster, Adam DePencier, a fellow Anglican chaplain, had been recruiting candidates for the Anglican ministry from the soldiers without his knowledge or permission. DePencier had just sent him a haughty note claiming that his higher ecclesiastical rank put him above the control of the director of Chaplain Services, who was only a canon in the Anglican church. It was a mistake: Almond was quite capable of bringing all his authority overseas to bear. Although a bishop ecclesiastically outranked a canon of the church, in the CEF, if that canon was a colonel and the bishop merely a lieutenant-colonel, the colonel always got his way. Almond replied: "I consider that you are the Anglican Bishop of the Army, so far as your Episcopal office is concerned, in the field, but you have no control over our chaplains, and no connection with them officially except through me; and in no way do you represent the Bishops in Canada officially. You are here because I asked for you, and not because the Bishops sent you."[1] Such was the way of the army officer, albeit an Anglican priest. Let other chaplains and ecclesiasts take note.

During his first year in office Almond forged a highly visible, versatile, and disciplined religious agency that earned the confidence and respect of most senior officers. The director also demonstrated remarkable skill at winning the confidence of the churches in Canada, which not only raised the public profile of the chaplaincy at home but also politically strengthened his hand in dealing with the army and other agencies overseas. As victory on the continent drew nigh in the early months of 1918, Almond focused his attention on the future, convinced that his men had earned the right to lead the Canadian Protestant churches in post-war reconstruction. It was this conviction, in fact, that propelled the service into the most prominent controversy of Almond's administration – its rivalry with the YMCA. By the end of 1917, thanks to Almond, Arthur Currie's attitude to the service had changed from impatience to appreciation. In 1919, just before leaving for Canada, he responded to Almond's final reports with a lengthy tribute to the Chaplain Service and a promise to back the padres in any of their post-war endeavours.[2] Almond could feel, with some justification, that the padres had worked out their own salvation. Between 1917 and 1919, despite home church neglect, government manipulation, their own ignorance, inexperience, and some byzantine intrigues, the Chaplain Service had ceased to be a flock of parsons and had become a professional service.

BETWEEN FEBRUARY AND MAY 1917 Almond's attention was centred upon giving the Chaplain Service a thorough house-cleaning. Benefiting from the experience of the hapless Steacy, he straightened out administrative muddles, harmonized denominational discord, and implemented personnel policies that solved many of the problems of that earlier regime. In doing this he was able to count on the government's support, disgusted as it was with the state of the service. It appeared that Almond had the confidence of the Canadian churches as well, judging by the general approval of his appointment voiced in the religious press, especially by fellow Anglicans.[3] In fact, none of the other denominations, even the Roman Catholic, objected to Steacy's replacement by another Anglican.

With Burke out of the way, the new director turned to solving the problems the former had created in England. Settling the Roman Catholic turmoil in the service was facilitated by having Workman take over all Canadian Roman Catholic chaplaincy matters, aided by Francis L. French (another 1914 original) as McGreer's Catholic counterpart at Corps. This reassured Canadian Roman Catholics.[4] Thus, while Almond remained sole head of an interdenominational Canadian Chaplain Service, Catholics were given internally an autonomous parallel administration, placed under the working authority of an assistant director of their own church, and, with John O'Gorman advising Doherty, enjoyed direct access to the Cabinet.[5] During the previous regime the director had remained aloof from his staff, holed up in his Oxford Circus office in London. Almond, however, made regular inspections of his commands. He visited the Corps in the Vimy sector, discussing reinforcement and policy with McGreer, Father French, and the senior chaplains and consulting with senior officers and Lieutenant-General Julian Byng, the Corps commander.[6] Along the way he mended broken fences with British chaplaincy authorities, who were relieved to have done with Steacy and were eager to commence work with as congenial and sensible a head as Almond.[7]

After setting these measures to work, Almond devoted the rest of February and March to visiting Canadian camps and hospitals in England, meeting senior chaplains and conferring with commanding officers in order to unravel tangles left over from the Steacy administration. His constant refrain was that such muddles would not happen again.[8] He dismissed a Methodist chaplain suspended from ministry by his denomination, and vetoed attempts by another Methodist, with Steacy's connivance, to change his denomination to Anglican, and sent him packing.[9] Almond issued a stern warning to his staff: "Chaplains while representing a religious body in Canada have not the privilege of changing their religious affiliation while in the Chaplaincy of the CEF." Under him, principles such as denominational boundaries as well as home church control over chaplain personnel were sacrosanct.[10] Proselytization by Roman Catholics, Anglicans, or other denominations was now forbidden.[11]

Almond then dealt with the cases of several chaplains with bad reputations who had never been disciplined. The notorious alcoholic who had come to England with one of the French Canadian battalions was quietly shipped home.[12] Wells, senior chaplain at Shorncliffe, reminded him of the presence of at least four Anglican chaplains whose reputations had neutralized their effectiveness, though Steacy had given them all second chances. Almond immediately demanded from two either their resignations or transferral to combatant ranks. The remaining pair were treated more leniently, owing to extenuating circumstances.[13] He thus reversed Steacy's face-saving policy of recalling chaplain failures from France and keeping them on in Britain as if nothing untoward had happened. Assistant Director McGreer was ordered to investigate and report upon any chaplain who needed to be returned from the continent.[14]

As he dealt with such loose ends, Almond took stock of the situation in England. By the summer of 1917 over 125,000 Canadians would be training in England, in camps ranging in size from 7,000 to 33,000 troops, spread from Salisbury Plain to Wales.[15] The Overseas Military Forces of Canada had spawned a number of special units and auxiliary services, from the Canadian Forestry Corps to the Canadian Training School at Bexhill-on-Sea: all wanted chaplains. The Forestry Corps, operating lumber camps in the forested regions of France and the

United Kingdom, required at least twenty. Furthermore, the growing number of casualties recuperating in England required more hospital chaplains: by the end of 1917 the twenty-five Canadian hospital units operating in England required almost sixty chaplains alone, while several thousand Canadians scattered across the United Kingdom, undergoing treatment in British hospitals, were yet without Canadian visitors.[16]

Such burgeoning growth could easily employ nearly two hundred clergymen in England alone.[17] In addition, Almond never forgot how the Canadian Corps would play a major role in the British 1917 offensives. His staff at the front would require many more reinforcements. Almond soon made urgent requests to have more chaplains sent from Canada. Besides the perennial Roman Catholic shortage, there still were too few Anglicans.[18] It was time to reorganize the service and set new policies in place. A month after Almond set to work, General Richard Turner promulgated Routine Order No. 822, the new Chaplain Service blueprint. Almond was placed in command of 276 chaplains: 102 Anglicans, 53 Roman Catholics, 58 Presbyterians, 33 Methodists, 14 Baptists, 2 Congregationalists, 1 Russian Orthodox, and 13 reinforcements from various denominations. Four assistant directors, with ranks of lieutenant-colonel, represented Roman Catholic, Anglican, Presbyterian, and Baptist communions.[19] Each division would have 17 chaplains, the Cavalry Brigade 3, as would general hospitals, casualty clearing stations, and stationary hospitals. The base camps at LeHavre and Rouen employed another 7. In England, training camps rated a chaplain for each thousand Protestant troops of a denomination and a priest for every five hundred Roman Catholics. General hospitals were manned by 3, stationary hospitals by 2 chaplains. Special hospitals of more than three hundred beds rated 2 padres, smaller hospitals 1.[20] Almond thus acquired the long-needed establishment to facilitate staff and reinforcement planning.

In the process the director also established a galaxy of loyal and capable subordinates around him. Anglicans occupied the most senior tier, yet each other major denomination was given equal access to Almond through its most senior representatives. Catholics looked to Workman and French, while William Beattie as ADCS, England, represented Presbyterians, with John Howard MacDonald as Almond's adviser on Baptist matters. When Methodists inevitably complained that they had been left out, Almond found a similar position for George Fallis, making him senior chaplain of the new Fifth Division at Witley Camp. Fallis, a young Ontario-born Methodist who had spent his first years in the ministry in British Columbia, had caught Almond's eye as a promising padre in Flanders in 1915. Sharing

Almond's vision of the revival that might come from the war, he became the DCS's most trusted Methodist lieutenant.[21] By this time the number of chaplains at Corps had reached nearly eighty, with almost fifty more under Fallis.[22] At the end of 1917 the British authorized another assistant directorship for the forestry, hospital, and support units on lines of communication in France. Fallis then took over as assistant for England, while Beattie went to the new position in France.[23]

Chaplain Service administration made another key advance in April 1917, when Turner and his staff gave Almond authority to send overage, unfit, worn-out, or inefficient chaplains working in England back to Canada for discharge. Almond immediately called in reports on ineffective chaplains from his senior chaplains.[24] Within a few weeks a steady trickle of spent chaplains were leaving for Canada, opening up vacancies to be filled by younger, healthier, or more efficient clergymen.[25] Staff quality in France and Flanders needed attention. Almond and McGreer rotated burned-out or unfit chaplains from France and the Corps back to England for recuperation or repatriation. This also exposed more chaplains to every sphere of action and varying aspects of overseas service, fitting them for post-war ministry to veterans of every branch of the army.[26] It was also an effective way of relieving the frustration of padres who had served in England since 1915 or 1916 and wanted a tour at the front. The resulting high rate of chaplain replacement, both immediately and after the 1917 offensives, soon ended most complaints from impatient chaplains in England.[27]

Almond also dealt with insubordination (not as prevalent as in the last days of Steacy's tenure) firmly, as ambitious or fractious individuals were threatened with repatriation. Chaplain complaints about his administration were investigated immediately and the critic either vindicated or rebuked.[28] As in Steacy's day, the home front nevertheless complicated manpower and chaplain morale problems as parish and denominational recalls or appeals from anxious next-of-kin still forced Almond to transfer back to England or repatriate at least one of his staff monthly.[29] In an age before the government of Canada was prepared to offer assistance to dependents of overseas officers, Almond found that only the most urgent military need (such as the German spring offensive of 1918) was sufficient grounds to veto or postpone a "compassionate" recall.[30] Bishops and congregations still issued resignation ultimatums to their long-lost padres, forcing Almond to bargain, cajole, or plead with them to keep his best workers.

Unlike Steacy, Almond made few promises he could not keep. Charges of denominational favouritism were forestalled by having the most senior chaplains of each communion deal with their own. In promotion matters Almond adhered firmly to the principles of denominational balance and seniority, which kept peace, in the main, with both his staff and the Canadian denominations.[31] His position of familiarity and trust with the Overseas Forces ministers (both George Perley and later A.E. Kemp), General Turner, and churchmen at home freed him to deal with occasional wire-pulling padres: chaplains who stepped over the bounds of military propriety were firmly, even curtly put in place.[32] On a more positive tack, Almond earned the allegiance of his own staff by backing them when local commanders interfered with or undermined their work. Whether it was fighting the establishment of a wet canteen for officer cadets or challenging rumours of inefficiency started by hostile commanders, the chaplains learned that they could count on their director for support.[33]

Outside the service, commanding officers found the new director much more efficient and obliging than Steacy. When they objected to a particular chaplain's being stationed in their command, Almond, unlike his predecessor, almost never overruled or ignored such requests, even when he privately judged them unjustified or other chaplains defended their colleagues. Such subordination of service prerogatives to local officers and willingness to accede to their wishes did much to mute the open criticism of the service among those used to dealing with Steacy.[34]

The director made little progress, however, in race and minority relations. Knowing the prevalent attitude of officers and men to non-whites, he was relieved when the specially recruited black construction battalion (from western Ontario and the Maritimes) was ordered by Headquarters to keep its African Baptist minister, W.A. White. He knew that white Canadian troops would not have accepted him.[35] Unfortunately, nothing satisfactory could be done for the Métis chaplain, an Anglican missionary who had come to England with his native recruits from the West. Almond tried to have him taken on as an itinerant chaplain to Indian detachments in France but found that Headquarters had banned such "roving commissions." The director was therefore forced to send him back to Canada for discharge after arranging for his employment with a British Columbia mission.[36] While the director was sympathetic to the proposal of appointing a Canadian Jewish chaplain overseas, there were no concentrations of Jewish troops large enough to merit one, according to Ottawa.[37]

Back in London, Almond left the traditionally sensitive matter of Roman Catholic administration to his new Catholic deputy. Workman proved especially gifted at clearing up Burke's legacies, such as posting a Belgian priest to Canada's only French-speaking unit (Quebec's Twenty-second Battalion) when their original padre was recalled to England. Almond's apology and Workman's dispatch of a French Canadian priest did much to improve matters. Similarly, Workman quickly found another Gaelic-speaking Cape Bretonner for outraged Gaelic-speaking Nova Scotians.[38] His dispatch of four recently arrived priests to France appeased critics at the front. His presence facilitated Almond's dealing with Catholic indiscipline, for the DCS could leave such sensitive matters to be dealt with by his able and tough-minded assistant.[39] Workman carefully weeded out any priests too eccentric or outspoken to fit into active military life. Certainly his counterpart at Corps, Father French, shared his viewpoint: "I must say that a man liable to take a glass too much or who cannot get up in the morning, or who is liable to disagree with officers in command must not be sent over here. God knows we have trouble enough without them."[40] Workman also had to deal with the occasional confidence-man trying to wangle an appointment, as Jesuit William Hingston pointed out concerning a certain "Sapper Lloyd": "I know a good deal about Sapper Benedict Lloyd. Late 150th Battalion; late Irish Rangers, late novice Dominican, late novice Society of Jesus ... he is the cheekiest beggar I have ever met, his marks being the religious communities ... The Dominicans were more taken in than we, if that's any satisfaction."[41] Sapper Lloyd remained in the ranks.[42]

In the metropolitan London area Almond created a special branch of the service, employing a dozen padres and with its own senior chaplain. Visiting hospitals and managing a number of social-service activities with YMCA, Red Cross, and, later, Knights of Columbus facilities, the London-area staff achieved high visibility, also meeting leave trains, conducting tours, and even conducting late-night "street patrols" to look out for Canadian revellers in difficulties.[43] So successful was the London work that, in the last year of the war, similar measures were taken by one Canadian chaplain stationed in Glasgow and another in Edinburgh.[44] Another area needing attention was the administrative network in France. After determined lobbying Almond attached chaplains to Forestry Corps, tunnelling companies, and railroad and labour detachments outside the Corps. By the summer of 1917 there were almost as many chaplains with these units as there were at Corps.[45] In December 1917 Almond successfully persuaded military authorities to free his staff from British supervision. The Canadians thus created another Chaplain Service Assistant Directorate, with corresponding Catholic deputy, for line-of-communications chaplains. The Canadian branch of GHQ thus brought all Canadian chaplains at the base camps and hospitals, as well as those with the Cavalry Brigade, clearing stations, and other special units, satisfactorily under Almond's supervision.[46]

The DCS also experimented with another method of augmenting his manpower: Steacy's proposal to draft clergymen serving in the ranks. Many had applied for promotion and transfer to the Chaplain Service: Anglicans and Methodists were serving as Medical Corps stretcher-bearers or orderlies, while some Methodists and Presbyterians had enlisted as combatants. Many had battlefield experience or were recuperating from wounds, and some had received decorations for bravery. Under Steacy only a handful of such applications had been accepted, but Almond, believing that these men would be especially well equipped by their experiences to understand the common soldier, arranged for over fifty to be taken on strength. In fact, until the spring of 1918 this became his favourite way of acquiring reinforcements.[47]

The new service seemed to bear a charmed life, though complaints still occurred. Perhaps the most serious charge made against the service under Almond involved the Canadian general election of 1917. Most chaplains openly expressed their pro-conscription and Union government sympathies when on leave, but Liberal sympathizers complained that the chaplains were also campaigning for the Union government among the overseas troops.[48] During the polling, Liberal scrutineers complained that the chaplains used church parades and voluntary services for electioneering. The most famous case occurred at Witley Camp, when W.T.R. Preston charged that church services in the Fifth Division were characterized by direct chaplain appeals to vote for Union government and for conscription.[49] The adjutant-general sharply inquired about such compromising measures, but Almond and Wells, now Witley senior chaplain, flatly denied the charge.[50] Officially, the army reported to the outraged Liberals that their charges were unfounded. Unofficially, many officers approved of the "heroic work" chaplains in England and France were doing, visiting their units and getting men out to vote, acting as scrutineers, and guiding election officials to convalescent soldiers.[51] Thus testifying to their dedication to winning the war, the service began to earn back the respect of the senior officers.

ALMOND DID MORE than consolidate the overseas service. By implementing a diplomatic campaign, he secured the co-operation and support of the denominational authorities on the home front. He had seen that much of Steacy's ineffectiveness lay in his lack of a strong civilian political base from which to negotiate with army authorities and government officials as well as to counter hostile critics. When he turned to the question of linking the chaplaincy with the home churches, Almond quickly discovered that the Canadian denominations were now anxious to become more directly connected, through the Chaplain Service, with the army overseas. The opportunity would not be wasted. The pains of war had gone deeper into the hearts of Canadians than ever before, jarring the complacency that had lulled churchmen into taking little interest in chaplains' affairs. By the end of 1916 most denominational squabbling was over, replaced by a search for ways to regain contact with and control over the clergymen in uniform as well as to prepare for the return of the troops. At the prompting and with the guidance of the Almond administration, the denominations began to co-ordinate their war work directly with their chaplains as well as with each other.

A sense of moral emergency generated the first concerted actions undertaken by chaplains and churches. In spite of repeated outcries against the wet canteen and the daily rum ration, Canadian denominations individually had not convinced the British government or Canadian army authorities to abandon such military traditions.[52] In the winter of 1917 the spectre of venereal disease and strong drink tempting Canadian troops was raised by confidential chaplain reports that their lectures and sermons against vice were undermined by military policy.[53] The Presbyterian Military Service Board, the Methodist Army and Navy Board, and "Spectator" for the first time took united action, demanding that Britain implement prohibition, redouble military and chaplaincy educational campaigns against sexual immorality, and strictly enforce laws against soliciting in the vicinity of military camps. Churches instructed chaplains to make confidential evaluations of moral problems among the overseas soldiers. The subsequent public outcry in Canada was followed by the bombardment of overseas military and political authorities with letters and petitions. Public denials by officials of the government and military officers seemed to have little soothing effect.[54]

The controversy provoked by the chaplains paid dividends to the Canadian Chaplain Service because Almond realized it was in an excellent position to reassure the churches. One of his first measures was to invite denominational leaders to visit the troops overseas, meet with their chaplains, and tour the Canadian front. Although officer critics initially attacked these "Cook's tours," chaplains argued that direct contact with home leaders empowered the service. The government needed someone to disarm church critics and the chaplains needed churchmen on their side if they hoped to gain stronger army influence. The first visit, by Methodist S.D. Chown in the summer of

1917, was a remarkable success. Chown warmly endorsed the Chaplain Service in his interviews with military officers and, back in Canada, defended the army against criticism from certain quarters. His words of commendation were music to the ears of a politically beleaguered government and a Chaplain Service consolidating its position in the overseas military forces.[55] Eventually, leaders of all the major Canadian denominations were brought overseas under Chaplain Service auspices. Bishop Fallon visited Canadian hospital units raided by German bombers and conducted funerals of nurses who had been killed in the raids. His outspoken testimony made excellent propaganda for the government as well as the Chaplain Service.[56]

At the same time, the director's own monthly reports to Lt-Gen. R.E.W. Turner, Almond's commander, furnished the government with much useful ammunition to defeat alarmists at home. These stressed that chaplains undertook recreation projects for soldiers as well as preaching against immorality.[57] To Almond, however, the greatest benefit such efforts reaped for the service was the political support of his work secured from the Canadian churches. Roman Catholic Bishops Fallon and Gauthier had their low opinion of the service transformed.[58] Almond and Workman also won Fallon's support for a Canadian branch in Ottawa, while Presbyterian Moderator John Neil and Bishop Richardson of Fredericton also enlisted in Almond's camp after their visits. Denominational leaders returned virtually commissioned by the chaplains to support the DCS.[59] Almond also sent the war home to the churches. George Fallis and Clarence Mackinnon were sent to Canada as Chaplain Service apologists, addressing congregations and briefing denominational leaders on the exploits, policies, and needs of their chaplains overseas. The chaplains took collections for service social work overseas and categorically refuted "the alarmist reports of moral decadence of the Canadian soldiery." Equally important, the Fallis and Mackinnon missions rallied more Canadian church leaders to the cause of opening a Chaplain Service branch in Canada.[60]

Such diplomacy paid dividends in 1918. General S.C. Mewburn acceded to the combined Protestant and Roman Catholic initiative, for Workman and O'Gorman too had been lobbying Bishop Fallon. In March 1918 the Cabinet adopted Almond's proposal, and by June, Mewburn had appointed William Beattie, a Presbyterian original who had been Almond's senior assistant director, as the director of the new service in Ottawa.[61] Much of the new agency's organization and procedure was adopted from Almond's administration. While a Protestant was to be director, Catholics would have their own independent counterpart with the rank of lieutenant-colonel. Again, Catholic divisions over the war affected who received that post. John O'Gorman declared English-speaking Catholicism's opposition to a French Canadian chaplain: "A Frenchman will ruin us – the French anti-war, anti-enlist campaign being more than the country can stand."[62] Eventually Adolph L. Sylvestre of Montreal, another 1914 original with bilingual credentials, was agreed upon. His arrival soon after Beattie's appointment, and meetings with the Canadian hierarchy, assured the government of Catholic support.[63]

By the end of June 1918 Beattie was hard at work in Ottawa. Two Protestant ADCs positions were created: Lt-Cols. G.H. Williams, based in Toronto, and Harold McCausland, in Calgary, supervised between them eleven senior chaplains and fifty chaplains in Canadian camps, depots, and hospitals. Beattie's command grew to a peak of sixty-six by demobilization.[64] He also urged the different Protestant denominations to speak with one voice in Ottawa by creating a federated war service council. Such would be essential backing in his negotiations with the government.[65] Fortunately for him, Catholic matters were ably sorted out by Sylvestre and the hierarchy. Previously, Catholic chaplains had been offered by their bishops to Bishop Fallon (if English-speaking) or Archbishop Bruchési (if French-speaking), then appointed by the government. In August, Bishop Emard of Valleyfield became the Canadian "episcopus castrensis," with Sylvestre as his vicar-general for Canada and Workman for chaplains overseas. Emard also took over from Bruchési the work of recruiting French Canadian pastors.[66] To Canadian overseas priests the creation of such a formal organization was a welcome if unfamiliar innovation. Father Ronald MacGillivray wryly recalled, "many of our chaplains if they ever heard of an Episcopus Castrensis thought it was a town in South America."[67]

Unfortunately for the future rapport between local pastors and the Chaplain Service, Beattie's organization now assumed their ministry – and capitation allowances – to Canadian camps and hospitals. Beattie strictly adhered to the policy that only his chaplains should carry out official military ministries. Civilian clerics were incensed at losing their duties and allowances at stations where Beattie located chaplains.[68] Although delicate negotiation and judicious granting of a chaplaincy to especially deserving cases smoothed out most ecclesiastical ruptures, the now unpaid "officiating clergymen" would have their revenge when Beattie was fighting to save the service from complete demobilization in 1920.[69]

Almond's initiative bore fruit in the last months of the war. Previous reinforcement and replacement problems soon disappeared under Beattie's able hands. Owing to strict adherence to the age limit of forty-five, younger and more active men than before served overseas and on troop transports.[70] Whenever a replacement was needed overseas, Beattie despatched one of his command, appointing another waiting clergyman to take his place. In the same way, padres returning from overseas yet unable to take up civilian parishes immediately could count on a more gradual demobilization, including temporary employment. Whenever possible Beattie employed returned veterans as most acceptable to the soldiers in training and in hospitals. Thus, chaplains returning to Canada from overseas were customarily retained in Canadian service ranks for several weeks before final demobilization.[71]

As victory approached, Presbyterians and Anglicans belatedly responded to Beattie's Chaplain Service prodding, resulting in the Presbyterian National Service Commission, specially commissioned to assist its chaplains both in war and in demobilization work, and the General Synod of the Anglican church's War Service Commission, which was to supervise chaplains, post-war veterans, and social-service matters.[72] In time the churchmen even followed Beattie's proposal to create the Federal War Service Commission of the Churches in Canada. Unfortunately, this came too late to do much for the Chaplain Service. The first meeting was not held until 21 November 1918.[73] As the year of Allied victory drew to a close, the Canadian churches completed their progression (shepherded, at each stage, by the Chaplain Service) from complacent enthusiasts to mobilized and co-ordinated agencies. The service might need such co-ordinated political influence in order to survive the period of demobilization. As events unfolded, however, at the critical moment such political and ecclesiastical influence was not forthcoming.

WHILE IN CANADA during the spring of 1918 Almond took stock of his work. Generally his policies had been successful: his branch had earned respect and co-operation from army authorities, based on their improved efficiency. To Almond, popularity with the troops was the result of success with the officers first. Chaplains had to work within the accepted military system of discipline, administration, and command. Consequently, his only disappointment had been with some chaplains taken from the ranks who retained a private's scepticism towards officers. While this made them more sympathetic to the men, it often cost them their brother officers' trust.[74] Whatever critics said, even those among his own staff, to Almond the chaplain was an officer and needed to keep that identity at all costs.

But in the late spring of 1918 Almond was looking beyond the victory offensive. It was time to plan for the crucial work of drawing the returning soldiers back towards the churches that so many had scorned before the war. Only the chaplains who had been overseas, he believed, had the experience and wide contact with the troops that would be necessary for the task, and only they had an intimate understanding of the men's points of view. The civilian clergy, he was convinced, owed the chaplains a great debt, one they might repay by giving returning padres the respect and positions of leadership they deserved in the post-war reconstruction.[75] No other ecclesiastical branch, department, or agency should be allowed to get in the way of the post-war padres' influence. Consequently, he viewed the aggressive YMCA with distrust and, in early 1918, open alarm. While the accusations and recriminations exchanged between the CCS and the Y did neither organization any credit, they reveal the enthusiastic and ambitious conceptions each held of its wartime role and post-war influence. In fixing their eyes on the future, both agencies jostled each other in the present. The resulting feud did Almond little credit and created much bad feeling between church and association after the war.

Since arriving on Salisbury Plain with the First Contingent, the Y had developed an extensive canteen and recreation-hut program, both in English camps and hospitals and with Canadian troops on the continent. In fact, by the last year of the war the Y's operations, which included daily Bible studies and evening evangelistic services conducted by the hut secretary, employed half as many "secretaries" and officers in each division and camp as did the Chaplain Service. YMCA personnel were officially placed on divisional rosters right alongside the chaplains. This was hailed by Y workers as a tribute to the work of an unofficial and interdenominational laymen's organization. For some of the chaplains, however, the Y's persistent expansion of its operation and its penetration into the CEF administration caused no little alarm.[76]

By the end of the Steacy regime, co-operation was turning into competition. The Chaplain Service had developed its own social-service department of canteens and cinemas, which critics charged overlapped with the Y's program. Nevertheless, Almond was loath to relinquish the increasingly popular social-service work. He and many chaplains also resented the Y's bringing evangelists from Canada to conduct independent crusades in the Corps. The Shorncliffe chaplains complained that military regulations made such activities strictly chaplain's work, and boycotted the meetings. Some chaplains complained that the Y seemed bent on becoming an independent, non-denominational church after the war. Almond, through military channels at the Corps, prevented the evangelists from conducting their services at the front. The association naturally resented chaplains' objections to what had been part of its militia tradition for two generations.[77]

Chaplain Service and YMCA talks sorted out few of their differences. While the division of hospital social work was satisfactorily negotiated, the question of YMCA religious work remained unsettled overseas: an uneasy truce was in effect at the time Almond took over as DCS.[78] Chaplains still resented the association's claim to be the most popular religious agency with the troops and envied its establishment of nearly three hundred soldiers as support staff. This situation was not improved by those Canadian churchmen who heaped praise on the association while giving little attention to their own chaplains.[79] Returned chaplains fuelled Almond's suspicions of the association with alarming reports of what enthusiastic YMCA speakers were actually telling audiences in Canada. Thurlow Fraser, a Presbyterian chaplain just back from the war, gave the gist of one such address:

> Here in Canada what the Church and the chaplains are doing is of no account ... The Y.M.C.A. is everything ... W.A. Cameron addressed great gatherings from Halifax to Victoria on "The Religion of the Trenches" and kindred themes. You know how near he got to the trenches. In all this the Y. is built up as the only agency which is working for the uplift of the soldier ... I was told by people ... that Cameron and the other speakers never once mentioned that there were chaplains at the front ... I challenged T.F. Best ... He replied that he did not know that we had canteens there at all; that he had never heard of them. That did not go down easy with any man who had been working the canteens around Bully-Grenay through that bitter weather in January and February ... The church at home knows almost nothing of what its representatives are doing over there, and makes no attempt to make their work known to the public.[80]

New tensions arose in France, where Canon Scott complained late in 1917 about unauthorized YMCA evangelistic services in the First Division.[81] In retaliation the Y denied chaplains the use of their huts for Anglican worship and social-service work. Chaplains complained to Corps Headquarters, which reminded the Y that army regulations gave the chaplains the right to control all religious work in the divisions. The association might bar padres from its facilities, but it had no authority to conduct services without Assistant Director McGreer's permission.[82] The episode created a bad impression at the Corps and settled nothing. Naturally, the Y resented such claims to monopoly.

McGreer, for his part, wanted the Chaplain Service to absorb the association's Corps work entirely.[83] Significantly, senior officers sided with the chaplains.

General Currie met with McGreer and YMCA head C.W. Bishop, ruling that association work had to come under chaplain authority. The Y bowed to Currie's wishes, but Bishop rejected any attempt to merge the two organizations.[84] The situation among Canadian units elsewhere in France also left something to be desired. While CCS-YMCA co-operation at the Canadian base camps remained excellent, elsewhere – in the field hospitals, Forestry Corps, and other auxiliary depots – mutual suspicion reigned and accusations of bad faith broke out. In one Forestry Corps district Chaplain Service films were shown on one side of the camp while Y shows went on the other.[85] Meanwhile, at the Corps, tensions continued during the winter of 1917–18 over association efforts to direct chaplain Edmund Oliver's education work.

In the spring the conflict spread to Canada, where Anglican churchmen attacked the Y's para-church nature for weakening the hold of the churches. Almond reinforced these doubts when he visited Canada in May and, galled by Y advertising at Chaplain Service expense, railed against association attempts to create a "substitute church."[86] He was further enraged by the massive publicity campaign for the association's fund-raising drive for $2.25 million, which put Chaplain Service welfare efforts completely in the shade. Perhaps the most offensive aspect of this campaign, however, was that Charles Gordon, an ex-chaplain speaking as a knowledgeable expert on affairs overseas, credited the Y with coming closer to the men than either churches or chaplains and with doing work the churches had failed to do. Further, Gordon depicted the Y as giving without expecting anything in return, personifying an undogmatic and open-ended charity that had more popular influence over the men than did the best-intentioned chaplains' efforts.[87] Chaplains were treated to the irony of their wives and families donating funds to the YMCA drive, unaware that their own husbands' Social Service Fund, initiated by Fallis the previous fall, needed their support.[88]

Almond felt honour-bound to refute these claims, and in private sessions with the church boards he voiced suspicions that the Y was not using its funds as advertised and suggested that the Canadian people demand a strict accounting before trusting the association with any more of its money. As far as Almond was concerned, the Y was not as interested in social service overseas as it was in empire-building at home for the future.[89] Although the debate led to an accord's being hammered out between Almond and Canadian heads of the association in Ottawa, the Ontario chapter of the Great War Veterans'

Association, with former padre C.E. Jeakins in the chair, officially censured the Y as a money-making parasite feeding off the men overseas.[90] This achieved nation-wide publicity when the *Toronto Star* identified Almond as the instigator of the censure. Almond denied the charge and demanded a retraction, in vain. The editor of the *Catholic Register* called for a government inquiry.[91] Some Montreal clergymen rushed a strong statement on Almond's behalf to a surprised and mystified Prime Minister Borden. Almond's denial to the Adjutant-General satisfied the prime minister, but chaplains who knew him well had their doubts.[92] The bishop of Montreal, generals such as Victor Odlum, even Kemp himself feared that Almond had gone too far.[93]

Now an alarmed Y leader in England, Major J.H. Wallace, appealed for an end to the fight. With his help Almond held a meeting with the association back in England to settle the matter.[94] The arrangement Almond and the Canadian heads had negotiated in Ottawa was accepted overseas. Wherever possible all social work was turned over to camp liaison officers and co-ordinators of joint work. To forestall further criticisms about self-advertisement, future writing paper would have both Chaplain Service and YMCA emblems on the letterhead. Chaplains were still allowed to be connected with social work, though the Y was responsible for equipment and its general supervision. Association workers were told that, while formal religious work was primarily chaplains' work, they were still to bring a religious message to the men they served.[95] Twelve days later the war ended. In the demobilization period, however, co-operation became the keynote of CCS-association relations during their joint "Canadian Citizenship Campaign," intended to prepare the troops for home reconstruction. Both groups were dedicated to bringing their shared concept of "Christian citizenship" to the men, through speakers from Canada and from the Chaplain Service. Even then, however, occasional complaints continued to surface from chaplains who found religious work going on in Y establishments without reference to the padres.[96]

Another joint YMCA and Chaplain Service venture that tested the enthusiasm and patience of both participating agencies was the Khaki University. During the winter of 1917, in the Fifth Canadian Division, the chaplains' practice of holding general lectures at YMCA meetings became, under the leadership of Presbyterian chaplain Clarence Mackinnon (former principal of Pine Hill Divinity College) more formal. By the end of 1917 the soldiers were taking a wide array of courses taught by chaplains in Y facilities.[97] The association invited H.M. Tory, president of the University of Alberta, to survey the prospects and develop a full-blown Y-sponsored educational scheme. Tory encountered Corps officers considering a similar educational program, led by chaplain E.H. Oliver, principal of the Presbyterian Theological College at Saskatoon. Oliver, a thirty-five-year-old graduate of Knox College and Columbia University, warmed to the prospect of starting up an extension school in the army.[98]

Oliver, Tory, and senior Corps officers agreed that Tory would become director of all overseas education, backed by the Canadian universities and the Y, with Mackinnon as deputy in charge of England, assisted by Harry Kent (another Presbyterian chaplain), and with Oliver in charge of France. Both chaplains would be on loan from the Chaplain Service and remain officially on Almond's staff, although responsible to Tory.[99] While Tory went back to Canada to raise funds, develop policy, and link up with Canadian universities, Almond asked General Turner to give the movement official recognition. Turner complied, creating a Military Education Committee consisting of Mackinnon, Gerald Birks, overseas director of the Canadian Y, and General G.C. MacDonald, representing Headquarters. Mackinnon became a full-time educationalist on loan from the Chaplain Service. Before long he had developed a number of other Khaki University classes in the rest of the Canadian camps of England.[100]

By then General Lipsett of the Third Division (with McGreer's and Oliver's help) already had his own scheme under way in France, bringing Oliver up from a base hospital to run an experimental school.[101] Using abandoned mine offices and storage bunkers as classrooms, with his assistant scrounging books and paper from various sources, Oliver canvassed teachers from Corps personnel while Thomas Best, South African War veteran and YMCA supervisor at the Corps, provided association facilities and materials. The result was so successful that Currie sanctioned the creation of the University of Vimy Ridge, with Oliver as officer in charge of technical and vocational education. The Y was assuming financial responsibilities for the Corps experiment and opening its huts for Oliver's hand-picked staff of chaplains and officers.[102] Oliver so impressed Currie that he appointed him Corps education officer. All Y educational work at the Corps was placed under the University of Vimy Ridge.[103]

Before long, however, tensions between Oliver, Tory, and the Y became apparent. Oliver insisted that his operation be neither as elitist nor as academic as many (including Tory) preferred. Oliver wanted his work primarily to equip soldiers for the practical problems of returning to civil life and the moral and spiritual challenges they would encounter when they returned to Canada.[104] Soon he was at loggerheads with Best and the association. The Y repeatedly informed him that the project was under Tory's – and the Y's – authority. When

Oliver ignored such directives, the Y withheld supplies and facilities. Oliver defiantly carried on without further Y "interference." Like Almond, he was determined that the Chaplain Service and the army, not the Y, would receive the credit for its educational work in France. McGreer, naturally, backed Oliver in the successive stormy interviews with Y officials.[105]

Eventually the Khaki University was formally established by order-in-council as the Educational Services Department of the Overseas Military Forces of Canada. This did not, however, end internecine conflict and misunderstandings. Almond had to remind Tory that Oliver and Mackinnon were still part of his command, only loaned to Educational Services.[106] Mackinnon, after a dispute with Tory, withdrew from the work in England and became Oliver's assistant in France, thus making the continental operation a more exclusively Chaplain Service enterprise. He was incensed when Tory announced the formation of a theological college in England without consulting the Chaplain Service or giving it a leading part in such a project.[107] As the education work wound down in the spring of 1919, Mackinnon complained that Tory's official account of the project did not give the Chaplain Service its share of credit. Oliver found himself in the awkward position of peacemaker between Mackinnon, Almond, and Tory, in General Turner's office.[108]

The turbulent story of Chaplain Service–YMCA relations can best be understood as the result of too much foresight. Both churchmen and Y representatives fought over their spheres of influence and the credit for educational work, not because they were merely glory-seeking but because they were intensely, even desperately concerned about the post-war nation and their influence upon it and in it. Public credit for wartime service and devotion, they believed, would encourage public respect and greater moral and spiritual influence upon veterans and their kin in the post-war nation. Both had similar, even overlapping moral national visions of the post-war world. Both refused, in the furious present, to risk their future influence by being left behind in the scramble to serve the troops and, in their gratitude, forge another link between religious faith and national morality.[109]

Ironically, the post-war years ultimately brought disillusionment to YMCA officials. As war fervour faded and donations dwindled, bitter veterans, former chaplains, and angry churchmen accused the Y of exploiting the soldier and hoarding or misappropriating wartime donations. They charged that its staff had been elitist, enjoying officers' privileges instead of identifying with the lowly private.[110] Some of the sharpest attacks were made by Anglican ex-chaplains, recalling wartime fears that the association intended to set itself up as a distinct sect in order to compete with the churches.[111] Bewildered Y officials blamed the Catholic hierarchy and the Knights of Columbus, the Salvation Army, and the Chaplain Service for spawning and spreading the rumours.[112] Thanks to the squabbling over religious prerogatives and recreational facilities overseas, the war had poisoned relations between the association and the churches for years to come, and serious damage had been done to the prestige of the association. Its bright dreams of playing a leading role in nurturing a generation of Christian citizens gradually faded.[113]

Unlike the feuding between the Protestant padres and the Y, relations between Catholic chaplains and their own welfare organization, the Knights of Columbus, were never a problem to Workman. By the end of 1916 Catholic chaplains, Canadian priests, and laymen had wanted a Catholic counterpart to the Y overseas. Workman's posting to London provided a knowledgeable priest to supervise directly from Chaplain Service Headquarters. After meeting with the apostolic delegate and the Ontario hierarchy, John O'Gorman approached the relatively small provincial chapters of the Knights of Columbus to shoulder the burden. The Canadian Knights saw in this an excellent opportunity to increase their public visibility and silence critics decrying lack of Catholic support for the war effort. As with the other denominations, the English-speaking church was anxious to be remembered after the war as a body that had done its share.[114] They soon raised over $80,000 dedicated to the construction of Catholic army huts in English camps, under direct chaplain supervision.

Through the summer of 1917, in the Canadian Catholic press, Workman and O'Gorman pleaded for funds to counter the potential threat of the YMCA and assist the chaplains.[115] The Knights sent their contributions directly to Workman and the chaplains, which, although adding to their work, effectively prevented any competition with the Chaplain Service and gave Catholic chaplains the control over welfare work that their Protestant counterparts had wanted.[116] O'Gorman, as secretary to the Knights' Catholic Army Huts Association, returned to chaplain's duty in England at the end of the year, allowing Workman to concentrate on military matters. The Chaplain Service provided him with an office at Headquarters. By that time a Knights of Columbus national war committee had been organized at home and an executive of chaplains created.[117] Through the winter of 1918 chapel huts were built in army camps and tents, recreation and religious goods sent to units in France, while a Canadian chaplain opened an office at the Catholic Club in Westminster Cathedral.[118] By April the London area boasted a full-sized Canadian Knights of Columbus club for soldiers on leave, with a resident chaplain able to patrol the streets countering "immoral" street influences. Padres repeatedly attributed higher communion turnouts to having their own chapel huts or tents.[119] Joint Protestant-Catholic services or lectures, however, were banned.[120] Thus, Chaplain Service social work as well as educational work, officially at least, proceeded on two clearly distinct if parallel denominational lines.

AFTER A HECTIC SUMMER and autumn the Armistice came, and demobilization work began in earnest. Almond was kept doubly busy returning members of his own command to their parishes while maintaining the morale-sustaining work of his department in France, Belgium, and England. Spare chaplains in France were rushed back to English embarkation camps as quickly as possible to help keep rowdy troops in order. Home church authorities were urged not to press for immediate return of too many chaplains.[121] Almond operated under considerable pressure from chaplains of those denominations, especially the Methodists, who were installed in parishes during the early summer meetings of their local conferences. The Canadian base in France, under General Embury, depended heavily on Fallis's line-of-communication chaplains – in Embury's words, "keeping those heroes happy."[122] John O'Gorman's work through the Catholic Army Huts Association also drew favourable attention, especially for his lavish free-distribution policy at the CAH canteen in the Le Havre embarkation camp, where Fathers John Knox and J.R. O'Gorman ably supported him.[123]

Perhaps the most challenging and, unexpectedly, exciting work done by chaplains involved toning down the unruliness of troops in England awaiting their return to Canada. Camps such as Kinmel Park, Ripon, and discharge depots at Buxton and Kirkdale swelled with boisterous troops, and chaplains hastily rushed in to keep them well behaved.[124] As early as January 1919 worried chaplains uneasily reported widespread unruliness in the camps.[125] Sailing delays and cancellations played havoc with their work and the tempers of the men. Then came the riots. In a series of violent confrontations, camp facilities were wrecked and shots fired, especially at Kinmel Park, where five men died and twenty-five more were wounded. What some chaplains and senior officers dreaded had come to pass: the mix of old sweats, conscripts, misfits, and barracks-lawyers had undermined discipline and dishonoured the Canadian forces overseas.

Whether or not the service played a significant role in restraining the violence or restoring order is difficult to tell. The chaplains' reports are replete with anecdotes and illustrations of chaplain influence tempering the actions of individuals and defusing tense situations. They were also relieved to note that the wrecking mobs left their recreational huts and chapels intact.[126] Also, a number of chaplains were cited by the camp commanders for their good work during the disturbances.[127]

By the end of April 1919, however, the bulk of Canadians left in Britain were speedily being shipped home, with chaplains on board each transport.[128] For the Chaplain Service the worst was over. Almond was able to detach chaplains for classes at British universities as they took advantage of the same education plans that once they had administered to the men under the Khaki University. Chaplains wishing to demobilize immediately in the United Kingdom were invited to apply to the DCS.[129] At the discharge depot in Buxton and at Kirkdale's No. 5 Canadian General Hospital, disabled Canadians, with their dependents, were interviewed by chaplains before departure. Until the end of May the Chaplain Service ran a hostel for dependents at Buxton and educational classes for hospitalized soldiers.[130] Only in early May 1919 did London Area social-service work close down, leaving a solitary chaplain manning the Beaver Hut in London. The Canadian embarkation camp at Le Havre held its final worship service in mid-May before shipping its last padres to England. By then Almond himself had departed for Montreal, leaving a deputy to clear up the last details and ship the record files back to Canada. His war was over.

4 Pilgrims: The Padre's Progress

Honourary Captain and the Reverend Edmund Oliver, Presbyterian chaplain to No. 3 Canadian General Hospital (then stationed at Boulogne), was bringing a routine day of work to an end with a brief service in the YMCA hut. Moments later, he encountered a ministry situation that had definitely not been included in his pastoral training at Knox College:

> As I was in the Evening Service ... an orderly burst in who flew up the aisle to me and whispered that Archibald, one of the Seriously Ill patients ... was dying in the Operating Theatre and the Colonel wanted me to come at once. I left the service at once and flew to the Operating Room ... He was a nice little chap that I had learned to love. I had been visiting him and praying with him for three or four weeks and I knew he was all right that way. "Jock," I said, "What is it, boy?" "Captain," he muttered, I'm fading awa', I'll no be there when you come in the mornin'." What could I do? I never felt so helpless in my life. Everybody had stood back to let me get to him. I just took one hand in mine, and placed my other on his brow and leaned down close to him and half comforted him half prayed with him, told him it would be all right, he was a brave boy – I think I grew a year older in a few minutes, but I helped to save the boy. His pulse grew better and he became quiet. Mrs. Nicholson placed him under ether, then I withdrew outside the door where I could hear the saw sawing off his leg. I saw him last night and this morning.[1]

Like Oliver in the operating room at No. 3 Hospital, few Canadian chaplains had any pre-war preparation for such emergencies. While some had been called to train wrecks, mine explosions, or accident scenes as part of their emergency parish duties, most had not tended men dying by the dozen in military wards or casualty clearing stations under shellfire. Some had been to the pre-war two-week militia camps, but few had endured months of dreary and drafty life in English army camps. Most had some summer student missionary experience with the hardy roughnecks and lonely women of the North and west, but few had spent years alone with some of the coarsest and frankly godless men who inhabited the industrial and frontier sectors of pre-war life.

Surprisingly, few of the men who put on King's uniform and left parish and pulpit for the Great War quailed at the prospect of their pilgrimage, or turned back readily from the road to the front. Drawing on whatever previous experience, training, and wisdom they brought with them, the padres felt and sometimes fumbled their way ahead. As they worked their passage from camp to clearing station, they also found their doubts and fears swallowed up in the unending needs of the men and in admiration of what they interpreted as the quiet heroism evidenced by so many of their flock. By inclination and training men of emotion, not analysis, the padres drawing closer to the front depended as much on their emotional bonds with their men as on prior training. Many drove themselves harder and criticized their charges less. Some idealized the soldier. Some began to see them not so much as charges or unruly sheep but as heroes and comrades, as fellow pilgrims setting out to touch the face of battle.

FROM THE MOMENT he heard the call to war the prospective chaplain encountered unfamiliar challenges and faced difficult decisions. He had to weigh the attraction of the chaplaincy against conflicting allegiances to his family and parish or religious superior. Most wives, reluctantly or otherwise, went along with their mate's decision. Ecclesiastical superiors, especially bishops straining to meet the demands of their dioceses, were often less accommodating. Even fellow parsons occasionally voiced quiet doubts about the propriety of Christian pastors going to war.[2] For most chaplains-to-be the Christian concept of vocation cut through the tangle of conflicting loyalties. Though few put it as simply as H.J. Latimer when he offered his services to the Methodist Army and Navy Board, many would have echoed his declaration: "I want to be a good soldier of Jesus. I want to be of service wherever he invites me."[3]

As clergymen, they were pledged to serve God and his Kingdom. As their relatives, neighbours, and especially parishioners flocked to the colours, they felt their calling extend to include military service in the nation's greatest enterprise. Family tradition as well as imperial nationalism and religious idealism also impelled some to offer their services.[4] If unable to receive appointment because their denomination happened to be overrepresented in the chaplaincy (as, by 1916, Methodist and Baptist ministers often discovered), many enlisted as soldiers or officers in combatant ranks and the medical corps. Such ministers chose to answer God's call by inspiring the men from alongside, without the privileges and, to some, limitations of military rank.[5]

The next step of the padre's progress consisted of securing a local unit commander's nomination and Ministry of Militia appointment. This usually led to some jostling among patriotic local clergymen until the denominational complexion of the unit, as well as the commanding officer's or minister of Militia's preferences, became known. Often, the clergyman who most assisted with recruiting was rewarded with a chaplaincy by the commanding officer, especially if his denomination formed the largest proportion of the unit. On appointment he was given the rank of honorary captain. This was both an asset and a liability; it gave him a definite place in army organization, with valuable rights and privileges, but it also placed the barrier of rank between him and the lowly privates. Army rank also placed the padre under military discipline, subjecting him to possible interference from above. Whether he liked it or not he was under the immediate control of military authorities: he was part of the military machine. While a few had qualms about their rank, most realized that they would have more status and independence (and consequently more freedom, they hoped, to get things done) as officers than as enlisted men or unranked parsons. Along with appointment came the task of assisting further in recruiting if the battalion were not up to strength.[6] Consequently, during the first two years of the war, when the majority of chaplains were appointed, most padres left Canada not only familiar with their own men but also personally responsible, at least in part, for their being in uniform.[7] Relatives often begged the departing padre to take care of the moral and spiritual well-being of their kin, a responsibility that later weighed heavily on many chaplain consciences.[8]

After appointment and the completion of recruiting, the green padre soon learned that preaching was the least time-consuming of his duties. He had to befriend the soldier in every way, from giving advice on how to deal with wives and sweethearts to appearing as a defence witness in military court. The notorious vices of the soldier, wine, women, and gambling, he and camp welfare workers tried to deal with by running recreational "stunts." This was vital work, even in the nominally dry Canadian camps, as local hotels and houses of ill repute (except in the most isolated camps) quickly sprang up in their vicinities.[9] Within a few weeks of donning khaki most chaplains realized that their task was too great and their duties too ill defined for one man. Although many officers envied the padre for apparently having so much time on his hands, the chaplain who filled his week with social and educational work soon found such ministries absorbing all his energy, time, and pay.[10]

To some chaplains the outdoor life of the army, free of mundane parish routine and the pettiness of civilian life, was a welcome time of masculine good fellowship and untrammelled opportunities to extend the influence and appeal of the church.[11] To others, the first weeks in the army quickly revealed how ignorant they were of military procedures, regulation drill, and army lore. Most regretted that the government did not provide some sort of chaplain's training. Many a padre, even those with previous experience in the militia, took a long time to live down his initial reputation as a well-intentioned bumbler.[12] Roman Catholic priests were outraged by inexperienced or inconsiderate Protestant officers who forced members of their flocks to attend church parades conducted by non–Roman Catholics.[13] Brigade services, involving up to five thousand troops at a time, made a strong visual impression and pleased the officers but defeated even the most leather-lunged preacher's efforts to make a spiritual point.[14] So did the lack of a sense of humour among commanding officers: W.A. Griesbach accosted the Forty-ninth Battalion's padre, W.A. Ball, after one evangelistic appeal during which he had pointed out that everyone, even the colonel, was a "miserable sinner." "Look here, Ball, you cut out this business of me being a miserable sinner. In the first place it isn't true. In the second place it is bad for discipline."[15] In bad weather, visiting the many sick led to some helpful interviews, but some soldiers did not recover from their illness or training injuries, leaving the padre with the as yet unfamiliar duty of notifying and consoling next of kin.[16] Nevertheless, as the weeks passed, most padres testified to feeling more and more that they belonged in the work.[17]

Whatever headaches his many small enterprises entailed, by the time he left Canada the average padre felt that he had a good knowledge of his flock and, given the pre-war masculine attitude towards religion, enjoyed a surprisingly close relationship with them. According to many chaplains, their men fell into three or four groups, each with its characteristic attitude towards padres and towards religion in general. First came the men most idealistic and sympathetic to religion. Many officers and initially many recruits were sons of the manse or of professionals and other community leaders. Also, many students and seminarians could be found in the ranks, especially those of the medical, artillery, and university-associated units, who shared similar upbringing, education, and social attitudes with the chaplain. Even those whose education and upbringing had led to agnosticism or religious scepticism usually shared a common moral world-view with the padre. This small group provided the chaplain with the most sympathetic component of his flock. Their presence and visibility, however, could also give the unwary padre a distorted impression of the typical soldier's idealism.[18]

Most chaplains realized that by far the majority of the flock consisted of men who in peacetime had strayed from the church or whose attachment to religion was nominal at best.[19] Rural battalions, however, had a large proportion of young men accustomed to paternal authority, and these soldiers tended to pose fewer disciplinary troubles for officers or moral failures for padres than the footloose, independent, and irreverent types from the factory, railyard, and waterfront.[20] As well, many units had a strong leavening of lumberjacks, trappers, miners, or cowpunchers, whose outlook on conventional religion and morality tested the patience of many a padre. Most units also contained much smaller numbers of sectarians, later dubbed fundamentalists, whose strong views and narrow perspective often made them the padre's most strident critics.[21]

If the men had not learned much of the padre's attitude towards the cause and their place in it from recruiting addresses or interviews, they soon learned more at divine service. While at Camp Hughes, Edmund Oliver preached to the Western Universities Battalion on the similarities between Marathon, the present war, and the revolutionary message of Jesus. Just as Greece had faced the "Asiatic menace" of Persia, so now Britain and her Dominions stood between Germany and Western civilization. Canada, Oliver proclaimed, was playing a crucial role in the latter-day Marathon. He also linked the world struggle with the message of the Atonement. Victory over evil was inevitable but could only be obtained arduously. Jesus, in fact, based redemption on conflict and sacrifice: "His supreme message was a Cross. Salvation comes through Calvary, life through death, redemption through sacrifice, civilization through fire." In this apocalyptic war Canada had to learn a new idealism, tried by fire. Personal morality and patriotic idealism were inseparably linked: "Prometheus stole fire from heaven. The Master flung fire upon earth. Today we are fighting for civilization, we are fighting for the Christ. He fights best who keeps clean."[22]

Most of Oliver's illustrations would have carried little weight in other, less well-educated units, but to even the lowliest rural or toughest city battalion, the padre preached the same mixture of personal consecration, moral purity, duty, and self-sacrifice.[23] Whether with simple biblical imagery or melodramatic anecdotes, the chaplains continually drew these motifs together in their preaching, whether in camp, garrison, or troopship. If the common soldier had never heard of Marathon, he had heard of Gideon and the Midianites or, at least, of David and Goliath: Congregationalist Harold Horsey, preaching to Ottawa's Thirty-eight Battalion (then on garrison duty in Bermuda), linked the young David's battle for freedom with their own crusade. The war, to him, "was a world wide movement for democracy." He characterized the British cause as "spiritual at heart and calling for the best men have to give ... The British were, by God's Grace, the leaders of modern democracy." The padre, "citing St. Paul and the Christian propaganda; Cromwell and the ideal of a free Commonwealth ... appealed for every man's personal contribution to the spirit of the Regiment, emphasizing the necessity for discipline as the dominating factor of success."[24]

As departure overseas approached, the chaplain and his flock also confronted the permanent separation from kin and entry into a harsher school of discipline. Letters to wives, parents, and children reassured them of the correctness of their decision to enlist, the righteousness of the cause, and the hope that victory would make future wars unnecessary.[25] The battalion, battery, or hospital unit would then entrain for the port of departure. Chaplains often had their first serious disillusionment with the men during the train ride, as the troops piled out of their carriages at each stop to procure whatever local alcohol was available. Benedict Murdoch, a New Brunswick priest, watched with mixed emotions his men stagger aboard the train after a brief stopover: "I felt terribly disenheartened, and I wondered if the people thought that the men had been drinking so during the summer ... The other thought was that I was grateful to God for having chosen me to minister to them. For surely they needed a priest." The following Sunday he persuaded over two hundred of his men to take a temperance pledge (excluding, however, the rum issue, "which under these circumstances could be considered medicine").[26]

At last the battalion, medical unit, or battery boarded ship for England. Depending upon the weather and the ship, the passage lasted from ten to twenty days. Most chaplains realized that this period presented a unique opportunity for them. Some soldiers proved more amenable to serious discussions; others were more willing to drop by his cabin when their bunkmates and friends were not looking. Protestant chaplains seized every opportunity to hold evening evangelistic meetings, while Roman Catholic padres celebrated mass daily, hearing confessions in their cabins each evening. Bible classes and lectures usually made up part of the daytime work. Visiting the sick bay, passing out recreation supplies, sometimes running magic lantern or film shows occupied all the chaplain's spare time.[27] On ship the chaplains soon discovered that gambling and surreptitious drinking persisted as serious problems. Consequently, they became more apprehensive as they considered the temptations of England, especially the controversial presence of the wet canteen.[28]

LANDFALL IN ENGLAND usually brought a brief period of leave, an interview with the director, and the first of several rude shocks. The padre generally left his inaugural interview with the DCS silently chagrined and disappointed. Either he had learned that the unit he had poured his energy into for several months was to be broken up, or (under Steacy) he had been told that there were already too many chaplains of his denomination in England and he might be repatriated.[29] At this turn of events some chaplains felt their idealism and enthusiasm fade into disappointment and bitterness. A few days later these men had resigned and were boarding ship for Canada. For the remainder, a few weeks of suspense and temporary service at one of the large camps would be followed by reposting to a new unit and unfamiliar troops, to wait their turn for a vacancy in France. Most of the new arrivals seemed, at least to observers, to take this in stride, but inwardly they fumed at service administration and mourned being cut off from the men they knew and had counted on accompanying to the front.[30] Consequently, most chaplains who came to England prior to 1917 bore a strong sense of grievance directed at the government or, more often, at Steacy, whom they accused of inefficiency and bad faith.[31]

Camp, base, and depot ministries, whether in England or in France, presented chaplains with some of their greatest challenges as well as disappointments. For many, settling into a new unit after being severed from their home battalion initially meant several weeks of loneliness. In the mess, fellow officers might be aloof and commanders preoccupied or brusque. The men in the ranks too were more distant and wary, if not contemptuous of parsons and churches in general. The transience of army life continually undermined the chaplain's attempts to win acceptance or moral influence. Before he got to know his men very well, they were posted elsewhere in England or sent as reinforcements to the base camps in France. There, if anything, the transiency rate was even greater, as drafts were kept at LeHavre or Rouen for only a few days before moving on. Oliver found his camp service with very discouraging: "The 19th Reserve Battalion is a kind of funnel through which drafts are passed ... It is hard to keep up much enthusiasm for a funnel. For the very essence of a funnel is to have the heart taken out of it."[32]

In their camp work chaplains often noted that the attitude of some of the men had changed for the worse. Faced with weeks of drills, marches, and lectures, medical inspections, bad food, and continual rain, the average soldier lost much of his initial enthusiasm for army life. Here, if not earlier in his pilgrimage, a chaplain learned that soldiers reserved the term "Padre" only for individuals who had earned their respect. In more common use (out of the chaplain's hearing) was the contemptuous epithet "— Parson." In the training and base camps too gathered the army types who, in many a chaplain's view, undermined his moral and religious influence: the professional slackers or incompetents, burned-out officers, brutal NCOs, and barracks-room lawyers determined never to see the front. As a result, chaplains had to combat more petty spite, mindless regulation, bureaucratic manipulation, and bitterness in camp and base work than in most other postings.[33] Before long many chaplains were warning relatives and church leaders back home that the initial press reports of revival breaking out among the men in khaki had been greatly exaggerated.[34]

In England most discovered that the moral climate of the camps was anything but encouraging. Already separated from home and friends by several thousand miles and many months, the men missed the companionship of "decent women" (as the padres put it) and often resorted to the "most unsavoury relationships" with those who lived on the boundaries of each camp. The endemic gambling and the presence of wet canteens in the camps also presented particularly alarming and persistent challenges.[35] Camp life placed the chaplain in one of the army's most drab and monotonous environments, facing men deprived of the exhilaration or fear of action with some of the weakest weapons in his arsenal. The most entertaining concert party, uplifting lecturer, competitive whist tournament, or enthusiastic service seemed to make little impression on men who seemed far more interested in beer-drinking and gambling.[36] The toleration of wet canteens in the camps, in spite of repeated complaints by chaplains to local military authorities, added to the depressing lack of official support in the padre's battle against intemperance.[37]

The prevalence of public houses and hotels in the vicinity of most camps also led to frequent requests from the Bramshott and Shorncliffe camp chaplains to their commanders (and even British politicians) to post such premises out of bounds to Canadian troops.[38] Neither military nor civil authorities, however, proved sympathetic to such appeals. Camp authorities – when they were not offended by the implied criticism of the discipline of their commands – wisely emphasized the impracticalities of enforcement and threw the challenge back to the padres. General Ashton told Shorncliffe's senior chaplain, George Wells, "I am afraid it is a grave indictment of your own Services, and an acknowledgement of your inability to cope with your duties, that your Resolution should appeal for disciplinary measures. I have always felt that the duty of a Chaplain does not begin and end on Sunday, but that he should obtain such an influence in his Unit, that the officers and other ranks with whom he is associated will lend him every assistance to control the very conditions under discussion."[39] Senior chaplains parried with the impossibility of achieving such a hold on men when training and reserve units had such high transiency rates and officers so little sympathy for the unit chaplain. After all, few indeed were still in contact with the men they knew best – those of their original units.[40]

Such exchanges usually brought out another common chaplain grievance – the low military priority of parade service. Wells complained: "We find, for example, that even the orders for Divine Service on Sundays are not carried out according to regulations. Seldom do the Officers attend and Inspections, Pay Parades, Range Practice or any similar duty very often unnecessarily interferes with Church Parade. In fact any order may at any time take precedence over that for the Church. My point in this is, that if those in authority do not pay heed to orders from Headquarters we can hardly expect them to pay much attention to the requests of a Chaplain."[41] In fact, the church parade's effectiveness remained a bone of contention between chaplains and many commanders, besides stirring up general resentment among the troops. This became evident in resentful soldiers' muttering and grumbling: on Salisbury Plain, a chaplain distributing Bibles supposedly asked what he should do with his last Bible; a wary sergeant-major immediately growled, "The man who tells the chaplain what he can do with that book gets field punishment." E.G. Black recalled a similar moment when his battery had just arrived in England. An unpopular padre "delivered a very sincere homily in which he exhorted us all to be good boys, very good boys indeed, because, as he said, 'In six months every man within sound of my voice will be either killed or wounded.' He paused for effect and we gaped at him in astonishment. Then someone at the back, in a stage whisper that could have been heard one hundred yards away, said, 'Holy … *jumping* … Jesus!'"[42]

If there was any event in army life where chaplains, soldiers, and officers were at cross-purposes, it was the parade service. Both in camp and at the Corps, compulsory church parades generated deep resentment on the part of the soldiers. As may be seen from the following comments by a theological student in the ranks, the best sermon in the world could hardly dent the shell of resentment such practices created in even the most religious soldier:

There is certainly more discipline than divinity about a Church Parade. The men have to turn out shaved and spotless – with gleaming buttons, polished boots, belts and badges. All this means work. They then have to fall in a good half-hour or three-quarters before the service begins, to be inspected – first by their platoon commanders, then by their company commanders, and lastly by the commanding officer or his adjutant. As a rule this is not got through without a good deal of cursing on the part of the sergeants and more than one "ticking off" by one or other of the officers. This is the prelude to "Divine Service." When all these disciplinary measures have been carried out, the men are marched to church, where they are, more often than not, preached "at," or talked to in a way that would be an insult to the intelligence of an Eskimo. These are a few of the reasons for the soldier's dislike of Church Parade. The soldier's religion! AH, THAT IS A DIFFERENT MATTER ENTIRELY: A MATTER WITH WHICH HIS ATTITUDE TOWARDS CHURCH PARADE HAS NOTHING WHATEVER TO DO.[43]

Commanding officers, while required by army regulations to be sympathetic to the padres' point of view, often saw church parades as a convenient occasion for COs to address the entire unit. Depending upon its previous performance and disciplinary state, these post-sermon addresses might run from commendations to threats and abuse. Many a padre felt the good of his sermon was undone by such performances. Chaplains, for their part, depended on the parade in order to address the entire unit, including its irreligious elements. Soldiers who would never have given the chaplain a hearing voluntarily, it was hoped, might gain some benefit from the compulsory service. Chaplains were rarely willing to admit that, under such circumstances, any hope of gaining a fair hearing presumed extraordinary divine intervention. Even after camp and Corps experience, many chaplains still insisted that the men did not resent the compulsion of the church parades, only the spit and polish that accompanied it.[44]

While aware of the padre's concerns, not every commanding officer shared his point of view. Thus, the parade issue often became the cause of a chaplain's falling out with his unit CO (a not infrequent aspect of camp or depot service). Getting along with the CO was the chaplain's greatest concern, as church services and recreational events fell under his authority. Without a CO's sympathy and co-operation the best-intentioned and most talented chaplain was circumscribed in his influence and limited to holding voluntary services and keeping out of the way. "It is wise not to insist too much upon one's rights as a chaplain. On the other hand one cannot afford to have his work not treated with the same respect as another officer, and I insist upon it as far as I am concerned," Edmund Oliver confided to his wife. Usually, the more experience a chaplain had with army regulations and usages, the more success he had in securing the CO's help. While the local senior chaplain could be summoned up to overrule recalcitrant unit commanders in camps such as Shorncliffe or Bramshott, in the far-flung Forestry Corps or line-of-communications depots the padre had to rely on his own diplomatic skill or force of personality to assert Chaplain Service rights.[45]

More than one CO was convinced that chaplains were indeed religious busybodies and that parade services were resented by the men. Such commanders felt that the most good a padre could do was to run the games room and canteen. "Colonel Sharman, the commandant ... summoned us to vent his views on chaplains and their work. I am pretty sure that well at the back of his head he has a rooted notion that chaplains are meant to be amusement purveyors or soup experts or cigarette distributors. He was given to understand in no minced words, that a priest's first consideration and sole obligation was care of souls," seethed H.S. Laws after meeting one CO.[46] Others were convinced that only voluntary services should trouble the soldier's one day of rest, or that any interested men should be sent off to attend village churches on their own.[47] In such circumstances the wise chaplain fought the impulse to insist upon his rights and offered instead to submit reports to his senior chaplain through the CO's office, as well as promising not to let religious services interfere with unit training or (in the case of Forestry and Labour units) productivity.

In spite of such tactics, many commanders had little time or sympathy for Chaplain Service rights and prerogatives. In such cases it did not always help matters for the frustrated chaplain to turn King's Regulations on hostile or apathetic authorities. The experienced chaplain avoided thus putting commanders and adjutants on the defensive, but occasionally one new to a unit or whose patience was exhausted provoked a confrontation. Then he might find regulations turned against him by exasperated and wily officers fed up with parsons tilting at windmills. Whenever possible such collisions were fended off by the cool-headedness and quick thinking of the senior chaplain. If such mediation failed, the chaplain was often effectively ruled out of order or humiliated by officers better versed in army law and military procedure. When the Roman Catholic chaplain of Sandling Camp demanded a court of inquiry after an incoming draft were quarantined (and their church parade cancelled), then sent to the wet canteen, camp officers arranged for the hearing to put the padre firmly in his place. The medical officer testified that measles was spread by crowds assembled in a confined space, such as the church hut, while there was no medical evidence that the disease was spread by inanimate objects, such as cups or bottles. Furthermore, beer, not hard liquor, was served in wet canteens. Witnesses testified that drunkenness was never in evidence there. The scrupulous court found the chaplain's charges unfounded and decided that proper procedure had, in fact, been followed. The result almost always was the defeat of the padre and humiliation of the Chaplain Service, forcing Beattie, Workman, or Almond to transfer the incumbent chaplain to another posting.[48]

While parade services sometimes led to serious problems, the chaplain found in recreation work his greatest satisfactions. Because of the drab environment and bleak nature of army life, recreation huts, with their pianos, civilian female staff (which made the men mind their language and their manners), good food, and games drew flocks of soldiers not employed in duties or training. The huts also became strategic locations for a padre to ply his trade. In these establishments religious and recreational enterprises mingled, usually with the chaplains running Bible studies and conducting voluntary services each evening and on Sunday nights. Each night as much as one-tenth of a camp's total population might remain for voluntary devotional services, which became for senior chaplains an indicator of the amount of true religion in the ranks.[49] Later in the war these huts became classrooms for education work, especially the Khaki University, with chaplains acting as teachers. To many chaplains the huts thus became oases for satisfying personal work and cheerful conversation with groups of men who otherwise seemed distant and aloof.[50]

Although greatly facilitating the padre's work, the hut routine had its challenges and could easily be wrecked by the insensitive way some chaplains worked. Many soldiers resented the practice adopted in some huts of offering concerts or variety shows in the evenings with prayer or evangelistic services tacked on to the end, before the men could make their escape. The sight of hymn books and the padre speeding to the stage could then provoke either a virtual stampede or sullen silence. Nevertheless, because chaplains cited occasions when men applauded or praised these "good-night" exercises, such obvious baiting, in spite of the objections of soldiers and some chaplains, continued throughout the war. Wiser chaplains, including those with experience of France, believed that the concerts often backfired, arguing that to soldiers, cakes and prayers went together better than concerts and prayers.[51] Chaplains also encountered at the counter or tables of the huts an erstwhile ally whom most eventually regarded as a nuisance – the sectarian fanatic (usually a private), whose critique of the padre's lukewarm preaching and liberal views were at times amusing but sometimes exasperating.

In England even the best hut program was not sufficient to divert the soldier from temptation. Most of the Canadian camps were near London, the fabled city of amusements and vice. Even padres in France and Flanders were concerned about the moral perils and temptations to their men while on London leave. While chaplains and the majority of better-paid Canadian soldiers sought out famous churches or historical landmarks, many had other destinations.[52] Between the lines of most camp sermons or lectures lay chaplain anxiety concerning the temptations of London leave. Later in the war, when David Warner took over the London-area branch of the Chaplain Service, this problem and that of the many Canadians in hospitals scattered across the city were addressed. In the meantime, some chaplains organized excursion parties to London in order to keep a fatherly eye on the soldiers.[53] Usually two Salvation Army chaplains and a Roman Catholic priest spent their evenings on "street patrol," steering lost or intoxicated soldiers back to their billets, helping out those who had been robbed or had otherwise run into trouble, and sometimes breaking up fights among Canadian and other Dominion troops. Occasionally they interceded with the London police on a soldier's behalf. Most importantly to Almond and the senior chaplain, they were a deterrent to young soldiers open to the solicitations of London prostitutes. Almond turned a deaf ear to critics who resented such "interference," pointing to incidents where soldiers welcomed and thanked chaplains on street patrol for their assistance. The loud approbation of Canadian church leaders also stifled military and government criticism of such zealotry.[54]

Nevertheless, the problem of sexual immorality and the rising incidence of venereal diseases in the CEF, in both England and France, led the chaplains into sharp and prolonged conflict with Canadian army authorities and individual medical officers. By the end of 1916 the latter were convinced that sermons and educational lectures had proved ineffective in combating the spread of these afflictions. As a result Canadian medical officers generally supported the distribution of prophylactic packets of contraceptive devices and antiseptics, with advice on their correct use, at the conclusion of morality lectures to the troops. "Post-exposure prophylaxis," already deemed more effective than moralizing by the British Army Medical Corps, quickly became routine in the Canadian camps and in London, in the so-called blue-light depots. When padres objected both to the lectures and to the medical officers' proposal to use educational films that "advised the troops to commit immorality as long as they cleanse themselves after," the medical officers flatly told them that they took orders from the Medical, not the Chaplain Service.[55] The Roman Catholic chaplains unanimously opposed the prophylactic campaign: Workman condemned such tactics as "incentives to vice ... Not for one moment would the fathers and mothers of our men tolerate it." He also praised the United States Navy's ban on condom distribution. Almond relayed their opposition to General Turner, demanding that more effort be put into traditional persuasion tactics and that stiffer penalties be enforced for contracting the disease. Workman and his Roman Catholic colleagues also asked Cardinal Bourne and the British hierarchy to intercede with British politicians, but with little effect on Canadian practice.[56] To medical officers, it was disappointing and frustrating to have padres quashing some of their most realistic projects to fight disease.

Fighting VD was among the camp padre's most inglorious chores. In many other related tasks, not always as satisfying as hospital or as glamorous as combat work, camp padres were busy men. They filled days with everything from visiting the sick to running errands for those in quarantine or military prison. It was in visiting the latter that most encountered their first "conscientious objectors" undergoing punishment for their refusal to obey orders. At this stage of their pilgrimage few chaplains had much patience for the objectors' pacifist views, for often they were based on radical religious or apolitical beliefs that padres regarded as socially irresponsible.[57] Appearing at orderly-room disciplinary hearings provided an opportunity for the chaplain to defend a soldier unjustly accused or to counsel moderation when a heavy-handed officer meted out sentence. Occasionally, at the base in France, padres investigated complaints that military prison guards were subjecting prisoners to brutality.[58]

A few played a prominent role in the unit by assisting in training or running foreign-language and literacy courses. The danger of such employment lay in its potential to preoccupy the chaplain and use up time better allotted to visiting or being visited in his rooms by soldiers with spiritual concerns. Setting up reading-rooms, planning concerts or games nights, and lecturing drafts on the perils of venereal disease and drunkenness easily became cold-blooded, routinized activities, sometimes requiring so much attention to procedure that the padre had little time to talk to the men individually. But camp chaplains usually found that most men did not want to talk unless some personal need drove them to seek out the padre.[59] Sometimes it seemed that only illness or family problems brought the soldier to seek advice or offer appreciation to the chaplain, so it became natural for beginners to believe that their best work was done in hospital visiting.[60]

Forestry and railway detachments had other frustrations. Military forestry imposed the same hard labour, isolation, and moral pitfalls in France and England as in Canada. Railway troop work near the front offered more excitement but also the stress of working exposed to heavy shelling. Many soldiers became dissatisfied with performing dangerous but non-combatant hard labour without the glamour of service with the famous Corps units. Lumber and railway men tried to carry on their spending and drinking habits acquired in the peace-time trades but encountered the heavy hand of military discipline. Ghastly accidents at sawmill, cutting, or construction sites seemed even more pointless than if they had occurred in action. Chaplains commonly complained that work in such units was something of a dead end, a diversion from the pilgrimage to the trenches, and a pasture for the aging, incompetent, or timid. Therefore, most padres disdained forestry and railway work and desperately tried to get into the Corps chaplaincy.

Wherever the posting, Sunday was anything but a day of rest. In order to give every unit the opportunity of worship, every chaplain had to hold several services each Sunday morning and occasionally in the afternoon. This made Sundays a hectic race from headquarters to headquarters as padres realized that nothing would sour both the commanding officer's and the soldier's attitude to parades sooner than to keep them waiting.[61] Parades were compulsory but participation in communion was not; thus some padres and senior chaplains gauged the level of religious interest by counting how many officers and men actually took communion. For Anglicans and non-conformists the number was not always encouraging, as frequently fewer than a tenth of their men took part.[62] Even Roman Catholic chaplains contrasted the fine turn-outs for devotional exercises (such as the dedication of a brigade's entire Roman Catholic component to the Sacred Heart) with the unwillingness of individuals to come to confession and assist at mass.[63]

The chaplain's preaching underwent some minor adjustments at the base but generally maintained the blend of personal and national crusading that required the soldier's individual commitment to both Christ and the war effort. National themes dominated on special occasions but did not disappear even when the more prosaic routine of calling for personal purity and good discipline was placed front and centre.[64] In routine sermons given at the training camps, chaplains encouraged the military and Christian virtues: duty, honour, purity, loyalty, and the Cause.[65] In the Bramshott soldiers' canteen David Christie, a Presbyterian, preached messages virtually identical with those of George Fallis, a Methodist who had preached there three years previously. References to the Empire and Canada led to recalling the prayers and hopes of loved ones, which led to appeals to the troops to be true to "their honoured Lord by purity and soberness ... by consecration to the man Christ Jesus."[66]

In time most of the soldiers were posted to the Corps or lines of communication in France. Their departure, especially if for the front, was always an occasion of mixed emotions on the part of the chaplain. On such occasions Edward Burwash, son of the Fenian raids hero, preached "of sacrifice for freedom and justice, and we commended them to the care and companionship of that 'greater man' who gave his life that others might be free."[67] Communion services seemed especially meaningful, as were the farewell addresses given by officers and chaplains. Perhaps the greatest challenge of the occasion was the prayer and benediction pronounced by the chaplain over the men about to go to the front. Finally, he would accompany his men to the railway station, cheerily wishing the men well or soberly reminding some that they would certainly need their religion where they were going.[68]

While few chaplains regretted leaving camp ministry, fewer wrote off the experience as disillusioning. In spite of its many disappointments, such work had its compensating rewards. Most reported that evangelistic work conducted in the huts continued to harvest a steady trickle of conversions or recommitments to Christianity.[69] In the camps, too, chaplains had maintained contact with a type of soldier common in the Great War who offered encouragement and assistance: the ministers, deacons, probationers, and seminarians in the ranks. These could be relied upon to devote their spare time to holding religious discussions, assisting at the recreation huts, and managing some of the many and diverse unofficial chaplain's duties when they were absent. Camp transiency was not always the rule (especially in camps such as Witley, where the Fifth Division was quartered for several months), and consequently some chaplains came to know their men exceptionally well. Because of its high religious interest, Witley camp was considered by Almond, Fallis, and Beattie a model unit for the breaking in and training of effective chaplains. Andrew Robb and H.J. Latimer, Methodist chaplains at Witley, reported that camp and hut work there exceeded their highest expectations, as so many men were open to evangelistic efforts. Among the already converted as well Robb believed devotional fervour ran high: "Testimony services were the best fellowship meetings I have been in. There was a spontaneity and heartiness in the testimony of soldiers I have never seen not even in our Conference Love Feasts." Latimer wrote, "There are no signs of fear among the men but a quiet thoughtfulness ... I believe many of our boys are quietly fighting out the great battle of life alone almost and if we chaplains could only touch the spot at the right moment many victories would be recorded for 'Him' on the borders of France."[70] It was at camps like Witley that the rumours of revival overseas gained more substance.

After a few months in his camp posting, the call would come to the chaplain to proceed to hospital or Corps duty himself. After the arrival of the order warning him to proceed, a few hours of hectic packing were followed by a hasty departure.[71] Often there was little time to say goodbye to friends made at hut and chapel, and the men whose lives he knew he had tangibly affected. The presence of such men in the ranks and the encouragement they offered the chaplain assumed even greater significance as he drew nearer to battle. And it was with a clear knowledge that they were leaving safety that most padres headed east. If not, they were often reminded by those seeing them off. Benedict Murdoch managed to set aside a few days for a retreat at Parkminster Carthusian Monastery. As he departed for the front, the retreat master assured Murdoch that he and his men were in their prayers. "I felt a strange feeling of security on hearing these words, but as I left the Monastery gates and turned to say farewell to the old monk, I felt a distinct sinking of my heart. 'Perhaps,' he said rapturously, 'you'll be a martyr.'"[72]

AFTER CAMP WORK came a period of employment in England (at Canadian convalescent hospitals) or at the Canadian general and stationary field hospitals on the coast of France. Usually after a few months at one or the other came the long-awaited transfer to the casualty clearing stations a few miles behind the front. As the chaplain progressed from one type of hospital to the next, he faced new challenges and experienced a profound alteration in his understanding of and relationship with the men to whom he ministered. Along the way he also encountered some of the most intense and yet consoling experiences of his career.[73]

Scattered across England were the convalescent hospitals. Each had at least one chaplain, while the larger units were allotted three: Roman Catholic, Church of England, and non-conformist. Here the chaplain first encountered the challenge of systematic ward visitation. As he gained experience, the average padre realized that hospital work was one of the most emotionally gruelling duties of the war, requiring tact, sensitivity, a sense of humour, and personal warmth (attributes not shared by all chaplains). Each soldier required personal attention. Amputees and blind soldiers needed whatever spiritual assistance the padre could offer in accepting and dealing with their disability. A padre had to gauge carefully the proportion of conversation devoted to religion or to other subjects. He also had to be conscientious, for few soldiers forgave the padre who overlooked or passed by a patient of another denomination without at least a kind word. As a typical ward held up to sixty patients, if he wanted to get through at least one ward each day, the padre had his work cut out for him.[74]

Hospital work brought other strains, especially during offensives, when an apparently endless stream of new patients poured into hospitals at all hours. Because they were always on call from the medical staff, hospital chaplains frequently remarked on the longer hours of duty and greater fatigue they felt.[75] Chaplains also saw the physical and, more disturbing, mental havoc that combat played on the men they had bid farewell to in camp a few months previously. For the first time, encountering shell-shock cases, they saw something of the psychological damage modern warfare causes.[76] Writing letters to relatives, relating the last hours of a recently deceased patient, was always a taxing process, especially during the great offensives, when wards were packed with seriously wounded or dying men. Most chaplains were well aware that the morale of the home front was in part dependent on their letters of consolation. Equally challenging were the letters to kin of soldiers who were permanently disabled. Often it was the chaplain who was asked to break the news that the returning soldier needed an example of patience, acceptance, and courage at home in order to rebuild his shattered life.[77]

In spite of its strains, after enduring the arid and mundane duties of camp ministry many chaplains found hospital postings a welcome change. Soldiers could be approached as individuals, conversation moved to religious concerns more readily, and the men showed more gratitude for their efforts and attention. To the chaplain the typical patient seemed more open to religious influence when recuperating from wounds than at any other stage of military service.[78] There were other new and welcome features to hospital work. In spite of their wounds and disabilities, the cheerfulness and courage shown by most of the patients encouraged and inspired chaplains jaded by the apathy and frustrations of camp work.[79] Hospital padres' reports continually point to the quiet courage and heroic endurance they witnessed in the wards, which seem always to have diminished their own sense of fatigue and discouragement. If most chaplains felt that they gave more in terms of energy and spirit to hospital work, most also felt that they received there more inspiration and true encouragement.[80]

Nevertheless, some hospital postings in England were unpopular with the average chaplain. These included the Canadian venereal disease hospitals set up by 1917 at Etchinghill, Cambridge, and Bramshott. While most chaplains were involved in efforts to warn men off fornication and adultery, they seldom had much patience or sympathy for the men who contracted venereal diseases, viewing them as moral failures who perhaps deserved their affliction and the humiliation and depression that often accompanied it. A few padres, however, proved more compassionate and responsive. At Etchinghill, Arthur Skerry found that many patients sought his counsel after chapel service: "Those who are very depressed and hysterical I take at once to our nerve specialist ... I believe we have prevented several suicides ... The whole aim of my work is to help a man regain his self respect with an optimistic attitude, without minimizing his mistake."[81] Too often, chaplains like Skerry complained, their peers were unable to do more than resort to moralizing and criticism.[82] Consequently, the chaplain who could sympathize with such patients and achieve some rapport with or influence on them was highly prized by the Chaplain Service.[83]

A special type of chaplain was also desired for English hospitals dealing with crippled or disabled soldiers on their way back to Canada. Soldiers destined to return to France congregated at Epsom, but Liverpool's Kirkdale Hospital (No. 5 Canadian General) and the Canadian discharge depot in Buxton collected disabled soldiers and those being sent home for discharge. Padres were attached to these units to give counsel and guidance. The Kirkdale senior chaplain reported an average of twenty soldiers a day dropping by his office: "'Go to the Chaplain' continues to be the advice given on all hands when anyone is in difficulty. There is no denying our usefulness here, and, by our exercising careful judgement in dealing with each case, our championship in any cause is respected." In these units, where bored and increasingly active patients awaited passage home, the chaplains conducted unusually aggressive social work.[84] At Buxton, where there was not much for the men to do, frequent breaches of discipline occurred, and the chaplain often found himself consulting with the commandant in the orderly room. The chaplains were sought out constantly by soldiers with personal problems that needed sorting out before returning to Canada. In 1917 Bruce Hunter, at Buxton, had at least ten marriage authorization or "personal difficulty" (dubbed "woman trouble") interviews a day. Along with commanding officers, the padres became self-appointed immigration agents, filtering out women who were considered undesirable in Canada or else extricating an injured party from one form of confidence trick or another used on them by a Canadian soldier.[85]

While some chaplains did not proceed any further forward in their wartime work, for many, hospital work in the base areas such as LeHavre, Boulogne, Etaples, and Rouen was an intermediate stop between duties in England and the casualty clearing station at the front. Even the doomed Canadian hospital ship *Llandoverry Castle*, bringing wounded back to England, needed a duty padre. One Canadian chaplain, Donald MacPhail, a Presbyterian, went down with the ship when it was torpedoed in 1918.[86] For most the stepped-up pace of the ward work was the first challenge. At the same time, however, they were stimulated by the greater intensity and simplicity of devotional life with troops so recently wounded. Referring to the willing response many gave to his offer to pray with them, Oliver wrote, "It is wonderful how the poor wounded fellows appreciate it. I have never yet had a refusal ... Religion is a very vital element in the life of a man who is near unto death."[87] Although staff and convalescents were sometimes suspicious and resentful of interfering padres, many patients welcomed their presence and night prayers, "when the lights are shaded and the ward is quietest, when they are not made conspicuous and there are no distracting interests and noises," as a Methodist padre put it.[88]

In times of activity at the front, chaplains put in long hours in the wards with the seriously or dangerously ill, normally of their own denomination, though in very hectic times casualties of other communions came under their care as well. During such periods padres went without sleep; the wards became blurs of pale faces and bandages, which changed daily as men were evacuated to England or else buried. Occasionally, when all medical means had been exhausted in rallying a patient, the doctor summoned the padre to do whatever he could. This confronted chaplains such as Oliver with the most stressful moments of their ministry, when they were summoned to the operating theatre to rally men whose will to live had virtually disappeared.

Daily there were funeral services to be read for men who had not rallied or had died of complications. Hospitals close to the Channel could be visited by relatives of the most critically ill, which visits often ended with the padre accompanying relatives back from the cemetery, offering words of consolation and reassurance. To his relief the YMCA occasionally sent a matron to assist Oliver in comforting mothers who had spent their sons' last hours at the bedside. One occasion, preparing for a funeral, Oliver was met by the Catholic padre, who was burying one of his charges. They read their services in succession, the Roman Catholic priest silently reading part of his service during

Oliver's in order to shorten the elderly woman's ordeal. Before she left, she placed one of her two bouquets of flowers on the second coffin, on behalf of the Catholic soldier's absent mother. Oliver wrote, "Such is the cost of war. I thank God, Rita, our lads are only babes."[89] Next-of-kin letters often took every spare moment for weeks after an offensive ended. For the hospital chaplain, who was usually expected to give grieving relatives reassuring information on the condition and state of mind of their men, phrasing these letters was often agonizingly difficult: "Can you imagine a harder job than writing to their wives? Such wounds as I never saw."[90]

The usual establishment of three chaplains for each hospital of several hundred beds was constantly in danger of being overwhelmed by the magnitude of their parish. The inexhaustible human need led many chaplains to try to serve day and night. "There is absolutely no limit to the work to be accomplished," wrote Oliver, who marvelled at the devotion of Anglican colleague Cecil Owen as they toiled over massive British casualties at Passchendaele. On top of his exceptionally heavy Anglican caseload, who often desired communion, Owen always finished his day with a "midnight peregrination" of the wards to see if his men were settling for the night.[91] During the Passchendaele offensive the sheer numbers of wounded coming into the receiving rooms and the gravity of their condition nauseated green padres and left the most hardened chaplains in tears.[92] In momentary respites, the day's events brought forth their rawest emotions, rarely confided as frankly to their kin as in Edmund Oliver's letters to his wife:

> Today was a heart breaking day. I saw such great gaping wounds, strips of legs, of arms, heads swollen out of all shape through having been shot, trench feet, broken thighs, that one can never forget such sights. You say some people criticized me for coming over here and leaving you behind. No one feels more distressed over leaving you than I do, but if I am to be worthy of my boy's mother I had to do it. My conscience commanded me. And if I can help just a little in this welter of suffering of bruised and maimed lives, and can comfort the dying by prayers and by any word of consolation I don't care a fig what any carping critic may say in Saskatoon. Perhaps that same critic might be doing better by a little war service too. I have two boys that are dying this minute, both with fractured femurs and gaping wounds. To go into a ward where a convoy of such material in human suffering is, to watch the sisters washing and dressing the wounds, and hear the ill-repressed groans of agony, – well, I couldn't have done it a year ago but I can endure it now – even the smell of it – and get down close to him to pray or to get a message for home, and I am glad to say I can keep cool and it doesn't excite me now when a man dies. I think it ought to make me a better Principal, a better Christian

and perhaps, – who knows? – a better husband and father. I didn't know there could be such suffering in the world – but it'll be over some day.[93]

Base hospital duty was rarely disturbed by the enemy. But in 1917 and especially during the spring of 1918 even these relatively cloistered areas were exposed to active air operations, and several Canadian hospitals were bombed by German aircraft. Chaplains had billets blown down around them and found bullet or shrapnel holes in their wards and chapels. A number of nurses and patients were killed and two chaplains seriously wounded during these attacks. As a result, on clear nights the padres were expected to be in the wards conducting evening prayers and settling the men, who were especially uneasy during air raids.[94]

As the chaplain progressed from field hospital further towards the front, he encountered perhaps the most intensely draining avenue of service open to Canadian chaplains. Even routine shelling of the line often triggered hectic activity at the advanced casualty clearing stations, usually posted around five miles behind the fighting and therefore liable to long-range German artillery barrage. Charles Masters, an Anglican chaplain from Ontario, had just arrived from England at No. 1 Casualty Clearing Station at Bailleul when a shipment of wounded arrived. His initiation was brief and brutal: "I dumped my kit in a corner, pulled off my coat, rolled up my sleeves and went to work with the rest. Throughout the long hours of the night, there was no halt or respite. Such was my initiation into active service. There was not even time to feel shocked at the sight of so much blood. Indeed one was so absorbed in caring for and alleviating the sufferings of wounded men as to have little time to ponder one's own feelings."[95] Often the emotional strain of such work was not felt until the next day. For such chaplains the closer proximity to combat added new and particularly sharp experience to chaplaincy work, some of it pleasant, most not. Wounds were fresh and ghastly. Patients were often comatose or in great pain. Gas gangrene smells were more evident, as were the odours of the poison gases from the uniforms of men just in from combat. During the worst days of some offensives as many as three-quarters of the men brought in did not live to see the base hospital.

Cases were sorted into three groups: there were those who needed immediate surgery, those who could stand evacuation to the base hospitals, and those whose wounds were beyond effective treatment. The latter were given palliative care, usually in the most comfortable ward of the unit, washed and sedated, closely attended by nurses and chaplain until they died.[96] Padres had to adjust to being turned out of bed at all hours to deal with men whose lives were flickering out even as they were being treated. Men affected by mustard gas were blinded and unable to write, while many more were missing limbs or digits. Taking last messages, giving communion, and writing hundreds of letters to bereaved relatives all required the chaplain's best efforts. Sending off personal effects was also often left to the padre, who sometimes went through them to ensure that nothing might be left among their contents to cause unnecessary heartache or disappointment to next of kin.[97]

It was a common procedure for chaplains new to France to be posted to clearing stations for a few months before they were permitted to go to the fighting units. In theory this was supposed to acclimatize them to the horrors of the front. As chaplain John Callan, who served several months in one such station, observed afterwards, the actual effect was often the reverse: "There was no place on all the front more likely to make him dread the fighting than the casualty clearing station ... Every day he saw men sadly wounded come from the line; day and night he heard the moans of the maimed; the smell of gas-gangrene was never absent from his nostrils; the pictures of agony never faded from his mind. He learned to think of the front as a place were men were shattered and mangled, for all who came from it had suffered hurt."[98] At the clearing station the padre could not escape overwork and nervous exhaustion. There was always another soldier in pain who needed easing, an errand to run, a letter to write, beside what he was already doing officially for the unit's medical staff. Worship services, prayers, and bedside vigils were often punctuated by incoming shellfire. Conversations with bitter and anxious soldiers were emotionally draining. It became increasingly difficult for a number of chaplains to utter certain conventional graveside phrases, such as "It has pleased Almighty God to take ...," without silent protest at the apparent injustice of such a conception of providence. The constant demands for alleviation of physical and emotional suffering almost always created an irresistible temptation to overdo the work on the wards.

The sense that the men were, at this stage in their lives, most open to religious influences drove many chaplains to pace their work emotionally instead of rationally. As Callan observed, the result usually was eventual collapse. "Few chaplains could do such work conscientiously for many months without a change, and the one who added to his overburdened day by attending to units of fit men in his vicinity was wise. The very sight of men who were sound and whole seemed to give him strength."[99] For many, however, this was not enough. As a result, casualty clearing stations became the site of many nervous and physical breakdowns among chaplains in France. In these cases the commander of the medical unit, whenever he detected a padre becoming too wrought up over badly wounded men, would recommend his transfer back to England for rest and recuperation.[100]

If there were intense strains, there was also intense satisfaction at the clearing stations. Chaplains found the slightly wounded and still conscious casualties receptive, and grateful for their offers to write letters of reassurance to friends and relatives. At the deathbed of many a soldier chaplains found confirmation of "the soul's good salvation" with which to reassure relatives. A Presbyterian chaplain reported, "One feels, yes knows, that he is doing something worthwhile to minister to the dying as we have so often, to do so takes tact and skill but is adequate compensation to know that you have been able to fortify these brave fellows as they fight their last great battle."[101] One of the hardest tasks for any chaplain anywhere was writing letters to relatives of the dead and dying. Chaplains at the front and with medical units were never free of this responsibility. What could one say to make sense of the loss to loved ones miles away? Chaplains writing next-of-kin letters found it hard to resist the temptation to lie about the specific circumstances of a patient's life or death. They felt responsible, at least in part, for the morale, the emotional and spiritual well-being of the bereaved. Hence, every word needed to be carefully weighed for its effect upon the recipient. Chaplains, however, repeatedly testified that what bolstered their morale in moments such as these were the replies that grateful relatives sent the padre. Callan recalled, "If the work of writing to the relatives was so sad that most men would do anything rather than compose such letters, the replies received were more than compensation." Relatives often replied to the padre's letters, indicating that whatever he had done had been warmly appreciated. Many letters were couched in the same language and written from the same religious perspective as his. Such letters were of great encouragement. Charles Masters recalled, "After gas attacks, it taxed the powers of the chaplain to write a message of comfort to each man's people. But few were missed. Among my treasured possessions are letters from every part of the British Empire in answer to these messages."[102]

Thus, for the compassionate chaplain, clearing station work most often increased the depth and power of his sympathy with and admiration for the soldiers. So Callan wrote, after one harrowing day in the wards:

> It is the day of God. It is a day when the tattered robe of Christ is being hemmed together by bleeding hands. It is a day when through all the clouds and horrors of war, the Christ is claiming His own and seeing of the travail

of His soul ... And if we, here, at the heart of this great upheaval, hear with disgust the petty and bitter acrimonies of sectarian strife, which still prevail at home, and think with sorrow that not all the blood which has been shed has cemented the breaches in the walls of the Church of God, our comfort is, that they who quarrel ... do so in ignorance; for they have not looked on life and death as we have; they have not seen the mean and petty trifles burned in the flame of finer things; they have not been where the voice of God is thundering – they have not known.[103]

Witnessing such heroic suffering moved many chaplains, not towards renunciation but instead to reaffirmation of the crusading and idealizing beliefs of previous preaching. After a day on the wards Presbyterian Arthur Burch was so caught up in the crusading mentality that he easily described the soldier who died in such a righteous cause, especially him whose death resulted from rescuing comrades, as "one of God's elect." Fellow Presbyterian Thomas McAffee, working at No. 3 CCCS, expressed similar views in admiration of the uncomplaining wounded, "many of whom are made perfect through suffering."[104] As the August 1918 offensive heralded success for the Allies, the crusading rhetoric reached new levels of intensity. Among the Methodists, Robert Scarlett wrote that his casualty clearing station was ready to receive "our brave heroic wounded boys who are driving the diabolical enemy of civilization back to his lair."[105] The heroism of "Tommy," he added, was a living rebuke to the narrow peacetime bigotry and self-righteousness of the churches. To him the soldiers were being cleansed of bigotry and narrow sectarianism in this "Great World War of Freedom against cruel slavery" and would have no patience for old-fashioned creeds or sectarian divisions after the war. As he surveyed the mounting casualties, Scarlett vowed that the dead would be avenged by demanding unconditional surrender from "the Prussian Beast."[106]

Often at this stage of their pilgrimage chaplains found themselves contrasting petty political controversies and slack social attitudes at home with the unequivocal realities they faced in their work. Chaplains consequently supported every policy that prosecuted the war more effectively. Padre calls for volunteers soon became demands for conscription by 1916. The next year Union government also received their endorsement.[107] English-speaking chaplains, whatever their pre-war political allegiances, tended to deplore the attitude of Wilfrid Laurier and the Liberals towards the conscription question, criticizing French Canada for its lack of moral resolution and half-heartedness in the cause. Thus, in the 1917 federal election they did not hesitate to urge spouses (who were exercising their franchise for the first time) and other relatives to forsake the Liberals and vote for Robert Borden's Union government. The war had transformed the moral universe of these padres, leaving them convinced that nothing less than all-encompassing reform was called for by the carnage and sacrifices they witnessed towards the front.[108] In spite of the increasingly stressful duties they performed, the padres grew even more relentless in their pursuit of final victory and a permanent end to the horrors of war.

To many of Canada's Great War chaplains the frustrations and hardships they encountered at each stage of the journey to the front were refining trials in a life-transforming pilgrimage. While some found the strain of overseas service more than they could bear, few reported that such experiences led to disillusionment with their cause or a crisis of faith. Instead most chaplains found that their camp, depot, and hospital service, in spite of the psychic strains, had a consolidating rather than a shattering effect on their beliefs. In their progress towards the front chaplains passed, in fact, through a powerful psychological process in which they increasingly identified themselves with the soldier, idealized his character, and ascribed a sacramental quality to his endurance and loyalty. In sharing the trials and spiritual experiences of the men in the forward hospitals and in the field, some padres bonded so intensely with their men that they acquired a somewhat distorted perception of soldier piety and, perhaps, of the cause they served. If most soldiers were not spiritually revived by their war, many padres clearly were. Their initial idealism was toughened into a commitment not to break faith, which they took from there to the next station in their pilgrimage: the front.

5 Soldiers: The Service in the Field

On 25 September 1916, under a broiling sun and desultory German shelling, a small group of Canadian soldiers gathered around a grave somewhere near the French town of Albert. The Anglican chaplain, fresh from a posting with the field ambulance, kept his service as brief as possible, for the Sixth Brigade men with him were preparing for another attack on the German line that night. As the service ended, a shell exploded close behind. The men dropped to the ground as iron fragments slapped the ground around them. A moment later the soldiers climbed to their feet. But not the padre – his legs would not move. At the field ambulance, medics dressed the small wound on his back and shipped him back to a British hospital for surgery, where, five days later, the doctors broke the news: the shell fragment had punched through his backbone and severed the spinal cord. Webster Harris would be paralysed for the rest of his life. Doctors were optimistic that he would live, but over the winter visiting chaplains remarked that Harris's health was deteriorating. The doctors attributed his decline to "complications." His wife arrived from Red Deer, where Harris had taken a parish after graduating from Toronto's Trinity College in 1910. In the first week of May 1917 Harris's fellow chaplains with the Canadian Corps were notified that he was dead.[1]

By war's end three more Canadian chaplains had been killed by enemy fire and dozens wounded or disabled by active service. Yet in 1914 or 1915 the odds of a padre's being killed or wounded were very low indeed, thanks to British army policy. By 1918, however, the Canadians had helped to change that. While those in authority wrestled with the problems of Chaplain Service administration, Canadian padres at the front worked their way from the back fringes to the centre of the zone of battle. Not content with serving only the worship and war needs of the soldiers, the padres also operated canteens, cinema tents, recreation rooms, and coffee stalls within range of enemy guns. Consequently, official respect for the Chaplain Service at the Corps grew, while its presence under fire was eventually taken for granted by the troops. By 1918, when the service was allotted a place in the first attacking waves, it was evident that a profound shift in the relationship between army and chaplaincy had occurred among the Canadians. The padres had done more than fulfil the original mandate from General Hughes. From being regarded, in 1914, as awkward and perhaps unnecessary baggage, the service had become a valued front-line auxiliary of the Canadian Corps.

THE BRITISH HAD worked out the basic administration of the Chaplains' Department on the continent by the time the Canadians arrived in Flanders in the winter of 1915. The Adjutant-General's Branch created senior chaplaincies for divisions, corps, and armies. A command structure for Anglicans, Protestants, Jews, and Roman Catholics was developed on the continent. Chaplains were given an official place in the structure of the field army and allowed to live with the medical and administrative units in the rear. By 1915 their official place in the BEF had been established.[2] But Dominion and individual British chaplains found the results far from satisfactory. Throughout 1915 all British chaplains (including Canadian) were officially banned from the trenches. Regulations stipulated that they were not to go beyond the advanced dressing stations operated by the field ambulances two or three miles behind the front line. That was considered dangerous enough for padres, as such stations often received attention from the German medium artillery.[3] As in 1914, chaplains were still under orders to stay with the medical men during weekdays, preach on Sundays, and keep away from the fighting. The last thing generals wanted was a parson wandering along the line wringing his hands and getting in the way. Therefore, brigadiers and senior chaplains ordered the padres to stay back, where they could minister to a greater number of men than if they were up at an isolated part of the fighting. Such attitudes were held by a few British chaplains themselves, who saw their prime usefulness in trench warfare manifest behind the line, where the men were wounded, sick, bored, or lonely.[4]

Before long, however, a number of padres had been reprimanded for coming up to the trenches. They denied that chaplains got in the way or, if wounded, distracted stretcher-bearers from tending to more important combatants. When brigadiers objected that having a padre killed or wounded in front of the men would be bad for morale, chaplains replied that only by taking the same risks as the men could they have any influence over their soldiers. They had seen that chaplains who obeyed their brigadiers and stayed out of the line obviously lost respect with the troops. British chaplain T.B. Hardy, twice decorated with the Victoria Cross before meeting his death in action, bluntly told new chaplains, "The line is the key to the whole thing. Work in the front line and they will listen to you. If you stay back, you are wasting your time. Men will forgive anything but lack of courage and devotion."[5] To these chaplains, a padre or two carried out of the line feet first might, in fact, be good for morale. Over the weeks commanders grudgingly changed their minds, though they still forbade trench work in offensive operations or intense enemy activity. This, however, was still deemed too restrictive by many chaplains who wanted permission to roam the lines, even under fire. The debate, therefore, was well under way when Steacy's Canadian padres arrived in Flanders.[6]

The Canadian padres would, however, play a role in settling the issue, led by a remarkable chaplain who was not even supposed to be in Flanders. Concealing himself among the men was a stowaway. Canon Frederick George Scott had been moved to a hospital unit in England, but, determined not to be separated from the fighting troops and with the connivance of his brigadier, he smuggled himself on board a transport and evaded army officials until he got to Flanders. Here the brigade major caught up to him but agreed to let him stay with the Third Brigade on the promise that Scott would report to a hospital unit when it arrived in France. Scott later admitted, "I never knew when it did come to France, for I never asked. 'Sufficient unto the day is the evil thereof' was my motto. I held on to my job at the front."[7] In this manner one of the most unlikely chaplaincy candidates launched an outstanding career overseas. Adopted by the Fourteenth Battalion, the canon acted as the Third Brigade's unauthorized extra chaplain.

Scott's success in stretching army regulations soon became part of the legend growing up around him. Other chaplains, perhaps because they were under closer supervision by their commanders, found military service somewhat more confining. Canadian brigade chaplains usually marched up with the men at night, held short prayers and communion services, and buried the dead, but did not enter the trenches themselves.[8] Soon, however, many Canadian chaplains quietly began asking their commanders to wink at occasional visits to their men when the front was quiet, or at night. Scott simply ignored regulations, counting on charming his way out of awkward trench encounters with outraged superiors. His sense of humour and zeal for action soon made him a welcome guest in the line. Eventually his enthusiasm and popularity made it too difficult for even Steacy to rebuke or remove him, and other brigadiers found it increasingly difficult to discipline their own padres who imitated him.[9]

After some weeks learning trench lore, the First Canadian Division celebrated Easter while moving to a new part of the line near Ypres. Scott and his fellow Christian chaplains thought how fitting it was that the volunteers be reminded of self-sacrifice.[10] On 22 April the Germans attacked behind a cloud of chlorine gas, throwing the Canadians into a confused, bloody, and costly struggle to preserve the Allied line. The Second Battle of Ypres was the chaplains' baptism of fire. In the chaos of battle, where rear areas became firing zones and support troops found themselves holding sections of the front line, the regulations about chaplains were simply disregarded. Steacy, working at a hospital in Aire, was thirty miles from the Ypres salient. Chaplains with medical units were swamped by an endless procession of wounded and gassed in their dressing stations, while the three brigade chaplains, with Almond and Canon Scott, were "happily a law unto themselves, and were able to go wherever the need was apparent."[11] This brought them to the forward area directly under German bombardment. By instinct they drifted to places where traffic to and from the firing zone converged: the pontoon bridge over the Yser Canal, the isolated regimental aid posts in St Julien, and the advanced dressing stations in St Jean, where, in streets choked with refugees, wounded, and reinforcements, they loaded ambulances, directed traffic, and guided stragglers to lost brigade headquarters. They plundered French dumps for rations and comforted the wounded and dying. At night they often accompanied stealthy burial parties working behind the trenches.[12]

The chaplains also helped to allay the panic of soldiers encountering a new weapon. Scott forced one recruit to swear not to tell the men in the rear that poison gas was being used against them. To steady some troops preparing to storm a German position at bayonet point, he passed down the line telling them "that they had a chance to do a bigger thing for Canada that night than had ever been done before. 'It was a great day for Canada, boys,' I said. The words afterwards became a watchword, for the men said that whenever I told them that, it meant that half of them were going to be killed." His work at dressing stations – reassuring the anxious, praising the wounded, taking last messages from the dying, and dispensing cigarettes and communion as appropriate – also won the approval of the medical officers and ambulance staff. Despite official doubts, Canadian chaplains proved to be anything but timid parsons: the good impression they made began to open the way to a more active role.[13]

After Ypres, Canadian padres were given considerably more latitude in interpreting regulations. Brigade chaplains were now allowed to use forward dugouts for Sunday services, although Canon Scott, when he tried to work with the wounded there during the weekdays, earned a tongue-lashing from his brigadier.[14] Nevertheless, he continued his ramblings, breaking the monotony of censoring letters and "parish visitation" in the billets with nighttime forays into the line. Later in the spring some chaplains were permitted to work forward of the dressing stations during offensive operations, taking down hastily dictated wills and last messages as well as praying with the dying. Canadian chaplains for the first time were nominated for battle honours. Further evidence that they were getting closer to combat appeared in the casualty lists when shells critically wounded two Canadian chaplains.[15] Nevertheless, the lure of work in the line drew the chaplains back, as more commanders permitted, even encouraged their padres to visit their units' positions for small meetings and communion services.[16]

By the summer of 1915 a number of Canadian chaplains had made bending regulations a trench routine, though individuals were still rebuked by officers scrupulously upholding regulations. During the following months, while the Canadians occupied the same Flemish sector, there was little fighting, and, until the autumn, the trenches were dry. Scott and his colleagues were issued horses, increasing their mobility. The slower pace of military life allowed chaplains to become better known as counsellors, confidants, and social conveners. Sundays, however, were hectic: after the German desecration of French and Belgian churches became known, the British Army denied the use of French churches to any non-Roman Catholic padres, forcing them to hold widely dispersed outdoor services (one chaplain had up to eleven services a Sunday).[17] The rear area would be full of men out of the line, and officers looked to the chaplains to help keep them out of trouble. Many began "non-religious" work, setting up libraries or games rooms, organizing sports, and passing out "comforts" from the Red Cross or church groups in Canada. The need to entertain idle First Division troops first inspired Arthur McGreer, an Anglican, to organize a concert troupe. He was so successful that the chaplains were asked to entertain the entire division. By the autumn the concert organization had become a permanent and distinctive aspect of Canadian chaplaincy work.[18]

Canon Scott continued his own unique contributions to morale, camping in the support area, holding morning communion services, mingling with the soldiers at their evening concerts, and passing out cigarettes. He continued his rambles, "having absolute liberty in wandering through the trenches." Thus, by autumn he was well known throughout the division, a powerful asset when Steacy was promoted to command the Chaplain Service: Scott became senior chaplain of the First Division.[19] Other chaplains also took up peripatetic ministries during the summer. The two Catholic priests responsible for the entire First Division found it absolutely necessary to move from one brigade to another in order to cover their vast field. The situation was not improved by the formation of the Canadian Corps, as the Second Canadian Division brought only two Catholic priests with it. The strain of hearing the confessions and giving sacraments to the Roman Catholics of two divisions began to wear out the four Canadian priests.[20]

Despite understaffing, however, as 1915 drew to a close the Canadian chaplains had made significant progress in the field. They had much more freedom to fraternize with the fighting men in and out of the line, and acquired new respectability.[21] Arthur Woods, senior chaplain of the recently arrived Third Canadian Division, reported:

> A word might be said in reference to the attitude of both officers and men towards the Army Chaplain. It will be remembered that at the beginning of things the Chaplain was looked upon as so much unnecessary baggage – to put the matter bluntly – and FIVE per Division were thought to be sufficient ... It was seen anyhow that after all the padre was of some use in the army on active service. The officers and men were quick to see that he intended to be one of themselves, and as far as possible play the game. So today we find that every Battalion Commander wants his Padre. And no one is more welcome in the trenches than the padre.[22]

By this time, under Deputy Chaplain General L. Gwynne, a similar process was beginning to occur in the British Army, though the Canadians believed that their chaplaincy remained less denominational and more intimately involved with their men throughout the war.[23] After arduous service and continuous testing of regulations, Canadian officers were being persuaded that they could count on the padres after all.

STEACY'S DEPARTURE FOR LONDON and Almond's promotion to Corps ADCS had brought Canon Scott, by then perhaps the most popular chaplain among "the Valcartier originals," to the senior chaplaincy of the First Division. With William Beattie at Second Division, Arthur Woods at Third, and Alexander Gordon's arrival at Fourth in mid-1916, the Corps chaplaincy was headed by five experienced and energetic clerics. Almond now commanded over fifty Canadian padres. With such an enlarged capacity for ministry and four experienced lieutenants to tend the divisions, he sought new ways to increase Chaplain Service visibility and effectiveness. McGreer's First Division concert party had been such a hit that the authorities asked the chaplains to entertain the whole Corps. Almond, mindful of the growing visibility of the YMCA, jumped at the chance. McGreer's enterprise became the Chaplain's Social Service Department under a "Corps chaplain," Alan Shatford (a Montreal Anglican sharing Almond's interest in social Christianity). Shatford soon opened a Corps theatre, charging admission for nightly concerts and giving free matinées. Before long a "Soldier's Institute" canteen, also operated by the Chaplain Service, appeared next door.[24] When autumn rains turned trenches into ditches, the Chaplain Service borrowed $3,500 from the Canadian government to expand the canteen, cinema, and concert programs. The Canadian Boy Scouts donated a huge tent (chapel, cinema, concert hall, and canteen, depending on the occasion) that held a thousand men. By Christmas, Shatford was scrounging spare transportation staff and equipment from all over the Corps to service his growing operation.[25]

By Easter 1916 the chaplains had acquired considerable experience in entertaining troops and running recreation centres. Their right to live in the line with their men under fire, however, remained in dispute. When Almond took command of the Corps chaplaincy, they were still officially forbidden to work ahead of the advanced dressing stations. While Scott and others defiantly visited the trenches in lulls, even the canon kept out of senior officers' sight during raids and heavy shelling.[26] In March 1916 General Alderson permitted Beattie's staff to take part in the St Eloi operation, assisting medical officers and comforting the wounded in regimental aid posts as well as dressing stations.[27] Fortunately for Almond and his staff, this trend was encouraged by the next Corps commander, Julian Byng. When he raised the issue of Gordon's Fourth Division staff going into the line, Almond discovered that Byng emphatically agreed with him on the proper place for padres: "Reference to Brigade chaplains visiting trenches, when the Brigade is in. I wish to say that Sir Julian Byng, Corps Commander, congratulated me on the fact that he had met SEVERAL chaplains in the trenches, and he thinks the chaplains must be seen by the men at the posts of danger if they are to have telling influence. I desire the utmost freedom for the CHAPLAINS in carrying out their duties to the troops … There is no question with either the 1st, 2nd or 3rd Divisions as to the chaplains visiting the trenches."[28]

With Byng's backing Almond overcame the most conservative commander's resistance. Chaplains routinely bunked with the medical officer when their units were in the line, and all were encouraged to live in the trenches. The padres paid a price for their persistence: before long two chaplains had been disabled by shell wounds and had to be returned to Canada. Nevertheless, Third Division chaplains proudly reported General Mercer's comment to Senior Chaplain Woods, "Woods, your chaplains are all men instead of preachers."[29] When the Germans unexpectedly pounced on the Third Division at Mount Sorrel, A.G. Wilken, Anglican chaplain to the Canadian Mounted Rifles Brigade, brought forward stretcher-bearers and ration and ammunition parties to CMR headquarters and was taken prisoner when it was overrun by the enemy.[30] Almond sent his brigade chaplains into the regimental aid posts located in the shelled zone, leaving only the ambulance-unit chaplains to tend the dressing stations. Chaplains served in ways unheard of since Ypres, scrambling across recaptured ground to maintain contact between aid posts, Headquarters, and support units. Working in dressing station and aid post by day, at night they organized and guided stretcher parties, often hip-deep in water or mud, through shrapnel barrages, trying to get wounded out of the firing line or off the open ground where they had fallen. Many conducted ration and ammunition parties back to the line. Any time left over was devoted to burials.[31]

Mount Sorrel settled the Canadian discussion about padres up front, in offensive as well as in holding actions.[32] The spring setbacks of St Eloi and Mount Sorrel also wrought a marked change in Canadian psychology: Scott sensed the casual attitude of superiority over the Germans had been shaken. It was becoming clear that brash amateurs could not get by on enthusiasm and daring alone.[33] The trench war begun in the autumn of 1914 had now entered a new phase dominated by one principle: attrition. The demands this type of combat made upon the soldier's will in turn made morale of compelling concern to the commanders. Their interest in any expedient that sustained the will to combat grew, so that even the most hardened general no longer neglected the role his chaplains might play. As the senior chaplain on the spot, Almond was determined not to let the army down, and as the Corps prepared for the Somme, he urged Steacy to increase his divisional establishments from eleven or twelve to seventeen chaplains each. It was then that Steacy's ineffectiveness and indifference to Catholic needs convinced Almond that the DCS would have to be replaced.[34] There was, however, one encouraging development: the British Adjutant-General's Branch officially withdrew its order forbidding chaplains to go forward of the dressing stations. Senior chaplains had complete freedom to post their staff to any part of the battlefield.[35] By this time a Canadian chaplain had earned the first Chaplain Service decoration. Ambrose Madden, a Roman Catholic, was awarded the Military Cross for tending wounded under heavy German fire.[36]

At the Somme, Canadian chaplains learned grim lessons, bidding farewell to hundreds of men who did not return and struggling with heat, rain, mud, and exhaustion. During the First Division's skirmishing before Pozières, two of Scott's chaplains, George Wood and John O'Gorman, were wounded while getting casualties off the field.[37] When the Second and Third divisions captured Courcellette, three more chaplains earned Military Crosses for risking their lives under fire. Harris received his ghastly wound. Chaplains worked round the clock at the Albert schoolhouse, the main dressing station, making the wounded comfortable as they awaited treatment and taking down last requests, giving last rites, and writing letters to next of kin. Other brigade padres worked in the heat and rain under canvas at the tent dressing station on Tara Hill, where walking wounded were treated.[38] After several costly and futile Canadian attacks, the Fourth Division captured Regina Trench as torrential rain ended the offensive.

The Somme was a harrowing experience for both chaplains and soldiers.[39] The optimism of the early summer had given way to grim pugnacity. "The army had set its teeth and was out to battle in grim earnest … one cannot write of that awful time unmoved," recalled Scott.[40] Nevertheless, chaplains faithfully assisted medical officers and stretcher-bearers, also holding services in dressing-station dugouts and ruined cellars. Several reported narrow escapes from shellfire, including Channel Hepburn, who was buried under four feet of earth when shelling caved in his aid post. A few minutes later, as Hepburn lost consciousness, nearby sentries dug him and the MO out of the sodden chalk. "Seems funny for a padre to bury himself in this way," he later mused to his wife. Though Hepburn appeared to shake off the immediate effects of his ordeal, within a few months he was rotated back to England, nerves and body worn out.[41]

Later, two more chaplains received Military Crosses for daring rescue work on the Somme. Senior chaplains learned how to co-operate more effectively with harried medical staff as doctors demanded their co-operation in shifting padres to where the greatest number of wounded or dying were gathered.[42] Further forward, chaplain and fighting man had served in the line, run risks, and been wounded there together. German shelling disabled several chaplains.[43] One of the padres brought back a blood-soaked notebook he had found in a shellhole beside a dead Canadian: "Through the blood and mud I deciphered his last message. 'Got it in the neck – Find Pay Book and Will at Record Office.' Then in a hurried and wavering hand he wrote his great Confession of Faith – 'God is Good – God is Love – God bless Moth –' the last word 'Mother' was never finished."[44]

At the Somme, Almond's Social Service Department investment paid rich dividends in soldier appreciation. At the Albert brickfield, where units rested, it operated a cinema in the Boy Scout tent, organized sports, and held services. A new feature pioneered on the Somme was the coffee stall. In the Contalmaison dressing station (nicknamed "Casualty Corner") the Australians turned over an old coffee-making machine to the Canadian chaplains. Accordingly, day and night, Chaplain Service coffee was served in cups made of cigarette tins.[45] Soon Chaplain Service coffee stalls appeared wherever trench routes met the roads, at advanced dressing and casualty clearing stations, even in Pozières (where coffee, tea, biscuits, and cigarettes were distributed), fewer than 1,500 yards from the front line. Unlike its canteens, Chaplain Service coffee stalls did not accept payment from the soldiers, as cinema and canteen profits were diverted to the stall expenses. Enterprising chaplains began setting them up in support trenches wherever a few cans of boiling water could conveniently be located. Officers asked chaplains to site them closer to their units in the line. Almond and Shatford made them an indispensable feature of Chaplain Service work.[46]

The Canadians finished 1916 in the relatively calm Lens-Arras sector, where they endured another wet and ugly winter in the trenches. By then the Corps chaplains had acquired a prominent battlefield role. Almond and his senior chaplains believed, with some justification, that the service had a far better reputation in the army than it had begun with. Now unit commanders invited the chaplains into the line and service heads counted on their presence and assistance.[47] The men gave them more respect and attention. But what had been pioneered in 1916 had still to be perfected. It had been a year of progress, but there was a price to be paid. Besides losses from wounds, seven chaplains had been evacuated from the Corps for health reasons ranging from exhaustion to "shell shock."[48] The stresses of 1916 had also weakened the internal harmony of the Chaplain Service. Chaplains in France, led by Almond and the Catholics, were determined to have Steacy's failures and betrayals ended before the next round of fighting began.

In the meantime there was another Christmas to celebrate. Canon Scott now found his services held a strong note of pathos for him. Who knew which of the men so cheerfully or solemnly appearing before him would be killed in the next week? But one had to encourage hope.

On New Year's Eve, in the cinema at Bruay he held a Watch Night service. He told the officers and men that 1917 would be "the year of the victory":

> I told the men that somewhere in the pages of the book which we were opening that night lay hidden the tremendous secret of our success or failure … After the Benediction I went down to the door and shook hands with as many of the men as I could, and wished them a Happy New Year … At ten minutes to twelve we sat in silence, while the band played Chopin's Funeral March. It was almost too moving, for once again the vision came before us of the terrible battlefields of the Somme and the faces that had gone. Then we all rose, and there was a brief moment for silent prayer. At midnight the bugles of the 14th Battalion sounded the Last Post, and at the close the band struck up the hymn "O God Our Help in Ages Past." A mighty chorus of voices joined in the well known strains … No one who was at that service will ever forget it. As we found out, the trail before us was longer than we had expected, and the next New Year's Eve found many of us, though, alas, not all, in that theatre once more, still awaiting the issue of the conflict.[49]

THE CHAPLAINS WERE RELIEVED to be clear of the Somme. Shatford reopened the cinema and established small canteens near the front line. The Chaplain Service and YMCA held evangelistic meetings in the evenings. Unit chaplains converted ruined buildings into chapels and theatres. In the largest billets Scott gave lectures on Allied war aims.[50] In the trenches the chaplains continued to enjoy good relations with their units, often being invited to live in the line, though dugout space was in very short supply. During the winter's fierce trench raiding the Canadian chaplains were willingly accommodated in brigade headquarters and advanced dressing stations, while many, at the request of unit commanders, went further up to battalion aid posts. Coffee stalls were also set up just behind the forward trenches during the raids. Unit commanders even scheduled more regular church parades.[51]

The Canadians had come to the Arras sector to capture Vimy Ridge. While Corps and divisional officers pondered their Somme experiences and laid their plans, the Chaplain Service took stock and replaced worn-out personnel, having learned that the Somme fight had convinced one of the Corps chaplains that war itself was unjust. Robert Shires, a Bishop's University–trained Anglican, resigned his commission. He was, significantly, the only Canadian chaplain to do so during the war.[52] After a few tense days of infighting, Almond replaced Steacy and brought Workman back to London as his Catholic adviser. McGreer became Corps ADCS, with Father Francis French as his Catholic deputy.[53] McGreer's divisional seniors began demanding weekly reports from all chaplains. Remembering Mount Sorrel, McGreer ordered senior chaplains to make contingency disposition plans so that each chaplain knew in advance exactly where he ought to be in a crisis. The old days of the senior chaplain's giving a few verbal instructions and a slap on the shoulder to each padre on his staff had given way to written reports, detailed itineraries, marked maps, and timetables.[54]

Working from a little hut near Corps headquarters, McGreer and French consulted with other service heads, especially the Medical Corps, learning where dressing stations, ambulance-loading points, and aid posts would be located and where there would be room for the Chaplain Service. Divisional authorities notified the service of intended battery and brigade positions, and the engineers designated chapel space in the tunnels under the ridge and construction materials for coffee stalls.[55] Chaplains would not only bid the soldiers Godspeed from their own trenches, but many would follow them across no man's land to work in the aid posts set up in captured trenches.[56] The tunnels that honeycombed the ridge occupied a prominent place in their reports and recollections. Scott held services for his men secure in the Maison Blanche complex. Overhead the exposed terrain was dotted with faded red and blue scraps of uniform clinging to the skeletons of French troops uncovered by rain and shelling. Nevertheless, chaplains back in the rest areas occasionally wished that they had tunnel protection for their services: at least one open-air church parade was cut short by strafing from a German fighter plane.[57]

On 20 March 1917 Allied artillery began their preparatory firing on Vimy Ridge. Military duties kept most soldiers occupied, but chaplains made special efforts to have their men come to voluntary communion: both religious and military schedules included it as an assault preliminary.[58] After sunset on 8 April the attacking brigades moved up into assembly trenches and the mouths of the tunnels, waiting for the dawn. The chaplains supplied many with hot drinks brewed at nearby coffee stalls.[59] At 5:30 a.m. the barrage lifted. As each objective was overrun, regimental aid posts and advanced headquarters were set up in captured dugouts. Chaplains participated in more of the battle than ever before. Over half were deployed in the regimental aid posts set up in the Canadian tunnels, or went forward into captured dugouts. Every division had at least one chaplain supervising coffee stalls in the assembly trenches and tunnels, and another posted to every divisional burial party scouring the field.[60] The remaining chaplains, about a third from each division, were stationed between one-half and three miles behind the start line, at the advanced and main dressing stations operated by the Canadian Field Ambulances.

George Wood and David Robertson, chaplains with battalions in the First Division, both began their Vimy action in the assembly trenches behind the Canadian line, dishing out coffee to troops from cookers in Elbe trench. As the First Brigade went over the top, Wood accompanied battalion Headquarters through the German counter-barrage towards the German line. Robertson went underground to work in aid posts in Bentata and Zivy tunnels. Wood's party was decimated by shelling and he was left behind, momentarily giving first aid while the CO went on. With gauze, bandages, and iodine Wood dressed fifteen wounded men and got them started back on stretchers borne by German prisoners. Until noon he worked with the MO at other temporary aid posts, but by evening he was busy in an aid post on the secondary objective east of the village of Thélus. In a packed dugout under the German trenches near Bois Carré he bound wounds and cared for the dying without respite for the next two days. He fed and supplied hot drinks to wounded and passersby with German rations, took names and home addresses, prayed, and buried the dead of the Fourth and Thirty-first battalions. By then Robertson had arrived, after two days underground passing out cocoa, binding wounds, and praying with the dying. During lulls in the shelling Robertson scoured the surrounding ground for wounded who might have escaped notice in the snow and sleet. Organizing stretcher-bearers, he got the mingled Canadian and German casualties he found carried to the rear. After a day further forward in a German dugout, so poorly ventilated that candles would not stay lit, he moved into Bois Carré to relieve Wood. By then the aid post had become a field ambulance dressing station, heavily shelled and visited by a steady stream of wounded. Five days after the assault began Robertson was setting up an advanced aid post in the railway embankment east of Farbus, supporting an attack on Arleux. Though withdrawn two days later, it was another week before his battalion was regathered for worship: he took as his text "The Good Shepherd giveth his life for the sheep."[61]

At Vimy senior chaplains exerted more control over the deployment of their padres than before. Like chess players they placed each of their dozen chaplains in whatever role needed playing in their division, rotating or reassigning them as their own philosophy or experience dictated. Canon Scott, for example, put over half of his chaplains in the forward regimental aid posts. The Second Division's senior chaplain, Louis Moffit, put more along the evacuation route behind the original Canadian line. Like Scott, Alexander Gordon attached more of his Fourth Division staff men to forward aid posts than to dressing stations and, also believing that senior chaplains should oversee the staff from the front, left the most junior chaplain in charge of his office and came up to live at an aid post. In all divisions Roman Catholic padres stationed themselves at the central dressing stations, hoping to minister to a larger number than if located at one of the isolated aid posts.[62]

The chaplains' reports of Vimy Ridge (the first of their reports to be systematically preserved) reveal the heightened stress and emotional tension that resulted from closer proximity to the fighting. Many eventually made the crossing of no man's land to assist at the regimental aid posts, where more time was spent in treating wounds than in prayer or counsel.[63] When medical officers were wounded or called away, padres were left in charge for hours or days at a time. Many combed adjacent shellholes and trenches for wounded Germans or Canadians who had been missed by the stretcher-bearers. Directing stretcher parties and carrying back the wounded, often under heavy shelling or sniper fire, punctuated their work. Later, they set up temporary burial grounds, often reinterring the remains of French soldiers who had fallen in earlier attacks.[64] Further back, field ambulance chaplains worked at collecting points where the wounded were given enough treatment to see them safely to the hospitals. Here men often arrived in a dying condition, and the padres spent more time in prayer than those at the regimental aid posts. They also supplied hot drinks, scrounged blankets for the wounded lying on the frozen ground, took last messages, and loaded ambulances with stretchers. Artillery chaplains roamed the gun pits.[65]

Taking Vimy Ridge did not end Canadian offensive operations that spring, and chaplains served in the aid posts during the battles for Arleux and Fresnoy.[66] Besides operations, of course, there was still much to be done in the burial of the many dead recovered from the battlefield. Finally, at the end of June 1917, the chaplains conducted thanksgiving and memorial services on the ridge.[67] It had been an exciting and exhausting spring, and the chaplains reaped praises from General Byng on down. So did the Social Service Department: its Boy Scout tent cinema was in constant operation, punctured by enemy fire and twice relocated when German shelling became too persistent. As usual, the forward coffee stalls had been very popular.[68] On 1 July 1917 the Corps celebrated the fiftieth anniversary of Confederation, and, as the day fell on a Sunday, the chaplains played a more prominent role than usual. Scott found himself the only member present at the First Division's Dominion Day service who could actually remember 1 July 1867. The next day the Chaplain Service social-service group conducted the Canadian Corps track and field competition.[69]

During the summer of 1917 Arthur Currie became the Canadian Corps commander. Like Byng, he was concerned that the chaplains should maintain the morale of the men at a high pitch. He had no use for clergymen, civilian or otherwise, whose conception of Christianity precluded resolute commitment to the job of fighting the Germans.[70] As a result, his response to McGreer's and Almond's plans to put as many padres as possible into the firing zone was entirely sympathetic. Currie planned to capture a valuable landmark north of Lens (designated Hill 70). His plan called for the same close artillery and infantry co-operation perfected at Vimy. The Chaplain Service was asked to encourage the gunners during the assault. As preparations for the Hill 70 attack continued, two of the chaplains visiting gunpits were wounded by German counter-battery firing.[71] Below Hill 70 the trenches gave poor shelter, so Scott posted his chaplains to the cellars and tunnels beneath the ruins of local villages. In one underground dressing station near Loos he set up a canteen and chapel and a recreation room as well, where boxing matches were held – an attraction also used by Britain's most famous chaplain, Geoffrey Studdert-Kennedy (better known as "Woodbine Willie").[72] McGreer received timely reinforcements when the British raised the divisional establishment from eleven to seventeen chaplains.

Currie considered Hill 70 the fiercest engagement the Canadians had taken part in up to that time. Certainly the seventy-one Corps chaplains found the pace demanding. They kept several coffee stalls as far forward as possible, in ammunition and ration dumps, lines-of-communication trenches, and aid posts. As at Vimy, these became bases from which chaplains scouring the open ground for casualties could refill their thermos flasks for the wounded. Five stalls were almost constantly under fire, in locations unsafe enough that two soldiers helping to operate them were killed and another wounded.[73]

The fighting, in the August heat, was characterized by such heavy barrages that evacuation of the wounded was particularly hazardous. Scott deployed all brigade chaplains at their regimental aid posts while others visited the gunpits, encountering German mustard gas for the first time. The gunners worked without gas masks in order to fire more accurately: Scott accordingly discarded his, in order to be recognized by the gunners. Between midnight and 7 a.m. on the first day, he visited forty-eight gun positions of the First and Second Artillery brigades.[74] His brigade padres, such as Edward Graham, spent the entire three-day battle at aid posts hastily set up in German dugouts. On the last day he was found on the final objective, burying as many of the unit's dead as he could.[75] Scott's emphasis on his chaplains' being with the men where they fell did not work as well for Catholics, however, as the solitary priest of each brigade could not serve at two or three battalion aid posts simultaneously. Father Madden, for example, made it through the barrage to the busiest of his aid posts, but became too busy to visit the others. He spent the worst day dressing wounded in the open, as stretchers could not be brought down into the captured dugouts. After Hill 70 he reported that immediate burial of the dead in summer was vital, as bodies decomposed more rapidly than at Vimy in the spring.[76]

Madden's experience confirmed the views of other senior chaplains who disagreed with Canon Scott's insistence on keeping his chaplains as far forward as possible. The Second Division's Louis Moffit stationed his padres at the dressing stations further back, concentrating on the line of evacuation and divisional artillery sites.[77] Judging by his reports and marked trench maps, Alexander Gordon sided with Scott: led by their athletic and hard-driving senior chaplain, Fourth Division padres were propelled into the thick of the engagement. Gordon circulated chaplains throughout the various zones of activity, so that all took turns at the heaviest assignments.[78] The chaplains of the Third Division faced the more humdrum tasks of a division in reserve, managing cemetery services and assisting at casualty clearing stations or stretcher relay posts.[79] Although the opposing strategies chosen by Moffit and Scott revealed a growing divergence of opinion between senior chaplains, all faced a fundamental quandary. Deploying a small staff across a divisional area, each was forced to choose between the immediate quality of chaplaincy care to individuals where they fell and the greatest quantity of wounded who could be seen. To Scott, Moffit's policy likely meant that more men would die in the forward zone without the clergy. Moffit, for his part, believed that his staff, by covering areas where traffic to the rear converged, saw more of the men who would live.[80] The debate was not resolved by the experiences at Hill 70 and recurred in the 1918 campaign.

After the battle the Canadians settled down to garrison duties on the Vimy front. Off-duty soldiers flocked to the busy Canadian zone around Barlin, where the Chaplain Service Social Service branch and the YMCA had established canteens. In order to transport, distribute, and protect the growing volume of Social Service Department goods as well as to operate its facilities, McGreer employed at least sixty soldiers who were not fit for front-line duty.[81] Woods, senior chaplain of the Third Division, hoped that the chaplain vacancies created by the summer's stress would be made good very soon. There were urgent reasons for this. The First Army commander had the Corps chaplains to tea one afternoon and lavished praise on them. In a way, he was saying farewell. A few days later, the Canadians were on their way north, to Ypres.[82]

THE CANADIAN ZONE at Ypres bordered on the site of their 1915 engagement, but there were very few familiar landmarks left between Gravenstafel Ridge and Passchendaele in the autumn of 1917. Only the roads remained, now the focus of intense pressure under the combined assaults of German shells and driving rain. Nearly half of the approaches to Passchendaele were covered in water or deep mud. For the men, getting to the line was a nightmare journey along slippery "duckboards," usually at night and under fire. For the stretcher-bearers it meant hours of dangerous and exhausting labour, requiring six of them to carry out one living man, groping their way past discarded dead green with rot. Scattered among the blasted ridges and hollows were little concrete shelters built by the Germans for machine-gunners to shelter from the British barrage. If the characteristic feature of Vimy had been the tunnels, for the padres at Passchendaele it was these "pillboxes." The only safe shelter above ground (and water) level, they became by default the favoured location for unit headquarters and regimental aid posts.

George Kilpatrick and George Pringle found that the mud was so deep that enemy shells lost much of their effect. Though medical staff and padres usually had to wade knee-deep in ground water, which collected in pillboxes, they were the only alternative to working in mud deep enough for wounded men to drown in.[83] Kilpatrick found himself burying men working in the burial parties, as well as numerous German dead left behind in earlier attacks. At a nearby aid post sat fellow Presbyterian Robert Thompson, temporarily blinded by mustard gas. During his battalion's attack Kilpatrick ran the aid post while the medical officer set up another on the right flank. He was impressed with the stoutness of the German defences, especially as shells bounced off his own pillbox. He soon had too many wounded to fit into the tiny space under the five-foot concrete carapace. Several casualties, including one German in agony "from a terrible case of gas gangrene," were killed by near-misses.[84]

Such terrain forced senior chaplains to drop the highly orchestrated Vimy methods. Realizing that the troops often took two extra days just getting in or out of the line, Moffit, Gordon, and Woods put their brigade chaplains in the forward area with their own units, reducing the number at the dressing stations. Once a padre had made his way to his post, he was more or less on his own for the rest of the action, except for short trips to perform burials or pick up supplies, but at least he was able to comfort the wounded and dying during the long wait for evacuation.[85] This, however, would not do for the Catholics. With only three or four in each division, they were unwilling to be isolated at aid posts and worked instead at the dressing stations, where wounded were brought together under their care.[86]

Passchendaele made it abundantly clear that the current allotment of only four priests to a division was far too small for the special needs of dying Catholics.[87] The Fourth Division's Roderick MacDonnell and William Murray found that they were wanted everywhere along the evacuation route. MacDonnell stayed at the dressing station while Murray patrolled the muddy approaches, visiting dying men at the relay and ambulance posts further up. German shelling was ferocious. Even getting out after the battle was over was hazardous. After shelling, gas, and lack of sleep and food for three days, Ronald MacGillivray's party picked their way back along a heavily bombarded escape route: "The dead were lying on both sides of the board walk, and wounded men would call to us from shell holes asking if we had a stretcher."[88]

For many of the brigade chaplains Passchendaele was marked by paradoxes of mercy in the midst of the most merciless campaign they had known. In broad daylight Thomas Stewart, chaplain to the First Canadian Mounted Rifles, was allowed, under a large Red Cross flag, to bring back the wounded almost from the enemy line, pausing only when stray shells landed close by. William Davis distinguished himself by wandering across no man's land with a white handkerchief on a walking-stick, locating wounded left behind during a failed attack on the German line. Floundering through the mud, he would place a rifle with the casualty's helmet, German or Canadian, balanced on top to help each side's stretcher-bearers. During a lull he presided over an informal truce. Under his direction German and Canadian stretcher-bearers carried each other's wounded to a neutral pillbox for first aid and exchange. Both Stewart and Davis, along with Robert Thompson of the Fourth Canadian Field Artillery, received Military Crosses for their work at Passchendaele.[89]

To earn his Military Cross, Thomas Colwell spent two days clearing his unit's stinking trenches and shellholes of wounded. Assisting stretcher-bearers, he bound wounds, dug shelter trenches, guided a blinded soldier caught in cross-fire to safety, and supervised evacuation efforts. Under a Red Cross flag he dragged wounded out of shellholes in no man's land before they drowned. During the day a dud German shell landed under his feet, leaving him breathless and disoriented, but on the way back to the aid post he found a dying soldier who wanted his company. That afternoon Colwell spent three more hours in a shellhole filled with sixteen wounded men dragged there by an undersized "bantam" stretcher-bearer. Shellfire kept throwing mud and water into their position, so Colwell rigged up groundsheets to cover the seriously wounded. It was dangerous work: the first bearer party he sent to the rear was wiped out before his eyes by a direct hit. Colwell took the next stretcher party himself, carrying a "pathetic casualty who had lost a leg to shellfire." The night was spent scouring the region for wounded left behind, the next day burying the dead, though "chased by shelling."[90] George Kilpatrick and George Pringle, with the Forty-second and Forty-third Battalions, experienced relentless shelling on and around their pillboxes, often killing the men who could not be fitted inside. Kilpatrick carried medical supplies up to the aid post and took charge of evacuation work when other officers were killed. Pringle spent his tour of duty inside a flooded pillbox, where wounded on stretchers lay with their backs in the water. Both admitted that the four sleepless days and nights were the most terrible they had yet experienced.[91]

Back of the line, the Chaplain Service and the Red Cross for the first time teamed up with the YMCA. The Red Cross supplied goods, transport, and coffee in the hospitals, while the Chaplain Service and the Y, under Shatford's direction, served coffee, cocoa, and tea to those going back and forth to the line from the advanced dressing stations. The wounded, medics, and bearer parties warmly appreciated the hot drinks, food, stoves and fuel, clothing and cigarettes available from the service.[92] Shatford and Alfred Steele, his Salvation Army assistant, got their cinema tent (concealed in an old building) operating in the shelled area and scraped together concerts for the men at the Vlamertinghe and Vrandhoeck depots. For the first time a Knights of Columbus–Catholic Army Hut tent was also deployed in each division, with a fifth set aside for the Twenty-second Battalion.[93]

Passchendaele was taken on 6 November. As the winter weather closed down offensive operations for 1917, the Canadians withdrew to Vimy. While most chaplains caught up on correspondence with next of kin, Gordon remained on the battlefield, aided by Anglican chaplain and friend Harold McCausland, burying the last Canadian dead. Several chaplains had been wounded during the attacks, three too severely to return to the Corps.[94] As one year before, a harrowing offensive was followed by a busy Christmas program in familiar Vimy. The coffee stalls reappeared in support and even front-line trenches, while padres fitted up recreation rooms, showed films, organized concerts and plays, ordered magazines, and held services.[95] There was diversion in the election campaign and the opportunity to vote for Borden's Union government – most chaplains had few scruples about urging their men to vote for conscription and victory.[96] Bishop DePencier, then chaplain to a Canadian hospital in France, came up to receive soldiers sponsored by their padres into full communion with the Anglican church.[97] New Year's Day brought back memories of both the heights and depths of the previous year, as the Honours List included awards for fourteen Canadian chaplains.[98]

Chaplain Service authorities valued these citations for bravery highly, though individual chaplains doubted that medals won a soldier's respect. Instead, they turned to soul-winning by social service, at Currie's request joining with the Red Cross and YMCA to run an officers' hostel at Corps Headquarters.[99] With Currie's permission, General Lipsett and Third Division chaplains conducted their "citizenship school" for soldiers lacking formal education.[100] Scott welcomed the return to the quiet sector, where conditions permitted his rambling through the trenches – "parish visiting in the slums," he called it: "It was great fun to go into the saps and surprise the two or three men who were on guard in them," even during shelling or German trench raids. Such appearances added to the Canon Scott lore of the Corps, as did his humorous monologues and "War Outlook" talks.[101] Other chaplains, too, spent extended periods in the line. One, Ambrose Madden, was wounded for the second time by shrapnel during a tour of Hill 70 trenches.[102] Few, however, ever achieved the prominence of Scott.

On 21 March 1918 the German army struck at the Allied line in Picardy, commencing the offensive anticipated since the Russian army's collapse. On 5 April the Germans reached a point just ten miles east of Amiens. By then the British had established an emergency defence line manned by hastily assembled detachments from several forces, including the Canadians. The Canadian chaplains spent an anxious Easter in the trenches with their units, their special services cancelled by the emergency. Senior chaplains drew up their own "secret orders" for chaplains in the event of a German breakthrough.[103] Canadian units were spread out along the ten-mile gap between Hill 70 and Arras for weeks, usually under very heavy German bombardment. In one of these gunnery duels Father Rosario Crochetire, chaplain to the Twenty-second Battalion, died when his dressing station near Arras was obliterated by shelling.[104]

Chaplains spent more time in advanced aid posts as the Germans bombarded support trenches heavily. Maurice de la Taille, a Jesuit priest with the Canadian Cavalry Brigade, came upon some wounded Catholics in a field ambulance. One soldier with serious facial wounds, asked if he wanted communion, wrote "Yes" in his own blood on the side of the horse ambulance. Confessions and mass, noted the Roman Catholic priests wryly, were better attended and more fervent when accompanied by near-misses.[105] Such proximity to the shelling, however, increased casualties among the chaplains. Father Arthur Coté of the Ninth Brigade was wounded during one of these raids but remained on duty. Another was returned to England after a nervous breakdown. Three Anglican chaplains were evacuated to England with severe shell wounds.

As the German offensive waned, the Canadians began preparations for the summer offensives. McGreer was joined at Corps Headquarters by Father Francis French, an intrepid priest from Pembroke, respected by all his colleagues for his unstinting devotion to dying Catholics. The service, with eighty chaplains at the Corps and fifty more on the lines of communication, had come a long way from the first dozen padres of 1915.[106] During the coming campaign it reached the midst of the battlefield. Among the chaplains, the old debate over the front line resumed. Arthur Creegan, with the Third Brigade, urged McGreer to deploy chaplains ahead of the regimental aid posts, in the attacking waves. He had found that most seriously wounded men arrived at the crowded and hectic aid posts comatose or already in shock, too late for the most vital spiritual work. He urged that padres go out with the stretcher-bearers, ministering to casualties where they fell, and brushed aside objections that too many chaplains would "come to grief": it could only raise Chaplain Service influence if a few more became casualties.[107] He got his wish. While padres carried on their recreation work and prepared for battle, McGreer, French, and the senior chaplains contemplated a strategy for the final offensives.[108]

Knowing that heavy fighting lay in the immediate future, there was an urgency in the chaplains' religious work. George Wells, new senior chaplain of the Second Division, persuaded senior officers to enforce officer attendance at church parades. Never one to shirk a difficult task or turn a blind eye to regulations, he also had divisional authorities crack down on the "blasphemous and foul language" so widely in use, and stepped up the intermittent war on illicit gambling that the padres waged in the divisions.[109] On a more friendly tack, chaplains conducted informal outdoor Bible classes, urging men to pledge allegiance to Christ and Church. At the end of May, Roman Catholics hosted Bishop Fallon, who addressed the chaplains and troops on the issues of faith and war.[110] His church's efforts crossed denominational lines with the Catholic Holy Name Society campaign for the voluntary suppression of profanity. Roderick MacDonnell, a Canadian Benedictine with the Twelfth Brigade, distributed the society's pamphlet to all ranks, with General Currie's and his divisional commanders' endorsements printed on its cover. Later that fall, chaplains going through the effects of both Catholic and Protestant dead often came across signed Holy Name Society pledge cards.[111]

The summer saw the popularity of Canon Scott soar to new heights. When army authorities withdrew chaplains' horses, he acquired a motorcycle and side-car from the Motor Machine Gun Brigade. Scott's machine became a familiar and somewhat comical sight rattling up the St Pol road at forty-five kilometres an hour, with a box of hymn-books and a portable altar strapped on the back. He had his name painted on the side-car fender, in order, he claimed, to prevent its theft. When Scott broke up some gambling among the troops that summer, however, they took revenge on him by stealing the hymn-books.[112]

On 15 July 1918 the Canadians returned to the line. The preceding weeks had seen the conclusion of a number of activities, including the spring classes of the University of Vimy Ridge: Oliver proclaimed a "holiday" for the duration of active fighting. In the last few days Canadian senior chaplains, Scott and Gordon in particular, were pleased to explain to new American chaplains how things were done in the Corps.[113] There was a final religious exercise for the padres to perform as the Canadians tensed for battle. August 4 was the fourth anniversary of the war, and a day of prayer was held for the success of the Allies.[114] Battle was imminent.

ON THE NIGHT of 7 August 1918 Canadian chaplains quietly slipped into position in Gentelles Wood, east of Amiens. Just after 4 a.m. the barrage opened. Three Canadian divisions, along with Australian and French troops, attacked the German lines. At Amiens, Canadian chaplains' work called for hasty improvisation, as Headquarters's security restrictions excluded the service from advance planning. Nevertheless, eighteen chaplains, a quarter of the Corps staff, went over the top with their battalions, while the remainder covered the Corps area. More chaplains had immediate access to the men when and where they were hit.[115] For padres the open fields of tall ripening grain remained a major concern, for they concealed both determined German machine-gunners and wounded Canadians. The padres helped to clear off the casualties, often with teams of prisoners they had collected. Most important to them was finding the seriously wounded or dying before, too late, they arrived at the regimental aid posts. Looking back, B. Whitaker reported that, deployed in this fashion, "No wounded man passed through the advanced area without seeing a chaplain. The work of ministering to their units justified any risks taken."[116] Even the death of William Davis, hit by shellfire while evacuating casualties at Caix, did not deter chaplains such as Creegan, who with many others felt vindicated in their advocacy of complete front-line commitment.[117]

Davis, who had seemed to bear a charmed life at Passchendaele, was buried with other fallen officers of the Fourth Canadian Mounted Regiment in a communal cemetery near Quesnel.[118]

At Amiens reports came in of padres leading men on to final objectives when combat officers became casualties, occasionally receiving the surrender of parties of the enemy and giving last rites to dying Germans.[119] Several close calls with death resulted from mingling with the attacking waves and aiding the wounded in the open. In the words of Roman Catholic chaplain Miles Thompkins, "I got my tail nearly shot off ... Certainly if I had a tail it would have been 'na poo.'" Surprisingly, only three other chaplains besides Davis became casualties.[120] One was a senior chaplain: Alexander Gordon, crossing a ridge with the Fifty-fourth Battalion, was bowled over by a burst of machine-gun fire. His wound bound with captured shell dressings (and lace curtain trim from a nearby German dugout), Gordon was bundled to the rear. Ambrose Madden won his second decoration (the DSO) for tending wounded during the attack on Caix. He was wounded too, for the third time since enlistment, and only saw action with the Second Brigade again in October.[121] Concentrating his efforts on stretcher cases (because walking wounded would see a priest at the casualty clearing station), Roman Catholic chaplain William Murray was sniped at as well as shelled for three days and nights, but his greatest annoyance, he reported later, was the practice of some bearers of removing all identification from the dead, making it impossible to sort out Roman Catholics from Protestants.[122]

The Amiens precedent was followed throughout the rest of the campaign. Canadian troops advanced east of Arras, broke through very heavy German defences between the Drocourt-Queant lines, and crossed the Canal du Nord. During these almost continuous operations senior chaplains simply carried on the Amiens methods, for they had no time to reorganize their workers. Father French began sending over half of his twenty priests up with the medical staff and bearers. As at Amiens, a number of padres were left to move about the Corps area as "free lances."[123] Twenty accompanied their units in the opening assault, while artillery chaplains visited the guns, buried the dead, and held services among the wagon lines. Most brigade chaplains' reports resembled that of George Taylor, Seventh Brigade, who accompanied his men to the attack on 28 August 1918:

> The line was extremely difficult owing to the nature of the ground, and we lost many men and officers by sniping. While I was dressing a man he got wounded in the arm a second time by a sniper working near us. Later in the afternoon when I went forward with "D" Company to the attack on Jig-Saw

Wood, we were driven to shell holes by snipers from a place which we thought clear of the enemy. I had two water-bottles full of hot coffee, and ran among the men giving this to them as long as it lasted. The want of water made this doubly acceptable. By 3 o'clock the company had gained its objective, but we had lost heavily. I went back and took a party of sixty prisoners forward to carry out the wounded. So intense was the gunfire that we could not do much for the first two hours. In this time four of the party had been killed. At dark I went forward with the Medical Officer, and we rested until the moon rose and then brought out the remainder of our wounded.[124]

Despite heavy sniping, Edward Graham's work getting to casualties in the open led to extraordinary recognition during the Canal du Nord crossing. Graham modestly stated that his rescue work encouraged stragglers and distracted others from looting. In fact, on 29 August 1918, followed on hands and knees by a wounded batman muttering imprecations because his London leave was lost, harassed by snipers, waving a handkerchief, and dragging a stretcher, Graham displayed either the daring or the suicidal indifference that won him a nomination for the Victoria Cross. That day he rescued five Twenty-second Battalion wounded from the German barbed wire in broad daylight.[125]

Reconstructing Chaplain Service work in those last weeks becomes difficult as the pace of combat, the short respites, the strain of constant movement, wounds, and illness all made the orderly compiling of reports impossible. Few parade services could be held; here and there small groups gathered for prayers and benedictions, often interrupted by German fire. In the end the bulk of the chaplains' efforts was dedicated to the wounded and dying.[126] The senior chaplains continued to post from one-third to half their staff in the forward areas or with attacking units. Catholic chaplains rotated between dressing stations and their units or took turns hearing confessions and celebrating mass in local churches (or the open air) for reserve troops. Priests and Protestants with the attacking waves alike reported that they were more successful in ministering to the dying in the field than at the dressing stations, though this often led to being under direct enemy fire.[127] Having been so involved in the final days of the advance, senior chaplains found it especially satisfying that, led by Father Thomas McCarthy of the Seventh Brigade, the Chaplain Service too entered Mons with the leading Canadian units.[128]

By 11 November the chaplains had learned that open warfare called for even more physical and emotional resilience than trench fighting. Chaplains of middle age or beyond, who had managed well enough previously, began to burn out at a growing rate.[129] From the beginning of September to the Armistice the mood in the chaplains' reports shifted from optimism to grim endurance as the excitement and stress of open warfare ground them down physically and emotionally. Unlike Vimy or Passchendaele, progress was measured in miles, not yards, but in a similar span of days just as many were killed or wounded as in the old bloodbaths.[130] The Chaplain Service paid a high price for its work in the forward areas. While nine padres received medals for heroism, eight were wounded and four rendered ineffective by battlefield exhaustion.[131] In the fifty days' campaigning between 22 August and 11 October, Chaplain Service attrition at Corps reached thirteen out of seventy-three (17.8 per cent), a considerable casualty rate for non-combatant officers.[132] Medical reports reveal that padres had been coming to the front of the battlefield since 1916, when four chaplains were hit by shellfire. During the next year, gas and enemy shells laid aside another eight. In 1918, however, four Canadian chaplains received gunshot wounds, which, along with German shrapnel, gas, and aerial bombing, raised the total of wounded padres that last year to seventeen.

With the Armistice came release from the tension and strain of combat. The chaplains were soon wrestling, however, with the challenges of ministering to troops in an army of occupation. While the Third and Fourth Divisions settled temporarily in Belgium, the First and Second marched with the British Second Army into Germany. McGreer urged Almond not to transfer or recall Corps chaplains during this period, as those who had been with the units under fire would have the best moral influence on them at this time. Already he was hearing alarming reports from his senior chaplains of what some of the troops, with time on their hands, secure from sudden death and surrounded by grateful civilian women, were doing. He brought Edmund Oliver back up to Corps Headquarters to revive the educational scheme. Soon the Khaki University was back in operation, with so many chaplains working as education officers that Shatford complained they had insufficient time for religious work.[133]

For chaplains in Germany the situation was somewhat less alarming. Many units received regimental and royal colours, which were consecrated by the divisional and unit chaplains at presentation. Education work continued to occupy much of their time, along with recreational work and religious counselling. Celebrating Christmas in conquered Germany was especially meaningful. Chaplains with student memories of the university at Bonn found the Second Division's divine services held in its chapel especially ironic: now the students had punished their teachers, who had so proudly grasped for world domination.[134]

In the early weeks of the new year the divisions in Germany were withdrawn to Huy and Namur, back in Belgium.

From the padres' perspective the arrival of two more divisions in Belgium presented one of the greatest moral challenges of the war, as Belgian women fraternized more freely with the liberators than did the German women. Some padres arranged tours of nearby Waterloo. Memorial services were held, and more king's and regimental colours were presented. The men were told to live up to the high standard achieved in the fighting, and the Holy Name Society campaigned for more members. Catholics taught Khaki U courses, prepared Christmas services, set up reading rooms and Catholic army hut tents; but by the early spring of 1919 the Roman Catholic padres were thoroughly alarmed at the sagging morals of their charges. It was a relief in mid-March to have the First and Third Divisions return to Britain. Still, the behaviour and morale of the Second and especially the Fourth Division, which had been in Belgium the longest, remained troublesome.[135] All concerned were therefore relieved by the decision to move the Canadians back to England in April. Equally glad to depart were the chaplains – to the Canadian Infantry Works Company, at work moving and reinterring the Canadian dead scattered across the old Somme battlefield. Months after the Armistice it seemed that the last rites of the campaign remained those set aside for the dead. That duty done, in the spring of 1919 the last Canadian padres departed for England.

As McGreer and his remaining chaplains turned homeward, they brought to a close the battlefield exploits of the Canadian Chaplain Service. In successive phases since the summer of 1915 the Canadian Corps chaplaincy had moved from the fringes to the front of the battlefield. In each the chaplains had pursued the inexorable logic of their wartime pastoral ministry. They had insisted upon becoming the soldier's companion in every phase of his existence. In the face of death the chaplains had not accepted their original assignment to the rear. Neither would they forfeit the respect and influence that would, they early realized, be awarded by the men exclusively to those who shared in every risk and stress of battle. As a result, instead of producing a few outstanding Friar Tucks and a flock of tepid followers, by 1918 the Corps chaplaincy consisted of a group of hardened professionals under senior chaplain tacticians of growing skill and aggressiveness. By then they had won their battle for acceptance on their own terms. Many shared with fellow officers and men the glory and also the physical and mental costs of victory as, for the rest of their lives, they relived the exaltation and despair of their pilgrimage overseas and back.

6 Comrades: To Touch the Face of Battle

> As one looks back upon it, the surface things of that life have drifted away, and the great things that one remembers are the self-sacrifice, the living comradeship, and the unquestioning faith in the eternal rightness of right and duty which characterized those who were striving to the death for the salvation of the world. This glorious vision of the nobility of human nature sustained the chaplain through many discouragements and difficulties ... I have often sat on my horse on rainy nights near Hill 63, and watched the battalions going up to the line ... At such times, the sordid life has been transfigured before me. The hill was no longer Hill 63, but it was the hill of Calvary. The burden laid upon the men was no longer the heavy soldier's pack, but it was the cross of Christ, and, as the weary tramp of the men splashed in the mud, I said to myself, "Each one has fulfilled the law of life, and has taken up his cross and is following Christ."[1]

The mundane and sordid daily aspects of army life at the front routinely frustrated and exasperated the cleric in uniform. Sometimes padres were very angry men. Yet Scott's meditation at Hill 63 reveals the love and fear that blended with their other emotions. Horrible wounds, death, inhumane military justice, soldierly compassion, and increasing admiration for the men rebelled against their own deep commitment to victory in the cause that had brought them all to the front in the first place. Yet for almost every chaplain the resolution of these inner turmoils lay not in renouncing the war or the beliefs that impelled them to touch the face of battle. Instead, the powerful union of love and anger, mixed with growing admiration of the men and identification with them, forged in the padre the white-hot conviction that they must win the war and make the world anew in the peace. Then their weapons would be their gospel and the returned man, whom they had come to know and love. Only a few realized that they loved their idealized soldier-pilgrims not wisely but too well, and that, once the challenging circumstances of the front were behind them, their men might not be as willing as they expected to carry on the crusade back home.

THE GOAL OF MOST Great War chaplains was the front. Whenever there were casualties or transfers among the Corps chaplains, the call would go in for one of the casualty clearing station or field hospital chaplains to proceed to the ADCS at Corps as quickly as possible. A few hours later, after hastily packing (and briefing his successor on the spiritual terrain he was now leaving), the padre chosen was on his way to Corps Headquarters. Upon arrival at McGreer's office, he would be taken over to the field ambulance, artillery brigade, or battalion in the infantry brigade where he would make his personal headquarters.[2] Officially the padre belonged to a brigade or ambulance, not its smaller components. The unit he called home was supposed to be primarily for food and lodging, but most chaplains shared in the life of "their" battalion, adopting regimental dress and cap badges.[3]

Breaking into the close circle of fellow officers was the new padre's first test. Without a good working relationship with them (especially the commander, adjutant, and medical officer) he would continually be marginalized, even rejected. More than once Almond or McGreer was asked by a CO to transfer a padre who had failed "to get a grip on the unit."[4] Yet he had to avoid becoming too dependent on the officers' mess. The new padre needed to establish both a good reputation among and rapport with the men in the ranks. This involved more than securing a private billet where soldiers could confidentially meet him and then sitting back to wait for visitors. Nor was the parade service necessarily the best opportunity to win acceptance. Usually making some contribution to the recreational or social life of the unit first broke the ice.[5] So did taking part in unit training and route marches, assisting stragglers with their burdensome kit. George Fallis, while with the Canadian Mounted Rifles, found that the men had little respect for chaplains who rode in the mess cart at the rear of the column.[6]

When out of the line, billet-visiting and getting into religious discussion with the men seemed to help to familiarize padres with those troops who were at least willing to talk. Though some enlisted men and NCOs resented his intrusion on their privacy, most chaplains reported that the soldiers in billets were friendly and responsive to the chaplain who showed a sense of humour and kept his sermons short.[7] Experienced chaplains soon learned that what the men actually said about them after such visits did not always coincide with their own impressions. They often found that the critical figure in getting to know their unit was their own servant, or batman. Most chaplains depended upon his monitoring of regimental moods and gossip. The typical chaplain thus viewed losing a good batman as a real blow to his ability to monitor the state of the unit.[8] Batmen also acted as trench guides and advisers until the chaplain got used to its dangers.

The chaplain's routine between offensives was dominated by visiting billets, counselling soldiers, censoring or writing letters (to next of kin or wounded unit members), organizing games, and planning services. Perhaps one of the most mind-numbing duties that brother officers passed off to chaplains was the censoring of the unit's letters, a process of reading through every personal piece of mail the unit generated, crossing or cutting out any references to military topics. None the less, many chaplains found the task a useful way of getting to know their men. One rather high-handed Anglican chaplain recalled, "A fellow wrote four appallingly mushy letters to four girls in the same town, all identical, protesting to each that he loved her alone. The censor put every one in the wrong envelope. The next mail to this Lothario must have been interesting."[9] When in the line a chaplain visited as many sections of the trenches as possible, usually ending his tour at the aid post, spending the night with the medical officer. Work at the front demanded a strong physique. Much of the average padre's day was spent walking (especially after the chaplains' horses were taken away by a frugal quartermaster-general early in 1918) from one unit to another or up to the line and back.[10] His bicycle, intended to replace horses, usually proved useless on French roads in wet weather. This was a special hardship for Roman Catholics, who were supposed to fast before serving mass.[11] Thus most padres fought a stubborn rear-guard action against having their horses taken away or replaced by broken-down nags. When an artillery chaplain lost his prized mount, he was offered a small mule by a battery commander. When the chaplain objected, his CO remarked, "Now, Padre, there was a much better man than you rode into Jerusalem on a similar mount, and I am afraid you will have to be satisfied with what we have offered you."[12]

Roman Catholic chaplains also found themselves taking responsibility for French civilians whose priests had been conscripted. Occasionally officers complained to Father French that his staff were too busy with civilians to be able to meet military needs.[13] Because of the way German troops had desecrated Catholic churches in 1914, British and Canadian non–Roman Catholic chaplains were denied the use of local parish churches and were thus forced to hold numerous and widely dispersed services out of doors. The positive side of this situation was its tendency to put the chaplain in contact with smaller groups of men, helping him to get to know the troops somewhat better, as long as he could stand the pace.[14] Artillery chaplains had even more ground to cover as they moved from battery to battery within the brigade. Field ambulance chaplains usually had all they could manage with their home unit's dressing stations; in the great offensives the senior chaplain would attach infantry chaplains whose brigades were not in action to the dressing stations to lend them a hand.

Unless the new arrival had the misfortune to arrive in mid-offensive, however, his first impression of Corps work was that of anticlimax. Battle was not continuous. In fact, much more time was spent on the prosaic and mundane, which often appeared less vital and materially useful. All Canadian Corps chaplains were expected every Monday to submit reports, with interesting anecdotes, to McGreer. Dissidents who criticized such reports as self-advertising got a stiff rebuke: "Some day the History of this war will be written and the only possible source of information that can be drawn on ... will be our files, and if all the files have no more on them than your report of last month, there will be nothing to write about in connection with our service. One must forget his own individuality in the better interests of the Canadian Chaplain Services." The chaplain duly wrote, "Visited the lines" or "Visited the guns" or "Arranged Sunday services," but what lay behind these few words ranged from ten-mile hikes visiting outlying detachments to hour-long interviews with troubled officers and NCOs or long evenings of correspondence, censoring, private talks, and visits to the billets.[15]

Here as elsewhere life had its peculiar headaches. The problem of fitting worship into military life became even more acute in the field as battle or its preliminaries played havoc with church parade schedules.[16] Brigade-strength services, usually held on ceremonial occasions such as 1 July, always caused muted padre resentment, for frustrated preachers could never make themselves heard, even in the calmest weather, addressing a square of several thousand men.[17] To army officers, Sundays, when the battalions were "in rest", provided excellent opportunities to shift their units to new billets without disrupting weekday training. As a result, constantly disrupted church parade arrangements at the front were one of the several vexations that tempted the padre to profanity:

A Brigade service was arranged to take place at 10 a.m. Sunday 8th at which the Senior Chaplain was to preach. The form of Service was specially printed for the occasion ... I arranged to give several officers and men a Communion service at 8. Found that the C. of E.'s could only parade at 8:30, so cancelled the Communion Service at 8 and arranged parade for 8:30. At noon Saturday was informed C. of E.'s could not parade at 8:30, so cancelled parade at 8:30 and reinstated service at 8. At 4 p.m. Saturday was requested to hold Parade for 54th Battalion, who had been instructed to ask me. – Arranged a parade for 8:30 and cancelled the Communion at 8. At 10 p.m. Saturday was notified that Brigade could not spare the time to 54th Battalion to hold a Church Service. So cancelled Parade and got as many as possible notified of Holy Communion – 3rd time of asking – at 8 o'clock. Only a few could be reached. Hurried to Brigade Parade – "No Parades Today." Had small service in p.m. with a few men and sang some hymns ... Would it not be lawful, highly expedient to interview the powers that be – and which therefore are presumably ordained of God – and request or admonish that Sunday should be left free from "schools for bombing", etc. etc. – for the best welfare of officers and men and for true efficiency?[18]

The wise padre, however, tried to take such interruptions in stride, especially if the church parade was being pre-empted by such popular activities as visits by the paymaster or trips to the baths.[19] By the time chaplains reached the Corps, most were well aware of the silent resentment felt especially by junior officers and the men at church parade and tried various techniques to soften the harsh disciplinary atmosphere of the service. In 1917 Canadian chaplains were assisted by a British Army order encouraging units to break ranks and gather around the chaplain in a semicircle.[20] Canadian chaplains welcomed the more informal atmosphere: Alexander Gordon told his father, "The only formation suitable for a hearty church service is no formation at all." Some learned from Gordon the tricks necessary to catch the attention of a sullen congregation: "So, when the chaplain had announced his text, 'Oh, come, let us worship'; he began, – 'I think I hear you fellows saying, "Why the blankety blank do we have to turn out for worship? What the dash dash is the use of church parade?" "Instantly, every man sat up, and for a quarter of an hour, while the chaplain preached, he was given the closest attention."[21] Even with the best of intentions, however, Gordon and his colleagues often found themselves ignored as the men, especially at the back of the congregation, dozed fitfully or craned their necks to watch patrolling aircraft or the exciting dogfights going on over their heads.[22] Scott once had a billet prayer service interrupted by a fistfight at the other end of the barn. His solution to the distraction was to take the congregation over to watch the fight, then, when the excitement was over, recall his men to prayer: "I told the men that nothing helped so much to make a service bright and hearty as the inclusion of a fight, and that when I returned to Canada, if at any time my congregation was listless or sleepy, I would arrange a fight on the other side of the street to which we could adjourn and from which we should return with renewed spiritual fervour."[23]

In all his work the chaplain at the Corps faced the difficult question of how his efficiency was to be measured. Touring horse lines, batteries, and trenches, striking up conversations, keeping an open door, and turning a hand to every mundane task that officers found distasteful all were intended to break down the barriers between clergymen and military men and demonstrate the church's interest in and concern for their welfare. All were attempts to prove to the men that the padre was trying to break through the privileges of his rank and elevated status to touch the lives and consciences of his men. Yet the same activities could keep a chaplain so busy with well-doing that other men would complain of his inaccessibility. Nevertheless, most chaplains believed that in social-service work they successfully broke down the peacetime barriers between the average man and the cleric. Even more valued was their freedom to visit the trenches and accompany the men into action. Repeatedly the chaplains reported that, unlike peacetime parish work, army life made it impossible for chaplains to be written off by the men as privileged and aloof from their real life and concerns.[24]

Nevertheless, most admitted that whatever extracurricular activities they took on, it was what they did to prepare the men and sustain them for battle that counted most. Such pre-battle preliminaries followed a recognizable pattern. The chaplains conducted evening voluntary services and held services of Holy Communion as frequently as possible. Roman Catholics customarily would be ordered to attend confession and mass (which was taken by the men as a sure sign that action was imminent).[25] One day would be spent with the medical officer and adjutant, finding out the unit's deployment for battle, where the aid posts, dressing stations, and coffee stalls would be located. The number of men coming for confidential talks might increase, while some soldiers would leave sealed letters with the chaplain, to be sent to relatives in the event of death in battle.

Depending on the time available and the disposition of the officers, a unit parade service would be scheduled as close as possible to the departure time for the line. Viewed from their side of the altar, such services were emotionally charged and often exhilarating for chaplains.[26] According to them, the men seemed more reverent, receptive, and devoted at such solemn occasions as the chaplains touched emotions neglected since childhood and buried deep in the soldiers' memories. Denominational considerations, age, and social class seemed especially irrelevant, transcended by the common purpose of worship and communion.[27] Roman Catholic soldiers and chaplains found themselves deeply moved by the pronouncement of General Absolution *in articulo mortis* ("in danger of death") on the eve of battle: "Next comes our chaplain, who says, 'My children, tomorrow you will meet the enemy. You will do your duty and fight bravely, as you have always done. But, let there be no illusion. Many of you will return in safety, but there are some who will return no more. And so I give you general absolution.' As he speaks, the voice of our good chaplain breaks with emotion. The battalion kneels; and the priest's hand makes over us the sign of the Cross. Kneeling on the grass, with emotion in my soul, I offer my life in sacrifice, if God so wills."[28]

At such times the obvious devotion of individuals made a deep impression on many chaplains and gave them a rewarding sense of belonging with and being appreciated by the men. After Passchendaele, one Catholic chaplain recalled:

> Even as I write this report, I can in fancy see their eager faces and hear their sincere, "Good-bye Father, Pray for me." These words kept ringing in my ears yesterday as I said Mass for the noble boys we left in Belgium. The life of a chaplain is usually a hard one, and as he struggles along, the indifference of those who should know better frequently causes him to ask the old question, '*cui bono*?' But on the other hand when he sees the courage of his men and their trust in God, when he receives back to the fold men who for years scoffed at religion; when men not of his faith grasp his hand and ask to be remembered by him as they go to face death, he is amply rewarded for his toil. I would not exchange these few hours in the mud and cold for years of peaceful parish work.[29]

Most wished some of the intensity of battlefield services could be transferred to peacetime worship in their old parishes. Memories of such services took on a special poignancy for the chaplain after action, when, as he wrote notification letters to soldiers' families, he recalled their last communion.

There was some discussion among the chaplains about what they ought to accomplish in these pre-battle devotions. How was a chaplain supposed to prepare men for battle? Early in the war senior officers had wanted the chaplains out of the way so as not to frighten or demoralize the men. Chaplains responded that their prayers steadied them, helped them to relax, and diverted them from morbid introspection.[30] Canon Scott, before the Vimy assault, emphasized the steadying effect of a clear conscience on the soldier's fighting morale. Pre-battle worship imparted a sense of absolution and spiritual tranquillity. In spite of training and discipline, each soldier remained an individual whose will had to be strengthened by "religion and right thinking ... To those that need it, and there are many, the assurance of pardoned sins through the Blood of Christ, gives a cheerfulness, a hope and a Divine courage in the face of death which military training alone cannot secure." The chaplain put the soldier in "the highest religious state" to commit himself to the self-sacrificing decisions and deeds of war. Social-service work, to Scott, was secondary to the chaplaincy's "real work in the army, and its value as a military asset, which lies in deeper things."[31]

Underlying such a philosophy were the assumptions of pre-war idealism that moral courage and spiritual devotion would triumph over the most discouraging physical circumstances. In their complete deference to the cause, few chaplains had deep sympathy for the men who occasionally approached them seeking assistance to be transferred to the rear or left behind during an attack. Scott had a strong reply to such expressions of fear, revealing the moral universe within which most chaplains functioned:

> I asked him what right he had to pray such a prayer. He was really asking God to make another do what he would not do himself. The prayer was selfish and wrong, and he could not expect God to answer it. The right prayer to pray was that, if he was called to go over the parapet God would give him the strength to do his duty ... I told him that he had the chance of his life to make himself a man. In the past he had been more or less a weakling, he could now, by the help of God, rise up in the strength of his manhood and become a hero ... His mother and sisters no doubt had loved him and taken care of him in the past, but they would love him far more if he did his duty now, "For," I said, "All women love a brave man." I told him to take as his text, "I can do all things through Christ which strengtheneth me," and I made him repeat it after me several times. I saw that the young fellow was pulling himself together, and he shook hands with me and told me he would go up to the line and take his chance with the rest – and he did.[32]

With such high expectations and strong imperatives, few chaplains felt equipped to deal with men whose self-control had entirely evaporated and who fell under military discipline for cowardice.

As zero hour approached, chaplains faced their own mixture of anticipation and suspense while they took up pre-bombardment positions: worries about the success of the attack, casualty rates, and personal safety.[33] Among the many prayers, some admitted, were their own petitions not to lose, or even appear to lose, their nerve.[34] These anxieties the padre usually bore alone: Scott, while admitting that his own emotions were in turmoil before battle, did his best not to let them show. "It was not wise for a chaplain to do anything which looked as if he was taking matters too seriously. It was the duty of everyone to forget private feelings in the one absorbing desire to kill off the enemy … I took great care not to let the men know that I ever was moved by … sentimentalism. We were out to fight the Germans, and on that one object we had to concentrate all our thoughts to the obliteration of private emotions."[35] Corps chaplains, especially in the early days of the war, often had the mixed blessing of knowing or having recruited many of the men going into attack. Knowing the families as well as the men themselves made concern over their fate and grief when he buried them exceptionally stressful.[36] Scott always took himself to some part of the line where he could watch the barrage and pray for victory. Other chaplains wandered through the trenches holding voluntary prayers with the men, passing on encouraging war news, or hurrying to the aid posts with the doctors.[37]

In the aid post, dressing station, or at the side of the wounded in the open, the Corps chaplains found more of the emotional strains and exaltation, fatigue and admiration for the spirit of the men that they had earlier glimpsed in the hospitals and clearing stations. They felt the tense helplessness of being under bombardment, overwhelmed by odours of poison gas, explosive fumes, and dead flesh. At times medical personnel needed rest or encouragement.[38] For days without much rest or sleep, accompanied by the hiss of acetylene lamps and the smell of blood and death, they concentrated on tending to the wounded and dying, guiding or directing stretcher-bearers, or conducting burials. Sometimes these latter missions of mercy became nightmares as the bearer parties they directed were cut up by shelling, leading more than one chaplain to blame himself for sending men to their deaths.[39] After their tours in the dressing stations, most echoed George Kilpatrick, who remarked to his senior chaplain after Passchendaele: "I saw deeper into the inferno of pain which our boys go thro' than ever before."[40] Edward Graham reported, after Hill 70, that he had come "out of the line with a deepened respect and admiration for fighting men and stretcher bearers and with a satisfying sense of having been of some use to them."[41] Repeatedly chaplains remarked on the courage, cheerfulness, and comradeship shown by their men. Inevitably their admiration for the heroism they witnessed increased their sympathy for and identification with the troops. After Vimy Ridge, George Wood wrote, "the wonderful bravery, endurance and self-sacrifice of the men at the front filled me with amazement and thanksgiving. Lads have come from the farm and shop and factory to show how heroes endure inexpressible hardships and peril. We who do our work in comparative comfort can truly admire the spirit of the men who go over the top. Such sacrifice cannot be in vain."[42]

Deathbed interviews and strong impressions of the courage, stoicism, and endurance of the suffering stretched the emotional reserves of most chaplains to the limit and, paradoxically, inspired them at the same time.[43] The chaplains found in these moments strong confirmation of their beliefs as dying men made their act of contrition, asked for baptism, or gave last messages for their relatives. Especially moving to Roman Catholics were the deaths of officers and men whom they had personally reconciled with the church after years of peacetime neglect. During the 1918 German offensive Benedict Murdoch asked a dying Catholic Highlander: "What will I tell your people at home?' ... 'Tell them –' he laboured a little for breath – 'tell them,' he repeated, 'I had the priest!'"[44] Then, as in clearing station or hospital work, the aftermath of battle meant several days of letter-writing, reassuring relatives that their men had died in the faith, sacrificially, with the attendance of the clergy and in good cheer. In their letters the padres repeatedly emphasized that their men had died not only for a great cause but also for their friends and families. As one Roman Catholic chaplain put it: "I feel sure that Our Saviour has accepted his sacrifice and rewarded him for that greatest of all acts of Charity, to give one's life for others." A few weeks later the grateful and mostly idealistic replies from relatives reaffirmed the padre's faith in the cause and his sense of purpose as a soldiers' pastor.[45]

Nevertheless, for many chaplains the emotional and physical demands of duty proved too much. Between April 1916 and war's end, nineteen Canadian chaplains were relieved of duty or hospitalized for "neurasthenia" or nervous collapse. Two of these cases involved padres who had suffered from shell shock as stretcher-bearers in the ranks. Fifty-one chaplains, many of them middle-aged, were hospitalized, transferred to less arduous duty, or repatriated to Canada because of exhaustion or collapse. Between March 1915 and March 1919 eighty-three chaplains were hospitalized overseas for at least one week before returning to duty. Many had been diagnosed with what today would be considered stress-related illnesses such as ulcers, infections, dysentery, heart complaints, psoriasis, tuberculosis, and bronchitis, while a number at the front also suffered from "trench fever."[46]

At the front some chaplains seemed to bear the immediate brunt of combat well, then broke down in the quieter interludes.[47] Others found the suspense and strain of high-explosive barrages left them paralysed with fear and anxiety. Most often the symptoms of combat fatigue followed a regular pattern that the perceptive senior chaplain could recognize and act upon.[48] Such cases usually cropped up in the aftermath of a major attack or during a prolonged period of action. After the Somme, Vimy, Hill 70, Passchendaele, and especially during the continuous strain of the last three months of the war, McGreer or French was continually replacing chaplains here and there who had broken down or were on the verge of collapsing psychologically. Geoffrey D'Easum requested a transfer to the rear after the heavy fighting of 1918: "At Cambrai ... five of us were walking in together ... A shell hit the front man directly and only his legs were left hanging in the wire – the other three were killed, among them a very gallant man and dear friend. We were in a very tight place together at Amiens and he would have given his life for me – although he was an R.C. God rest his soul. I know that these experiences are common, but this one, coming on top of several others (I was with C company at Arras when a bomb got 66 of us) has left me rather wobbly. Still, I WOULD PREFER TO STAY WITH MY BOYS in France than to work in England."[49]

These chaplains who had used up their reserves of courage and energy broke down in gradual stages, the crisis often preceded by numerous physical symptoms or illnesses. Over a period of a few weeks or months reports from these chaplains gradually lost their initial optimism and became characterized by complaints and fault-finding. Quarrels between officers and chaplains increased in frequency and intensity. Such chaplains often became insomniacs. Stresses that had formerly been taken in stride, such as aerial bombing or routine shelling, now left them unsettled and tense.[50] In many cases in which chaplains approached a breakdown, such irritability gave way to depression, emotional numbness, and carelessness under fire, which soldiers and fellow officers sometimes mistook for complete self-abandonment. More experienced officers recognized such behaviour as symptoms of impending nervous breakdown.[51]

IT WAS IN BOTH the mundane and the traumatic circumstances of Corps life that the chaplain was expected to find and impart inspiration. This brought him to the challenge of preaching. If there was one occasion when the padre had the ear of the army, it was when he preached. Yet if there was one congregation that tended to be indifferent or resentful, it was a military unit at church parade. To be forced to go to church seemed to the men a fundamental violation of the very democracy they were fighting for. Even the most observant and dedicated Christian in the ranks found compulsory church parade a farce.[52] The challenge of getting the soldier's attention was an especially daunting prospect at the front. While in the line the padre's parish lived in the presence of sudden and anonymous death, dealt from afar by a hidden foe. In rest or in support the men lived in squalid conditions, which discouraged preachers from being clever.[53] At the same time, field sermons had tacit constraints, for the padre had to meet the expectations of brother officers and army authorities, who did not consider a church parade the place for unsettling the minds of the men by posing difficult questions or balancing paradoxes. To them the chaplain was only supposed to impart with conviction the virtues of duty, obedience, sacrifice, and courage. Yet the padres knew that the men quickly detected insincerity.

The padres usually began by stressing Christian ethics, urging the men to be a good Christian soldiers, well behaved and morally clean. Second, chaplains preached on brotherly love and comradeship.[54] On the eve of battle, however, the call for courage and obedience as well as the reminder of God's providence and protection became central to field preaching.[55] With sudden death imminent, the consolatory aspects of the faith grew in importance and appeal. With sure pastoral instincts, most chaplains on the eve or aftermath of battle guided their men to consider the central significance of the Cross and the Resurrection. After Vimy, as they counted their losses, David Robertson led the Second Brigade survivors to consider the text, "The Good Shepherd Giveth His Life for His Sheep."[56] Isaac Naylor, a Methodist, reported that Holy Week 1918 had proved an excellent occasion to remind soldiers of the message of the Cross and Christ's sacrifice, "in the days of crisis and suffering through which we have been passing as an Empire." It was a special opportunity for a padre to "come to grips with a man just at that period when he is most impressed with the message of the Cross."[57] Certainly the chaplains were rewarded when they encouraged the soldiers, in dugouts or before they went into battle, to call upon their faith for protection and courage. The hope of heaven seemed more relevant than ever to both soldier and chaplain.[58] Hepburn described to his wife a post–Vimy Ridge service he conducted with his unit: "You should have heard the men sing … 'And now oh Father mindful of thy love.' I am not very emotional as a rule but sometimes the men over here make me feel the reality of things tremendously. Of course at other times the profane language and obscene talk, etc., make me discouraged and sorry but the real worth is there if only we can get in touch with it and hold it, and I have had many experiences with men here which are nothing less than sacred to me."[59]

But there was more to trench preaching than saddlebag evangelism and the consolations of salvation by trust in Jesus. Never far absent – taken for granted, in fact, as the natural extension of even the most personal devotional talk – lay its ultimate realization in the urgent national cause at hand. After the most harrowing battlefield experience, ostensibly a denial of all the most idealistic and optimistic preaching, chaplains often led the soldier from his personal trust in Christ, his comrade of the trenches, to mobilization under the manly Christ, captain of world regeneration.

On a dreary October day in 1917 about one hundred men of the Forty-third Battalion emerged intact from its part in the Passchendaele offensive. The following Sunday morning, in a ploughed field near Poperinghe, George Pringle held a brief service: a prayer for the mourners back home, a thanksgiving hymn and a few cheerful words, then the benediction.[60] That night he was invited by about thirty NCOs and men to tell some tales of his Klondike missionary days. Pringle talked about the expert Yukon guides he had known and linked his midwinter trust in them to the soldiers' pressing need to trust in Christ. Now, in his congregation's bitterness, doubt, and confusion about God, suffering, and so-called Christian civilization, he urged them to follow Christ, for only he had the credentials to guide the trail they were taking. Jesus knew the right trail, having travelled it himself to the end. He was willing, strong, and able to get them over its roughest parts. He would never leave them behind. Christ was upright, compassionate, and affable, a guide they could confide in. Jesus they could trust intuitively, without blind credulity or formal education. He was more than guide and comrade. He was the Saviour who rescued from death and put his disciples on the Godward side of the watershed of sin and death.[61]

Despite the presence of such devotional elements, Pringle's message that night had a larger regenerative context. He dealt simply and directly with the two main objections he knew his men had to religion. He told them to treat their scepticism about the Bible as he dealt with stray buttons found in Yukon bachelors' porridge. They could be set aside while eating, then identified, examined, and critically put in their proper perspective later. He reminded them that the Psalmists and Prophets railed as angrily against hypocrisy, selfishness, war, and injustice as they did. Jesus himself showed that one could not be right with God without leaving room in his heart for others. A Christian must be deeply interested in social reform. "You can't follow Christ and forget your brother, for the trail of Christ is the trail of self-sacrifice for others." Pringle told his men that taking Jesus for their guide meant taking him as their captain in the earthly as well as heavenly cause of the Kingdom.[62] For such chaplains the concepts of personal and national regeneration remained unshakeably linked, even after the most harrowing experiences.

Even in the communion sermon were mingled personal and public consecrational motifs. For chaplains trained in the school of historical criticism before the war, communion regained its New Testament meaning as a pledge of service, a memorial of Christ's death in which soldiers not only drew strength and assurance from him but drew it for consecrated service on earth. Thomas Colwell, who had also been in the trenches at Passchendaele, preached soon after of Christ and consecration in both personal and national terms. Communion, properly understood, was a memorial of Christ's sacrifice for the soldiers present. Their participation in it was a public act of gratitude and personal consecration to him. They knew better than anyone back home what sacrifice was: "There never was a time when men appreciated more the sacrifices of our Saviour. That soldier who has seen the muddy water of some shell hole become red with his own blood has learned to appreciate the supreme sacrifice of his Lord." Yet Colwell knew from long experience that most soldiers would not come forward because they were hesitant to pledge themselves so unreservedly to the absolute standard the sacrament required. Jesus, however, he told the men, welcomed even the most imperfect and unstable to his table. Colwell urged his flock not to hesitate: all "who have turned their feet toward the Heavenly City even though with faltering steps they follow the footsteps of their Master on the pathway of sacrifice and service" were enjoined to come forward. In this means of grace, he promised, there was to be found for them healing, strength, hope, and purity.

The message was not yet finished. Colwell reminded the men that one day there would be national remembrance of their sacrifices overseas. He recalled the Somme, Vimy, Hill 70, and Passchendaele and spoke of the shame and ignominy of those who had not done their share in the great cause. As he wove together the Cross and their own battlefield Golgotha with the Last Supper and their field communion, Colwell firmly placed his devotional and evangelistic appeal within the framework of their war for the Kingdom of God.[63] Thus, taking communion testified to their Christianity and their faithfulness unto death. To Colwell as to Canon Scott the packsack became their Cross and the trench their Golgotha, their march the *via dolorosa* and their death a triumph and redemption as they were all consecrated to Christ and the salvation of society. In the case of Canon Scott, such sentiments burst out of his poem "Requiescat," scribbled after his ramblings in Flanders across the First Divisional area in 1915:

In lonely watches night by night,
Great visions burst upon my sight,
For down the stretches of the sky
The hosts of dead go marching by ...

The anguish and the pain have passed,
And peace hath come to them at last.
But in the stern looks linger still
The iron purpose and the will.

Dear Christ, who reign'st above the flood
Of human tears and human blood,
A weary road these men have trod,
O house them in the home of God.[64]

Recent scholars have suggested that many chaplains abandoned the themes of moral and political crusade when they encountered the cynicism and horror of the front line. According to these studies, chaplains found it impossible to maintain their optimistic idealism in the face of battle. David Marshall, for instance, observes that padres turned instead to themes of personal devotion, stressing the comfort and salvation awaiting individuals who committed themselves to Christ. The front was judged to be the place not to harp about saving civilization but to encourage the saving of individual souls from the wreck of civilization.[65] This portrait of the preacher, however, is distorted by the assumption that crusading beliefs inherently contradicted the evangelical and devotional preaching close to the line. Certainly the patriotic metaphors and crusading language of the sermons encountered in the rear area were substantially pared away at the front because padres knew the the men's scorn for the florid imagery and clichés of home-front preaching. The evidence indicates that most chaplains simplified and abbreviated their preaching to suit field conditions and the needs of their men. Nevertheless, while the routine preaching fare was devotional and often centred upon personal consecration, the conceptual framework upon which the weekly homily hung was the compelling necessity of the cause, with all its religious and national significance. Almost every field sermon, even the most simple communion homily, drew and linked together the personal consecration of each soldier and the common consecration of all to the cause of humanity that they served in this war.[66] Like many of the clergy at home the chaplains interpreted the war within the framework of providential history informed by their biblical studies, colleagues, and professors.[67] If anything, padres were the least disposed by their circumstances or the needs of their flocks to tinker with such a helpful theological matrix.

Further, every special service in the field, whether after battle or on the anniversary of war's outbreak, whether at cemetery commemorations or on national holidays, portrayed the national and world significance of the cause as well as the implications of the war for every soldier attending.[68] Chaplains reassured the troops that they were indeed fighting for "a new Heaven and a new Earth."[69] The soldier repeatedly heard that the living owed a debt to the fallen, who had died for their safety and freedom. Those who had been killed in war had become martyrs for national righteousness.[70] While searching the battlefield after an engagement at Passchendaele, Colwell came across a Canadian soldier equipped as a sniper,

> on his knees, his rifle still clasped in both hands and pointed at the enemy, his head slightly bowed, but his spirit as the men say not irreverently had gone "West." To bury him you have to take the rifle out of his hands, the only means he had to safeguard his home and country. He might have taken cover and been safe but death found him, "A soldier on his job" – 2nd C.M.R. address – Realizing what it meant, I went over to him and put my hand on his steel helmet and said, "Good old Boy." Our Church is doing much, I'm sure and perhaps the truth is that only as we place these men in our debt by some small service, can we help to save them for God and for our country's future.

Two months later Colwell told the Army and Navy Board, "The men are paying a big price here, so that Christianity may be saved, those conditions necessary for its growth, and that freedom may not perish from the earth. It still is grandly true that these men like our Saviour, march along the stony pavement of stern duty to the completion of a task which demands the sacrifices of supermen."[71]

Occasionally Catholic chaplains, who usually scorned the facile identification of death in battle with salvation that some Protestants proclaimed, in their own way implied a similar conclusion. Adrian Beausoleil, who spent a year in the French army as a soldier-priest before becoming a Canadian chaplain, used to tell his men before battle or a raid that they were indeed fighting for God's cause: "He will not forsake you, not one hair will fall from your head without His permission. He has a splendid reward for those who might fall, were you my own brothers, I would say, 'Go to it. God bless you.'"[72] Most Roman Catholic homilies, however, remained exhortations to make better use of the sacraments and not to neglect devotional exercises. In their field and dressing station work the Catholic chaplains repeatedly urged men in dire straits "to make a good act of contrition" before preparing themselves for death.[73]

In the aftermath of battle the padre also faced men who had had time to think and question the fundamental truths to which they clung in adversity. As one Methodist put it, the most frequent question put to the padre was "Why?"[74] Why, if God was on their side, did so much bad weather play havoc with Allied offensives? Why were so many good men killed and so many evidently worse survive? To such familiar queries, the wisest response was to reinterpret providence: perhaps the bad weather had saved them from worse disasters, he replied. After all, had good weather allowed them to overextend their advance and be defeated, then they would have wanted to know why God had not sent bad weather to save them. Besides, no one knew how much God interfered with natural laws in order to work his will. God allowed good men to die because they were needed for service in heaven. Death was promotion, in fact, to higher service. Bad men lived to have another chance. In the face of adverse circumstances the padre reminded them that God's ways were mysterious but ultimately good.[75]

Some chaplains in private allowed themselves to think about the same questions. Their sense of identification and the strong bonding that took place with the men sometimes placed them in spiritual dilemmas, caught between their compassion and the stern demands of military duty. At least one, Robert Shires, an Anglican, found after the Somme that he could no longer reconcile his Christian profession with his role as military chaplain. Almond advised British authorities that Shires was "a Conscientious Objector and claims that he is unable to consistently preach Christianity to the troops. I consider that his present mental attitude makes his position in the Field either one of hypocrisy or very dangerous to the morale of our troops."[76] Shires offered his resignation, stating simply, "I have been led to feel that Christianity, as I understand it, does not fit very well with the War." He was quietly transferred to England, released from the Chaplain Service, and sent home to Canada.[77] Shires was the only Canadian chaplain to renounce his vocation openly. The remainder soldiered on, in spite of trauma, frustration, or spiritual setbacks. Rather than abandon the struggle, most chaplains dealt with the situational paradoxes of their duties by adopting a crusading mentality. This resolution was often placed under great strain when the padre who had completely bonded with his men found them to be victims of the military justice system, incompetent generalship, or the callous disregard of civilian leaders.

One hectic night on the Somme, Canon Scott was on duty at the dressing station in the Albert schoolhouse:

A man was brought in who looked very pale and asked me piteously to get him some water ... I got him taken into the dressing room, and turned away for a moment to look after some fresh arrivals. Then I went back towards the table ... They had uncovered him, and, from the look on the faces of the attendants round about, I saw that some specially ghastly wound was disclosed ... Beyond this awful sight I saw the white face turning from side to side, and the parched lips asking for water. The man, thank God, did not suffer very acutely, as the shock had been so great, but he was perfectly conscious. The case was hopeless, so they kindly and tenderly covered him up, and he was carried out into the room set apart for the dying ... When the sergeant came in to have the body removed ... he drew the man's paybook from his pocket, and there we found that for some offence he had been given a long period of field punishment, and his pay was cut down to seventy cents a day. For seventy cents a day he had come as a voluntary soldier to fight in the great war, and for seventy cents a day he had died this horrible death. I told the sergeant that I felt like dipping that page of the man's paybook in his blood to blot out the memory of the past.[78]

Perhaps the most harrowing of the chaplain's duties, however, lay in preparing the condemned soldier for death by firing squad. Here, more than in any other experience, the padre bore the emotional brunt of army discipline.[79] A padre was detailed to each of the twenty-five Canadians executed, to accompany him during the last twelve hours of his life. These sleepless nights locked in with the accused, culminating in the dawn execution of the sentence, created some of the chaplains' worst personal as well as vocational inner conflicts. Here the life of one was sacrificed for the many, not in atonement but as a warning. The army followed the logic of Caiaphas, not Jesus: a volunteer's exhaustion of nerve required his involuntary death at the hands of men from his own unit. Here the padre saw that the object of military law was not to give justice to individuals but to maintain discipline. The army treated cowardice or desertion as a moral failure, not as the involuntary result of physical or mental collapse.[80]

The padre's goal in these circumstances was to divert the condemned's bitterness and self-pity into acceptance of his sentence and instil in him the courage to die at peace with God and man.[81] Then followed counsel to "try to look beyond the present to the great hope which lay before us in another life. I pointed out that he had just one chance left to prove his courage and set himself right before the world. I urged him to go out and meet death bravely with sense unclouded, and advised him not to take any brandy," recalled Scott.[82] Often this required hasty religious instruction, baptism, and first – and last – communion. When this took place the chaplain could feel some satisfaction with his ministry, but this was not always the case. The chaplain pronounced a benediction on the blindfolded figure and, after execution of the sentence, was expected to address the firing squad.[83] Funeral rites finished his work.

Senior officers reassured chaplains that those executed were repeat offenders and that only the most extreme cases were condemned, but padres such as Scott often went to extreme lengths to appeal for commutation. He won praise even among the most hardened veterans for his midnight tramp to army Headquarters, getting generals out of bed in a vain attempt to have one such sentence suspended.[84] Nevertheless, padre memories of this most hideous form of death lingered. Depression, then anger, left some padres seething with suppressed rage. Caught between their own complete deference to the iron discipline of the military cause and post-war realities, many could only vent their anger on the stay-at-homes: "If this book should fall into the hands of any man who, from cowardice, shirked his duty in the war, and stayed at home, let him reflect that, but for the frustration of justice, he ought to have been sitting that morning, blindfolded and handcuffed, beside the prisoner on the box. HE was one of the originals and a volunteer," wrote Scott.[85] More than one brigade chaplain quailed at this stern duty, forcing authorities on at least two occasions to call in the divisional senior chaplain to assist or stand in for them.[86] Even the most hardened chaplain took at least a day afterwards to pull himself together.[87] The unfortunate priest of the Twenty-second Battalion, who had already performed this duty twice, warned that two similar sentences were pending asked for a transfer back to England. Such responsibilities, after a heavy season of front-line action, had drained dry his reserve of courage.[88]

FEW CHAPLAINS DIRECTLY PARTICIPATED in such stressful trials. For the majority, routine work followed a familiar pattern of interviews, games, sermons, lectures, and trips to canteens or coffee stalls. While the work soon seemed well in hand, over an extended period of time the rapport with the men might imperceptibly grow cooler and more distant. Often, when the padre felt most at home with his fellow officers, observers from senior chaplains to batmen would warn that his reputation with the men was beginning to suffer. Occasionally senior chaplains, at the request of the unit CO, would transfer padres to new battalions in order to give them a fresh challenge. Giving up a place in a unit that felt like home was a sacrifice not every chaplain made with good grace, yet some, such as Harold McCausland after

Passchendaele, were perceptive and courageous enough to request it themselves:

> I am growing convinced that I am steadily losing touch with my battalion, as far as the NCOs and men are concerned. I feel that, mentally, they label me – and with no little justification – 'For Officers Only.' In some way or other, and very gradually, I have managed to become so engrossed with various activities connected with the battalion, that now I have practically no time to be among the men. I think I am working for the men, but this work seems only to keep me from them. Previously, for instance, I would go among the men to get personally their own stories of casualties. Now I am forced to send out a form of report to be filled in by the Company Commanders. Formerly it was my delight to go among the men with magazines and other things sent me for them. Now the great heap of things before me as I write will have to get to them through the Platoon Commander and the Quartermaster stores. Possibly this will help you see that, although my work has greatly increased, the work which appealed to me and told most has been on the steady decline. Just now I feel this very keenly because of the arrival of new men, who only know me as the sort of Padre who never comes among his men. I am confident that a new man, free to go his own way, is a vital necessity here.[89]

Then the pilgrimage turned the chaplain back towards the base or to another unit, to begin the cycle yet again.

Few chaplains underwent such experiences for long without undergoing gradual but profound emotional transformations. Several, such as Scott and Gordon, went beyond anxiety for and sympathy with their men to the point of eliminating the distinction between non-combatants and combatants, wishing to take some part in the fighting themselves. As senior chaplain of the Fourth Division, Gordon supported one Anglican chaplain's request for transfer to the artillery "because I think fighting quite as much a clergyman's job as preaching. It is for my superior to decide … When will our people learn that Bosche leaders have no sense of honour or chivalry, that when we deal with them as with human beings they only laugh up their sleeve, and think us fools?"[90] Scott confessed in his post-war memoirs: "It was a horrible thought that our men were up there bearing the brunt of German fury and hatred … The men whom I knew so well, young, strong and full of hope and life … were now up in that poisoned atmosphere and under the hideous hail of bullets and shells. The thought almost drove a chaplain to madness. One felt so powerless and longed to be up and doing. Not once or twice in the Great War, have I longed to be a combatant officer with enemy scalps to my credit."[91]

Sometimes, ironically, the same chaplains found themselves ministering to dying Germans they came upon in newly captured trenches and dugouts. On such occasions they found an unexpected spirit of compassion stirring in them: "As they happened to be Roman Catholics, I took off the Crucifix which I wore round my neck and gave it to them. They would put up their trembling hands and clasp it lovingly, and kiss it, while I began the Lord's Prayer in German. This happened many times that day. One man who had a hideous wound in the abdomen was most grateful, and when he handed me back the crucifix he took my hand and kissed it. It was so strange to think that an hour before, had we met, we should have been deadly enemies."[92] While combing the shellholes of Vimy Ridge, David Robertson encountered another such casualty: "halfway down the entrance of a partially caved in German dugout; I saw a man sitting, his head bowed, and hands folded, and by his side a prayer-book. I got no answer when I called, so I crawled down, for I felt sure he was still praying. He must have died so a little time before. He was a little German. Peace to him."[93] Others, having seen less of the front, found it more difficult to minister to prisoners of war, although many chaplains felt obliged by their calling to give whatever aid and succour they could to a defeated enemy.[94]

In other ways Corps chaplains revealed how closely they had identified with their men. Several chaplains repeatedly turned down offers of promotion or transfer in order to remain at the front. After a few months in the trenches, padres such as Scott found leave in London a profoundly disorienting experience.[95] While critical of stay-at-home civilians, most chaplains officially expressed confidence in the high command, although one, Albert Andrew, was arrested and threatened with court martial for criticisms expressed to a Canadian reporter after the Armistice. McGreer and Almond, with George Kilpatrick's assistance, managed to have his case deferred, assisted by Andrew's having just received the Military Cross.[96] Other chaplains found themselves breaking various regulations in order to assist the men and avoid the stigma of enjoying the privileges of rank. Perhaps the best-known examples involved sharing automobile rides with stragglers along the busy roads of France. Both Scott and George Fallis broke regulations rather than have the men see a padre pass by without offering a ride. When Fallis was confronted by General Byng, his only defence was, "Sir, I'm a rotten soldier but a good padre."[97] Scott's spoofing of regulations became one of his best tactics for winning the attention of the troops, although he made it clear that military discipline itself was beyond question. Occasionally the front-line chaplains were known to let off steam in the direction of their own rear-area authorities, although few followed the example of Robert Ridgeway, who stamped out of one chaplains' meeting after a senior chaplain advised him and his colleagues to curry favour with commanders in order to increase their influence. According to one witness, Ridgeway's parting remark was: "Damn the general, a chaplain's first duty is to his men!"[98]

What may have disturbed observers, especially at home, was the tendency of chaplains overseas to become extreme critics of their home churches. The alienation of chaplains from their ecclesiastical authorities ranged from chiding them for their lax attitudes towards the importance of overseas work to damning them for recalling them away from the trenches.[99] The Methodist Army and Navy Board's T.A. Moore was appalled at the anger directed towards the home church by some chaplains, especially when the board tried to recall them (as part of Almond's plan to have more clergymen get chaplain's experience) from their units or use their reports as propaganda.[100] At least one Anglican chaplain publicly criticized the prohibitionists on the home front who wanted to deny the rum ration to the troops. Better the purist first abolish war itself, Robert Renison charged, than hypocritically deny a little comfort to the man who was risking his life in the front line.[101]

Such outbursts, while unsettling to churchmen or senior chaplains, were usually accepted by most observers as the occasional product of war-worn emotions. Most chaplains, after letting off steam and after a few days' sleep, agreed. In spite of the exhaustion and frustrations of active service, most turned homeward in 1919 with optimism. Immediately after their return to peacetime work, chaplains, almost to a man, testified that their years overseas had been highly rewarding. Most reported that the war had been an edifying, deepening, and refining experience for them. Many had surprised themselves by adjusting so well to military life and bearing up to the strain of service. The spiritual rewards were, for most, matched by the personal satisfactions and the lasting comradeship experienced overseas, which the padres hoped to enjoy in post-war life. In spite of the trials and stresses, few would have objected to Alexander Gordon's perspective, which he shared with his father in 1919:

> As I have often said, the work of an army chaplain is easier than that of a minister in an ordinary charge, whether a home-mission or self-sustaining. He has not financial worry, he usually has a horse and groom; he is sure of his congregation, one made up of strong young men. That any minister would covet; he has no loneliness but any amount of company that are soldiers and gentlemen; he is responsible only to his superiors, and he is never badgered by unreasonable cranks or by old women of either sex. In

fact, if he has any fitness for life in the army in wartime, he has just the best kind of life and is at liberty to do his work as he sees fit, without interference from annoyance. I have never enjoyed any part of my life more than that spent in the army.[102]

The typical chaplain viewed his war as a personal as well as a national victory. Having steeled himself for the worst, the parson had allowed himself to be submerged in the army and, to his relief, had emerged as "the padre" – one who had found the arduous pilgrimage to the trenches not merely bearable but eventually a triumph. In many a padre's estimation, he returned now to Canada with a new identity, powerful memories, firm friendships, and high hopes for his future work. To most, one of the most promising outcomes of the victory had been those months of comradeship with the soldiers, the sense of having been useful and appreciated by the troops, of having made their own way through perils and pitfalls to create a new identity for the clergy and the church in the minds of Canada's bravest men. Overseas the padres had sustained themselves with the hope of winning greater influence on the life of the nation by earning the respect and loyalty of the soldiers. While individual padres had fallen by the wayside or failed to measure up to the stern standard of war, most chaplains believed that they had won the hearts of the troops and that their own characters, transformed by rising to the challenge of the front, would remain so for the rest of their lives.

Yet the chaplains' perspective, however comprehensive they thought it, was in fact greatly limited. Many aspects of army life tended to give them a misleading perspective on both their own standing in the eyes of the men and the effect of war on their faith. In the process of serving at the Corps many chaplains so identified with their men in their suffering that they often based their sweeping generalizations on atypical anecdotes. They saw themselves, thus, through a glass darkly. The padre actually dwelt, in army life, at the intersection of two circles, one the small and brotherly officers' mess, the other the large, often anonymous or shifting population of the unit. Most officers shared a similar education, upbringing, and outlook with the chaplain. Many, even the most free-thinking, nevertheless shared a world-view (albeit shorn of much of the religious colouring) similar to his. But the chaplain faced a very different social grouping in the ranks. Except for the ordained or student clergymen, most soldiers had neither the education nor the willingness to view life in idealized terms. While many units had devout or at least religiously observant laymen in the ranks, the bulk of the unit consisted of men who were largely indifferent to the padre and voluntarily kept out of his way. Even the chaplain who won the confidence of a few individuals usually found he was meeting many of the same men each visit.

Considered realistically, the average chaplain voluntarily met with fewer than a quarter of an average-sized unit. In everyday battalion life, well over half of a unit rarely saw or communicated with a chaplain. A ring of sympathetic or encouraging soldiers and officers thus easily came to insulate the average chaplain from the rest. Few occasions allowed the padre to cut through this blanket of associations. In parade preaching, the cards were stacked against him by circumstances and army custom. His voluntary services only attracted the soldiers already interested. His social-service work, however, might show some that the clergyman was of some practical use. Most importantly, courage and devotion shown in the line could win him the grudging respect of most of the men who benefited from it in one way or another. But battle was a discontinuous process. Weeks might go by at the front without the men seeing or conversing with the chaplain.

The same, however, was not true in the hospital or clearing station. There the men were the padre's constant concern and were perhaps most appreciative because they were most needy of whatever encouragement he offered. Here the reserve between soldier and chaplain had the greatest chance of breaking down. But hospital contact, as the patients recuperated, always ended with the soldier returning home to Canada or to his unit, back to the arid and tension-ridden padre-soldier routine of normal army life. Chaplains who predicted great post-war spiritual harvests after working in the aid posts, casualty clearing stations, and field hospitals seem sometimes to have forgotten that the desperately wounded soldiers who confronted their situation with faith and courage were more often buried than returned to Canada. Tragically, a padre's greatest harvest was left behind after the war in the cemeteries of Flanders and France.

Chaplains thus were particularly liable to delusion. In the enthusiasm of recruitment and first-unit life, it was easy for them to set up an optimistic mental framework that was supported by their experience. In camp the chaplain might, despite his growing understanding of the low level of common religiosity, point to his hut work and other satisfying endeavours to support his optimism. In hospital work his emotions were daily validated by intense spiritual experiences and the unnaturally malleable nature of the wounded patient. Fresh from such energizing and confirming episodes, dominated by empathy, he entered front-line work, where he identified with the men in their service and sacrifice. In fighting his way into the front line, developing a supplementary social-service practice, and eventually making a place for himself on the battlefield, he came to share enough of the dangers and stresses, exhilaration and tensions to confirm him in the conviction that he had succeeded in identifying both himself and the church with the cause of the private, whom he grew to admire and idealize.

The chaplain, however, in such an emotionally and physically demanding situation was himself seeking support as much as he was trying to give it. Thus a padre's pilgrimage was inevitably shaped by his own expectations and needs. So too was it shaped by his pre-war education and outlook. In the journey to war he found what he needed. Few indeed of the padres seem to have suspected that their vision might be a wartime illusion. Although a few suggested that such was the case, the majority could not conceive of the possibility that, in identifying with the men and throwing themselves completely into the fray, they had been as much bemused as enlightened by the school of battle.

7 Preachers: The Voice of Consolation and Prophecy

By daybreak on 11 November 1918 Canadians of the Seventh Brigade had cleared Mons of German soldiers. Later that week two religious services marked its liberation. The first, a memorial service for Canadians killed during the last hours of the war, was held in the cathedral on 16 November. George Kilpatrick, now senior chaplain of the Third Division, a Presbyterian, triumphantly proclaimed:

Already the light of world peace is before us … All barriers of creed and station are swept aside in the joy of this liberation which is shortly to become the foundation stone of enduring peace … Not alone by force of arms has victory been gained … but first to last because in this business we have been allied with Eternal Righteousness. This is the first secret of victory. God confronting the forces of Evil and working through our human agencies enlisted in His Service, has brought us at last through the Valley of the Shadow to the Dawn of peace. We are still too close to the Great Drama of world war to read aright the meaning, yet even now we may see that through the fiery crucible of battle has come a golden heritage and, out of that which seemed all evil, certain Treasure has been given to the world. We have finally learned the truth that there ARE things greater than wealth can buy … Liberty, and Justice, Compassion – Service, these Great Ideals once but names have knocked at the door of men's lives and touched great and humble alike … Shall we not then, thank God for the Vision "of the things which cannot be shaken," for that Revelation is the strength of which we shall prove better citizens of the Empire and worthier subjects of our God … We worship here, a company of men redeemed by the gift of their lives. For them – and they are not far from us – we lift our hearts to God with a gratitude which can only find true expression in our deeper consecration of life itself ... It is the way of Love; virile, constructive, reconciling Love. We who have witnessed the collapse of a military system fired by the LOVE OF POWER, are called to create a brotherhood inspired by the POWER OF LOVE ... I admit your criticism ... "This is the sheerest Idealism" ... We are all Idealists at heart and a Renaissance of National Idealism alone can solve the problems of World Politics ... we who have fought "to make the world safe for Democracy" are confronted by this truth, that Democracy itself can never be safe and can never survive without the "vision of an Ideal State which Christians call the Kingdom of God" ... After Thanksgiving comes Dedication, ... The Kingdom of God needs us.[1]

For Kilpatrick, one of the youngest Corps chaplains, it was a considerable distinction to have been chosen to speak. Nevertheless, he had earned the right by three years' distinguished service. Both his idealism and his evangelism were echoed by distinguished Protestant chaplains throughout the Corps. On the following day, at the second thanksgiving service Alan Shatford, an Anglican who had been at the front since 1915, preached an almost identical sermon to 1,600 Canadian soldiers.[2] Kilpatrick and Shatford spoke for more than the chaplains of their respective communions. Both based their sermons on the theological foundation that chaplains of all non–Roman Catholic denominations had laid since 1914. Now that message of consolation and prophecy had been vindicated. Out of evil, God's instruments had wrought good. Providence had prepared the way: the time had come to bring the regenerative crusade home. Within a decade, however, events would invest almost every sentence of these unwitting oracles with a heavy irony.[3]

Since the 1960s churchmen and scholars have debated the Great War's impact upon Canadian religious history. While some have sampled declarations by overseas chaplains from one or two denominations, none has mapped the contours of wartime preaching for the chaplaincy as a whole.[4] Nor have they compared the chaplains' public writings and preaching with their private utterances to home church leaders as they moved from home front to England, on to the front, and again towards home. As an approach to a more general profile, this chapter will survey, in the context of their overseas service and their educational background, the writing and preaching of Anglican and non-conformist Canadian chaplains only. Roman Catholic chaplains left few theological statements in the public record or military archives. Protestants, by contrast, repeatedly alluded to war's effect on their views of providence, Christology, evangelism, and the mission of the church. Judging by both their public preaching and their private reports, instead of shattering their beliefs, the war entrenched more deeply their prior vision of ecclesiastical reform and national righteousness. Since the 1890s most Protestant padres-to-be had united their personal religious experience with theological optimism, philosophical idealism, and liberal nationalism, forging a resilient armour against even the horrors of the Great War. The pre-war years of these men, from their college days to maturity, shaped a model of providence that assumed critical significance overseas – regenerative struggle for the Kingdom of God.

FROM THE OUTSET, prophetic and consoling themes dominated chaplains' messages. To them, Germany's wanton aggression justified full British and Canadian participation in the European struggle. Assisting Britain was more than a colonial duty; it was Canada's entry on the world stage as a mature nation. After early reports of German atrocities, chaplain rhetoric went beyond patriotic to apocalyptic levels. The war became a duel between the kingdoms of God and Satan. To Charles Gordon, Canada's duty stood revealed "clear as the morning sun above the prairie rim … With a clear conscience and a steadfast heart we can invoke the God, not of battles, but the God of Righteousness and Truth to our aid."[5] By the end of 1915, after the sinking of the *Lusitania*, Lord Bryce's report on German atrocities, and the Ypres gas attack, the chaplains were convinced that Germany had become a moral and spiritual abomination. The Kaiser wore the "brand of Cain."[6] Wilmot Clarke, chaplain and recruiter for the 235th Battalion, warned central Ontario Methodists: "God will never give His blessing and favour to the man or church that does not go forth to aid the cause of Him who breaketh the oppressor in pieces. This is a holy war. Again there rings across our land the ancient call, 'Who is on the Lord's Side?' Let Methodists in these Counties answer the call of duty and ANSWER IT NOW!"[7]

Such rhetoric was not the exclusive preserve of Protestantism. At the height of the war it unexpectedly crossed ethnic as well as denominational lines. John O'Gorman told his Ottawa congregation that the only way in which Canada would stay out of the war was by seceding from the British Empire. Loyal Irish Canadian sacrifices might even shame England into granting Ireland Home Rule. But most compelling was the absolute righteousness of the cause. Dodging enlistment was "undoubtedly a sin … Every able-bodied Canadian bachelor, who is not detained by a more urgent duty, is in conscience bound to enlist … Catholics of Canada, your Catholicity is now being tested by the white fire of sacrifice. A census will be taken of the shirkers of Canada.

Every good Catholic in that number will be a scandal to the Church." Although such preaching outraged most French Canadian churchmen, many other Ontario and Maritime Roman Catholics, following the lead of an increasingly nationalistic English-speaking hierarchy, echoed the newly minted chaplain's proclamation.[8]

In spite of the appalling casualties of the Somme, chaplains remained unrelenting in their passion to defeat Germany, and their crusading outlook seemed undampened by trench experience. After eight months at the front Richard Macnamara reminded fellow Anglicans that Germany was the most diabolical nation in history. Reverting to paganism, she had been stopped in the nick of time only by the sacrifices of the rest of Christendom. Canadians must make sure that such a war would never recur. Then from this Armageddon would issue a new world order of light and universal brotherhood.[9] Other front-line padres echoed him. Back from the Somme, Charles Gordon affirmed the prophetic vision. In the trenches, he and his men had experienced the reality of God's presence and his providential plan for the war. He had seen the war strip away materialism and individualism, teach Christian love and comradeship, erode denominationalism by throwing Protestants and Roman Catholics together in common cause. Padres learned not to worry about soldiers' external vices (such as smoking or drinking the rum ration) and to struggle instead to strengthen their innately Christian character.[10] The sacrifice of such men demanded that the living take responsibility for completing their mission. Gordon challenged the nation to rededicate itself, recalling Christ's warning to those who looked back: "I do assure you before God there is only one thing for Canadians to be at ... Anything that helps the war is right. Anything that hinders it is wrong. Any man who hinders Canada from seeing her way and from ploughing her furrow is a man – what about him? Unfit for the Kingdom of God."[11]

Victory in the field encouraged the chaplains. From the shadow of Vimy Ridge, Canon Scott dared Canadians to abandon their "disgusting, selfish lives ... Every man must put his shoulder to the wheel, even if it is a chariot of fire."[12] As the 1918 Allied offensive heralded Allied victory, crusading rhetoric reached new levels.[13] Occasionally harshness dominated, especially when chaplains encountered German violations of war conventions, French and Belgian war orphans, or devastated areas of occupation. Robert Renison, then a hospital chaplain attending a memorial service for soldiers and nurses killed in German bombing of Canadian hospitals, prophesied divine retribution: "Let them who, by kneeling at the devil's feet, thought to win the world, weep – ay, let them weep." On the road to Mons, vindication remained the dominant emotion. Renison, marching with the Twenty-first Battalion into Belgium, wrote: "Everyone saw the genuine gratitude of a nation delivered from slavery ... Turkey had surrendered unconditionally, Austria-Hungary was already vanishing for ever after a thousand years of chequered history, during which she had been consistently the enemy of Human Progress."[14]

Even in war's darker moments the padres balanced harsh rhetoric with a consoling millennial hope. They reassured Canadians that God always brought good out of evil. Out of war's suffering would come personal, even national regeneration. John Pringle spoke for many when he assured Canadians that the troops did not want the war to end until "it ends right, with righteousness dominant through our victory and with its proper place in our own and the world's life." He encouraged them to trust in Providence: "The nations and the church will come out of this furnace purified, surely. The things that are essential and the things, wood, hay stubble, ... that are not essential, will take their proper place in the hearts and lives of men." English-speaking Roman Catholics, in their own way, agreed. Although many, with Benedict Murdoch, viewed the war as an outcome of the Reformation and God's judgment on modernity, many pointed to the war's beneficial effect upon personal piety. John O'Gorman pointed to the providential work the war did for the Empire, Ireland, and the Catholic faith. Militarism was destroyed and Catholic liberty preserved by the English-speaking democracies. European secularization and Prussian Lutheranism had been checked. France, Italy, and Belgium were being saved from atheism, undergoing Catholic renewal in their suffering. Even the new nations the Allies promised to create would have Catholic majorities.[15]

Most padres based their optimism upon the religious transformation they believed was occurring among the troops. In France and Flanders a purer Christianity was being imprinted on a generation of Canada's bravest and best. Wounded or dying, the men instinctively fell back on their childhood faith for comfort and relief. Their superficial profanity concealed a deeper religiosity and fierce moral commitment that the padres had grown to respect. Scornful of institutional religion but drawn to the figure of Christ and his crucifixion, the men generously answered calls for self-consecration. The soldiers now understood better than those at home the meaning of the Cross. Such men were moral crusaders with a new social vision. Their unwavering passion for justice and truth, their willingness to die so that others would enjoy peace and liberty, their love for comrades and mercifulness even for the wounded enemy, all led padres to hope that they would bring home this hard-won discipleship to regenerate Canada and the world.

For many chaplains Canada's participation in the world conflict was the providential opportunity to realize the pre-war national gospel. On 1 July 1917 William Beattie preached to a mixed congregation of soldiers and civilians in St Columba's Presbyterian Church in London. Like David Inglis in 1866, he took for his text "He shall have Dominion from Sea to Sea." Why had the Canadians proved so formidable in battle?

I believe it is because they have caught the vision of an unconquerable soul ... But unconquerable only when it has caught the vision and spirit of Christ ... Please God 100,000 men or more shall return to Canada at the close of this war. Men back from the very jaws of death, men who have learned something of the power and promise of the unconquerable soul. Men who have fought to maintain in Europe and in all the world the right to live. Shall we, when we return to yonder home land, be less zealous for high ideals? If we discipline ourselves in the things of Principle – High Honour and Courage – if we yield ourselves to the sweet sentiments that gather around the home, and if we cultivate an exalted Faith in the goodness and wisdom of God and the saving Power of His son, Jesus Christ, then shall the song ... be a song not merely of prophecy, but one of Holy Covenant ... And we in Canada shall have done our bit to hasten the day when His Dominion shall be from sea to sea, and from the river unto the ends of the earth.[16]

To many padres the war had caused an unprecedented levelling and unifying of the Canadians overseas. Edmund Oliver, writing in *Social Welfare*, warned Canadians at home that the men had been converted from a mass of individuals to a powerful and cohesive social force:

They are gathering ideas, and at the same time they are gathering the courage, the force, and the power of co-operation that will carry those ideas into effect ... They are not going back to be content with the old order ... We are only blind if we do not see ahead of us profound social upheavals and new political adjustments ... In the days to come we must be knit together with a sense of social service in a democracy that is diligent and refined. We must advance with the spirit of truth, unfrightened liberty; honouring toil, demanding justice, shrinking from no sacrifice, confident of the eternal verities, and, daring, in every department of life, to battle with brain and brawn against wanton wrong and wilful waste and wicked war.[17]

Chaplains repeatedly warned their co-religionists at home that the church's greatest challenge lay in attracting and harnessing this unvarnished virtue when the men finally came home.[18]

As a result, from the beginning of 1917 Anglican, Presbyterian, and Methodist chaplains in particular called for domestic ecclesiastical reforms. The churches needed a rigorous house-cleaning if they hoped to attract the veteran back to the fold. While not all those returning were revived saints – in fact, conceded one Methodist, a minority were incorrigible renegades – the chaplains asked churchmen to heed their advice and help the veteran to realize in Canada the gospel of the trenches.[19] The men viewed churches as socially cold, the clergy as aloof, censorious, and sanctimonious. The church obviously should give laymen more leadership and sponsor wholesome recreation – dances, card parties, and film shows in church halls. The men craved the social fellowship of army comradeship and wanted the churches to quit their bickering.[20] Methodist and Presbyterian chaplains testified that the Christianity of the trenches proved the validity of church union.[21] Some Anglicans as well favoured broader denominational co-operation, while a few were bold enough to call for general ecumenical reunion.[22]

Moreover, chaplains contended, worship services needed to recapture the sense of simplicity and reality felt overseas. Doctrine needed revision or translation into more modern language to which veterans could subscribe. In particular, the old evangelical doctrines of innate depravity and damnation must be abandoned. The war had taught soldiers, and many padres, that men were innately good, noble, and capable of self-sacrifice. If teachers at home could not accept such an optimistic anthropology, then they would be rejected, "if only," as one Anglican chaplain put it, "for the very simple reason that THE MEN ALREADY BELIEVE IT THEMSELVES. THEY know whereof they are made if theologians do not."[23] The doctrine of hell had no power, wrote a Methodist chaplain, over men who had overcome its earthly equivalent. Another added that even the Apostle's Creed contained supernatural statements that the troops considered irrelevant. Let the men, therefore, work out their own beliefs in their own words.[24] Anglicans characteristically wrote of Prayer Book revision, shorter services, more powerful preaching, and better adult Christian education on contemporary issues.[25]

After living closely with the men, chaplains claimed that only pastors with the most modern training and manly attributes would win the veteran's respect. Anglicans and Methodists in particular recommended that future candidates for the ministry be better screened for intelligence, health, sociability, and secular experience as well as orthodoxy or piety. Seminarians needed training in sociology, economics, and politics, not ancient languages and dogmatics. Of course, the best candidates for the ministry would come from the returned men themselves, for the veteran had no use for stay-at-home students or clergymen.[26] Finally, the Canadian churches had to embrace the most ambitious and practical social-reform agenda possible, speak out for veterans' rights, and demand education and vocational training for the returned man.[27]

This call was loudly echoed by some Anglican chaplains trying to rouse an apparently somnolent denomination to the vision of the social gospel.[28] Churches must appeal to the veteran's innate idealism, patriotism, hero worship, and sense of comradeship. If they could show him that the church was the one peacetime institution that embodied the highest values for which he had fought, he would be irresistibly drawn back into the fold. The old institutions and dogmas, the aging leadership and hallowed traditions had to be renovated or scrapped. In this process, who but the returned chaplains could give the correct type of leadership? As one Methodist chaplain boldly put it: "There will be some good folk who will probably shake their heads and say that chaplains have come back with some dangerous and erroneous views. Some, doubtless, will think that we have, in fact, gone to the devil. Now we, on the contrary, unworthy as we are, believe that we are nearer God, and that we know and sympathize with men more than ever was the case in pre-war days. I am sure that we are humbler."[29] As the war drew to a victorious close and church leaders turned to the problems of reconstruction, the chaplains' message took on a note of even greater urgency. The veterans were by nature impatient. If the Canadian churches failed to capture their allegiance now, they might be lost forever.

CHAPLAINS OVERSEAS MADE more than the religious and secular press their pulpit. Protestants reinforced public declarations with confidential reports to denominational leaders. Methodist and Presbyterian chaplains constantly made suggestions to their military service boards. During the summer of 1918, after Roman Catholic chaplains demurred, Almond and his Protestant lieutenants set out to instruct home church officials in the name of the rest of the Chaplain Service. Anglicans led the way. From the early days of the war Francis Moore, David Warner, and Alan Shatford among others had followed closely the theological debate in the Mother Church over the meaning of the conflict. The controversy stirred up therein by the National Mission of Repentance and Hope, as well as the strong critique of the church voiced by many BEF chaplains, had spawned several committees and resulted in at least one publication attempting to bring the message from the front home to British ecclesiastical leaders.[30] In August 1918 Warner, with Almond's sponsorship, dispatched a seven-part questionnaire to all Canadian Church of England chaplains overseas and others already back in Canada. Aided by senior chaplains, his digest of the sixty-odd responses was endorsed by two-thirds of Canadian Anglican chaplains overseas. Almond confidentially dispatched it to the Canadian bishops. While promising not to release the report to the press, he urged the hierarchy to seize this great opportunity to take the lead in Canadian reconstruction. Over half of the CEF was at least nominally Anglican. Clearly this church and its chaplains were in a strategic position to influence Canadian life. He asked the bishops to give sympathetic consideration to their chaplains' submission.[31]

The report bluntly announced that the pre-war church had failed to win and hold men.[32] Many of the troops completely refused to follow the church's moral or religious teachings. Nevertheless, many others had been drawn into the war on the side of right by the moral residue of Christianity shaping their personal or national ideals and social instincts. Still, the general level of commitment to the regular church, as well as the amount of religious knowledge among the men, was appallingly low. Most knew little of major church doctrines, nor did they realize that such were at the root of their inarticulate morality. Ignorance of what she truly stood for, however, was only one explanation of the failure of the pre-war church. The chaplains reported that the men rejected otherworldly or pessimistic dogmas and were baffled by or bored with archaic liturgy.[33]

Anglican chaplains charged that the leadership of the church had grown out of touch with the nation's men. Soldiers dismissed the clergy as professionalized, distant from everyday life, and often effeminate. Chaplains now understood their view that parsons were bookish bumblers, weak leaders, and poor speakers. Chaplains wanted better training in modern social science and business management. Anglicans wrote that their church colleges needed to acquaint seminarians with "the position of Modern Science," adding athletic and institutional training in settlement and club work to their curricula. Clergymen needed the intensity of training demanded by professions such as medicine and law.[34] Churches catered more to women, little children, and the aged, not men or youth. Parishes were controlled by elderly men and women, while parish life was impersonal or cliquish, quite the opposite, pointed out the padres, to the regimental comradeship of the army. That comradeship ought to be transplanted to the parish. The men detested denominational differences and favoured ecumenical co-operation, even organic church union.[35] Anglicans at home might find this problematic, but, chaplains warned, if their church hoped to have any impact on the returned soldier, she at least had to drop the old exclusiveness.[36]

Finally, the men were repelled by church social and political conservatism: its apathy towards questions of economic, social, and industrial life. Warner's survey was, perhaps, a probe for fellow Christian Socialists in the chaplaincy.[37] Significantly, over half blamed much of the religious indifference among their army flocks on church callousness to social and industrial problems and its overt sympathy for capitalism.[38] Consequently, the church had little credibility with the men. The chaplains, however, claimed that their identification with the men had earned the church a sympathetic hearing. If church leaders heeded their prophetic word, the veterans might throw their lot in with the church. Priests with sociological and political training, armed with the vision from overseas, could become its shock troops to lead the nation to righteousness.[39]

Warner and Almond's report to the bishops made it plain that the calls to reform from chaplains writing in the church press were more than the fulminations of a radical minority. The survey was endorsed by an impressively large number of priests, whose age and region of origin, combined with prior seminary training, revealed a broad reform concern among Canadian Anglican padres. Most were relatively younger, predominantly from western missionary fields (which employed many English clergy) or from dioceses where immigration, urbanization, and industrial conditions had encouraged them to grapple with the tenets of Canadian Social Christianity, especially the dioceses of Montreal and Rupert's Land.[40] Long military service or battle experience evidently did not drum the reforming urge out of a padre or predispose him to conservatism. Forty-six of the eighty-five signatures to the report came from chaplains with Corps service (including fifteen who had previously been in the ranks), while others were those of men of proven competence working in hospitals, camps, and lines-of-communication depots. In fact military service may have reinforced or confirmed ideals and convictions previously instilled by university and seminary. Whether they drew inspiration from liberal idealism, evangelical muscular Christianity, or from corporate conservatism, many Anglican chaplains now echoed the aspirations and agenda of Christians of other denominations. To Almond, Warner, Moore, Shatford, and others it was not too late to kindle the social passion in the Canadian Anglican church:

> As for the vision itself, it is the establishment of the Kingdom of God, which involves nothing less than the penetration of every sphere of life in our wider Dominion with Christian Principles. And to do this our Church must take a

larger place than ever before in Politics, in Industry and in the social problems of the people. "Deference to wealth," especially by the Clergy, should not be a possible criticism in the years to come, and "the workers" must be made to feel that the whole Christian Church is not only with them, but leads them in their demand for a living wage, and for healthy conditions of labour and life. In other words, it must be made patent to the world that the Church has a mission, and one that is concerned not only with the life to come, but with life here and now. The abolition of social wrongs, and the creation of a righteous social order must have an equal place in the Church's programme with that of individual redemption from moral and spiritual depravity or the ministrations of the means of grace to the Church's children.

There was one overriding lesson to be drawn from their war experience: "Only when men see that the Church is concerned with their whole life, with their social and physical condition, not less than their spiritual state, will they be likely to respond to her efforts to win them."[41]

Soon Almond gave chaplains from other Protestant denominations their chance. He readily agreed to a similar project undertaken by Edmund Oliver and Harold Kent on behalf of the non-conformist chaplains. Warner and Kent drew up a twelve-part questionnaire and dispatched it to Presbyterians, Methodists, Congregationalists, and Baptists. The text of this Chaplain Service questionnaire is reproduced in Appendix 2. Although based on premises similar to those of the Anglican report, this survey probed for more specific information. The first five questions requested criticisms of the pre-war flaws in church organization, life, and doctrine. The second five sought specific recommendations for improvement in these areas, while the final two invited summary conclusions based on the prophetic vision of repentance and the program of renewal that arose from the war.[42] Almond appointed representatives of each denomination to summarize the responses and to transmit the results to their respective churches.[43] After the war ended, those chaplains would meet under Almond's leadership to compose a joint message for publication in the Canadian churches. The response rate for this survey was disappointingly lower than that conducted by the Anglicans, as the final offensive of the war was under way and few chaplains from the fighting units had the time or interest to answer the questionnaire. Only half of the manuscript responses to this survey, most written by camp and hospital chaplains in England or on the continent, made their way back to London. To the frustration of historians and archivists, except for the twenty-seven Presbyterian and one Baptist responses that Kent preserved in Chaplain Service files, the remainder cannot be located.

Although all Methodist chaplains were sent copies of the questionnaire, T.A. Wilson told Kent that only one-third of them had come back by the end of 1918.[44] Nevertheless, Almond concluded, the committee would proceed.[45]

The Presbyterian responses closely resembled those of the Anglicans. Most Presbyterians agreed that their church had lost touch with many of its men before the war. The majority blamed the church more than the men.[46] Some estimated that from half to three-quarters of their men knew nothing of the adult Catechism or Westminster Confession. There were, however, reasons to hope that the pre-war slide could be reversed. Like the Anglicans, some Presbyterians argued that the piety nurtured in many of the men by their mothers still had a crucial influence on them as adults.[47] The war had reawakened in many soldiers a childhood faith that, the chaplains believed, would not die out after demobilization. Once they were persuaded that the "meek and mild" Saviour of pre-war days was a pernicious fallacy, most soldiers developed greater respect and admiration for Jesus Christ, a transformation that chaplains claimed was an essential preliminary in coming to faith. There now existed a great opportunity for the church to tap the spring of idealism welling up in the men through a vigorous program of enlightened propaganda, institutional reform, and national leadership on social, economic, and political issues. Most chaplains believed that widespread ignorance of what the churches really stood for was the greatest barrier to evangelism among the veterans. They also suggested that, now that many knew clergymen as chaplains, critics of the clergy might be won back to the churches.[48]

The Presbyterian padres pointed out a program similar to that advised by the Anglicans for their home church, as doctrine, clerical training, and social ministries all came under heavy criticism. Like the Anglicans, these chaplains found the men critical of their church's social conservatism and lack of warm fellowship. Presbyterian chaplains too were convinced that their denomination had failed to catch the overseas vision. Only by declaring another crusade at home could the victory won overseas benefit the churches.[49] Naturally, the best clergymen to lead this crusade were the returned chaplains, who had learned first-hand how much military organization and efficiency could tone up the effectiveness of national life.[50] The home clergy were poor leaders, with antiquated training and little influence, timid preachers because they were dependent upon voluntary offerings. As their professional status in Canadian society declined, the clergy failed to attract aggressive and capable candidates, while churches refused to pay enough to attract or keep the competent and ambitious.[51]

A few Presbyterian chaplains urged that the laity be equipped for and given a larger role in social and religious church work, for Christianity had to be thrust into the life of the nation. The church needed to give religious education by extension courses, as well as church-sponsored social and political ethics courses. Industrial and parliamentary chaplaincies were needed. More clergymen, and the main denominations, had to enter the political process directly. Formal union between the churches and lay organizations such as the YMCA was a necessity.[52] The churches must overcome internal class divisions, abandon their rich patrons, and sacrificially embrace the cause of the poor.[53] Here the Anglican and Presbyterian chaplains' recommendations merged into a united vision of the realization of the Kingdom in Canada.

In other ways, however, the Presbyterian survey reflected the distinctive preoccupations of Canadian Presbyterianism. This was especially true of the vexed question of organic church union. Almost all Presbyterian chaplains reported that the war had demonstrated its urgent necessity. Thanks to the editors of their ecclesiastical journals, the Presbyterian chaplains had already become a highly visible pro-union faction. Now Oliver, Frank Forster, Alexander Cornett, Robert Campbell, and George Kilpatrick added their voices to the chorus for union from overseas. To George Little church union was the best method of conserving and dedicating the moral devotion raised up by the war to the peacetime crusade for the Kingdom of God. Alexander Cornett called for complete Protestant union after the war, even leaving open the door for eventual admission of "Rome."[54] Of the remainder of the Presbyterians, only a handful were sceptical enough to suggest that federation or co-operation would be the most expedient form of church union to pursue after the war.[55]

Presbyterians were somewhat more critical of the content of pre-war theology than were Anglicans. Several ministers, in fact, called for a radical paring away of obsolete dogmas and wide-ranging revision of the Creed. They claimed that many fellow clergymen were forced into hypocrisy when church authorities required them to subscribe to the Westminster Confession, now undermined by modern thought. Both the seventeenth-century concepts and the seventeenth-century language of Presbyterian diehards seemed foreign and strange, while crank conservatives, with their pessimistic view of mankind and "ludicrous theories of eschatology," were ridiculed by soldiers and embarrassed the chaplains.[56] Along with the reform of traditional beliefs, some advocated borrowing an Anglican and Roman Catholic practice made popular by the war: frequent communion. These rejected the old Presbyterian view that sacramentalism was superstitious and called for the church to restore to communion its ancient meaning as a pledge of service, not otherworldly ritual.

Evidently many of the Presbyterians had found overseas the confirmation of the national gospel they proclaimed before the war. Whether the same was true of the other denominations consulted for the chaplains' message to the churches is difficult to say. Only one Baptist response, from McMaster-trained Henry Mullowney, remains in Chaplain Service files. Mullowney had challenged fellow Baptists to embrace the social gospel before the war. In 1917, as a padre overseas, he stirred up conservatives at home with his criticisms of Baptist dogmatism, pessimism, and the traditional Baptist view of conversion.[57] He heartily endorsed both the critique and the suggestions offered by his Anglican and Presbyterian colleagues, and offered with some advice specifically for his own denomination. He too criticized denominationalism, questioning even such distinct Baptist tenets as the separation of church and state and baptism by immersion. In light of his overseas experience, much of the touting of "Baptist distinctives" at home was ecclesiastical "hot air about Denominational prejudices."[58] Like the Anglicans and Presbyterians, Mullowney was optimistic about the opportunity the war offered the churches. He confidently assured John MacDonald: "We must put the Empire of Jesus Christ in our minds, our hearts and actions ... It seems to me that the present crisis has prepared the people of Canada for a large programme in Constructive Statesmanship within the Churches. Our own denomination I feel certain is ready for grappling in dead earnest with the problems of the nation."[59]

The reform vision was not, however, something all chaplains shared. And this point needs to be underscored. Some chaplains challenged both the assumptions and the conclusions of the reform advocates. John Magwood, a Methodist, while agreeing that the Kingdom of God was at hand, asserted that the Kingdom was not a political or social order but a personal gift. The war had brought many individuals to repentance and had marshalled a civilization to fight for right, but, he insisted in the *Christian Guardian*, salvation was of Christ, not social reform.[60] A few weeks later Edward Graham, a thirty-eight-year-old Mount Allison University graduate whose combat record as a South African CMR trooper as well as padre to the Thirteenth Battalion should have given his views greater weight with the Army and Navy Board, confidentially vented his dissatisfaction with the crusading and optimistic pronouncements of both chaplains and denominational leaders. The war was just but not holy, he argued:

That's all Tommy rot to me. Most of us here know ourselves and the fight too well to presume to identify it with the cause of Jesus ... It is true we have our orators pointing to the Union Jack and shouting "Jehovah my Banner" ... but most of us, for one reason or another, would prefer that the Union Jack, for all its crosses, should be mingled less freely with the emblems of our religion. My reason is that it lowers the standard of Jesus. Yet I believe it is every Christian's duty and privilege to contribute ... to the winning of this war, not as a Christian, but as a citizen of our warring country – not presuming to identify, in our case, that which is Caesar's with that which is Christ's.[61]

Graham denied that overseas experience transformed the souls of soldiers or the capacities and insight of chaplains. Neither traditional Methodist doctrine nor his own prior experience as soldier or chaplain bore out such premises. Neither experience had especially fitted him "for leadership or social reconstruction":

Much have I wondered at the respect given to opinions of soldiers on all sorts of subjects, and at the expectation that they will have gained special wisdom and disinterestedness in the future ordering of our country's affairs. I oppose all this pious sort of reverence for these splendid fighters. Let them be reverenced by all means but don't think that soldiering will make Solomons and Jonathans of them, or that even the chaplains will have been transformed into anything very much different from what they were. If the Church's power of leadership is in danger it will never be restored by men sent here for "experience."[62]

The response to his jeremiad was anything but appreciative. The board replied that he had been the only chaplain to voice such peculiar sentiments, which they ascribed to his prolonged period of arduous service.[63]

Among the Anglicans, two chaplains challenged the consensus. George Wells warned against expecting too much from the allegedly purifying catharsis of combat. Many men would come back after the war with the same vices (evidenced by the venereal disease rate among troops landing in England) that they had carried from home. In fact, he warned, overseas experience bred misplaced optimism instead of sober realism. Wells told readers of the *Canadian Churchman* that allowing radical Anglican chaplains to force their reconstruction agenda upon the home church without waiting for the bishops would be disastrous. The war had taught him that unity and caution took precedence over innovation and individual genius. Besides, he argued, padres were not innately better equipped by their experiences to lead a peacetime denomination. War service was an abnormal interlude in one's priestly life, not its central spiritual experience. Ecclesiastical leadership qualifications, especially of ex-soldiers, ought not to be premised first upon war service. "There has been far too much," he wrote, "of glorifying of the Canadian Soldier by our returned chaplains and not enough of the plain truth." A hopeful statement that they might become a blessing after the war was "more likely to meet the approval of all the Chaplains as a whole – who have lived with the men here – and more likely to gain the sympathy of the good people at home who must live with them in the future." As to the revival felt in the army, "the chaplains as a whole are not convinced of that and some Senior Chaplains – or at least one – know that as a matter of fact the attitude of officers and men towards services of any kind is about the same as it has been all along."[64]

Evidently, Wells was not an isolated or marginal critic. In fact, after the Armistice a small dissenting movement arose among Anglicans with the Canadian Corps. In February 1919, while the Corps was still in occupation, Almond submitted drafts of the proposed chaplains' message to padres in the field for approval. Arthur Creegan (who had replaced Scott as senior chaplain, First Division) and McGreer led conservative colleagues in a defence of Anglicanism's distinctiveness against the call for church union and revision of the liturgy.[65] Creegan, Wells, and some of their subordinates also opposed a revised draft: Creegan reminded Almond that his faction did not want Anglican distinctives discarded just to achieve church union. Army life had stifled denominationalism, indeed, but only for the duration of the war.[66] After lengthy talks the Corps chaplains passed the revised statement, with the proviso that the message indicate that its views were not entirely unanimous. Against the loud testimony of the majority, however, the objections of a handful of their colleagues had little chance of making a lasting impression.[67]

Two final protests crossed Almond's desk in the spring. George Broughall, a fifty-year-old graduate of Toronto's Trinity College, echoed Wells's denial that chaplains had a special revelation to pass on home, nor did he like the message's emphasis on the implied failure of the church. The irreligion of the Canadian soldier was his own responsibility, not the church's. Broughall opposed any doctrinal revision in the light of modern thought. He rejected entirely any suggestion that military experience had proved the viability or correctness of church union schemes, and he strongly objected to the call for the church to solve the social and industrial problems of Canadian society. The institutional church's mission was to shepherd Canadians into another world, though Christians "as individuals, should be keenly interested in all that affects the social welfare of the community and ... their attitude should be determined by their Christian principles."[68] J.C. Wilson, a Maritime Baptist, also rejected most of the premises underlying the proposed message. To him regeneration was an individual, not a national possibility. The church had often failed in its duty, but this duty was to individuals, not society. He sympathized with the passion for national and social righteousness but doubted that the padres, when back in Canada, would stick by anyone "who dares to give it a practical application."[69] He resented the stress on ecumenical unity after his own difficulties with Anglican exclusiveness in the army. He suspected that any Anglican enthusiasm for unity came from the assumption that their church would take precedence again. Wilson found ulterior motives in the call for fewer "popular" sermons and less dependence by ministers upon voluntary contributions. A strong Baptist, he read these as subtle moves to state-church privileges. Rather than complete organic unity, Wilson wanted the freedom of dissent and principle that co-operation, not union, offered.

Wilson's theological outlook thus made it impossible for him to accept the message. Statements that field conditions made the atmosphere of worship impossible, he said, were made only by padres who thought one had to worship in chapels. Personal witness and knowledge of the men made worship real, not liturgy or written prayers. Why supplement the Creed or modernize doctrines? The Creed was a crutch that many men would do better without in their personal belief. The stress on the church leader to become more involved in his people's daily life was fine, but not if that meant lowering his personal standards or outward witness. The ministry was not a profession like medicine or law, and the section on ministerial education and training was fundamentally flawed in presenting it as such. "In proportion as the Christian Church uses such a method in approaching possible entrants for her ministry", he observed, "she will forfeit her prestige, power and prospects." Wilson criticized padres who had been shocked by the ignorance of Christianity overseas. Any pastor doing personal work before the war knew this. This "lesson" of the war only revealed that many clergymen had no prior knowledge of the common man. Finally, Wilson denied that the war was a crusade and that the soldiers were advancing the Kingdom of God. "Does this position allow the anaemic and puerile teaching that all who fell in action secured their future by virtue of that sacrifice, irrespective of the antecedents of the moment? If so then insofar as that is true the Faith of the New Testament has not only continued unbroken, not only been vindicated, but its very foundations have been shattered." Nevertheless, Wilson's criticisms, like Broughall's, did not neutralize the outspoken approval of the message from supporters of his own denomination such as Mullowney or the more moderate MacDonald.[70] Nor did other padres join with them in protest against the summaries of war lessons proposed by their leaders.

THE MAJORITY OF PADRES ACTIVELY refused to let criticism or contradictory evidence check their high hopes. Their interest in such confident proclamations had been evident at chaplains' conferences held by the BEF in 1917 and 1918. The Army Chaplains' Department hosted two week-long retreats, combining recreation with stimulating addresses by leading religious thinkers. In all, sixty-five Canadian Anglican and non-conformist chaplains from the Corps attended these special sessions.[71] The Canadians arrived in a hopeful frame of mind, yet many shared the caution of an Anglican about to go on retreat: "One can speak to Chaplain after Chaplain and find the same dissatisfaction with the existing state of things, and desire to better it. Now and again one meets an extremist who would spoil the whole movement by his sweeping condemnation of all things that now are. We do not need destruction, we need reorientation, and it may take place so quietly that not a murmur is heard."[72] It was a desire to test and affirm, not to deny their intellectual foundations, that shaped the padres' response to the sessions held in Aire, France.

Presbyterians such as George Pringle and George Kilpatrick were impressed by Dr John Kelman, an Edinburgh theologian, who remarked that the soldier came to God "in a ... sense, without a theology ... It is the Christ way he has found unknowingly ... Christians must be comrades. Differences among churches are not fundamental, but temperamental ... After the war will come our opportunity for leadership ... If we lose the people then we'll not easily win them again." They praised an address by Alan Shatford, who called for simplification of dogma and church union, even at the expense of hallowed Anglican institutions.[73] Joseph Tupper assured readers of the *Canadian Churchman* that Shatford's and Kelman's addresses were well received even by British chaplains. The padres were challenged by Kelman's advice to exalt the roles of the Saviour as Comrade and Sacrifice to the men, who truly understood the significance of those themes in the trenches. Then the preacher, as "propagandist of the Kingdom of Heaven," might help the post-war world find resurrection after its international Calvary.[74] Shatford argued that "a new era for the Church" had been inaugurated by the war. He called for a widely unified, comprehensive response to the war from the whole Christian church to make the world the Kingdom of God. The soldiers were at the forefront of a great awakening, which the church, led by its chaplains, must capture and lead, establishing universal democracy. Broad church union must be implemented, at least by federation if not by organic union. Concluding with the example of the Old Testament prophets as civil guardians, Shatford urged his colleagues to take up the torch of regeneration when they returned at the head of their veterans.[75]

At the next retreat Bishop Brent, Canadian-born Episcopalian and leading American army chaplain, delivered a rousing message in the same vein as Shatford's. At the retreats chaplains also discussed the books that had most influenced their thinking. They urged churchmen to read T.R. Glover's *The Jesus of History* and William James's *The Varieties of Religious Experience* in order to prepare themselves for the coming work.[76] Methodist chaplains were delighted to hear George Jackson (who had returned to Britain after the controversy over his modernist preaching in Toronto) tell them of his reflections upon Job, the honest doubter, whose denial of false faith in tribulation was archetypical of all suffering Christians in the course of their war. Jackson concluded his message with a prophetic forecast of the great triumph of faith that would come, as it had for Job, when the travail of faith was complete, though in their case it would be the greater final triumph over war of world brotherhood in Christendom.[77]

Other speakers at the second conference included G. Campbell Morgan, F.B. Meyer, and T.R. Glover. Morgan pointed out that the war was a catastrophe from one point of view, but also a chastening and renewing blessing. His realism about the dark nature of the war contrasted greatly with his optimism about the eventual triumph of God in history, through the Cross. Meyer portrayed a triumphalist vision of the victory of the spiritual over material forces, the fulfilment of God's historical plan to bring the Kingdom to earth. Drawing on his own research, Glover emphasized the moral manliness and activism of the apostle.[78] On leave, the Methodist chaplains agreed with their British counterparts who preached, on Victory Sunday, that all history was the redemptive process and progress of God's children.[79]

A similar blend of advanced liberal scholarship and evangelical fervour became evident when many chaplains dealt with the subject of Christ. From the beginning of the war YMCA workers and chaplains had emphasized the masculine and militant characteristics of "the Jesus of History," opposing what they saw as the pre-war stereotype of a "meek and mild" Saviour.[80] Chaplains such as George Fallis preached that, while Jesus was known as the Prince of Peace, he should also be recognized as the "Prince of Justice and Righteousness."[81] Similarly, Walter Rauschenbusch's *The Social Principles of Jesus* and Harry Emerson Fosdick's *The Manhood of the Master* became the basis of many a Canadian chaplain's Bible study or discussion group.[82] After the Armistice both books became part of the curriculum of the joint Chaplain Service-YMCA Citizenship Campaign, which was intended to indoctrinate returning veterans with the ideals of the Kingdom of God.[83] Throughout the war many Canadian chaplains drew on Fosdick's view that the Jesus of history was not the effeminate and otherworldly martyr of Sunday-school convention but a joyful, vigorous, and brotherly comrade of active men. Jesus revealed to the men of his own day and to those now in the trenches the supreme value of service for others. His hope never wavered "in the victory of right over wrong." He was sympathetic to the poor and victimized, indignant at injustice and corruption. Jesus waged a tireless campaign on behalf of his Father's Kingdom, was capable of wrath, and was ferocious on behalf of others. Like Jesus, the Christian's love was to be fearless, uncomplaining, and unabated in the face of discouragement – indeed, just like that of the soldier who sticks to his duty. In the cause of his Father's Kingdom, Jesus was the model patriot.[84]

Fosdick's book was especially helpful to chaplains because of its emphasis on the militant personality of Jesus. As Allied victory drew near, however, Walter Rauschenbusch's work gave timely emphasis to Jesus' social crusade. Despite his emphatic rejection of war as a method of realizing the Kingdom, chaplains eagerly drew upon his portrait of Jesus' zeal for the highest ethical, economic, and political principles of brotherhood. In the struggle for the Kingdom of God, Rauschenbusch argued, even patriotism, if it was marked by brotherly love and inclusiveness, was superior to selfish, crude, and materialistic nationalism. While the present war seemed a mockery of Jesus' millennial hope, Rauschenbusch, drawing upon William James, called on his readers to rally to the cause of the Kingdom of God as a "moral substitute for war." Even the temporary abandonment of Christ's pacifism (as a desperate measure in the battle for world salvation) was worth it if the Right ultimately was victorious. While warning that victory was only achieved by voluntarily self-sacrifice (the "Cross as a Social Principle"), Rauschenbusch called on all modern Christians to join in the combat to bring the Kingdom of God to realization in the post-war world.[85] To many Canadian chaplains such sentiments were ideally suited to guide the men in their return to civilian life. To them the only way to accomplish the great task of regenerating post-war society was through the power of a personal commitment to the militant, manly, and world-changing Saviour. Righteous citizenship could only be accomplished by righteous men.[86]

At the same time the Canadian chaplains, while using the work of well-known modernists and social gospellers, nevertheless did not relinquish their pre-war conviction of the metaphysical uniqueness of Jesus Christ. In fact, part of the special attractiveness of Fosdick's or Rauschenbusch's studies of Jesus was their evident basis in the religious experience and devotional life of their authors. While chaplains were drawn to the Jesus of history's humanity and sympathy, therefore, most continued to portray Jesus as the divine Son of God. While eager to make Jesus more human, comradely, and relevant to their men, very few were willing to strip him of divinity. Throughout the war chaplains such as George Kilpatrick and Edward Burwash found in their war and the faith of their men both the divine power and presence of the saving Son of God and the sympathy and humanity of the suffering Jesus of history. Writing in the spring of 1918, George Kilpatrick reassured his father that "for four years the figure of the Christ has been very busy on the battlefield saving men. His unseen but living Presence has still its ancient power to strengthen and uphold ... Personally I can say truly it has been possible in some experiences of the front to realize almost the visible Presence of Him who gave us the promise 'Lo I am with you always' ... The true Jesus of history is today the Christ of the Trenches, and there is great reinforcement in His companionship ... Could there be a higher honour or a truer joy than to present to the men who know all about friendship, the comradeship of the man of Galilee – who was also the Son of God?"[87]

Such a blending of personal faith, idealism, and the sordid realities of trench life and death also characterized the approach of many chaplains preaching about the Atonement. Having been raised in churches and families where the conventional limited view of the Atonement had already given way to an emphasis upon the free offer of grace to all who trusted in Christ, and having bonded so closely with their army flocks, it became imperative for chaplains to link the human suffering of the trenches with the sufferings of Christ. In the trenches most padres realized that their pre-war view of the Atonement and its accompanying model of salvation based on nurture and reconsecration required virtually no modification to meet war conditions.[88] In fact, the war perhaps made it easier for such a process to take place as soldiers fell back on their childhood faith (instilled in the home or at Sunday school) when faced with the perils and trials of their own little Calvary, the trenches. Rather than emphasize the older view of human depravity as innate and God's violated justice requiring satisfaction (which had come under repeated attack in the Protestantism of the English-speaking world in the preceding century), many

Canadian Protestant chaplains emphasized the soul's freedom, when moved by an appreciation of the sufferings of Christ on its behalf, to reach out to God and obtain grace. For these chaplains evangelism became less and less the preaching of sin and demand for repentance, more and more the tapping of childhood faith, admiration, and love for Jesus. The war had proven to them that old-fashioned ideas of "conversion" had been superseded by newer models.[89]

The effect of the Cross upon the believer, many padres suggested, could now be appreciated more than ever by the soldiers bearing their burdens daily in the trenches and ultimately being called to sacrifice their own lives for the sake of their loved ones. While some older and more pessimistic chaplains continued to preach Jesus as divine Saviour and to call upon the soldiers in faith to repudiate all their past and present works entirely, many other padres portrayed the state of the men in the trenches and the vision of Christ on the Cross as linked, even as two points on the same continuum. To chaplains such as Colwell, Kilpatrick, and many of their Presbyterian and Methodist colleagues, Jesus Christ and the Cross remained the "secret of a padre's point of contact" with his men.[90] Hence the urgency that Kilpatrick and his fellow chaplains felt in waiting for the church at home to grasp this truth and make it central to the days of reconstruction to come.[91]

To many chaplains the power of this deepened appreciation of the Cross and Jesus Christ among the soldiers overseas would continue to mould lives and nations after the war was over. Thus, in the spring of 1918 George Kilpatrick, whose ability to articulate such sentiments led to his selection to preach the victory sermon at Mons, tried to sum up, on behalf of the many Canadian Protestant chaplains, the continuity between their pre-war faith, their experience overseas, and their hopes for the future:

> In the experience of war we have been face to face with no theoretical analysis of the atonement's meaning but with a great demonstration of its truth that through sacrifice comes life, and that love, be it of country or of friend will stop at nothing to bring salvation ... Life has been redeemed – made safe – for us by the sacrifice of our men and surely there is close kinship between their sacrifice and that of Jesus Christ ... These rough wooden crosses which line the fields of France and Flanders are not by accident the symbols of sacrifice, for they mark the resting place of those who "loved not their lives unto death" and who in their dying caught something of the spirit of our Master. We who have lived in the years of the Great War may make no claim to complete understanding of the atonement, or the fullness of Divine Love, but at least we have seen with our own eyes the demonstration of our Master's

word, "Greater Love hath no man than this – that a man lay down his life for his friend" ... The preaching of the atonement will hereafter fall on the ears of men and women who because of their experience will find in it a new and deep significance ... On the battlefront Christ has been very busy these past years ... He knows what it is to have the sacrifice rejected and the gift spurned and they too shall learn in after days that men too easily forget that life has been redeemed not with "corruptible things" – but with "precious blood." We cannot expect that out of the tumult there will emerge ready made a new world. The salvation of men only began with the sacrifice of Christ and today we are only laying the foundations of a new and sweeter world ... Our task is very clear. We have to testify in life to our fidelity to those great principles for which men daily die, that from these honoured dead we take increased devotion to that cause for which they gave the last full measure of devotion – that we highly resolve that these dead shall not have died in vain. Only thus shall we keep faith with them and take our place in the progressive redemption of mankind.[92]

With unconscious irony Kilpatrick and many of his colleagues had blended their religious experience with the most harrowing crusade of the previous century – the American war against slavery – linking their war and its significance with Lincoln's Gettysburg commemoration two generations before. Kilpatrick could not know that the years to come would prove as disappointing as the Reconstruction years proved to be for veterans of the American Civil War. Kilpatrick spoke the Canadian Protestant padres' hopes: to pour from war's fiery crucible a redeemed nation, capable of realizing their pre-war theories, ideals, and visions in a renewed Dominion. In order to grasp the adamant strength of this vision, inquirers must seek its source in the pre-war seminary and theological training of the men who became the Canadian padres.

WHILE MANY CANADIAN CLERGYMEN in the years 1897–1914 were being introduced to militia ways and ideals, many more were finishing their education or launching careers in Canadian classrooms, missions, and pulpits. The seminary had always played a decisive role in equipping clergymen for Christian service, especially in Presbyterian, Roman Catholic and Anglican circles. In the years before the war the Methodist and Baptist churches too placed greater emphasis upon training an educated clergy. Because denominational authorities tried to send only those considered best qualified to influence the young men joining the Canadian Expeditionary Force, their younger, more active, and better-educated members received the greater number of chaplaincy nominations. As a result, most Protestants serving as Canadian chaplains shared a strikingly broad consensus about their faith and the war.[93] Roman Catholic chaplains also shared a common religious vision, but theirs was rather different from that of the Protestants and was fractured by ethnic and language differences within their fold as well. In order, then, to understand how most Protestant chaplains had been equipped for battle, some attention must be given to the tendencies and dominant motifs of pre-war Canadian and Old World religious thought.

By the end of the nineteenth century many Protestant leaders and educators were convinced that the times demanded a new breed of Christian leadership. Christianity had undergone great tribulation in the nineteenth century as canons of the faith were subjected to criticism by scholars, scientists, and sceptics. New sources of authority challenged biblical and theological propositions and raised doubts about the providence of God and the mission and character of the church. New industrial and social forces challenged Christianity's hold upon European and North American culture. Fortunately, to many Protestants, the church had passed the peak of the crisis and found the resources to triumph over the forces of secularization. The course of the Great War revealed that such efforts to preserve and extend the faith had an obvious influence on Protestants in the Canadian Chaplain Service as they weighed their civilian convictions in the balance of war. In camps and trenches these men would test their pre-war views on authority, providence, and the national significance of their faith. Events proved that, for them, there was a powerful link between classroom, pulpit, and the war.

Perhaps the most widespread controversy among theologians and educators before the war was the battle over religious authority. The majority of Protestant clergymen destined to become Canadian Great War chaplains were trained and led by a generation that believed it had met and overcome the challenges of naturalistic evolution, scientific inquiry, and biblical criticism. Drawing upon the work of British mentors mediating German scholarship to the English-speaking world, Canadian Protestant theologians by the 1890s were confident that they had indeed answered the forces of doubt.[94] Darwinism, most now believed, had been tamed by substituting providential for naturalistic evolution. The apologetical writings of Henry Drummond, explaining evolution as God's principle for natural and human progress, achieved wide distribution among English-speaking Protestants and reassured many a Christian beset by doubts.[95] Drummond argued that all natural and social laws expressed the same supernatural principle – God's benevolent, sacrificial love. Pictured in virile, activist language, this nerved thinking Christians to greater moral and spiritual effort for good. Struggle on behalf of others, Drummond taught, was demonstrated unconsciously by the material in nature and consciously in practice by men and women of faith, for they all drew on the ideal originating in the mind of God. Beyond family love, he went on, human history and social organization followed a similar dynamic as the world evolved towards a grander realization of Christian fraternity.[96]

Significantly, most Presbyterian chaplains, especially those educated at Pine Hill, Knox, Queen's, and McGill colleges, had absorbed this view by 1914.[97] Other challenges to authority from science, it was believed, might be overcome by the disciplined use of Baconian science and empirical methods. To Nathanael Burwash, who personally or through former students shaped the education of almost every Methodist Great War chaplain, all truth was open to patient, reverent criticism based on inductive methods. Such, he contended, confirmed and extended rather than undermined traditional evangelical religious experience: the result proved to be "the old truth in its evangelical fullness." Thus the natural and social sciences, rightly conducted, served as handmaidens to religion. Dogmatic accretions would be pruned from creeds and practices of all the denominations to expose the historical and timeless nature of original Christianity. Progress and piety were consciously linked and updated by the efforts of conscientious biblical and theological scholars, whether Presbyterian, Methodist, or Baptist. The dominant note in their studies and preaching was the vindication of the old evangelical experience by the new methods and conclusions of secular thought.[98]

More important to the young seminarians and laymen, however, was the challenge to authority posed by German critical biblical scholarship. Rather than rejecting the Old Testament scholarship of Julius Wellhausen or that of the New Testament scholar Albrecht Ritschl, however, British and Canadian authorities, using their empirical assumptions, drew deeply on their methods but selectively discarded their conclusions when they contradicted the canons of faith and religious experience. For them higher criticism was a vitally useful tool in their apologetic for Christianity in a questioning age.[99] In Presbyterian and Anglican schools, where biblical exegesis had been a traditional exercise, then in Methodist and Baptist colleges such as Victoria (where after 1874 it was made mandatory for all seminarians by Burwash) and McMaster, a new picture of the Bible's original message and the origins and destiny of the church arose. The new scholarly methods were readily embraced as tools with which to prune away traditional dogmatic accretions and free the timeless essence of the faith from its historical contamination by the church.[100] Students of the Old Testament prophets and the Psalms, such as Knox College's J.E. McFadyen, absorbed the writings of George Adam Smith and imparted to their students a renewed appreciation of the growth of monotheism and the passion for national holiness of the Israelites. Especially interesting was the powerful influence that the small band of prophets evidently had on the life of their nation. Their patriotism was declared their greatest contribution to social ethics, as was their conviction of the sacred nature of Israel's history. In the Old Testament prophets' proclamations of the divine mission of an elect nation, Canadian as well as British preachers found ready inspiration for their own generation. Canadian Protestants wrestling with the national ills of the Laurier period were inspired by their fearless castigation of wealth and power and vision of national regeneration.[101]

Critical study of the New Testament and the early church was deemed essential for the modern ministerial student. Here, just as the German critics' dangerous naturalism had been excised, so the denial of Christ's divinity and resurrection were carefully set aside. British and Canadian scholars instead emphatically pointed out the metaphysical uniqueness of Jesus and his continuing divine power to seek and save lost men.[102] Nevertheless, Canadian students easily adapted the critics' understanding of Jesus' preaching and exemplary ethical holiness to their own needs.[103] Jesus, as militant prophet of the Kingdom of God with a social as well as personal gospel, attracted great interest. Two generations of biblical criticism had given Canadian churchmen a Saviour ideally suited for bringing in the Kingdom on earth as in heaven. Jesus, it was emphasized, was the fearless enemy of evil and injustice, advocate of the downtrodden, and militant prophet of national righteousness.[104] The story of the early church, stripped by Adolf Harnack of dogmatic accretions and presented in progressive terms by his interpreters, also appealed to many young Presbyterians taking a year or two of postgraduate study in Berlin.[105] Many graduates of other Protestant denominations selectively adapted Harnack's account of the history of church doctrine from their reading.

These adjustments in biblical emphasis were directly linked to the special emphasis on the dynamic role of God's providence in human and religious history. The battle between reason and Revelation led to the questioning of God's guidance of human events. Here Anglican and Presbyterian students in particular were irresistibly drawn to the philosophical idealism expounded in Britain by T.H. Green of Oxford and his Glasgow colleagues, Edward and John Caird.[106] Like Drummond, students in Presbyterian, Anglican, and Congregational seminaries found in neo-Hegelian Idealism a philosophical system that reinforced their moralistic and optimistic interpretation of providence, that made sense of the tendencies of the age without undermining their religious experience or Christian faith. It was considered by many to be an ideal apologetical and missionary framework with which to take the Evangel into the new century.[107] To these students the central meaning of history lay in the progress of ideas and humanity towards unity, harmony, and freedom. History, rightly interpreted, became the unfolding of the triumph of the spiritual over the material as God, in history and through the Christian church, transcended and informed evolving nature. Such a view of God's immanent instead of transcendent providence interpreted all reality as "the expression of a rational Divine principle which was God." In an age of obvious technological, intellectual, religious, and political progress, no lack of evidence prevented these students from believing that Western society was indeed moving human civilization towards world brotherhood, as the human spirit, made in the image of God, rationalized nature, God's visible garment, through obeying the dictates of duty, the voice of God in the conscience.[108]

Here the Caird brothers and their Canadian disciples – John Watson at Queen's, George Paxton Young at Toronto University, T.B. Kilpatrick at Knox, George Blewett at Victoria, and I.G. Matthews at McMaster – found a valuable role for the historical study of religion, tracing the course of human efforts to realize such high principles in the past. To Watson and Kilpatrick, for example, Jesus had taught the ethical ideals "that were the highest form of religious consciousness and morality expressed in the history of the human race," the fatherhood of God and the brotherhood of Man. Thus, men and women who identified themselves with the divine purpose aided the progression towards organic wholeness and the harmony of world brotherhood – the earthly realization of the Kingdom of God. The nation-state played an important role in this blend of individualism and collectivism in providing the proper conditions for human fulfilment and eliminating the competition that exploited the weak. Thus would the competitive ethic be supplanted by the higher ethic of co-operation. All of this, the Cairds' followers lectured, was the result of the power of ideas.[109]

For Canadian Methodists, who were perhaps less drawn to Idealism because of its pantheistic overtones, the acceptance of the inductive method of church history led to their pursuit of providence by a similar route.[110] Canadian Methodists based their progressive and optimistic view of church history, from primitive Christianity through decline and renewal by Luther, Calvin, Knox, Wesley, and the Evangelicals of the previous generation, on the same scholarly basis as did their British or German mentors, adding the nationalistic hope that Canada would play a leading role in this triumphal process.[111]

This evolving world-view, combined with the post-millennial eschatology embraced by much of the educated ministry, led to strong anticipations of the coming of the Kingdom of Christ as the culmination of Christendom's evangelization of the world. In the nineteenth-century fires of purification the church had at last been shorn of obsolete dogma and credalism by biblical criticism and historical theology. The doctrines of the Atonement and Incarnation had been harmonized with scientific and intellectual progress. Thus the Gospel was re-equipped to penetrate throughout secular culture. This process was seen as conservative, preserving the historical essence of the central doctrines of the Christian church as its many branches moved closer towards federation or even organic reunion. The Church in the twentieth century, it was expectantly proclaimed, would triumph over the last barriers to complete realization of the Kingdom of God on earth. All the forces of history, tended by a dynamic and benevolent providence, could only advance the coming of the post-millennial vision of a regenerated earth. Canada, the Idealists believed, had been equipped with the political, racial, and religious traditions that would play a leading role in this process.[112]

IN THE DECADES before the war many Protestant clergymen in the classrooms, press, and parishes of the Dominion were joined by colleagues armed with similar or sympathetic convictions brought from their studies in Britain or the United States. They created an ambitious consensus among clergymen on the role of religion in private and national life. Although leaders were deeply concerned about the corrosive impact of "relativism," which threatened to becalm the evangelical movement, the major Protestant denominations (though led by Presbyterians and Methodists) forged "national gospels," which became more forcefully advocated in the months before the war.[113] In the decade before 1914 Protestant reformers focused attention on the national transformation wrought by immigration, industrialization, and urbanization, beginning a program of education and persuasion that they hoped would revitalize religion and lead towards the redemption of the young country. Fundamental to this campaign, by the outbreak of the war, was the creation of a national voice of righteousness by denominational union or federation, which, it was hoped, would create a distinctive Canadian national Protestant church, extending the faith's vital impulse first to the nation, then to the world.[114] The full impact of changing social, intellectual, and cultural currents after 1900 would not become evident until after the Great War, but in the midst of their careers as contemporary prophets of national as well as personal regeneration, by 1910 leading Protestant clergymen were urgently proclaiming that the time had come to rise up and possess the land. Evangelicals, borrowing a phrase from William James, spoke of a world where the virtues of war were being harnessed to overthrow social evils and usher in national righteousness. Others issued evangelical calls to battle on the side of providence.[115] Adopting the language and imagery of battle, the clergy of Canada were already setting about the task of kindling the moral equivalent of war in their congregations when overtaken by the events of August 1914.

Nor were such progressive and dynamic processes without their secular parallels. During this period similar values, while not always founded on religious authorities but nevertheless reinforcing their values, were part of the public discourse of the nation. By the last decade of the peace, imperialism had brought its own politically urgent synthesis of idealism and progressivism to the fore. Among the Canadian imperialists, many of them clergymen such as George Grant, the sense of imperial mission was an extension of the same values proclaimed as the national agenda of the churchmen.[116] Their idealism was a fundamental link between the two groups, as was their Whig view of history and the similarly high value they placed on self-sacrifice and work. A federated British Empire, led by a reformed Canada, accepting the responsibility of acting as God's instrument to civilize the world, was the deeply cherished vision of both groups.[117] Sharing so many values with the imperialists, the Protestant clergy became idealistic prophets of imperial nationalism, with its sense of mission and its social-reform conscience. Both groups understood war as a beneficial process if waged for a just cause rather than territorial aggrandizement. War could easily be rationalized as a benevolent if brutal process of civilization, as furthering the spread of Protestant religion and British concepts of justice. For such visionaries the military way became a school for character, imparting the values of duty, service, and self-sacrifice that were already being emphasized by the clergy. Here lay a major point of convergence between the course charted by a Sam Hughes and the clergy of Canada. Even William James's desire to find war's moral equivalent appeared in the imperialist's call for the great nations to uphold international obligations and defend the weaker ones.[118]

By the beginning of the First World War a powerful consensus existed among leading Protestants. An imperial-nationalist vision and optimistic vocabulary were shared by many Protestant clergymen, intellectuals, politicians, and social reformers. Secular conceptions of duty, sacrifice, progress, and imperial mission mingled with the passion of preachers to extend the kingdom of God to every land and nation. Young men heard the call to service in classrooms and churches across the nation, from leaders who increasingly emphasized the essentially Christian nature of Canadian character and national destiny. Whatever blessing or misfortunes providence dispensed, whatever loss of conviction the evangelical consensus had seemed to feel in the pre-war years, the time had come, in an age when men's hearts grew cold, to rally against the allies of evil and decay.

Among Canadian Roman Catholic clergymen, however, the pre-war years were filled with turmoil and tension, more often ethnic and linguistic than theological in nature. English, Irish, and Scottish-bred priests shared the same Thomist theological training, anti-Protestant apologetical views, and outspoken critique of modernity as their French-Canadian counterparts. Both denounced the materialism and secularism of Canadian life, the growth of socialism and suffragism. Ironically, both were convinced of the urgent need to involve the church in the nation's social and political problems. In fact, it was this commitment that led to their collision. While French Canadian churchmen defended their language and mission to preserve ultramontane Catholicism in North America, English-speaking priests demanded a larger share in the leadership of the national church and openly promoted the adoption of English as the language of North American Catholicism.

During the last few years of peace this barely concealed schism within the church flared into mutual denunciation. In 1910 the English and French-speaking portions of Canadian Catholicism were rocked by controversy when England's highest Roman Catholic prelate, Monsignor Bourne of Westminster, addressing the Twelfth Eucharistic Congress of the North American church in Montreal, pleaded for the adoption of English as the language of the North American church. Henri Bourassa's ringing rejection of Bourne's appeal echoed the rallying cry of Ontario's French-speaking Roman Catholics defending the cause of bilingual education in their province. There the archenemy of bilingualism appeared in the form of a fellow churchman, Bishop Michael Fallon of London, who became spokesman for Ontario Catholics determined to promote separate schools but at the expense of the French language. This controversy reached the boiling point in 1912, when the Ontario government passed educational regulations intended to phase French-language instruction out of its separate schools.[119] While moderates tried in vain to maintain the appearance of unity and Catholic periodicals attempted to paper over the cracks in the walls of the church, the issues of language and conflicting nationalisms continued to polarize church factions.[120]

By 1914, therefore, the Canadian Roman Catholic church was sharply divided on ethnic and linguistic lines. French-Canadian clergymen, preoccupied with the nationalist question as well as the problems of industrial and economic modernization of their province, fixed their vision and activities firmly on *la survivance*, on parish and diocesan concerns, while their hierarchy stood poised to strike out at English-speaking critics, especially of their own denomination.[121] For their part, Fallon, the Ontario hierarchy, and like-minded bishops in the Maritimes and the west, committed to maintaining their influence within the growing church and the Canadian community, struggled to realize their own vision for the church, a vision that appeared very similar to that of non-Catholic imperial nationalists of the day. For to Fallon and his fellow clerics, although often of Irish extraction, the British Empire remained the best vehicle for the Christianization of the world and the progress of the race. Anything that stood in its way or threatened to undermine its influence, from French-Canadian nationalism to German or Japanese imperialism, had to be opposed.[122] While he had his doubts about the French Canadians, as war clouds gathered across the Atlantic, Sam Hughes knew he could count on men of Fallon's stamp in the coming crisis.

Although they had criticized aspects of theological education and organization in light of their overseas experience, the wartime utterances of the Canadian Anglican and other Protestant chaplains illustrate that, in their view, prior religious experience and seminary training had served them well during the war. Their high resistance to disillusionment, their optimism and unambiguous preaching indicate that their pre-war convictions formed a strong yet flexible matrix within which to contain, if not resolve, their personal experiences and trials of faith. Their religious experience and theological studies had given these chaplains a model of history and providence well-suited to crusading nationalism, as well as a language suitable to rationalizing and softening the cruel paradoxes of war, ennobling death and destruction as sacrifice. Their Old Testament training stood as a prophetic model for their role as clergymen serving in war time, preaching and prophesying personal and national regeneration. Similarly, their New Testament studies supplied them with a Christology and a renewed appreciation for activist Christianity well suited to waging a regenerative war with perseverance and patience.

These considerations energized their preaching to the troops, both at the special services of commemoration and celebration held for the troops and in the more routine preaching regimen of the weekly parade and informal services. The devotional emphasis became more pointed and more poignant the closer the padre and his flock came the front line. Nevertheless, the padre did not discard the cosmic religious framework that he had limned for the folks at home. Even in France there were numerous military occasions when he and the troops expected the most vibrant patriotism and crusading idealism. The anniversary of the war's outbreak, Easter, Dominion Day, New Year's Eve, the anniversaries of the Ypres gas attack, Vimy Ridge, and the Somme, as well as other patriotic occasions all were opportunities to blend the devotional theme with the patriotic and crusading motifs. Thus it becomes apparent that, underneath all the pietist and evangelistic content of the routine front-line, practical exhortations to the troops, there was, in the minds of padres at least, an implicit cosmic theological framework for their war – the great national crusade for the winning of the Kingdom of God on earth.

War service thus brought out in almost every padre the latent reformer and confirmed in their idealism those already calling for national, social, and religious reform before the war. The war became for many chaplains the great sanctifying experience of the modern church, which would bring the Master's mission to fruition with international regeneration. It had to be this way. The debates in seminary, the new complexities of formal criticism in classroom or study were left behind or brushed aside in the urgency of war and the need for clarity and certainty.[123] No war in history had involved such massive forces, such mighty continents, so many peoples and nations, and called forth the utmost in national courage, brotherhood, and altruistic devotion. No war had been so clearly caused by the greed of one or two corrupt and aging political systems. Surely defeating them once and for all would throw down the last barrier to the millennium of peace and brotherhood foreseen by the Master?

So in war's dark crucible each denomination's "national gospel" found renewed power and immediacy. For the church militant as much as home-front clerics, the Great War became a providential opportunity to convert Canadians to the padres' pre-war vision of idealism and national reform. Even the few who objected to the sentimentalism and hyperpatriotism colouring wartime Christianity nevertheless testified that their own convictions had survived the fires of war intact. Almost all intended to bring their own regenerative vision home to revive the churches and, consequently, the nation. Time would reveal that the wartime vision was unable to weather the decades of debate to come, yet for the padres, war neither shattered the old nor created unique theologies. Instead, it entrenched a prior vision of righteousness that tried to wrestle the war into the padres' pre-existent world-view. Nor was there much in military life or combat service to challenge the padres' interpretation, for everything they saw and heard could be rationalized into their own gospel with deceptive ease. Few indeed were the padres who sensed that they had been ineffective in winning the men to their own point of view, or that the noble transformation in character wrought by war could not last into the peace. In that sense, most Protestant padres unwittingly took the Great War and fashioned it in their own image.

8 Veterans: A Peace Endured

Looking back, with nearly a decade of hopes and disappointments behind him, Will Bird, formerly a Forty-second Battalion Highlander, later a Nova Scotian journalist, began his personal chronicle of war. In 1930 a small run of *And We Go On* was released to the Canadian reading public, with moderate financial success. While he rejected the style ("putrid with so-called realism") of Charles Yale Harrison's portrayal of the Western Front in *Generals Die in Bed*, Bird, too, bluntly challenged the clichés and facile rhetoric of officers and war leaders whose words seemed so hollow after a decade of peace. Bird did not spare the padres:

"Where's the padre?" asked the Student. "Before I came over I fancied that they were always with the soldiers, helping the wounded ones and having little services every chance they got". "Don't," said Tommy, "start that argument. I was a member of the Methodist Church when I enlisted. Now I don't know or care about anything connected with it. Preachers and padres are not any better than brass hats. They're out of touch with the men, and they've lost their hold." "Don't you believe in God?" asked the Student. "I do," said Tommy gravely and reverently. "If I didn't I'd quit everything. But I'm going to have my own belief in my own way. It's all going to be between Him and me, and no preacher is going to have anything to do with it. They tell you it's wrong to hate another man, wrong to kill a man, and that's a commandment, and yet they get up in pulpits and out on church parades and tell you that we're fighting for the Lord and talk as if the Germans were devils, and that it's all right to kill them. Bah – padres, I'm sick of them. They say just what the brass hats want them to say, there's not a sincere man among them. If there was he'd be out between the lines trying to stop both sides from killing each other."

Later, in an English camp, Bird's friend again has the last word with a chaplain trying to detain him for a short service:

"No," said Tommy, "I don't want to hear any more twaddle. I've had to go on church parades but this isn't compulsory, and once I'm out of this rig no man will ever make me listen to your stuff." The Padre tried to argue. "We're going to teach a real gospel now," he said. "The war's over and we're going to, first of all, prove to the people what a horrible crime it is." "Don't do that," cried Tommy. "You'll lose the few you've still got if you turn hypocrite. The war hasn't changed. If it's wrong now it was wrong in '14, and what did you shout then?" The padre's eyes flooded full. He could not talk.[1]

For many chaplains two decades of peace proved more arduous than the war years. As they returned from the crusade, Almond and his Protestant staff called for a church renewal in their home communions, but their clarion call met with a lukewarm response. Before long the apparent solidarity of the chaplains themselves eroded as they found themselves on conflicting sides of a number of peacetime debates, for wartime idealism and millennial expectations were continually challenged by domestic social and ecclesiastical conflict, veteran disaffection, and international developments escalating towards another world conflict. In 1919 chaplains saw themselves as radical agents of renewal. In the crises of the peace, however, they often sided with the forces of moderation and shunned Canadians, even fellow chaplains, more radical than themselves. By the 1930s even ex-soldiers seemed to turn on them. Eventually a few padres questioned or renounced their initial vision, but in the last years of the peace most clung faithfully to their beliefs and offered themselves again for national service in 1939.

AFTER DEMOBILIZATION, ex-chaplains faced the sometimes traumatic process of resettlement. In their first civilian weeks most felt emotionally and physically exhausted. For some there were visits to be made to their comrades' next-of-kin, discharging last requests and deathbed vows.[2] While many eagerly anticipated getting back to their pre-war situations, others doubted their ability to settle down again to the old routine. Changes had to be made in both church and nation, and they were going to take the lead.[3]

Many chaplains accordingly turned aside from careers in the church, searching for better social-service opportunities or escape from the confines and insecurities of ecclesiastical life. Caught between demobilization and the lack of a parish, Alfred Lavell, for example, chose a career with the Parole Board of Ontario. Within a few weeks he was joined by Baptist chaplain Joseph Grimshaw. Back in Edmonton, Kenneth McLeod took up work with the provincial government, rising to the post of superintendent of child welfare by 1937. Only then did he take a parish in the United Church of Canada.[4] Others pursued business opportunities. Some accepted parishes in the United States or Great Britain. Among the first was Frank Vipond, who had in vain lobbied churchmen on behalf of returning Anglican priests. Methodists and Presbyterians also moved to parishes in the United States.[5] Thus, in spite of Almond's and Beattie's hopes to retain the chaplains as a national asset, their influence on Canadian conditions was waning.[6] From Beattie's perspective, one of the greatest losses was Baptist Henry Mullowney, one of the most outspoken supporters of the 1918 surveys and the Chaplains' Message. After finishing his law degree in Great Britain, Mullowney went to California to pursue a legal career.[7]

Roman Catholic chaplains, by contrast, found their transition back to civilian work facilitated by Workman, Sylvestre, and Bishop Morrison, who closely co-ordinated their demobilization work.[8] Chaplains recruited from outside the country usually returned to their original foreign stations. Others returned to their overseas mission fields, such as China and Argentina.[9] In the Maritimes, however, three of Bishop Morrison's priests, Michael Gillis, Archibald MacDonald, and Miles Thompkins, embarked on a unique project of social betterment, lending their assistance to the growing co-operative movement based at St Francis Xavier University. MacDonald and Thompkins, after post-war study at Ontario's agricultural college at Guelph, returned to teach improved farm management at the university, while Gillis aggressively promoted the university's adult extension department.[10]

For many of those who returned to Canada, however, getting ecclesiastical employment remained their immediate concern, eased by temporary employment in Beattie's Canadian branch of the Chaplain Service before final demobilization. This was Beattie's way of helping those taken on at the end of the war to complete the full year's service that qualified them for demobilization pay and benefits. Not all could be accommodated in this fashion, however, as Beattie was ordered to cut staff sharply after the Armistice.[11] A few chaplains found it easier to cling to their army postings rather than take the plunge back into civilian life. These, to Beattie's frustration and disgust, lobbied fiercely with politicians or generals to be retained.[12] Other chaplains gradually worked their way back into Canadian life by undertaking veterans' hospital postings. Several moved from that branch to the Department of Soldiers' Civil Re-establishment as hospital chaplains.[13] A few, mostly from the Methodist branch, spent their last weeks in uniform on propaganda speaking tours, addressing congregations or veterans' groups on the lessons of the war and prospects for the peace.[14] Others worked for a short time with returning soldiers at demobilization stations such as Montreal or Halifax on behalf of their denomination's national service commission or assisting immigration chaplains' work.[15]

Methodist chaplains proved more difficult to resettle than those of any other denomination, as their discharges rarely coincided with the annual stationing made at summer conference meetings. In June 1919, Methodists fearing discharge after conference meetings cried alarm to the Army and Navy Board.[16] Even those Beattie discharged well before the 1919 stationing faced hardship until the summer, forcing them to ask for temporary employment by the General Conference. Fortunately, most were temporarily employed by the Board of Evangelism and Social Service until the next conference.[17]

Anglicans, too, had difficulties, as bishops replied to their requests with reports of few vacancies awaiting their return, except for rural and mission charges. Long before, a sharp exchange in the *Churchman* indicated the attitude of some to the return of overseas competitors. When bishops were asked to settle returned chaplains in large parishes where they could wield wider influence, an angry civilian priest challenged the assumption that chaplains deserved special privileges.[18] Chaplains demobilized before their agreements with priests holding their old parishes ran out occasionally found their bishops begging Beattie to keep them a little longer, but Ottawa decreed that this made them a public charge.[19] In order to get a post quickly, several Anglican and Presbyterian chaplains demobilized in England to accept British parishes.[20] Others entered British universities to complete their education or pursue graduate studies before returning to Canada. McGreer, studying at Oxford, was eventually called to Bishop's University as principal. Louis Moffit and William Graham took up teaching at Winnipeg's United College.[21] Most of these chaplains, however, prepared for humbler roles. George Fallis, for his part, took himself off to the University of Chicago Divinity School, including a season at Hull House, before returning to a British Columbia parish.[22]

By the end of 1919, while many were successfully adjusting to home life and work, not all were content with their civilian lot. For some the year had been one of disappointment, frustration, and bitterness.[23]

Beattie heard complaints from demobilized chaplains that they were at a considerable disadvantage when competing for preaching calls against clergymen who had remained at home. They found no vacancies in diocese, presbytery, or conference and learned to their dismay that no extraordinary efforts would be made to find one for them and their families. Their only option was the poorly paid isolation of home mission work, or else to leave the church for secular jobs.[24] Some turned on their churches, accusing them of neglecting the returned chaplain, even of attempting to stifle their prophetic role in the church by forcing them to the margins of the ministry.[25] A few took out their disappointments and bitterness on Almond or Beattie personally. Often these were chaplains who had returned under a cloud or with some report of inefficiency overseas behind them, which they now saw prejudicing their applications for parishes at home.[26]

Occasionally, though, the anguish and frustration overseas blended with the disappointments of home with special bitterness. This was the experience of William Lyon, an Anglican who had brought a number of Mohawk and Cayuga Iroquois men from his Ontario mission into the 114th Battalion before sailing for England in 1916. As usual under the Hughes regime, his contact with them was broken when the unit was broken up and he was sent off to camp and hospital ministry, "selling matches and collecting the pennies from a Pool Table" in Etaples, France. There he agitated vainly for a posting to the Pioneer battalion where his converts were serving, despite McGreer's ruling that he was too old for dangerous duty. Finally, Beattie and Fallis found him a chaplaincy in the Canadian Railroad Troops, operating under German shellfire. Returning to Canada, Lyon explained to Beattie that his native veterans now had little interest in the church since they had come back from France. This he blamed on McGreer and the army, which had discredited "both me and my Indian brethren … many of whom sleep in the soil of France … who went down to their graves, without a word of comfort from a 'Black Coat,' as they call a clergyman … Ten long months were those dear boys without any spiritual help or comfort … I only wish that that Colonel had to follow up the Indian work – for he would learn what a stumbling block he has been to the Cause – 'better that a mill-stone were hanged about his neck.'" To Lyon, the indifference and hostility that he met with from Iroquois veterans came from their resentment that in the hour of danger they had not been given a chaplain who spoke their language. "Years of faithful labour have been lost, and not in this generation shall we be able to reclaim the ground lost in this War," he told Beattie.[27]

While Lyon contemplated the ruins of his missionary work, even those settling into familiar parishes found that things were not always easy. Renison was completely disoriented by peacetime life in Hamilton. "I felt I could never preach again. I came home to my family, now composed of two sons. At first the baby's cries reminded me of the wounded and dying on the battlefields." He wrestled with the paradoxes of his experience, depressed by the juxtaposition of individual heroism with mass destruction and haunted by the thought that war might recur. It took a few weeks' holiday with his wife before "I was able to adjust myself to the world I had known before going overseas."[28] He was one of the few padres to admit publicly that, in spite of their idealism and forceful preaching, there lay beneath the surface some mental or emotional turmoil. For others there were times when the old emotions came back with a shock, as Thomas Colwell found one night in 1919 in a Pacific gale, when the motor of his missionary boat failed: "It was like a night in the trenches, a miserable, anxious time in the dense darkness."[29]

For some, old wounds, for others ruined constitutions rendered them incapable of church work.[30] Some tried moving to American branches of their denominations, to take parishes in Florida or California.[31] Still others died of war's debilitating after-effects. During the 1930s early death removed some of the most famous and influential chaplains, including Edmund Oliver and John O'Gorman, from the Canadian scene. Many had daily and annual reminders of the price they had paid for their war service from their own bodies, as fragments of long-buried shrapnel worked themselves out of their flesh, and a few strapped on artificial limbs each morning. Sometimes a padre was unable to escape war memories: on 28 August 1926 Charles Whitaker, a British Columbia United Church minister who had served as both stretcher-bearer and chaplain overseas, rented a small boat, rowed out into the Pacific, and was not seen again. A few days later the boat, with his wallet, coat, and walking-stick, was found drifting in English Bay.[32]

For those who could not make the adjustment to civilian life and hoped to carry on their careers in the army, there was no going back. Throughout 1919 and 1920 ex-chaplains unable to settle into civilian ministry inquired about getting back into the Chaplain Service or its British equivalents.[33] The addition of a few more ships to the navy prompted offers to serve in a naval chaplaincy.[34] Beattie struggled to save the service from demobilization, but the war had barely ended when senior Militia officers recommended returning to the pre-war capitation system – that is, paying clerics a service fee based on attendance at worship.[35] Beattie and his senior chaplain in Winnipeg argued that both militia and naval garrisons as well as returned men needed a permanent chaplaincy. In a time of labour and civil unrest, the presence of uniformed chaplains who had the veterans' trust would be essential in keeping them in order.[36] As a result, Beattie's staff was, for the time being, left intact. Almond's overseas efforts were stymied by S.C. Mewburn and Kemp, who employed a few for the Department of Soldiers' Civil Re-establishment veterans hospitals but made no promises about a permanent force.[37]

Beattie lobbied with Halifax officers, who agreed that educational and social needs, especially among under-age and illiterate recruits, required the services of a permanent chaplaincy. The old system fostered religious indifference among the troops and neglect by local churches. Beattie gratefully included these views in his brief to the minister of Militia, requesting a small permanent chaplains' force.[38] Then sympathetic commanders and General Mewburn met with the Cabinet. The minister of Finance quashed all plans for a chaplaincy. Mewburn was directed to demobilize every available soldier as speedily as possible, and in January 1920 the adjutant-general authorized the return of the capitation system in depots across the country. Beattie's tiny staff of five, along with the dozen or so chaplains in the Department of Soldiers' Civil Re-establishment hospitals, were all that remained of the service.[39] Facing ecclesiastical complaints and without the staff even to care for soldiers still convalescing in military hospitals, Beattie began designating civilians as officiating clergymen.[40]

Beattie tried to organize ecclesiastical support, discovering, however, that most clerics wanted their pre-war monthly service fees back. Undaunted, he pressed the adjutant-general to consider the growing dissatisfaction among the Halifax Catholic clergy as well as high desertion rates among new recruits.[41] The adjutant-general obligingly recommended a chaplains' force of nine for the Permanent Militia.[42] This recommendation, however, was refused by the politicians. So were attempts to have a naval chaplaincy created for the small fleet. The minister told Beattie that the ships were too small and that the capitation system would serve.[43] Denied permission to transfer his remaining staff to the DSCR, Beattie was reduced to pleading that three be retained until the spring of 1921.[44] He vainly appealed to church heads, but the Federal War Service Commission, of which he had expected so much, was no longer active. Pragmatic church leaders accepted the government's economic arguments and the return to civilian ministry. The Federal Council of Churches failed to take action. On 31 December 1920 the Canadian Chaplain Service was disbanded.[45]

Over the next two decades the CCS eked out a shadowy existence in the Non-Permanent Active Militia. On 1 June 1921, a new CCS was organized, with an establishment of two hundred part-time officers:

one for each infantry battalion, regiment of cavalry, artillery brigade, or machine-gun battalion. Ranks remained honorary.[46] A corps reserve was not organized for the service until 1924. The next year Canadian Officer's Training Contingent units at the larger universities were each authorized one chaplain.[47] In 1927 signal battalions were allotted chaplains, as was each divisional or district engineering headquarters two years later.[48] During 1931 the service was officially allied with the Royal Army Chaplains Department, by royal authority. From that date, except for various dress regulations, the Chaplain Service disappeared from Militia orders until September 1939.[49]

AS THE PERMANENT Chaplain Service dwindled, the wartime vision burst upon the home churches with questionable effect. During the spring of 1919 Protestant clergymen across the Dominion discovered an extraordinary packet in their daily mail. In it was a letter from Alan Shatford and George Kilpatrick, on behalf of the Chaplain Service, asking them to read the enclosed "Chaplains' Message to the Churches of Canada" to their congregations on the second Sunday morning in June.[50] While most clergymen could guess the general contents of the message from the chaplains' wartime statements, many must have been somewhat startled by its forthright recommendations and forceful tone:

> We, the Chaplains of the Overseas Forces of Canada, have had an honour and an opportunity given to few. We therefore believe it is our duty to set before the Church convictions concerning the work of the Kingdom of God which result from our experience in war. This we do, not presumptuously with the thought that our positions as Chaplains invest us with a certain authority, but solely because as your trustees in the service of God there has been given to us in war an experience, the interpretation of which we regard as a debt to be discharged in humility and with fidelity.

The war had not shattered, but vindicated their faith. The gospel had not failed, nor had the Canadian church entirely failed, either in her support during the war or in the preceding years of toil and teaching. "The Church … has been in a measure true to the Spirit and the mission of our Lord." But now a new and "definite challenge" lay in her path: rededicating Canadians to a refined vision of the church's mission in society. The war had given chaplains a glimpse of that new vision. In all, nine areas of church life and teaching needed immediate reform.

First, the church needed to reconsider her purpose in "the great epoch of reconstruction, upon which we are now entering": nothing less than "the establishment of the Kingdom of God on earth." The great vehicle for this divine transformation was to be the church:

> Believing as we do, that the Kingdom of God is a social order as well as a personal gift, we see here a clear call for the Church to identify herself with every aspect of human life ... And this is our hope, that men will be more ready to become acquainted with Christ and that hereafter the message of His redeeming Love may have a familiar note in the ears of those who in war have learned to worship and to honour enduring love and limitless sacrifice.

Next, the Chaplains' Message turned to the ordained ministry. Revival must begin at the top, with greater clerical professionalisation and training. The churches must recruit the best-educated leaders and make the ministry an attractive profession to young men, confronting them with "the challenge of the Ministry as offering scope for the widest and the most effective service." They must be educated for at least seven years beyond secondary school, in colleges that were affiliated and accredited with the public universities. They must be made skilful preachers, able to share the concerns and win the respect of "strong and vigorous men" among the veterans and the working classes.[51]

The Message was not confined to the clergy alone; the church also had an educational responsibility. Because pre-war family Bible-reading and traditional Sunday-school teaching had declined in quality and because ministers had abandoned "deep teaching" for "popular sermons," thousands of soldiers had not even an elementary knowledge of the Christian faith. Out of ignorance they associated Christianity with obsolete institutions, puritanism, and hypocrisy. The church seemed irrelevant, even harmful. Chaplains believed that many would return to the church if only they learned what she really stood for. They called for improved prophetic teaching from the pulpit, more mature and challenging Christian-education programs for adults, and more careful recruitment and training of Sunday school teachers. The churches' dogma, too, needed to be supplemented and clarified. Even the Apostles' Creed was archaic and ought to be reinterpreted "in terms of present knowledge." Judging by the soldiers overseas, modern men neither understood nor repeated it unreservedly. What was needed was

> a new presentation of Christian Truth. And by "new" we mean in terms of modern knowledge ... Not only are there the newer conceptions of God, Man,

and the Universe, but Providence and Prayer, Salvation, Heaven and Hell require a fresh presentation in the Church's teaching ... The official doctrine of the Church seems at variance with the facts of life and the deepest prompting of the human heart. If the Church would guide the thought of men, she must take account of these two criterions of truth ... For only as her message rings true to life and experience will she remain the leader and inspirer of mankind.[52]

For most men overseas, the impetus to worship and many of its traditional practices had been shorn of their obsolete conventions. Consequently, the padres called for hymn- and prayer-book modernization. The soldiers

feel that many of our hymns and prayers do not really express their desires. The very phraseology is foreign to their thought and speech. They will not continue to repeat forms, no matter how ancient and sanctified they may be, if these are no longer a vehicle for the soul's true longing. It seems to us imperative that something should be done to eliminate obsolete expressions, recast phraseology and make needed verbal changes in our forms of prayer and praise in order that our public worship may become more real and true. Chaplains from non-liturgical churches testified to the value of liturgical forms when judiciously used ... On the other hand, the value of informal and spontaneous worship has been impressed upon those whose experience previously had been confined to a liturgy ... The Church should therefore provide for greater elasticity in her public worship.

Some painful lessons had been learned overseas about Holy Communion. While some soldiers welcomed it, most abstained from taking part, said the chaplains, through a sense of unworthiness or because they felt that participation obligated them to more "serious" living. Too many soldiers regarded the sacrament as a preparation for death or a pre-battle talisman, while many others held back, convinced that calling upon God only in the face of danger was a sign of cowardice. An encouraging sign, however, had been their appreciation of the "deep social significance to the Lord's Supper": many participants "sought out a comrade to accompany them to the altar; it was the hour of communion and comradeship." Therefore, chaplains recommended that churches both give more emphasis to communion as a means of grace and celebrate it more often while fostering a more joyful atmosphere around the table as a special commemoration of fellowship. "Perhaps in this way we may sustain and deepen the sense of comradeship so remarkably exhibited during the tragic months of the war."[53]

The rest of the Chaplains' Message was devoted to affirming prior chaplains' statements on church union, the churches' social programs, and their attitudes to veterans. The war had confirmed for most padres the pressing need for a broadly conceived church union. Chaplains had allowed men of all denominations to come to communion. They had held united parade services (where non-Roman Catholics were led in worship by chaplains of other churches), and they had presented a united front on soldier welfare and religious extension work in the army: "These things we have done and our practice has certainly not been to the detriment of religion ... The great majority [of chaplains] would urge therefore, in the interests alike of a better understanding between the Churches and of the effective carrying out of the work of the Kingdom of God, that what has been their practice under active service conditions should be authoritatively sanctioned when they return to Canada, and become the general practice of the church."[54]

The chaplains pointed proudly to their social-service work. It had taught them that the church's ministry was to bodies and souls alike:

> As time passed we became concerned with every phase of the soldier's life ... This enlargement of our duty has greatly increased the respect of the men for the Chaplains' Department. It has won for the Church a deeper sympathy, and opened up the way for a more intimate and spiritual ministry ... We are convinced that the Church should now branch out into larger social activities. The problems of pleasure and entertainment, of housing and hygiene, of capital and labour, of civic and moral reform, of national development, are her concern, and she must lay hold of every organization established for their solution. We need to recover something of the passion for civic and national righteousness which stirred the hearts of the ancient prophets ... The Kingdom of God is a social organization, and we must become passionate prophets in the new City of God.[55]

As part of this vision, and out of awkward experiences in England and France, a new and potentially controversial relationship with the YMCA was deemed essential. The chaplains called for closer consultation with the church by the Y; in future it must have more clergymen representing their churches on the board of directors at national and local levels.[56]

After a ringing tribute to the innate religiosity of the soldier, the chaplains challenged the church to bring the millennial vision to pass in post-war Canada. Churches must honour and materially assist veterans. They had to proclaim their dedication to the social justice that would make Canada a truly redeemed nation:

Too long has the impression prevailed that the Church has always been on the side of vested interests. If the Churches expect to deal with the great opportunity offered by hundreds of thousands of soldiers returning to civil life, with its work and its problems, they must be ready to concern themselves actively in securing for these men economic, social and political justice ... In order to win their allegiance the Church must take up the Cross and lead the way.

Such grand aims, the chaplains concluded, could be achieved if the idealism and great vision of the war years could be transferred into peacetime. Again, William James's phrase expressed what the Great War chaplains desired of the peace. This hunger for national holiness – a "moral equivalent to war" – must be displayed by the Canadian church:

It belongs to the Church so to confront men with the Jesus of History that they shall hear His accents, and catch something of the fire of His Spirit and the passion of His Faith. Our men will not be slow to give themselves to the greatest cause that ever challenged the heart of man or to follow the peerless Leader in the heroisms of active service for His Kingdom ... The vision of the Church, however, is not alone of the "far-off Divine event"; it is also of a day when the manhood of the world shall be rallied to the service of God and our fellowman, when all gifts of life shall be consecrated to the task of ushering in that reign of peace which, conceived in honour and born of justice, is dedicated to the establishment of His rule among men.[57]

The Message loudly echoed salient points of the non-Catholic denominations' pre-war "national gospel." To Almond and its authors (George Kilpatrick, Clarence Mackinnon, David Warner, Francis Moore, Arthur McGreer, and Alan Shatford), the Message offered to throw the combined weight of all non-Catholic chaplains into the post-war struggle to realize the gospel of regeneration.[58] Although composed entirely by Presbyterians and Anglicans, an impressive list of signatures followed, including other representatives of all the major denominations employed overseas. Arthur Creegan, George Wells, and Channel Hepburn represented the many Anglicans of Social Christian orientation in the service; John MacDonald represented the Baptists, while Philip Smith signed for the Congregationalists; Edmund Oliver, Harold Kent, and Alexander Cornett gave the message impressive Presbyterian backing, and George Fallis signed as the representative Methodist. Kilpatrick and Shatford, therefore, delivered the Chaplains' Message, the fruit of so many surveys and discussions in the closing days of the war, to Canadians with high hopes. Its reception by the home churches, however, was unexpectedly discouraging. Instead of a universal readiness to rise up and possess the land, the chaplains found the churches apparently dominated by the urge to get over the war as quickly as possible. Few Canadians, indeed, were even listening for such a clarion call to action.

FROM THE PERSPECTIVE of the home denominations the Chaplains' Message could hardly have arrived at a more inopportune time than the spring of 1919. During the winter the nation seemed torn between those desiring an immediate realization of every wartime objective and those determined to restore the country to pre-war ways. National attention was already focused on the west, where labour demanded recognition of its sacrifices. The clarion note of the Message was sounded to a church already contemplating with alarm the prospect of post-war adventures.

For Kilpatrick and Shatford difficulties began with the Anglican reception. By the time Shatford arrived home, fellow churchmen were divided over the real lessons of the war and the prophetic insight of its participants. In the *Canadian Churchman* chaplains such as Moore, Warner, and Frank Vipond attacked home-front critics who viewed the war as having spiritually stunted the religious growth of the soldier and limited the post-war influence of the padres.[59] At the same time, both the editor and "Spectator" grew impatient with overseas prophets. The *Churchman*'s advice to padres was to get over their abnormal experience as quickly and quietly as possible, just as the veterans were supposed to welcome the return to normal civilian conventions of work and worship.[60]

It was into such a tense ecclesiastical as well as social atmosphere that Shatford came with the final text of the Message. The official reception was anything but encouraging. Both the Anglican hierarchy and the War Service Commission of the General Synod flatly refused to endorse the Message and vetoed the Federal War Service Commission's proposal to promulgate it on behalf of all the non-Roman Catholic churches.[61] Shatford glumly reported to Almond that the bishops not only refused to endorse the message but refused to let it be read in public or even be circulated confidentially among the clergy. With his daughter's assistance, Shatford privately mailed 1,800 copies to Anglican priests, but the lack of support from the hierarchy was telling.[62]

Shatford hoped for a better reception from the church press. The editor of the *Churchman*, R.W. Allin, was the first to take public notice of the Message, but he gave little evidence of sympathy or full understanding of its intent. After loosely paraphrasing the report and favourably quoting a few passages, he commented with alarm that in attacking the Apostles' Creed the padres had missed the mark. His lasting impression of the Message was that while there was much good in it, wartime emotion had clouded its meaning and diminished its lasting usefulness.[63] "Spectator" fastened on two minor criticisms of traditional evangelistic and Sunday-school methods, pronouncing them mere confirmations of what older ministers had always known. As for the rest of the Message's contents, Spectator thought them more suitable "for the clergy and Church councils" than congregations. Almost as an afterthought, he characterized the Message as a "wise and courageous" effort, which he was sure would bear fruit.[64]

The chaplains could hardly miss the import of such damningly faint praise. Instead of becoming reformers and counsellors, over the following months Anglican chaplains were reduced to essayists and minor prophets, reading lectures or making reports to colleagues at alumni gatherings, which were heard with sympathy and respect but little practical response.[65] Nor could the Anglican chaplains hope to maintain any official status or cohesiveness as an institution in the post-war church. By September 1919 the General Synod was closing its books on the war and its chaplaincy as the War Service Commission disbanded, turning its remaining work over to the Council for Social Service.[66]

Nevertheless, reading the Lambeth Conference report one year later, Shatford still hoped that the returned chaplains could make as great an impression on the Canadian church as had the British in theirs. Nor would future ministers-in-training be neglected. With Beattie rendering official assistance from Ottawa, copies of the Chaplains' Message were sent out to the theological faculties of McMaster, Queen's, and Victoria universities, as well as the colleges of the Congregationalists, Presbyterians, and Methodists in Montreal, at Knox College in Toronto, and the Presbyterian colleges in Halifax, Saskatoon, Edmonton, and Vancouver.[67] Whatever the heads of churches did with the Message, Beattie was determined to get the word out to as many clergymen and potential clergymen as possible.

Shatford soon learned that the reception given the Message by the other communions was only somewhat kinder. During the summer of 1919 Kilpatrick reported that it had been favourably received by the Presbyterians, Methodists, and Congregationalists. In fact the Presbyterian General Assembly (which had just elected a chaplain, John Pringle, as moderator) devoted a special sitting to hearing optimistic reports of the work overseas from returned chaplains, who confirmed most statements of the Chaplains' Message.[68] The General Assembly agreed to circulate the Message, without comment, to every congregation in Canada and reimbursed Kilpatrick for the expenses incurred in promoting it. Delegates sympathetically heard William Beattie plead with the presbyteries to help employ ministers who had resigned their churches for overseas service, while the National Service Commission proposed methods of linking returning soldiers with local churches.[69]

Methodists published a condensed version in the *Christian Guardian*, placing special emphasis upon the call for a new social program and the Message's blend of evangelical and idealistic sentiments.[70] Officially, that church too affirmed its chaplains' view. An Army and Navy Board special commission returned to Canada convinced that the men overseas were happy with the work of the home front during the war. The men, they argued, had grown sympathetic to prohibition once they received from the commission the facts about improved national morality and efficiency resulting from the ban. The commission was relieved to discover that probationers and chaplains were not alienated from the church and were eager to return to circuit and college.[71] Such encouraging reports gave them hope that the word from the front would have greater weight in these communions than with the Anglicans. Even the Baptists of Ontario and Quebec published the Message during July 1919.[72]

Unfortunately for the chaplains of the Protestant communions, such praise accomplished little more than the non-promulgation by the Anglicans. While sympathetic enough to have the Message published, except for expressing concern for the resettlement of the veteran, little was done by any of the Protestant churches to follow its recommendations. Instead, their attention fastened on reeling the returned fish into the local church and diverting restless veterans from dissatisfactions with civilian life.[73] Securing veterans' benefits and socializing the soldier took priority over internal reform. Even padres were concerned more with the return to peacetime normalcy than with mobilizing another crusade. Speaking for the Presbyterians, A.S. Grant warned Beattie that the church's National Service Committee was running out of funds and momentum. As in other denominations, the returns from the collection plate were meagre: only $8,544.42 of a projected $60,000 budget was received by the committee in 1919. Thus many projects proposed by the church and the chaplains could not be undertaken.[74] Similar news came from the other churches, which subsequently curtailed the plans of the combined Federal War Service Commission that Beattie and the churches had formed at the end of the war.[75]

Over the remainder of 1919, after some feeble efforts to create veterans' affairs committees, the churches dismantled their military service boards. The Methodists disbanded in October 1919, handing last-minute duties over to the Social Service and Evangelism Department, while the editor of the *Canadian Baptist* worried that even the returned soldiers' issue was now largely being overlooked by his denomination.[76] By the 1920 General Assembly the Presbyterian National Service Commission recommended its own discontinuation and the turning over of any business remaining to the regular standing boards of the church.[77] By then the official prospect of realizing any of the goals of the Message seemed about to vanish into thin air, leaving the wartime vision of the chaplains a statement instead of a program.

In fact the undercutting of the Chaplains' Message had not resulted entirely from apathetic church governments and parishioners whose idealism and pocketbooks were exhausted. Most of the chaplains themselves proved far less radical in practice than in preaching. In their work with demobilizing soldiers and in their opposition to social and political radicalism they gave practical evidence of a conservatism that belied their own rhetoric. While a few ex-chaplains, led by Canon Scott, declared sympathy with the discontented veterans in Winnipeg during the 1919 General Strike, padres still in uniform were universally alarmed and repelled by the disputes in Winnipeg and British Columbia.

Scott heard of the strikes while mingling with returning troops in Quebec City. He smuggled himself on to a troop train and arrived unannounced in Winnipeg in early June. Although he stated that he had come to mediate between disputing veterans, his public statements in support of the strikers appalled those opposed to the strike, in particular Brigadier-General H.J.B. Ketchen, Militia commander in the Winnipeg District (and an unofficial adviser of the anti-strike Citizens' Committee). Ketchen alerted Militia Headquarters, which replied that Scott was absent without leave from his Quebec garrison post and should be ordered to return to Quebec "for medical treatment immediately." Scott was bundled on to an eastbound train by Militia officials. After his return to Quebec, the local Militia commander demanded an explanation from the chaplain for his absence without leave. Scott argued that it was a military necessity to ease veteran tension caused by the Winnipeg dispute. There the matter was allowed to rest, and thus ended Canada's most famous chaplain's brush with veteran unrest.

Given the potential gravity of such a charge, Militia authorities believed that Scott had been treated with unusual consideration, unavoidable because of his reputation among soldiers and his public stature. But Scott was not the only padre in Winnipeg who raised his voice on labour's behalf during the rowdy spring of 1919. Ex-chaplain David Christie, a Presbyterian, spoke out in favour of the strikers and criticized the Citizens' Committee for its use of the churches to recruit strike police. John Murray, an Anglican ex-chaplain who before the war had opposed the General Synod's plan to create a Council of Social Service, now declared his sympathy with strike objectives, though he still rejected the sympathetic strike as a legitimate labour tactic.[78] Significantly, the veterans involved in the strike responded enthusiastically to Scott's speeches at public rallies, suggesting that some of them, at least, were looking for leaders such as their old padres to inspire them again in the crisis of that Winnipeg spring. Perhaps, too, their response explains army eagerness to scotch the canon's self-appointed ministry in any way possible.

Nor were all padres as eager to lead the men along a radical road to reform. Many other chaplains, such as Charles Gordon, emphatically rejected the strikers and their veteran supporters. Foreseeing worker discontent, during the spring Beattie's assistant director in Toronto, G.H. Williams, a Methodist, held meetings with returned men employed in local industry "with a view to stabilise the men's thought and interest in their work. In such cases the men have all been called from duty and an opportunity given to address them collectively. The general unrest experienced by the returned men is largely psychological, and with sympathetic interest and encouragement will soon disappear."[79] Those serving in Winnipeg during the strike, however, believed charges that the strike was a One Big Union–cum–Bolshevik conspiracy. As a result, Beattie's western staff struggled to retain the confidence of the veterans still in uniform or under medical treatment and to keep them out of the strike. Hospital chaplain Frank Bushfield's magazine the *Threshold* condemned the strike and portrayed it as a result of foreign and Bolshevik agitation.[80] The "Red Triangle Hut" operated by the YMCA in Winnipeg became the headquarters of chaplain efforts to "offset false propaganda." The Winnipeg Mititary District senior chaplain held talks with the troops mingling at the hut "in an effort to show them the unrewardness [sic] of the sympathetic strike and thus prevent them from being led away by the 'Red' propaganda of the strike leaders."[81]

Further west, the senior chaplain in Alberta undertook a speaking tour for the anti-radical Great War Veterans' Association (GWVA), addressing veterans in mining towns.[82] Perhaps the most sustained effort outside of Winnipeg took place in Vancouver, where labour unrest in early June also prompted the GWVA to request the padres' intervention on the side of law and order. Here Charles Whitaker, a Methodist chaplain on light duty while recovering from leg wounds, earned the lion's share of the credit for persuading the GWVA in British Columbia to condemn the Vancouver strike and endorse the stand of the city council.[83] As a result, Whitaker became the head of the British Columbia GWVA until 1922.

Alarmed at the Bolshevik Revolution and the rising tide of civil war in Russia, the Canadian government had contributed an infantry brigade to the Allied force sent to Siberia in late 1918. With it William Beattie sent six hand-picked chaplains, including Western Front veterans such as Harold McCausland, George Farquhar, and Harold Clarke. By June 1919 they were back in Canada, their Siberian interlude in the war against Communism having come to an end, but with another struggle against the Red Peril still under way. Thanks to Farquhar's Siberian Expeditionary Force reports and a vivid depiction before the Presbyterian General Assembly of his experience of the Russian Revolution, Beattie rushed Farquhar out of Winnipeg on to a speaking tour of eastern GWVA chapters and veterans' hospitals. Farquhar was convinced that "our press and people do not appear to understand the situation as evidenced by a wire of sympathy from a Canadian organization to the Bolsheviki ... To give to them the real facts of the case would do the country a service and prevent the confusion of Bolshevism and Socialism, the cause of so much sympathy with the most vicious form of anarchy."[84] Beattie wanted these views circulated to a much wider audience, as the DCS and other officers considered them an especially effective antidote to the "extremist propaganda" afoot among veterans in the country that summer.[85]

By the end of 1919 most chaplains had made their attitude to veteran radicalism plain. In spite of the prominent publicity given Scott's Winnipeg intervention and the sympathy shown labour and veterans by several ex-chaplains, the majority had thrown themselves into the campaign to stem the tide of radicalism. Many padres had already joined the most moderate of the veterans' groups, such as the Great War Veterans' Association. They supported the GWVA Dominion command's open censure of the Winnipeg strike and its anti-bonus position during the bitter dispute between the government and veterans demanding a war-service gratuity.[86] By 1921, when Douglas Haig proposed Canadian participation in his British Empire Service League, chaplains joined with the remaining moderate veterans to shift their organizations' emphasis from social reform to the more pragmatic role of lobbying governments on behalf of disabled and pensioner veterans' interests. Out of this centre group emerged the Canadian Legion, a union of veterans' groups (at least two of which were ex-chaplain-led) that attracted many ex-chaplains over the next decade.[87] In these and other local endeavours the majority of chaplains made it plain that, as ex-chaplains, ex-officers, and anti-radicals, their sympathies did not lie with the bitter populism or radicalism of some veterans from the ranks.[88]

DESPITE THE SURGE in labour radicalism and the reflexive conservative response of many chaplains to that unrest, life for the majority of padres had to go on. And it was in the week-to-week work of parish and pulpit that many attempted to infuse their message with some of the ardour of their wartime vision. For Edmund Oliver, back from the war, the time of civilian dedication had arrived. Righteousness had been established on earth. He reminded Canadians of the *Lusitania*, the execution of nurse Cavell, and the use of poison gas by Germany. Rather than take revenge on Germany, however, he called on Canadians to make "the day of Thanksgiving ... the day of Dedication ... Across the wastes of Flanders and the ruins of Artois I see written one brief word – Calvary. It is an exegesis in blood. Shall modern Golgotha lack the Easter triumph? Surely the nations of the world will rise into a new life ... Let us dedicate ourselves to take up their task, whose pioneers and pathfinders for the New Day, the Day that dawned when the student of Sarajevo fired the shot that was heard around the world."[89] Charles Gordon, back in his Winnipeg pulpit, appealed both to the thought of Henry Drummond and to his own war experiences to call on apathetic Presbyterians to declare war on social and personal sin. Despite the bitter after-shocks of the strike still being felt in Winnipeg, he urged businessmen and students to fight off the depression and apathy that he sensed had arisen after, if not because of the war.[90]

Nor were these the sentiments of Presbyterians alone. Renison, back in his Hamilton Anglican pulpit, even as he struggled with the personal emotional difficulties of demobilization, preached the same message to his congregation and published the same sentiments in an appendix to J.C. Hopkins' patriotic commemoration *Canada at War*.[91] For Renison the horrors of battle could only be justified if the Old World learned from its New World saviours how to break the cycle of war after war. Charles Masters depicted the war service and sacrifices of fellow Wycliffe College alumni in similar terms.[92] Alan Shatford, back in his St James', Montreal, pulpit, continued to proclaim the blend of idealism, social Christianity, and British patriotism that had characterized his pre-war and overseas preaching.[93]

This optimistic note was echoed in other ways than articles, sermons, and novels. Canon Scott, settling back into parish life, put his recollections and convictions into print in *The Great War As I Saw It*

(1921). Nothing overseas or in war's aftermath prompted him to question the settled conviction that the war had been a crusade that offered Canadians a providential opportunity to realize a higher level of national righteousness.[94] William Beattie, too, attempted to chronicle and to interpret the work of all the chaplains in his manuscript on the history of the service (1921), commissioned by the government. In his history he reiterated the standard motifs and interpretations of the war – the soldiers as moral and spiritual Galahads, the chaplains as reincarnated Friar Tucks – in order to emphasize his main argument: the moral and spiritual worth of the chaplains as advisers to the veterans and reconstructors of Canadian life.[95] Beattie's account was crafted to support the recommendations of the Chaplains' Message, with its call for church unity, social programs, and ecclesiastical reform.[96] Unfortunately for him, Militia and government authorities judged his work too cliché-ridden for publication.

Clearly, the immediate post-war years had not been easy for the returned padres. Whether because of the rising social turmoil on the one hand or the lukewarm reception given their Message by church officials on the other, or because of their own inability to help their flocks make the transition to peacetime society, everything seemed to dampen the effect of their wartime message. Those who struggled to retain its urgency did so in the face of a society that was becoming indifferent.[97]

HAVING MET THE CHALLENGES of rising worker radicalism, most ex-chaplains settled into the work of church and parish. It was in this setting that they attempted to salvage what they could of the vision. Yet even this modest achievement would be denied most by internecine battles fought over the nature of the church, the nature of peace, and the best manner of realizing it. Just as finding their careers endangered by the war made their triumph overseas ring hollow in the ensuing decades, so larger concerns bore disappointments. The great ecumenical hope faded into dissension and unfulfilment. So did the millennial expectation that war had been eliminated. By the beginning of the 1930s the bright prospects of 1919 had indeed faded into riddles and frustrations.[98]

Not long after their return it became clear to many non–Roman Catholic chaplains that the achievement of broad church union was going to take more time and effort than they had expected. As labour and farm reform movements rose and fell, and social service seemed more and more the preserve of government and secular social workers, church union, for non-Anglican Protestants, at least, was still viewed as the single most effective project remaining with which to get on with establishing the Kingdom. Unfortunately, events proved that the ecumenical optimism of the chaplains could not overcome either the barriers of episcopal ordination or the refusal of the Presbyterian church to die. Whatever the sympathy of Anglican chaplains to the vision, ecclesiastically, Anglican disinterest in the project was apparent to Presbyterians and Methodists as early as 1923, when a frustrated J.E. Ward (a Toronto rector who had served as a chaplain) was reduced to issuing on his own initiative a general call for national church union.[99] By then the former denominations were distracted enough by the schism that yawned within the Presbyterian fold. It was also evident that ex-chaplains would be found on both sides of the union chasm.

During the Great War the matter of church union seemed to be settled for Presbyterian ministers overseas. Unionists repeatedly assured Presbyterians that the chaplains and clergy in uniform were, as a result of their army experience, universally in favour of union. At the General Assembly of 1915 William Beattie's and John Pringle's telegrams reinforced this impression, encouraging unionists such as W.T. Herridge (appearing in his militia chaplain's uniform) to claim all the chaplains overseas as pro-union. Anti-unionists, however, resented this exploitation of patriotic emotionalism by their opponents, but their claims that the views of at least several chaplains had been misrepresented by Beattie and others were dismissed as foundationless.[100] In fact, throughout the war unionists and anti-unionists both claimed that the war was vindicating their position on the question, unionists calling it the providential evidence to go ahead, antis viewing it as a warning to halt and reconsider. During 1917 other chaplains, such as Robert Taylor and George Kilpatrick, continued to declare that the war made union inevitable.[101] In 1917 friction between the factions favouring organic union and the antis became so alarming that moderates, led by ex-chaplain Thurlow Fraser, successfully negotiated a truce for the duration of the war and two years after. During this period it became apparent that a significant portion of the clergy, including several chaplains, favoured a federative model of church union and were reluctant to press on to organic fusion with the Methodists and Congregationalists.[102]

By 1918 the Presbyterians in charge of the chaplain survey had concluded that roughly half their chaplains, while agreeing that denominational differences had been proven obsolete in army practice, in fact favoured federation over organic union.[103] These men were not prepared to see Presbyterianism die in order to achieve ecumenical efficiency. Nevertheless, between 1921 and the fission of

1925 the struggle between unionists and antis forced many of the federationists to a crucial choice. Contrary to the unionists' claim, many CEF and leading militia chaplains were repelled by the uncompromising attitude and coercive tactics of unionist colleagues such as Charles Gordon, John Pringle, William Beattie, George Kilpatrick, and Edmund Oliver. When D.R. Drummond, himself a militia chaplain, proposed his federation scheme as a compromise in 1923, the refusal of the unionists to reconsider the previous decisions of the General Assembly drove many of the moderate chaplains back over the anti-unionist line.[104] Even Ebeneezer McLaren (who had taken a role in the last Presbyterian union of 1875), a chaplain who had previously favoured union, by 1923 had joined Daniel Gordon and others in withdrawing his support.[105] By then William McConnell, another wartime federationist, had been converted into the spokesman of the anti-union Presbyterian Church Association and, with the assistance of other erstwhile federationists such as Alexander Gordon and John McCaskill, was working for the survival of their denomination. McConnell now used the war as an argument against proceeding with union: he argued that so many Presbyterian members had been overseas during the 1915–16 union controversy that a third denominational vote was required to authorize union. He was confronted by other former chaplains like Oliver, Charles Gordon, and Donald Macgregor, who debated him in church meetings in northern Ontario and western Canada.[106] In 1924 it was Oliver who briefed provincial and federal legislators on the unionist cause and claimed much of the credit for fathering the United Church. Finally, in June 1925 the final parting of the ways took place. By then many more ex-chaplains had elected to remain Presbyterians than might have so chosen in 1919. Of the ninety-three Presbyterian ex-chaplains in Canada at the time of union, thirty-six remained with the original church, while fifty-seven, led by Mackinnon, Gordon, and Oliver, proceeded into union.[107] Some, such as George Kilpatrick and George Farquhar, departed at a considerable price, their churches having remained Presbyterian.

Nevertheless, the immediate results of church union, achieved at such a cost, did not prove as encouraging as its proponents had hoped. After such a cost in effort and harmony United Church leaders found their new denomination apparently lethargic and cautious rather than invigorated and ambitious. Charles Gordon and Clarence Mackinnon, Edmund Oliver, James Faulds, and other ex-chaplains who took a share in leading the church often felt the need to pummel its members into wakefulness at the opportunities before them. Mackinnon and Oliver especially made passionate addresses, breathing new life into the rhetoric of their wartime idealism in their efforts to stimulate the young church.[108] Rather than accelerating the realization of the war's highest hopes, the sacrifices of the union fight left deep scars and doubts, just as the failure of prohibition and the economic crisis of the Great Depression struck at the prospects of the Kingdom of God.[109] By the end of the first decade of the peace, the fruits of the union crusade seemed disappointingly meagre. The apparent wartime interdenominational consensus of the padres had proved too delicate to flourish in the peace. Instead of a new ecumenical dawn, the padres had experienced or witnessed some of the most bitter dissension possible, especially in Presbyterian ranks.

Nor did ex-chaplains maintain a united point of view on the matter of war and peace in these decades. In the early years of the peace non-Anglicans threw their influence behind colleagues attacking military cadet training in the schools. As presbyteries and conferences passed resolutions condemning war, however, many Anglicans found it difficult to renounce either past or future defensive measures.[110] Some chaplains aligned themselves with liberal internationalists in the United Church, who foresaw peace arising from the ruins of Europe through the League of Nations. During the 1920s some prominent ex-chaplains advocated international arbitration and disarmament treaties in order to outlaw war. As members of the League of Nations Society they condemned arms producers as "merchants of death" and urged Canadians to work actively, through education and public service, for world brotherhood. George Fallis travelled across the United States addressing Rotary Club and Chautauqua Association meetings on "the problem of World Peace." Attacking both isolationism and competitive nationalism, Fallis tried to persuade Americans to help the League of Nations succeed: "fighting must be supplanted by negotiation." In 1929 he joined Henry Wise Wood on the Chautauqua Peace River circuit, again lecturing on "the Pulse of Peace": education, tolerance, and international goodwill.[111]

In Montreal, Alan Shatford joined other liberal clergymen, led by W.A. Gifford, in calling for Christians in future to be sceptical of patriotism and battle cries based on the cruel and barbaric passages of the Old Testament. The non-violence and forgiveness of the spirit of Jesus had to be spread through Christian love and service. Instead of accepting war as inevitable, North American Christians were called to renounce isolationism and military preparedness at the same time. The churches must instead prepare to educate and persuade their communities to renounce war as an instrument of national policy, teaching them that war debased those who appeal to it, even in the cause of right. Thus, many hoped, Christians could oppose militarism at home and join hands with liberals throughout the world to prevent another fatal conflagration.[112]

At the same time, some chaplains found Canadians apathetic about the prospects of the League of Nations, wary of international commitments that might lead them to fight again on its behalf. The League, without United States participation, seemed to many Canadians doomed to fail. Even the Canadian chapters of the League of Nations Society were internally divided on the issues of non-resistance and sanctions against war. Charles Gordon found, with Beattie and Fallis, that his passionate advocacy of the League made little lasting impression on his Canadian audiences. Equally disappointing was the internal bickering and virtual paralysis of the League itself. To some, only the churches of the member nations, by rekindling the moral passion of the war years in the service of peace, could save the League.[113]

Thus, while many could join in the condemnation of war, few chaplains seemed attracted to the absolute pacifism of the radical non-resisters. Among the leading Canadian pacifists of the 1930s only one ex-chaplain, R. Eddis Fairbairn (whose war service had been rendered in the Bermuda garrisons), maintained a consistently radical critique of all forms of violence. Back in his Yale divinity professorship, however, Douglas Macintosh strongly denounced military service (and his own chaplain rhetoric) as he probed weak points in pre-war liberal theology. As a result, his refusal to bear arms in America's defence prevented him from becoming an American citizen.[114] At least one other ex-chaplain, also a Baptist, deliberately left Canada after the Second World War broke out in order to avoid participation in another war. When he heard that the Canadian Officers' Training Corps had been welcomed on the McMaster University campus, F.G. Poole sadly rebuked university officials from his home in the neutral United States: "I write freely as a former war veteran and chaplain, disillusioned by the enterprise of Government in this futile effort to solve national and international problems by the use of arms ... Surely we had a right to expect something better from the Church this time. Surely this is no way to bring in the Kingdom of Peace and Goodwill, nor an evidence of courage and sacrifice for God and Humanity."[115] Such lonely advocates won few Canadian adherents as the decade drew to a close.

While at first most Canadian chaplains sympathized with the moral persuasion and moral indignation of churchmen who hoped to educate Canadians into making disarmament and world harmony their cause, as the increasingly turbulent decade of the 1930s wore on the main body of ex-chaplains firmly aligned themselves on the side of preparedness.[116] Although chaplains such as Charles Gordon refused to despair, they could bring nothing new to the increasingly strident peace debates. He readily declared himself a deluded participant in the Great War and condemned his own facile crusading sermons. By 1936 an explosion similar to 1914 seemed to be brewing, threatening to impede the bringing in of the Kingdom of God. From his pulpit Gordon vowed never again to take part in or abet war. Yet, while hating war, he could not help pointing out that some nations must police "criminal" nations. In such cases armies were acting as the "enemies of war," preserving the world from greater evils. And he still had faith that the Christian nations of the League would succeed in spreading peace and goodwill, which would ultimately bring an end to war.[117] James Faulds echoed Gordon, although he contended that peace could not come without international righteousness, leaving open the possibility of resorting to force in self-defence.[118]

In these same years other chaplains began to attack the rhetoric of their war-hating colleagues. While some, such as William Beattie, still denounced munitions manufacturers at League of Nations Society gatherings, others, such as Harry Kent (still serving as militia chaplain to the local Kingston regiment), as principal of Queen's Theological College denounced United Church radical pacifists as naïve and irresponsible. Though the issue of collective security in the face of fascist and imperial challenges remained a bone of contention among them, these quietly put aside their idealistic hope of the previous decade and prepared for battle. Others were making their views known by their deeds. Many ex-chaplains who had never renounced defensive war as being against the will of God revisited the armouries and associated themselves with the regiments. Among them was George Fallis, who mused, "There is so much more to peace than holding indignation meetings against war."[119] Before these developments, however, the chaplains had to weather what to them was perhaps the cruellest disappointment of all, bitter public denunciation by articulate and angry veterans.

AS SOLDIER ATTITUDES to their war shifted in the post-war decades, so did their estimation of the padres. In the Canadian war literature emerging in the 1920s the chaplains fared more or less well at the hands of the veterans who authored it. At first most Canadian war books followed, in slightly more subdued garb, the patriotic and optimistic themes that had been part of wartime propaganda. Wide-eyed personal accounts and heroic panegyrics were gradually replaced by sober books of commemoration and comradeship, usually written by officers. Many simply reproduced the portrait of the chaplain that had emerged from works published while the war was being fought.[120]

Over the next few years the battalion histories gave a standard view of the chaplain. Most were officer-subscribed products of the chronicler tradition, based upon the regimental war diary and other official documents. The chaplain would be allotted two or three paragraphs: if he earned any citations or decorations, they would be mentioned and his role as a fellow officer and contributor to unit life noted. Usually he was portrayed as the medical officer's alter ego, the spiritual affairs officer who was brave, devoted, patriotic, and above all useful, whether with the MO in the aid post, censoring letters, umpiring a baseball game, passing out cigarettes, or managing bearer parties.[121] In outstanding examples of this genre, brave chaplains were regarded with extreme warmth, as "more man than cleric," at least by the officers.[122]

By 1930, however, this narrative tradition began to change. More personal recollections of junior officers and ex-privates injected anger and bitterness into the literature. The change in perspective immediately changed the image of the chaplaincy. In the ex-private's opinion the padre now seemed an irrelevancy at best, an obscenity at worst. Such angry rejoinders to the predictable and platitudinous literature of reassurance and commemoration first appeared in the regimental history of the 102nd Battalion published in 1919. L.M. Gould's *From B.C. to Basieux* is a lonely forerunner of the denunciations that began in Canada (as in Europe) about the end of the 1920s. The memories of the Somme rankle this soldier's account of religion as he recounts the subsequent church service's cancellation because of the weather: "Thank God sometimes for the rain: these Church Parades on active service, especially when called in the Forward Area, were the grimmest and ghastliest of Service jokes, and were provocative of more blasphemy and discontent than any active operation." This angry tone continues with a very bitter assessment of army religion and officer mentality:

> The following day was a Sunday, and the conflicting claims of godliness and cleanliness caused a terrible fiasco, owing to the well-meant endeavours of the officiating chaplain to harmonise the two. "If your men have to go the baths," said he, "well and good: I know that the baths are the first consideration; but let them come into the Church Service on their way back." The chaplain was right, from the point of view of common sense and Christianity, but, sad to relate, it fell out that a party of Brass Hats thought well to attend Divine Service that morning and anyone who had experience of Brass Hats and their way of looking at things will readily understand the consternation caused in their

breasts when sundry members of the 102nd turned up with no puttees on their legs, but with towels hanging around their necks. It is entirely contrary to K.R. & O. for an enlisted man to worship his Creator unless he is properly dressed, and the Brass Hats did not fail to register their opinions in the quarters where such registration might be expected to do the most good. But what a blessing it is that some of us have been endowed with a sense of humour and with backs akin to those of ducks!

In this account the YMCA carries off most of the laurels. The one chaplain who is credited with redeeming the padre in the eyes of the battalion is Roman Catholic padre Charles Fallon, whose athletic prowess and fearless devotion to the wounded in the 1918 battles won tribute. "It is certainly true that if we had more chaplains in the Corps of the type of Capt. C.A. Fallon the Cause of Religion would have benefited: he was not merely a chaplain and a good fellow out of the line: he figured that a chaplain had his uses when fighting was going on."[123]

Gould's hostility, nevertheless, remained very much a minority sentiment in Canadian war literature until the late 1920s, when W.B. Kerr and a few others struck out at the patriotic smugness of earlier memoirs. Although Kerr recognized that there were exceptions – most notably Canon Scott – his account of the underside of war from the perspective of the artillery is critical of most chaplains:

Each Brigade had a chaplain; ours stayed at the wagon lines and held services there Sunday morning; rarely, if ever, did we see any of them at the guns … Most kept well out of danger, made friends only with the officers, knew nothing of the men, they who ought to have acted as a link between the commissioned and the non-commissioned ranks with the confidence of both. The chief interest of some seemed to be in getting themselves promoted or moved back to England or the base; such conduct was viewed with disgust and regarded as entirely unworthy of the men's profession.[124]

Kerr noted that, while the chaplains had at times helped to improve the quality of life of the units by running canteens and social work, for the most part they had failed in their religious role.[125]

Given the chaplains' high expectations of the peace and the idealistic war ideology that they held before the men, one might expect a strong cynicism from disappointed veterans after a decade of waiting for the founding of the Kingdom of Heaven on earth. As this disillusionment reached the reading public towards the end of the 1920s, it was immediately apparent that the padre had become one of the easiest targets to strike at when the patriotic memory of the war faded and disillusionment became bitterness. This note of denunciation came to dominate later Canadian war literature, beginning with the appearance of the writings of Charles Yale Harrison and Will Bird.

Harrison's account of his service with the Fourteenth Canadian Battalion was highly acclaimed as the first "authentic" account of the war by a private. His narrative struck at all the patriotic and sentimental traditions of the war and its growing hagiography of the men in the trenches. Most of the soldiers were godless, cynical, and profane. Religious soldiers were a minority, consisting mainly of millennial cranks whose narrow morality and censoriousness drew constant ridicule from the men. The religion of such men, to Harrison, had no influence on the men, who found them hypocritical and usually cowards at critical moments. God is portrayed as yet another general, an evil, authoritarian figure who sends men to die and abandons them to the shelling. Prayer makes the men uneasy and irritable, for it seems to draw enemy fire. To Harrison, chaplains are irrelevant, fatuous, and either dishonest or cowards. The men are not idealistic or reverent but earthy and calloused. For them, after a barrage, parade service is a puny and pathetic exercise.[126]

Bird's lesser-known *And We Go On*, while sustaining the tone of denunciation, delivers a much more detailed and penetrating account of both religion in the ranks and the chaplains who represented it in battalion life (in 1969 a carefully edited and gentler version was published as *Ghosts Have Warm Hands*). Church parades are impositions, futile in effectiveness because they are compulsory and often become tacit battles of will between officers and resentful soldiers. The padres generally were not respected and usually shunned.[127] Readers are told that in the infantry, "padres, as a rule, were scorned, for only sincerity could live with the 'other ranks,' and they knew, whatever the showing, that he was not one of them. Our own padre was not disliked. Sometimes on the crater line he came at night with cigarettes and warm drinks and talked with a private, but he was apart from the men, and usually with, perhaps through circumstances, an officer [the Medical Officer] whom the majority cordially hated."[128] Indeed, one of Bird's characters (Tommy) seems to embody the hostility of the author towards padres in general and their ministry in particular. Bird's recollections are worthy of attention for several reasons. We know his battalion – the Forty-second – his private thoughts, those he places in the mouths of his comrades; we even know the hated medical officer's name – and we know who was his padre. He was George Kilpatrick, DSO, a central figure in the framing of the Chaplains' Message.[129]

Evidently the padres had exaggerated their wartime influence. Few indeed were the soldier-writers who admitted that the padres had won them over to an idealistic point of view. All the same, was this loud repudiation by memorialists an adequate indication of the chaplain's real stature in the army? Between the literatures of wartime hyperbole and post-war disillusionment remains a significant body of soldiers' published and private diaries and letters, as well as the confidential reports of individual chaplains. Out of this often neglected material emerges a more complex but also more convincing picture of the padre with the men that has often escaped notice by scholars and veterans in recent years.

Although a great deal more research is needed in the area of Great War religious influences upon men in battle, the religious culture of the CEF overseas was far from monolithic.[130] Besides the obvious differences in worship and doctrine between Protestants and Roman Catholics, there were also individual variations in belief, arising from different levels of education, social background, and ethnic culture as well as variations in the basic religious knowledge of the troops. Similarly, the attitude of officers, especially those not promoted from the ranks, was often very different from that of the men. While propagandists and churchmen spoke optimistically of revival in the trenches and bitter veterans later rated religion of no comfort and padres a nuisance, other Canadian officers and men seem to have had a wide middle range of responses to the padre, ranging from appreciative to ambivalent.[131]

Most appreciative were the religiously inclined officers and men. Repeatedly chaplains encountered fellow clergymen in the officers' mess and in the ranks, besides the many students and seminarians who had volunteered to serve overseas. Many soldiers, especially in the first years of the war, had indeed volunteered out of a sense of duty or idealism that had a religious basis. Such soldiers naturally came to the attention of the hard-pressed padre and most often gave encouragement and assistance to him whenever army life permitted. These were the soldiers who criticized the rum ration, who salted their letters with quotations from Dostoevsky, Browning, Henry Drummond, or Bishop Lightfoot, and who expressed their convictions in the same language and philosophical vein as the padres.[132] Their presence and many statements of sympathy with the themes both of crusade and of personal consecration emphasized by the padres were continually noted in chaplains' reports and statements to the public.

Nevertheless, while sympathetic to the padre, such soldiers could also be his sharpest critics, if only because they considered themselves fellow workers in the vineyard. Having seen the problems of the padre's appeal to the men from below, they tried to warn chaplains and home churchmen that the optimistic predictions of the chaplains were unrealistic. They knew and confessed that their dogged ferocity in the line was as much hot hatred, rage, and fear as idealism and devotion to God and the Kingdom.[133] They also sympathized with the critique of religion voiced by the more outspoken soldiers and admitted that many of the older tenets of their childhood faith were being scoured by the abrasive effects of army life. After service in the CEF, students such as James Endicott or James Mutchmor, while taking up post-war careers in the church, sometimes found their priorities and fundamental convictions changed by their overseas service, which confirmed the critique of a William James or the paradoxes of an S.H. Hooke at Victoria College.[134] Significantly, it was this cohort of seminarians and recent ordinands before 1914 who had been most exposed to scholarly criticism and the challenges to the evangelical consensus posed by "relativism."[135] Younger men than the generation of Burwash, Chown, or even George Fallis, they found it far more difficult to view the war as their padres did. Some students felt the harrowing effects of war more immediately than others. Often these seemed more open to post-war disillusionment than did the chaplains, who had already been among the working clergy before the war. In Canada and Australia many seminary students who served overseas never returned to complete their studies for a career in the clergy. Principal Samuel Dyde of Queen's Theological College, for example, found that most of his students who had taken up arms did not return to finish their courses after the war.[136]

At the opposite end of the spectrum from this small group of sympathizers lay the larger but perhaps not dominant collection of sceptics and cynics. These men ranged in intellectual level and religious perspective from the educated atheist or agnostic to the most rough and calloused type from the Canadian hinterland, dockyard, or slum. Thomas Dinesen, an upper-class Dane serving with the Forty-second Battalion, expressed his scepticism in the language of Kantian metaphysics, but his resentment of church parade captured the feelings of many others in his battalion, as did his contempt for dogmatic evangelism and chaplain moralizing.[137] Serving alongside him were other tough-minded pragmatists who, like Private Donald Fraser of the Thirty-first Battalion, fatalistically thrust worry and fear aside, and seem never to have thought of, much less cared about, the padres. Such soldiers ruthlessly pared away religious sentiment and emotionalism from their front-line philosophy, viewing men who took up religion as morbid and bad for morale. Padres, to them, were irrelevant, even – especially if they harped on preparing one's self for death – resented.[138] More customary among the men in the ranks was the blunt contempt for padres held by men who brought their anger against and alienation from the clergy into the army with them, who saw parsons either as spokesmen for the social and economic elite or, as Will Bird and his friend Tommy found them, as hypocritical in preaching holy war while representing the Christian gospel. While some soldiers liked the padres, many more found them a nuisance, especially if their moralizing presence got in the way of the soldiers' illicit activities or evident ambition to leave no woman in France untouched.[139] To them, padres were "for officers only" and, unless they proved themselves in battle (like Scott) or in some way advocated the common soldier's point of view, were beneath contempt.

Somewhere between the rhetoric of the hardened atheist and the fulsome idealist, however, lay the views of what was probably the largest proportion of the men, the uncommitted or disillusioned but not entirely irreligious. These soldiers, Dinesen was surprised to find, did not question the existence of God, even after prolonged combat experience, though neither would they trust themselves to an exclusive dogmatic, denominational, or moralistic variety of Christianity. If religiously tolerant, they were also impatient with blank atheism. While intolerant of the fanatics and wary of the padre, such men nevertheless found an irreligious view unthinkable.[140] Many men, unable to fathom the ironies and tragedies they faced, consciously or subconsciously ignored the great spiritual questions the war posed. Many did not allow themselves to think about such issues while overseas – they were part of that other life that soldiers had left behind and hardly dared to think of.[141] Unwilling to take communion, for it would commit them to a moral standard they were unable or unwilling to follow, they nevertheless were found praying in barrages and before going over the top. After a safe return from battle, while a few would be made more thoughtful by their experience, many more slipped back into their usual materialistic and morally rough-and-ready life, dodging the padre and ducking services until the prospect of combat, death, illness, or marital infidelity in the family at home brought them surreptitiously to the padre's tent door.[142] It was this component of the padre's parish, malleable, profane, yet capable of high comradeship and great sacrifice, that he expected so much from – and that, in retrospect, expected so much from him.

THUS THE PADRE'S WARTIME stature and influence were largely determined by the type of man he was dealing with. While war may not have turned sceptics into believers or believers into atheists, it probably did encourage in the majority of soldiers an agnostic tendency that kept them from trusting unreservedly in the padre or his message yet did not prevent them from drawing upon his acts and words of encouragement whenever they were needed. These same men, however, when the crisis had passed, might shrug off their having turned to the padre as an act of weakness. As many padres realized, or learned the hard way after the war, many a soldier who had once called upon them for succour, advice, or encouragement was not willing to admit it afterwards, especially in front of other men.

In the interwar years this tendency was magnified by the massive disparity between the padres' idealistic preaching and post-war realities. In fact, the depth of feeling in some post-war denunciations might well have been the product of a disappointed war-time hope for what the chaplains had prophesied overseas. Certainly, from the vantage point of the 1920s the hyperbolic preaching of a Kilpatrick or a Shatford could only elicit contempt from the disillusioned veteran. But the accompanying assertion by many that they had seen through the padres, shunned them, and repudiated their efforts while at the front must be weighed against the decade of frustration and disillusionment that followed their return to Canada. Thus, if there were fewer true believers in the army than the padres believed, neither were there as many atheists as veterans have claimed. To many Canadian soldiers of 1914–19 the padre had indeed been important at one time or another. Given the high expectations of the peace that the chaplains had encouraged the men to entertain, inevitably there was great bitterness among veterans after a decade of waiting for the Kingdom of God to arrive. By then the padre was an easy target. Thus the topics of padres and religion continue to be the cause of lively and generally injudicious pronouncements in Canadian war literature and Legion branches. To recapture the mutual dependence that chaplains and fighting men enjoyed in the Great War, the historian must reach back past the psychological watershed of that first peacetime decade.

From the beginning of the 1930s Canadian war literature flows in two opposed streams so far as padres are concerned. A.J. Lapointe's *Soldier of Quebec* returned to the devout, crusading soldier and padre as brother-priest motifs, but for each book of this nature there can be found a handful that echo Kerr or Bird.[143] Even the nurses had their say when Mary Clint in 1934 shrewdly pointed out that the unity and co-operation between denominations seen among the padres and soldiers was not produced by religious revival but by a common patriotism. Padres and churchmen who thought otherwise she referred to the contemporary debate in Canada over the church-union controversy. It was the Cause that united in wartime, not the Faith, she concluded, remarking: "One might suggest, however, that in another war *all* chaplains should be specially selected to honour their creed and cloth."[144] As war clouds gathered in Europe, however, the angry tone subsided and the literature became more restrained once again.[145]

By then the Great Depression had dealt a major blow to any remaining post-war optimism. Some chaplains watched their financial security turn to ashes in the crash of 1929. Others found their salaries shrinking and opportunities diminishing over the following months. While many, with Francis Moore, Canon Scott, and Edmund Oliver, busied themselves with speaking out for the impoverished worker or farm family, others confronted the spectre of a world where insecurity and injustice seemed again poised to take dominion.[146] Some chaplains, however, such as Arthur Priest and George Wells, sided with the forces of conservatism, condemning labour radicalism and rebuking parsons who attacked capitalism.[147] This ambivalence towards the past appeared on several occasions as the world lurched towards another world war. In Toronto destitute soldiers angrily appealed for the chaplains to denounce wealth from the pulpits of their comfortable parishes: "We beseech the men who made their chaplaincies the most humane, the most fraternal, and, therefore the most Christian of the War's services, to come to our aid again, because there is not only a great hope, but also a great danger in their position as priests and pastors in the Church ... They will know, more keenly than we can, the difficulty, where rich men congregate, of bearing witness constantly to the imperious need for social reconstruction which must mean financial reconstruction. We want them, above all, to show us how the strong, true thing, can be said strongly, and the brave changes in profit-making be bravely made, and religion and citizens be fitly joined together."[148]

At the same time, many veterans strove to rekindle the comradely glow they had once known. Wherever they gathered, the chaplains among them, even as they affirmed the verities of the past, now struggled to salvage something for the future. In 1934, during the Canadian Corps reunion in Toronto, Canon Scott called for rededication to the great cause of their youth.[149] In 1936 came another such commemorative occasion. During the veterans' pilgrimage to Vimy, and especially at the dedication of the war memorial on Hill 145, the chaplains' words of commemoration betrayed divided minds and hearts. A.E. Deschamps, auxiliary bishop of Montreal and lieutenant-colonel in the Militia, spoke in the traditional vein of the men who had died for others and who, in practising "the higher form of Christian Charity ... will live again in the heavenly home."[150] Speaking for the United Church, George Fallis, in a paraphrase from the New Testament letter to the Hebrews, portrayed the dead as heroes and martyrs of the Christian faith and called for rededication from the surviving crusaders:

They were shot, bayoneted, gassed, slain with Artillery shrapnel and machine gun, bombed from the skies. They wandered about in gas masks, living in dugouts and ditches, being tormented with vermin. They were thirsty. They were hungry. They were cold and frost-bitten. They were imprisoned. They were separated from their loved ones. And these, all having given a good report, through faith died not having reached their glorious goals, God having provided that we should finish the task and make real their vision of a world swayed by peace and brotherhood. Without us their vision fades. Today on these slopes of Vimy a deathless army urges us on. To us they throw the torch. This monument is a fresh pledge that we shall not break faith.[151]

A few minutes earlier, however, the men had heard another ex-chaplain with longer and closer experience of the front and its human wreckage, who had left a son buried in France, voice the uncertainties of many a veteran nerving himself for the future:

Returning to France and Flanders' Fields gives us a feeling that we are treading on sacred ground as we think of the countless thousands who lie sleeping here. To many who thought that the Great War would end war, we can only say that One, and only One, can make men live together in love and peace. We must educate our children in the finer aspects of courage and sacrifice which emerged during the war so that they will remember the heroism and the deeper lessons which should have resulted from it.[152]

By 1939 such hopes were in ashes. The circle had closed. As Canada declared war against Germany, only one ex-CEF chaplain joined in the "Witness against War" statement organized by members of the United Church.[153] By then many ex-chaplains had been serving in the militia for years. Others, led now by Kent, Kilpatrick, Fallis, George Wells, and Alexander Gordon, grimly volunteered for active service. On 18 October 1939 Bishops George Wells (Anglican) and C.A. Nelligan (Roman Catholic) were appointed heads of their respective branches of the Canadian Active Service Force Chaplain Service.[154] A new and yet all-too-familiar phase of their pilgrimage had begun.

9 Conclusion

The story of the Canadian Great War army chaplaincy is a study in irony. The two decades after the Armistice proved manifestly incongruous to many of the men who had so optimistically prophesied about it in 1918. To the leaders of the Chaplain Service, especially Almond, Fallis, Beattie, Oliver, Kilpatrick, Shatford, and Warner, it had won an institutional war for professional recognition and administrative independence in the CEF. Personally, many chaplains could point to their successful pilgrimage to touch the face of battle while preserving faith and ideals intact. Theologically, most returned endowed with a prophetic vocation and message of national consequence. Some still believed that their hold on returned men was strong. In 1919 chaplains anticipated careers where their experience and expertise would profoundly influence the Canadian churches in the coming years. Before long, however, their hopes were awash in waves of post-war change and controversy. Instead of solidarity and success, padres and soldiers experienced the profound dislocation and loneliness of resettlement in an environment that provided neither the structure nor the intensity that might have allowed their wartime transformation to endure. How could the solidarity and dedication that characterized a fighting force under fire survive when its members were scattered across a society that no longer valued its very reason for existence? How could the padres, scattered by their own denominations and suffering the same isolation and loneliness as their men, transform a church or a nation that no longer valued their vision or experience?

Though neglected in peacetime, by 1919 the institution of the military chaplaincy had nevertheless come of age in Canada. The initial policy of Canadian governments had been characterized by justifiable wariness on the matter of denominational pluralism and reluctance to grant any status further than that of honorary regimental officer. During the Great War this tentativeness gave way to an acknowledgment of both the chaplaincy's intrinsic usefulness and the legitimacy of the Canadian churches' playing a role in its operation. This shift was not, however, achieved easily. In the first years of the war the chaplaincy suffered greatly from the minister of Militia's erratic and often cynical despotism. The churches, too, by their complacency and competitiveness, contributed to the sorry state of the chaplaincy administration under its first DCS. During the critical year of 1917, however, the chaplains, led by Almond, Workman, and O'Gorman, worked out their own salvation from the Hughes system, escaping government domination and mobilizing the churches on their own behalf. The churches, alarmed and directed by their chaplains, claimed a greater role in the administration of the chaplaincy. As a result the state acknowledged the need to refer to the churches. Yet while, under Almond, the Chaplain Service was virtually self-directed, it nevertheless remained firmly within the sphere of influence of its original sponsor, the Canadian military establishment. As long as Almond was DCS, it was clear to all that the chaplaincy was dedicated to supporting the mission and efficiency of the Canadian army. While the government's role of original and dominant sponsor had been qualified and diluted, the chaplaincy had not been handed over to the Canadian churches.

Given their wartime successes, chaplains naturally expected to maintain some permanent and distinct status in the post-war Canadian forces. Instead, the service fell victim to a government bent on return to pre-war methods and found itself cut adrift by churches equally bent on return to normalcy. After all its achievements and successes overseas, by 1921 the chaplaincy, as an institution in the Canadian forces, had been returned to its pre-war status and disorganization. Nevertheless, it did not lose all the ground it had won overseas, as was evident in 1939, when it was reconstituted for active service with relative ease (if not entirely without controversy). Significantly, in this mobilization the churches played a much greater role than in 1914. The Roman Catholic and Protestant branches were laid out on the basis of the lessons learned in the Great War, with each branch parallel but distinct and autonomous. The controversial relationship between social welfare and chaplains' services was also resolved by the creation of a distinct auxiliary branch that in no way competed with the chaplains. Some lessons at least had been learned from the Great War experience.

For the Great War chaplains, personally and theologically, some ironic lessons also had to be learned in the post-war years. Overseas the chaplains had won their fight with commanders over serving in the trenches. They had taken an officer's share in the war, and many had paid the price of victory in health, career, and outlook. Nevertheless, they had found the experiences of their pilgrimage generally consolidating, not shattering their prior world-view or personal faith. They had discovered in fact that they arrived in the war already equipped from pre-war days with the concepts and vocabulary well suited, in their eyes, to greet and guide the men in the great national undertaking. Rather than feeling theologically inadequate, many chaplains felt that a vital missing ingredient of religious experience had now been granted them, and through them to the Canadian people. In Victorian and Edwardian Canada, how indeed could a theology of sacrifice otherwise be realized by the clergymen of Canada's major denominations? The clergy might describe the ideal of sacrifice in the abstract, but, except for those engaged in foreign or home missions, how could they experience its most profound teachings? In an age when the church was in danger of no longer reaching and gripping society, the trenches offered the missing experiential ingredient for the padres both to realize their faith and to take hold of Canadian men's souls.

The padres had confidence in their theology and apologetic, but many also conceded that the men had not, before the war, experienced conversion or revival. It was this experience, not the doctrine, that was lacking in the pre-war church and nation. In the army, however, the war offered both the chaplains and the men a chance to experience self-sacrifice. By 1918, while many a padre conceded that some men were still largely untouched, others indubitably had been converted or spiritually revived in the trenches. The padres could remain hopeful that the men as veterans might still see in their war the missing ingredient to their faith, as a reformed and purified church reached out to them. The church thus had to be readied to gather in the ripe harvest – hence the optimistic content and tone of the Chaplains' Message and the sense of urgency among the padres as the war drew to a close.

Ironically, the first few months of the peace, then the hollow decades that followed proved the few critics among the padres more prescient than the majority. The padres were confronted with a different reality: that if some soldiers had indeed been touched by God overseas, many others were still cynical and bitter. The men seemed to have been left unconvinced by the padres' optimistic preaching. For chaplains the war might have been a regenerative crucible, but the peace certainly was not. Some concluded ruefully that war left many men spiritually as it found them. They were confronted with the possibility that, in sharing the trials and spiritual experiences of the men in hospitals and in the field, they had bonded so intensely with their men that they had acquired a distorted perception of soldier piety and revival. In permitting the example and statements of a pious few to typify the many, they had misread raw human courage and plain bloody-mindedness for Christian self-sacrifice and moral heroism. Thus deafened and blinded to the soldiers' true spiritual attitude and the warnings of the few clear-eyed critics among their own number, the padres did not see that a sceptical, if not agnostic temper was the spiritual norm for many troops.

Yet others, perhaps, had been transformed. Padres had, after all, encountered admirable soldiers whose qualities of self-sacrifice and dedication to the cause were indeed an inspiration to them. What the padres learned from the peace, perhaps, was that such a transformation is not permanent or indelible: heroic faith is summoned by heroic circumstances, not the isolated, competitive, and self-centred realities of peacetime Canada. Such darker conclusions had few spokesmen in 1919. The ensuing years, however, taught a humiliating lesson that certainly altered the style and rhetoric of the Canadian military chaplaincy in the next world conflict. By then the ministry and message of the Great War were fast becoming poignant memories, remembered by a few each November with the setting of the sun and drawing down of window blinds. The second great war soon relegated the hopes of the first into a separate compartment of the national memory, about which Canadians still feel ambivalent. Like the smells and touch of an old uniform, bent photographs, and crumbling newspaper clippings, the Great War ministry became a legacy of dreams and hopes loved and lost. The age of Canadian warrior-priests had passed.

Appendices

APPENDIX ONE
Nominal List of Canadian Great War Chaplains

Name	Denom.	Canada	England	MEF*	France/Belgium
		Location of service			
Abbott, Brinley	CE		X		X
Allen, Hugh James	CE		X	X	X
Allison, Wallace Crosbie	CE		X		X
Almond, John Macpherson	CE		X		X
Ambrose, George Michael	CE		X		X
Anderson, Frederick Wm.	Pres	X	X		X
Andrew, Albert Edward	CE		X		X
Andrews, George Hubert	CE		X	X	X
Andrews, Thomas Wesley F.	Meth	X			
Appleyard, Edward	CE		X		X
Archer, William Lawrence	CE	X			X
Armitage, W.J.	CE	X			
Armitage, William Ramsay	CE	X	X		X
Armstrong, Adam	Meth	X	X		X
Arts, Joseph	RC		X	X	
Askey, William**	CE	X			
Baines, Ernest	Meth		X		
Ball, W.A.R.	CE	X	X		X
Barnett, John Hilary	Pres	X	X		

Note: This list does not include Canadian chaplains who served in British, American, or other armed forces in the First World War.

* Mediterranean Expeditionary Force
** Siberian Expeditionary Force
*** Chinese Labour Corps

Name	Denom.	Location of service			
		Canada	England	MEF*	France/Belgium
Barrow, Gore Munbee	CE	X	X		X
Barton, William	CE		X		X
Bayley, W.H.	CE		X		X
Baynes-Reid, William L.	CE	X	X		X
Beattie, John Alexander	Pres		X		X
Beattie, William	Pres	X	X		X
Beausoleil, Adrian F.	RC	X	X		X
Belford, J. Franklin	CE	X	X		
Béliveau, Hector L.	RC	X			
BellSmith, Frederick M.	Meth	X			
Ben-Oliel, Herbert A.	CE		X		X
Benson, Rowland	Bapt	X			
Biggs, Ernest Robert John	CE	X	X		X
Bischlager, Arthur	CE		X		X
Blake, Henry Thomas	CE		X		X
Bouillon, Joseph George	RC	X	X		X
Boulden, Charles Howard	CE	X	X		X
Bowen, John Campbell	Bapt	X	X		X
Boyle, Victor Osmond	CE	X			
Bradley, John Leo	RC		X		X
Bridgman, Wellington	Meth	X			
Bromwich, Henry Wm.	Meth		X		
Broughall, G.H.	CE		X		X
Brown, Thomas Crawford	P/M	X			
Bruce, Harry	CE		X		X
Bruce, Thomas Langlois	CE		X		X
Brydges, Ralph Lionel	CE	X	X		X
Buck, Frank Hepworth	CE		X		X
Buckland, Alfred W.	CE		X		X
Buckland, Caleb Henry	CE	X	X		X
Bucklee, Harry	CE	X			
Bullock, C.S.	Unit	X	X		
Bullock, Gerald W.	CE		X		X
Bulteel, Reginald Herbert	CE	X			
Burch, Arthur Lafayette	Pres	X	X		X
Burgess, Edwin Harcus	Pres		X		
Burgess-Browne, Ethelbert	CE	X	X		X
Burke, Alfred Edward	RC		X		
Burnett, Herbert William	Meth	X	X		X
Burns, Robert Newton	Meth	X	X		X
Burwash, Edw. Moore J.	Meth	X	X		X
Bushfield, Frank	Meth	X	X		
Callan, John Joseph,	CE		X		X
Calvin, J.	Meth	X			
Cameron, Donald Ewing	Pres		X		
Cameron, Duncan Peter	Meth	X	X		

Name	Denom.	Location of service: Canada	England	MEF*	France/Belgium
Campbell, George Ira	Meth	X	X		X
Campbell, J.	Pres	X			
Campbell, Robert Morrison	Pres	X	X		
Cannon, Wallis Edward	RC	X	X		
Carleton, William Burler	RC		X		X
Carlisle, Arthur	CE	X			X
Carroll, William	S Army	X	X		X
Carruthers, Christopher	CE	X	X		X
Carson, Roy Livingstone	CE		X		X
Cassap, William Henry	CE		X		X
Cassmore, George Stacey	Meth	X			
Caswell, Wm. Cocker B.	Meth		X		
Cawley, Herbert	CE	X	X		X
Chambers, Edmund	Meth		X		
Chapman, F.C.	CE		X		X
Chartier, Charles Eduard	RC	X	X		X
Chessire, Howard Stanley	CE		X		X
Christie, David Wallace	Pres		X		X
Church, Edward Fredrick	Meth	X	X		X
Clarke, George Arthur	Bapt		X		X
Clarke, Harry Bertram**	Meth	X	X		X
Clarke, Wilmot Gereau	Meth	X	X		X
Coburn, John	Meth	X	X		
Coffin, R.L.	Pres	X			
Colwell, Thomas Collins	Meth	X	X		X
Comeau, Isaac Daly	RC	X			
Compton, Samuel Moore J.	Pres	X	X	X	X
Comyn-Ching, John Morton	CE		X		X
Conron, Matthew English	Meth	X	X		X
Cook, Albert	Bapt	X	X		X
Cooney, Thomas L.	RC	X			
Corcoran, William Tillman	RC	X	X		
Cornett, Alexander Dow	Pres		X		X
Costello, Fred. Raymond	RC	X	X		X
Costello, Paul	RC	X	X		X
Coté, Arthur Basil	RC		X		X
Coté, Georges Jules	RC	X	X		X
Coulthurst, Percy	CE		X		X
Creegan, Alfred Henry	CE		X		X
Crochetière, Rosario G.	RC	X	X		X
Cumming, C.R.	CE		X		X
Curran, Thomas Patrick	RC		X		X
Dadson, Thomas McCosh**	Bapt				
Daniel, Ivor James Edward	RC	X	X		X
Davidson, John Cheyne	CE	X	X		X
Davies, John Arthur	CE	X			

Name	Denom.	Canada	England	MEF*	France/Belgium
		Location of service			
Davis, William Henry	ce		X		X
Daw, Samuel	CE	X	X		
Day, Robert Booker	CE		X	X	X
Deacon, Sidney Coles	CE		X		X
D'Easum, Geoffrey Cyril	CE	X	X		X
de la Taille, Maurice	RC		X		X
Denoon, Alexander Hugh	Pres	X	X		X
DePencier, Adam Urias	CE		X		X
Desjardins, Joseph Jules	RC		X		X
Desjardins, Joseph N.	RC		X		X
Dix, George McLaren	Pres	X	X		X
Dodds, Thomas	Pres	X	X		X
Doe, Edward Gordon	RC		X		X
Doyle, Bernard Steven J.	RC		X		X
Doyon, Constant Victor C.	RC	X	X		X
Drummond, D.R.	Pres	X			
Ducharme, Joseph Anthime	RC	X	X		
Dumas, Joseph	RC	X			
Duncan, George Petric	Pres	X	X		X
Dunne, Leonard J.	Bapt		X		
Dyde, S.W.	Pres	X			
Dykes, Philip John	CE	X	X		X
Earp, Ernest Charles	CE	X	X		X
Edmison, George Alexander	Pres	X	X		X
Elliott, Joseph	Pres	X	X		X
Elliott-Baker, Frank Wm.	CE		X		X
Emmet, Arthur George	CE	X	X		X
Emsley, William Henry	Meth	X	X		X
Fairfull, James Kilgour	Bapt	X	X		
Fallis, George	Meth	X	X		X
Fallon, Charles Augustine	RC		X		X
Fallon, James	RC		X		X
Farquhar, George Alex**	Pres	X	X		X
Farrell, Allan Caton	Meth		X		X
Faulds, James	Pres		X		X
Ferguson, William A.	CE		X		X
Fisher, Walter Francis O.	CE		X		X
Fitzgerald, W.F.	CE	X			
Florence, E. Watering	CE	X	X		
Foreman, Clarence Wardlaw	CE	X	X		X
Foster, Duncan Ernest	Pres	X			
Forster, Frank Graham	Pres	X	X		X
Fortier, James Adolphe	RC	X	X		X
Fox, Charles George	CE		X		X

Name	Denom.	Location of service			
		Canada	England	MEF*	France/Belgium
Fraser, Thurlow	Pres		X		X
French, Francis Lawrence	RC		X		X
Frost, Francis George	CE		X		X
Frost, Harry Arthur	Meth		X	X	
Fulton, R.G.	Meth	X			
Garbutt, John	Meth	X	X		X
Gaudet, Joseph Jean Vital	RC	X	X		X
Gavreau, Germain	RC		X		X
Gibson, John Elias	CE	X	X		X
Gibson, John George	Meth		X	X	
Gillis, Michael	RC	X	X		X
Gilmour, Joseph Leeming	Bapt	X			
Godfrey, William Stephen	Meth	X	X		X
Goforth, Paul	Pres	X			
Goodrow, William George	RC	X	X		
Gordon, Alex. MacLennan	Pres	X	X		X
Gordon, Charles William	Pres		X		X
Gornall, Herbert Thomas	Meth	X	X		X
Graham, Archibald	Pres	X	X		
Graham, Edw. Ernest	Meth		X	X	X
Graham, Fred. Taylor	Meth	X			
Graham, James Richard	Pres	X	X		X
Graham, William Creighton	Meth	X	X		X
Gray, George John	CE		X		X
Greene, Allan Dallas	CE	X	X		X
Greene, Heber Kerr H.	CE		X		X
Grimshaw, Jospeh Baker	Bapt	X	X		X
Gronlid, Hjalmar Oliver	Luth	X			
Guay, Edward	RC		X		X
Guthrie, Donald	Pres		X		X
Hagar, Arthur Edmund	Meth	X	X		X
Hale, J.	Meth	X			
Hamel, Georges Antoine	RC	X	X		X
Hamilton, William John	Pres		X		X
Hann, Solomon Wye	Meth	X			
Harden, Arthur	Meth		X		X
Harkness, Nelson Alex.	Bapt	X			
Harper, Frank Cecil	Pres	X			
Harris, Webster Henry F.	CE				X
Harrison, Ralph Douglas	CE	X	X		X
Harrison, Thomas	Pres	X	X		X
Harston, Ernest	Meth		X		X
Hawks, Edward	RC		X		X
Hawthorne, Sydney	CE	X	X		

Name	Denom.	Location of service			
		Canada	England	MEF*	France/Belgium
Hay, Robert James	CE	X	X		X
Hedley, Charles Wilkinson	CE	X	X		X
Hepburn, Channel G.	CE		X		X
Herbert, Robert	CE	X	X		X
Hetherington, A. Joseph	RC	X	X		
Hicks, George O. Walder	Pres		X		
Hilton, Ronald	CE	X	X		
Hinchliffe, Joshua	CE	X	X		X
Hindley, George Joseph	Cong		X		X
Hingston, William Hales	RC	X	X		X
Hodgkinson, J.	CE		X		X
Holman, John Holman	CE		X		X
Hooper, Ed. Bertram	CE	X	X		X
Horne, Charles Wyrne E.	CE		X		X
Horsey, Harold Irwin	Cong	X	X		X
Howard, A. L.	Pres	X			
Howard, Roger S. Wm.	CE	X			
Howie, Robert	Pres		X		X
Hughes, Ed. William	CE		X		X
Hughes, S.J.	Meth	X			
Hunter, John Bruce	Meth	X	X		X
Hussey, Thomas Peter	RC		X		X
Hyde, James	Pres		X		
Hyde, T.B.	Cong	X			
Ingles, George Leicester	CE		X		
Irwin, Robert Joseph	Meth	X	X		X
Jackson, Marcus Harry	CE		X		
Jeakins, Charles Ed.	CE	X	X		X
Johnston, Eric Franklin	Meth		X		X
Johnston, John Wesley	Pres	X	X		X
Johnston, Robert	Pres	X			
Johnston, T.W.	Meth	X			
Jolicœur, Simeon	RC		X		X
Jones, I. James	CE	X	X		X
Jones-Bateman, W.	CE		X		
Kalestinoff, Alexis	R Orth		X		
Kain, Roy Joseph	CE	X			
Kelly, William Joseph	RC		X		X
Kelly, William Terrence	RC		X		
Kelley, Patrick James	RC		X		X
Kent, Harry Arnold	Pres		X		
Kennedy, John R.	CE		X		X
Kenny, Henry Bruce	Meth	X			
Keough, William Taylor	Meth		X		X

Name	Denom.	Location of service			
		Canada	England	MEF*	France/Belgium
Kerby, George W.	Meth	X			
Ketterson, Alexander	CE	X	X		X
Kidd, William Ennis	CE	X	X		X
Killoran, James Patrick	RC	X			X
Kilpatrick, George G.D.	Pres	X	X		X
Knight, Linley Arthur	CE		X		X
Knox, John	RC		X		X
Kuhring, Adolph Gustav	CE	X	X	X	X
Labonté, Arthur James	RC	X	X		X
Lacouture, Onesime Phil.	RC	X		X	
Lamarre, Antoine Ambrose	RC	X	X		
Lambert, Robert Kerr	Meth	X	X		X
Lambert, Sidney Elizah	Meth	X			
Lane, David James	Pres	X	X		
Laronde, Louis	CE		X		
Latimer, Herbert J.	Meth	X	X		X
Lavell, Alfred Edward	Meth	X	X	X	
Lawrence, Channing Gordon	CE	X	X		X
Lawrence, William Levi L.	Meth		X		
Laws, Ernest	RC		X		
Laws, Harold Stewart	CE	X	X		X
Lawson, George Albert	Bapt	X	X		
Lemoine, Nathaniel	CE	X			
Lester, Charles Valentine	CE		X		
Letang, Henry Edward	RC		X		X
Lewis, Owen Gurney	CE	X			
Little, George Albert	Pres		X		X
Lizotte, Joseph Oscar	RC	X	X	X	
Lochead, John	Pres		X		X
Lockary, Francis Michael	RC	X	X		X
Lorymer, William Tindale	Bapt	X	X		
Lowry, Lorenzo Patrick	RC		X		X
Lyon, William Percy	CE	X	X		X
McAfee, Thomas	Pres	X	X		X
McAlpine, Walter Sym	Bapt		X		
McCallion, Hugh Joseph	RC		X		
McCaskill, John James	Pres	X	X		X
McCausland, Harold**	CE	X	X		X
McCarthy, Thomas M.	RC		X		X
McColl, Allan McDougall	Pres		X		X
McConnell, William F.	Pres		X	X	X
MacDonald, Alexander John	Pres	X	X		X
MacDonald, Archibald B.	RC	X	X		X
MacDonald, Ewen John	RC		X		X
MacDonald, George Alfred	Pres	X	X		X

Name	Denom.	Location of service			
		Canada	England	MEF*	France/Belgium
McDonald, I.H.	Pres	X			
MacDonald, John Howard	Bapt	X	X		X
MacDonald, Joseph William	CE	X	X	X	
MacDonald, Pius Augustine	RC	X	X		X
MacDonald, Ronald	RC	X	X		X
MacDonnell, Roderick A.	RC	X	X		X
MacEachern, Norman Allan	Pres	X	X		X
McElhiney, John Alexander	S Army	X			
MacFarlane, Hugh Henry	Pres		X		X
MacFarlane, J.A.	Pres	X			
MacGillivray, Angus H.	Pres	X	X		
MacGillivray, John M	S Army	X			
MacGillivray, John Milton	Pres	X	X		X
MacGillivray, Norman H.	Pres	X	X		X
MacGillivray, Ronald C.	RC		X		X
McGonigle, Thomas George	CE	X	X		X
McGreer, Arthur Huffman	CE		X		X
McGregor, Donald Campbell	Pres	X			
McInnis, John Lewis	Pres		X		X
MacIntosh, C.C.	Pres	X			
Macintosh, Douglas Clyde	Bapt		X		
McKay, Callum N. Miller	Pres	X	X		X
McKegney, Samuel E.	CE		X		X
Mackinnon, Clarence	Pres	X	X		X
Mackinnon, George Alex.	Pres	X			
Mackinnon, Murdock A.	Pres	X			
Mackintosh, Archibald C.	CE		X		X
McLaren, Ebeneezer Duncan	Pres		X		X
McLean, John Albert H.	Pres	X	X		
McLeod, Kenneth Campbell	Pres	X	X		X
MacLeod, Ronald	Pres	X	X		
MacLurg, A.	Pres	X			
McMillan, J.W.	Pres	X			
McNab, John	Pres	X			
McNairn, William Wallace	Pres		X		X
Macnamara, Richard	CE		X		X
MacPhail, Donald George	Pres		X		X
Macpherson, Donald	RC		X	X	X
McQuillan, Patrick	RC	X	X		X
Madden, Ambrose	RC	X			X
Magner, Alan Kenneth	Pres		X		
Magwood, John Wesley	Meth	X			
Magwood, Wilberforce T.D.	Meth		X		X
Maltais, Ludovic	RC		X		X
Marsden, T.	CE		X		
Marshall, David Huggie	Pres	X	X		X
Martin, James Campbell	Pres	X	X		

Name	Denom.	Canada	England	MEF*	France/Belgium
		Location of service			
Martin, Samuel Angus	Meth	X	X		
Martin, William George	Meth		X		
Masters, Charles Keith	CE		X		X
May, William Hubert	Pres		X		
Meagher, James Vincent	RC	X	X		X
Megaw, John Wesley	Pres	X			
Melvin, James Wilfred	Meth		X		X
Metcalfe, W.	CE	X			
Miller, James Sime	Pres	X	X		X
Mitchell, George Stewart	Pres		X		X
Moffit, Louis Wilfred	Meth		X		X
Montgomery, Henry	CE	X	X		
Moore, Arthur H.	CE	X			
Moore, Francis John	CE	X	X		X
Moore, Robert John	RC		X		X
Moorehead, William Henry	CE	X	X		X
Morgan, William Henry	CE		X		
Morris, John Fergusson G.	Meth	X			
Morrow, John D'ole	Pres	X	X		X
Morton, Stanley Edgar	CE	X			
Morse, Charles Knolton	Bapt		X		
Mosley, T.A.	Meth		X		
Mothersill, John Elmore	Pres		X		X
Mullowney, Henry Strachan	Bapt	X	X		X
Muncaster, William Henry	Pres	X	X		X
Munro, George T.	Pres	X	X		X
Murchison, James Moore	Meth		X		
Murdoch, Benedict Joseph	RC	X	X		X
Murphy, Edward Patrick	RC	X			
Murray, John Oswald	CE		X		X
Murray, William Leo	RC		X		X
Mutch, John Maurice	Pres	X	X		
Naylor, Isaac Breamwell	Meth	X	X		X
Newcombe, Harley Coleman	Bapt	X	X		
Nicholson, Harry Luscombe	CE	X			
Nicholson, James Francis	RC		X		X
Nicoll, Charles K.	Pres		X		
Nobles, Harry Roscoe	Bapt		X		
O'Brien, Michael Thomas**	RC	X			
O'Gorman, Charles Devlin	RC		X		X
O'Gorman, John Joseph	RC	X	X		X
O'Gorman, John Robert	RC		X		X
O'Gorman, Michael Joseph	RC		X		X
O'Hare, Peter Francis	RC	X			
Oke, Charles Samuel	Pres	X	X		X

Name	Denom.	Location of service			
		Canada	England	MEF*	France/Belgium
Oliver, Daniel	Pres	X	X		X
Oliver, Edmund Henry	Pres	X	X		X
O'Leary, Peter M.	RC		X		X
Olivier, Jacques Marie**	RC	X			
Omond, Malcolm N.	Pres	X	X		X
O'Reilly, James Joseph	RC		X		X
Orton, Arnot Stanley	Pres	X			
Osbourne, Thomas Arthur	Meth	X	X		
O'Sullivan, Thomas	RC	X	X		X
Ovsianitsky, John	R. Orth.	X	X		
Owen, Cecil Caldbeck	CE	X	X		X
Paquin, Julian	RC	X	X	X	X
Parker, William Fowler	Bapt	X	X		X
Patterson, Thomas Allan	Pres		X		X
Paulin, James Burnside	Pres	X	X		X
Payne, A. Beauchamp	CE		X		X
Peacock, Harold Dobson	CE	X	X		X
Pearson, Harry Mitchell	Pres	X			
Penfold, Robert	S. Army	X		X	
Petrie, John Alexander	Pres		X		X
Phaneuf, Francois Maurice	RC	X	X		
Pickett, Michael Joseph	RC		X		X
Pickup, Harold Richard	Pres	X	X		X
Pinnington, Edward F.	CE	X	X		X
Piper, F.C.	CE		X	X	
Pirot, Julius	RC		X		X
Planet, Edward Henry	RC		X		X
Plews, George Walton	Meth	X	X		X
Poole, Frederick Gifford	Bapt	X	X		X
Porter, Frederick Seely	Bapt	X	X		X
Priest, Arthur Harding	CE		X		X
Pringle, George Charles	Pres		X		X
Pringle, John	Pres		X		X
Procunier, Charles Ault	CE		X		
Pugsley, Ernest Edgar	Meth		X		X
Pugsley, George	CE	X	X		X
Pullinger, Bertram Wallis	CE	X	X		X
Rae, Victor Guest	Pres		X		
Ralston, James Oates	Pres	X	X		X
Reed, Christopher	CE		X		X
Reid, Andrew Dunn	Pres	X	X		X
Renison, Robert John	CE		X		X
Reycraft, John Franklin	Meth	X			
Richardson, John Alex.	CE		X		

Name	Denom.	Location of service			
		Canada	England	MEF*	France/Belgium
Riddiford, Walton Charles	Bapt	X	X		X
Ridgeway, Robert Weston	CE		X		X
Robb, Andrew David	Meth	X	X		X
Robertson, David. Ed. D.	CE		X		X
Robertson, Harold Deek***	Meth				
Robertson, William	CE	X	X		X
Robinson, Charles Bryan	S Army	X	X		
Roche, Joseph Lawrence	RC	X			
Rollins, James	Pres		X		X
Rooney, Joseph	RC		X		X
Ross, David Graham	Bapt	X	X		X
Runnells, Arthur Elie	Meth		X		X
Sammon, John Joseph	RC	X	X		
Sarkissian, Samuel H.	CE	X			
Sawers, Frederick John	CE	X			
Scarlett, Robert Arthur	Meth	X	X		X
Scott, Frederick George	CE		X		X
Seaman, William Frederick	CE	X	X		X
Selkirk, J.H.	Pres		X		
Shatford, Alan P.	CE		X		X
Shelley, Charles Walter	Pres	X	X	X	
Sherring, Frederick G.	CE	X	X		X
Shires, Robert John	CE	X	X		X
Shirley, John Alvin	CE	X			
Shore, Henry M.	CE	X	X		X
Sigouin, Leon	RC	X			
Singleton, Wilfred B.	CE		X		X
Skerry, Arthur Lindsay	CE		X		
Smith, Philip Merton	Cong		X		X
Smith, W.B.	Pres	X			
Smyth, James	Meth		X		
Sparks, Wm. Hamilton H.	CE	X	X	X	X
Sparling, Charles Ashbury	CE	X			
Spencer, Clarence R.	CE		X		X
Spencer, Robert Almon	Meth		X		
Spiddell, Joseph Dimock	Bapt		X		X
Stafford, Roy Percival	Meth		X		
Staley, Melville Daniel	RC		X		X
Stanton, Austin	RC		X		X
Starr, George Lothrop	CE		X		
Steacy, Richard Henry	CE		X		X
Steele, Alfred	S Army	X	X		X
Stephenson, Fred. Lambert	CE	X	X		X
Stewart, Thomas Hudson	CE	X	X		X
Stuart, Cecil James S.	CE		X		X

Name	Denom.	Location of service			
		Canada	England	MEF*	France/Belgium
Suckling, William Thorley	CE	X	X		
Summers, Donald James	RC	X			
Swindlehurst, Frederick	CE		X		
Sylvestre, Ludger Adolph	RC	X	X		X
Taylor, George Claremont	Pres		X		X
Taylor, Hugh Daniel	Meth		X		X
Taylor, Robert Bruce	Pres		X		X
Taylor, William John	CE	X			
Thackery, Joseph	Cong	X			
Thomas, Herbert Edgar	Meth	X	X		
Thomas, John Henry	CE	X	X		X
Thomas, Turberville	CE		X		X
Thompkins, Miles Nicholas	RC		X		X
Thompson, Basil W.	Meth	X			
Thompson, Robert Fleming	Pres	X	X		X
Thompson, T.J.	Pres	X	X	X	
Thornton, William Henry	RC		X		X
Tibbits, S. John Knox	CE	X	X		X
Tolmie, J.C.	Pres	X			
Trench, Albert Charles	CE		X		
Tully, Joseph	CE		X		X
Tupper, Joseph Freeman	CE	X	X		X
Tyler, C.M.	Meth	X			
Vipond, Frank	CE		X		X
Walker, William Robert	CE	X	X		X
Wallace, J.M.	Pres	X			
Wallace, Thomas George	CE	X	X		X
Wallace, William Fulton	CE	X	X		X
Walsh, William	Meth	X			
Walton, Thompson	S. Army	X		X	
Ward, James Edward	CE	X			
Warner, David Victor	CE		X		X
Watts, John Ord	Pres	X	X		X
Wayman, John Wright	CE		X		X
Wells, George Anderson	CE		X		X
Whalley, Clement K.	CE		X		X
Whillans, James	Pres		X		X
Whitaker, B.L.	CE		X	X	X
Whitaker, George David	CE		X	X	X
White, Francis Paul	RC		X		X
White, James Hunter	Pres		X		X
White, William Andrew	Bapt	X	X		X
White, William Charles	CE		X		
White, William George	S. Army	X			

Name	Denom.	Location of service			
		Canada	England	MEF*	France/Belgium
Whittaker, Charles W.	Meth	X	X		X
Wilken, Allan Giles	CE		X		X
Wilkinson, Samuel	Meth		X		X
Williams, Frederick	Meth		X		
Williams, Cecil Grosvenor	Meth	X			
Williams, George Henry	Meth	X			
Williamson, Frederick	CE		X		X
Wilson, J.C.	Bapt	X	X		X
Wilson, T.A.	Meth	X	X		X
Wiseman, John Franklin	CE	X	X		
Wood, A.B.W.	RC		X		X
Wood, George W.	Pres		X		X
Woodcock, Herbert F.D.	CE		X		X
Woods, Albert W.	CE	X	X		X
Workman, Wolston Thomas	RC		X		X
Wright, George	CE		X		X
Wright, John Henry	Meth		X		X
Young, Edward Hudson	ce		X	X	X
Young, W. Harold	Meth		X		

Sources:

Smith, G.Oswald, ed. *University of Toronto Roll of Service.*

Canadian Almanac and Directory, 1914–19.

Acta Victoriana.

National Archives of Canada. Ministry of Militia and Defence. Canadian Chaplain Service Records, 1914–20.

Presbyterian Church in Canada. *Acts and Proceedings of the General Assembly of the Presbyterian Church in Canada*, 1914–19.

United Church Archives. Methodist Army and Navy Board Records, 1915–19.

APPENDIX TWO
Chaplain Service Questionnaire, 1918

Office of Director of Chaplain Svcs.,
O/S Military Forces of Canada,
Oxford Circus House, 245 Oxford St.
London, W.1.

August 20th 1918

You have for a considerable period been serving as a Chaplain in the Overseas Forces. Under different circumstances you have been brought into close touch with great numbers of men of all conditions. This experience will have enabled you to form convictions regarding the work of the Church that should be of great value not only to yourself but also to others who are earnest workers for the Kingdom.

The Director of Chaplain Services is anxious that no one should feel that his work as a Chaplain has been accomplished when he has merely interpreted the message of the Church to the soldiers. There still remains the no less important task of interpreting the soldiers, the war and its lessons to the Church at home. It is the Director's aim that the Chaplain Services should gather up the inspiration and lessons which the war has afforded our Chaplains Overseas and place these at the service of our Brethren in the Ministry at home who have not been so fortunate as to share directly in this great work. Our experience has been meaningful to us. We should endeavour to make that experience meaningful and helpful to the Churches in Canada. To this end the Chaplain Services has undertaken a two-fold task: –

(1. For the Various Denominations.)

The D.C.S. has appointed a committee to represent each Denomination who will solicit an expression of opinion from the Chaplains in that particular Denomination. The accompanying questionnaire has been drawn up with a view to enabling the Chaplains to voice their judgment on the matters referred to them. On the basis of the answers received the Denominational committees will prepare each for its own Church an intimate and direct message. You will therefore prepare careful answers to the questions that are herewith sent to you.

(2. For the Church at Large.)

The D.C.S. has appointed a committee representing all the non–Roman Catholic Churches to prepare a deliverance based upon these answers which will give expression to the great common convictions regarding Church Work and Christian Service that the war has led us to form. The answers to the questionnaire should reach this office not later than September 30th, 1918.

The Chaplains having enjoyed the unique experience should have a special message for the Churches at home. This will contribute materially towards arousing them to a realization of the greatness of the task when the soldiers return. And perhaps this realization of the greatness of that task more than anything else will kindle in young men of suitable gifts a desire to dedicate their lives to the Christian Ministry. To this end the Director is anxious not only that this questionnaire should receive the most careful attention but also that the Chaplains should cultivate opportunities for presenting to outstanding young men the claims of the Christian Ministry as a life work and calling.

J. H. MacDonald, Major
A.D.C.S.,
for D.C.S., O.M.F.C.

QUESTIONNAIRE:

1. Does our church appear to you in a measure to have failed to win and hold men? If so:
(a) In what particular?
(b) To what extent?
(c) For what reason?

2. Have you found in your personal dealings with men that there has been a neglect of definite Christian instruction in the fundamentals of religion? If so, specify.

3. Do our men seem to believe that our Church has not dealt effectively and sympathetically with the problems of practical life?

4. To what extent have you found Denominational differences a hindrance in your work among men?

5. What are considered in the Army to be the chief sources of ineffectiveness:
(a) In the Church?
(b) In the Ministry?

6. In what way can our Churches develop a Christian Fellowship as vital and intimate as the present comradeship in arms?

7. Does your experience show that the Communion in our Church should receive greater emphasis than is the case at present?

8. Has your experience with the Church Parades and Sunday Services convinced you that our Church Services would be improved by giving the Congregation an opportunity more largely to participate in the public worship?

9. Has your experience as a Chaplain revealed any way in which the training of our Ministry can be improved? If so, particularize.

10. The energy, devotion and sacrifice which have been put into the War should be conserved and dedicated more definitely to the work of the Kingdom of God.
(a) How can this best be brought home to the individual?
(b) How can the Church best magnify the calling of the Ministry and make the most effective appeal to suitable young men?

11. The war has revealed the necessity of large vision and wise direction for the attainment of great objectives.
(a) Has the Church caught a similar vision?
(b) What suggestion have you to offer?

12. What suggestions in the way of constructive statesmanship have you to offer from your observations and experience which are not covered by the above questions?

Source: NA, Chaplain Service Records, vol. 4663, Questionnaire file.

APPENDIX THREE
Canadian Militia Chaplaincy Growth, 1896–1914

Table 1
Militia Chaplains, 1897–1914, by Denomination

Year	*CE*	*Pres.*	*RC*	*Meth.*	*Bapt.*	*?*	*Total*
1896	1	1					2
1897	13	4	1			1	19
1898	25	8	3				36
1899	33	6	4	1	1	2	47
1900	37	12	5	2	1	1	58
1901	42	13	7	2	1	1	66
1902	44	14	8	3			69
1903	43*	12	9	4		2	68
1904	50	17	11	4			82
1905	53	20	11	5			89
1906	55	19	12	5		1	92
1907	56	20	13	6		1	96
1908	66	21	13	6		1	107
1909	69	23	13	5		2	112
1910	69	21	14	5	1		111
1911	72	25	15	3	1	4	120
1912	77	25	16	3	2	3	127
1913	76	28	16	4	2	6	132
1914	92	31	19	5	2	3	150

* Add 2 South African War padres (unattached), which raises the Anglican total for 1903 to 45.
Source: Canadian Almanac and Directory, 1897–1915 (Toronto: Copp Clark 1896–1916), passim.

Table 2
Pre-War Chaplaincy Growth

Militia units 1897–1914: Served by chaplains of only one denomination

	CE	*Pres.*	*RC*	*Meth.*	*Total*
Cavalry	27	5		3	36
Infantry	53	21	17	3	108
Artillery	6	4	1		11

"New" Militia units, 1903–14: Chaplain denomination

	CE	*Pres.*	*RC*	*Meth.*	*Total*
Cavalry	17	3		1	21
Infantry	17	9	9	1	36
Artillery	5	2			7

"Western Canada" Militia units, 1897–1914: Chaplain denomination

	CE	*Pres.*	*RC*	*Meth.*	*Total*
Cavalry	11	4		1	16
Infantry	11	7		1	19
Artillery	1				1

Source: Canadian Almanac and Directory, 1897–1915 (Toronto: Copp Clark 1896–1916), passim.

Notes

ABBREVIATIONS

ADCS	Assistant Director of Chaplain Services
CAR	*Canadian Annual Review*
CCS	Canadian Chaplain Service
CEF	Canadian Expeditionary Force
CFC	Canadian Forestry Corps
CHAP	Canadian Historical Association *Papers*
CHR	*Canadian Historical Review*
CRT	Canadian Railroad Troops
DCS	Director of Chaplain Services
DSO	Distinguished Service Order
JCS	*Journal of Canadian Studies*
MC	Military Cross
OC	Officer Commanding
OMFC	Overseas Military Forces of Canada
NA	National Archives of Canada
PANS	Public Archives of Nova Scotia
QUA	Queen's University Archives
QQ	*Queen's Quarterly*
RC	Roman Catholic
SR	*Sciences religieuses/Studies in Religion*
UCA	United Church Archives
USA	University of Saskatchewan Archives

INTRODUCTION

1 UCA, Nathanael Burwash Collection, box 28, file 630, unpublished biographical draft, chapter X, 9–11, 15–16. For details of the battle and Inglis's role in it, see Capt. John A. Macdonald, *Troublous Times in Canada*, 46–51, 239–41, and Capt. F.H. McCallum, "Experiences of a Queen's Own Rifleman at Ridgeway," 24–9.

2 UCA, Burwash biography, 10–11, 15–17. See also McCallum, "Experiences," 28. Marguerite Van Die points out that Ensign MacEachern's experience of "brighter evidence" during his dying prayers became for Burwash a decisive example of the "witness of the Spirit"; see *An Evangelical Mind*, 60.

3 Queen's University, Douglas Library, Jackman Collection, Rev. David Inglis, *Righteousness Exalteth a Nation: A Thanksgiving Sermon*, 12 pp.

4 NA, MG 30 E 4, William Beattie Papers, "History of the Canadian Chaplain Services" (hereafter, Beattie, "History"), unpublished ms, 345 pp. In 1923 A.F. Duguid, recently appointed official war historian, recommended that the Beattie manuscript undergo major revision, which evidently did not take place; see NA, Department of National Defence, Headquarters Central Registry, vol. 1742, D.H.S.-46-26, Duguid to G. Kilpatrick, 9 Nov. 1923.

5 F.G. Scott, *The Great War As I Saw It*; also "The Chaplain Services," in *Canada at War*, 6:116–36; and B.J. Murdoch, *The Red Vineyard.*

6 See C.W. Gordon, *Postscript to Adventure*; George Fallis, *A Padre's Pilgrimage*; and George Anderson Wells with J.C. Wells, *The Fighting Bishop.*

7 J.R. O'Gorman, "Canadian Catholic Chaplains in the Great War," *Canadian Catholic Historical Association Report, 1939–1940*, 71–84; and his *Soldiers of Christ: Canadian Catholic Chaplains, 1914–1919*. See also W.T. Steven, *In This Sign.*

8 The most recent study of post-war Canadian chaplaincy developments is Major A. Fowler's "The Adaptation of the Ecclesiastical Hierarchy to Military Bureaucracy, 1945–1968: The Pursuit of Assumed Status," MA, Carleton University 1991. On the naval chaplaincy, see W.E.L. Smith, *The Naval Chaplain in the Days of Sail* and *The Naval Chaplain and His Parish*; and Pierre Doyon, "Aumôniers Catholiques dans la marine royale du Canada de 1939 à nos jours," MA, University of Ottawa 1968. See also Jacques Castonguay, *Unsung Mission: History of the Chaplaincy Service (RC of the RCAF)*; and R.J. Ogle, "The Inception, History and Growth of Canadian Military Chaplains' Faculties," in *The Faculties of Canadian Military Chaplains.* On Protestant branch developments, see C.D. Edward Aitken, "The Background and Development of the Royal Canadian Army Chaplains' Corps (Protestant)," B.Litt., Pine Hill Divinity Hall, Halifax 1965.

9 The one reference to chaplains consisted of a footnote dedicated to Canada's most famous chaplain, Canon F.G. Scott; see G.W.L. Nicholson, *Canadian Expeditionary Force, 1914–1919*, 451. An almost identical tribute may be found in Larry Worthington, *Amid the Guns Below*, 41–2.

10 See J.R. O'Gorman, "Canadian Catholic Chaplains," 72–3, 80–1. In fact, during the 1940 federal election Ernest Lapointe, while campaigning in Quebec, contrasted his party's creation of a distinct Roman Catholic branch under a bilingual chief with the anti-Catholic policy followed by Borden's government in the First World War. See J.L. Granatstein, *Canada's War*, 88, 110.

11 Henry Borden, *Robert L. Borden: Letters to Limbo*, 147–8.

12 Desmond Morton, *A Peculiar Kind of Politics*, 99, 114–16.

13 M. Bliss, "The Methodist Church and World War I", *CHR*, (Sept. 1968): 213–33; J.W. Grant, *The Churches in the Canadian Era*; A.R. Allen, *The Social Passion*; E.A. Pulker, *We Stand on Their Shoulders*; and John S. Moir, *Enduring Witness*, 208–9.

14 J.H. Thompson, "'The Beginning of Our Regeneration,'" *CHAP*, (1972): 227–45. See also E.A. Christie, "The Attitudes and Opinions of the Presbyterian Church in Canada with Respect to Public Affairs and Social Problems, 1875–1925," MA, University of Toronto 1956, 117–24; and Brian Fraser, *The Social Uplifters*.

15 Mark McGowan, "'We are all Canadians': A Social, Religious and Cultural Portrait of Toronto's English-Speaking Roman Catholics, 1890–1920," PhD, University of Toronto 1988.

16 David Marshall, *Secularizing the Faith*, and his "Methodism Embattled," *CHR* (Mar. 1986): 48–64.

17 Michael Gauvreau, *The Evangelical Century*, and his "War, Culture and the Problem of Religious Certainty," *Journal of the Canadian Church Historical Society* (Apr. 1987): 12–31.

18 For German Lutheran padres, see Albrecht Schbel, *300 Jahrre Evangelische Soldatenseelsorge*. On the United States Army chaplaincy, see Roy J. Honeywell, *Chaplains of the United States Army*; and Earl F. Stover, *Up from Handymen*. For accounts of the American chaplains in the American Revolution and Civil War, see E.F. Williams, "Soldiers of God: the Chaplains of the Revolutionary War," PhD, Texas Christian University 1972; and Drew Gilpin Faust, "Christian Soldiers: The Meaning of Revivalism in the Confederate Army," *Journal of Southern History* (Feb. 1987): 63–90.

19 Ray Abrams, *Preachers Present Arms*.

20 Gordon Zahn, *The Military Chaplaincy: A Study of Role Tension in the Royal Air Force*. Zahn, a Roman Catholic pacifist, charged chaplains of the Royal Air Force with tacitly resolving the conflict between Christianity and war by endorsing the military way and abandoning a cardinal

tenet of Christianity, that of absolute pacifism. Zahn's work has been countered by Clarence Abercrombie, a sociologist with previous experience as an officer in the United States Army, in *The Military Chaplain.*

21 Robert Graves, *Good-bye to All That,* 157–9; see also 183–4, 195, 200; Guy Chapman, *A Passionate Prodigality,* 50–1, 117, 166–7; and C.E. Montague, *Disenchantment,* 66–79.

22 P. Middleton Brumwell, *The Army Chaplain*; A.C. Dow, *Ministers to the Soldiers of Scotland*; and John Smyth, *In This Sign Conquer.*

23 John Ellis, *Eye-Deep in Hell,* 155–6; and Alan Lloyd, *The War in the Trenches,* 133–9. See also Jane Leonard, "The Catholic Chaplaincy," in David Fitzpatrick, ed., *Ireland and the First World War,* 10–11.

24 Albert Marrin, *The Last Crusade: The Church of England in the First World War,* 118–39, 186–92, 202–15.

25 Alan Wilkinson, *The Church of England and the First World War,* 110–92. Much of Wilkinson's portrait of the Church of England is based on Marrin's.

26 Michael McKernan, *Australian Churches at War,* 7–39, 68–79, 109–26, 172–8.

27 Michael McKernan, "Clergy in Khaki: The Chaplain in the Australian Imperial Force, 1914–1918," *Journal of the Royal Australian Historical Society* (Dec. 1978): 145–66.

CHAPTER ONE

1 *Canadian Churchman,* 9 Apr. 1885; see also *Presbyterian Witness,* 2 May 1885, 1; *Canadian Churchman,* 28 May 1885, 342.

2 *Canadian Churchman,* 23 Apr. 1885.

3 Carol M. Whitfield, *Tommy Atkins: The British Soldier in Canada, 1759–1870,* 111–12, 183–8. During the War of 1812 the Royal Army employed at least thirteen Anglican clergymen in the Canadas. During the American invasions of 1813 two Lower Canadian Roman Catholic priests received temporary chaplaincies to French Canadian militia regiments; see L.H. Irving, ed., *Officers of the British Forces in Canada during the War of 1812,* 20, 35, 102.

4 Smyth, *In This Sign Conquer,* 21–114.

5 31 Victoria, c.XL, sect. 17.

6 Cartier selected R. Stewart Patterson and Father Marie-Joseph Royer, an Oblate acquaintance from Ottawa, as chaplains, but he had to insist upon these "highly important" appointments before the governor general and militia commander relented. NA, Militia and Defence (RG 9), Reports and Memoranda, vol. 35, Returns and Answers to Parliament, 1870 file, R. Ross memo, 16 Apr. 1870; see also Cartier to Governor General, 28 Apr., and Lindsay to Governor General, 30 Apr. 1870; and *Canada Gazette,* 17 May 1870.

7 Ryerson charged that Cartier allowed a dozen French Canadian priests to go with the expedition while refusing to allow even one Wesleyan chaplaincy: *Toronto Globe,* 21 May 1870, 2; see also 9–10 June 1870; and *Presbyterian Witness,* 18 June 1870, 197. See also UCA, Egerton Ryerson Papers, box 6, Correspondence, 1870, Punshon to Cartier, 23 Apr. 1870.

8 Cartier claimed "there was no Protestant denomination amongst whom he had so many personal friends as the Methodists, in Montreal especially": *House of Commons Debates,* 20, 26 Feb. 1871, col. 55, c. 164–75; see also *Canadian Sessional Paper 35,* 1871.

9 Ryerson to Campbell, *Toronto Globe,* 18 June 1870. See also C.B. Sissons, *Egerton Ryerson,* 578–82. Punshon restated this view: Punshon to Cartier, 11 Nov. 1870, in *Sessional Paper 35,* 9–10.

10 Nevertheless, Militia Headquarters still recognized only three denominations: Presbyterian, Roman Catholic, and "the Established Church." *Regulations and Orders for the Canadian Militia, 1879,* paras. 355–9.

11 NA, RG 9, Deputy Minister's Correspondence, vol. 77, file 05982, Rev. J. Renaud to Col. W. Powell, 23 May 1884, D'Orsonnens to Powell and margin, 6 June 1884.

12 The commander of the Ninth Battalion arranged for Abbé F.X. Faguy to follow from Quebec, joining his unit in time for the northern Ontario crossing. G. Beauregard, *Le 9me Bataillon au Nord-Ouest,* 6, 14. In Montreal officers of the Sixty-fifth sought out Oblate Father Philemon Prévost.

13 Ouimet to Caron, 1 Apr. 1885, in D. Morton and R.H. Roy, *Telegrams of the Northwest Campaign of 1885,* Champlain Society XLVII, 66; see also E.R.J. Chambers, *Histoire du 65me Régiment Carabiniers Mont-Royal,* 94.

14 Caron to Ouimet, 2 Apr. 1885, in Morton and Roy, *Telegrams,* 73. Prévost caught the Sixty-fifth's train and was led from car to car to be introduced to the men by the commander. C.R. Daoust, *Cent-vingt jours de service actif,* 22.

15 George Lloyd and T.W. Acheson thus served as both soldiers and preachers, although Lloyd was not ordained until after he was wounded at Cut Knife Hill: see W.T. Barnard, *Queen's Own Rifles of Canada 1860–1960,* 33, 49, 58, 62; also General Synod Archives of the Anglican Church in Canada, G.E. Lloyd Papers. On the Alberta force, see T.B. Strange, *Gunner Jingo's Jubilee,* 434–5, 462, 476–7, 510. See also C.A. Boulton, *Reminiscences of the Northwest Rebellions,* 323, 372. For McDougall's correspondence with his wife during the campaign, see QUA, John McDougall Papers.

16 D.M. Gordon, "Reminiscences of the Northwest Campaign of 1885," *Queen's Quarterly* 1 (1903): 9. See also Frederick Middleton, *The Suppression of the Rebellion in the Northwest Territories of Canada, 1885,* ed. G.H. Needler, 17, 39.

17 NA, RG 9, Adjutant General's Correspondence, vol. 92, file 09584, "Extract given to deputation of Presbyterian clergy by the Minister, 20-4-'85."

18 Just as Middleton wisely advised Caron not to have more than one clergyman of each denomination in the same brigade: "Reminiscences," 9; also QUA, D.M. Gordon Papers, box 12, Gordon Journal, 29 Apr.–5 May 1885. See also Middleton to Caron, 1 May 1885, in Morton and Roy, 227.

19 In the end the only religious scandal of the campaign concerned the rumour that Protestant soldiers of the Sixty-fifth had been forced to march in a Corpus Christi procession in Edmonton. Caron to Ouimet and replies, 3–6 July 1885, in Morton and Roy, 371. See also *Presbyterian Witness*, 9 May 1885, 1.

20 Bishop Sweatman tried wangling an appointment directly from Caron and the prime minister: see Morton and Roy, 212–13. Deputy Minister Panet notified Whitcombe that he would have to be invited by the Royal Grenadiers, a Toronto regiment. Church authorities sent a suggestive telegram to the commander and hustled him on to a westbound train. Panet to Caron, 28 Apr. and Caron to Whitcombe, 28 Apr. 1885, Morton and Roy, 217; and *Canadian Churchman*, 7 May 1885, 291 and 295.

21 Oblivious of Baptist sensibilities, he suggested that only the Presbyterian, Methodist, Catholic, and Anglican denominations needed to send chaplains: *Christian Guardian*, 22 Apr. 1885, 8.

22 *Christian Guardian*, 29 Apr. 1885, 4; also NA, RG 9, Deputy Minister's Correspondence, vol. 159, file A1900. Even veterans such as Rev. Horace Mussen found the phrase "this gentleman has not been selected by any regiment" the death-knell of their hopes: NA, RG 9, Adjutant General's Correspondence, vol. 93, 09667, Mussen to Adjutant General, 25 Apr. 1885. For a complete list of Northwest Rebellion chaplains, see NA, RG 9, Deputy Minister's Correspondence, vol. 161, A1900 and A1968 1/2, Chaplains' List; also *Presbyterian Witness*, 2 May 1885, 1, 23, 164, and 29 May 1885, 172.

23 The following were appointed chaplains and/or received campaign medals for their service:

Name	*Denomination*	*Unit*
Ball, W.S.	CE	7th Fusiliers
Barclay, J.	Pres.	Montreal Garrison Artillery
Faguy, F.-X.	RC	9th Voltigeurs
Gordon, D.M.	Pres.	90th Winnipeg Rifles
Gilmore, G.	CE	Lorne and Simcoe Battalion
Lloyd, G.E.	CE	Queen's Own Rifles

Name	*Denomination*	*Unit*
Mackay, W.	CE	Alberta Field Force
Mackenzie, W.P.	Pres.	Alberta Field Force
McDougall, J.	Meth.	Alberta Field Force
Pitblado, C.	Pres.	Halifax Battalion
Prévost, P.	RC	65th Carabiniers
Quinnez, C.	CE	Midland Battalion
Rowland, W.	Pres.	91st Battalion
Whitcombe, C.E.	CE	10th Royal Grenadiers

See NA, Militia and Defence, 11a5, vol. 11, Northwest Rebellion medal list.

24 Faguy shuttled back and forth between headquarters at Gleichen and the outposts at Humboldt and Crowfoot. Getting to all the detachments for worship and mass on the same day proved too much for the padre – the Crowfoot detachment spent a few Sundays "like true pagans." Beauregard, *Le 9me Bataillon*, 67; also 23, 28, 47–8.

25 D.M. Gordon, "Reminiscences," *QQ* 1:15, 12. This stood his son, Alexander, in good stead when he served as chaplain to the First Canadian Division. See A.B. Tucker, *The Battle Glory of Canada*, 67; see also QUA, Gordon Diary, 10 May 1885; and Middleton, *Suppression*, 57.

26 According to Strange, Prévost wanted to administer last rites on the spot. The general persuaded him to wait until they were out of range. Chambers, *65me*, 114; see also Strange, *Jubilee*, 492.

27 Gordon began afternoon Bible readings, making evangelistic efforts that stressed the active and manly nature of the Christian calling: QUA, Gordon Diary, 5, 14, 21, 25, 28 June 1885. He found it progressively harder to "get them to settle down to an evening service, as I found even in the case of some of our Sunday Services": Gordon Diary, 8–9 June 1885.

28 Father Faguy's winning personality won his unit's affection. Beauregard praised him as a model chaplain: *9me*, 41–2, 53–6, 72. Other attempts to improve morale involved organizing sports. Gordon helped to write and direct a play that the Ninetieth eventually performed in Winnipeg: see "Reminiscences," 19; also QUA, Gordon Diary, 9 June 1885.

29 Whitcombe insisted that his morning service was for Anglicans only. Sometimes in the evening a united service with voluntary attendance was held. Gordon sighed, "I do like to see Christians worshipping together, and I would rather build bridges to unite people than dig ditches to separate them. However the other side preferred it otherwise." QUA, Gordon Journal, 5 June 1885.

30 Gordon, "Reminiscences," 20.

31 *Christian Guardian*, 22 July 1885, 1; also NA, RG 9, Deputy Minister's Correspondence, vol. 164, A2170, Strange to Presbyterian Missionary Society, June 1885.

32 Former chaplains Whitcombe and Lloyd kept up their connections with the Royal Grenadiers and Queen's Own Rifles until both were called to other pulpits. D.M. Gordon did the same for the Ninetieth. E.J. Chambers, *The Royal Grenadiers*, 81; and Chambers, *The 90th Regiment*, 59, 69; see also Barnard, *Queen's Own Rifles*, 71. Military District 8's 1886 summer camp employed a clergyman as chaplain: see Canada, Department of Militia and Defence, Sessional Paper 6, 1886, Report of the D.O.C., M.D. 8, 9 Nov. 1885.

33 The Fredericton Infantry School commandant attempted, unsuccessfully, to recruit one of his own: NA, RG 9, Adjutant-General's Correspondence, vol. 94, file 09892, School Commandant to Adjutant General, 9 May 1885. In Winnipeg the local commander of the Mounted Infantry school tried to pay D.M. Gordon, several Catholic and Anglican priests, and a Methodist minister for their ministry, but was forbidden by regulations: NA, RG 9, Deputy Minister's Correspondence, vol. 252, A3656, petition of 26 Feb. 1886, and reply 6 May; also O.C. Winnipeg School to Panet, 12 May 1886. See also RG 9, Deputy Minister's Correspondence, vol. 275, A6864, Father Guay to O.C., M.D. 7, 27 June 1887, and reply 28 June 1887.

34 See clippings from *La Minerve*, *L'Etendard*, *Franco-Canadien*, and the predictable reply in the English-language *Saint John News*, in NA, RG 9, Deputy Minister's Correspondence, vol. 273, A6679, correspondence dated 24 May 1886, 31 Jan., 9 May, 15 June, and 1 Aug. 1887; also 9 Apr. 1888. Aubry eventually dropped his case: see ibid., vol. 303, A8705, newspaper clippings from *La Minerve*, 24 Oct., *L'Etendard*, 26 Oct., 3 Nov. 1888, *Franco-Canadien*, 26 Oct., and *St John News*, 26, 29 Oct. 1888.

35 In 1894 the Prince of Wales's Regiment tried without success to have Bishop Bond and Dean Carmichael gazetted as lieutenant-colonels on the strength of their services since the 1860s: NA, RG 9, Deputy Minister's Correspondence, vol. 338, A10986, Lt-Col. Butler to Deputy Minister, 18 June 1894, and reply. Montreal's Sixty-fifth continued to have an *aumônier*, named by the archbishop himself; after Prévost's death, he chose a former Papal Zouave, Jesuit J.G. Garceau. E.J. Chambers, *Histoire du 65me Regiment Carabiniers Mont-Royal*, 29, 143–4.

36 NA, RG 9, Deputy Minister's Correspondence, vol. 373, 13304, Lt-Col. Roy to Panet, 31 Mar., and reply 2 Apr. 1894.

37 Toronto's Forty-eight Highlanders struck up a relationship with D.J. Macdonnell, minister of St Andrew's Presbyterian Church, and in 1892 he became their unofficial padre. That year observers noted that

Hamilton's Thirteenth Regiment had an Anglican priest with it, Rev. G.A. Forneret. Alexander Fraser, *The 48th Highlanders of Toronto*, 44–5.

38 NA, RG 9, Deputy Minister's Correspondence, vol. 383, 14019, written to Deputy Minister, 16 May 1894 and 20 May 1895; also G.O.C. report, 25 May 1895.

39 Thus A.H. Baldwin became the first of many militia "padres": see E.J. Chambers, *The Royal Grenadiers*, 90. See also Chambers, *65*[me], 144.

40 *Militia General Orders*, Ottawa, 1 Oct. 1897.

41 When Lt-Col. D'Orsonnens authorized a stoppage in pay of one dollar from each soldier at St Jean for the local clergyman of his denomination, Ottawa disallowed the order. Colonel Powell emphasized that the permanent force was too small, too religiously diverse, and too dispersed for any form of permanent force chaplaincy. NA, RG 9, Deputy Minister's Correspondence, vol. 382, 13941, Powell to Deputy Minister, 19 Apr. 1895.

42 NA, RG 9, Deputy Minister's Correspondence, vol. 427, 18810, Rev. W. Williamson to Deputy Minister and reply, 2 Oct. 1899.

43 *Militia General Orders*, 211, Ottawa, 14 Oct. 1899.

44 W. Magney, "The Methodist Church and the National Gospel," *United Church of Canada Archives Bulletin* #20 (1968): 46. See also *Methodist Magazine and Review*, Feb. 1900, 190–3, and UCA, Albert Carman Papers, box 8, file 35, Militia and Defence to Carman, 20 Oct. 1899.

45 Fullerton was already known to the local militia for his services to the artillery there: NA, RG 9, Adjutant-General's Correspondence, vol. 307, 85352, D.O.C., M.D. 12, to Ottawa, 23 Oct. 1899; *Presbyterian Witness*, 14, 11 Nov. 1899.

46 NA, RG 9, Records of Active Service, vol. 27, Miscellaneous file, Borden to Chief Staff Officer, 25 Oct. 1899. On YMCA militia work, see Murray Ross, *The YMCA in Canada*, 112–14, 270–1.

47 NA, RG 9, II A 3, vol. 27, Misc. file, G.O.C. to Deputy Minister, 29 Oct. 1899.

48 NA, Otter Papers, vol. 1, file 4, G.O.C. to Deputy Minister, 29 Oct. 1899; see also Supplementary Report, *Canada Sessional Paper 35a*, 1900, 8; and PANS, F. Borden Papers, MG 2, vol. 92, pp. 349, 372, 375, Borden to Fullerton, 26 Oct. 1899. According to Borden's letter to the YMCA, Barrie would go as welfare officer "with the understanding that no responsibility be taken by this Department … after arrival in South Africa, nor can any assurance be held out that he will be able to accompany the troops" on operations. NA, W.D. Otter Papers, vol. 1, file 4, Deputy Minister to Gzowski, 25 Oct. 1899; also RG 9, Deputy Minister's Correspondence, vol. 428, 17855, Borden to G.O.C., 25 Oct. 1899.

49 NA, Otter Papers, vol. 1, file 1, Casimir Gzowski to Otter, 27 Oct. 1899.

50 A.J. Balfour, to *Canadian Churchman*, published 23 Nov. 1899, 715, 25 Jan. 1900. Years later George E. Lloyd wrote Almond, "I wonder if you ever knew that you took the place I was expecting and thought I was appointed to ... The Bishop told me afterwards how that was done or we should have had no chaplain at all." NA, RG 9, Canadian Chaplain Service Records, vol. 4631, G.E. Lloyd file, Lloyd to Almond, 16 Mar. 1917. See also NA, RG 9, II A 3, vol. 27, Miscellaneous file, G.O.C. to Deputy Minister, 1 Nov. 1899; and Royal Canadian Regiment file, G.O.C. to Commander, South Africa, 2 Nov. 1899.

51 See Canada, *House of Commons Debates*, 19, 21 June 1900, 7971; also *Canadian Churchman*, 9, 30 Nov. 1899, 691. On the large Anglican showing among the Royal Canadians, see S.M. Brown, *With the Royal Canadians*, 32; also Russell C. Hubly, *"G" Company, or Everyday Life of the R.C.R.*, 15.

52 *Canadian Churchman*, 15 Feb. 1900.

53 Carman Miller, in his article "A Preliminary Analysis of the Socio-economic Composition of Canada's South African War Contingents," *Histoire Sociale/Social History* (1975): 225, gives the corrected denominational proportions of the R.C.R.:

Denomination	*% of Complement*
RC	15.4
Meth.	13.3
Pres.	20.3
CE	42.5

54 NA, RG 9, Deputy Minister's Correspondence, vol. 431, 18037, Pinault to Sinnett, and to Cox, 11 Jan. 1900; also *Militia General Orders*, 6, Jan. 1900, 5. The YMCA added the noted Ontario athlete Thomas F. Best: NA, RG 9, Adjutant-General's Correspondence, vol. 312, 87465, telegram and letter of 5 Jan. 1900; Ross, *YMCA*, 271.

55 UCA, Carman Papers, boxes 9 and 10, files 31, 37, 38, Carman to Borden, 30 Dec. 1899, and Borden to Carman, 2 Feb. 1900; also various applications to Carman, 1–3 Jan. 1900. Lane took the precaution of applying through his militia commander, capitalizing on his previous experience as chaplain to British forces in Halifax and Bermuda. See also NA, RG 9, Adjutant-General's Correspondence, vol. 312, 87246, Lane to O.C. Ninety-third Militia Regiment, 26 Dec. 1899; and Deputy Minister's Correspondence, vol. 430, 18013, Borden to Lane, 3 Jan. 1900 and reply. His letters home are quoted from by G. Labat, *Le Livre d'or*, 103–6.

56 UCA, Carman Papers, box 10, file 38, Heustis to Carman, 3 Feb. 1900.

57 Ibid., Lane to Carman, 6 Feb. 1900. Lane wrote, "A chaplain not already acquainted with inner circles might have gone to Cape Town only to be told to return by the next boat. I feel satisfied that we have made a very important bit of history, the precedent now established beyond cavil will point the way for all time to come." Ibid., Lane to Carman, 3 Feb. 1900. Having had similar experiences while an imperial chaplain in Bermuda, Lane was satisfied that he had won a great victory for dissenter rights. Local Methodist official S.F. Heustis, however, was disturbed by Lane's insistence upon commissioned rank and privileges as dangerous to his clerical status. Ibid., box 10, file 38, Heustis to Carman, 6 Feb. 1900.

58 *Presbyterian Witness*, 27 Jan., 24 Feb. 1900. The denominational census made Lane's aggressiveness appear a little ridiculous, since less than an eighth of the force was Methodist. Miller establishes the percentages of the denominations represented as:

Denomination	*% of Complement*
RC	9.3
Meth.	14.3
Pres.	20.8
CE	46.7

See "A Preliminary Analysis," 225, and *Presbyterian Witness*, 27 Jan. 1900, 28.

59 Desmond Morton, *The Canadian General*, 166, 174–6; also NA, Otter Papers, vol. 1, file 1, Chief Staff Officer to Otter, 29 Oct., article 14, and G.O.C. Canadian Militia to G.O.C. South Africa, 30 Oct. 1899.

60 NA, RG 9, Deputy Minister's Correspondence, vol. 432, 18173, G.O.C. to Major L.F. Pinault, Militia Deputy Minister, 18 Dec. 1899, and Otter to Pinault, 8, 26 Jan. 1900. As a result the chaplains went unpaid until the early spring of 1900: ibid., Pinault to High Commissioner, 6 Mar. 1900 and reply of 23 Mar., also Records of Active Service, vol. 34, R.C.R. War Diary, 1, 30 Jan. 1900; and vol. 32, Otter to G.O.C., Canadian Militia, 4 May 1900. See also NA, Otter Papers, vol. 1, file 5, Otter to Chief Staff Officer, 25 Jan. and reply, 15 Mar. 1900.

61 Carman Miller, "Chums in Arms," *Histoire Sociale/Social History* (Nov. 1985): 359–73.

62 NA, Otter Papers, vol. 1, file 4, Otter to Molly Otter, 14 June 1900.

63 Almond made a small impression by joining in sports: Brown, *Royal Canadians*, 251; also NA, Otter Papers, Notebooks and Diaries, Otter Diary, 13 Apr. 1900. Among the Catholics, however, O'Leary made a

favourable impression, at least on the French Canadians, with his cheerful and encouraging sermons: Labat, *Le Livre d'or,* 92.

64 Colonel Otter evidently preferred to leave them behind tending sick and stragglers on the route marches across the veldt: NA, RG 9, Records of Active Service, vol. 32, Otter to Canadian G.O.C., 11 May, 28 July 1900; also vol. 34, Commander's Diary, R.C.R., 1 Oct. 1900. Otter found little in his South African experience to alter his conviction that padres were of little military use except for divine service: see W.D. Otter, *Otter's Guide,* 9th ed., 1914, 27, 45, 71.

65 In June Otter disciplined a padre "for being beastly drunk for three days and using the Hospital wines to aid him in keeping up his jamboree. I shall try to induce him to go the Cape and reform, though he wants to do that here with the regiment – it is rather sad." Since Fullerton and O'Leary were not in Springs at the time of the incident, circumstantial evidence points to Almond as the culprit: NA, Otter Papers, vol. 1, file 1, Otter to Molly Otter, 26 June 1900. Compare this with "J.M. Almond," in Morgan, *Canadian Men and Women of the Time,* 20–1.

66 "Too much can not be said of the Catholic chaplain and his work; ... That church must have realized what a grand opportunity was given, and I admire the way in which the opportunity was seized and turned to account. To those who were unbelievers on the field, the work of the chaplain must have been a powerful argument in favour of Catholicism. It is a pity that the Protestant churches were not equally alive to the great opening for the example of true Christian character. How is it that while England and America are resounding with the praise of this Catholic, we hear nothing of the other two chaplains? How is it that every soldier of the R.C.R., be he Catholic or Protestant, bestows honour on him, but dismisses with a shrug of the shoulders the mention of the others? How is it that the Protestant church is loud in praise of the Catholic chaplain, but has no words of commendation for her own?" Hubly, *Everyday Life,* 56.

67 Gaston Labat, *Le Livre d'or,* 128; also 134, 46–60, 52, 62, 128–31.

68 Brown, *Royal Canadians,* 191; also NA, RG 9, Records of Active Service, vol. 32, Otter to G.O.C. Canadian Militia, 23 Feb. 1900. According to the Otter diaries, only O'Leary left Belmont with the battalion, Almond having been ill and Fullerton away. Brown reports, however, that Almond did come along for this part of the journey. He caught up to the regiment again at Bloemfontein. See NA, Otter Papers, Notebooks and Diaries, 12 Feb. 1900.

69 Brown, *Royal Canadians,* 204; Morton, *Canadian General,* 120, 201. At Paardeberg O'Leary's recklessness won favourable mention in Otter's

dispatches: NA, RG 9, Records of Active Service, vol. 32, Otter to G.O.C. Canadian Militia, 26 Feb. and 1 Mar. 1900. Ironically, Otter's reports reached Canada because a chaplain, perhaps Fullerton, paid the cable costs: see Morton, *Canadian General*, 207. In the words of T.G. Marquis: "Then there was that noble self-sacrificing priest, Father O'Leary, who has time and time again in this war proved himself worthy of the Victoria Cross. Than he there was no braver soldier in South Africa. Wherever a wounded man needed succour he was there; where a dying lad needed to be shrived he was to be found. Out of the firing line he could not keep, and his escapes were miraculous. Dangers, privations, hardship affected him but lightly; his only thought was for the men he had come to Africa to sustain and comfort in the hour of danger and sickness, and the only commander he heeded was his duty. He was courting death in the firing line that bloody Sunday in February, but death passed him by; and yet how close it came." T.G. Marquis, *Canada's Sons on Kopje and Veldt*, 241–2; also see William Hart-McHarg, *From Quebec to Pretoria with the Royal Canadian Regiment*, 113–14.

70 NA, RG 9, Records of Active Service, vol. 32, Otter to G.O.C., Canadians, 30 Mar. and 24 Aug. 1900; also Morton, *Canadian General*, 210–12.

71 Morton, *Canadian General*, xviii, xix, 17, 177–8. The association chose Barrie and Best for their evangelistic skill, see Ross, *Y.M.C.A.*, 271–3.

72 Barrie evidently used a letter of introduction from the British commander-in-chief, Lord Roberts, as authorization to accompany the Royal Canadians, in spite of Otter's wishes: see Ross, *Y.M.C.A.*, 272.

73 Hubly, *Everyday Life*, 54–6; also Hart-McHarg, *From Quebec to Pretoria*, 69.

74 E.W.B. Morrison, *With the Guns in South Africa*, 30, 36; also 21, 45, 59, 121; NA, RG 9, Records of Active Service, vol. 32, Reports and Orders of R.C.A., Jan.–Feb. 1900. On the debate caused by this policy within the Army Chaplains' Department, see Smyth, *In This Sign Conquer*, 133–44.

75 When Sinnett was not with the troops, he seems to have been visiting casualties along the line of communications: NA, RG 9, Records of Active Service, vol. 33, War Diary of 2nd C.M.R.s, 29 July, 12–30 Sept. 1900. He was present at some critical moments in the campaign, taking service just before the advance to Johannesburg and officiating at the burials of men such as Lieutenant Chalmers: T.G. Marquis, *Canada's sons*, 440.

76 NA, RG 9, Records of Active Service, vol. 33, "D" and "E" Battery Records, 12–14 Aug. 1900, and J.L. Biggar to Col. Lessard, 17 Aug. 1900. Sinnett and Lane managed to stay with their cavalry units somewhat longer. Sinnett, Lane, and Best also found other ways to endear themselves to the officers by picking up edible items to spice up mess

fare. Morrison, *With the Guns,* 168; and NA, RG 9, Records of Active Service, vol. 33, Diary Brigade Staff, R.C.A., 5 Sept. 1900, and War Diary of the 2nd C.M.R.s, 3 July, 14 Aug., 16 Sept. 1900; also *Canadian Sessional Paper 35a.* See also NA, Albert Hilder Papers, MG 30, E 300, "Memoirs of the Royal Canadian Dragoons, South Africa," 83, 109; and Labat, *Le Livre d'or,* 118, Lt. J.E. Burch letter, 8 May 1900. See also Morrison, *With the Guns,* 29–30, 105, 212–13, 237–8, 300–1.

77 "P.M. O'Leary," in Morgan, *Canadian Men and Women of the Time,* 868; also Carman Miller, "A Preliminary Analysis ... Contingents," 226.

78 J.C. Wells, *The Fighting Bishop,* 70–1. See also W.T. Steven, *In This Sign,* 6.

79 W. Beahen, "A Citizen's Army: The Growth and Development of the Canadian Militia, 1904–1914," PhD, University of Ottawa 1979, 223.

80 Lane reported to Methodist authorities that, after a few days at camp with his regiment, an Anglican chaplain came in "and assumed ecclesiastical preference." He suggested that Canadian Methodists copy their American cousins by creating an army and navy board to back up their chaplains with the weight of the denomination. To him the dispute also demonstrated the need for a rank structure. UCA, Albert Carman Papers, box 11, file 61, Lane to Carman, 3 Dec. 1903.

81 Chaplains who served ten years or less became honorary captains, those with more than ten years' service honorary majors. The privilege of corresponding independently with the recognized head of their own church was modelled on British practice. *Militia General Orders,* 138, Sept., 1903; *King's Regulations and Orders for the Canadian Militia,* 1910, paras. 1058–9, 1366. When with their units outside the camps they could wear their padre's badge on normal clerical dress. Ibid., 231, Nov. 1905; Chambers, *The Queen's Own Rifles of Canada,* 142; Barnard, *The Queen's Own Rifles,* 79–80, 89, 97; and Chambers, *The Royal Grenadiers,* 94–5. The Militia Department also provided separate forms of service for Catholics and Protestants to use at colour consecrations.

82 Of the initial appointees, 15 were from central and western Ontario and 2 from the Maritimes. Only 2 came from French-speaking Quebec. Anglicans were the most numerous at 13, with 4 Presbyterians making up the next largest group. By 1914, of 150 militia chaplaincies, Anglicans led the way with 92, Presbyterians 31, Catholics 19, with 5 Methodists and 2 Baptists bringing up the rear. These proportions correspond closely with the total who served between 1897 and 1914. Of 254 militia chaplains, only 10 were Methodists and 4 Baptists. Of the 23 pre-war Catholic chaplains, all but 2 were of French Canadian lineage. Two regiments did not acquire chaplains until 1910, when both selected Anglicans. The sturdy pagans of the Fifty-third and Fifty-eighth Regiments apparently never acquired padres.

According to the census, Roman Catholicism remained the largest denomination in Canada, followed by the Methodists, Presbyterians, and Anglicans. See *Fifth Census of Canada*, 1913, 2–3.

83 Twenty-seven cavalry units exclusively selected Anglicans. The Methodists supplied three. The absence of French-speaking cavalry chaplains can be explained by the virtual non-existence of French-speaking units. According to Beahen, only one squadron of the Alberta Mounted Rifles was French-speaking: see "A Citizen's Army," 240–2. Older regiments, led by such Protestant traditionalists as the Toronto Denisons, were little more inviting to English-speaking priests. When George Denison was asked by a trooper to be listed by whatever denomination did credit to his squadron, he replied, "Very well, you will go to church with me," and put him down Church of England. "After that a number of the men said that they had been in the habit of attending other churches, but to put them down Church of England": *Soldiering in Canada*, 267–8. Evidently other militia officers adopted the same practice.

84 Fifty-three infantry regiments always employed Anglican chaplains.

85 Over thirty regiments from this area exclusively selected Anglican chaplains before the war.

86 Ross McCormack, "Cloth Caps and Jobs: The Ethnicity of English Immigrants in Canada, 1900–1914," in J.M. Bumsted, ed., *Interpreting Canada's Past*, 2: 183–4. Of the 60–odd units reorganized or founded after 1903, the Anglican church held the chaplaincies of 39. Again, no Catholic priests and only 1 Methodist minister (in the Fourteenth Hussars) secured lasting appointment. Of the 37 units west of Kenora, 22 were "C of E." Again, no Roman Catholic and only 2 Methodist padres (Thirty-second Light Horse and Sixtieth Regiment) were appointed. Among the infantry of the west, however, the Presbyterians made a stronger showing, especially in units such as Winnipeg's Seventy-ninth Highlanders (with Presbyterian author C.W. Gordon as its chaplain); 3 western Cavalry troops exclusively appointed Presbyterian chaplains. See Beahen, "A Citizen's Army," 192–6, 200, and the Militia and Clergy of Canada lists in *The Canadian Almanac and Directory*, 1898–1915.

87 Seventeen regiments, sixteen of them from Quebec, exclusively nominated Catholic priests. Except for the oldest of the French-speaking units, many had no chaplain listed at all until just before war's outbreak.

88 After taking over the Militia ministry, Hughes forbade Quebec regiments to march in religious processions. In 1914, after a storm of protest, he permitted Montreal's Sixty-fifth Regiment (which had been founded as an escort for the bishop of Montreal) to take part in the

Corpus Christi procession without arms: Beahen, "A Citizen's Army," 240–8; and Desmond Morton, "French-Canadians and the Canadian Militia, 1868–1914," *Histoire Sociale/Social History* (Apr. 1969): 45.

89 Only three infantry regiments, one in Ontario and two in Nova Scotia, exclusively employed Methodists. New Brunswick and Nova Scotia also supplied the occasional Baptist.

90 It would be interesting to investigate whether or not the faint opposition to the Boer War that was felt in some Methodist circles still coloured their clergy's view of militia service. See Carman Miller, "English-Canadian Opposition to the South African War," CHR (Dec. 1974): 433–5; and William Magney, "The Methodist Church and the National Gospel," 46. As late as 1910 some districts petitioned the General Conference to denounce the armaments race and endorse the arbitration meetings being held at the Hague: UCA, General Conference Papers, Petition of the Uxbridge District, 1910.

91 See Carman Miller, "A Socio-economic Analysis," *Histoire Sociale/Social History* (1974): 222–3, 226, 229.

92 Information has been accumulated on 76 of the pre-war chaplains. The denominational proportions of the sample correspond closely with the chaplain population, except that information on only the most prominent Catholic, P.M. O'Leary, was accessible. Of 254 militia chaplains, 156 were Anglican, 53 Presbyterian, and 29 Roman Catholic, with 10 Methodists and 4 Baptists. Of the sample, 54 Anglicans, 17 Presbyterians, 3 Methodists, 1 Catholic, and 1 Baptist were discovered. The sample describes only prominent clergymen. Many were of more humble station. Some were recent immigrants, especially the Anglicans, as the Canadian church still recruited many of its clergy from the motherland.

93 Although 19 were born in Britain, only 9 were educated and trained there; 38 were Canadian-born and 52 were educated in Canada.

94 At least 20 were commissioned when over forty-five years of age, and half had been ordained for more than fifteen years at the time they became chaplains. Another explanation for the comparatively high number of older men in the chaplaincy is that the pulpits of traditional "garrison churches" were occupied by more experienced and accomplished men, while more junior clergymen began in smaller curacies and missions.

95 Morgan, *Canadian Men and Women*, 740; Matheson was assisted by Rev. J.O. Murray, his curate, in serving the Ninetieth.

96 On church union, see "W.T. Herridge," in Morgan, *Canadian Men and Women*, 528. The Anglican chaplain to the Ninth Mississauga Horse led the local Anti-treating League and denounced "Bridge-whist as one of the most abominable gambling games in the country." This padre did

not last long. See "L.E. Skey," ibid., 1029. Two other prohibitionist padres were George Lloyd and J.C. Tolmie, a Windsor Presbyterian. See J.C. Hopkins, *Canadian Annual Review* (1914), 452, 640, 726.

97 Perhaps the most active in this respect was James Barclay of Montreal's St Paul's Presbyterian Church, described by G.M. Rose as a member of "the Charles Kingsley school," proving to young men that Christianity, manliness, and social service went together, in battle, society, or on the playing field. See G.M. Rose, *A Cyclopedia of Canadian Biography*, 124; see also "J. Barclay," "W.W. Bolton," "W.T. Herridge," and "G.L. Starr" in Morgan, *Canadian Men and Women*, 58–9, 117, 528, 1055.

98 G.L. Starr, an Anglican, had earned militia certificates in infantry and cavalry and commanded a company of the Forty-first Regiment from 1890 to 1896 before retiring from the active list with the rank of major. After ordination he joined the Fourteenth Regiment as chaplain. See Morgan, "G.L. Starr," in *Canadian Men and Women*, 1055. Chaplains E.H. Capp, Henry Montgomery, and South African padre J.M. Almond were chosen to lead their respective South African Veterans' Associations. Almond was president and co-founder of the Montreal Last Post Association. See Morgan, "E.H. Capp," 198; "H. Montgomery," 816, and "J.M. Almond," 20–1. See also H.F. Wood and John Swettenham, *Silent Witnesses*, 203–4.

99 "A.C. Hill," in Morgan, *Canadian Men and Women*, 534. Almost one-third of the regiments listed in 1914 had the same chaplain for ten years or more. Of these 51, 20 had served at least fifteen years and 6 had been chaplains for eighteen years, serving actively from their 1897 appointment until the call came for the European war.

100 Morgan, "Thurlow Fraser," *Canadian Men and Women*, 420–1. G.M. Grant was chaplain to the Forty-seventh Regiment from 1897 to his death: see Carl Berger, *The Sense of Power*, 25–33. W. Witten (whose chaplain proposals guided Borden in 1897), Anglican chaplain to the Thirty-fifth Simcoe Foresters, was "looking to the organic and organized federation of the Empire – the Empire governed by a parliament, with representatives from every portion of the self-governing colonies." See "W. Witten" in Morgan, 1811. Canon F.G. Scott, chaplain of the Eigth Royal Rifles, openly opposed Reciprocity during the 1911 election. See "F.G. Scott" in Morgan, 1003. Canon A.P. Shatford, of Montreal's Third Victoria Rifles, proclaimed: "Today ... it is Canada for the world, and we think of England as the centre of an Empire which tends to the solidarity of the human race and the universal brotherhood of man." See "A.P. Shatford" in Morgan, 2012; see also "A.E. Welch," 1155.

101 W.H. Aston, *History of the 21st Regiment Essex Fusiliers of Windsor*, 34–5; see also A. Fraser, *The 48th Highlanders of Toronto: Canadian Militia*, 42.

102 R.C. Johnstone of the Ninetieth Winnipeg Rifles, an Anglican, was described in this manner by the regimental historian: see E.J. Chambers, *The 90th Regiment*, 71. See also Fraser, *48th*, 42, 74, 93: and Chambers, *Histoire du 65ᵐᵉ Régiment*, 144.

103 Before 1900 this had led to a number of local confrontations between temperance societies, vendors and militiamen. See Jean-Yves Gravel, *L'Armée du Québec: un Portrait Social*, 85–6.

104 Ross, *Y.M.C.A. in Canada*, 111–14. They had not been as welcome in Quebec camps, where their evangelical Protestantism offended many Catholics: see Gravel, *L'Armée*, 87–8.

105 Henceforth, Hughes decreed, "liquor and beer would be banished from militia camps. The women of Canada would know that their sons would be safe from alcohol's temptation. If Hughes could manage it, the two weeks under canvas with the county regiment would no longer be a boozy *rite de passage* for Canada's rural youth." Desmond Morton, *A Peculiar Kind of Politics*, 16; and Beahen, *Citizens' Army*, 216–22. To the delight of some troopers, at least one militia chaplain publicly opposed Hughes. W.T. Herridge, Presbyterian chaplain to Ottawa's Princess Louise Dragoon Guards, preached at the 1914 camp that prohibition had a negative effect on morals. See H.M. Jackson, *The Princess Louise Dragoon Guards*, 41. See also Ronald G. Haycock, *Sam Hughes*, 145.

106 See General Order #112, 1912, and 1910 *Militia Regulations*, para. 191; see also Haycock, *Sam Hughes*, 138–9.

107 H. Steele, *The Long Ride*, 26. It was also a good opportunity for a commander to get his unit some more drill and ceremonial practice: see Gravel, *L'Armée*, 103. See also Paul Hutchison, *Canada's Black Watch*, 37, 40, 53; John Quigley, *A Century of Rifles*, 18; and J.D. Sinclair, *The Queen's Own Cameron Highlanders of Canada, 25th Anniversary Souvenir*, 14. The parades of the Quebec Catholic units also drew heavily on the ceremonial linking of church and nation, with the officers serving the battalion padre at mass, and the proceeds of the offering went to the charities of the church: see Gravel, *L'Armée*, 103–4.

108 Fraser, *The 48th Highlanders*, 44, 38, 42, 60, 74.

109 Chambers, *65ᵐᵉ*, 130; see also Barnard, *Queen's Own*, 89. For a similar prayer of consecration used at the 1892 dedication of a Toronto regiment's colours, see Fraser, *48th Highlanders*, 46–7.

110 Silver, *The French Canadian Idea of Confederation*, 153–9, 224–34; see also Tom Sinclair-Faulkner, "'God's Flower of Hope': The Religious Matrix of Quebec's *Indépendantisme*," in *Canadian Issues* (1985): 368–72.

111 "Le Chapelain, en quelques mots, nous déclara que nous devions être fiers de cette action et comme chrétiens et comme bons citoyens, une action telle que nos ancêtres avaient accoutumé d'accompli quant,

découvrant des pays nouveaux, ils y plantaient une croix, pour marquer que la barbarie devait être soumise à la foi et la croix", Chambers, *65me*, 104; see also Strange, 462–3; Daoust, *Cent-vingt jours*, 81; and Sinclair-Faulkner, "God"s Flower of Hope," 370–2. In July 1888 the commander of the Quebec Voltigeurs told a reporter that "it has been the militia which has been the guardian of our religion, our language and our laws": Gravel, *L'Armée*, 104.

112 Nathanael Burwash echoed them: see Berger, *Sense of Power*, 230, 249–251. See also Morton, *Canada and War*, 49.

113 J. Farrell, "Michael Francis Fallon," *Canadian Catholic Historical Association Report* (1968): 80–1.

114 UCA, *Minutes of Conferences*, 1896–1901. See also UCA, Methodist Army and Navy Board, box 3, file 52, S.F. Dixon Correspondence, Dixon to Moore, 27 Aug. 1914.

115 After the South African War, however, some militia mobilization plans included chaplains, though no procedure was defined for recruiting and appointing them for expeditionary forces. Lord Dundonald, Militia GOC in 1903, proposed four padres for every division and ten for each army corps, with two for each cavalry brigade. QUA, Dundonald Papers (mic. reel 131), "Final Draft of an Infantry Division," 30–1, 9 Feb. 1903. See also *Canada Sessional Paper* 130 (1905): 13; NA, RG 9, *Militia Council Minutes*, 23 Dec. 1909, para. 1028, and 29 May 1906, paras. 949–51.

116 Ibid., 1905, paras. 1089–90, 1249.

117 R.C. Fetherstonhaugh and G.R. Stevens, *The Royal Canadian Regiment*, 1:192.

118 Robert Borden, *Robert Laird Borden: his Memoirs*, vol. 1, ed. by Henry Borden, 450–1; see also G.W.L. Nicholson, *Canadian Expeditionary Force*, 5–6. Regarding Hughes and the press, see A.F. Duguid, *Official History of the Canadian Forces in the Great War, 1914–1919*, vol. 1, pt 1, 4.

119 F.G. Scott, *Great War*, 15, 17; Nicholson, *C.E.F.*, 17.

120 Wells, *The Fighting Bishop*, 145–6. Harry Frost wrote, "At Victoria College we came to believe that a need and qualifications to meet that need constituted a call. I volunteered." *Christian Guardian*, 11 Nov. 1914, 11.

121 *Canadian Churchman*, 6 Aug. 1914. The chaplains preached on topics as varied as an anagram of Christian virtues drawn from the shoulder-badge initials of the Princess Patricia's Canadian Light Infantry, "the guardian wall of fire" (preached to the Halifax garrison), and "despotism versus constitutionalism." Archdeacon Cody gave his benediction to the Queen's Own Rifles before its draft left Toronto: ibid., 20 Aug.–3 Sept., 1, 15 Oct. 1914, 667.

122 Quoted in John H. Thompson, *The Harvests of War*, 29.

123 *Christian Guardian*, 2 Sept. 1914, 2. See also *Canadian Churchman*, 20 Aug., 3 Sept. 1914; for other public proclamations favouring Canada's participation in the war made by prominent churchmen and religious periodicals, see J.C. Hopkins, *CAR* (1914): 286–9.

124 *Catholic Register*, 13 Aug., 17, 24 Sept. 1914. Borden's leading Catholic Cabinet minister at the time, C.J. Doherty, played a leading role in getting the support of the hierarchy: see Rene Durocher, "Henri Bourassa, les évêques et la guerre," *CHAP* (1971): 248–54.

125 Scott, *Great War*, 17.

126 Strength Proposal Table of 10 Aug. 1914, in Privy Council Records PC2080, reproduced in Duguid, *Official History*, vol. 1, pt 2, 38; also UCA, Methodist Army-Navy Board Papers, box 3, file 48, Hughes to Moore, 11 Aug. 1914. By the end of the month over seventy offers of service had reached church headquarters. Chown reported that there were at least twelve candidates for every proposed Methodist chaplaincy: UCA, Methodist Army-Navy Board Papers, box 3, file 48, Moore to Hughes, 21, 25 Aug. 1914, and box 3, file 5, S.D. Chown to Moore, 31 Aug. 1914.

127 UCA, Army-Navy Board, box 4, file 89, Lane to Moore, 15 Aug. 1914, and box 6, file 146, Moffit to Carman, 20 Aug. 1914.

128 Ibid., box 9, file 232, Bushfield to Moore, 23 Aug., 4 Sept. 1914. Passed over in the selection of chaplains for the early contingents, Bushfield enlisted as a sergeant in an Alberta battalion. He was promoted to a chaplaincy later in the war.

129 *Canadian Churchman*, 10, 17 Sept. and 1 Oct. 1914; see also 8 Oct. 1914, 653.

130 J. McWilliams and R. James Steele, *The Suicide Battalion*, 14–18; Scott, *Great War*, 17. See also Desmond Morton, *A Peculiar Kind of Politics*, 20.

131 Most militia chaplains bade farewell to their men at the armoury: J.A. Currie, *The Red Watch: With the First Canadian Division in Flanders*, 35, 39. Whether or not a militia chaplain went with the draft also depended upon the preferences of his unit commander. George Wells and his old commander were distantly related and on friendly terms: Wells, *Fighting Bishop*, 128. Others, however, were not as welcome. Canon Scott found that his new commander had brought along his own chaplain, and "it was plainly evident that I was not wanted." He eventually found a home in the Fourteenth Battalion. Scott, *Great War*, 19.

132 Some would later transfer to the Chaplain Service: NA, MG 30 E 4, William Beattie Collection, typewritten manuscript history of the Chaplain Service, 1922 (hereafter Beattie, "History"), 14; also RG 9, Chaplain Service Records, vol. 4620, R.B. Day file; also Harry Frost, *Christian Guardian*, 11 Nov. 1914, 11.

133 Militia List, 1914, and General Order 42, 6 Aug. 1914, and Valcartier Camp Order 241, 2 Sept. 1914, and Valcartier Field State of 3 Sept. 1914, in Duguid, *Official History*, Appendices, 29 and 54; also W. Murray, *History of the 2nd Canadian Battalion*, 7.

134 George Ingles, curate of St George's, Toronto, and chaplain of the Queen's Own Rifles, intended to accompany his men to Valcartier but was instructed not to come, as too many clergymen were already in camp. *Canadian Churchman*, 3 Sept. 1914.

135 *Canadian Churchman*, 24 Sept. 1914, 623; *Canada*, 5 Sept. 1914, 330; also Alan Capon, *His Faults Lie Gently: The Incredible Sam Hughes*, 70; and Morton, *A Peculiar Kind of Politics*, 20. Catholic volunteers heard that Hughes had locked horns with the archbishop of Quebec, and blamed it on the minister's Orangeism: C.L. Flick, *'Just What Happened,'* 36.

136 UCA, Methodist Army-Navy Board, box 44, file 48, Moore to Hughes, 14 Sept. and Steacy to Moore, 19 Sept. 1914; also box 3, file 52, S.F. Dixon Correspondence, Dixon letters of 27 Aug., 1 Sept. 1914.

137 Wells, *Fighting Bishop*, 150.

138 At Valcartier denominations chosen could be one of Church of England, Presbyterian, Wesleyan, Baptist or Congregational, Other Protestant, Roman Catholic, or Jewish: see Duguid, *Official History*, Appendices, 59.

139 NA, RG 24 C1, vol. 1811, GAQ 3-9-1, Hughes to War Office, 3 Sept. 1914, H.Q. C.593-2-1, 101; ideas such as these may have prompted the six Salvation Army hopefuls to volunteer "also to assist cooking and other camp duties on active service." See *Canada*, 5 Sept. 1914, 330.

140 Wells, *Fighting Bishop*, 150.

141 Hughes "was especially interesting and terrible to us chaplains, because … no one could find out whether he was going to take us or not. The chaplains were in consequence very polite when inadvertently they found themselves in his august presence. I was clad in a private's uniform … and I was most punctilious in the matter of saluting General Hughes whenever we chanced to meet." Scott, *Great War*, 17, 19–21. Another obstacle some ministers encountered was Hughes's stipulation that married men would not be accepted without their spouse's consent. At least one Methodist minister interested in serving was disqualified on this account: see UCA, Methodist Army/Navy Board papers, box 7, file 174, W.C. Graham letters.

142 *Canadian Churchman*, 8 Oct. 1914, 653, and 15 Oct. 1914, 664. See also *Canadian Baptist*, 19 Nov. 1914.

143 NA, RG 9, Chaplain Service Records, vol. 4642, A. Skerry file, Whitaker to Steacy, 19 Sept. 1914.

144 A.M. Gordon, Presbyterian chaplain to the Fourth Brigade and son of Riel Rebellion chaplain D.M. Gordon, recorded these initial impressions: "The duties of a chaplain, as far as I can learn, are not laid down exactly, but if he keeps his eyes open, he will soon find that, like Aaron Wilbur's acquaintances with London public houses, they are 'intrusive and peculiar.' Preaching on Sundays is one of them, but only one of them. His first business is to identify himself as closely as he can with the life of the troops." QUA, A.M. Gordon Papers, box 2, Diary of Sept.–Oct. 1914, 4–6.

145 Beattie, "History," 14; Wells, *Fighting Bishop*, 150. A.W. Woods attended all unit parades, took part in route marches, and reported success on the rifle range. "Being an expert rifleman I have been able to assist the green shots in some measure." NA, RG 9, Chaplain Service Records, vol. 4642, Skerry file, Woods to Steacy, 19 Sept. 1914.

146 Ibid., Beattie to Steacy, and Almond to Steacy, 19 Sept. 1914.

147 Scott, *Great War*, 17–23; also Duguid, *Official History*, vol. 1, pt 1, 91. The service also was reported in *Canada*, 26 Sept. 1914, 413.

148 NA, RG 24 C1, vol. 1811, GAQ 3-9-1, Militia Order 463, 14 Oct. 1914.

149 Wells, *Fighting Bishop*, 150. On Hughes's penchant for South African veterans, see Haycock, *Sam Hughes*.

150 Pringle, as a well-known missionary in the Yukon, had acted as the Yukon Field Force padre, visiting detachments of soldiers along with the miners. One friend Pringle made in this way was the young Captain H.E. Burstall. see UCA, John Pringle Papers, 71, Pringle to Rev. Mr Cochrane (Presbyterian Home Missions Committee head), 17 Aug. 1898; also A.L. Disher, "The March of the Yukon Field Force," *Beaver* (Fall 1962): 9.

151 Gordon's well-known Conservative politics probably helped. QUA, D.M. Gordon Papers, box 2, 1919 correspondence, A.M. Gordon to D.M. Gordon, 14 Jan. and 4 May 1919.

152 On Steacy and the Cadet Committee, see *Canadian Almanac and Directory for 1915*, 143. See also NA, Chaplain Service Records, vol. 4622, W.H. Emsley file.

153 See the Anglican Church of Canada, Ottawa Diocesan Archives, Bishop John Charles Roper Papers. One, G.L. Ingles, died of meningitis on Salisbury Plain. *Canada*, 24 Oct. 1914, 92, is the earliest source that lists all the First Contingent chaplain appointments. Some Anglican appointments were announced in the *Canadian Churchman*, 10 Sept. 1914, 588.

154 C.F. Winter, *Lieutenant-General the Hon. Sir Sam Hughes*, 144–5. Hughes was probably pleased with the interview, but Canon Scott's account is strongly ironic: "I do not know what the feelings of the others were, but I had an impression that we were rather an awkward squad, neither fish, flesh nor fowl ... From his manner I inferred that he looked upon us as

a kind of auxiliary and quite dispensable sanitary section." Scott, *Great War,* 22, 53.

155 Capon, *His Faults,* 14. On Hughes and his obtuseness on sensitive religious issues, see Haycock, "Sam Hughes," 103–5, and *Canadian Annual Review* (1907): 408, 473–4. Editor A.E. Burke openly asked the obvious: "Is Sam Hughes Sane?" *Catholic Register,* 8 Oct. 1914.

156 *CAR* (1914): 202, 218, 138–45; also *Christian Guardian,* 2 Sept. 1914, 7; *CAR* (1912): 117–19, 285, 293; and (1913): 216–18, 284–5.

157 Haycock, "Sam Hughes," 177–8, 180, 328–9; and also J. English, *The Decline of Politics,* 96–100.

158 Ken Cameron, *History of No. 1 General Hospital, Canadian Expeditionary Force,* 24.

CHAPTER TWO

1 NA, Chaplain Service Records, vol. 4648, D.C.S. England, 1915–19 file, Currie to Steacy, 20 Sept. 1915.

2 Canon Scott, now First Division Senior Chaplain, had at least three of his ten staff in this state of indecision. He convinced them that their true duty lay with the Corps. NA, Chaplain Service Records, vol. 4646, A.W. Woods file, Woods to Steacy, 11 Sept. 1915. NA, Overseas Minister's Records, vol. 24, file 7-4-2, Alderson to Carson, 9 Sept. 1915, and Hughes to Carson, 18 Dec. 1915.

3 NA, Chaplain Service Records, vol. 4648, D.C.S., 1917–18 file, Turner to Almond, 20 Jan. 1917.

4 Gordon spent hours chatting with the men, taking part in all training and even trying out the automatic pistols carried by his fellow officers, while John Pringle entertained informal gatherings with tales of his missionary days on the Klondike. See QUA, Gordon Papers, vol. 2, Diary of Atlantic Crossing, Sept.–Oct. 1914; and *Presbyterian,* 1 June 1916, 521. See A.F. Duguid, *Official History,* vol. 1, pt 1, 106; also, L.W. Moffit, "With the Canadian Troops," *Christian Guardian,* 4 Nov. 1914. Gordon quickly learned to adapt his service to suit the Anglican majority that turned up for service. See also Scott, *Great War,* 26–9; and Harry A. Frost, "Leaves from a Chaplain's Diary," *Christian Guardian,* 11 Nov. 1914, 11–12.

5 Beattie, "History," 15. Beattie, a Presbyterian chaplain, even agreed to hold the bids of his ship's daily sweepstakes on the convoy's progress. See UCA, Gordon Papers, ibid., and F.C. Curry, *From the St. Lawrence to the Yser with the 1st Canadian Brigade,* 39.

6 H.A. Frost, *Christian Guardian,* 12 Jan. 1915, 11–12; Beattie, "History," 18; Duguid, *Official History,* pt 1, 139–40. See also Scott, *Great War,* 30; and *Presbyterian,* 1 June 1916, 521.

7 A.F. Duguid, *Official History*, pt 2, 136; *Presbyterian Witness*, 7 Nov. 1914; *Presbyterian*, 18 Mar. 1915, 289; and *Canadian Baptist*, 5 Nov. 1914, 1 Apr. 1915. See also J.C. Hopkins, *CAR* (1914): 202, 206–7, 471; *CAR* (1915): 187–8, 192; and Fetherstonhaugh, *The 13th Battalion*, 22.

8 Scott, *Great War*, 31. Usually the chaplains reassured relatives at home of the many ways in which they and the soldier's welfare associations were rivalling the canteens in appeal. H.A. Frost, "Notes," *Christian Guardian*, 12 Jan. 1915, 11–12. For examples of padre protest, see William Beattie, *Presbyterian*, 4 Feb. 1915, 120.

9 George C. Nasmith, *On the Fringe of the Great Fight*, 60.

10 For Steacy it was an especially happy Christmas, as he married the daughter of a prominent Australian family. A.M. Gordon stood by as his best man. *Canada*, 2 Jan. 1915, 9.

11 Scott, *Great War*, 32; also *Canada*, 16 Jan. 1915, 2 Jan. 1915, 7–8; also R.C. Fetherstonhaugh, *Royal Montreal Regiment*, 20.

12 Beattie, "History," 38. Rabbi Michael Adler went to Flanders with the Canadians, although he was officially attached to a nearby British casualty clearing station, and for at least the next year he was considered the Jewish chaplain to Canadians. Adler proved too busy to visit on a weekly basis, however, so Jewish troops were usually sent to the nearest synagogue. In England senior chaplains arranged facilities for visits by the Jewish chaplain in London. NA, Chaplain Service Records, vol. 4655, Jewish Troops file, Adler to Steacy, 30 Oct. 1914 and reply; also vol. 4659, DCS file, Routine Orders, 1st Canadian Division, 439, 14 Mar. 1916; also R.C. Fetherstonhaugh, *The Royal Montreal Regiment*, 212. See also Chaplain Service Records, vol. 4646, T.A. Wilson file, Wilson to DCS, 31 Jan. 1916; and vol. 4627. The Salvation Army quickly dispatched its first military chaplain, Robert Penfold, to England. NA, RG 9 III B 1, vol. 392, C-15-1, Canadian Adjutant-General to Alderson, 25 Nov. 1914.

13 *CAR* (1914): 292; also Cameron, *History of #1 General Hospital*, 77, 104, 131; and Goodspeed, *Battle Royal: A History of the Royal Regiment of Canada*, 83; *Canadian Churchman*, 7 Jan. 1915.

14 UCA, Methodist Army/Navy Board, box 8, file 216, T.A. Moore to Rev. D.P. Cameron, 19 Feb. 1915.

15 Scott, *Great War*, 34; also NA, RG 9 III B 1, vol. 392, C-15-1, War Office to Alderson, 2–3 Feb. 1915. NA, RG 9 III B 1, vol. 392, C-15-1, Alderson to A.D.M.S., 22 Dec. 1914. Evidently a divisional allotment of five chaplains existed in the German army throughout the war: see Ellis, *Eye-Deep in Hell*, 155–6.

16 *Canadian Churchman*, 11 Feb. 1915, 93; Beattie, "History," 21; NA, Militia and Defence, Chaplain Service Records, vol. 4651, Establishments

file, Steacy to Hughes, 14 June 1915; and Morton, *A Peculiar Kind of Politics*, 25–6.

17 Beattie, "History," 21; also *Canada*, 6 Feb. 1915, 153. An officer back from the front advised the Canadians that the chaplains really belonged with the field ambulances, "for, from the work, it's very evident, that it is at that point that the chaplains are required, almost more than anywhere else." NA, RG 9 III B 1, vol. 392, C-15-1, Col. Jones to Quartermaster-General, Canadians, 9 Dec. 1914, and Steacy's reply, 12 Dec. 1914.

18 NA, RG 9 III B 1, vol. 392, C-15-1, Alderson to War Office, 6 Jan. 1915; also Beattie, "History," 22; and M.B. Clint, *Our Bit*, 23. NA, Chaplain Service Records, vol. 4626, J.B. Grimshaw file, McGreer to Principal Chaplain, BEF, 3 Mar. 1917; also RG 9 III B 1, vol. 392, C-15-1, 12 Feb. 1915; *Canadian Baptist*, 25 Feb. 1915, 9; 6 May 1915, 9.

19 UCA, Methodist Army/Navy Board Papers, box 2, file 34, Frost to Chown, 21 Jan. 1915; *cf* Frost, "Notes From a Chaplain's Diary," *Christian Guardian*, 19 May 1915, 9–10.

20 NA, RG 9 III B 1, vol. 392, C-15-1, W.T. Workman to Col. MacDonald, War Office, 6 Feb. 1915.

21 For example, see *Canadian Churchman*, 4 Feb. 1915, 73; 6 May 1915, 286; 27 May 1915, 337; and 24 June 1915, 397; *Canadian Baptist*, 1 Apr. 1915, 1. Such behaviour was reflected in the practice of rival denominational papers each claiming that its clergymen were the camp "senior chaplains": *Canadian Baptist*, 10 Dec. 1914, 9; and 17 Dec. 8; and *Canadian Churchman*, 6 May 1915, 281. During the spring the Salvation Army's field secretary lobbied long and hard with militia authorities for his camp workers to receive independent commissions and permission to wear khaki instead of Salvation Army blue. Hughes stipulated, however, that only army representatives officially approved as overseas battalion chaplains had that right. NA, Department of Militia and Defence, Central Headquarters Registry, vol. 1819, file HQ 33-1-231-5.

22 NA, Department of National Defence, Central Headquarters Registry, vol. 4331, M.D. 2 file, 34-2-24-1, Rev. J.R. Maclean Report; and vol. 306, HQ 33-1-233, petition of Toronto Committee of Religious Workers to General Hodgins and Sam Hughes, 13, 21 Apr. 1915. NA, Department of National Defence, Central Headquarters Registry, vol. 4410, files 1 and 2. The Methodists were determined that Williams receive the same rank and seniority as Charles W. Gordon, who had just become a battalion chaplain and major. Williams finished the war a lieutenant-colonel. *Christian Guardian*, 8 July 1915, 434.

23 *CAR* (1915): 347; also Donald Santor, *Canadians at War*, 38; *CAR* (1915): 346–7; Presbyterian Church in Canada, *Acts and Proceedings*,

1915, 18, 30, 59. On the impact of these developments in Canada, especially the west, see John H. Thompson, *The Harvests of War*, 31–8. A similar process of escalation was taking place among the Australian and British churches at the same time: see McKernan, *Australian Churches at War*, 28–39, 63–7; and Marrin, *The Last Crusade*, 119–42.

24 Quoted in Brian Scott, "The *Western Outlook* and *Western Baptist* and Baptist Social Christianity, 1908–1922," in Canadian Society of Church History, *Papers* (1983), 8–9. See also *Canadian Baptist*, 19 Aug. 1915, 1. The pre-war anti-militarism of McMaster University, which boycotted the Canadian Defence League's cadet training, now gave way to the view that "the bearing of arms, the training of cadets, and the raising of an army of Christian soldiers, once considered so abhorrent, were now justified by the enormity overseas." See C.M. Johnston, *McMaster University*, vol. 1, 129–31. On the adoption of crusading by the Baptist Convention of Ontario and Quebec, see S.R. Ramlochan, "The Baptists of Ontario and World War I", student paper (1973), Canadian Baptist Archives, McMaster Divinity School, 6–18.

25 Church of England in Canada, *General Synod of the Church of England in Canada, 7th Session*, 95, 132. The Presbyterian Board of Social Service and Evangelism was more concerned about evangelistic services for soldiers training in Canada than for those already overseas: *Presbyterian*, 25 Mar.. 1915.

26 *Canadian Churchman*, 15 July 1914, 447; and 15 Aug. 1915, 493.

27 CAR (1915): 289, 339–40. The pastoral letter of 23 Sept. 1914 is reproduced in *Catholic Register*, 22 Oct. 1914.

28 On Doherty's crucial role, see Durocher, "Henri Bourassa, les évêques et la guerre de 1914–1918," CHAP (1971): 254–69.

29 Marilyn Barber, "The Ontario Bilingual Schools Issue, 1910–1916," 40, 103–4. See also CAR (1915): 288–9, where both Bruchési and Bégin urged the rural clergy to take its political guidance from the hierarchy and not from lay politicians. Most French Canadians, already convinced that the English hierarchy was "imperialist," resented Fallon, Gauthier, and McNeil on both the language and the conscription issues throughout the war. See Durocher, "Henri Bourassa," 264–9.

30 Mark McGowan, "The De-greening of the Irish," CHAP (1989): 119–22, 139–40.

31 Durocher, "Henri Bourassa," 256, and *Catholic Register*, 25 Mar. 1915. On the Irish-Canadian Catholics, see McGowan, "De-greening," 139–40, and Robin Burns, "The Montreal Irish and the Great War," *Canadian Catholic Historical Studies* 52 (1985): 67–81.

32 Significantly, of 102 Canadian Roman Catholic chaplains employed by the Chaplain Service in the Great War, only 35 bore French Canadian surnames or came from dioceses of French Canada. By contrast,

67 priests bore English, Irish, or Scottish surnames. All chaplains selected for the CCS spoke at least two modern languages, in theory French and English, though some English-speaking priests spoke better German than French, and some French Canadian chaplains spoke very halting English. Not all priests came from the secular clergy. At least twenty-four were drawn from the religious orders: 8 Oblates, 5 Jesuits, 4 Franciscans, 3 Dominicans, 2 Redemptorists, 2 Basilians, 1 Sulpician, and 1 Benedictine. See J.R. O'Gorman, *Soldiers of Christ*, 7–8; also Durocher, "Henri Bourassa" 256.

33 *Catholic Register*, 29 Apr. 1915. See also 13 May 1915, 22 Oct. 1914, 13 Aug. 1914, 3–24 Sept. 1914, 4 Mar. 1915, 17 June 1915.

34 Official confirmation of this was made to the editor of the *Hamilton Times* by the deputy minister of Militia, reporting on total enlistments to 31 March 1915. NA, Department of Militia and Defence, Central Headquarters Registry, vol. 1294, file HQ 593-1-77, Deputy Minister to Hugh Humphrey, 19 June 1916. See *Christian Guardian*, 2, 16 Dec. 1914; also *CAR* (1915): 341–2. The following were the official totals:

Denomination	*Enlistment*
CE	17,187
Meth.	2,539
Pres.	8,704
RC	4,526
Bapt. / Cong.	1,451
Jewish	47
Other	1,613
Total	36,267

Source: A.F. Duguid, *Official History*, vol. 1, appendices, 58. Duguid notes that the incorrect total is in the original government document.

35 Bishop Bidwell (Diocese of Ontario) remarked in July, "I hope that this debt, owed by the nation to the Anglican Church, will not be forgotten." *CAR* (1915): 342–5, for this and similar utterances from Archbishop S.P. Matheson. Compare *Christian Guardian*, 31 Mar. 1915, 2. Chown countered, "The genius of our Church has been to emphasize the paramount importance of spiritual life and to care for the social welfare of the people. This war, coming so suddenly upon us, caught us unprepared to take our full part in the military programme which immediately became imperative. We are not dominated by that cast of thought which comes from State Church traditions and aspirations. In order that we may fully meet our patriotic obligations we must make special efforts to spur into abounding practical activity the fund of

latent loyalty of which we are surely possessed in equal degree with the other Churches of Canada." S.D. Chown, 16 Nov. 1915, quoted in *CAR* (1915): 342.

36 NA, RG 9 III B 1, vol. 392, file C-15-1, Whitaker to Piper and Carson, 12 Feb. 1915; also RG 9, Overseas Minister's Records, vol. 24, files 7-4-2, O.C., Shorncliffe to Carson, 15 Feb. 1915, and Carson to Hughes, 15 Feb.; also Beattie, "History," 31; and Frost, "Notes," in *Christian Guardian*, 19 May 1915, 10.

37 NA, RG 9, Overseas Minister's Records, vol. 24, files 7-4-2, G.O.C., Shorncliffe to Carson, 28 July 1915, and Piper to O.C. Shorncliffe, 29–31 July 1915.

38 NA, RG 9, Overseas Minister's Records, vol. 24, ser. 7-4-4, Bayley to Carson, 14 Aug. 1915; ser. 7-4-2, Carson to MacDougall, 30 July 1915, and Bayley to Carson, 3 Aug. 1915; also *Canadian Churchman*, 22 Apr. 1915, 252–3.

39 Methodists were among the first to complain. Frost described the situation to T.A. Moore. Louis Moffit, the only Canadian Methodist yet to cross the Channel to France, had not been posted to the First Division but instead to a hospital unit in the rear, where he ministered mostly to British casualties. Frost charged Steacy with deliberately putting Moffit out of reach of the Methodist soldiers under fire, especially as several Anglicans, two Presbyterians, three Catholics, and a Baptist already were with the division. Both Moffit and Frost had vainly protested this decision.

40 Frost also accused Steacy of refusing other Methodists a turn in France: UCA, Methodist Church, Army and Navy Board, box 5, file 123, Frost to Moore, 12 May 1915.

41 NA, RG 9, Overseas Minister's Records, vol. 24, files 7-4-7, Hughes to Carson, 5 June 1915.

42 UCA, Methodist Army Navy Board, box 5, file 123, Frost to Moore, 5 July 1915. According to Frost, at the time of his letter Moffit had still been at the hospital and Emsley in England. Shortly after this Emsley, another Presbyterian minister, and a Catholic priest had been "virtually smuggled across" by No. 1 Canadian General Hospital, with Piper's connivance. In June the queries by Carson and Hughes also triggered Moffit's transfer to the First Brigade and Emsley's to the clearing station. See ibid., Frost to Moore, 19 July 1915.

43 UCA, Methodist Army and Navy Board, box 4, file 91, letters of H.E. Thomas, 24 Dec. 1914, 3 Mar. 1915.

44 NA, RG 9, Overseas Minister's Records, vol. 24, files 7-4-2, Steacy to Carson, 12 July 1915 and reply 23 July; also files 7-4-6, Steacy to Hughes, 19 July 1915; and *CAR* (1915): 190–1.

45 Duguid, *Official History*, vol. 1, Appendices, 430; see also *Canadian Churchman*, 26 Aug. 1915, 545; NA, RG 9, Overseas Minister's Records,

vol. 24, file 7-4-2, Carson to Ottawa, 14 Aug. and reply 18 Aug. 1915; Duguid, *Official History*, pt 2, 426; RG 9, Overseas Minister's Records, vol. 24, files 7-4-6, Carson to Alderson, 20 Aug. 1915, and Alderson to Carson, 9 Feb. 1916.

46 NA, Militia and Defence, Overseas Minister's Records, vol. 24, file 7-4-2, Steacy to J.W. Carson, 9 Sept. 1915.

47 Thus Steacy retained the services of effective chaplains such as John Pringle and George Wells: NA, Chaplain Service Records, vol. 4645, Wells file, 4639, Pringle file and 4615, Almond file. However, A.B. Payne was forced to resign his commission: see vol. 4638, Payne file.

48 Apparently, British Anglicans were incensed by Hughes's dispatch of these workers with official chaplains' commissions: *Canadian Churchman*, 14 Oct. 1915, 658. Carson informed Hughes, "We are giving these officers ... every possible encouragement but the British War Office will not recognize them as chaplains. We have pulled every possible string but without results. Do you wish me to take the matter up further?" NA, Overseas Minister's Records, vol. 24, file 7-4-3, Carson to Hughes, 8 Oct. 1915. See also Chaplain Service Records, vol. 4674, D.C.S. London-Steacy file, Hughes to Carson, 8 Oct., and Steacy to Hughes, 22 Oct. 1915.

49 This had been suggested by Hughes's first Salvation Army chaplain, Robert Penfold, as a detour around the War Office; such a policy had been adopted by the Australian and New Zealand Corps. NA, Chaplain Service Records, vol. 4638, Penfold file, Penfold to Steacy, n.d. See also Beattie, "History," 294–5; and NA, Overseas Minister's Records, vol. 24, 7-4-3, Carson to General J.C. MacDougall, 28 Oct. 1915. See also Chaplain Service Records, vol. 4642, A. Steele file, Routine Order 3392, 4 Nov. 1915.

50 Neither Steacy nor Almond, as Anglicans, entirely sympathized with the decision to grant recognition to the sectarian Army. Neither, however, offered their opinion to the minister of Militia. Both remaining Salvationists were retained in England pending a vacancy in France. One served as a chaplain; the other became a combatant officer and was killed in September 1917. Beattie, "History," 295. In 1916 Salvationists, complaining that many of their members overseas had been falsely designated Anglicans, asked to have more chaplains in France. Steacy replied that, until the War Office changed its mind, the Canadians were fortunate to have one at the base. See also NA, Overseas Minister's Records, vol. 24, 7-4-3, Hughes to Carson, 26 Jan. 1916; F. Morris to Carson, 14 July 1916; Steacy to Carson, 1 Aug. and Morris to Hughes, 3 Aug. 1916. See also Chaplain Service Records, vol. 4673, Salvation Army files.

51 In words reminiscent of Egerton Ryerson in 1870, Presbyterian John Pringle reminded the minister that Canada had no privileged state church: NA, Overseas Minister's Records, vol. 24, 7-4-2, Pringle to Hughes, 3 Sept. 1915. On Bayley's contempt for non-Anglicans, see Chaplain Service Records, vol. 4616, Bayley file, Bayley to Steacy, 8, 10, 30 Oct. and 25 Nov. 1915. Carson warned Generals Sam Steele and J.C. MacDougall: "My absolute orders from the Minister were, and still are, that a non-conformist was to be our Senior Chaplain in Shorncliffe ... I do not know why you have held up this appointment, but I assure your that the Minister would be anything but pleased if the matter were to come to his ears." NA, Overseas Minister's Records, vol. 24, 7-4-4, Carson to MacDougall, 12 Oct. 1915, and Carson to Steele, 12 Oct. 1915; and vol. 24, 7-4-4, Carson to Hughes, 10 Nov. 1915 and reply. See also Chaplain Service Records, vol. 4616, Bayley file, Steacy to Col. Reid, Director of Recruiting and Organization, 12 Nov. 1915; also vol. 4618, D.P. Cameron file, Cameron to Steacy, 3 Dec. 1915. The incident revealed the byzantine nature of the Hughes administration. A similar letter by a Presbyterian warned Steacy, as a brother Orangeman ("There are certain persons that would rejoice if we were both found together with a knife through the heart"), to beware the treachery of his assistants. Another argued against Gordon's candidacy because of his widely known Liberal connections. See Chaplain Service Records, vol. 4618, E.H. Burgess file, Burgess to Steacy, 15 Jan. 1916; also vol. 4672, Shorncliffe file 2, T.A. Patterson to Steacy, n.d. (1915); also vol. 4622, D. Guthrie file, Guthrie to Steacy, 14 Jan. 1916.

52 NA, Overseas Minister's Records, vol. 24, 7-4-4, Steele to Carson, 24 Jan. 1916, and Steacy to Carson, 24 Jan. 1916.

53 For a more complete description of the creation of the CEF, see Desmond Morton, *A Peculiar Kind of Politics*, xi, 44–5. Nearly every clerical offer of service made to Militia Headquarters was redirected to the nearest battalion recruiting centre with instructions to approach the commanding officer. If this method created local discontent (especially among Methodists), urgent appeals to Hughes or members of Parliament often resulted in the minister's appointing his own favourite to the coveted chaplaincy. NA, Department of National Defence, Central Headquarters Registry, vol. 4410, file 1, passim.

54 According to Canadian Headquarters, the actual overseas strength by denomination was as follows:

Denomination	*Strength (Overseas)*
CE	45,088
Meth.	7,021
Pres.	22,696
RC	11,835

Denomination	*Strength (Overseas)*
Bapt. / Cong.	3,441
Jewish	122
Other	4,923
Total	95,126

See NA, Department of National Defence, Central Headquarters Registry, vol. 1249, HQ 593-1-77, Record Officer to Military Secretary, Militia and Defence, 29 Oct. 1915.

55 NA, Overseas Minister's Records, vol. 24, file 7-4-5, Steacy to Carson, 9 Sept. 1915; also Chaplain Service Records, vol. 4648, D.C.S., England, 1917 file, Almond to Steacy, 17 Sept. and 27 Nov. 1915.

56 NA, Overseas Minister's Records, vol. 24, 7-4-2, Hughes to Carson, 14, 23 Oct. 1915, Hughes to Carson, 4 Dec. 1915; Steacy to Carson, 28 Jan. 1916.

57 When he took office, Bayley had made the alarming discovery that Shorncliffe, with its thousands of Canadian soldiers awaiting the call to the front, depended on a solitary priest for its Roman Catholic inhabitants. NA, Militia and Defence, III B 1, vol. 600, file C-33-2, Shorncliffe Church Parades file, W.H. Bayley to Canadian Headquarters, 11 Aug. 1915.

58 NA, Militia and Defence, Chaplain Service Records, vol. 4643, A.L. Sylvestre file, Sylvestre to Steacy, 5, 16, 28 July and 25 Oct. 1915. A year later Bishop Fallon's brother, chaplain James Fallon, reminded Steacy that Hughes must be told to recruit English- as well as French-speaking priests for the Irish and Scottish Canadian Catholics overseas. Ibid., vol. 4623, Fallon file, Fallon to Steacy, 2 Sept. 1916.

59 When Steacy consulted CEF officials, he learned that the Fifth Brigade was 42 per cent Roman Catholic, 31 per cent Anglican, and 7 per cent Baptist and Congregationalist. The remainder were supposed to be Presbyterian and Methodist. Of the 1,791 Roman Catholics, about 38 per cent were considered English-speaking. NA, Militia and Defence, III B 1, vol. 1106, file N-2-4, Steacy to D.A.A.G., Pay and Records Office, 3 Sept. and reply 18 Sept. 1915. In November, Beattie reported that the Fifth Brigade was only 29 per cent Anglican, 45 per cent Roman Catholic, and 26 per cent non-conformist. To minister to the brigade, Beattie had available only one Roman Catholic and two Anglican chaplains. NA, Chaplain Service Records, vol. 4616, William Beattie file, Beattie to Steacy, 1 Nov. 1915.

60 *Catholic Register*, 16 Sept. 1915, 4.

61 Ibid., 30 Sept. 1915, 4.

62 NA, Overseas Minister's Records, vol. 24, file 7-4-5, Steacy to Carson, 23 Sept. 1915, and Carson to Steacy, 29 Nov. 1915. Also vol. 24, file 7-4-2, Steacy to Carson, 29 Jan. and reply 16 Feb. 1916.

63 "I would almost think that it would be resented, and I would go further and say properly resented, by the Minister if we undertook to tell him what he should do with his own organization in Canada. The establishments that we want to make up for the Minister are establishments in England and not in Canada, and I think that part of the work had better be left pending,", wrote Hughes's "special representative." NA, Overseas Minister's Records, vol. 24, file 7-4-2, Carson to Reid and Steacy, 17 Mar. 1916. For Steacy's proposal, see NA, Militia and Defence, III B 1, vol. 473, file 0-134-1, 1st Contingent file, Steacy and F.A. Reid to Carson, 16 Mar. 1916.

64 After obtaining clearance from Carson, Steacy advised G.A. Wells of his plan in early 1916: "If it comes to a decision between taking a full-fledged clergyman out of the ranks or sending home to Canada for one, other things being equal, we shall always take the man from the ranks." NA, Chaplain Service Records, vol. 4671, Shorncliffe Camp file, Steacy to Wells, Feb. 1916. See also NA, Overseas Minister's Records, vol. 24, 7-4-2, Steacy to J.W. Carson, 30 Nov. 1915. Steacy only used this method six times, though his successor as DCS employed it more freely, in order to recruit chaplains already familiar with life in the ranks.

65 F.A. Walker, *Catholic Education and Politics in Ontario*, 279. See also McGowan, "The Degreening of the Irish," 137–8.

66 Burke, recently made apostolic prothonotary, was wearing the purple stock: *Catholic Register*, 12 Aug. 1915. See J.C. Hopkins, *CAR* (1915): 207–14, 340; and *Canada*, 25 Sept., 13 Nov. 1915. See also *Canadian Baptist*, 12 Aug. 1915, 8; and NA, RG 9 III C 15, vol. 4618, A.E. Burke file, Confidential Report by Almond to General R.E.W. Turner, 1 May 1917; Carson to Hughes, n.d., and reply 24 Sept. 1915; and Carson to MacDougall, 27–8 Sept. 1915.

67 Ibid., Carson to Hughes, and replies 4, 10 Oct. 1915. See also *Canada*, 15 Nov. 1915, 188. See also NA, RG 9 III C 15, vol. 4618, Burke file, G. Wells to Steacy, 21 Mar. 1916.

68 *CAR* (1915): 340; NA, RG 9 III C 15, vol. 4618, Burke file, *Canada Gazette* clipping, "Canadian Chaplaincy"; Burke to Steacy, 29 Sept. 1915; NA, Overseas Minister's Records, RG 9 III A 1, vol. 24, file 7-4-5, Steacy to Hughes, 23 Sept. 1915 and reply 29 Nov. 1915. See also Steacy to Carson, 29 Jan. and reply 16 Feb. 1916; Chaplain Service Records, vol. 4618, Burke file, Burke to Steacy, 15 Nov. 1915; vol. 4650, Perley Correspondence, Burke to Perley, 1 Dec. 1915. See also vol. 4618, Burke file, Hughes to MacDougall, 2 Dec. 1915, and Carson to Hughes, Dec. 1915.

69 NA, RG 9 III C 15, vol. 4643, A.L. Sylvestre file, Sylvestre to Steacy, 24 Mar. 1915; also Sylvestre to Steacy, 17 Feb., 3 Mar., 12 Apr. 1916.

70 NA, RG 9 III C 15, vol. 4643, Sylvestre file, Sylvestre to Steacy, 7 May 1916; and NA, RG 9 III A 1, vol. 24, 7-4-1, Carson to Steacy, 16 May 1916.

71 *Canadian Churchman*, 15 June 1916, 383.

72 NA, RG 9 III C 15, vol. 4649, Bishop of Antigonish file, Morrison to Borden, 23 Mar. 1916.

73 Ibid., vol. 4674, D.C.S. London–Steacy file, Steacy to Perley, 17 Apr. 1916; Steacy to Morrison, 18 Apr. 1916; and Burke to Steacy, 17 Apr. 1916.

74 Ibid., Burke to Borden, 17 Apr. 1916. *Catholic Register*, 26 May 1916. Burke addressed two further reassuring letters to Bishop Morrison: NA, RG 9 III C 15, vol. 4618, Burke file, Burke to Morrison, 15, 22 June 1916.

75 NA, RG 9 III C 15, vol. 4651, Establishments file, Almond to Steacy, 13 Apr. 1916; RG 9 III A 1, vol. 24, file 7-4-5, Steacy to Carson, 30 May, and Carson to Workman, 30 May 1916.

76 NA, RG 9 III C 15, vol. 4636, O'Gorman file, O'Gorman to Burke, 22 June 1916.

77 Ibid., vol. 4636, O'Gorman file, O'Gorman to Steacy, 26 June 1916.

78 Ibid., vol. 4615, Almond file, Almond to Steacy, 4 Oct. 1916, and reply 6 Oct. 1916.

79 Ibid., vol. 4647, Workman file, Workman to Steacy, 1 July 1916.

80 Ibid., vol. 4618, Burke file, Workman to Morrison, 26 July 1916.

81 Ibid, vol. 4636, O'Gorman file, Catholic Canadian Corps chaplains to Almond, 31 July 1916.

82 Ibid., vol. 4647, Workman file, Workman to Perley, 23 Nov. 1916.

83 Ibid., vol. 4629, A.E. Kemp file, Fallon to Kemp, 22 Dec. 1916.

84 For example, see NA, Chaplain Service Records, vol. 4617, C.H. Buckland file, Buckland to Steacy, n.d. (spring 1916), and vol. 4616, William Beattie file, Beattie to Steacy, 20 Dec. 1916. To the director's chagrin, most of the recalls came for Anglicans whose vestry councils at home seemed unable to function without their priest, or whose temporary replacements proved incapable of keeping a congregation together. See NA, Chaplain Service Records, vol. 4617, C.H. Buckland file, Steacy to Buckland, 29 Aug. 1916; and vol. 4640, C. Reed file, Reed to Steacy, 18 Sept. 1916.

85 The War Office recommended that all Canadian chaplains be made aware that they were expected to serve at least twelve months or the duration of the war. NA, Overseas Minister's Records, vol. 24, file 7-4-2, Steacy to Carson, n.d. (Nov. 1915), and War Office to Carson, 18 Nov. 1915. Several padres voluntarily resigned their parishes in order to carry on unhampered overseas by such home responsibilities. For example, see NA, Chaplain Service Records, vol. 4641, Shatford

file. One unfortunate chaplain, E.B. Hooper, lost his parish when, in spite of Steacy's strong intervention on his behalf, he ignored the Anglican bishop of Fredericton's ultimatum to forget the war and come home. "Many people in Canada run away with the erroneous idea because a chaplain is not serving at the front, he might as well be back with his parish," wrote Steacy. "There is no greater heresy than that ... From my point of view I would have some sense of shame for my church in Canada if such a man as Captain Hooper is proving himself to be, should be obliged to resign his charge." NA, Chaplain Service Records, vol. 4627, E.B. Hooper file, Steacy to Bishop of Fredericton, 19 Sept. 1916.

86 NA, Chaplain Service Records, vol. 4616, J.F. Belford file, Commander, Canadian Railroad Troops, Purfleet, to Steacy, 18 Jan. 1917. For example, see NA, Chaplain Service Records, vol. 4615, Abbott file, Commander, #1 Canadian General Hospital, to Steacy, 7 Feb. 1916. One commander bitterly reminded Steacy that six chaplains had been posted to and then removed from his medical unit in just over six months: NA, Chaplain Service Records, vol. 4634, R.C. MacGillivray file, Commander Canadian Convalescent Hospital, Epsom, to D.C.S., 21 Aug. 1916. See also NA, Chaplain Service Records, vol. 4617, Bradley file.

87 In the meantime, the transplanted padre discovered that battalion officers plainly felt he was occupying a post that belonged to a Canadian, and asked for a transfer back to the British Army. Almond then received an angry letter from the British principal chaplain in France, who demanded that the Canadians take better care of officers loaned them as a courtesy when their own administration failed. This temporarily ended the exchange of chaplain personnel between the two armies. NA, Chaplain Service Records, vol. 4619, H.B. Clarke file, Steacy to British Adjutant-General, Mar. 1916; also vol. 4615, A. Alexander file, Principal Chaplain J. Simms to Almond, 24 Apr. 1916.

88 Steacy was ordered to cut his Presbyterian surplus as quickly as possible, leaving him to complain bitterly about his lack of control over reinforcements. NA, Overseas Minister's Records, vol. 24, 7-4-2, Steacy to Carson, 20 Sept. 1916; also Chaplain Service Records, vol. 4619, J.W. Carson file, Steacy to Carson, 26 Oct. 1916, and memorandum dated 21 Nov. 1916. NA, Chaplain Service Records, vol. 4634, 4635, N.H. MacGillivray files, Steacy to Carson, 13 Sept. 1916; vol. 4632, W.H. May file, May to Steacy, 11 Dec. 1916; vol. 4636, J.A.H. McLean file, McLean to Steacy, 26 Dec. 1916; vol. 4621, George Dix file, Dix to Steacy, 15 Dec. 1916; vol. 4621, A.H. Denoon file, Denoon to Steacy, 15 Dec. 1916.

89 This episode plainly demonstrated the problems Hughes's multiple appointments caused. Three chaplains were Roman Catholic, four

Anglican, and none non-conformist. NA, Department of National Defence, Central Headquarters Registry, vol. 1377, HQ 593-6-1, O.C., Nova Scotian Highland Brigade to D.A.A.G., Aldershot Camp, Nova Scotia, 22 Sept. 1916. See also Overseas Minister's Records, vol. 24, 7-4-11, A.J. Archibald to Hughes, 28 Aug. 1916, and Steacy to Carson, 2 Nov. 1916; also vol. 4631, Lorymer file.

90 NA, Chaplain Service Records, vol. 4671, Shorncliffe file 1, Wells to Steacy, 15 Jan. 1917.

91 Canada's only Unitarian chaplain during the First World War also received his appointment this way (although only half of 1 per cent of the recruits belonged to that church), having been selected for Hughes's "American Legion" recruiting scheme and sent to England with its solitary contributing unit. He found employment in the London command doing work with venereal disease patients until after the war. See Chaplain Service Records, vol. 4617, C.S. Bullock file; vol. 4620, P. Coulthurst file, Coulthurst to Steacy, 29 Aug. 1916; press clipping; and vol. 4633, Mullowney file. Others made their way to Hughes while on tour in Britain: "While not in favour of parsons rambling in, yet Elliott is a good fellow. Therefore please post him." NA, Chaplain Service Records, vol. 4622, Elliott file, Hughes to Carson, 15 Dec. 1915, or Chaplain Service Records, vol. 4628, E.W. Hughes file. On Steacy's favouritism, see NA, Chaplain Service Records, vol. 4617, Burnett file, and UCA, Methodist Army and Navy Board, box 4, file 91, H.E. Thomas to T.A. Moore, 5 Jan. 1916.

92 J.W. Carson's 1915 recommendation to Hughes of one candidate is especially revealing: "I had a visit yesterday from Col. Steacy, our very genial Director of Chaplain Services … and in this connection I would like to say to you that I have a very good friend in the person of the Rev. —, who would give his eye teeth to get over here … A genial Irishman, a red hot Orangeman … He is a man's man in every sense of the word, a genial jovial man who brings sunshine wherever he goes, and you would make no mistake in appointing him a chaplain." NA, Overseas Minister's Records, vol. 24, file 7-4-2, Carson to Hughes, 27 Nov. 1915. The same qualifications commended T.A. Patterson's application to the minister of Militia: NA, Chaplain Service Records, vol. 4638, Patterson file.

93 NA, Chaplain Service Records, vol. 4631, Lizotte file, O.C., Salonika, to War Office, 12 Oct. 1916; Report of Senior Roman Catholic Chaplain, Salonika, Oct. 1916; and vol. 4656, Mediterranean Expeditionary Force file, W.H. Sparks report to Steacy, 10 Aug. 1916. After the war the details of the affair were published by the widow of one of the Catholic physicians at No. 4: see J.J. Mackenzie, *Number 4 Canadian Hospital*, ed. Kathleen Mackenzie, 96–102.

94 The Presbyterians in particular desired that two Hughes appointees proving unable to get along with both the officers and men overseas be sent home. J.G. Shearer informed Steacy that the Presbyterian Board of Military Service was "anxious that for the future no appointments should be made of Presbyterian Chaplains, unless these have been endorsed by the Board." NA, Chaplain Service Records, vol. 4618, Burgess file, Shearer to Steacy, 5 July 1916; and vol. 4638, Patterson file, Patterson to Steacy, June 1916. For examples of Steacy's clinging to chaplains already under discipline at home for pre-war ecclesiastical misdeeds, see NA, Chaplain Service Records, vol. 4623, Florence file, also vol. 4618, Cameron file. In the latter case Steacy finally did suggest to the defaulter that he either go home and answer the charges against him or else transfer to the combatant ranks and clear his name by heroism. See also UCA, Methodist Army and Navy Board, box 8, file 216.

95 Steacy used at least one chaplain who was unfit for active duty as a shuttling replacement for hospital vacancies. Despite the chaplain's bad back, physical weakness, and crippling arthritis, Steacy ruthlessly used him to plug holes in his command during the fall of 1916. See NA, Chaplain Service Records, vol. 4637, T.A. Osbourne file.

96 In at least one case the D.C.S. even ordered a commander who referred to chaplains as a burden, to tear up all correspondence on file in which he had slighted the honour of the Chaplain Service. See NA, Chaplain Service Records, vol. 4623, E.W. Florence file, Steacy to Commander, #1 Canadian Depot, 10 July 1916. This was in marked contrast to the speedy dismissal of one Roman Catholic at the very beginning of his term in office: see NA, Chaplain Service Records, vol. 4615. One of the most glaring drunkenness cases, that of the chaplain to the Forty-first Battalion, has been noted by Desmond Morton: see "The Short, Unhappy Life of the 41st Battalion," *QQ* 81: 74, 78.

97 NA, Chaplain Service Records, vol. 4631, Lester file, Wells to Steacy, 12 May 1916, 8 June 1916, and vol. 4642, Wells to Steacy, Dec. 1916; also vol. 4631, Lizotte file, and vol. 4617, Wells to Steacy, 1 Feb. 1917.

98 The previous appointment of William Beattie, a Presbyterian, to the head of the Second Division chaplains Steacy dismissed as a courtesy, not a right, granted that church. NA, Overseas Minister's Records, vol. 24, file 7-4-9, Steacy to Carson, 4 May 1916; Watson to Steacy, 6 May 1916; Steacy to Carson, 15 May 1916; and vol. 4621, Daniel file, Watson to Steacy, 31 July 1916; also vol. 4641, Ross file. See also NA, Overseas Minister's Records, vol. 24, 7-4-9, Watson to Carson, 17 July; Carson to Steacy, 26 July 1916; see also Chaplain Service Records, vol. 4619, Carson file, Carson to Steacy, 17 July 1916.

99 As Bishop Taylor Smith, the Chaplain General, advised Steacy, "When selecting men for the front I want you to leave the posting of them to

the D.C.G. on the other side, who will consult your Canadian Senior Chaplain to the Forces, Canon Almond. I find from experience that they know best just what they require." NA, Chaplain Service Records, vol. 4652, Establishments file, Taylor Smith to Steacy, 1 Feb. 1916.

100 NA, Chaplain Service Records, vol. 4641, Shatford file, Shatford to Steacy, 11 Oct. 1915, and reply, 12 Oct. The DCS tangled with General Headquarters over the posting of Canada's solitary Anglican bishop overseas, A.U. DePencier. Steacy sent DePencier, then a captain, to a front-line casualty clearing station. Deputy Chaplain General Gwynne, however, believed him more useful posted further back and sent him to a Canadian base hospital unit. Steacy immediately protested: "I am not going to permit a Bishop of the Church in Canada to be crowded into a corner," he warned, "or to be elbowed out of the Canadian zone." Ibid., vol. 4621, A.U. DePencier file, Steacy to Adjutant-General, 1 June 1916.

101 Canadian officers, for example, could not understand why Steacy wanted more padres for training units in England than were currently at the front. NA, Militia and Defence, III B 1, vol. 424, E-197-1, Establishments, Chaplain Services file, D.A.A.G. to Steacy, 26 Feb. 1916. Almond strongly objected to Steacy's tendency to give him men such as this unpromising candidate: "He does not possess the qualities so absolutely essential in a chaplain, the power of grip as a Preacher, and what is really more important, he is not equipped socially for mixing with officers and men. Please keep the standard up. The work calls for strong men, physically, mentally and spiritually. It is all so vitally important ... I fully realize your difficulties, as you have not the choice of men sent over from Canada, and I deeply sympathize with you, but if we are going to win out, there must be choice made somewhere." NA, Chaplain Service Records, vol. 4616, J.A. Beattie file, Almond to Steacy, 10 Mar. 1916.

102 NA, Chaplain Service Records, vol. 4615, Almond file, Steacy to A.W. Currie, 13 Nov. 1915.

103 NA, Chaplain Service Records, vol. 4652, Establishments file, Steacy to War Office, 2 Aug. 1916. NA, Chaplain Service Records, vol. 4652, Establishments file, Almond to Steacy, 21 Jan. 1917. Almond's view was supported by similar advice from Canon Scott and Charles Gordon. Vol. 4651, Establishments file, Gordon and Scott to Steacy, 4 July 1916; also vol. 4664, A.D.C.S. France file, Almond to Steacy, 27 June 1916.

104 NA, Chaplain Service Records, vol. 4664, A.D.C.S. France file, Almond to Steacy, 27 Dec. 1915.

105 Almond angrily warned Steacy: "The responsibility rests somewhere in England and the Chaplains of the Canadian Corps feel the situation keenly. I beg to request that this failure to fill vacancies be thoroughly investigated." NA, Chaplain Service Records, vol. 4651, Establishments

file, Almond to Steacy, 30 May 1916; vol. 4615, Abbott file, Abbott to Steacy, 12 Feb. 1916. See also vol. 4663, Organization file, Almond to Steacy, 8 Oct. 1916. Almond was disgusted by Steacy's meddling, and when the DCS sent an Anglican priest to a French Canadian medical unit operating in France so that the chaplain could finish his doctoral thesis for the University of Paris, he rebelled. Almond ordered the parson to take Corps duty, and when he demurred, ordered him back to England. Steacy was outraged, and the padre appealed to George Perley, but Almond held his ground, forcing Steacy to yield. NA, Chaplain Service Records, vol. 4615, Almond file, Almond to Steacy, 21 Nov. 1916; vol. 4664, A.D.C.S., France file, Almond to Steacy, 14 Jan. 1917; vol. 4615, Almond file, Almond to Steacy, 22 Oct. 1916, 19 Dec. 1916; and vol. 4647, Young file, Almond to Perley, 17 Mar. 1917.

106 NA, Overseas Minister's Records, vol. 24, file 7-4-8, Steacy, E.A. Burke, W.H. Emsley, J.H. MacDonald, and G. Farquhar to Hughes, 3 Aug. 1916.

107 "Where is the delay? ... We are almost blind looking for the promised increase of establishment. When do you propose sending these men over? Before long, I imagine, we shall be thinking of other things than increased establishment, and I am most anxious to have things settled at once," NA, Chaplain Service Records, vol. 4615, Almond file, Almond to Steacy, 19 Jan. 1917; also vol. 4652, Army Council memo, 9 Dec. 1916.

108 NA, Chaplain Service Records, vol. 4664, A.D.C.S., France, Almond to Steacy, 8 Jan. 1917.

109 NA, Chaplain Service Records, vol. 4648, D.C.S. file 6, Adjutant-General to Steacy, 15 Jan. 1917.

110 For examples of previous Methodist attacks on moral conditions overseas, see *Christian Guardian*, 24 Mar. 1915, 29.

111 UCA, Methodist Army and Navy Board, box 3, file 44, General Correspondence re Chaplains, Memo regarding Chaplaincy, Interview with Sir Sam Hughes, 26 Nov. 1915.

112 *Christian Guardian*, 9 Feb. 1916. UCA, Methodist Army and Navy Board, box 1, Minutes, 1, 8 Dec. 1915, 18 Feb. and 8 May 1916. See also Regulations re Combatant Ministers and Probationers, ibid., 15 Dec. 1915.

113 Although a number of chaplains replied that such frequent reports were an unwarranted burden, the first such letters were read to the board in March 1916. UCA, Methodist Army and Navy Board, box 1, Minutes, 10 Mar. 1916.

114 E.E. Graham complained of their interests being left up to the good will "or caprice of our Anglican Director and his so-called Assistant". UCA, Methodist Army and Navy Board, box 4, 82, E.E. Graham to

T.A. Moore, 14 Feb. 1917. W.C. Graham resigned his commission and returning to theological education work in Canada. He told Moore, "I am convinced that our entire department needs a rude shaking up." UCA, Methodist Army and Navy Board, box 7, file 174, Graham to Moore, 12 Jan. 1917. See also ibid., box 5, file 124, John Garbutt to T.A. Moore, 1 Feb. 1917.

115 Chown publicly claimed that Militia and Defence forms with the title "Wesleyan" confused "thousands" of recruits, who were recorded by careless or unscrupulous officers as "Protestant" – that is, in army parlance, Church of England. *Christian Guardian*, 19 Jan. 1916, 2; also UCA, Methodist Army and Navy Board, box 1, Minutes, 10 Jan. and 2 Feb. 1916. "Unfortunately," Moore commented, "too many of the Commanding Officers are of the Episcopalian Church, and until our church took recent action no Chaplain could be appointed without the consent of the Commanding Officer." He privately conceded to fellow Methodists, "The fact that Methodist ministers have not allied themselves closely with the Army during the past years, has militated very much against us. Very few of our ministers were Chaplains to the local regiments before the war broke out, and on account of the clergy of other denominations holding these positions, we found ourselves with a very serious handicap when we came to make appointments." Ibid., Moore to C.W. Watch, 17 Dec. 1915.

116 UCA, Methodist Army and Navy Board, box 1, Minutes, 10 Jan. and 2 Feb., 15 May, and 5 Sept. 1916 meetings. See also UCA, Methodist Army and Navy Board, box 5, Circular letters file, S.D. Chown and T.A. Moore circular letter, 22 Dec. 1915.

117 *Canadian Churchman*, 29 June 1916, 411. The returns, supplied by Militia Headquarters, were as follows:

Denomination	*Men Overseas*	*Total Enlistments*
CE	75,394	124,688
Meth.	18,164	18,418
Pres.	41,029	63,146
RC	26,143	32,836
Bapt. / Cong.	8,519	10,325
Jewish	376	376
Others	6,637	13,155
Total	176,262	263,111

See NA, Department of National Defence, Central Headquarters Registry, vol. 1249, HQ 593-1-77, Headquarters to Bishop of Huron, June 1916. See also *Canadian Churchman*, 6 July 1916, 424, and 31 Aug. 1916.

118 *Canadian Churchman*, 15 June 1916, 383. See also "British Fair Play" to editor, *Canadian Churchman*, 21 Sept. 1916, 609. In Toronto, Colonel Logie complained that he could not stop Ottawa from overriding local unit commanders' nominations and appointing Hughes's own candidates. NA, Department of National Defence, Central Headquarters Registry, vol. 4410, file 2, Military District #2 Chaplains' files, Logie to J.P. Falconer, 24 Mar. 1916.

119 The editor had been informed by Headquarters of the following appointments:

Denomination	*Enlistments Overseas*	*Chaplaincies*
CE	165,145	93
Pres.	70,671	56
RC	51,426	37
Meth.	35,908	30
Bapt. / Cong.	18,458	14
Jewish	851	2
Other	12,469	60
Total	354,928	232

Canadian Churchman, 7 Sept. 1916, 567, and 15 June 1916, 383. Australian Anglicans, too, considered their chaplaincy interests endangered by their government's initial chaplain quotas. Before the war the Australian Defence Department agreed to appoint chaplains in proportion to their denomination's representation in the national census. As in Canada, a few months into the war it was clear that Anglicans were enlisting out of all proportion to other national denominations. Australian churchmen were eventually successful in having their share of the chaplaincies increased. Ultimately, like the CEF, the AIF was almost 50 per cent Church of England. See McKernan, "Clergy in Khaki," 145–6, and *Australian Churches at War*, 40–1.

120 *Canadian Churchman*, 27 Apr. 1916, 264; 21 Sept. 1916, 600; 3 Aug. 1916, 488. By this time, "Spectator" had been made aware that the Presbyterians had chosen the former course. *Canadian Churchman*, 21 Sept. 1916, 609; and 5 Oct. 1916, 632. UCA, Methodist Army and Navy Board, box 1, Minutes, Apr. 1916.

121 The Australian government solved its chaplaincy denominational problems by giving each communion its own chaplains' branch, complete with its own chaplain-general. As each denomination remained autonomous, official denominational bickering over rights, appointments, and prerogatives was kept to a minimum. See McKernan, "Clergy in Khaki," 146–7.

122 Presbyterian Church in Canada, *Acts and Proceedings* (1916), 20, 59, 93, 100–1, 106, 163. The committee included several prominent social reformers, including J.G. Shearer and Murdoch Mackinnon, as well as militia chaplain W.T. Herridge and returned chaplain R.B. Taylor. See *Presbyterian*, 6 July 1916, 7–8. See also NA, Militia and Defence, Chaplain Service Records, vol. 4619, Burgess file, William Beattie to J.G. Shearer, and Shearer to Hughes, 5 July 1916. Over the following months this committee undertook many of the same measures as had the Methodists, ranging from demanding more Presbyterian appointments to requiring its chaplains to take their own census of enlistments. *Acts and Proceedings* (1917), 545.

123 The shortage of chaplains in western training camps and Hughes's neglect of religious ministry for the recuits (he had left for England without making any provision for the summer) especially galled the Presbyterians, who handed on a secret report from E.H. Oliver to the Army and Navy Board. See UCA, Methodist Army and Navy Board Papers, box 1, Minutes, 26 June 1916, 15 Dec. 1916. By then the Army and Navy Board had become alarmed by news that Steacy continued to employ a minister who had been suspended from the ministry by his home conference and that an unnecessary and unemployable surplus of Methodist chaplains was accumulating in England. UCA, Methodist Army and Navy Board, box 1, Minutes, 26 June, 5 Sept. 1916, and 15 Dec. 1916.

124 NA, MG 30, D 20, vol. 2, J.J. O'Gorman Papers, Doherty to O'Gorman, 13 Jan. 1917; also RG 9, III A 1, vol. 104, Roman Catholics file, Borden to Perley, Doherty to Perley, 3, 11, 17 Jan. 1917. See also O'Gorman Papers, vol. 2, Perley to Workman, 23 Jan. 1917.

125 NA, MG 27, II D 12, George Perley Papers, vol. 8, file 244, Borden to Perley "from Doherty," 28 Jan. 1917, and Perley to Borden "for Doherty," 31 Jan. 1917. See also NA, RG 9 III A 1, vol. 104, Roman Catholics file, Perley to Doherty, 27 Jan., and Gauthier to Kemp "for Perley," 1 Feb. 1917; also Morrison to Perley, 12 Feb. 1917.

126 NA, George Perley Papers, vol. 8, file 244, Borden to Perley, 28 Jan. 1917, and Burke to Perley, 2 Feb. 1917; also Perley to Borden, 31 Jan., 1, 3 Feb. 1917. O'Gorman reassured Workman, "Burke's objections to you are amusing, and unintentionally complimentary, for you were baptized a Catholic if not by a Catholic and formally became a Catholic before the age of reason. Burke himself was a pagan for about a week! You are as much a Canadian as the majority of Canadians overseas." NA, RG 9 III C 15, vol. 4643, J.J. O'Gorman file, O'Gorman to Workman, 24 Mar. 1917.

127 NA, RG 9 III C 15, vol. 4636, O'Gorman file, O'Gorman to Workman, 28 Feb. 1917.

128 "Were it not for his political pull, and the deference which is shown to his purple stock (which deference he shamefully abuses)," fumed O'Gorman, "he would have long since been court-martialled, as are all imposters in the Army." NA, Chaplain Service Records, vol. 4636, J.J. O'Gorman to Archbishop Gauthier and Archbishop McNeil, also Bishops Fallon, Ryan, and Morrison and Apostolic Delegate, 11 Sept. 1917. Bishop Ryan of Pembroke, on behalf of the Ontario hierarchy, advised the prime minister, "I think he is deservedly not a *persona grata* to the Catholic Chaplains." NA, Kemp Papers, vol. 118, file 110, Ryan to Borden, 14 Sept. 1917. When he returned to Ottawa, Burke tried to go to Washington and advise the United States Army on its chaplaincy. A warning from O'Gorman and the Ontario hierarchy to Fr Francis O'Hern, the American cleric in charge of recruiting Roman Catholic chaplains, sufficed to keep the erratic Burke at arm's length, though not before more opposition questions in the House of Commons embarrassed the government. NA, Chaplain Service Records, vol. 4636, J.J. O'Gorman file, Workman to O'Gorman, 3 July. See also O'Gorman to Workman, 21 July 1917, and NA, A.E. Kemp Papers, vol. 118, file 10, Chaplain Service, O'Gorman to Kemp, 25 July 1917. British criticisms of Burke, along with O'Gorman's letter and Almond's confidential report, were forwarded to Borden: see Chaplain Service Records, vol. 4636, O'Gorman file. See also House of Commons, *Debates*, 1917, 15 Aug. 4511, and 12 Sept. 1917, 5704; also House of Commons, *Orders for the Day*, 18 Aug., nos. 21 and 18; 20 Aug. 1917, clippings in Kemp Papers, vol. 118, file 10, Chaplains Service. See also Chaplain Service Papers, vol. 4637, P.M. O'Leary file, O'Leary to Workman, 20 Aug. 1917.

129 Almond informed Workman (still at Corps Headquarters), "Be prepared to leave France on short notice. Hand over to McGreer. I'm trying to have you and Beattie recalled before I go over to France. I'm keeping a stiff upper lip and *Turner* is supporting me to the hilt. I'm tired; but once you and Beattie are back here I shall be greatly relieved. I have written the Principal Chaplain re the recall of you and Beattie. NA, Chaplain Service Records, vol. 4647, Workman file, Almond to Workman, 10 Feb. 1917.

130 NA, Perley Papers, vol. 8, file 245, Kemp to Perley, 2 Mar. 1917. See also Perley to Borden, 12 Feb. 1917.

131 "I'm taking over the position of D.C.S. tomorrow," Almond informed Workman; "in the meantime carry on … I'm taking up tomorrow with the Adjutant General the establishment of the A.D.C.S., Deputy A.D.C.S., and Corps Chaplain. I believe they referred the nomination of a Senior Roman Catholic in England to the Roman Catholic authorities in Canada. There is nothing definite; but believe me, you will be

or I shall be back in my old job … I have not enjoyed the past ten days, and the atmosphere was terrible, you can imagine the suspicion, however, I have a clear conscience." NA, Chaplain Service Records, vol. 4647, Workman file, Almond to Workman, 12 Feb. 1917.

132 Though these requests were opposed by Burke and Allied elements overseas, Almond informed Workman: "I'm having a stiff fight, but I am keeping my jaw set – Premier Borden is coming over and I'm to interview him re Senior Roman Catholic. Your church recommends you or F.L. French. Beattie is putting up a hard fight." NA, Chaplain Service Records, vol. 4647, Workman file, Almond to Workman, 19 Feb., 7 Mar. 1917.

CHAPTER THREE

1 NA, Chaplain Service Records, vol. 4621, DePencier files, Almond to DePencier, 16 Dec. 1918.

2 NA, Chaplain Service Records, vol. 4648, DCS files, England, 1915–19, Currie to Almond, 3 May 1919; also Currie to Almond, 8 Nov. 1917 and 18 Oct. 1918.

3 *Canadian Churchman*, 29 Mar. 1917.

4 *Catholic Register*, 8 Feb. 1917, 10. "These appointments will not surprise anyone who is in touch with our Catholic chaplains. Since the beginning of the war the principal handicap our chaplains were under, apart from lack of sufficient numbers, was that there was no Senior Catholic Chaplain in England. All matters relating to Catholic chaplains were in the hands of a Protestant … For some peculiar reason Canadian Catholics have up to the present never had in England the Senior Chaplain to which they were entitled. Father Workman's appointment is then a very necessary and welcome one." *Catholic Register*, 15 Mar. 1917.

5 "You will of course be independent of Almond in all Catholic matters, and will deal officially through Perley with the government," O'Gorman reassured Workman; "Catholic Canada looks to you now. You have the authority; don't be afraid to exercise it. Doherty and me will look to you in all things concerning the chaplains." NA, Chaplain Service Records, vol. 4636, J.J. O'Gorman file, O'Gorman to Workman, 28 Feb. 1917.

6 NA, Chaplain Service Records, vol. 4615, Almond file, Almond report of Apr. 1917.

7 "Whatever qualifications Mr. Steacy had as a clergyman … he was very deficient in administrative capacity and in consequence gave a great deal of unnecessary trouble … The relationship between our office and the H.Q. of the Canadian Corps have been of a most cordial

nature owing to the perfect understanding between Canon Almond and ourselves," wrote Bishop L.W. Gwynne, deputy chaplain-general. See NA, Chaplain Service Records, vol. 4615, Almond file, 25 Apr. 1917. Principal Chaplain J. Simms agreed: "From the arrival of your corps until the removal of Colonel Steacy I never felt that things were in a satisfactory condition ... Since Colonel Almond has been appointed, the outlook is much brighter ... May I say further that I hope Mgr. Burke will not be encouraged to visit France in the future. So far as I know, he has no authority to represent his Church in the manner he professes to do." NA, MG 27 II D 9, Kemp Papers, vol. 118, file 10, Chaplain Service, 1915–18, Simms to Perley, 30 Apr. 1917.

8 "This is irregular, but I can assure you that it will not happen under the present administration. Please allow the question to drop." NA, Chaplain Service Records, vol. 4648, file 5, D.C.S., England, 1917, Almond to D.A.D.W., Canadian Corps, 19 Feb. 1917. In such cases, Workman informed the director, adopting face-saving expedients usually permitted Canadian administrative errors to be corrected, "rather than have to explain matters to the Principal Chaplain, as there are still several of Steacy's muddles worrying him." NA, ibid., Workman to Almond, 3 Mar. 1917; also vol. 4628, H.I. Horsey file, Mar. 1917. Almond's reforms were hampered by his discovery that Steacy had lost or destroyed some essential administrative records. Almond's housekeeping, therefore, included restocking depleted files with duplicates from the records left at Corps. He informed McGreer, "There are not more than a dozen letters on my own file in this office." NA, Chaplain Service Records, vol. 4648, D.C.S., England, 1917 file, McGreer to Almond, 4 Apr. 1917, and reply, 15 Apr. 1917.

9 *Canada*, 28 Apr. 1917, 105. See also NA, Chaplain Service Records, vol. 4618, D.P. Cameron file. On the denominational switch, see NA, Chaplain Service Records, vol. 4617, W. Bromwich file, Bromwich to Steacy, 4 Nov. 1916, and Bromwich to Archbishop of Canterbury, 1 Dec. 1916. Almond only learned of the situation from an Anglican senior chaplain's chance remark: UCA, Methodist Army and Navy Board, vol. 3, Minutes, 9 Apr. 1917. During Methodist leader S.D. Chown's visit to Almond's headquarters in London, arrangements were made to send the defaulting chaplain packing, on "compassionate grounds," back to Canada: NA, Chaplain Service Records, vol. 4617, W. Bromwich file, 25 May 1917. The Board also ordered the chaplain to resign from the Methodist ministry and join the Anglican Church: see UCA, Methodist Army and Navy Board, box 1, Minutes, 15 May 1917.

10 NA, Chaplain Service Records, vol. 4617, Bromwich file, Almond to Adjutant-General, 13 Mar. 1917.

11 Even denominational jibes made in confidential reports would no longer be overlooked, as an Anglican senior chaplain learned when he dismissed the term "Protestant" as an unworthy "German title." See Almond to G.M. Ambrose, 15 Feb. 1917, and reply, NA, Chaplain Service Records, vol. 4669, Bramshott Camp file.

12 Officially, he was reported as burned-out by "arduous service." *Canada*, 10 Mar. 1917, 283; also NA, Chaplain Service Records, J.O. Lizotte file; see also Morton, "The Short, Unhappy Life of the 41st Battalion," *QQ* (81): 74, 78.

13 In one case, involving a Valcartier appointee, Almond pointed out that the padre had suffered from alcohol dependence before the war. See Wells to Almond, 21 Feb. 1917, NA, Chaplain Service Records, vol. 4642, A. Skerry file. Two men with good militia and South African War records he treated more leniently. Both promised not to drink again, were reposted in England, and served with distinction there until demobilization. See Wells to Almond, 25 May 1917, NA, Chaplain Service Records, vol. 4617, E. Biggs file.

14 Thus Almond was enabled to deal intelligently with queries from the adjutant-general concerning chaplains with stained reputations still in England. Almond declared, "I am not going to make England a dumping ground for chaplains ... No chaplain will be permitted to return to England without every detail being reported upon, even if it involves a Court Martial in France." NA, Chaplain Service Records, vol. 4648, D.C.S., London, file 5, Almond to McGreer, 14 Mar. 1917. This included requesting an officer of the Adjutant-General's Branch to investigate one charge against a chaplain: see vol. 4648, D.C.S., London, file 6, Beattie to Major McInnis, 26 Mar. 1917.

15 George Wells, Shorncliffe Camp's senior chaplain, complained in April that he had nine chaplains too many in his command. Two months later, however, he was short seven. NA, Chaplain Service Records, vol. 4671, Shorncliffe Camp file, Wells to Almond, April–June 1917 reports. On average Shorncliffe required over thirty chaplains. Bramshott employed sixteen (four Anglican, four Presbyterian, three Methodist, three Baptists, a Roman Catholic, and a Salvation Army representative). See NA, Chaplain Service Records, vol. 4669, Bramshott file, Ambrose to Almond, 1 May 1917. Larger camps and depots included Salisbury Plain, Shorncliffe, Seaford, Bramshott, Witley, Hastings, Crowborough, Shoreham, Purfleet, Rhyl, Ripon, and Kinmel Park. Smaller concentrations, such as Epson, Borden and Frensham Pond, Sunningdale, and Ashford, also required chaplains during the summer months. See Beattie, "History," 157.

16 Each general hospital required three (Anglican, Catholic, and "nonconformist"); stationary hospitals each required two (Catholic and

Protestant); while ten "special hospitals" each employed at least two. See Beattie, "History," 189. Almond ordered senior chaplains to have all Canadians hospitalized within twelve miles of their headquarters to be visited by chaplains. NA, Chaplain Service Records, vol. 4658, Routine Orders, Director of Chaplain Services, London, 16 Apr. 1917. Eventually, itinerating chaplains were posted to eleven designated areas, centred on major cities with concentrations of hospital units, while over thirty English civilian clerics, mostly Roman Catholic (known as "officiating clergymen"), were asked to oversee the hospitals and smaller camps nearest them. See Beattie, "History," 189–90, 210–11, and Chaplain Service Records, vol. 4675, Card Index, officiating clergymen, list (United Kingdom).

17 Even the troopships needed chaplains, argued the director, as "in this period of submarine warfare the presence of the right chaplain on board ship shall do a great deal for the morale of the troops." NA, Chaplain Service Records, vol. 4648, D.C.S., London, file 6, Almond to Director of Personal Service, O.M.F.C., 1 Mar. 1917.

18 NA, Chaplain Service Records, vol. 4616, William Barton file, Almond to O.C., #3 Canadian General Hospital, 1 Mar. 1917.

19 Almond's establishment for the Canadians contrasts highly with that of the Australians. Although the AIF at its peak employed sixty battalions (twelve more than the Canadians), it did not have as many support or auxiliary units as the CEF. Consequently, the maximum number of Australian padres overseas hovered around one hundred, even at the peak of AIF growth. There was also considerably higher circulation among the Australians owing to the practice of having many chaplains serve for one year, then be rotated home. Thus 414 Australian clergymen served as chaplains (compared to 447 Canadians) overseas, among them 175 Anglicans (42 per cent), 86 Roman Catholics (20.7 per cent), 70 Presbyterians (17 per cent), 54 Methodists (13 per cent), and 27 other Protestants (6.5 per cent). See McKernan, *Australian Churches at War*, 41–2. Despite their dissimilar establishment and manpower policy, the Canadian denominational proportions were surprisingly close: 166 Anglicans (37 per cent), 84 Roman Catholics (19 per cent), 98 Presbyterians (22 per cent), 64 Methodists (14 per cent), 24 Baptists (5 per cent), and 11 (2.5 per cent) other denominations.

20 A small support staff of five clerks was also authorized: see Routine Order 822, by Major-General R.E.W. Turner, Commanding Canadian Forces in the British Isles, 15 Mar. 1917, reproduced in Beattie, "History," 4–6.

21 Somewhat to the chagrin of fellow Methodist chaplains and the alarm of Methodist leader S.D. Chown, who feared that Fallis was too much

under Almond's Anglican influences. NA, Chaplain Service Records, vol. 4648, file 2, DCS, 1918–19, Order of 4 July 1918.

22 These postings were announced in March, See *Canada*, 10 Mar. 1917, 283; on Fallis see NA, Chaplain Service Records, vol. 4623, Fallis file.

23 Fallis was then made responsible for conducting all social service work in England and on the lines of communication. Beattie, "History," 6, quotes OMFC Routine Order 3124, 13 Dec. 1917.

24 Almond predicted that as many as five chaplains per month might be weeded out of the army this way: see NA, Militia and Defence, Overseas Minister's Papers, vol. 75, 10-8-26, Almond to Adjutant-General, 5 Apr. 1917. See also Chaplain Service Records, vol. 4647, D.C.S., file 6, George Perley and Almond to E. Kemp, 23 Apr. 1917; Almond briefing to senior chaplains, 10 Oct. 1917, NA, Chaplain Service Records, vol. 4650, Conferences file.

25 *Canada*, 14 Apr. 1917, 49. Almond designated seven for such disposal on his first gradation list: NA, Chaplain Service Records, vol. 4658, Nominal Rolls file, 4 May 1917. Ten more departed in June: *Canada*, 23 June 1917, 344; 30 June 1917, 371. Denominationally redundant chaplains were also returned. Almond arranged for the most determined to have one month's duty in France or Belgium before their return to Canada. Thus, the recipients of such "Cook's Tours" could say that they had actually seen the trenches. This policy proved unpopular with soldiers and chaplains already at the front and was soon discontinued. NA, Chaplain Service Records, vol. 4618, Bushfield file; vol. 4636, Newcombe file. On "Cook's tours," see also vol. 4616, Belford file. In the following months a handful of misconduct cases led to two outright dismissals of Hughes appointees from the service. NA, Chaplain Service Records, vols. 4615, 4624 (Abbott and Fox). Cases of chaplain inefficiency were dealt with more gently. In one case Almond moved a padre to a smaller camp where he could do less harm. NA, Chaplain Service Records, vol. 4619, Carson file. For the sake of one incompetent's family, Almond posted him to a small hospital where, it was hoped, he could do little harm and where, in fact, he performed adequately for the duration. NA, Chaplain Service Records, vol. 4618, Burgess file, Almond to Adjutant-General, O.M.F.C., 1 Feb. 1919.

26 NA, Chaplain's Service Records, vol. 4615, Almond file, Almond to McGreer, 20 Apr. 1917.

27 "Our chaplains are getting across to the Front much more quickly now than heretofore," E.H. Oliver told his wife. See USA, Oliver Papers, Oliver to Rita Oliver, 20 June 1917. On the seasonal "housecleaning" Almond and McGreer systematically engaged in, see NA, Chaplain

Service Records, vol. 4648, D.C.S., file 5, Almond to McGreer, n.d. (autumn 1917).

28 One, on the strength of his Hughes connection, protested McGreer's posting him to siege artillery. Backed by Almond, McGreer replied, "There is only one way by which a chaplain may remain with the Canadian Corps and that is by carrying out orders without protests!" McGreer to Hughes, 26 May 1917, NA, Chaplain Service Records, vol. 4628, E. Hughes file. In the one open attack upon his administration by a Corps chaplain, in May 1917, Almond and McGreer discovered that the heart of the matter lay in Canon Scott's somewhat disorderly management of the First Division. After appeasing the chaplain, they agreed, however, not to rebuke Scott. McGreer commented, "It is well known to you, as it is to the rest of us ... that Canon Scott is not strong in matters of administration but it is equally well known that as a chaplain he probably accomplishes more for the benefit of the men than the majority of chaplains in the field." McGreer to Almond, 18 June 1917, NA, Chaplain Service Records, vol. 4624, J.E. Gibson file.

29 NA, Chaplain Service Records, vol. 4622, Edmison file.

30 NA, Chaplain Service Records, vol. 4658, Routine Orders, D.C.S. London file, 29 Apr. 1918.

31 For example, H.S. Mullowney's explosion at Almond's posting him to the rear was left to fellow Baptist J.H. MacDonald to deal with. See NA, Chaplain Service Records, vol. 4633, Mullowney file; also see Almond to George Wood, 31 Aug. 1918, NA, Chaplain Service Records, vol. 4646, Wood file. George Kilpatrick had been appointed senior chaplain of the Third Division over Wood's head. Wood grudgingly accepted Almond's explanation.

32 For example, see Almond to G.M. Ambrose, 3 Apr. 1918, NA, Chaplain Service Records, vol. 4615, Ambrose file; also Almond to L.W. Moffit, 12 July 1918, vol. 4632, Moffit file; also vol. 4616, J.A. Beattie file.

33 See E.H. Oliver to Almond, 16 Aug. 1917, and Beattie to General R. Turner, 20 Aug. 1917, NA, Chaplain Service Records, vol. 4670, Hastings file; and Almond to J.J. Callan, 6 May 1917, vol. 4618, Callan file.

34 So did Almond's rapid dismissal of the most flagrant examples of chaplains who were unable to get along with their commanders, as in the case of two Presbyterian chaplains who had made themselves completely unwelcome in this manner. He sent the worst case home, ostensibly because of "arduous service," although his church board was notified of the true situation: see NA, Chaplain Service Records, vol. 4638, Patterson file; NA, Chaplain Service Records, vol. 4619, Compton file; also vol. 4643, Harrison file; vol. 4630, Laws file; vol. 4633, Muncaster file.

35 Captain W.A. White, of the African Baptist church in Truro, had to be taken on strength as a surplus chaplain, for, as J. MacDonald, Almond's Baptist adviser noted, no one knew what effect having a black chaplain overseas might have on the predominantly white Canadian Expeditionary Force. NA, Chaplain Service Records, vol. 4648, D.C.S., London, file 6, MacDonald to Almond, Apr. 1917. Almond explained to Headquarters, "A coloured chaplain can only be of use with coloured troops." Almond to Headquarters, O.M.F.C., 18 Dec. 1918, NA, Chaplain Service Records, vol. 4645, W.A. White file. White reported that he was unable to win acceptance in adjacent units, even though they were without chaplains at the time. Ibid., vol. 4665, Reports, France file, White to McGreer, 20 July 1917.

36 See Almond to Headquarters, O.M.F.C., 11 Jan. 1918, NA, Chaplain Service Records, vol. 4630, L. Laronde file.

37 The proposal was made by Canadian Rabbi H. Abramowitz of Quebec, who argued that the Military Service Act would bring in larger numbers of Jewish troops. Since the British already employed eight and the Australians one Jewish chaplain, it was time for the Canadians to follow suit. Ottawa appointed Abramowitz honourary chaplain to the Quebec and Valcartier troops. NA, Chaplain Service Records, vol. 4665, Jewish Chaplains file, Abramowitz to Mewburn, Jan. 1918, and Almond to Mewburn, 22 Feb. 1918.

38 NA, Chaplain Service Records, vol. 4674, A.D.C.S., RC, London file, 185th Battalion officers to DCS, 26 Apr. 1917 and reply; on the Fifth Brigade's demand, see vols. 4634, 4635, R.C. MacGillivray files, Almond to Bishop of Antigonish, 5 Mar. 1917. The angry Twenty-second Battalion, according to Father French, took some time to cool down. NA, Chaplain Service Records, vol. 4648, D.C.S. file 6, Workman to Adjutant-General, O.M.F.C., 29 Mar. 1917; also vol. 4639, Pirot file, Almond to Rawlinson, 5 Mar. 1917; on the situation in the Twenty-second, see French to Workman, 17 Mar. 1917.

39 When the British assistant principal chaplain in France, Father Rawlinson, discovered a Canadian priest neglecting his duty, Workman deftly arranged for the defaulter's bishop to recall him, sparing the necessity of a court martial and further embarrassment to the service. In another case a transfer back to England and a severe dressing-down brought the careless offender to heel. NA, Chaplain Service Records, vol. 4646, W.T. Workman file, Workman to Almond, 21 Mar. 1917; also vol. 4621, Desjardins file, Principal Chaplain to Almond, 21 Dec. 1916. Even Bishop M.F. Fallon's brother (an ally against Burke) was not spared admonitions for unmilitary behaviour. See NA, Chaplain Service Records, vol. 4623, J.P. Fallon file. Workman took him to task

for transmitting Catholic chaplains' complaints to Bishop Fallon, whose excessive protests to Headquarters alienated senior officers from the Chaplain Service. See Workman to J.P. Fallon, Mar. 1917.

40 NA, Chaplain Service Records, vol. 4628, D.C.S. Reports, file 7, F.L. French to Workman.

41 NA, Chaplain Service Records, vol. 4627, W.H. Hingston file, Hingston to Workman, 2 Feb. 1918.

42 Workman's efficiency continued to smooth Catholic-Protestant relations throughout the remainder of the war. He responded quickly, for instance, to Prince Edward Island priests who feared that Catholic Micmacs and enlisted men from the island were attending evangelistic talks by the YMCA. NA, Overseas Minister's Papers, vol. 75, Rev. J.A. MacDonald to E. Kemp, 1 Feb. 1917; also Workman to Almond, 21 Mar. 1917; Almond to George Perley, same date. See also NA, Chaplain Service Records, file 4622, W.H. Emsley file, Workman press release and letter to D. Jones, editor of the *Pembroke Observer*, July 1918. Rumours that Catholic boys were being encouraged to change denominations prompted sharp warnings to Protestant senior chaplains that such proselytizing was not permitted in the CEF. NA, Chaplain Service Records, vol. 4617, A. Bischlager file, Workman to William Beattie, 21 Mar. 1917. So did complaints that commanding officers refused to provide opportunities for Roman Catholics to participate at mass. Workman was never loath to bring the full weight of regulations to bear on any officer who obstructed Catholic rights. NA, Chaplain Service Records, vol. 4623, J.P. Fallon files, Workman to Fallon, 2 Feb. 1918.

43 Almond's reports to Turner emphasized how chaplains "helped them to spend their furlough in the Metropolis to the best advantage and are at the same time kept out of the way of many insidious temptations to which they might otherwise be liable." See NA, MG 30 E 46, R.E.W. Turner Papers, vol. 4, D.C.S. Monthly Precis Report, Aug. 1917. Chaplains also arranged for London families to open their homes on weekends in order to entertain Canadian officers and men. An information booth at Victoria Station was manned by a chaplain. NA, Chaplain Service Records, vol. 4649, D.C.S. file 18.

44 *Canada*, 5 May 1917, 138; also NA, Chaplain Service Records, vol. 4670, London Area files. Under a "Home Church" program initiated by the Chaplain Service, Headquarters troops were adopted by city congregations. Chaplains also wrote letters to the home churches of soldiers being demobilized, so that the men would receive church assistance when they returned. As the Canadians were the only contingent offering such chaplain services in London, often other colonials, including Newfoundland troops, requested their assistance. See NA,

Turner Papers, vol. 6, file 28, for an extensive collection of London-area senior chaplain reports to Turner between early 1917 and June 1919; also Beattie, "History," 170–5.

45 Initially, J.R. O'Gorman complained, only one priest had been working with the eight railroad troops battalions. NA, Overseas Minister's Records, O'Gorman to Perley, 10, 31 July 1917. Eventually the government permitted one Roman Catholic and two Protestant chaplains to every three thousand railroad troops: ibid., Chaplain Service Records, vol. 4670, Purfleet file, McGreer and Almond letters, Aug.–Oct. 1917, and Beattie, "History," 141. Canadian Forestry Corps troops in France, for example, took on three chaplains during 1917, but an additional twelve were on duty by the end of hostilities. See C.W. Bird and J.B. Davies, *Canadian Forestry Corps*, 39. By the summer Almond reported sixty-two chaplains on the lines of communication, while seventy-one were posted to the Corps: NA, Chaplain Service Records, vol. 4648, D.C.S. file 8, Almond to Turner, 27 Aug. 1917.

46 Not that the British gave up control easily – in fact, Almond had already received a snooty blast from his erstwhile ally, the principal chaplain, for allowing a Canadian Anglican bishop to meet with non-Anglican Canadians at the base without his permission. See NA, Chaplain Service Records, vol. 4648, D.C.S. file 4, McGreer to Almond, 13 Aug. 1917; Headquarters, O.M.F.C. Routine Order 3124, 13 Dec. 1917, in Beattie, "History," 6. William Beattie was dispatched to the continent as the new A.D.C.S., succeeded by George Fallis in the spring of 1918. NA, Chaplain Service Records, vol. 4649, D.C.S. files 1 and 4, Beattie, Fallis, and Almond correspondence. John O'Gorman became Fallis's Roman Catholic deputy at the new Canadian Section of GHQ in early 1918. Beattie, "History," 137–8. In June, Headquarters gave the Forestry Corps a senior chaplain, W.F. McConnell, a Presbyterian, who reported to Fallis on the extensive and scattered religious work to Canadians in the forested areas of France. NA, Chaplain Service Records, vol. 4635, McConnell file. See also Desmond Morton, *A Peculiar Kind of Politics*, 161.

47 In all, sixty such appointments were made during the war, fifty-four under Almond. Almost half of the chaplains appointed in this way came from the medical corps, the rest from combatant or auxiliary ranks. Half were Anglicans, the remainder equally divided between Methodists and Presbyterians, with two Baptists and a Congregationalist also receiving commissions. For example, see NA, Chaplain Service Records, vol. 4634, J.H. MacDonald file, MacDonald to Canadian applicant, 30 Oct. 1917. Only a dozen such promotions were made after May 1918, mostly during the last weeks of the war, when chaplain losses demanded replacement from the pool of clergymen already overseas. In other

cases of urgent need Almond and Workman recruited stray chaplains from other imperial contingents even remotely connected with or interested in Canada, including the Australians. Father H.S. Laws thus was recruited by Workman in March 1918, when Bishop Fallon could not provide an English-speaking priest from Canada. See NA, Chaplain Service Records, vol. 4630, Laws file.

48 Almond and other prominent chaplains, such as Charles Gordon, Canon Scott, and John Pringle, aired such sentiments in the Canadian press for months. For a private correspondence example, see NA, Chaplain Service Records, vol. 4625, W.C. Graham file, Nov. 1917.

49 Desmond Morton, "Polling the Soldier Vote," *JCS*, (Nov. 1975): 39–58. See also Morton, *Peculiar Kind of Politics*, 141 n 62.

50 NA, Chaplain Service Records, vol. 4672, Witley Camp file, A.J. Cameron to D.C.S., 4 Dec. 1917; also Wells to Almond, 6 Dec. 1917. On Brigadier General Thacker's ban on electioneering, see vol. 4648, D.C.S. file 8, Thacker circular letter, 3 Dec. 1917.

51 NA, Chaplain Service Records, vol. 4648, D.C.S. file 4, McGreer to Almond, 8 Dec. 1917; also vol. 4665, Reports, Senior Chaplains, England, Sr Chaplain, London Area, Dec. 1917. One hospital chaplain in England reported, "I did not hesitate to use my opportunities of placing before the men, the vital issues so plainly involved in the election in which they had the privilege and duty of voting. As a loyal Canadian I could not do otherwise, and many a lad thanked me for having made so clear the issues ... The result of the elections is known, and here it was received with every demonstration of joy." NA, Chaplain Service Records, vol. 4669, Hospitals, E.B. Hooper report of Dec. 1917. On the chaplains' campaigning for Union government at Corps, see Dr J. Hayes to A. McCurdy, 18 Dec. 1917, quoted in Morton, *Peculiar Kind of Politics*, 143 n 71.

52 For examples of Methodist attacks on the wet canteen and rum ration, see *Christian Guardian*, 24 Mar. 1915, 29, and 22 Sept. 1917, 9–10; and UCA, Methodist Army and Navy Board, box 1, Minutes, 8 Dec. 1915 and 21 Nov. 1917.

53 *Canadian Churchman*, 21 Dec. 1916, 819. See anonymous Presbyterian chaplain, Shorncliffe Camp, to Presbyterian Moderator, 29 Dec. 1916, copy in UCA, Methodist Army and Navy Board, box 3, file 64. The Methodist chaplain to the new Canadian VD hospital in Etchinghill, R.A. Scarlett, cited medical officers to the effect that over seven thousand Canadian men had been infected, that syphilis treatment methods (developed more to return men to action than to eradicate the disease completely) were imperfect, and that significant numbers of men would suffer relapses after demobilization. He predicted a postwar population of about twenty thousand ex-sufferers potentially

capable of infecting their families in future. Scarlett to T.A. Moore, 28 Jan. 1917, in UCA, Methodist Army and Navy Board, box 7, file 198, Scarlett file, and box 3, file 64.

54 Hopkins, *Canada at War,* 119; see also Report of the Board of Military Service, Presbyterian Church in Canada, *Acts and Proceedings* (1917), 546; UCA, Methodist Army and Navy Board, box 1, Minutes, 18–19 Mar. 1917; Andrew Baird and J.G. Shearer to Lloyd George, 19 Jan. 1917, copy in UCA, Methodist Army and Navy Board, box 3, file 64, Conditions in England file. "Spectator" called on the House of Bishops to verify twith chaplains the hair-raising stories that were filtering back to Canada; *Canadian Churchman,* 25 Jan. 1917, 52. Women's groups discussed withdrawing their support for recruiting. On similar responses by the Australian churches to overseas reports, see McKernan, *Australian Churches at War,* 68–71.

55 Chown told the Social Service Council of Canada, "the Canadian troops Overseas show absolutely no sign of deterioration." Hopkins, *Canada at War,* 120; see also Hopkins, *CAR* (1917): 512–13. Almond and Fallis prudently secured permission for Chown to wear military uniform: UCA, S.D. Chown Papers, box 10, file 1218, Chown to T.A. Moore, 23 June 1917. See also NA, Chaplain Service Records, vol. 4619, Chown file, and UCA, Methodist Army and Navy Board, box 2, file 41. A copy of his report was dispatched to George Perley: see NA, Militia and Defence, Overseas Minister's Papers, vol. 75, Chown to Perley, 2 Aug. 1917. See also W.B. Caswell, in *Christian Guardian,* 24 Oct. 1917.

56 *Catholic Register,* 22 Aug. 19 Sept. 1918. Others included the moderator of the Canadian Presbyterian church and the Anglican bishop of Fredericton. See William Beattie, "History," 282–3, NA, Chaplain Service Records, vol. 4674, J.A. Richardson file; see also Richardson's address to synod on his return, *Canadian Churchman,* 28 Apr. 1918. Another official hosted by the Chaplain Service during the summer of 1918 was Canon H.J. Cody, an Anglican priest who was Ontario minister of Education: see Chaplain Service Records, vol. 4619, Cody file.

57 *Montreal Gazette,* 6 June 1918, 6. Government officials supported wide publication of Almond's January report (which featured Chaplain Service work in VD hospitals) to "offset the wide-spread slanders regarding the moral conditions under which our soldiers overseas live." General W. Gwatkin noted, "Elsewhere I have pointed out that under the guise of religion, humanity and social betterment, much mischief is being done; and the best, perhaps the only way to undo it is through the agency of counter propaganda." See Hamilton to Nichols, 25 May 1918; also Gwatkin and Minister of Militia's endorsement on the margin, NA, Department of National Defence, Central Headquarters Registry,

vol. 2547, HQ-2069-G, vol. 1. Australian chaplain reports were also used to reassure home folk: see McKernan, "Clergy in Khaki," 150–4.

58 Fallon, on his return to Canada, publicly praised Almond and McGreer for their fairness and consideration extended to Catholic chaplains. Both bishops, according to Beattie, "expressed themselves delighted with the zeal and success of the chaplains, and with the fair and harmonious manner in which the Chaplain Service was conducted." Beattie, "History," 283; also *Catholic Register,* 19 Sept. 1918.

59 NA, Chaplain Service Records, vol. 4641, A.E. Runnells file, Almond to Runnells, 20 Feb. 1919; see also Beattie, "History," 286. See also NA, MG 30, R.E.W. Turner Papers, vol. 4, D.C.S. Reports of Jan., Feb., and Sept. 1918; Chaplain's Service Records, vol. 4623, Bishop Fallon file; Beattie, "History," 280–2. As the war drew to a close, A.S. Grant, representing the new Federal War Service Commission of the Canadian churches, T.A. Moore, and S.D. Chown toured Europe to learn of military and Chaplain Service demobilization plans.

60 Beattie, "History," 207. See *Canadian Churchman,* 4 Oct., 27 Dec. 1917. Fallis raised $50,000 during his tour. NA, Chaplain Service Records, vol. 4623, Fallis file, and vol. 4673, Social Services file 10, Anglican Bishop of Ontario circular letter, Fallis circular letter, Sept. 1917. See also *Christian Guardian,* 2 Jan. 1918 and 1 May 1918, and *Presbyterian Witness,* 20 Dec. 1917, 584. On Mackinnon, see NA, Chaplain Service Records, vol. 4634, Mackinnon file; also *Christian Guardian,* 19 June 1918, 15. In an Ottawa meeting between government and church heads, Fallis lobbied for talks on creating such a Canadian branch. On Fallis's tour, see his Sept. 1918 report to Almond, NA, Chaplain Service Records, vol. 4674, Major G.O. Fallis file. Fallis claimed to have given nearly fifty addresses to about fifty thousand people during his seven weeks in Canada: see NA, Turner Papers, D.C.S. Report, Nov. 1917.

61 UCA, Methodist Army and Navy Board Papers, box 1, Minutes, 18 Feb. 1918. Almond seems first to have broached the subject with overseas authorities in July 1917: see NA, Militia and Defence, Overseas Minister's Papers, vol. 75, file 10-8-26, Almond to Turner, 24 July 1917. For Ottawa's initial rebuffs, see *Canadian Churchman,* 29 Mar., 26 Apr. 1917, and 2, 23 Aug., 4 Oct. 1917. See also vol. 4636, J. O'Gorman file, O'Gorman to the Archbishops and Bishops of Ontario, 4 Oct. 1917, and vol. 4623, Bishop Fallon file, Fallon to Workman, 17 Nov. 1917. NA, Militia and Defence, Overseas Minister's Papers, vol. 75, file 10-8-26, Almond to Kemp, 18 Feb. 1918; Kemp to Mewburn, 23 Feb. 1918, and Mewburn to Kemp, 20 Mar. 1918; Chaplain Service Records, vol. 4615, Almond file, Almond to Turner, 2 Apr. 1918; *Canadian Churchman,* 23 May 1918. See also Almond and Mewburn to

Kemp, 4 May 1918; Kemp, R. Turner, and Adjutant-General Thacker to Mewburn, 15 May; Mewburn to Kemp, 29 May 1918; and *Canada*, 8 June 1918, 284. See also *Canadian Churchman*, 13 June 1918; "Spectator", in ibid., 29 Aug. 1918.

62 NA, Chaplain Service Records, vol. 4636, J. O'Gorman file, O'Gorman to Workman, 30 July 1917.

63 Beattie, "History," 314.

64 Of this number Beattie employed, sixty-six served overseas before demobilization: Beattie, "History," 7–8, 310–11. See also NA, Chaplain Service Records, vol. 4652, Establishments file, Clerk of Privy Council, 17 June 1918; *Catholic Register*, 19 Sept. 1918. Of those first appointed, nineteen were Anglican, ten Roman Catholic, twelve Methodist, eight Presbyterian, two Congregationalist and one Baptist. NA, Militia and Defence, Canadian Headquarters, Ottawa, Routine Order 1040, 9 Sept. 1918.

65 Beattie, "History," 313.

66 Beattie, "History," 209–10. See also NA, Chaplain Service Records, vol. 4622, Bishop Emard file.

67 Quoted in R.J. Ogle, *The Faculties of Canadian Military Chaplains*, 12 n 38.

68 Where such appointments had been matters of patronage, such as at the St Jean, Quebec, garrison and on the west coast, Beattie became the target of very intense priestly wrath and some political pressure. He held his ground. See NA, Chaplain Service Records, vol. 4632, A.H. Moore file; vol. 4649, D.C.S. Ottawa file 7, Nov. 1918–Feb. 1919.

69 Such as in the Maritimes, especially in Halifax, where he gave appointments to both the Catholic and Anglican "honorary chaplains" appointed in 1915. Ibid., vol. 4657, Military District 6 file, Beattie to G.O.C., M.D. 6, 29 July 1918. Beattie did provide free rations and transport for the unpaid volunteers: see NA, Chaplain Service Records, vol. 4663, Officiating Clergy file, Beattie to Adjutant-General, 14 Aug. 1918. See also Beattie, "History," 312.

70 A few over-age clerics and chaplains were employed in more sedentary postings in Canada: see, for example, NA, Chaplain Service Records, vol. 4624, Fraser file, A.S. Grant to Beattie, 24 Aug. 1918 and reply; also vol. 4637, Owen file.

71 Beattie, "History," 308–10. For a brief description of Beattie's early work, see Canada, House of Commons, *European War, Memorandum #5, The Work of the Department of Militia and Defence, from 1 January 1918 to 31 October 1918*, 42–5.

72 *Presbyterian and Westminster*, 3 Oct., 21 Nov., and 12 Dec. 1918 issues. See also *Canadian Churchman*, 2, 23 Aug. 1917. Almond had often been vexed by the lack of co-ordinated Anglican direction, especially

in personnel matters. At one point he complained to the bishop of Ontario: "Year after year has gone by with scarce a word from the Church at home, except to make application for the recall of a chaplain who was doing particularly good work. It is not surprising that there may have crept into our minds an occasional question as to whether Canadian churchmen really appreciated the magnitude and importance of the great moral and social problems we are endeavouring to solve." Almond to Bishop of Ontario, 15 Mar. 1918, NA, Chaplain Service Records, vol. 4649, Bishop of Ontario file.

73 Although Bishop Roper, Almond, and DePencier were made honorary members, the Anglican committee gave little thought to chaplaincy, only demobilization and reconstruction. Minutes of the War Service Commission of the Church of England in Canada, 25 Oct. 1918, in Anglican Church of Canada, General Synod Archives (GSA), Council for Social Services, box 8, War Service Commission Reports, 1918–20, A.S. Grant to G.L. Starr, 27 Sept. 1918. The commission agreed to approach the Catholic church in the local ecclesiastical province with a view to securing their co-operation, but no reply was made before the commission disbanded. UCA, Methodist Army and Navy Board, box 1, file 4, Minutes, 22 Nov. 1918, and Minutes of the Organization of the Federal War Service Commission of the Churches in Canada, 21 Nov. 1918.

74 Almond told the Methodist board: "It was thought that these men who had signed up and went over the parapet would make better chaplains ... but they do not measure up to the Chaplains appointed direct. The ideal Chaplain must be a man who can get hold of the officers first. It works from up down. You get the officer, you get his men. You must have a man who can go into the officers' mess, be a man and talk to them. His whole attitude is such that they are glad to have him there, and they will follow him." UCA, Methodist Army and Navy Board, box 1, Minutes, 30 Apr. 1918.

75 "This in ten years' time will probably bring about, if not absolute Church Union, a spirit of Christianity that will measure up to the spirit of the Master," 30 Apr. 1918, UCA, Army and Navy Board, box 1, Minutes.

76 On YMCA establishments in the Corps, see Bishop, *The Canadian Y.M.C.A.*, 66–7, 100, 179. By war's end the Chaplain Service had employed 447 clergymen overseas. In comparison, the Y had employed 407 association secretaries and overseas officers. See Bishop, 397–409; and Beattie, "History," 197–8.

77 In fact some Y workers felt that critics and rival agencies too often tried to cash in on activities that the Y undertook at its own expense. See Ross, *The Y.M.C.A. in Canada*, 286–7; Bishop, 180–1. See NA, Chaplain Service Records, vols. 4646, Wilson file, Nov. 1915; 4616,

Ben-Oliel file, Jan. 1918; and 4627, Hooper file, Nov. 1917, for chaplain complaints about YMCA attempts to monopolize recreational work. Between October 1916 and March 1919 Baptists John MacNeil and W.A. Cameron, Anglicans H.P. Abbot and L.E. Skey, Presbyterian George C. Pidgeon, and Methodist J.E. Hughson successively led crusades throughout the Canadian YMCA network overseas. C.W. Bishop, *Canadian Y.M.C.A.*, 110–12, 136, 170–2.

78 Bishop, *The Canadian Y.M.C.A.*, 111–12, 133. During 1918 chaplains still resented the affluent and aggressive Y's encroachments on work in their territory. NA, Chaplain Service Records, vol. 4635, J.W. MacDonald file, Jan. 1918. As a rule, work in English camps and hospitals, as well as in the London area, proceeded without friction for the duration of the war. See NA, Chaplain Service Records, vol. 4673, Y.M.C.A. file, Almond memo, 28 January 1918; Senior Chaplain, London Area, to Almond, May 1918–Febr. 1919 reports. The one exception was in Liverpool, at No. 5 Canadian General Hospital, where the senior chaplain, an Anglican, refused to permit any joint work. NA, Chaplain Service Records, vol. 4669, Chaplain Reports, Hospitals, H. Ben-Oliel to Beattie, 22 June 1918.

79 For example, see *Canadian Churchman*, 4 May 1916, 2, and Bishop, The *Canadian Y.M.C.A.*, 260. By then, including workers and staff in England, the Y overseas amounted to 140 officers and 745 other ranks.

80 NA, Chaplain Service Records, vol. 4624, Fraser file, Fraser to William Beattie, A.D.C.S., 10 Aug. 1917. A few months later, in response to former chaplain Albert Carlisle's query, Almond wrote, "I share in some degrees your view of the Y.M.C.A. They have undoubtedly done good work but have made it appear in Canada that they are the whole cheese." Ibid., vol. 4619, Carlisle file, Almond to Carlisle, 17 Nov. 1917. George Fallis confirmed these reports during his Canadian tour. NA, Chaplain Service Records, vol. 4673, Social Services file, Fallis to Almond, 7 Sept. 1917. Almond complained to McGreer, "The Y.M.C.A. because of their extensive advertising have caught the imagination of the Canadian people and seem to have put it all over us." Ibid., vol. 4648, D.C.S., file 4, Almond to McGreer, 9 Nov. 1917.

81 Corps authorities subsequently informed the association that future religious work had to be sanctioned by A.D.C.S. McGreer. NA, Chaplain Service Records, vol. 4673, Y.M.C.A. file, D.A.A.G., Corps to Y.M.C.A., Corps, 14 Sept. 1917.

82 NA, Chaplain Service Records, vol. 4673, Y.M.C.A. file, D.A.A.G., Corps to Y.M.C.A. office, Corps; also McGreer to Almond, 25 Sept. 1917. Almond subsequently reminded the association's overseas head, Gerald Birks, that the Chaplain Service ought to supply or at least approve the clergymen brought over for special services and that both

McGreer and the divisional senior chaplains had to be consulted before any religious program could be undertaken at the Corps. NA, MG 30, R.E.W. Turner Papers, vol. 9, file 60: Y.M.C.A. and Chaplains, Almond to Birks, 2 Oct. 1917.

83 NA, Chaplain Service Records, vol. 4673, Y.M.C.A. file, McGreer to Almond, 26 Apr. 1918. Evidently, the minimum McGreer desired was the D.C.S. sitting on the overseas Y Council, supervising all religious and social work. He believed that church officials originally should have demanded that the Y co-operate with the service, since most of its funds originated with the church folk of Canada. The money being spent by the Y should be controlled by the denominational representatives, "who have been appointed to look after the religious work of the Expeditionary Force." NA, Chaplain Service Records, vol. 4648, D.C.S. file 4, McGreer to Almond, 4 Jan. 1918.

84 Thus McGreer interpreted Currie's ruling. NA, Chaplain Service Records, vol. 4673, Y.M.C.A. file, McGreer and Shatford to Almond, 17 Mar. 1917; McGreer to Almond, 18 Mar. 1918; and vol. 4664, A.D.C.S. Reports, France, McGreer report for Feb.–Mar. 1918, Bishop to J.H. MacDonald, 13 Apr. 1918; also mimeographed letter, Major Wallace, Y.M.C.A., to all Y.M.C.A. officers, n.d.

85 UCA, Methodist Army and Navy Board Collection, box 5, file 105, W.T. Keough to T.A. Moore, 27 Jan. 1919. NA, Chaplain Service Records, vol. 4668, Canadian Forestry Corps, file 1, W.F. McConnell to Fallis, 27 Aug. 1918, and Fallis reply, 3 Sept. 1918; also Fallis to Sr Officer, Y.M.C.A., Canadian Corps, 3 Sept. 1918. See also NA, Chaplain Service Records, vol. 4668, Chaplain Reports, file 21, Renison to Fallis, 14 June 1918.

86 NA, Chaplain Service Records, vol. 4615, Almond file, Almond to Beattie, 8 May 1918. Almond's views came up at an inter-church meeting where he had presented his case for a Canadian branch of the service. UCA, Methodist Army and Navy Board, box 1, Minutes, 22 Apr., 6 May 1918. See also *CAR* (1918): 457, and *Canadian Churchman*, 19 July, 2; 23 Aug. 1917. See *Canada*, Apr.–June 1918, passim, especially 1 June 1918, 258; also "In this great positive campaign of organized Christianity, too much cannot be said of the Y.M.C.A.," C.R. Carrie, "Organized Christianity with the Canadians in France," *Presbyterian and Westminster*, 11 Apr. 1918, 348–9. Carrie, a returned association officer, commends both chaplain and Y secretary contributions, but awards the Y the lion's share of credit as it has the "greatest share of the work" – the social and religious interests of the men to the rear. Ironically, his article also appeared in the Anglican *Canadian Churchman*, 2 May 1918.

87 The campaign also carried, in successive weeks, endorsement by a number of prominent Canadian churchmen and portrayed the work

of Y coffee stalls as the only ones in operation at the Corps. See *Christian Guardian*, 17, 24 Apr., 1 May 1918. In contrast to these massive advertisements, the Chaplain Service received half a page, shared with the Methodist Army and Navy Board's appeal for funds. In fine print at the foot of the page the Y's C.W. Bishop endorsed the Chaplain Service appeal, assuring churchmen that there was no duplication of effort overseas. NA, Chaplain Service Records, vol. 4615, Almond file, Almond to William Beattie, 8 May 1918; see also *Canadian Baptist*, 11 Apr. 1918, 7. McGreer exploded in wrath when he saw the Gordon interview: "I would like to emphasize the fact that there is no officer in the field who has more intimate association with the men in all their varied activities than the chaplain ... By those who know the facts this cannot be regarded as other than an unfair and undeserving misrepresentation of the ministers on active service for whom their churches are making great sacrifices in order that they may remain with the men who so urgently need their ministrations." NA, Chaplain Service Records, vol. 4664, A.D.C.S. Reports, France, McGreer to Almond, 21 May 1918.

88 USA, Oliver Papers, Oliver to Rita Oliver, 17 June 1918.

89 "The Y has no business to be trying to raise $2,500,000 in Canada. They are not spending it on the Field. They are making money on the Field. Either their business management is rotten, or else they are making a mint of money ... The Chaplains believe that the Y.M.C.A. has a proper place and are sorry to oppose them in any way, but they are trying to take upon themselves the responsibility of becoming the spiritual dictators, not only in France, but here ... Others look upon the Y.M.C.A. as a new brand of religion ... They won't do it in France or in England. They are second to the Chaplain Service, and we can hold our own." Almond to the Army and Navy Board on 30 Apr. 1918, UCA, Methodist Army and Navy Board, box 1, Minutes.

90 *CAR* (1918): 587, 596; on Jeakins's election as GWVA head, see *Canadian Churchman*, 24 May 1917, 326.

91 "It is claimed also by the veterans that the Y.M.C.A. gave itself the credit of inaugurating the Vimy Ridge University, a work done entirely by the chaplain service ... This condemnation of the Y.M.C.A. coming from delegates representing 12,000 returned soldiers, and inspired by a senior chaplain, is a very serious matter and demands the immediate attention of the proper authority." *Catholic Register*, 30 May 1918; also NA, Chaplain Service Records, vol. 4673, Y.M.C.A. file, John Brown to Almond, 28 May 1918, and Almond to Editor, *Toronto Star*, same date; the story also ran, according to Chaplain Service files, in Ottawa, Montreal, Hamilton, and other Toronto newspapers between 10 and 25 May 1918.

92 NA, Militia and Defence, Overseas Minister's Records, vol. 78, file 10-8-52, *Canada Gazette*, 15 June 1918, 245, 263; also letters of D.J. Fraser, G.P. Duncan, and R.W. Kicki to Borden, 13–18 May 1918; Kemp to Mewburn, 1 June 1918 and reply; Chaplain Service Records, vol. 4673, Y.M.C.A. file, Canadian Adjutant-General to Almond, and reply, 18 June 1918; QUA, D.M. Gordon Papers, box 2, 1918 Correspondence, A.M. Gordon to D.M. Gordon, 29 May and 21 June 1918. See also Frank Carrel, *Impressions of War*, 71, 195–6.

93 NA, Chaplain Service files, vol. 4649, D.C.S. file 13, Bishop of Montreal to Almond, 11 June 1918 and reply. The bishop conceded that he too was growing tired of the association's "pure-proud attitude," in a 10 June letter to Almond. USA, Oliver Papers, Oliver to Rita Oliver, 15 June 1918. In writing to his friend A.M. Gordon, Odlum went so far as to suggest that Almond had lost his mental balance on returning home: see NA, Chaplain Service Records, vol. 4673, Y.M.C.A. file, Odlum to A.M. Gordon, 5 June 1916; also vol. 4648, D.C.S. file 2, Almond to McGreer, 24 July 1918.

94 To him it was "the scandal to our common faith, and a new betrayal of our Lord. It's full of menace to the kingdom of God both now in our army and in the future in Canada after the war ... If the official representatives of the church, you of the clergy, and me more especially of the laity cannot present a united front there is something radically wrong ... We must find a way out." NA, Chaplain Service Records, vol. 4673, Y.M.C.A. file, Wallace to Almond, 31 July 1918; McGreer to Almond, 16 Sept. 1918 and reply.

95 Ibid., memo of Y.M.C.A. C.C.S. meeting, signed by Gerald Birks, Y.M.C.A., and Almond, D.C.S., 30 Oct. 1918; also Beattie, "History," 292–3; and Ross, *The Y.M.C.A. in Canada*, 287–9.

96 "It does seem to me that there is just a little effort to usurp the work of a chaplain." See NA, Chaplain Service Records, vol. 4628, J.B. Hunter file, Hunter to Almond, 5 Mar. 1919; Bishop, *The Canadian Y.M.C.A.*, 173, 265. See also NA, Chaplain Service Records, vol. 4668, C.F.C. file #2, W.C. Riddiford to W.F. McConnell, 10 Nov. 1918; and vol. 4629, A.E. Kemp file, Kemp to Almond, 19 Oct. 1918, where the minister expresses his preference for padre speakers from the front over "well-meaning" idealists from Canada. Complaints emanated from Headquarters in Ottawa, too, until it was explained that the program originated with the Y. See NA, Department of National Defence, Headquarters Central Registry, vol. 441, HQ 54-21-1-160. *Canadian Churchman*, 10 Oct. 1918, 646.

97 Beattie, "History," 287–8; NA, Chaplain Service Records, vol. 4665, Reports, Senior Chaplains, England file, George Fallis reports, Jan.

1917–Sept. 1917; Mackinnon to Fallis, 17 Oct. 1917. See also NA, Chaplain Service Records, vol. 4629, Kent file.

98 Since 1908 Tory had made the University of Alberta a Canadian byword in adult and extension education: see Mario Creet, "H.M. Tory and the Secularization of the Canadian Universities," *QQ* (winter 1981): 726. Tory also invited Oliver to leave chaplain's work and join the Y as an educational director: USA, Oliver Papers, Oliver to Rita Oliver, 30 July 1917.

99 USA, Oliver Papers, Oliver to Rita Oliver, 27 Nov. 1917; on Mackinnon and G.A. Wells's irritation at giving up control to Tory and the Y in 1917, see Wells, *Fighting Bishop*, 178.

100 The committee was struck on 25 Oct. 1917: Beattie, "History," 287–8. C.W. Bishop, *Y.M.C.A. in the Great War*, 188–92.

101 USA, Oliver Papers, Oliver to Rita Oliver, 1–5 Dec. 1917.

102 See Canadian Corps Routine Order 1580, 17 Dec. 1917, in Beattie, "History," 289; USA, Oliver Papers, Syllabus of the University of Vimy Ridge, and Oliver to Rita Oliver, 7–9 Jan. 1918. See also Almond's D.C.S. reports to General Turner, Jan. 1918, in NA, MG 30, Turner Papers, 2575–2576.

103 USA, Oliver Papers, University of Vimy Ridge Syllabus, 2–4; Beattie, "History," 288; USA, Oliver Papers, Oliver to Rita Oliver, 7 Dec. 1917; C.W. Bishop, *Y.M.C.A. in the Great War*, 198.

104 NA, Chaplain Service Records, vol. 4651, Education file, Oliver to Almond, 21 Dec. 1917. After the war, Oliver wrote, "it was not designed primarily to give University courses at all, nor even to meet the needs of Undergraduates … The University was really a school of efficiency and citizenship, a sort of combination of an Agricultural High School and a Technical School." NA, MG 30, E 25, Oliver Papers, Lt-Col. E.H. Oliver, Assistant Director Educational Services, O.M.F.C. to Canadian War Records Office, Report on Education in France, 29 Apr. 1919, 2.

105 "It nettles the Y.M.C.A., for they like to get everything under their wing … McGreer told me later that I saved the educational movement in France." USA, E.H. Oliver Papers, Oliver to Rita Oliver, 27–30 Dec. 1917. See also Oliver to Rita Oliver, 1, 9, 26 Jan. 1918.

106 Although nominally under Tory, in the new structure Oliver had working autonomy over all education work on the continent, not just at Corps. Under this establishment Tory became a full colonel, with Oliver and Mackinnon, his two assistant directors (ADES), promoted to lieutenant-colonels. NA, Chaplain Service Records, vol. 4637, E. Oliver file.

107 USA, Oliver Papers, Oliver to Rita Oliver, 7 Aug., 27 Sept., 4 Nov. 1918. Mackinnon was responsible for work in Forestry Corps: NA,

Chaplain Service Records, vol. 4634, C. Mackinnon file; vol. 4648, A.D.C.S. Reports, file 2, McGreer to Almond, 17 Dec. 1918. Oliver fumed, "Tory is surrounded by a coterie of McGill men who constitute a mutual admiration society." USA, Oliver Papers, Oliver to Rita Oliver, 18–19 Dec. 1918, 21 Jan. 1919.

108 USA, Oliver Papers, Oliver to Rita Oliver, 9, 18 Mar. 1919. As usual, these claims appeared in articles prepared by Y.M.C.A. officers for the religious press. See John L. Love: "It was the sagacious leaders of the Canadian Y.M.C.A., ever on the alert to further the welfare of the fighting forces, who tended and nourished and directed into practical channels the scholastic aspirations of the soldiers. In co-operation with the chaplains and military authorities they prayed and planned, and contrived a way." In "The Most Wonderful University in the World: Canada's Khaki College," *Christian Guardian*, 24 Apr. 1919, 18. On YMCA claims, see Bishop, *Canadian Y.M.C.A.*, 197–8, and *CAR* (1971): 456. Compare with NA, Chaplain Service Records, vol. 4651, Education file, Mackinnon to Almond, 20 Feb. 1918; also J.B. Hunter to Almond, 18 Jan. 1919.

109 "As we have pointed out above, the great crisis for Christianity lies, not in the past but in the future when the days of reconstruction shall have begun. If in those days the principles of Christ, without which there can be no lasting peace, are to become really effective, it will need the united effort of all men of goodwill. If under the stress of war and active service conditions we can satisfactorily work out the place of the Y.M.C.A. in the life of the Church as the common organ of all the churches for certain forms of social effort a great and lasting contribution will have been made to the future welfare of our Nation." Joint YMCA-CCS statement, 30 Oct. 1918, printed in Bishop, *Canadian Y.M.C.A.*, 185.

110 Ross, *Y.M.C.A. in Canada*, 291–2.

111 *Canadian Churchman*, 23 Oct. 1919. Most notable in 1919 was this exchange between Rev. J. Callan, employed by the Y, and Rev. S.E. McKegney, both ex-chaplains. Callan reported to the general secretary of the National Council that "a strong prejudice against the Y.M.C.A. exists in Canada." Callan to C.W. Bishop, June 1919, quoted in Ross, *Y.M.C.A. in Canada*, 292.

112 This was made plausible by Bishop M.F. Fallon's public criticism of the association from his London diocese in 1922, where he referred to attached from Anglican as well as Catholic chaplains on the association's secularizing influence. Ross credits Catholic chaplain complaints of Protestant proselytization overseas, as well as previous papal denunciation, for Fallon's outburst: *Y.M.C.A. in Canada*, 292, 315.

113 Ibid., 294, 312–16, 320–1.

114 For Workman's and O'Gorman's letters, as well as editorials, hierarchical endorsements, and campaign advertisements, see *Catholic Register*, 5 July, 2, 23, 30 Aug., 6, 20 Sept. 1917. See also Daniel and Casey, *For God and Country*, 15.

115 *Catholic Register*, 30 Aug. 1917; Daniel and Casey, *For God and Country*, 11–19.

116 NA, Chaplain Service Records, vol. 4623, Bishop Fallon file.

117 Workman was made president, French, at Corps, his vice-president, with John O'Gorman, John Knox, and P.M.H. Casgrain his secretary and deputies. Sylvestre remained the Canadian director. See Beattie, "History," 219.

118 *Catholic Register*, 24, 31 Jan. 1918.

119 Ibid., 25 Apr. 1918; also E. Laws to Workman, 10 Aug. 1918, NA, Chaplain Service Records, vol. 4666, Reports, file 4.

120 NA, Chaplain Service Records, vol. 4658, Routine Orders, D.C.S., London file, 25 Nov. 1918; and O'Gorman to Almond, 22 Nov. 1918, ibid., vol. 4663, Reconstruction file.

121 For example, see Workman to Bishop of Antigonish on behalf of M.N. Thompkins, Jan. 1919, NA, Chaplain Service Records, vol. 4644, Thompkins file; vol. 4656, A.D.C.S. Reports file, Workman to Sylvestre, 19, 30 Dec. 1918; vol. 4634, P.A. MacDonald, and vol. 4641, A.B.W. Wood files.

122 Fallis, *Padre's Pilgrimage*, 93; also NA, Chaplain Service Records, vol. 4631, C. Mackinnon file, Fallis to Mackinnon, 27 Mar. 1919.

123 Beattie, "History," 222; O'Gorman overrode Workman's objections that such largesse would bankrupt the fund. O'Gorman claimed it was too urgent an opportunity to win soldier good will to be missed. See O'Gorman to Workman, 20 Jan. 1919, NA, Chaplain Service Records, vol. 4637, J.R. O'Gorman file, vol. 4636, J.J. O'Gorman file. See also vol. 4648, D.C.S., England file, Workman-O'Gorman correspondence, Feb. 1919.

124 By March 1919, for example, Kinmel Park employed seventeen chaplains, as many as in a full division. See Senior Chaplain to O. C., Kinmel Park, NA, Militia and Defence, III B 1, vol. 1708, Kinmel Park Chaplaincy file. On the government's concern about keeping order during demobilization, see Morton, *Peculiar Kind of Politics*, 180–1.

125 For example, see NA, Chaplain Service Records, vol. 4631, L.P. Lowry file; vol. 4625, C.W. Foreman file; vol. 4646, ADCS, RC file, A.B.W. Wood to Workman, 29 Jan. 1919.

126 Ibid., Senior Chaplain report to O.C., Kinmel Park, 27 Mar. 1919. On the Kinmel riot, see Chaplain Service Records, vol. 4621, Daniel file, Daniel to Workman, 7 Mar. 1919; also vol. 4665, R.C. Chaplains Reports, Mar. 1919 report by A.A. Lamarre.

127 NA, Chaplain Service Records, vol. 4615, H.J. Allen file; vol. 4640, Riddiford file; and vol. 4638, Peacock, for similar work at Witley, and vol. 4642, Spiddell, for Seaford work.

128 For the work of chaplains in camps and on returning transports, see Canada, Department of Militia and Defence, *The Return of the Troops,* 60–3, also 25, 49.

129 Routine Orders, Canadian Chaplain Service, 28 Apr. 1919, in NA, Chaplain Service Records, vol. 4658, Routine Orders, D.C.S., London file.

130 NA, MG 30, Turner Papers, D.C.S. Monthly Reports, May 1919.

CHAPTER FOUR

1 UCA, Oliver Papers, Oliver to Rita Oliver, 1 Oct. 1917.

2 Benedict Murdoch, a New Brunswick Roman Catholic, discovered that some colleagues disapproved of his eagerness to enlist. Among those least impressed by his new vocation was his own bishop, whom Murdoch had not consulted before publicly pledging to go overseas with the 132nd battalion. "One morning I received a letter from the Bishop telling me plainly and firmly that he wished me to keep quiet, and not to talk so much about going to the front until I should know whether or not I would be permitted to go." After the commanding officer interviewed the bishop, Murdoch was allowed to proceed. *Red Vineyard,* 11–15.

3 UCA, Methodist Army and Navy Board, box 5, file 127, H.J. Latimer to T.A. Moore, 29 Dec. 1915.

4 Methodists as well as Presbyterians and Anglicans felt the pull of such traditions. Nathanael Burwash's son Edward felt compelled to volunteer largely because of his father's service against the Fenians. UCA, Methodist Army and Navy Board, box 15, file 346, Recollections of E.M. Burwash. W.G. Clarke, Methodist minister in Bowmanville, Ontario, claimed that his grandfather had been a veteran of Waterloo and his mother's family of Loyalist stock. "I am bound to Great Britain's fortunes. But more I believe that Great Britain's fortunes are inseparably linked with the cause of humanity, liberty and Christian civilization in this world struggle." UCA, Methodist Army and Navy Board, vol. 5, file 122, Chaplain Correspondence, W.G. Clarke to T.A. Moore, 17 Feb. 1916.

5 Walter McAlpine, a McMaster-trained Baptist, recalled, "I noticed the men who were answering the call. They needed a man among them who could help them morally, and I believed I was called of God to fill this place, so I enlisted as a private in the 136th Battalion." He was a sergeant by the time he was promoted to the chaplaincy in 1916. See

Canadian Baptist Archives, McMaster Divinity College, W.S. McAlpine file, autobiographical m, 14 Feb. 1950. The Eleventh Canadian Field Ambulance recruited ten ordained ministers into its ranks before leaving Canada in early 1916: see *Diary of the Eleventh Canadian Field Ambulance*, 11.

6 N.H. Macgillivray (a Presbyterian) helped to recruit much of the Ninety-first Battalion from Elgin County, Ontario: see NA, Chaplain Service Records, vol. 4635, Macgillivray file. Edmund Oliver, likewise, became chaplain of the 196th Western Universities Battalion, which included many of his own students: ibid., vol. 4637, Oliver file. M.E. Conron, a Methodist, helped to recruit the 140th Battalion in New Brunswick: ibid., vol. 4620. J.F. Tupper was chief recruiting officer in Pictou County before joining as chaplain: ibid., vol. 4644. D.G. MacPhail, another Presbyterian, was active as recruiter in Haldimand County, Ontario, before going overseas: ibid., vol. 4634.

7 UCA, Methodist Army and Navy Board, box 4, file 79, Harold Clarke to T.A. Moore, 29 June 1916.

8 The most striking example of this was Charles Gordon's Forty-third Battalion, where over three hundred members came from his own parish of St Stephen's Presbyterian Church, Winnipeg: *Postscript to Adventure*, 213.

9 William E. Chajkowsky, *History of Camp Borden, 1916–1918*, 59–60. On chaplain attempts to combat this, see John Coburn, "Life at Camp Borden," *Christian Guardian*, 6 Sept. 1916, 20. See also T.C. Colwell, "One Chaplain's Work," *Christian Guardian*, 19 July 1916; USA, Oliver Papers, Correspondence, 1916–19, Oliver to Rita Oliver, 23, 29 June, 6 July 1916. Many spent their afternoons out on the ranges, learning to shoot with the troops. USA, Oliver Papers, Oliver to Rita Oliver, 20 July, 14 September: "Today I surprised myself by really doing well on the pistol range … I think that in an Emergency I could manage a German."

10 Oliver spent over three hundred dollars of his own pay, along with private donations by other citizens of Saskatoon and Regina, in erecting a recreation tent complete with stoves and rented piano, a five-hundred-volume library, and a gramophone. USA, Oliver Papers, Oliver to Rita Oliver, 28, 30 July, 15 Aug., 15, 27 Sept. 1916. As he confided to his wife, "A chaplain can be more useful here than I realized." Ibid., 26 July 1916.

11 "Many men who had passed long years away from the sacraments had come into the white bell tent … and, kneeling there, had been reconciled after many years estrangement from God." Murdoch, *Red Vineyard*, 24–9. C.J. Williams, a Methodist recruiting for his battalion near Peterborough, assured T.A. Moore: "Tis Grand to be a chaplain and to

go with the men to the front, such good lads at heart, helping them to live like gentlemen and if needs be to die like men … Oh! Doctor, let ministers measure up to the stature of men NOW and Methodism is safe. Be human and sit where these men sit. Give me a live minister from a field and I will show you a batch of recruits from that circuit for 'the Flag.'" UCA, Methodist Army and Navy Board, box 2, file 34, Williams to Moore, 18 Mar. 1916.

12 British and Canadian chaplains repeated this complaint, which was not addressed until after the war. See Beattie, "History," 246; and George Birmingham (J.O. Hannay), *A Padre in France*, 52–3, 56. Only thirty-seven Canadian chaplains had experience as militia chaplains before the war.

13 Usually the priest marched into the adjutant's office and pointed out in army regulations where it stated that Roman Catholics were not to attend non-Catholic services if unit parades. See Murdoch, *Red Vineyard*, 26–8.

14 USA, Oliver Papers, Oliver to Rita Oliver, 10 July and 7 Oct. 1916.

15 G.R. Stevens, *A City Goes to War*, 165.

16 "One of the Manitoba students died here," Oliver confided to his wife. "I visited him a couple of hours before his death, and then was detailed to meet his mother at the station. Fortunately for me his brother came instead and I found my task much easier than I had anticipated. It is hard enough to write a letter to people under these circumstances but to meet them is a little too difficult." USA, Oliver Papers, Oliver to Rita Oliver, 11 July 1916.

17 USA, ibid., Oliver to Rita Oliver, 15 Oct. 1916. In correspondence with his wife Oliver repeatedly testified that the many little ventures and minor successes of his summer at Camp Hughes confirmed his sometimes shaky sense of vocation, as he proved to himself that "a chaplain can do something" to win and hold the respect of his men. USA, Oliver Papers, Oliver to Rita Oliver, 13 July 1916.

18 A sampling of the sentiments of such soldiers can be found in the letters to Miss C. Burkholder, secretary of St Stephen's College, in the college papers, 1914–18: see University of Alberta Archives, St Stephen's College Papers, box 4.

19 Keith Fallis, the son of a missionary, found that his idealistic "attitude was not typical … of any but a small, idealistic group of students, of people who came from teachers' families or preachers' families. That was one of the first shocks to me. We had a few fellows around who had been over … and who were doing some of the training. And they were cynical and scornful – 'You'll get over THAT when you get over there' – if you expressed any idealistic feeling about the war. The average fellow in the army was rather a coarse and to some extent brutal-minded

fellow. I went down to Ottawa to Landsdowne Park to train – of all my fellow soldiers, eight out of ten seemed to me to have no other interest except finding a girl for the night. I came from a sheltered family." Quoted in D. Read, *The Great War and Canadian Society*, 98–9.

20 Ibid., 98–9, 117–18.

21 Fallis, *A Padre's Pilgrimage*, 69–71.

22 USA, Oliver Papers, "A Preachment by the Padre," in *Western Universities Battalion* (unit newsletter), 21 Oct. 1916, 2. M. Gauvreau mistakes this sermon as one of Oliver's overseas addresses: *Evangelical Century*, 260.

23 Roman Catholic padres, too, devoted much attention to the morality issue, as reports from Valcartier and Petawawa indicate. NA, Chaplain Service Records, vol. 4665, Reports, R.C. Chaplains, Canada file; and Murdoch, *Red Vineyard*, 25, 29.

24 "Who can define the precious thing we call sacrifice? ... Is it worth while? Yes, a thousand times yes and more for all we hold dear – the best of the ages – is in the balance, and my comrades, Britons never shall be slaves. We ... stand today for the freedom and security of the weaker nations. We stand willing to sacrifice and to die if need be to make men free. Yes! It is our honour to contribute our personal quota to this, the biggest movement of the age; the establishing of democracy and lasting peace among the nations of men." NA, MG 30 E 153, Journal, 38th Battalion, C.E.F., by Rev. and Chaplain H.I. Horsey. Oliver told his battalion before it embarked for England: "In this contest Heaven is not a neutral. Heaven is not too proud to fight ... Why do we share in the struggles of Heaven? Because we share in its aspirations. We fight Germany because in Canada we too prize liberty. We too want to see the constituted self-government, even of little nations, respected." *CAR* (1916): 438. During the crossing he preached on "Gideon as a hero of national service." Gideon's "Public Morality ... Personal Religion ... Patriotic Devotion ... and Disciplined Service" gave him the victory. It was the same sermon he had preached to his Saskatoon congregation before enlisting. USA, Oliver Papers, Oliver to wife, 6 Nov. 1916.

25 "I want you to feel as I set sail that I have never doubted it was my duty to go. I want Murray to feel that when his country needed his daddy, that daddy did not flinch." USA, Oliver Papers, Oliver to Rita Oliver, 31 Oct. 1916; see also 10, 15 Oct. 10, 1916. After landing in England, Oliver reassured his wife: "I have no regrets that I came. I do not see how I could have done otherwise. Nevertheless it is my last war ... I am not in favour of peace yet, for it would be inconclusive it if came now, and one does not want peace now only to have Murray go to war when he grows up." Oliver to Rita Oliver, 17, 23 Dec. 1916.

26 Murdoch, *Red Vineyard*, 30–2. See also USA, Oliver Papers, Oliver to Rita Oliver, 26 Oct.–4 Nov. 1916.

27 Murdoch, *Red Vineyard*, 35–6. See also Beattie, "History," 229–32, and Anglican Church of Canada, Ottawa Diocesan Archives, Diary of Channel G. Hepburn, Aug. 1915.

28 "I fear the effects of the wet canteen. We can only do our best to minimize its effects." USA, Oliver Papers, Oliver to Rita Oliver, 5 Nov. 1916. Oliver broke up one gambling ring on board ship, operated by one of the ship's crew, as well as crewmen profiteering by charging the soldiers for better quality food. USA, Oliver Papers, ibid. Australian chaplains on their ten-week voyage to war often found their prolonged contact with the men a greater disillusionment than did the Canadians, as the effects of enlistment enthusiasm wore off and the crude, lewd, and vicious traits of some of the men emerged. See McKernan, "Clergy in Khaki," 148–9.

29 USA, Oliver Papers, Oliver to Rita Oliver, 2 Dec. 1916. Although, because of censorship, he refused to discuss with his wife the details of the breakup of the 196th, Oliver's letters vented his anger at the process, which he shared with dozens of other chaplains coming to England under Steacy's administration. See USA, Oliver Paper, Oliver to Rita Oliver, 12 Nov.–31 Dec. 1916 and 4, 23 Feb. 1917. See also NA, Chaplain Service Records, vol. 4625, W.L. Godfrey file. F.J. Moore bluntly informed Canadian readers that "when a chaplain arrives in England … he is extremely fortunate if he is allowed to remain with [his battalion] for more than a few days … Objections have been raised, rather naturally, against this arrangement, but since most battalions are sooner or later split up, the battalion chaplain loses his original men in any case." *Canadian Churchman*, 13 July 1916, 441.

30 To many padres such as Thomas Colwell, who had spent months with the 102nd Battalion in British Columbia, it was especially galling to have Steacy remove him from his battalion, on the eve of its joining the Fourth Division, in order to send another Methodist, Harold Clarke (who happened to have arrived in England earlier), to Flanders. UCA, Methodist Army and Navy Board, box 9, Colwell file, Colwell to Moore, 14 Aug. 1916.

31 Murdoch's bitterness was common among the chaplains to other units which suffered the same fate as his battalion. "I returned to Bramshott Camp a somewhat wiser man as to the workings of things military … I never should have offered my services as chaplain had I foreseen the catastrophe which had befallen us. I had counted on being with my men till the last. Before leaving for overseas many of the mothers of the lads had come to me and had told me what a great consolation it was to them to have the assurance that a Catholic priest would be with

their sons. Now I was not going with them." Murdoch, *Red Vineyard*, 44–6. It was cold comfort to be reassured by an Anglican that their men would receive adequate spiritual care from other chaplains.

32 USA, Oliver Papers, Oliver to Rita Oliver, 25 Jan. 1917. See also Oliver to Rita Oliver, 6 Feb. 1917.

33 Birmingham, *A Padre in France*, 18–21.

34 A.C. Farrell, a Methodist chaplain at Seaford, informed T.A. Moore that he did "not find any great manifestation of deep religious desire such as it was said the war was producing in the men in khaki and it was hoped it would. It may be in France later on, but not yet." UCA, Methodist Army and Navy Board, box 8, file 219, Farrell to Moore, 28 Dec. 1916.

35 Not every chaplain was as successful as Oliver in getting local police forces to "chase undesirable women out of town." USA, Oliver Papers, Oliver to Rita Oliver, 27 Apr.–3 May 1917. Both British and Canadian chaplains repeatedly ascribe similar qualities to these aspects of camp life. See Birmingham, *A Padre in France*, 64–76, 79–82, 123.

36 J. Pirot, a Roman Catholic chaplain with the Canadian Forestry Corps, complained: "Truly I don't like this work. Our men are just like civilians of old, far away from danger – and the ideals are rather low!" NA, Chaplains' Service Records, vol. 4639, Pirot file, Pirot to Workman, 22 Aug. 1918.

37 The most notable exception to this was the Bexhill officer's training school and the "Boy's Battalion" of under-age soldiers quartered there, where E.H. Oliver won the support of both commanding officers to ban the wet canteen. This move, however, cost Oliver the sympathy of many junior officers. USA, Oliver Papers, Oliver to Rita Oliver, 1, 5, 17 Aug. 1917.

38 See NA, Chaplain Service Records, vol. 4670, Crowborough file, E.D. MacLaren to Almond, 28 Mar. 1917. The most notable case was a resolution by George Wells and his thirty-three Shorncliffe chaplains asking Headquarters to clamp down on drunkenness, profanity, and the growing incidence of venereal disease in camp. They demanded that camp authorities place all public houses within five miles of the camp "out of bounds to all Canadians." NA, Militia and Defence, Shorncliffe Camp records, vol. 679, file E-173-2, Chaplains Establishment, Resolution of Shorncliffe Chaplains to G.O.C., Canadian Training Division, 1 Mar. 1917. In order to add to the pressure on army authorities the Shorncliffe chaplains sent a copy of their petition to the editor of the *Canadian Churchman*, which was published 29 Mar. 1917.

39 At Shorncliffe the CO firmly denied the January 1917 petition and pointed out that the bootlegging that would result from such a regulation would lead to greater abuses, as smuggling of hard liquor into

camp would increase, and while pubs and hotels were not bawdy houses, bootlegging dens were. General Ashton to Senior Chaplain George Wells, 12 Mar. 1917, ibid.

40 This was especially prevalent at Shorncliffe and Bramshott. Wells admitted to General Ashton: "We have to admit that we have not been able to cope with the evils of which we have complained, but we cannot admit that we have failed in our duties regarding them ... In cases where chaplains have come from Canada with their own Regiments, and where they are attached to permanent units in France, they can and do make a place for themselves among officers and men and receive loyal support in the work. But in Reserve Units, where moves are being continually made and *esprit de corps* is very little in evidence, we get very little support and find our work extremely difficult." Wells to Ashton, 22 Mar. 1917, ibid.; NA, Chaplain Service Records, vol. 4669, Bramshott file, Bramshott chaplains' petitions of 15 Nov. 1917 and 27 Mar. 1918; C.G. Hepburn to Almond, 29 Mar. 1918.

41 Wells to Ashton, 22 Mar. 1917, ibid.

42 *Unknown Soldiers*, 38, and E.G. Black, *I Want One Volunteer*, 93.

43 *Canadian Churchman*, 21 Nov. 1918, 756. See also *Presbyterian and Westminster*, 18 Oct. 1917, 374.

44 Clarence Mackinnon, *Reminiscences*, 200. See also USA, Oliver Papers, Oliver to Rita Oliver, 3 Dec. 1916. Roman Catholic chaplains remained the most adamant in insisting on the right of worship and attendance to the sacrament. See NA, Chaplain Service Records, vol. 4665, Reports, R.C. Chaplains, England file: "I should like to know whether Sunday church parade takes precedence over every other parade. For months past draft inspections parade has been held on Sundays, during church parade ... On the very day on which Catholics, leaving for France, should have an opportunity of receiving Holy Communion and being instructed by their chaplain, they are deprived of their privilege of hearing Mass ... Something drastic will have to be done, I am afraid, before the C.R.A. will realize that the Chaplain is a definite part of the military organization, and not a hanger-on or concession to public opinion." Se also NA, Chaplain Service Records, vol. 4630, H.S. Laws file, Laws to Workman, 1 Apr. 1918.

45 See USA, Oliver Papers, Oliver to Rita Oliver, 26 Mar. 1917, 2 July 1917.

46 NA, Chaplain Service Records, vol. 4630, Laws file, Laws to Workman, 1 Apr. 1918.

47 NA, Chaplain Service Records, vol. 4668, Canadian Forestry Corps, file 2, Major Kenny to C.W. Shelley, 4 Dec. 1918. See also Shelley to Almond, n.d. (1918).

48 See NA, Militia and Defence, C.E.F. Records, vol. 623, file C-217-2, Court of Inquiry, 28–29 March 1918, Church Services at Sandling, complaint by Honourary Captain C.A. Fallon, Headquarters, Shorncliffe.

49 NA, Chaplain Service Records, vol. 4665, Reports, Senior Chaplains, England file, A.D. Cornett to W. Beattie, 20 May–20 June 1918.

50 N.A. MacEachern, "Fifteen Months in an English Camp," *Christian Guardian*, 4 Jan. 1918, 7. This article also appeared in the *Canadian Churchman*, 20 Dec. 1917, and the *Presbyterian and Westminster*, 29 Nov. 1917, 507. Birmingham, *Padre in France*, 125–6. See also J.W. Whillans, *Presbyterian and Westminster*, 7 Feb. 1918.

51 Birmingham, 124–5. See also Beattie, "History," 162–3.

52 NA, Chaplain Service Records, vol. 4621, J.C. Davidson file, Almond to Davidson, 16 June 1917.

53 Beattie, "History," 164. See also NA, Chaplain Service Records, vol. 4642, Shore file; vol. 4620, Davis file; vol. 4633, Mosley file. Military authorities discouraged this practice, however, as officers and men complained that chaplains were obtaining more than their share of leave. They were ordered to leave things up to London welfare agencies. NA, Militia and Defence, Series III B1, vol. 2178, file C-12-26, vol. 2, J.C. MacDougall to G.O.C., Bramshott, 7 Oct. 1916.

54 "Through this agency, many unwary soldiers have been kept from the dangers to which they might otherwise have succumbed," Almond reported. Australian and Canadian troops especially were prone to brawling on back streets, sometimes with knives or razors. Ibid, Nov. 1917 and Jan., Apr. 1918 reports. See also T.A. Mosley to Warner, 18 Mar. 1918: "The statement has repeatedly been made, that the soldier resents what they call the interference of the chaplains, but from experience in London, both in this office, and on the street, I find that statement to be incorrect. Our men welcome the approach and help that we are always willing to render, and in many cases have sought assistance of the Chaplain while on patrol work on the streets."

55 Ian Casselman, "The Secret Plague: Venereal Disease in Early Twentieth Century Canada,", MA, Queen's University 1981, 151–4. See H.J. Latimer to Almond, 8 Aug. 1917, NA, Chaplain Service Records, vol. 4665, Reports, France file. See also M.H. Jackson to Almond, 25 Feb. 1918, NA, Chaplain Service Records, vol. 4628, Jackson file. For the MOs' perspective on the controversy, see Robin Kierstead, "The Canadian Military Medical Experience During the Great War, 1914–1918," MA, Queen's University 1982, 199–211. Australian chaplains and churchmen also came into conflict with military medical officials over prophylactic distribution: see McKernan, *Australian Churches*, 167–8.

56 John Knox to Workman, 25 Mar. 1918, NA, Chaplain Service Records, vol. 4629, Knox file. Workman to Almond, 12 Mar. 1918 and reply; see also Almond to General Turner, 12 Mar. 1918, NA, Chaplain Service Records, vol. 4647, W.T. Workman file. See also Workman, A.L. Sylvestre, John Knox, John O'Gorman, J.P. Fallon, M.N. Thompkins, William Hingston, and I.J.E. Daniel to Cardinal Bourne, 21 Mar. 1918, NA, Chaplain Service Records, vol. 4618, Bourne file.

57 "There is something peculiar in seeing a Conscientious Objector down on his knees sculling out the Klink or peeling potatoes all because he refuses to take a human life," Oliver wrote. His religious census of the camp prison's inmates included "one Seventh Day Adventist, One Salvation Army, some from the 'Peculiar People of Essex," four Anglican, one Methodist, one Plymouth Brethren, one Theosophist, three agnostics, one Presbyterian, one Unitarian, and three Doubtfuls." USA, Oliver Papers, Oliver to Rita Oliver, 12, 25 Dec. 1916; also 16 Nov., 29 Dec. 1916. For a Methodist chaplain's impatience with pacifists, see UCA, Methodist Army and Navy Board, box 4, file 82, E.E. Graham to Moore, Oct. 1916. By the spring of 1918, when conscripts began to arrive in England, chaplains reported a growing number of such sectarian pacifists who refused to obey orders. Some chaplains succeeded in persuading such men to transfer to the medical service as stretcher bearers: NA, Chaplain Service Records, vol. 4665, Reports, Sr. Chaplains, England, A.D. Cornett to Almond, 21 May 1918.

58 NA, Chaplain Service Records, vol. 4674, D.C.S. Correspondence with #1 Canadian Infantry Base Depot, O.C. to Almond, 22 July 1917. USA, Oliver Papers, Oliver to Rita Oliver, 16 July 1917; NA, Chaplain Service Papers, vol. 4629, Kent file, court martial summons, 24 June 1918, and ibid., vol. 4665, Reports, France, W.A. White report, 5–11 Sept. 1917; also J.W. Melvin report, 2 Aug. 1918; and A.D. Cornett report, 30 June 1917. H.S. Mullowney, a Baptist chaplain with the Canadian Forestry Corps, found his role as courtroom mediator taking up a great deal of his time. After the war, Mullowney pursued a legal career rather than return to the ministry: ibid, vol. 4668, C.F.C. file, Mullowney to W.F. McConnell, 18 Sept. 1918.

59 Consequently most chaplains were not satisfied with shared accommodation, even with other chaplains: see UCA, Oliver Papers, Oliver to Rita Oliver, 13 Dec. 1916 and 7, 23 Jan. 1917.

60 USA, Oliver Papers, Oliver to Rita Oliver, 4 Apr. 1917.

61 NA, Militia and Defence, ser. III B 1, vol. 600, c-33-2, Church Parades, Shorncliffe files, 1918–19; also Chaplain Service Records, vol. 4665, Reports, France file, Burgess Brown, 5 Sept. 1917.

62 While publicly chaplains such as George Fallis and Canon Scott appeared satisfied with such a low turn-out, in private Presbyterians

such as George Little and W.F. McConnell were appalled at this phenomenon. Compare *Christian Guardian,* 3 Nov. 1915, 22, and Scott, *Great War,* 243, with NA, Chaplains Service Records, vol. 4663, Questionnaire file, McConnell and Little responses.

63 On the largest such mass consecration, see *Catholic Register,* 14 June 1917. Roman Catholic chaplains frequently complained that rear-area troops were slacker in devotion and neglected the sacraments. NA, Chaplain Service Records, vol. 4665 Reports, R.C. Chaplains, England, Ronald MacDonald, 23 Mar. 1917. Yet some priests testified to a growing level of devotion, pointing to a number of baptisms, first communions, and conversions to Catholicism. NA, ibid., passim.

64 On Dominion Day 1917 Oliver pointedly contrasted the Canadian celebration of liberty and justice with the militarism of another nation celebrating on that day: the North German Confederation. USA, Oliver Papers, Oliver to wife, 25 June 1917. See also: "Germany's utterances this week in the matter of prosecuting the submarine war led me to preach a belligerent, or ...'blood and thunder' sermon this morning from Jeremiah 51:33, "The daughter of Babylon is like a threshing floor. It is time to thrash her." I took as my text, "It is time to thrash her," (4 Feb. 1917).

65 Oliver's last sermon to each group was usually based upon Paul's words to Timothy: "I charge you to keep your commission without stain." "It will be a kind of farewell shot at them," he informed his wife. USA, Oliver Papers, Oliver to wife, 19 Jan., also 18 June 1917. Methodist chaplain H.W. Burnett preached a similar series based on Ephesians, "The Moral and Spiritual Equipment of a Soldier," to his Bramshott charges: UCA, Methodist Army and Navy Board, box 2, file 34, Burnett to Moore, 7 Feb. 1916. Oliver's successor at Bexhill, Presbyterian S.J.M. Compton, also preached on similar themes: see NA, Chaplain Service Records, vol. 4649, Bexhill file, Compton's sermon of 6 Jan. 1918; and ibid., vol. 4619, Compton file, address of 20 Jan. 1918.

66 Compare Fallis, in *Christian Guardian,* 10 Nov. 1915, 29, with Christie, *Presbyterian and Westminster,* 27 June 1918, 620. Also see Alan Shatford to convalescent soldiers, "The Soldier's Duty," *Canada,* 25 Mar. 1916, 367. Even in Siberia, George Farquhar (who had seen service with the Fourth Division in France previously) reminded his Canadians to act in a way that would not shame their country, their comrades, or Jesus Christ. See Farquhar diary in A. Cameron, "Padre in Siberia," BA Honours thesis, Mount Allison University 1982, 134–5.

67 Burwash also reported that inquiries for confirmation, religious instruction, baptism, and prayer shot up on the eve of departure to the front. NA, Chaplains' Service Records, vol. 4665, Reports, France, Burwash

report of 31 Aug. 1917; see also vol. 4664, A.D.C.S. Reports, France file, Burwash to George Fallis, (summer 1918), and ibid., vol. 4617, C.H. Buckland file, Buckland to D.C.S., report of duties, Nov. 1915–July 1916.

68 J.C. Davidson, an Anglican, told his men, before they were drafted to France: "Comrades, your time of testing has come. Call up – or rather call down from Heaven all the powers given you of spirit and mind and body ... If you never did so before, get now into right connection with God and keep it up. You need your Religion now. Use it. Get into the way of leaning on Divine Help." NA, Chaplain Service Records, vol. 4621, Davidson file, Sermon to the 93rd Battalion, 5 Aug. 1916. Oliver preached to his cadets, "Whether we live or die, we are the Lord's." USA, Oliver Papers, Oliver to Rita Oliver, 14 Jan. 1917. On one of these occasions A.E. Lavell described his men for Methodists at home: "A fine lot of lads. They will not all come back. This is the sorrow of it. But they knew and they went, and this is the glory of it." Lavell, "How a Draft Left a Canadian Training Camp in England To Proceed to France," *Christian Guardian*, 17 Feb. 1917. See also Birmingham, *A Padre in France*, 105–8.

69 See UCA, Methodist Army and Navy Board, box 2, Burnett to T.A. Moore, 21 Jan., 7 Feb., and 27 Apr. 1916; also box 5, file 124, Garbutt to Moore.

70 NA, Chaplain Service Records, vol. 4616, Boulden file, 27 Mar. 1918; UCA, Methodist Army and Navy Board, box 6, file 165, Robb to Moore, 5 May 1917; also box 5, file 127, Latimer to Moore, 19 Oct. 1916. Some of the most optimistic assessments of religion in the camps came from Methodists in English camps. See UCA, Methodist Army and Navy Board, box 2, file 34, Extracts of Chaplains' Letters, Burnett to Moore, 21 Jan. 1916.

71 George Fallis, "Leaves from a Chaplain's Diary," *Christian Guardian*, 3 Nov. 1915.

72 Murdoch, *Red Vineyard*, 56.

73 For a British perspective, see Wilkinson, *Church of England and the First World War*, 138–68.

74 Certainly no other offence by a hospital chaplain received as much criticism from troops in England as being missed on a ward visit. For example, see *Canada*, 6 Oct. 1917, 18. See also Beattie, "History," 190–1, 236–7; NA, Chaplain Service Records, vol. 4635, McConnell report of Mar. 1917; George Pringle, "The Work of a Hospital Chaplain," *Presbyterian and Westminster*, 8 Feb. 1917, 168; and Anglican Ottawa Diocese Archives, Hepburn Papers, Diary, Oct.–Nov. 1915.

75 Beattie, "History," 191.

76 George Fallis, "Leaves from a Chaplain's Diary," *Christian Guardian*, 10 Nov. 1915, 29. J.W. Whillans, "Shell Shock," *Presbyterian and Westminster*, Jan. 1918, 143–4. Chaplains new to hospital work were not always so sympathetic, having been advised by doctors that many symptoms were feigned out of cowardice or produced by the subconscious and more or less easily cured by electrotherapy. See Murdoch, *Red Vineyard*, 89–93. On the Canadian treatment of shell shock, especially among the enlisted men, see Thomas Brown, "Shell Shock in the Canadian Expeditionary Force, 1914–1918: Canadian Psychiatry in the Great War," in Charles Rowland, *Health, Disease and Medicine*, 308–32.

77 Beattie, "History," 146–9.

78 "I like the hospital work best of all. One feels that he is able to do some real Christian work there." USA, Oliver Papers, Oliver to Rita Oliver, 18 Jan. 1917. Ernest Pugsley, a Methodist chaplain, cautiously echoed him: "There is no spirit of revival, but there certainly is a deep under current working amongst the men. They welcome our ministrations and there is no difficulty whatever in speaking to them of the great factors in life, providing ordinary tact and common sense is observed." NA, Chaplain Service Records, vol. 4668, Chaplain Reports, file 20, Pugsley to Fallis, 13 May 1918. See also vol. 4668, Chaplain Reports, file 23, Burgess Brown report of 16 Aug. 1918.

79 E. Burwash, "By the Wayside of War," *Christian Guardian*, 8 Aug. 1917, 9.

80 George Pringle, *Tillicums of the Trail*, 60–5; also NA, Chaplain Service Records, vol. 4675, Extracts from Chaplains' Reports file, Shatford report.

81 Beattie, "History," 193. Certainly Oliver felt this way when he moved from battle casualties to the VD ward: "When these cases come along I always feel that they have made a mess of their lives and bodies ... I pass them by for I cannot write home of them nor am I going to expose myself to accidental contact. Yet I imagine they have their better moments of remorse and need help even more than some others." USA, Oliver Papers, Oliver to Rita Oliver, 26 Nov. 1917.

82 NA, Chaplain Service Records, vol. 4633, J. Mothersill file, Mothersill to Beattie, July 1917 report. Mothersill served at the Cambridge VD hospital. On Skerry, see NA, Chaplain Service Records, vol. 4669, Chaplain Reports, Hospitals, Skerry to Almond, 16 Apr. 1918.

83 Almond consistently opposed the transfer to the front or recall to Canada of chaplains who proved adept at such ministry. NA, Chaplain Service Records, vol. 4633, Mothersill file; also vol. 4639, G. Plewes file.

84 Beattie, "History," 184–7. In Liverpool chaplains modelled their work after what was done in the London area, adding an extra emphasis to

adult vocational education for the disabled soldiers about to return to civilian life.

85 See NA, Chaplain Service Records, vol. 4654, Buxton file, Bruce Hunter reports. Cases of bigamy or illegitimacy had to be referred to the commandant after investigation by the padre. Straightening out these tangles required a great deal of letter-writing by the chaplain. Beattie, "History," 175–83; see also NA, Chaplain Service Records, vol. 4628, Hunter file, Hunter to Almond, 31 Aug., 17 Sept., 4 Oct. 1917; 20 Jan., 30 Apr. 1919. NA, Chaplain Service Records, vol. 4669, Chaplain Reports, Hospitals file, H. Ben-Oliel to Almond, 20 June 1918.

86 Almond had recently posted Donald MacPhail to the ship as padre when, on 27 June 1918, the ship was torpedoed by a German U-boat. His emergency posting was to assist the nurses. Their lifeboat was caught in the suction of the dying ship. MacPhail's body was recovered and buried by French civil authorities in December of that year. NA, Chaplain Service Records, vol. 4634, MacPhail file.

87 Beattie, "History," 145. See also USA, Oliver Papers, Oliver to Rita Oliver, 8 Sept., 6 Oct. 1917: "There is not a great deal of privacy. Under special circumstances a screen is put around a cot but when one wants to pray with a sick man he just kneels down simply beside the cot and so has worship with the patient." "It makes a man get down to some tremendous realities", Oliver confided to his wife: ibid., 12 Oct. 1917. On the pace at field hospitals, see NA, Chaplain Service Records, vol. 4665, Reports, R.C. Chaplains, France, R.J. Moore report, 31 Aug. 1918. See also Ottawa Anglican Diocese Archives, Hepburn Papers, Diary, Oct. 1915.

88 UCA, Methodist Army and Navy Board, box 4, file 82, E.E. Graham file, Graham to T.A. Moore, Oct. 1916. Not every hospital chaplain was as fortunate as Herbert Greene at No. 2 Canadian General Hospital, who was assisted in his work by a sympathetic nurses' aide: NA, Chaplains' Service Records, vol. 4665, Reports, France file, Greene Report, n.d. Often the chaplain found it necessary to live down the failures of a predecessor whose lack of devotion or personal quirks had soured the unit's view of the Chaplain Service: Murdoch, *Red Vineyard*, 76, 95–6. See also NA, Chaplain Service Records, vol. 4620, F.R. Costello file, Costello report of Feb.–May 1918. On the more hostile attitude of staff, see Costello file, Costello reports for Feb. to May 1918, and vol. 4621, G. C. D'Easum file, D'Easum to McGreer, Feb. 1918 reports.

89 USA, Oliver Papers, Oliver to Rita Oliver, 19, 29 Sept. 1917.

90 By 15 Oct. 1917 Oliver had written 233 letters in four days, mostly to mothers, as the dead had been too young to have wives. See USA, Oliver Papers, Oliver to Rita, 29 Oct. 1917. See also NA, Chaplain

Service Records, vol. 4665, Reports, France file, W.F. Parker to Almond, 30 Sept. 1917; also Robert Howie report, 30 Sept. 1917.

91 Oliver wondered if such inquiries disturbed the wards more than settled them. He turned in, when possible, at 9:30. See USA, Oliver Papers, Oliver to Rita Oliver, 15 Oct. 1917. Similar devotion during the 1916 fighting earned hospital commander's tributes for R.W. Ridgeway: see Fetherstonhaugh, *#3 Canadian General Hospital*, 53.

92 This was Owen's and Oliver's experience at No. 3 Canadian General Hospital during Oct. 1917. See USA, Oliver Papers, Oliver to Rita Oliver, 14 Oct. 1917.

93 Oliver's letters from No. 3 Canadian General Hospital indicate that this was his most harrowing posting overseas. See USA, Oliver Papers, Oliver to Rita Oliver, 18 Oct. 1917.

94 NA, Chaplain Service Records, vols. 464617, R.N. Burns, and 4634, W.F. Parker files. USA, Oliver Papers, Oliver to Rita Oliver, 11–12 Sept. 1917.

95 Charles Masters memoir, in the possession of his son, Donald C. Masters, of Guelph.

96 "Many times in the night to come, I would wish that the parents had known that their boy had at least the comfort of a decent bed, and a Padre standing by for his last hours," wrote a Canadian nurse serving in a casualty clearing station at the Somme. See K. Wilson-Simmie, *Lights Out!* 127–8; on the wartime development of the "triage" system, see Keegan, *Face of Battle*, 272.

97 J.J. Callan, *Canada at War*, 6:122.

98 Ibid.,.121, and Callan, "A Chaplain at a C.C.S.," *Canadian Churchman*, 12 Dec. 1918, 795, 808–10. Much the same philosophy applied to posting new chaplains to hospitals, then moving them closer to the fighting by way of the clearing stations. See UCA, Oliver Papers, Oliver to Rita Oliver, 7 Sept. 1917.

99 Callan, *Canada at War*, 122, also his "Work at a C.C.S.," *Canadian Churchman*, 12 Dec. 1918, 809.

100 NA, Chaplain Service Records, vol. 4633, Mosley file, O.C., #3 C.C.C.S., to George Fallis, 1 Nov. 1918. See also vol. 4640, Robertson file, Mar. 1918.

101 NA, Chaplain Service Records, vol. 4665, Chaplain Reports, France file, Denoon report, 1 Oct. 1917. Such phrases predominate in Baptist, Methodist, and Presbyterian chaplain reports, but similar phrases, couched in their denomination's conventions, can be located in Anglican and Roman Catholic reports as well: see NA, Chaplain Service Records, vol. 4665, Reports, France," W.F. Parker (Baptist) report, 30 Sept. 1917, and vol. 4668, Chaplain Reports, file 18, reports of 15, 30 Apr. 1918.

102 Callan, *Canada at War,* 123; also his "Work at a C.C.S.," 795; also C.K. Masters, Memoir, ms, 8–9; and Ottawa Anglican Diocese Archives, Hepburn Papers. See also NA, vol. 4668, Chaplain Reports, file 21, Robert Howie report, 16 June 1918. In addition, what kept many working effectively for extended periods of time was their admiration for the moral heroism of the wounded. Repeatedly chaplains and other medical staff credited their endurance to the moral example of their patients. As nurse Wilson-Simmie recalled: "When I became bitter, as I often did, and even doubted that there could be a God, I had only to witness what went on in that ward to come down off my high horse and see Christ by every bedside. They were so unselfish, so patient, so very brave, so very young." *Lights Out!* 127.

103 "Work at a C.C.S.," 810. For more subdued but equally sympathetic statements, see UCA, Methodist Army and Navy Board, box 9, Colwell file, Colwell to T.A. Moore, 28 Dec. 1916, or box 4, file 82, E.E. Graham to Moore, Nov.–Dec. 1916.

104 NA, Chaplain Service Records, vol. 4664, Reports, A.D.C.S., France, file 2, Burch to Fallis, n.d. (1918); also vol. 4665, Reports, France, Protestant, McAffee report, 31 July 1917. See also Ottawa Anglican Diocese Archives, Hepburn Papers, Diary, 12 Nov. 1915.

105 Ibid., vol. 4668, Chaplain Reports, file 23, Scarlett to Fallis, Aug. 1918. Similar themes dominate his May and June 1918 reports: ibid., file 22 and Scarlett's July 1918 report.

106 Ibid., vol. 4668, Chaplain Reports, file 20, Scarlett to Fallis, Oct. 1918. W.G. Clarke welcomed the Amiens victory as vindication of the righteousness of their cause. His thanksgiving service, with French civilians present, seemed especially appropriate as his men "gave emphasis to the common bonds of unity that bind into one the mighty people whose destinies are so inseparably identified with the triumph of humanity, democracy and the Kingdom of God on Earth." NA, Chaplain Service Records, vol. 4668, Chaplain Reports, file 23, Clarke to George Fallis, 15 Aug. 1918.

107 At the 1915 Presbyterian General Assembly, John Pringle's telegrams urged fellow churchmen to enlist. *CAR* (1915): 224, 346. In 1916 Robert Taylor, a Scottish-born Presbyterian minister back from six months with the Forty-second Battalion, called from his Montreal pulpit for conscription. R.M. Bray, "The Canadian Patriotic Response to the Great War," PhD, York 1977, 182. See John Almond, John Pringle, Harry Kent, E.D. McLaren, George Duncan, G.L. Starr, and W.H. Thornton echoing Charles Gordon's call for Union government with conscription. Kent advised Anglicans in Canada: "Cast politics to the winds, vote Union Government and Conscription." *Canadian Churchman,* 27 Sept. 1917, 623; also *CAR* (1917): 416, 556, 578, 635. See

also *Canadian Churchman*, 21 June 1917, 398; 27 Sept. 1917, 623. See also *Presbyterian and Westminster*, 12 July 1917, 52.

108 This was particularly noticeable among Presbyterians and Methodists who previously had voted Liberal. Between May and July 1917 Oliver moved from dismay at Liberal policy to outright abandonment of the party. USA, Oliver Papers, Oliver to Rita Oliver 29 May, 9, 22 June, 2, 19, 24 July 1917. Back in Canada, ex-chaplain William Graham reported that he was telling soldiers' wives that there was only one way to vote: "Conscription." NA, Chaplains' Service Records, vol. 4625, W.C. Graham file, Graham to Almond, 24 Nov. 1917.

CHAPTER FIVE

1 NA, Chaplain Service Records, vol. 4626, Harris file, and Ottawa Anglican Diocese Archives, Hepburn Papers, Diary, 12 Oct. 1916.

2 Smyth, *In This Sign Conquer*, 156–7, 162–3, 167.

3 Owen Creighton, *With the 29th Division in Gallipoli*, 32, 51; NA, RG 9 III B 1, vol. 919, file C-75-3, Principal Chaplains' Instructions to Chaplains, December, 1915; also Keegan, *The Face of Battle*, 272.

4 Owen Creighton, a British chaplain, explained: "At the time there was only one C. of E. chaplain to each brigade, in fact we had only three to the whole Division. The question was how we could be of greatest use to the greatest number of men. And it followed that if three regiments in a brigade were in an attack, being with any one of the three would make it impossible to do anything in the other two. The converging point for the wounded would be the advanced dressing station of the Field Ambulance to which we were attached." Later this policy was changed: Creighton, *With the 29th Division in Gallipoli*, 32–3.

5 Quoted in Dennis Winter, *Death's Men: Soldiers of the Great War*, 60.

6 Smyth, *In This Sign Conquer*, 164–6, 179–80. Unit medical officers also wanted to carry on forward medical work while their supervisors ordered them to remain in the rear. See Robin G. Kierstead, "The Canadian Military Medical Experience during the Great War, 1914–1918," MA, Queen's University 1982, 66–71.

7 Scott, *Great War*, 35–7.

8 NA, Chaplain Service Records, vol. 4659, DCS file, 1st Canadian Division, Routine Orders #27 and #32, 18 Feb. 1915. Scott, however, was making forays into the line by the end of February: "I was warned to keep myself in the background as it was said that the chaplains were not allowed in the front line ... I was immensely pleased at having at last got into the front line. Even if I were sent out I had at last seen the trenches." When Scott was accosted by a British general, instead of reporting him, he invited him to lunch. Scott, *Great War*, 37, 39. See

also Beattie, "History," 23–5; Gordon, *Postscript to Adventure*, 248, 251–2; and Currie, *"The Red Watch,"* 131.

9 Fetherstonhaugh, *14th Battalion*, 23, 28, 35.

10 Beattie, "History," 25; also Scott, *Great War*, 48–9. Scott led a voluntary Good Friday service in front of the town hall, where several hundred stood and worshipped while the racket of lorries and motorcycles threatened to drown out the sermon and songs. On Easter morning he fitted up a local hall with cross, lighted candles, and the ubiquitous Union Jack as altar cloth. Several communion services were held there that day, beginning at 6 a.m.

11 Beattie recalled that over five thousand casualties went through the Vlamertinghe medical stations, where the majority of the Canadian chaplains served during the action. Beattie, "History," 30. Alexander Gordon worked at the First Field Ambulance dressing stations: *Presbyterian*, 24 June 1915, 673–4.

12 Beattie, "History," 26–9. A. Gordon, *Presbyterian*, 24 June 1915, 674. Beattie, with the First Brigade, began the battle at the bridge, cheering the men on, it was said, with passages of Scripture, having short prayers with parties going forward, and helping to carry out the wounded. Later he won praise for getting rations up under fire. Tucker, *Battle Glory of Canada*, 104; William Perkins Bull, *From Brock to Currie*, 350; also *Canada in the Great World War*, 3:100.

13 Scott, *Great War*, 61–74; also Duguid, *Official History*, pt 1, 420. At the invitation of its commander, Scott remained with the ambulance for several days after the battle, only wandering back to his quasi-official home unit when the majority of the casualties had been taken off his hands. See also Fetherstonhaugh, *14th Battalion*, 48–9, and Gordon, *Presbyterian*, 24 June 1915, 674. Australian chaplains were also thrown into the midst of the fray at Gallipoli, where the confined Allied bridgehead merged battle and support areas. Unlike the Canadians, when the AIF was posted to Europe, Australian chaplains seem to have abided by the regulations that kept chaplains out of the line. Such a policy may have cost the AIF chaplains some of their initial popularity with the men. See McKernan, *Australian Churches at War*, 59. British chaplains at Gallipoli felt the same tensions. Creighton, too, became caught up in the fighting and spent more time visiting the forward positions. Other chaplains in his division went ashore in the initial landings. *With the 29th Division*, 32–4, 51, 65.

14 The general had ordered Scott not to come east of brigade headquarters on this occasion. The dugouts where he caught the canon, however, were almost a mile beyond it, a few hundred yards from the very front line, in an exposed position where horse ambulances only dared come up for the wounded after dark. The general threatened to send

Scott to a dreaded hospital posting but the chaplain still disregarded the order.

15 *Canadian Churchman*, 13 Jan. 1916, 29. See also NA, Chaplain Service Records, vol. 4617, A.W. Buckland file; vol. 4646, A.W. Woods file, Woods's report of 31 Dec. 1916; vol. 4616, Ball file; and *Canada*, 8 Apr. 1916, 35. While Ball was having his mutilated arm bandaged and splinted, the Forty-ninth Battalion's resident n'er do well quipped, "God, padre, How're the boys going to get to heaven now?" Stevens, *A City Goes to War*, 46.

16 Charles Masters' commander gave him permission to visit the units in the trenches, where he gave "continuous communion. The men came singly or in pairs, reverently partook of the sacred emblems of the Lord's Passion and went quietly back to duty, strengthened and refreshed for the grim burden of war." See C.K. Masters, Memoir, ms, 20. See also Ottawa Anglican Diocese Archives, Hepburn Papers, Diary, Feb.–June 1916, and Gordon, *Postscript*, 230ff, 242. Beattie, "History," 23–4, 33–4; Duguid, *Official History*, pt 2, Map 10; W.R. Jones, *Fighting the Hun from Saddle and Trench*, 62; Sir Andrew MacPhail, *The Medical Services*, 37; and Fetherstonhaugh, *13th Battalion*, 59.

17 Beattie, "History," 38. Scott, *Great War*, 90, 93–123. Conditions were so static in this sector that the First Division Engineers built a burlap and wood church hut (complete with bell and baptismal font), which was dedicated on St George's Day and used for Easter services. Scott, *Great War*, 132–3.

18 Beattie, "History," 119; also Scott, *Great War*, 109–11.

19 Duguid, *Appendices*, 431. Scott, *Great War*, 94–7; Fetherstonhaugh, *13th Battalion*, 66.

20 Sylvestre reported that, by July, the Third Brigade had been without a priest for some time, and he reckoned that the First had "not met a priest who understood English since Easter!" NA, Chaplain Service Records, vol. 4643, Sylvestre file, Sylvestre to Steacy, 5 July 1915. By then Sylvestre was exhausted, but Steacy could not find a replacement until autumn, when he recalled him to England. Ibid., Sylvestre to Steacy, 16, 28 July, 25 Oct. 1915.

21 "The rules which hitherto had fenced off the chaplains, as being officers, from easy intercourse with the men were being relaxed. Chaplains were being looked upon more as parish priests to their battalions. They could be visited freely by the men, and could also have meals with the men when they saw fit … Our chaplains had done splendid work, and I think I may say that, with one or two exceptions, they were idolized by their units." Scott, *Great War*, 99, 115. Eventually British authorities conceded that chaplains should live at brigade or battalion headquarters. See Royal Canadian Regiment Archives, Wolseley

Barracks, London, Ont., General Routine Orders, B.E.F., Adjutant-General's Branch, G.H.Q., 1 Dec. 1915; also NA, RG 9 III B 1, vol. 919, C-75-3, Principal Chaplains' Instructions to Chaplains, Dec. 1915.

22 NA, Chaplain Service Records, vol. 4646, Woods file, Woods report, 31 Dec. 1916; also Gordon, *Postscript to Adventure*, 228.

23 As Woods put it, "simpler and more effective"; on the British transition, see P.B. Clayton, *Tales of Talbot House in Poperinghe and Ypres*, 17–18.

24 Organizing general-interest lectures and distributing Canadian newspapers and magazines also became features of Shatford's Social-service work. A Nova Scotian by birth, Shatford was a graduate of King's College, Windsor. In 1906 he became curate of St James the Apostle in Montreal. Long before the war his preaching had drawn the attention of imperialists and social gospellers in the English-speaking Montreal community. See Morgan, *Canadian Men and Women of the Time* (1912), 1012.

25 Within twelve months the loan had been repaid. By Easter 1916 seventy thousand Canadian troops had attended Chaplain Service concerts. Beattie "History," 37, 42; Scott, *Great War*, 109–11. Shatford was relieved when Almond appointed the single Salvation Army chaplain permitted the Canadian Corps as his full-time assistant. On Salvationists at Corps, see NA, Chaplain Service Records, vol. 4619, Carroll file; vol. 4642, Steele file; and vol. 4638, Penfold file. On this period see also Shatford's report in *The Proceedings of the 8th General Synod of the Church of England in Canada*, 386–9.

26 Scott left his clerk in charge of the senior chaplain's office and went up the line for days, returning to divisional headquarters only for Sunday services: "I used to take comfort in remembering Poo Bah's song in *Mikado*, 'He never will be missed, he never will be missed.'" To the delight of the troops, Scott often brought along his dog. *Great War*, 118–21. Cecil Owen visited his Sixth Brigade charges in the line nearly every day of its tour, holding "trench funerals" for those killed by snipers or shells. NA, Chaplain Service Records, vol. 4637, Owen file, Owen to Steacy, 11 Oct. 1915. On Shatford's Christmas Day visits to the trenches, see Fetherstonhaugh, *The 24th Battalion*, 34. See also C. Masters memoir; Fallis, *A Padre's Pilgrimage*, 72, 75–9; and Wells, *Fighting Bishop*, 159.

27 One, William Walker, won high praise from the commander of the battalion he served. NA, Chaplain Service Records, vol. 4645, Walker file, O.C., 31st Battalion, to Steacy, Apr. 1916; also Beattie, "History," 39.

28 QUA, A.M. Gordon Papers, box 2, Correspondence, Military, Almond to Gordon, 22 June 1916. According to D. Macintire, a Canadian later killed at Vimy, Byng had a religious streak: see Pierre Berton, *Vimy*, 96.

29 A.M. Gordon, "A Chaplain at the Front," *QQ* (1919): 173. By this time similar debate was taking place between German officers and chaplains: see Schübel, 50–1. I thank Dr Douglas Dodds, Mr George Innis, and especially Mr Bernard Lindenblatt, German Army (retired), for their assistance in translating Schubel's book. Among the Canadians, A.W. Buckland, an Anglican, was concussed by a large shell, developing an ulcer soon afterwards, and was sent back to England. *Canadian Churchman*, 13 Jan. 1916, 29; also NA, Chaplain Service Records, vol. 4617, Buckland file. W. Ball, another Anglican, insisted on billeting with his unit's intelligence officer. When their dugout was shelled, he was wounded and partially buried. Another blast freed him but one arm was so mutilated that even after extensive therapy Ball could not continue as a chaplain and retired to a parish in England. NA, Chaplain Service Records, vol. 4646, A. Woods file, 31 Dec. 1916; vol. 4616, Ball file; also *Canada*, 8 Apr. 1916, 35.

30 Wilken remained the service's solitary chaplain in German captivity until March 1918, when he was repatriated through Holland to England. Beattie, "History," 40; NA, Chaplain Service Records, vol. 4646, Wilken file, Almond to Steacy, 6 June 1916, and vol. 4646, A.W. Woods file, report, 31 Dec. 1916, 3.

31 NA, Chaplain Service Records, vol. 4646, Wilken file, Almond to Steacy, 17 June 1916; also Fetherstonhaugh, *24th Battalion*, 160, 165. For an account of Mount Sorrel from an aid-post chaplain, see George Kilpatrick, "The Third Battle of Ypres," *Presbyterian*, 13 July 1916, 32–3. Beattie, "History," 40–1; also Masters ms, 11; and NA, Chaplain Service Records, vol. 4632, Masters file, Masters to Steacy, 2 July 1916. Alex Gordon was cited for leading stretcher-bearers in similar work for twelve hours under heavy shelling. Two bearers were killed and five wounded in this incident: QUA, Gordon Papers, box 2, Almond to Gordon. One chaplain, William Barton, was wounded but refused to be evacuated during the engagement, while W.H. Thornton, a Roman Catholic chaplain, was rendered permanently deaf when his casualty clearing station was shelled. NA, Chaplain Service Records, vol. 4616, Barton file, and vol. 4644, Thornton file. See also Ottawa Anglican Diocese Archives, Hepburn Papers, diary, May–July 1916.

32 Charles Gordon discusses these anxieties among his battalion officers during this battle. *Postscript to Adventure*, 248–52, 256.

33 Scott, *Great War*, 129–32; Urquhart, *Arthur Currie*, 112–14, 129.

34 Beattie, "History," 44. Though Almond did not get his divisional increase for some time, Steacy did send four padres – two Anglicans, a Baptist, and a Catholic – for temporary Corps duty during the summer offensive. NA, Chaplain Service Records, vol. 4621, Daniel file, Steacy to War Office, 4 July 1916.

35 "Some doubt appears to exist as to the position chaplains should occupy during active operations. It is considered that, provided their presence in no way hampers the operations in progress or in contemplation, no restrictions should be placed on their movements; and that chaplains should be encouraged to go where the Senior Chaplains, Church of England, Nonconformist and Roman Catholic, of divisions, decide that their services can be most advantageously employed, and where they can be of most use to the troops." Quoted in J. Edmonds, *History of the Great War Based on Official Documents*, 138. The existence of this ruling, unfortunately, has not had very much recognition or influence in the historiography of the Great War chaplaincies.

36 Madden, a forty-one-year-old Oblate from Vancouver, was attached to the Eighth Brigade at the time: "He assisted to dress wounds and conducted men who had been blinded to dressing stations. He did much to cheer up the men, and undoubtedly saved lives by digging men out of buried trenches." NA, Chaplain Service Records, vol. 4621, Madden file. See also *Canada*, 26 Aug. 1916, 246. The Military Cross had been instituted by Great Britain at the end of 1914 to recognize distinguished and meritorious combat service by junior officers.

37 G. Wood was wounded on 13 Sept. but returned to duty soon after. NA, Chaplain Service Records, vol. 4646, Wood file, report, 15 Sept. 1916. One week earlier O'Gorman had been crippled by shellfire while searching no man's land for casualties. He returned to Canada for recuperation and received the Military Cross. See Fetherstonhaugh, *Royal Montreal Rifles*, 111.

38 Nicholson, *C.E.F.*, 172. During these attacks Fifth Brigade chaplain William Kidd won an MC for assisting casualties under fire for three days without rest. *Canada*, 2 Dec. 1916, 295. Arthur McGreer was recommended for a DSO after carrying up supplies for wounded men and leading stretcher parties under fire so hot that several casualties were lost in the attempt – he eventually received an MC. Robert Thompson won his MC for taking care of wounded under fire. Ibid., 25 Nov. 1916, 258; Beattie, "History," 45; NA, Chaplain Service Records, vol. 4635, McGreer file, DSO recommendation, 23 Sept. 1916; on Thompson, see *Canada*, 2 Dec. 1916, 296.

39 Some appreciation of the devastating losses taken by the Canadians on that day can be gained from reading battalion accounts, especially Fetherstonhaugh, *13th Battalion*, 137–41; also C.B. Topp's *42nd Battalion*, 82–9. The latter account was extracted from the unit chaplain's diary. The Canadians suffered 24,029 casualties on the Somme: Nicholson, *C.E.F.*, 198.

40 Scott, *Great War*, 139–40.

41 Ottawa Anglican Diocese Archives, Hepburn Papers, Diary, Oct. 1916–Apr. 1917.

42 Alexander Gordon, in particular, encountered difficulty in deploying his too-few Roman Catholic chaplains effectively, as Medical Corps officials were reluctant to allow them room in the Courcellette aid posts during attacks. Gordon and Almond ensured this would not recur at Vimy the following April. NA, Chaplain Service Records, vol. 4665, Reports, R.C. Chaplains, Britain, file, unsigned report of Catholic chaplains' work at the Somme, Oct., 1916; also MacPhail, *Medical Services*, 86ff.

43 NA, Chaplain Service Records, vol. 4646, A. Woods file, Woods report, 31 Dec. 1916; vol. 4626, Harris file; also Masters ms, 22–6, and Beattie, "History," 51. Channel Hepburn, of the Ninth Canadian Field Ambulance, won an MC for his gallantry in caring for wounded under fire near Pozires. Despite being buried by a shell, he carried on until ordered to the rear by a medical officer. NA, Chaplain Service Records, vol. 4627, Hepburn file. J.A. Fortier, another Catholic serving with the Canadian Cavalry Brigade, subsequent to the fighting was also awarded an MC for tending wounded under fire. NA, Chaplain Service Records, vol. 4623, Fortier file.

44 Quoted in Beattie, "History," 50.

45 Beattie, "History," 44; Scott, *Great War*, 138.

46 Beattie, "History," 44, 50; also NA, Chaplain Service Records, vol. 4646, A.W. Woods file, Woods report, 31 Dec. 1916. The Third Division senior chaplain reported that officers and men were still talking about the coffee stalls long after the Canadians left the Somme. See also Church of England in Canada, *8th General Synod Report*, 386–8, and Gordon, "A Chaplain at the Front," *QQ* (1919): 175.

47 Scott, *Great War*, 144; and MacPhail, *Medical Services*, 86ff. See also Masters ms, 20, and *Canada*, 4 Nov. 1916, 162.

48 Long-range German artillery now made rear areas hazardous as well. NA, Chaplain Service Records, vol. 4646, A.W. Woods file, Woods report, 31 Dec. 1916. By Christmas two more padres had been removed to England after serious accidents. NA, Chaplain Service Records, vol. 4646, Williamson file, Workman to Steacy, 28 Oct. 1916. The fighting had taken its toll on senior chaplains: Beattie asked for relief. In early 1917 he left the Second Division for administrative work in England. NA, Chaplain Service Records, vol. 4616, W. Beattie file, Beattie to Steacy, 19 Oct. 1916.

49 Scott, *Great War*, 153–60.

50 Scott, *Great War*, 161–2; Beattie, "History," 51.

51 Alexander Gordon claimed that only one unit commander in his division still resisted weekly church parades. He withdrew all objections

when Gordon appealed to divisional authorities. NA, Chaplain Service Records, vol. 4667, Chaplain Reports, file 13, Gordon to McGreer, 17 Mar. 1917; Chaplain Reports, file 14, R.D. Harrison report, n.d., 1917.

52 NA, Chaplain Service Records, vol. 4641, Shires file, Shires to Almond, 6 Feb. 1917; vol. 4615, Almond file, Almond to Steacy, 19 Jan. 1917.

53 NA, Chaplain Service Records, vol. 4616, Barrow file, McGreer to Almond, Mar. 1917.

54 By this time similar measures were in force among the British chaplains, although not all chaplains were accompanying their troops into the front lines. See Smyth, *In This Sign Conquer*, 164–5.

55 MacPhail, *Medical Services*, 94–8. For an example of such negotiations, see NA, Chaplain Service Records, vol. 4667, Chaplain Reports, file 13, A. Gordon to A.A. and Q.M.G., 4th Division, 24 Mar. 1917.

56 On Vimy planning, see Herbert Fairlie Wood, *Vimy!* 86–8; also NA, Chaplain Service Records, vol. 4648, file 5, McGreer to D.C.S., 8 Apr. 1917.

57 Steele and McWilliams, *Suicide Battalion*, 75; also Scott, *Great War*, 162; Fetherstonhaugh, *13th Battalion*, 158–9; and Fetherstonhaugh, *14th Battalion*, 139.

58 Beattie, "History," 53; Scott, *Great War*, 165–7; Wood, *Vimy!* 127–8.

59 During these preparations Presbyterian chaplain James Paulin was hit by shell fragments and evacuated. He never returned to the Corps as months of therapy proved ineffective, and was eventually returned to Canada. Ironically, he was the only Chaplain Service casualty at Vimy Ridge.

60 According to McGreer, it was a matter of professional pride to Corps chaplains and burial officers to do a better job of clearing the field of dead at Vimy than had been possible at the Somme.

61 Wood and Robertson reports of Vimy Ridge, Beattie, "History," 54–9.

62 NA, Chaplain Service Records, vol. 4667, Chaplain Reports, file 13, Gordon report, Vimy Ridge.

63 As examples of such activities, see E.E. Graham report of 10 May 1917, and D. Robertson report, NA, Chaplain Service Records, vol. 4666, Vimy Ridge Reports file, also quoted in Beattie, "History," 56–9; also George Wood report, which is also quoted in Beattie, 54–6, and Chaplain Service Records, vol. 4667, Chaplain Reports, file 13, Gordon report of 4th Division Chaplains, Vimy Ridge.

64 Peebles and Singer, *History of the Thirty-First Battalion*, 213; also Gordon, "A Chaplain at the Front," *QQ* (1919): 173–4. George Kilpatrick, with the Third Division, reported that even German wounded were shot down at his side: Pierre Berton, *Vimy*, 256. See also NA, Chaplains' Service Records, vol. 4665, Reports, R.C. Chaplains, France file,

3rd Division Senior Chaplain's Reports; and Beattie, "History," 63–4. See also C.B. Topp, *42nd Battalion*, 382, 130–1.

65 NA, Chaplain Service Records, vol. 4667, Chaplain Reports, file 3, George Farquhar report; file 13, F.L. Stephenson report, 21 May 1917; vol. 4635, Harold McCausland file, Vimy Ridge report; Sr. Chaplain Moffit, 2nd Division report, Beattie, "History," 61–3.

66 Nicholson, *C.E.F.*, 270–7.

67 Fetherstonhaugh, *14th Battalion*, 153; also McWilliams and Steele, *Suicide Battalion*, 86. At the third of these services, with General Currie present, the army commander congratulated the troops. Beattie, "History," 69; Scott, *Great War*, 181.

68 General G.F. Farmer to McGreer, 7 May 1917, Beattie, "History," 70. See also Scott, *Great War*, 175, and *8th General Synod Report*, (1918) 389. Edward Appleyard won a Military Cross for his work evacuating wounded and burying the dead under German shellfire. Robert Ridgeway won his for taking over an abandoned aid post and supervising the evacuation of the wounded under fire. Ambrose Madden again won distinction for leading the rescue of a number of men left in the German barbed wire during the 29 April attack. Frederick Sherring and Ralph Harrison were nearly killed when their dressing stations took direct hits from German naval guns. NA, Chaplain Service Records, vol. 4675, Extracts of Chaplains' Reports file.

69 Competitors were served lunch by the Chaplain Service: Beattie, "History," 73. "Canada had travelled a long distance on the path of nationhood since that far off time, and now, after fifty years, I had the satisfaction of being with the great Canadian Army Corps on European soil, engaged in the biggest war of history ... The splendid body of men before me gave promise of Canada's progress and national glory in the future," Scott recalled. *Great War*, 189.

70 In January 1918 Currie responded to a request by Bishop Arthur F. Winnington-Ingram, British Anglican bishop of London, for an invitation to visit the Canadians by inquiring of Almond if the bishop "was one of those clergymen who believed that the proper thing to do in this war was to turn the other cheek if the Bosche hit you very hard on one. If such were his views it was not my intention to ask him, but I am told His Lordship is an entirely different sort of man ... I am sure his visit would do us all a great deal of good." NA, Chaplain Service Records, vol. 4648, D.C.S. file 1, A.W. Currie to Almond, 22 Jan. 1918.

71 One chaplain was hit by shellfire and, shell-shocked, returned to Canada. Two others, including the chaplain to the Twenty-second Battalion, were sent back to Canada after being diagnosed "neurasthenic."

NA, Chaplain Service Records, vol. 4648, file 7, French to Workman, 3 July 1917. Scott billeted with the gunners before the assault, using their pits and dugouts as his headquarters while visiting the batteries. Scott, *Great War,* 198ff. See also Fetherstonhaugh, *24th Battalion,* 154; and his *14th Battalion,* 161, 166, 168; Weatherbe, *Rideau to the Rhine,* 263; Lapointe, *Soldier of Quebec,* 54.

72 Scott, *Great War,* 192.

73 NA, MG 30 E 46, R. Turner Papers, vol. 4, 2274–5, D.C.S. Report to Turner for Aug. 1917. See also Beattie, "History," 74–5, 202.

74 Scott, *Great War,* 198ff.

75 Fetherstonhaugh, *13th Battalion,* 192, 195, 201; also NA, Chaplain Service Records, vol. 4665, Reports, France, Graham report of 12–19 Aug. 1917.

76 NA, Chaplain Service Records, vol. 4631, Lockary file, Hill 70 report; also Madden file, Madden report of 15–18 Aug. 1917.

77 This applied only to the Protestant staff. Moffit's trio of Catholic priests was spread as thinly as anyone's.

78 NA, Chaplain Service Records, vol. 4665, Reports, France file, Baynes-Reid report, 30 Aug. 1917, and vol. 4668, Chaplain Reports, file 5, Baynes-Reid to Gordon, 20 Aug. 1917. See also Beattie, "History," 75. For Gordon's maps, which give medical unit positions, evacuation routes, and unit headquarters locations, see QUA, A.M. Gordon Papers, box 6, Great Britain, War Office, General Staff Geographical Section, London 1917, map: France, (Lens), Edition 10A, scale: 1/20,000.

79 Although one chaplain in the division suffered a nervous breakdown during this period and was barred from the trenches by his unit commander. NA, ibid., vol. 4668, Chaplain Reports, file 15, J. Tupper to Woods, 26 Aug. 1917.

80 NA, Chaplain Service Records, vol. 4629, Kidd file, Kidd report, 9 Aug. 1917; also Corrigal, *20th Battalion,* 143–4. Moffit's padres, however, reported having much more time to speak with and minister to the casualties as they waited to be evacuated or to have their wounds dressed: ibid., vol. 4626, Hay file, 3 Sept. 1917 report. Moffit also put two chaplains in the rear to cover the artillery units, and had one of them also see to the burial party. He reported later that the coffee-stall operation had been especially successful.

81 General Currie sent McGreer's application to First Army headquarters, noting that sixty men of this type were already working for the chaplains. In the meantime the coffee stalls continued to operate, one just three hundred yards behind the front line. Beattie, "History," 76, 203, 207; NA, RG 9 III B 1, vol. 942, file E-102-3, McGreer to A.W. Currie, 4 Oct. 1917; and Currie to G.O.C., 1st Army, 4 Oct. 1917. Profits were spent on the troops, in hundred-franc gifts for infantry, artillery, and

engineer units for sporting goods as well as, throughout the rest of the Corps, for tennis and badminton rackets, musical instruments, baseball outfits, over five hundred books, fifty pounds of "edifying printed pictures" (to counter the lurid pin-ups that abounded), free magazines, and stationary.

82 Beattie, "History," 76; also NA, Chaplain Service Records, vol. 4668, Chaplain Reports, file 15, Woods to McGreer, aut. 1917.

83 Nicholson, *C.E.F.*, 312–13, 317; also Urquhart, *Arthur Currie*, 173–9. On Passchendaele, see Nicholson, *C.E.F.*, 318–27.

84 Kilpatrick report, Beattie, "History," 78; see also UCA, George Kilpatrick Papers, Kilpatrick to T.B. Kilpatrick, 6 Nov. 1917.

85 "As it turned out, this was really the only plan that could have been adopted." Ibid., vol. 4668, Chaplain Reports 15, Woods to A.D.C.S., Nov. 1917; Beattie, "History," 77; NA, Militia and Defence, 2nd Division Records, vol. 919, C-75-3 (Chaplain file), Moffit report of Passchendaele operations, 2nd Division chaplains, 22 Nov. 1917.

86 Ibid., vol. 4665, Reports, R.C. Chaplains, France, MacDonnell report, 26 Oct.–3 Nov. 1917.

87 Ibid., vol. 4665, Reports, R.C. Chaplains, France, R.C. MacGillivray to Senior Chaplain, Report of operations covering 3 Nov. 1917; Beattie, "History," 78–9.

88 MacGillivray report, ibid., and Beattie, "History," 80; also Chaplain Service Records, vol. 4623, M.F. Fallon file, Workman to Bishop Fallon, 5 Dec. 1917.

89 *Canada*, vol. 49, 9 Feb. 1918, 153; vol. 50, 4 May 1918, 130, 147; Bennett, *4th C.M.R.s*, 85–6; NA, Chaplain Service Records, vol. 4620, Davis file; vol. 4675, Extracts from Chaplains' Reports, Woods and Stewart to Almond, 22 Oct.-4 Nov. 1917 report.

90 "I was humbled, perhaps if I had been more careful or not so hasty in getting them off the poor fellows might have been spared," he reported. NA, Chaplain Service Records, vol. 4620, Colwell file, report of 11 Nov. 1917; and *Canada*, vol. 50, 4 May 1918, 130.

91 UCA, G. Kilpatrick Papers, box 1, Correspondence, Kilpatrick to T.B. Kilpatrick, 6 Nov. 1917; also Beattie, "History," 77–8; NA, Chaplain Service Records, vol. 4668, Chaplain Reports, files 15 and 16, Kilpatrick reports, 6, 20 Nov. 1917. On Pringle's experiences, see vol. 4639, Pringle file, report of 22 Oct.–4 Nov. 1917, and his *Tillicums of the Trail*, 127–34.

92 MacPhail, *Medical Services*, 102–3; and *Canada in the Great World War*, 4:209, 232. The nine coffee stalls set up at advanced dressing stations served up to 1,000 gallons of coffee and 1,200 gallons of other hot drinks to about 10,000 men daily. Three Chaplain Service canteens operated for a time but soon closed for lack of transport to bring in more supplies.

93 McGreer and Shatford were especially pleased by English observers' favourable comments on the stalls and other Canadian measures for clearing the field of wounded. NA, Chaplain Service Records, vol. 4648, file 4, McGreer to Almond, 7 Nov. 1917; also Shatford, in *8th General Synod Report* (1918), 389–93; Beattie, "History," 82; and Bennett, *4th C.M.R.s*, 75.

94 One of their number, suffering from combat stress and mental instability compounded by the effects of poison gas, tried to take his own life and was returned to England for observation and therapy. Chaplains R. Thompson, G. D'Easum and Father T. McCarthy all returned to the Corps after recovering from the effects of gas. Unitarian chaplain C.S. Bullock had been slightly wounded at Passchendaele, and two Catholic priests, F. Costello and L. Lowry, had to be returned to England, completely spent by the 1917 campaign. Workman reported that the last six months had entirely used up Costello's reserve of courage: "He never quavered as long as he was in the line." NA, Chaplain Service Records, vol. 4623, M.F. Fallon file, Workman to Fallon, 5 Dec. 1917; also vol. 4668, Chaplain Reports, file 16, Gordon to McGreer, late Nov. 1917.

95 NA, Chaplain Service Records, vol. 4675, Extracts of Chaplains' Reports, E. Graham report, Jan.–Mar., 1918. *Canada in the Great World War*, 5:5, 49, 54–5; Weatherbe, *Rideau to the Rhine*, 234; W.B. Kerr, *Shrieks and Crashes*, 200–1.

96 NA, Chaplain Service Records, vol. 4668, Chaplain Reports, file 16, H. Baynes-Reid to A.M. Gordon, Dec. 1917.

97 Scott's First Division padres alone presented around forty candidates. *Great War*, 234–5.

98 One padre received the DSO, eight others Military Crosses, while six were mentioned in despatches. The Distinguished Service Order was established in 1886 to recognize distinguished officer gallantry in the face of the enemy. One senior chaplain received a CMG: Beattie, "History," 84. The Order of St Michael and St George had been created in 1818 for extraordinary service to the British Empire, including the distinguished service of colonial officers in British military operations: see Arthur Jocelyn, *Awards of Honour*, 35–8.

99 Jocelyn, *Awards of Honour*, 20–1; *8th General Synod Report* (1918), 390; Beattie, "History," 84.

100 *Canada in the Great War*, 5:27–31, Bennett, *4th C.M.R.s*, 93.

101 Scott, *Great War*, 234–42.

102 NA, Chaplain Service Records, vol. 4631, Madden file, Madden to Workman, 15 Mar. 1918; *Canada*, vol. 49, 23 Mar. 1918, 334.

103 *Canada*, vol. 50, 18 May 1918, 183. See also Murdoch, *Red Vineyard*, 152–3, 168–75; Scott, *Great War*, 245–51; NA, Chaplain Service

Records, vol. 4666, Reports file 4, Gordon's Secret Orders to Chaplains, May–June 1918. See also his marked map in QUA, A.M. Gordon Papers, box 2, Great Britain, War Office, 1917, France (Arras), scale: 1/20,000, Edition 10A.

104 *Canada*, vol. 50, 13 Apr. 1918, 37, 51; also J. Chaballe, *Histoire Du 22e Bataillon Canadien-Français, 1914–1919*, 324–32.

105 Murdoch, *Red Vineyard*, 188–95.

106 Beattie, "History," 145.

107 NA, Chaplain Service Records, vol. 4665, Reports, France file, Creegan to McGreer, 19 Aug. 1917.

108 McGreer, nevertheless, badgered Almond for a larger establishment, as General Currie's reorganization of the Corps created more work than his present staff could handle. See NA, MG 30, R. Turner Papers, 2688–90, 2766, D.C.S. reports to Turner, for Mar.–Apr. 1918.

109 Wells, *Fighting Bishop*, 202–4. Corps chaplains found both gambling and profanity tempting them to become moral policemen. Gambling was officially outlawed, though the Corps chaplains still carried out two campaigns, one in mid-1917 and another a year later, of preaching and petitioning senior offices to root out Crown and Anchor (a popular game that the padres believed was rigged to fleece the unwary). NA, Chaplain Service Records, vol. 4648, Reports file 4, Corps Chaplains Meeting, 9 July 1917. See also vol. 4667, Chaplain Reports, file 14, E. Graham to McGreer, 29 July 1917; also Creegan to McGreer, 17 June 1917, and file 8, Wells report, 15 May 1918. Most chaplains followed a more relaxed code about profanity, rebuking only the most outrageous examples. See Callan, "Chaplain Services," in *Canada in the Great World War*, 128–9.

110 Fetherstonhaugh, *24th Battalion*, 214; Beattie, "History," 89.

111 Beattie, "History," 89, 214–18; Murdoch, *Red Vineyard*, 198.

112 Scott, *Great War*, 259–71.

113 Scott, *Great War*, 270; UCA, D.M. Gordon Papers, box 2, Correspondence, 1918, A. Gordon to W. Gordon, 1 Aug. 1918; NA, RG 9 III B 1, vol. 1000, P-124-3, vol. 1, McGreer to A Branch, Canadian Corps, 27 July 1918, and reply.

114 University of Western Ontario Archives, G.C. Markham Papers, "Memoir of Pte. C.G. Markham: The Last Hundred Days," 2.

115 NA, Chaplain Service Records, vol. 4666, Amiens, Battle Reports file, Moffit and Wells reports, and orders of 6 Aug. 1918. See also Wells, *Fighting Bishop*, 206–8.

116 NA, Chaplain Service Records, vol. 4674, Reports, A.D.C.S., Corps, McGreer's report, 8–18 Aug. 1918; Beattie, "History," 92–4, and Whitaker's report, 96. A. Gordon's maps of Amiens allow a close view of how his chaplains were deployed for the engagement. Every dressing

station, canteen, and coffee stall within reach of the division was clearly noted, allowing him to tour the area to check on his staff. His report was never completed, for he was wounded at the outset of the battle. QUA, A. Gordon Papers. Doctors, too, experimented with immediate battlefield transfusion at Amiens: see N. Guiou, *Transfusion*, 54.

117 NA, Chaplain Service Records, vol. 4667, Chaplain Reports, file 6, A.H. Creegan report of Canal du Nord engagement.

118 The previous May, Davis had turned down a request from his bishop to return to Canada: NA, Chaplain Service Records, vol. 4620, Davis file, L.W. Moffit to McGreer, Aug. 1918. See also Bennett, *4th C.M.R.s*, 122–3.

119 For example, see NA, Chaplain Service Records, vol. 4666, Amiens, Battle Reports file. See also W.J. Hamilton report, quoted in vol. 4675, Extracts of Chaplains' Reports, also quoted in Beattie, "History," 95, and Scott, *Great War*, 277–9. See also Murdoch, *Red Vineyard*, 242–3.

120 Arthur Priest, chaplain of the Tenth Brigade, was wounded but soon returned to duty. Father Desjardins of the Fifth Brigade was winded by a near miss, something considered a normal occupational nuisance. Beattie, "History," 98; NA, Chaplain Service Records, vol. 4665, Reports, R.C. Chaplains, France, French to Workman, 17 Aug. 1918; vol. 4644, Thompkins file, Thompkins to French, 23 Sept. 1918.

121 See NA, Chaplain Service Records, vol. 4631, Madden file; also *Canada*, vol. 53, 8 Feb. 1919, 168. According to witnesses, Gordon was accosted by the Fifty-fourth Battalion's commander with a shout, "Mr Gordon, what in hell are you doing up here?" As he paused, Gordon was struck down by indirect machine-gun fire. He eventually received a DSO. QUA, D.M. Gordon Papers, box 2, 1918 Correspondence, G.H. Gordon to D.M. Gordon, 24 Aug. 1918; also *Canada*, vol. 52, 7 Dec. 1918, 343.

122 Military Crosses were won by Father E.J. MacDonald and R. MacGillivray (bar to his MC): *Canada*, vol. 53, 18 Jan. 1919, 76; W. Boss, *The Stormont, Dundas and Glengarry Highlanders*, 129. Protestants winning MCs included George Wright, who rallied and led officer-less soldiers on to their objective before turning to the wounded: *Canada*, vol. 53, 18 Jan. 1919, 85. George Kilpatrick won his DSO for gallantry with the Forty-second Battalion wounded on Hill 102: Topp, *42nd Battalion, R.H.C.*, 282; *Canada*, vol. 53, 8 Feb. 1919, 168. R.W. Ridgeway won a bar to his MC for similar exploits with the Fifty-second Battalion: *Canada*, vol. 53, 18 Jan. 1919, 73. Other Fourth Division chaplains decorated included W.L. Baynes-Reid (DSO), Father W.L. Murray (MC), and G.C. D'Easum (MC): see *Canada*, vol. 53, 8 Feb. 1919, 167; vol. 52, 14 Dec. 1918, 368, 370. Social Service Department resources were again pooled with the Red Cross, YMCA, and Knights

of Columbus: Robert Renison, in Beattie, "History," 97. Also see his account "A Tale of Five Cities" in J.C. Hopkins, *Canada at War*, 369–70. Shatford proudly pointed out that the Social Service Department had not placed extra logistical demands on Corps transport. Only one officer and twelve second-category men brought supplies forward, by improvising equipment, hitchhiking rides on passing lorries, or temporarily borrowing trucks and wagons. Shatford report of Amiens, and Colwell report, in Beattie, "History," 94–7.

123 Beattie, "History," 103, 109, 111; also NA, Chaplain Service Records, vol. 4665, Reports, R.C. Chaplains, France, Letang report, Oct. 1918.

124 Taylor report, quoted in Beattie, "History," 107–8. See also 107, McKegney report. Other reports are found in NA, Chaplain Service Records, vol. 4666, Arras Battle Reports. See also Kilpatrick, in Beattie, "History," report of 26–28 Aug. 1918, 105.

125 NA, Chaplain Service Records, vol. 4667, Chaplain Reports, file 6, Graham report, 29 Sept. 1918. During the rescue Graham's batman lost part of his cheek from German sniping, which only subsided after they waved a Red Cross flag and a stretcher over their heads: NA, Chaplain Service Records, vol. 4625, Graham file; also William Beattie to Graham, 8 Jan. 1921 and reply. See also *Canada*, vol. 53, 8 Feb. 1919, 168; and Chaplain Service Records, vol. 4666, Arras Battle Reports file, Graham report.

126 Beattie, "History," 111, 116. NA, Chaplain Service Records, vol. 4666, Reports file 5, Senior Chaplain, 2nd Division, report of 15 Sept. 1918; vol. 4667, Chaplain Reports, file 8, Senior Chaplain, 4th Division Report, 18 Sept. 1918.

127 W.L. Murray report, quoted in Beattie, "History," 109–10. NA, Chaplain Service Records, vol. 4665, Reports, R.C. Chaplains, France, Letang report of Oct. 1918. At Cambrai, B.J. Murdoch found himself anointing two dying stretcher-bearers with a German field gun firing at his position over open sites: *Red Vineyard*, 290–1.

128 NA, Chaplain Service Records, vol. 4667, Chaplain Reports, file 11 (R.C., 1918), McCarthy report, 17 Nov. 1918.

129 As one chaplain admitted in his report, "I have been so busy that I cannot get caught up with my work, and at times – well – I would be glad to be relieved. I am rapidly becoming a 'crock.'" Beattie, "History," 111.

130 Artillery chaplain Callum McKay, working at an advanced dressing station near Inchy, was hit by a piece of shell that landed nearby. After finishing the dressing on the soldier he was tending, McKay bandaged himself and carried on. The station had no other chaplains in attendance at the time. An hour later, however, he was forced to retire to the nearest dressing station to have his wound attended to. "I was

sorry to have to leave the important point without any chaplains at so critical a time, but my wound bled so freely that I was compelled to do so," he explained to his senior chaplain. NA, Chaplain Service Records, vol. 4634, McKay file, McKay report of 27 Sept. 1918. The reports of his colleagues and many other Corps chaplains are assembled in NA, Chaplain Service Records, vol. 4666, Arras Battle Reports file.

131 Military Crosses were won by C.W. Whittaker, F.G. Sherring, W.R.R. Armitage, F.H. Buck, C.J.S. Stuart, J.B. Hunter, S.E. McKegney, and Fathers J. Nicholson, T. O'Sullivan, C.A. Fallon, W.L. Murray, and H.E. Letang. A.E. Andrew was cited on 30 Sept. J.F. Nicholson, T.H. Stewart, and H.R. Pickup were wounded during this period. C.N.M. McKay was wounded on 27 Sept., J.W. Whillans and Canon Scott on the 29th; E.E. Graham and Father M.N. Thompkins on 2 Oct. R.J. Renison, G.C. D'Easum, F.G. Frost, and B.J. Murdoch, who reported themselves or were reported exhausted, remained on duty, as their units were sent into rest until war's end. At one point the Twenty-second Battalion was temporarily without its French-speaking priest, who had been gassed. The only replacement at hand was a Gaelic-speaking Glengarry priest, Father Ewen MacDonald, who went over the top with them. NA, Chaplain Service Records, vol. 4665, Reports, R.C., France file, E.J. MacDonald report of 13 Oct. 1918. His superior considered MacDonald the closest approximation to a Quebec priest available.

132 The service lost another chaplain during this period when Eric Johnston, a Methodist who had joined the Corps for the battle of Amiens, collapsed from exhaustion and died of pneumonia in a British field hospital on 18 Nov. 1918. Canadian Corps casualties in these actions amounted to 30,806, or about 24 per cent, all ranks. 1,544 of these were officers. Nicholson, *C.E.F.*, 460.

133 NA, Chaplain Service Records, vol. 4648, file 2, McGreer to D.C.S., 18, 20 Nov. 1918; also Shatford to McGreer, 4 Dec. 1918, and vol. 4667, Chaplain Reports, file 6, McGreer to Almond, 20 Nov. 1918.

134 McGreer, quoted in Beattie, "History," 121. Also Fetherstonhaugh, *Royal Montreal Regiment*, 276–7; see also his *Royal Highlanders of Canada*, 312; Corrigall, *20th Battalion*, 298, 300.

135 NA, Chaplain Service Records, vol. 4665, Reports, R.C. Chaplains, France file. Various reports, espec. by P.J. Kelly, J.R. O'Gorman, and W.L. Murray. Shatford told an all-Corps padres' conference that about one hundred Canadian venereal disease cases a week were being diagnosed. He opposed, however, mass distribution of prophylactics. In March, O'Gorman approached Fourth Division authorities and demanded that obligatory lectures be given about the moral as well as medical dangers of illicit sex, with padres as well as medical officers in

charge. He asked that all Brussels public houses be closed at 11 p.m. and all local prostitutes interned. In his capacity as senior priest with the Canadians (Father French was in ill health), O'Gorman met with Cardinal Mercier, Belgium's most distinguished prelate, who agreed to hound Belgian civic officials. NA, Chaplain Service Records, vol. 4648, file 3, O'Gorman to Workman, 10–14 Mar. 1919.

CHAPTER SIX

1 Such sentiments had unexpected results on his wartime congregations: "I told the men this one day on church parade; and a corporal sometime afterwards said that, when next their battalion was moving up into the line, a young fellow beside him was swearing very hard over the amount of stuff he had to carry. My friend went over to him and said, 'Don't you know that Canon Scott told us that this really isn't a pack, but it's the Cross of Christ?' The lad stopped swearing at once, and took up his burden without a word." Scott, *Great War,* 117, 165–72.

2 Murdoch, *Red Vineyard,* 97–104.

3 Presbyterian George Pringle was asked, along with the doctor and the quartermaster, by the OC of the Forty-third Battalion to wear the battalion kilt and badges. Pringle wisely agreed. *Tillicums of the Trail,* 27–8. He considered himself fortunate to have been sent to such, in his words, "a classy unit." NA, Chaplain Service Records, vol. 4639, Pringle file, Pringle to Almond, 30 May 1918.

4 NA, Chaplain Service Records, vol. 4622, B.S.J. Doyle file. See also vol. 4646, F. Williamson file.

5 George Fallis was convinced that he did not win the acceptance of his first unit until he hit a winning home run in a brigade baseball tournament. "I was immediately made brigade sports officer." *A Padre's Pilgrimage,* 67–70. As Alexander Gordon told his father, sports remained a popular ice-breaker between padres and men whenever the units were out of the line: UCA, D. Gordon Papers, box 2, 1918 Correspondence, A. Gordon to D. Gordon, 13 June 1918.

6 Fallis, "Leaves from a Chaplain's Diary," *Christian Guardian,* 29 Dec. 1915, 19; 5 Apr. 1917, 17.

7 Ibid., 9 Feb. 1916, 30; 3 May 1916, 17. See also W.H. Burnett, *Christian Guardian,* 20 Sept. 1916, 21 Feb. 1917, 18.

8 Murdoch, *Red Vineyard,* 107, 119ff.

9 R.J. Renison, *One Day at a Time,* 105.

10 QUA, D. Gordon Papers, box 2, 1918 Correspondence, A. to D. Gordon, 13 May 1918. Although, as Beattie and many other chaplains who did not know how to ride recalled, it was a relief to be spared the frustration and, sometimes, danger of managing a horse, especially

under fire: NA, Chaplain Service Records, vol. 4643, J.H. Thomas file; also vol. 639, G.W. Plewes file. Horses, because of both the tetanus micro-organisms found in their manure and their own skittishness, were an occupational hazard for all soldiers at the front, including padres. Several were seriously injured in riding accidents during 1916–17. Beattie, "History," 246.

11 The removal of horses also added to the sense of isolation for the priests, who were scattered widely along a divisional front. Rarely did Roman Catholic chaplains get to meet or billet together. Murdoch, *Red Vineyard*, 192, 213–14, 235–7.

12 J.A. MacDonald, *Gun-Fire*, 89.

13 Murdoch, *Red Vineyard*, 42, 126–7, 139, 166.

14 Beattie, "History," 38. See also Fallis, *Christian Guardian*, 10 Nov. 1915, 9 Feb. 1916, and 3 May 1916.

15 During the war John Callan published a brief account for the SPCK, relating the "average" day of an artillery chaplain, which was printed in the *Canadian Churchman*, 9, 16 May 1918. He and Beattie both drew upon it for their post-war accounts. Senior chaplains, eager for eye-catching anecdotes giving their senior officers a more vivid picture of their work, occasionally criticized the overworked padres who employed such laconic terms. NA, Chaplain Service Records, vol. 4666, Reports file 5, George Wells to Eric Johnston, 24 Sept. 1918 and reply; NA, Chaplain Service Records, vol. 4619, Cassap file, Fallis to Cassap, 3 Aug. 1918.

16 Although religious services were ordered for the men attacking Vimy Ridge, Roman Catholic chaplains in the Fourth Division complained that Protestant unit commanders kept the men too busy getting ready for the battle. NA, Chaplain Service Records, vol. 4667, Chaplain Reports, file 13, Gordon to McGreer, 17 Mar. 1917. Similar complaints were made by the priests after the Armistice, when commanders judged that confession and worship services were not essential: NA, Chaplain Service Records, vol. 4667, Chaplain Reports, RC, file 11, Roderick MacDonnell report, 5 Apr. 1918; also William Carleton report, 23 June 1918; or Miles Thompkins report, 2 July 1918. Carleton, a Catholic, complained that getting commanders to schedule church parades now reminded him of the evil days under Steacy: see NA, Chaplain Service Records, vol. 4665, Reports, Roman Catholic Chaplains, France file, Carleton to French, 17 Nov. 1918.

17 NA, ibid., Chaplain Reports, file 14, Archer to McGreer, 8 July 1917; also Ridgeway to McGreer, 9 Aug. 1917.

18 Ibid., G.C. D'Easum to McGreer, 19 July 1917.

19 On such occasions, Scott recalled, the adjutants had a stock answer: "'Cleanliness is next to Godliness' … I used to look at the Adjutant,

and merely remark quietly, – the words of the Psalmist, 'I held my tongue with bit and bridle, while the ungodly was in my sight.'" *Great War,* 104. Others, such as Frederick Sherring, let off steam in the direction of their senior chaplain: "Everything is a washout … How effective do you expect my work to be under these conditions? How effective do you expect the G.O.C.'s message, on the use of bad language, to be?" NA, Chaplain Service Records, vol. 4667, Chaplain Reports, file 7, Sherring report, 29 Dec. 1918; also Malcolm Omond and Alan Shatford reports same date. See also vol. 4667, Reports, file 6, George Gray to Arthur Creegan, 18 Nov. 1918: "I feel more like quitting than ever before."

20 NA, RG 9, Canadian Corps Records, vol. P-109-3, First Army Circular 46, 20 Aug. 1917. By this time, in the German army, even in Prussian units, Lutheran chaplains had acknowledged similar difficulties with the compulsory church parade and were proposing the substitution of voluntary services. German army authorities only relented, however, during the period of restlessness and growing indiscipline at the end of the war. See Schbel, 50–1.

21 QUA, D. Gordon Papers, box 2, 1918 Correspondence, A. Gordon to D. Gordon, 13 May 1918, and Chaplain Service Conference Address, Ottawa, 1941, "Chaplain Experiences with the C.E.F," 3–4.

22 A photograph of one such incident, with the grinning rear ranks looking skyward, appears in Singer and Peebles, *31st Battalion,* 257. See also *Canada's Heroes in the Great World War,* vol. 1, photograph section, 3.

23 Scott, *Great War,* 102.

24 Beattie, "History," 123.

25 Before the Amiens attack, Third Brigade Catholics turned out in such large numbers that their chaplains heard confessions and dispensed the sacrament up to the last minute to soldiers already armed for battle. Murdoch, *Red Vineyard,* 238–40. See also Fetherstonhaugh, *Thirteenth Battalion,* 120.

26 George Fallis wrote, "Was ever a greater moment given to a minister to speak the gospel of comfort and cheer? … I spoke for five minutes on the text, "the eternal God is thy refuge." Then we bowed our heads in prayer for ourselves, our cause, our dear ones and the native land … There have been moments of great spiritual exaltation in my experience … but it is quite impossible to call to memory any time when the Infinite seemed so close … as when, about to face fearful odds, we bowed before the God and Father of us all." *Christian Guardian,* 9 Feb. 1916.

27 "The deep spiritual solemnity of the occasion was felt by all, as row upon row, men with uncovered heads bowed or knelt before the

Divine Presence. An holy awe had fallen ... The various attitudes and genuflexions of the men revealed their distinctive Christian nurture and training, albeit, over all there was a unity of spirit and purpose that told how really the one Body of Christ was manifested in this last solemn act of Christian worship" – so wrote Harold Horsey after the Thirty-eight Battalion's pre-Somme service. Beattie, "History," 45.

28 Lapointe, *Soldier of Quebec*, 54; Chaballe, *Histoire du 22e Bataillon Canadien-français*, 1:143, 290.

29 NA, Chaplain Service Records, vol. 4665, Reports, R.C., France, Roderick MacGillivray to French, 3 Nov. 1917. See also J.R. O'Gorman, "Canadian Catholic Chaplains," 76–7.

30 George Pringle, in Beattie, "History," 75.

31 "It is with pleasure," wrote Scott, "that one sees all our chaplains are conscious of this fact and because of this they have special power with the men." NA, Chaplain Service Records, vol. 4675, Extracts of Reports, Scott to McGreer, 28 May 1917.

32 Scott, *Great War*, 151–2. For an example of George Fallis's similar counsel to a soldier with a (correct) premonition of being wounded, see *Christian Guardian*, 18 Oct. 1916, 19.

33 George Pringle was seriously ill on the eve of Passchendaele but could not report sick because of the certain conviction the men of the Forty-third Battalion would assume he had lost his nerve. After consultation with the medical officer and "fifteen grains of aspirin," he went forward. *Tillicums of the Trail*, 151–3.

34 Rosario Crochetière, while chaplain of the Twenty-second Battalion, confided to a colleague that he was nearly paralysed with fear before every action. He was killed by a direct hit on his dressing station in the spring of 1918. J.R. O'Gorman, "Canadian Catholic Chaplains," *Canadian Catholic Historical Association Report* (1939–41), 75.

35 Scott, *Great War*, 80, 153.

36 Gordon, *Postscript*, 248–52, 256.

37 After Amiens, George MacDonald, with the Fifty-fourth Battalion, reported, "A word of cheer and Christian Hope means more than all else besides during these hours of danger; in this I felt that I was performing a duty as essential as a weapon of war." NA, Chaplain Service Records, vol. 4667, Chaplain Reports, file 8, MacDonald Report, 5 Oct. 1918. At Cambrai, James Whillans spent the night before an attack chatting with the men of his battalion, telling them encouraging war news, and discussing the coming battle "hopefully." "I spent a considerable time with some of these groups and passed on with a 'God Bless you boys' ... When the 10th Battalion passed forward into action I stood and shouted, 'Good old Tenth' telling the men the good news from Palestine and the Balkans and that things were going well up

ahead." NA, Chaplain Service Records, vol. 4667, Reports, file 6, Whillans to McGreer, report of 26 Sept.–8 Oct. 1918. See also Scott, *Great War,* 129–31.

38 Benedict Murdoch's two days at a dressing station near Cambrai are vividly described in *Red Vineyard,* 288–9. At one difficult point in the 1916 fighting, George Fallis was taken aside by one harried medical officer who ordered him to pray: *Padre's Pilgrimage,* 81; Nicholson, C.E.F., 154.

39 Murdoch, *Red Vineyard,* 258–63, 290. See also NA, Chaplain Service Records, vol. 4664, Reports, A.D.C.S., France, file 2, John Holman report. See also Thomas Colwell's Passchendaele experience, ibid, vol. 4620, Colwell file, Colwell report of 11 Nov. 1917.

40 NA, Chaplain Service Records, vol. 4668, Chaplain Reports, files 15 and 16, Kilpatrick reports of 6, 20 Nov. 1917. Compare these with his jaunty letter to his parents, calculated to disarm their worry. UCA, George G.D. Kilpatrick Papers, box 1, Correspondence, Kilpatrick to parents, 6 Nov. 1917.

41 NA, Chaplain Service Records, vol. 4665, Reports, France, Graham to McGreer, Aug. 1917.

42 "Many homes will be purer, and many hearts more sympathetic because of the thousands who have been, 'Obedient unto death.'" NA, Chaplain Service Records, vol. 4666, Reports file, Wood Vimy Ridge report; also Beattie, "History," 54–6. Watching the gunners toss aside their gas masks in order to fire more accurately in defence of the infantry at Hill 70, Scott wrote: "I felt myself to be such a slacker beside them, but I told them how gloriously they were carrying on, and how their work was appreciated by the infantry." *Great War,* 198ff.

43 "Could one ever grumble again at little hardships?" Beattie, "History," 81–3, quoting Charles Hedley's Passchendaele report.

44 Murdoch, *Red Vineyard,* 174; see also 220–2, 246, 266–9. Beattie, "History," 78–9. See also Fallis, "Leaves from a Chaplain's Diary," *Christian Guardian,* 18 Oct. 1916, 20.

45 Fallis, "Leaves," *Christian Guardian,* 11 Oct. 1916, 19. See also Arthur Labonte to Mrs W. Gorrell, *Catholic Register,* 31 May 1917. Presbyterian chaplain Robert Thompson, comforting the parents of a Methodist student killed in Flanders, wrote: "Although I am a stranger to you, please accept my sincere sympathy in your loss. Your boy like many another has given up his life for his friends." University of Western Ontario Regional Room Archives, Letters of Bombardier Ross Malcolm Taylor, 1915–16, Thompson to Mr Taylor, 8 Jan. 1916. Often the commanding officer of the battalion or battery would write reassuringly to relatives as well: see Fetherstonhaugh, *24th Battalion,* 187. For an example of a letter by Almond to a chaplain's widow, see NA, Chaplain

Service Records, vol. 4628, Eric Johnston file, Almond to Mrs Johnston, 19 Nov. 1918.

46 Canadian hospital chaplains in the Mediterranean suffered from dysentery, paratyphoid, and malaria. The influenza pandemics of 1918 and 1919 also hospitalized a number of chaplains, killing two, Charles Sparling and Roy Kain. Two additional chaplains, Joseph Elliott and William Emsley, died as a result of illnesses contracted in or aggravated by overseas service.

47 The few weeks after Passchendaele were marked by a handful of such chaplain collapses. NA, Chaplain Service Records, vol. 4623, M.F. Fallon file, Workman to Fallon, 5 Dec. 1917.

48 NA, Chaplain Service Records, vol. 4646, A. Woods file, Woods to Almond, 31 Dec. 1916. See also vol. 4645, Clement Whalley file, McGreer to Almond, Sept. 1917.

49 NA, Chaplain Service Records, vol. 4621, Geoffrey D'Easum file, D'Easum to Almond, 31 Oct. 1918.

50 NA, Chaplain Service Records, vol. 4643, Thomas Stewart file; vol. 4634, A. Mackintosh file; vol. 4665, Reports, R.C. Chaplains, France, B. Murdoch to F. French, 1 Sept. 1918. Murdoch's first symptoms of combat fatigue became evident when he was unable to relax on his second annual retreat at Parkminster Monastery: *Red Vineyard*, 216. His subsequent reports continued to show the progression of symptoms of nervous deterioration until his brigade was taken out of action two weeks before the Armistice. At that point he was dangerously close to collapse: ibid., 263.

51 After Passchendaele such near-suicidal indifference was especially marked in one chaplain's behaviour just prior to an attempt to shoot himself. NA, Chaplain Service Records, vol. 4622, Francis Elliott-Baker file, Anonymous Imperial Officer to Almond, 26 Nov. 1917; also Elliott-Baker to Almond, 24 Apr. 1918. Murdoch was behaving in the same manner just before his brigade was withdrawn from combat in October, 1918: see Murdoch, *Red Vineyard*, 293–8. See also Fetherstonhaugh, *14th R.M.R.*, 263–4.

52 For example, see the letters of St Stephen's College students and faculty to Miss Burkholder, in University of Alberta Archives, St Stephen's College Papers, box 4.

53 Oliver confessed, from the Eighth Canadian Field Ambulance, "One learns to become very direct and practical in his addresses out here, so I spoke to them on what it means to be a Christian." USA, Oliver Papers, Oliver to wife, 29 Apr. 1918.

54 Much of Oliver's "field preaching" continued in this vein, a far cry from his weekly orations at Bexhill. "I take some simple theme like 'Prayer,' 'Purpose,' 'Temptations,' and talk in a very practical straight-

forward way about it for a short time. I have three meetings every night." Ibid., 11 Apr. 1918.

55 For example, A. Wilken, preaching to the CMRS, reassured the men that "God is Love": Fallis, "Leaves from a Chaplain's Diary," *Christian Guardian,* 26 Apr. 1916, 17. Thomas Colwell, a Methodist with the Eighth Brigade at the Somme, held a brief open-air service in the trenches: "We sang 'Fight the Good Fight' and had a little prayer" for protection and courage. NA, Chaplain Service Records, vol. 4620, Colwell file, Colwell to A.D.C.S., 24 Oct. 1916. During the preparations for Vimy Ridge, W.L. Baynes-Reid emphasized the presence of God in his talks with the men. *Canadian Churchman,* 11 Mar. 1917. Harold Clarke, a Methodist, preached to the Eighty-fifth Battalion just before Passchendaele on the battalion motto. His text was: "Quit you like Men": "At the conclusion of the service the sacrament was administered. It was a most impressive service throughout and the address most excellent and appropriate," recalled the battalion historian. See Hayes, *The 85th in France and Flanders,* 85–6.

56 Beattie, "History," 70, Robertson report of 22 Apr. 1917. Arthur Emmett chose the Easter service that he held prior to Vimy Ridge to focus upon the Christian hope of the Resurrection. Murray, *History of the 2nd Battalion,* 162. The same considerations prompted padre McInnis of the Fourth Division after the heavy fighting around Cambrai in 1918: "What could one speak to such an audience at such a time but of the glory of the sacrificial life and of the 'Great Sacrifice'?" NA, Chaplain Service Records, vol. 4674, Reports to A.D.C.S., Corps file, McInnis to 4th Division Senior Chaplain, Oct. 1918.

57 NA, Chaplain Service Records, vol. 4668, Chaplain Reports, file 18, Naylor to Fallis, 25 Apr. 1918.

58 Beattie, "History," 32, refers to a 1915 pre-Festubert sermon: "In the midst of Death we are in Life." William Burnett reported, after his arrival at the Sixth Canadian Field Ambulance, "The troops are more serious and responsive in France – Easter's sermon is 'Immortality' – again stressing evangelical appeal and response of the men." UCA, Methodist Army and Navy Board, box 2, file 34, Extracts of Chaplains' Letters, Burnett to Moore, 27 Apr. 1916.

59 Ottawa Anglican Diocese Archives, Hepburn Papers, Diary, 13 May 1917.

60 Pringle was as war-weary and disturbed as his congregation, for he had been stationed at Waterloo pillbox, the regimental aid post, during the attack. Following a battle, officers preferred to hold a brief voluntary service after allowing the men to sleep in. It was the one occasion when the padre did not object to a service cancellation. Fallis, "Leaves from a Chaplain's Diary," *Christian Guardian,* 26 Apr. 1916. Usually the

next service, after reinforcements had been received, was declared a parade service in order that officers, chaplain, and men might familiarize themselves with each other.

61 The need to present to soldiers that Christ had entered the most ugly and harrowing experiences of earthly life as the ideal captain appeared in other chaplain messages, such as John Magwood's, *Christian Guardian*, 10 Oct. 1917. As British writers such as Donald Hankey and padres such as Geoffrey Studdert-Kennedy reminded their men, Jesus was not like the staff-officer who never came up to the trenches but, instead, like the beloved captain who led his men from the front and lived with his men in the line. See Hankey, *A Student in Arms*, 55–66; and Studdert-Kennedy, "The Religious Difficulties of the Private Soldier," in Macnutt, *The Church in the Furnace*, 390–1.

62 George Pringle, *Tillicums of the Trail*, 127–46.

63 UCA, Methodist Army and Navy Board, box 9, Colwell file, "In Remembrance of Me," Communion sermon for 3, 10 Feb. 1918.

64 Scott, *Great War*, 75. The poem also appeared in *Canada*, 26 June 1915, 354.

65 Marshall, *Secularizing the Faith*, chap. 6; also his "Methodism Embattled,", *CHR* (March 1985), 48–9.

66 Similar assumptions and themes dominated the preaching of Australian chaplains overseas: see McKernan, "Clergy in Khaki," 151–6, and *Australian Churches at War*, 55–7.

67 Gauvreau, *Evangelical Century*, 258–60.

68 Arthur Hagar, with the Canadian Railroad Troops, wrote: "A service under shell fire has not proven to be the least effective way of preaching the Gospel of the Kingdom ... We have good talks together and I am realizing now more than ever, that the big job before these men, and all our troops, is not the winning of a material victory, but the great moral conquest and regeneration that is to follow after, and for which, I firmly believe, this war is a preparation." NA, Chaplain Service Records, vol. 4668, Chaplain Reports, file 22, Hagar to Fallis, 16 July 1918.

69 Charles Hedley, "From a Chaplain's Diary," *Canadian Churchman*, 5 July 1917, 411.

70 So preached Father Edward Doe on Dominion Day 1916 at a Field Hospital in France: Cameron, *#1 Canadian General Hospital*, 288. In 1918 George Fallis and Robert Renison preached that the living thus have every cause to hope for their personal salvation; see Renison, in Hopkins, *Canada at War*, 141: "The preacher spoke of St. John's vision of a new heaven and a new earth and said that the gates of pearl were the gates of sacrifice. The new world which was even then opening before us had been reached through the death of those who had died four years before. He mentioned the fact that the Canadian Corps was

advancing along the historic line of the Mons retreat. Their voices seemed to cheer us from their resting place." See also Renison, "Memorial Day in France," *Canadian Churchman,* 8 Aug. 1918, 505; and his "In the Promised Land," *Canada,* 28 Dec. 1918, 429.

71 UCA, Methodist Army and Navy Board, box 9, file 233, Colwell to Moore, 20 Jan., 3, 10 Feb. 1918.

72 "These few words I know steadied the high strung nerves of those boys by putting them face to face with the reality and by showing them where help and eventually an immediate reward could be gotten." NA, Chaplain Service Records, vol. 4664, Reports, A.D.C.S., France, file 2, Beausoleil report, n.d. Not all Catholics, however, were so blunt. Murdoch seemed to stick to devotional motifs and illustrations. After battle he found the men easily moved by the contrast between their scarred souls and the renewable beauty of nature, which Murdoch likened to the forgiveness of God. *Red Vineyard,* 199–201.

73 Murdoch, *Red Vineyard,* 246. See also J.R. O'Gorman, *Soldiers of Christ,* 13–22, 25.

74 NA, Chaplain Service Records, vol. 4675, Extracts from Chaplains' Reports, G.I. Campbell report.

75 Callan, *Canadian Churchman,* 9, 16 May 1918.

76 NA, Chaplain Service Records, vol. 4641, Shires file, Almond to Steacy, 19 Jan. 1917.

77 Ibid., Shires to Steacy, 6 Feb. 1917. Almond, in his reply, allowed himself to be more sympathetic to Shires's scruples: "I quite understand your position, though I feel that you are doing the right thing" by resigning. Almond to Shires, 17 Feb. 1917. A graduate of Bishop's University, Shires was thirty-one at the time, somewhat younger than the average Canadian chaplain, and had been ordained only since 1912. He had enlisted as padre to the Sixtieth Battalion in 1915, while a rector in Alberta, and served at the Somme as an artillery chaplain. After the war he served in small Quebec and Ontario charges until, in 1933, he became rector of St Jude's Church, Toronto.

78 Scott, *Great War,* 140–2.

79 "There is nothing which brings home to the heart with such force the iron discipline of war as the execution of men who desert from the front line," wrote Canon Scott, echoing the universal sentiment of his colleagues. Scott, *Great War,* 210. See also Alan Shatford, who described it as his most painful experience of the war. NA, Chaplain Service Records, vol. 4675, Extracts from Chaplains' Reports file.

80 Twenty-three Canadian executions resulted from this charge; the remainder were for murder. Usually the condemned were repeat offenders. See Morton, "The Supreme Penalty: Canadian Deaths by Firing Squad in the First World War," *QQ* (Autumn 1972): 345–52.

81 "The man's mind was completely changed. The hard, steely indifference and the sense of wrong and injustice had passed away, and he was perfectly natural. I was so much impressed by it that while I was talking to him, I kept wondering if I could not even then, at that late hour, do something to avert the carrying out the sentence." Scott, *Great War,* 211.

82 Ibid., 213.

83 "I told them how deeply all ranks felt the occasion, and that nothing but the dire necessity of guarding the lives of the men in the front line from the panic and rout that might result, through the failure of one individual, compelled the taking of such measures of punishment. A young lad in the firing party utterly broke down." Scott, *Great War,* 214.

84 Scott, *Great War,* 211–13. See also *Unknown Soldiers,* 68.

85 Scott, *Great War,* 215.

86 Scott's own experience came about this way: *Great War,* 210, 212. On the case of a Second Division padre completely failing to do his duty, see Wells, *Fighting Bishop,* 200, where the chaplain begged Wells to take his place. "He said he knew what was expected of him but that he simply could not do it, and in that moment I felt he was far less of a man than the prisoner he should have tried to console," wrote Wells. He had the chaplain shipped back to England; see NA, Chaplain Service Records, vol. 4630.

87 NA, Chaplain Service Records, vol. 4651, War Diary, A.D.C.S. (Corps), 2 Mar. 1918; also Noyes, *Stretcher Bearers!* 113.

88 "It is well to say that it is my duty, but such a duty must not be imposed too often on the nerves and the conscience of the naive priest. My health is still good, but sleepless nights and sleepless days are running down my whole system, and I fear, not a shell shock, not cowardice, but weakness of body and mind ... For nothing in the world would I have it said that a priest was a coward in the field, not for myself, but for the sake of the Chaplains' Department. Pray for me and my boys, dear Father, that we may keep good and strong in the fulfilment of our duty." NA, Chaplain Service Records, vol. 4619, Charles Chartier to Workman, 21 July 1917. Chartier was unfortunate in coming to the Twenty-second at a point when the battalion's morale had been especially low and desertions high. As a result the battalion commander was determined to make an example of such cases and refused to appeal their sentences. Gagnon, *Le 22e Bataillon (Canadien-français), 1914–1919,* 279–95.

89 NA, Chaplain Service Records, vol. 4635, McCausland to McGreer, 29 Nov. 1917; for an earlier example, see Ottawa Anglican Diocese Archives, Hepburn Papers, Diary, Apr. 1917.

90 Ibid., 3 June 1918.

91 Scott, *Great War,* 64; see also 62, 66, 70, 197. For similar thoughts by a Methodist, see Fallis, "Leaves from a Chaplain's Diary," *Christian Guardian,* 5 Apr. 1916, 18.

92 Scott, *Great War,* 278–9. See also Murdoch, *Red Vineyard,* 242–3.

93 NA, Chaplain Service Records, vol. 4675, Extracts from Chaplains' Reports file.

94 Methodist Robert Burns had great difficulty overcoming hatred of the enemy, especially after working with gas casualties and witnessing the bombing of a Canadian hospital in Doullens. "In spite of these experiences I was able to develop enough Christianity to minister to thousands of German Prisoners in Prison Camps. I got German Hymnbooks and conducted worship with them. I gave them many a plain message as to the ideals of Christ and the moral might of character. More than once I ministered to them when dying and buried many of them in the prisoner's plot." NA, Chaplain Service Records, vol. 4675, Extracts from Chaplains' Reports file. For an example of similar work by a Roman Catholic chaplain, see *Catholic Register,* 25 May 1916.

95 Scott, *Great War,* 93, 240. See also Gordon, *Postscript,* 276. Robert Thompson refused two leave offers: NA, Chaplain Service Records, vol. 4644, Thompson file, 1 June 1917, Aug. 1918. He also refused promotion to Fourth Division senior chaplain, which would have taken him away from the artillery batteries: QUA, D. Gordon Papers, George MacDonald to A. Gordon, 14 Aug. 1918. William Kidd, too, refused promotion to senior chaplain when it became clear he would have to leave his original battalion: NA, Chaplain Service Records, vol. 4629, Kidd file, Mar. 1917.

96 McGreer advised Almond: "He used language which is commonly employed by officers of all ranks and I'm sure he never dreamt of all his statements being reported." NA, Chaplain Service Records, vol. 4648, Reports file 2, McGreer to Almond, 17 Dec. 1918. See also vol. 4667, Chaplain Reports file 7, Kilpatrick to McGreer, 26 Dec. 1918.

97 Fortunately for Fallis, Byng saw his point: "Those lads would think you were a H— of a padre had you passed them up in that cloudburst. I'll have the order amended not to include padres." *Padre's Pilgrimage,* 87–8; also Scott, *Great War,* 114–15.

98 Quoted in Callan, "The Canadian Chaplain Services," *Canada and the Great World War,* 6:133.

99 Presbyterian chaplains often complained that the General Assembly had neglected their interests, trailed behind the other churches in supporting them, and allowed incompetents to get into the system under Hughes. NA, Chaplain Service Records, vol. 4663, Questionnaire file, William McConnell, Samuel Compton replies. John McCaskill was

outraged with the "few Ecclesiastical joy-riders" whom Almond brought to "the fields of Armageddon": McCaskill to Harry Kent, 30 Sept. 1918.

100 Ernest Pugsley was among the first to denounce the board for neglecting chaplains and valuing home work above overseas ministry. UCA, Methodist Army and Navy Board, box 6, file 149, Pugsley file, Pugsley to editor *Christian Guardian*, 7 Jan. 1916. His angry letter was handed over to Moore without publication: Moore to Pugsley, 28 Jan. 1916. In 1918 Edward Burwash, William Burnett, John Wright, Edward Graham, and Robert Lambert angrily objected to being taken away from their men in order to give latecomers military credentials. See NA, Chaplain Service Records, vol. 4630, Lambert to Fallis, 20 May 1918. Having just survived Passchendaele, Graham was outraged by the florid propaganda of the board's annual report. To him the board had no idea of what the work was like overseas, and thus no business giving the home folk a sentimental portrait of the war. When the board advised him that he might be recalled from the Thirteenth Battalion virtually on the eve of the victory campaign, Graham warned that the men were fed up with the holy war rhetoric and optimistic hopes of revival among the troops that characterized its utterances. Graham also disagreed with the Service's critique of the YMCA. To him the management of both the Chaplain Service and the Army and Navy Board were completely out of touch with the true state of religious affairs at the front. By January 1918 Graham had attempted to leave the chaplaincy and serve as a combatant officer. His transfer, however, was vetoed by both Canon Scott and General Currie. UCA, Methodist Army and Navy Board, box 4, file 82, Graham to Moore, 10 Nov. 1917, 3 Jan., 23 Feb. 1918, and 17 June 1918.

101 Renison, in Hopkins, *Canada at War*, 393.

102 QUA, D. Gordon Papers, box 2, 1919 Correspondence, A. Gordon to D. Gordon, 4 May 1919.

CHAPTER SEVEN

1 NA, mg 30 E 158, George Kilpatrick Papers, Sermon delivered at Mons Service, 16 Nov. 1918. The italics are in the manuscript.

2 "Officers and men of the Canadian Corps, the world has been saved from a power that would have reversed the centuries and plunged us into the Dark Ages. We have been saved from an Ideal that would have wrecked all security and made freedom and peace impossible. We have been saved for the purpose of declaring by lip and life that Right is Might, that justice, liberty and truth are the ideals which make for the happiness of men. This "salvation is of the Lord." It is the Christian ideal. Ours is the solemn task to take what we have gained from

the war – the newer knowledge, the larger vision, the wider sympathy, the richer devotion and apply them to the building of a greater Canada. Then some future day there will come to us another triumph and we shall cry "Thanks be to God who giveth us the Victory, through our Lord Jesus Christ." NA, Chaplain Service Records, vol. 4674, A.D.C.S. Reports, Corps file. See also vol. 4667, file 6, for complete text of Shatford's sermon.

3 On Christmas Day 1918 Shatford preached again at Mons, telling his troops that the coming peace treaty would permanently eliminate war: "Our confidence is sure that it will be of such a nature as to guarantee complete immunity from war in the future ... For the acceptance of Peace Terms by all the nations will mean a New birth of Humanity, a fresh era for the world ... Our victory is the assurance that God has recognized the right." Shatford, "The Peace Quadrilateral," published sermon preached at Mons, 25 Dec. 1918.

4 David Marshall, *Secularizing the Faith,* 156–81; Michael Gauvreau, *Evangelical Century,* chap. 7; Richard Allen, *Social Passion,* chap. 3.

5 Gordon told Canadians that the Kaiser and "Prussian Junkertum" had flung their gauntlet in the teeth of "Christian civilization." Embracing Nietzsche's philosophy, she had lusted after "the Satanic glory of war." "Canada's Duty" (Winnipeg: Canadian Club 1914). This address, widely distributed, set the tone of Protestant religious propaganda for the duration of the war. See *Presbyterian Record,* Dec. 1914, 537–8; Hopkins, *Canadian Annual Review* (1914), 188–9; and *Presbyterian,* 13 Jan. 1916, 32. Some of Canon Scott's first diatribes appeared in Canadian newspapers as he sailed with the First Contingent: *Canadian Churchman,* 8 Oct. 1914. Methodist chaplains, too, expressed their conviction that God was with the Empire. See Harry Frost, *Christian Guardian,* 11 Nov. 1914, 11–12; and Louis Moffit, ibid., 4 Nov., 13.

6 Scott, *In the Battle Silences,* 10, 13, 31. For other Anglican responses, see chaplain Baynes-Reid's sermon to troops in Canada, *Canadian Churchman,* 6 May 1915, 287, and Renison's sermon "Germany in Nabaoth's Vineyard," ibid., 9 Mar. 1916, 151.

7 Clarke was one of many who used the Old Testament with telling effect: "As a Church, let us beware the fate of Meroz ... 'Curse ye Meroz, saith the angel of the Lord; curse ye bitterly the inhabitants thereof, because they came not to the help of the Lord, to the help of the Lord against the mighty.'" UCA, Methodist Army and Navy Board, box 5, file 122, Clarke file, recruiting pamphlet (1916), "The Methodist Church and the British Flag, by Capt. the Rev. W.G. Clarke, B.A., Chaplain 235th Battalion, C.E.F.," 2 pp. Preachers in the United Kingdom also cited the example of Meroz in their preaching to the undecided: see Marrin, *Last Crusade,* 132. Alexander Ketterson, a chaplain

with Orange Lodge as well as Anglican credentials, wrote: "Their deaths will not be in vain, for from their graves in France and Flanders will spring forth a nobler and a fuller life, which will be an incentive to others, like them, to do noble deeds ... Their deaths will also tend to solidify and strengthen the sentiment of loyal adhesion to the Motherland ... The noble Dead! Gallant soldiers, what a glorious death; brave Crusaders, you have died in a noble cause!" *On Active Service*, vii.

8 *Catholic Register*, 20 Jan. 1916, 4; also CAR (1916): 434–5. "For one cannot be a good Christian if one is a bad citizen. He who is disloyal to his country is disloyal to the Church. He who is only partially patriotic is only partially religious, for patriotism is a virtue." O'Gorman, in Donald Santor, *Canadians at War, 1914–1918*, 38. "Hence the policy adopted by the Irish-Canadians to fight Germans on the field of battle and British junkers in the council chamber of the Empire is one which fulfils our duties as the sons of Irishmen and the sons of Canada." O'Gorman, *Catholic Register*, 29 Mar. 1917, 1. Henri Bourassa complained to Bishop Gauthier about O'Gorman, with little effect. See Durocher, "Henri Bourassa, les évêques et la guerre de 1914–1918," CHAP (1971): 256.

9 The chaplain borrowed an appropriate title from Rudyard Kipling, "Things as they are": *Canadian Churchman*, 4 Jan. 1917, 7. Other chaplains, from various denominations, sent similar messages from France. W. Emsley (Meth.), *Canada*, 23 Oct. 1915, 93; John MacDonald (Bapt.), ibid., 25 Dec. 1915, 361, and 4 Jan. 1916, 7; also C. Shelley (Pres.), *Presbyterian*, 27 July 1916, 80; George Fallis (Meth.), *Christian Guardian*, 27 Oct. 1915, 9 and 29 Dec. 1915, 19; Harry Frost (Meth.), ibid., 13 Jan., 19 May 1915; W. Burnett, ibid., 20 Sept. 1916, and 21 Feb. 1917, 18; E. Burwash, ibid., 8 Aug. 1917, 9.

10 *Canada*, 20 Jan. 1917, 80; and *Vancouver Sun*, 29 Oct. 1917. Gordon said he now considered rum and cigarettes as vital as rifles for winning the war. This prompted wry comments on how war had cured the moralistic traits of Canada's most famous social gospeller. See Fred Paul, "Ralph Connor's Conversion," *Saturday Night*, Jan. 1917. I thank Joyce Sowby for this reference. See *Canadian Churchman*, 27 July 1916, 470, for Gordon on the subjects of front-line revival and ecumenicalism.

11 Charles Gordon, sermon, 13 Jan. 1917. See also his "Stripped to the Skin – An Address to the Ottawa Canadian Club, 23 January 1917," both in the possession of Ruth Gordon, Winnipeg. See also his statement: "Before Canada there is but one simple, single duty, and for every man, woman and child in Canada that duty is to plough this tearing, terrible furrow of war straight through to the end." In Hopkins, CAR (1917): 51, 416, 556. See also CAR (1916): 312.

12 *Canadian Churchman*, 29 Mar. 1917, 200.

13 See "The Bivouac of the Dead," *Canada*, 20 July 1918, 65. A.B.W. Wood pointedly described to Canadian Roman Catholics the aftermath of the air raids. *Catholic Register*, 22 Aug. 1918, 1–2.

14 *Canada*, 28 Nov. 1918, 429; also Matthew Conron, *Christian Guardian*, 11 Dec. 1918; and *Canadian Churchman*, 11 July 1918, 443; 16 Jan. 1919, 48; and 13 Mar. 1919, 165.

15 *Presbyterian*, 28 Oct. 1915, 417. Murdoch, *Red Vineyard*, 179–81. See also NA, Chaplain Service Records, vol. 4664, A.D.C.S. Reports, France, file 2, L. Maltais report, 1918; and A.B. Wood, *Catholic Register*, 25 July 1918, 2. For O'Gorman, see *Catholic Register*, 14 Nov. 1918, 2; also E. Hawks, ibid., 19 Sept. 1918, 6.

16 NA, RG 9 III D 1, vol. 4718, folder 113, file 29, Beattie at Dominion of Canada Jubilee Service, St Columba's Church, London, 1 July 1917. See also Macnamara, *Canadian Churchman*, 4 Jan. 1917, 8; Dean G.L. Starr, *Canadian Churchman*, 21 June 1917, 389; and E.C. Earp, address on Vimy Ridge in Toronto, reported in ibid., 2 Aug. 1917, 494. Canon Scott, too, portrayed "the Cause" in sacred terms and the soldiers as moral and spiritual Crusaders, even after two years roaming the battlefields; see his *In the Battle Silences*, 7, 10, 13, 16. To him, the war was leading the free nations upwards to eternal light; see his "To France," in George Perley, ed., *Canada in Khaki*, vol. 1.

17 Oliver, "Educational Reconstruction," *Social Welfare* 1, no. 2, (Fall 1918), clipping in USA, Oliver Papers, Clippings file.

18 See chaplains' addresses to the Anglican General Synod, *Canadian Churchman*, 19 Sept. 1918, 602, 609. See also David Christie, *Presbyterian and Westminster*, 27 June 1918, 620; Arthur Burch (Pres.), *Canadian Churchmen*, 26 July 1917, 478; Robert Taylor, *Presbyterian and Westminster*, 5 July 1917, 11–12, and 12 July 1917, 43–4; John MacNab, ibid., 5 Sept. 1918, 220–1; James Whillans, ibid., 6 Sept. 1917, 235–6, and July 1918; James Faulds, ibid., 3 May 1917, 522–3; and Anon., 5 Apr. 1917, 389. For Anglicans, see Francis Moore, *Canadian Churchman*, 11 Jan. 1917, 21; Adolph Kuhring, ibid., 25 Jan. 1917, 62; Joseph Tupper, ibid., 20 Dec. 1917; William Barton, ibid., 8 Nov. 1917, 718; Christopher Carruthers, ibid., 5 Sept. 1918, 575.

19 Alfred Lavell, "The Returning Soldier and the Church," *Christian Guardian*, 17 Apr. 1918, 9; 24 Apr. 1918, 9–10; and 1 May 1918, 9. See also Harold Frost, *Christian Guardian*, 20 Sept. 1918, 20–1; and Gustave Kuhring's remarks to a Hamilton congregation, *Canadian Churchman*, 7 Oct. 1918, 668.

20 Francis Moore, "After the War," *Canadian Churchman*, 11 Jan. 1917, 21, 28–9.

21 Charles Whittaker, *Christian Guardian*, 6 Feb. 1918, 8; *Presbyterian and Westminster*, 5 Sept. 1918. For John Pringle's and William Beattie's pro-Union remarks, see *Presbyterian*, 28 Oct. 1915, 417, and 1 June 1916, 521–22.

22 See Herbert Woodcock's remarks to the Anglican General Synod of 1918, *Canadian Churchman*, 19 Sept. 1918, 609.

23 Francis Moore, *Canadian Churchman*, 11 Jan. 1917; also Alfred Lavell, *Christian Guardian*, 13 May 1918, 9, and 9 Oct. 1918, 7–8. See also *Canadian Churchman*, 2 Aug. 1917, 492.

24 Lavell, *Christian Guardian*, 24 Apr. 1918, 10; also Whittaker, ibid., 6 Feb. 1918, 8–9.

25 Francis Moore, *Canadian Churchman*, 28 Dec. 1917; also Joseph Tupper, ibid., 26 Apr. 1917.

26 Lavell, *Christian Guardian*, 9 Oct. 1918, 7–8. See also Arthur Carlisle, *Canadian Churchman*, 11 Oct. 1917, 649, 656; comments of the Ontario Synod, ibid., 28 Nov. 1918; and *Presbyterian and Westminster*, 5 Sept. 1918.

27 "A Chaplain," "When the Men Come Home," *Presbyterian and Westminster*, 5 Sept. 1918, 213–14.

28 Francis Moore, *Canadian Churchman*, 11 Jan., 26 Apr., and 30 Aug. 1917. See also Joseph Tupper, ibid., 2 Aug. 1917, 492; 25 Oct. 1917, 683; 15 Nov. 1917, 731; 9 May 1918, 297. See also ibid., 3 Jan. 1918, 4–5, 14. On Moore, see *Canadian Churchman*, 15 Nov. 1917. If the nation did not heed the call of the new day, he warned, the Kingdom of God might be realized by the Labour Party instead of the Anglican Church. *Canadian Churchman*, 4 Apr. 1918, 217.

29 Lavell, *Christian Guardian*, 24 Apr. 1918.

30 Moore, a thirty-two-year-old priest trained at the University of Durham, had come to Toronto in 1912. He was to play a leading role in the social awakening of Toronto Anglicans after the war. On the response of the Mother Church to the war, see F.B. Macnutt, *The Church in the Furnace*. The institutional and intellectual response of the Church of England to the war has been described by both Albert Marrin, *The Last Crusade*, and Alan Wilkinson, *The Church of England and the First World War*.

31 Warner sent out 125 questionnaires and received 60 full-length replies. The digest report compiled by Warner and Senior Chaplains Wells (Second Division), Woods (Third Division), McGreer (ADCS), Shatford (Corps chaplain), Hepburn (Bramshott), and Moore (Epsom Camp) was endorsed by eighty-five priests. See NA, Chaplain Service Records, vol. 4663, Questionnaire file.

32 Only four of the sixty Anglicans who answered Warner's survey denied the failure of the pre-war churches. Warner asked the chaplains to list

the general faults of the denomination, its clergy and congregations, then to note any defects in their own training that had come to light overseas. Two questions probed the need to overcome denominational rivalry and "industrial problems". The seventh asked how the church could kindle in parish life the warm comradeship of the army.

33 The chaplains wanted these considerations to guide the Canadian church in the task of Prayer Book revision (already under way in a committee of the General Synod). The survey also called for priests to have the liberty "to make use of extemporary prayer." NA, Chaplain Service Records, vol. 4663, Questionnaire file, response to question 3.

34 Ibid., response to question 3. "More than anything else we believe it is the human agent that counts, and with the right men in the ministry, rightly trained, there need be little fear of the Church's future." NA, Chaplain Service Records, vol. 4663, Questionnaire file, printed letter of the eight Anglican senior chaplains to the Canadian bishops, 20 Aug. 1918, 2. In fact this issue led to detailed comment in the responses. The church had to lengthen its training period to at least five years for undergraduates and three for postgraduates. The bishops must amalgamate inefficient "partisan" colleges in each synod with seminaries federated with the provincial universities. NA, Chaplain Service Records, vol. 4663, Questionnaire file, Warner, "Summary of Answers to Questions asked in Circular Letter on the Men and the Church," questions 1, 2, 3, 6, Dec. 1917, by Anglican Chaplains of the Overseas Military Forces of Canada.

35 Ibid., Anglican Survey, response to question 5.

36 "Finally, we pray our Fathers in God to consider sympathetically the pressing need for closer co-operation between the Churches in Canada. We do not ask that history should be forgotten or that essential principles shall be ignored; but we Chaplains have found during these years of war that the fundamental things uniting us are more and greater than the things which account for our divisions ... And a prospect of Christian Unity has opened out before them, which they hope one day to see fulfilled. It would indeed be a thing to be deplored if, after sharing together in Christian worship and service we fell back to division and possibly hostile disagreement." Anglican Survey, ibid.

37 Before the war Warner had made at least one sustained effort (evidently with little success), while rector at Shelburne, to introduce Christian Socialism to fellow Nova Scotian Anglicans. See Warner, *The Church and Modern Socialism: An Essay.*

38 NA, Anglican Survey, response to question 4.

39 In the words of the preamble to the Anglican survey, "We believe that we know, to an extent quite impossible under normal conditions of parochial work, what the weaknesses of the Church are." NA, Chaplain

Service Records, vol. 4663, Questionnaire file, Warner and Almond letters of Nov. and Dec. 1917, and 1 Mar. 1918; and Almond to Canadian Bishops, 20 Aug. 1918.

40 Fifty-three were under fifty years of age. The diocese of Montreal had a reputation among Canadian Anglicans for harbouring clergymen with advanced social and ecclesiastical views. Warner came from Nova Scotia; Wells and Woods were from Rupert's Land; McGreer, Almond, and Shatford from Montreal; and Hepburn from Quebec. According to Pulker, the Montreal diocese under Bishop J.C. Farthing had, before as well as after the war, remained one of the strongholds of Anglican Social Christianity in Canada. *We Stand on Their Shoulders*, 57, 62–3, 93.

41 Ibid., 2–3.

42 NA, Chaplain Service Records, vol. 4663, Questionnaire file. See Appendix 2, above.

43 To avoid redundancy, Almond appointed McGreer, Wells, Hepburn, Shatford, Moore, and Warner to speak for Anglicans on the general Chaplains' Message Committee. Methodists were represented by T.A. Wilson and George Fallis, Presbyterians by Kent and Oliver, Baptists by John MacDonald, and Congregationalists by Philip Smith. Ibid. See also USA, Oliver Papers, Oliver to Rita, 28 Aug., 6 Sept. 1918.

44 Perhaps anticipating their resentment of another demand for a report, Kent urged them to be as detailed and comprehensive as possible: "There still remains the no less important task of interpreting the soldiers, the war and its lessons to the Church at home, … our Brethren in the Ministry … who have not been so fortunate as to share directly in this great work … We should endeavour to make that experience meaningful and helpful to the Churches in Canada … The Chaplains having enjoyed the unique experience should have a special message for the Churches at Home. This will contribute materially towards arousing them to a realization of the greatness of the task when the soldiers return." NA, Chaplain Service Records, vol. 4663, Questionnaire file, Preamble to Chaplain Service Questionnaire, 20 Aug. 1918.

45 NA, Chaplain Service Records, vol. 4669, Bramshott file, Kent to Wilson and reply, autumn 1918; also UCA, Methodist Army and Navy Board, box 10, file 258, Fallis to T.A. Moore, 26 Aug. 1918. Since then the Methodist manuscripts have disappeared.

46 Of the twenty-seven Presbyterians who replied, twenty endorsed this view, three partially agreed, and four bluntly refused to admit any blame on the church, holding the men entirely responsible for their own infidelity.

47 Oliver, George Pringle, and Alexander Macdonald, in particular, emphatically stated that many soldiers in times of crisis fell back on

the faith instilled in them by their mothers. To them, the residual piety found in many of the troops was perhaps the greatest asset of the church.

48 Victor Rae predicted that half of the men now alienated from the church might be won back by such reforms.

49 "The whole nation has suffered, 'For what?' For righteousness sake and the Kingdom of God. If the church can only rouse the people and get them to realize that this is what they suffered and died for during the period of the war, it is quite natural to suppose that they will have spirit enough to continue the fight ... Let the churches learn the lessons of the trenches, the brotherhood, the sharing, the 'Christian spirit' of the men." NA, Chaplain Service Records, vol. 4663, Question file, James White response.

50 Perhaps the most remarkable example of this was Oliver's response to the questionnaire, where he laid out in detail how the General Assembly would benefit from an ecclesiastical general staff, to serve as the executive branch of the Presbyterian system. Oliver's exhortation to the home denomination was, after winning the war overseas, to proclaim another war for social Christianity at home. Ibid., Oliver to Kent, 26 Aug. 1918. His response ran to twenty-six handwritten pages, hammering home one aspect after another of the war's vindication of his pre-war convictions. See also John Beattie, William McConnell, David Christie, and Ebenezer McLaren responses, and Victor Rae, James Faulds, John Macgillivray, and Harold Pickup to Kent. See also William McConnell response. Four-fifths of these chaplains flatly claimed that the men considered the church completely out of touch with their real lives.

51 Most of the chaplains (including Henry Mullowney, a Baptist) added that the clergyman of the future deserved a better salary as well as more respect as a professional from laymen. Some Presbyterians wanted seminarians to take business apprenticeships as a qualification for ordination, to give them "a better knowledge of human nature." NA, Chaplain Service Records, vol. 4668, C.F.C. file, Mullowney to MacDonald, 12 Sept. 1918.

52 Ibid., Faulds to Kent, 28 Sept. 1918; also Burgess to Kent, 30 Sept. 1918. See also Pickup response.

53 Ibid., George Pringle.

54 On Presbyterian support of union, see NA, Chaplain Service Records, vol. 4663, Questionnaire file. At the end of the war, of the twenty-six Presbyterians surveyed, only one completely opposed union under any circumstances. See NA, Chaplain Service Records, vol. 4663, Questionnaire file, Compton response.

55 These included Alexander Gordon, Harold Pickup, John McCaskill, James Faulds, and John Beattie. See also QUA, D. Gordon Papers,

1918 Correspondence, A. Gordon to George Pidgeon, 22 May 1918. On Beattie, Pickup, McCaskill, and Faulds, see NA, Chaplain Service Records, vol. 4663, Questionnaire file. Recent students of the Presbyterian church-union controversy have suggested that Presbyterian ministers who favoured union in 1925 tended to have in their background seminary training or post-graduate study in Britain or Europe, while older ministers without such study or with ties to American seminaries, such as Princeton, tended to oppose organic union. Evidently, service as a Great War chaplain either followed from similar idealism or tended to predispose a minister towards union. Significantly, most of the Presbyterian chaplains shared the same intellectual background as the former group. In fact, many of these chaplains, with intellectual ties to Glasgow (Faulds, Cornett, McColl), Edinburgh (Christie), and Berlin (Oliver, Kilpatrick), were among the most articulate advocates of union in 1925. See Clifford, "The Interpreters of the United Church of Canada," *Church History*, no. 2 (1977): 212–14. Two other Unionist chaplains had post-graduate work at Yale (Little) and Columbia (Oliver).

56 Oliver wanted all Presbyterian seminarians to have long training in modern biblical criticism, "to Kill a lot of freak notions about Criticism which our illiterate Evangelists parade as piety." Many of the younger Presbyterian chaplains suggested dispensing with subscription to the Westminster Standards at ordination, or even abandoning such "subordinate standards" entirely. See also Pickup, Muncaster, Watts, Cornett, Little, Campbell, Wright, Rae, and Christie responses. Only two respondents, Compton and Burgess, opposed any plan to modernize doctrine or deepen the influence of "the German Theology."

57 *Canadian Baptist*, 23 Aug. 1917, 4; response by J. McIntosh, 4 Oct. 1917; and Mullowney's rejoinder, 13 Dec. 1917, 3. In his pre-war sermon, Mullowney explicitly draws on Rauschenbusch's *Christianity and the Social Order*. See Mullowney, "A Plea for Social Justice," *Canadian Baptist*, 8 July 1915, 2.

58 "I think most of us realize that the much advertised principle of complete separation of Church and State is a mere chimera impractical and undesirable, the time has come for the churches of Canada to take a deeper and more intelligent interest in the Government of this country." NA, Chaplain Service Records, vol. 4668, C.F.C. file, Mullowney to MacDonald, 12 Sept. 1918. Like the Anglican and Presbyterian chaplains, Mullowney felt that the Baptist church needed to modernize the professional training of the clergy. Mullowney wanted all Baptist ministers trained to the standard of doctrine and outlook of McMaster University. Too many ministers, he felt, were being ordained without adequate professional training, especially in sociology and economics.

59 Ibid., Mullowney to MacDonald. A powerful Methodist affirmation of these sentiments came from Thomas Colwell, who also urged T.A. Moore to organize laymen's commercial co-operatives for the urban poor, effectively eliminating capitalism and benefiting the weak: "Undoubtedly it would be unpopular, but every new endeavour along right lines has been unpopular." UCA, Army and Navy Board, box 9, file 233, Colwell to Moore, 27 Dec. 1918.

60 *Christian Guardian,* 10 Oct. 1917, 7.

61 UCA, Methodist Army and Navy Board, box 4, file 82, Graham to T.A. Moore, 3 Jan. 1918. For an allusion to preaching based on the crosses found on the British flag, see Harry Frost, "Notes from a Chaplain's Diary," *Christian Guardian,* 29 May 1915, 9.

62 UCA, Methodist Army and Navy Board, box 4, file 82, Graham to Moore, 17 June 1918. Another Methodist challenged, with little effect, Almond's public statements about army revival overseas. John Smyth, principal of Montreal Methodist College, was dismissed as impertinent, as he had been in England for only a few weeks as chaplain to the Irish Canadian Rangers. See NA, Chaplain Service Records, vol. 4642, Smyth file, Oct. 1917, Almond correspondence.

63 UCA, Methodist Army and Navy Board, box 4, file 82, Graham file, T.A. Moore to Graham, 16 July 1918.

64 Wells, "The Church Must Face the Facts," *Canadian Churchman,* 13 June 1918, 379–80.

65 As McGreer described it to Almond: "As was to be expected … It isn't going to be easy to get a truly representative message, I'm afraid – particularly on the point of Church Unity. If we indicate the number who endorse each point dealt with, we shall guard against misrepresenting things to the people at home … Creegan and I were a minority opposed to the prevailing views advanced at yesterday's meeting." NA, Chaplain Service Records, vol. 4648, file 2, McGreer to Almond, 2 Jan. 1919.

66 "It must not be forgotten that the co-operation which existed amongst chaplains in the Canadian Overseas forces did away almost entirely with definite teaching on the distinctive doctrines of the Church, that if similar conditions obtained at home definiteness in religious teaching would largely cease … We feel that the chaplains in their message should pause before they make such a recommendation, lest religion generally, the cause of unity particularly, be injured rather than aided." NA, Chaplain Service Records, vol. 4675, Chaplains' Message file, Creegan to Almond, 1 Mar. 1919. On Wells's agreement, see ibid., Wells to Almond, 26 Feb. 1919.

67 The DCS found that more chaplains praised the sentiments of the message than opposed it. Methodist Wilberforce Magwood was rapturous

in his praise and revealed his own conviction that the Kingdom of God was coming soon as a result of the war. Ibid., vol. 4631, Magwood file, Magwood to Fallis, 17 Mar. 1919. Salvation Army chaplain Thompson Walton, after wide social-service experience in London and France, added his blessing. Ibid., vol. 4645, Walton file, Walton to Almond, 17 Mar. 1919.

68 Ibid., vol. 4618, Broughall file, Broughall to Almond, 18 Mar. 1919. Earlier in the summer William Lyon, another Anglican, echoed Broughall's call for doctrinal conservatism and simpler preaching, without affectation or catering to the fads of the day. The letter was placed on his personal file. See vol. 4631, Lyon file, Lyon to Fallis, 31 July 1918.

69 Wilson caught two contradictions in the message: once when it claimed that the Canadian masses were hungry for the Gospel but then argued that they were easily bored with current teaching, and again when it claimed that while it was hard to hold voluntary services, the men wanted to have more. "I fail to see how these statements can make a good impression."

70 Ibid., vol. 4646, Wilson file, Wilson to MacDonald, 17 Mar. 1919. On Mullowney's sympathies, see vol. 4668, Canadian Forestry Corps file, Mullowney to MacDonald, 12 Sept. 1918.

71 Roman Catholics evidently did not take part in these retreats, though individual priests often took their leave in English monasteries. Beattie, "History," 276.

72 *Canadian Churchman*, 2 Aug. 1917, 492.

73 Shatford, quoted by George Pringle, "Army Chaplains' Conference," *Presbyterian and Westminster*, 8 Nov. 1917, 447. Reflecting Kelman's address, Kilpatrick suggested that many of his men were dissatisfied with traditional creeds yet were sincerely groping for an adequate doctrinal statement of their deep belief in God. UCA, Kilpatrick Papers, box 1, Correspondence, Kilpatrick to T.B. Kilpatrick, 14 May 1918, 2–6. Many chaplains endorsed the similar portrait of "inarticulate" Christianity drawn by Donald Hankey in *A Student in Arms*, 89–102, and QUA, D. Gordon Papers, box 2, 1918 Correspondence, A. Gordon to G.C. Pidgeon, 22 May 1918.

74 For Kelman's effect, see UCA, Kilpatrick Papers, box 1, Correspondence, Kilpatrick to T.B. Kilpatrick, 14 May 1918. On Kelman's attack on dogmatism and his triumphalist views of providence and the war, see *The War and Preaching*, 7–9, 32–47, 100–20, 185–8. Aspects of his address were repeated in the portions Kilpatrick authored of the Chaplains' Message to the Churches in 1919.

75 They tended, however, to look at the question of ecumenical reunion in a much more gradual sense than those of other denominations. Significantly, Anglicans recalled Shatford's call for church union in

federative, not organic terms, as each denomination tended to see itself as most catholic! Tupper, "Chaplains Conferences," *Canadian Churchman*, 25 Oct. 1917, 1 Nov. 1917; also 8, 15, 22 Nov. 1917.

76 Tupper, *Canadian Churchman*, 22 Nov. 1917; 4 Apr. 1918, 217; 2 May 1918, 286; also 25 Apr., and 2 and 9 May 1918.

77 Moffit, *Christian Guardian*, 5 Jan. 1918, 2. Certainly the Methodist chaplains, predominantly Victoria College graduates, should have been predisposed to hear Jackson approvingly. Since 1900 Nathanael Burwash had been imparting similar views of biblical criticism and exegesis to his students. Van Die, *Evangelical Mind*, 102–8.

78 *Christian Guardian*, 12 June 1918, 18. Colwell had reported similar discussions among the padres at a First Army chaplains' conference in March 1918. UCA, Methodist Army and Navy Board, box 9, file 233, Colwell to Moore, 29 Apr. 1918.

79 M.E. Conron, *Christian Guardian*, 11 Dec. 1918.

80 George Kilpatrick blamed this pre-war sentimentality about Christ on bad theology and equally bad religious art. "In Glover's phrase, the 'Jesus of History' must be rediscovered and claimed if the manhood of the world is to be at His feet." UCA, Kilpatrick Papers, Kilpatrick to T.B. Kilpatrick, 14 May 1918, 8. Other Presbyterians, echoed Kilpatrick in their 1918 questionnaire responses. NA, Chaplain Service Records, vol. 4663, Questionnaire file, responses of Pickup, Burgess, White, Compton. Alexander Gordon echoed Kilpatrick's contempt for the sentimental pre-war portrait of Christ's personality: QUA, D. Gordon Papers, box 2, 1918 Correspondence, A. Gordon to D. Gordon, 22 May 1918.

81 "Leaves from a Chaplain's Diary," *Christian Guardian*, 27 Oct. 1915, 11.

82 NA, Chaplain Service Records, vol. 4667, Chaplain Reports, file 8, Harold Laws report of 13 May 1918. Throughout 1918 Hugh Taylor held informal discussions based on Fosdick, with his men in France on the personality of Jesus. Ibid., vol. 4665, Reports, France, Taylor report, summer 1918.

83 The YMCA and First Contingent chaplains had brought Fosdick's book with them from Valcartier, using it both on board ship and at Salisbury Plain. C.W. Bishop, *Y.M.C.A. and the Great War*, 25. See also Ross, *Y.M.C.A. in Canada*, 281. On Chaplain Service use of Fosdick and Rauschenbusch in 1918–19, see NA, Chaplain Service Records, vol. 4663, Reconstruction and Suggested Outline of Canadian Citizenship Program files; and Adam Armstrong, "A Chaplain's Work," *Christian Guardian*, 26 Mar. 1919, 15.

84 H.E. Fosdick, *The Manhood of the Master*, chap. 1. In the rest of the opening chapter Fosdick characterizes Jesus as embodying William James's concept of the "once-born" man. See James, *Varieties of Religious*

Experience, 78–81. On the militant aspects of Jesus's character, see Fosdick, 36–42 and chap. 4, 5, 8, and 12. See also Fosdick, 47–9 and 53–5, where Jesus is linked with Garibaldi and Napoleon.

85 Rauschenbusch, *The Social Principles of Jesus*, 12, 21, 26, 60, 151–6, 165, 180, 186.

86 So wrote Harry Nobles, a Baptist chaplain, in his pamphlet for the citizenship campaign. See "The New Canadian," Canadian Citizenship Series 10.

87 UCA, Kilpatrick Papers, box 1, Correspondence, Kilpatrick to T.B. Kilpatrick, 14 May 1918, 2–4. This view is discussed in the context of "taming" the experiences of trenchland by re-evaluating the old creed in terms of Christian "realism." Gauvreau, *Evangelical Century*, 262–5.

88 On the pre-war emphasis on mother-nurture in Methodist and Presbyterian revivalism, see Van Die, *Evangelical Mind*, chap. 1 and 4, and Brian Fraser, "The Christianization of Our Civilization," 74.

89 Callan, "Blood Brothers," *Canadian Churchman*, 9 Aug. 1917, 507–8. Such an advanced view of salvation occasionally drew sharp criticism from both ultra-conservative Protestants and Roman Catholics in Canada. See *Canadian Churchman*, 30 Aug. 1917, 560; also 6, 20 Sept., 15 Nov., and 13 Dec. 1917. The editor of the *Catholic Register* professed to be appalled at the adoption of such views by Presbyterian commentators on the war, lamenting that such a biblically-centred denomination had evidently abandoned the traditional conceptions of sin and salvation. *Catholic Register*, 12 Apr. 1917, 4. The debate over the newer forms of "conversion," or what should take its place, is explored in Phyllis Airhart's *Serving the Present Age.*

90 Christie, "A Soldiers' Meeting and Some Reflections," *Presbyterian and Westminster*, 27 June 1918, 620.

91 Kilpatrick, *Presbyterian and Westminster*, 26 Dec. 1918, 590. See also Presbyterian chaplains James Faulds, James Whillans, and David Christie, *Presbyterian and Westminster*, 6 Sept. 1917, 233–56; and Robert Taylor, ibid., 5 July 1917, 11–12, and 12 July 1917, 43–4. On the similarity of T.B. Kilpatrick's or J. McFadyen's Christological focus in their pre-war teaching, see Fraser, "Christianization of Our Civilization," 67. For them, as later for their students, the solutions to all problems of religion and morality were Christological – but a Christology seasoned by trench ministry. See Gauvreau, *Evangelical Century*, 262–4.

92 UCA, Kilpatrick Papers, box 1, Correspondence, Kilpatrick to T.B. Kilpatrick, 14 May 1918, 16–18.

93 Of the Canadian chaplains who served overseas in the Great War, 55 per cent are known to have been trained in Canadian seminaries. The remaining number presumably were trained in Great Britain, although a few chaplains emerged from colleges and seminaries in the

United States. Among the Anglicans, Trinity and Wycliffe Colleges in Toronto contributed fifty-six future chaplains, while Bishop's graduated a dozen, among them Canon Scott and John Almond. Anglican graduates of Huron, King's (Nova Scotia), and St John's (Winnipeg), as well as other diocesan colleges, became chaplains. Knox College in Toronto contributed thirty (almost one-third of the total) future Presbyterian chaplains, Queen's University Theological College twelve, and McGill's Presbyterian College ten. Eight Presbyterian Great War chaplains were graduates of Pine Hill Divinity College in Halifax. Among the Methodists, forty-one, or two-thirds of the graduates destined for chaplaincies, were graduates of Victoria College, while Montreal's and Winnipeg's Wesley Colleges produced ten more between them. Mount Allison graduated eight future Methodist chaplains. Half of the twenty-four Baptist chaplains to serve overseas were McMaster graduates, while others trained at Acadia and in American seminaries on the east coast. Less is known about Roman Catholic Great War chaplains-in-training, although Laval, the University of Ottawa, and St Michael's College in Toronto (after 1910), as well as diocesan seminaries in Quebec and the Maritimes and in Ireland, Belgium, and France, all contributed future Great War padres.

94 Michael Gauvreau, "The Taming of History: Reflections on the Canadian Methodist Encounter with Biblical Criticism, 1830–1890," CHR 65, no. 3 (Sept. 1984): 315–46, and *The Evangelical Century*; see also A.B. McKillop, *A Disciplined Intelligence*; Brian Fraser, *The Social Uplifters*; and Van Die, *An Evangelical Mind*.

95 On the taming of evolution in Canadian schools, see McKillop, *Disciplined Intelligence*, 94–5; among Presbyterians, Brian Fraser, *Social Uplifters*, 38–60; for Methodists, Gauvreau, *Evangelical Century*, 125–50, and Van Die, *Evangelical Mind*, 38–9.

96 See Fraser, "Christianization," 39–44.

97 On the wide impact of Drummond on the Protestant English-speaking world, especially Canadian Presbyterians, see ibid., 37–60. Fraser has illustrated this process in his study of T.B. Kilpatrick, professor at Knox College before the war. Significantly, his son George proved one of the most articulate and influential CEF chaplains: ibid., 38–60. On the role of Henry Drummond in the early studies of Edmund Oliver, Clarence Mackinnon, and Harry Kent, all chaplains destined for prominent educational careers in Canadian Presbyterian and United Churches, see Mackinnon, *A Life of Principal Oliver*, 57, and his own *Reminiscences*, 51–9.

98 Van Die, *Evangelical Mind*, 97–108, 113. Similar convictions were shared by the closely related Presbyterian colleges in Canada by this date: see Fraser, 270–1. By 1910, well over half the Methodist clergy in

training were at Victoria College or one of its allied colleges in the Maritimes or the west; on the role of Baconianism in Methodist colleges in Canada, see also Michael Gauvreau, "The Taming of History," 328–30. On similar impulses at McMaster, Acadia, and Brandon Baptist colleges, see C.M. Johnston, *McMaster University*, vol. 1, and G.A. Rawlyk, ed., *Canadian Baptists and Christian Higher Education.*

99 Gauvreau, "Taming," 331–2. For their reading of F.W. Farrar, J.B. Lightfoot, and Andrew Fairbairn, see Van Die, *Evangelical Mind*, 213–22; Gauvreau, "Taming," 338–40; Fraser, "Christianization," 28–9. Thus Canadian scholars such as Watson, T.B. Kilpatrick, and John Edgar McFadyen, teaching Presbyterian seminarians, could argue that higher criticism had a constructive rather than a destructive effect on faith and doctrine. Fraser, "Christianization," 28.

100 Van Die, *Evangelical Mind*, 96–101, 150–4; Gauvreau, *Evangelical Century*, chap. 4; and Fraser, "Christianization," 29–30. For similar developments among Baptists at McMaster, see Masters, *Protestant Colleges*, 9–16, and Johnston, *McMaster*, vol. 1, chap. 5.

101 Gauvreau, *Evangelical Century*, chap. 5. John McFadyen, professor of Old Testament at Knox College and a pupil of George Adam Smith, passed these ideals on to a generation of Presbyterian seminarians, many destined to become chaplains. The prophets, he taught, "stood closer to modern needs, and therefore mean more to modern preachers than the apostles because they expected to have some practical effect on the politics of their age." Fraser, "Christianization," 30, 34–8. On McFadyen's and Adolf Harnack's influence on Edmund Oliver, see Mackinnon, *Life of Oliver*, 81–2. In 1908 Principal A. Gandier of Knox College revised the seminary curriculum, adding social and ethical topics to biblical and theological studies. After 1909 Knox seminarians were required to do some type of social work as students: see Moir, *Enduring Witness*, 174–6, 184, 188–90.

102 Gauvreau, *Evangelical Century*, 201–14. See Fraser, "Christianization," 21–2, 265–6.

103 Gauvreau, *Evangelical Century*, 337–8; Van Die, *Evangelical Mind*, 106–7, 156–64, 187–8; Fraser, "Christianization," 453–4, 67–78.

104 "The values to be upheld by the public conscience were those found in the character of Christ – faithfulness, courage, patience, calmness and self-sacrifice," wrote Kilpatrick. See Fraser, "Christianization," 83.

105 Presbyterians destined to become Great War chaplains, such as Harold Kent, Edmund Oliver, George Kilpatrick, and Malcolm Omond, attended Harnack's lectures. Mackinnon, *Life of Oliver*, 82.

106 See Owen Chadwick, *The Victorian Church*, 57–111.

107 Fraser, 28ff. On the wide influence of Idealism in Canadian universities before the war, see Masters, *Protestant Church Colleges*, chap. 1, and

McKillop, *Disciplined Intelligence*, 184–96. On Idealism in Canadian Congregational colleges, especial Montreal Congregational College, see Silcox, *Church Union in Canada*, 133.

108 McKillop, *Disciplined Intelligence*, 191, and Fraser, "Christianization," 18–19, 60.

109 See Brian Fraser on Edward Caird and his influence on T.B. Kilpatrick, "Christianization," 57–76, also 22–3.

110 Gauvreau points out the Methodist distrust of Idealism and adaptation of historical biblical criticism before the war: see "Taming of History," 336 and note. E.M. Burwash's 1910 lecture "The New Theology" illustrates how such assumptions and accompanying methods percolated through to the generation of Methodist students who would become Great War chaplains. While critical of R.J. Campbell's philosophical idealism, Burwash, as he had learned from his father Nathanael, nevertheless maintained that, preceded by the requisite religious experience, reverent historical criticism was a valuable tool in understanding scripture and expressing religious truths.

111 Van Die, *Evangelical Mind*, 154–67, 170–7.

112 Ibid., 156–64, 166–76; Gauvreau, *Evangelical Century*, 322–4; also Richard Allen, "Providence to Progress," in *Canadian Issues* 7 (1985): 39–46.

113 M. Gauvreau, *Evangelical Century*, chap. 6, 218–28.

114 N. Keith Clifford, "His Dominion: A Vision in Crisis," SR (1973): 315–26; also B. Kiesekamp, "Presbyterian and Methodist Divines," SR (1973): 289–302. See also Van Die, *Evangelical Mind*, 166–74; Fraser, "Christianization," 224–6, 137–40, 145–50, 222–40, 274–5; William Magney, "The Methodist Church and the National Gospel," 71–87; Van Die, *Evangelical Mind*, 108–13, 137–41.

115 The well-known passage from *Varieties of Religious Experience* suggesting the value of a moral equivalent to war appeared in W.R. McIntosh's call to Presbyterian youth in 1911. While at the 1913 pre-General Assembly conference in Toronto, W.T. Herridge, a well-known Presbyterian minister and militia chaplain, presented the challenge to Christianize Canada in similar terms: see Fraser, "Christianization," 137, 150. While previous historians have evaluated the embattled language of the Canadian call for righteousness as defensive, one has recently emphasized its optimistic, progressive tone: see Van Die, *Evangelical Mind*, 173–6. On the growing familiarity with William James, see Airhart, *Serving the Present Age*, 98–102, 140–1.

116 For the religious idealism and reform ideals of G.M. Grant's and George Parkin's imperialism, see Berger, *The Sense of Power*, 31, 186–7, 225–40; see also McKillop, *Disciplined Intelligence*, 196–7, 206, 230.

117 Berger, *Sense of Power*, 30–1, 223–32, 262–4.

118 Ibid., 244, 250–6.

119 On Fallon and the education controversy, see J.K.A. Farrell, "Michael Francis Fallon," *Canadian Catholic Historical Association Report* (1968), 83–90; and Brown and Cook, *Canada, 1896–1921: A Nation Transformed*, 171–2, 254–62. See also Barber, "The Ontario Bilingual Schools Issue, 1910–1916," MA, Queen's University 1964.

120 Moir, "A Vision Shared? The *Catholic Register* and Canadian Identity before World War I," in *Canadian Issues* 7: 356–66.

121 Ryan, *The Clergy and Economic Growth in Quebec*, 257–302. See also Brown and Cook, *Canada, 1896–1921*, 127–43, 258–9.

122 Fallon spoke for a number of Canadian priests of Irish extraction (such as John O'Gorman and his colleagues), who sided with his critique of French Canadian nationalism and echoed his praise of the British Empire as the last barrier against social disorder and international evil. See Farrell, "Michael Francis Fallon," 77–81. Mark McGowan has examined the new nationalism of the English-speaking Catholics of the Toronto region in "We Are All Canadians," PhD, University of Toronto 1988.

123 Gauvreau, *Evangelical Century*, 229–39.

CHAPTER EIGHT

1 Will Bird, *And We Go On*, 337. Tommy dies the next day of influenza. See also 279–81, 297–300.

2 Wells found taking a smaller parish and several months of quiet necessary for his recovery. *Fighting Bishop*, 234. George Kilpatrick spent a month in Montreal, visiting relatives of Forty-second Battalion dead. When he had seen as many as possible, he was unable to take up work again without a long recuperation with his family. UCA, Kilpatrick Papers, Autobiography, "A Quiver Full of Arrows," 8–9.

3 QUA, D. Gordon Papers, box 2, 1918 Correspondence, A. Gordon to D. Gordon, 5 Nov. 1918. H.J. Latimer told the Methodist Army and Navy Board's T.A. Moore that, after three years at war, he felt he needed several months of quiet study before he could preach in a civilian church again. UCA, Methodist Army and Navy Board, box 5, file 127, Latimer file, Latimer to Moore, 3 Jan. 1919.

4 NA, Chaplain Service Records, vol. 4623, Forster file, and vol. 4628, Howie file. Grimshaw continued as a probation Officer in Toronto until retirement in 1940: see Canadian Baptist Archives, McMaster Divinity College, Grimshaw biographical file. UCA, Methodist Army and Navy Board, box 6, file 160, Lavell file, Lavell to Ernest Thomas, 24 Aug. 1919. On McLeod, see his papers in Alberta Provincial Archives.

5 There is no indication on Chaplain Service files whether or not Vipond chose to leave because of frustration at his Canadian reception. See NA, Chaplain Service Records, vol. 4644, Vipond file, Vipond to Beattie, Apr.–May 1919. He returned to Canada later in the decade. By 1927 Harold Frost and T.A. Mosley were firmly embedded in the American Congregational church. *New Outlook*, 2 Feb. 1927 and 21 Dec. 1927.

6 On Beattie's and Almond's wartime prediction of the value of keeping such clergymen in Canadian circles, see NA, Chaplain Service Records, vol. 4623, Fisher file, and vol. 4638, Peacock file. See also vol. 4615, Allen file; vol. 4623, Ferguson file; vol. 4624, Frost file; and vol. 4618, Blake file.

7 NA, Chaplains' Service Records, vol. 4633, Mullowney file. See also McMaster Baptist Archives, Mullowney biographical file.

8 NA, Chaplain Service Records, vol. 4634, MacDonald file, Workman to Morrison, Jan. 1919; also vol. 4641, Sammon file, and vol. 4635, McQuillan file.

9 NA, Chaplain Service Records, vol. 4626, Hawks file; vol. 4621, de la Taille file; and vol. 4621, Deacon file.

10 Alex F. Laidlaw, *The Campus and the Community*, 67ff.

11 NA, Chaplain Service Records, vol. 4633, Mosley file; vol. 4631, Magner file; and vol. 4622, Dykes file.

12 Sometimes such tactics resulted from the desperation of a chaplain without a charge. One Baptist put it bluntly: "I am a desperate man, and I am out of a job ... There are no churches vacant and it is winter." Eventually Beattie found him a temporary location in a Hamilton veterans' hospital. See Riddiford to Beattie, 1 June, 6 Dec. 1919, in NA, Chaplain Service Records, vol. 4640, Riddiford file. Occasionally such tactics forced Beattie to summon up the support of General W. Gwatkin, chief of General Staff: "This chaplain is entitled to wear the uniform so long as he is borne on the strength of the C.E.F., to which he clings like a limpet ... If, after he has been prized off the strength of the C.E.F., well and good." The chaplain was discharged. See NA, Chaplain Service Records, vol. 4618, Campbell file, Beattie to General W.T. Gunn, 18 Mar., 25 Apr. 1919. See also Beattie to Adjutant-General, 25 Apr. 1919, and W. Gwatkin to Adjutant-General.

13 NA, Chaplain Service Records, vol. 4625, J. Graham; vol. 4630, S. Lambert; vol. 4646, T. Wilson; and vol. 4639, George Pugsley. Cecil Owen, who had shared the arduous 1917 hospital duty with Oliver overseas, carried on this work at Vancouver's Shaughnessy military hospital. Renison, *One Day*, 125.

14 NA, Chaplain Service Records, vol. 4619, E.F. Church; vol. 4620, M.E. Conron; and vol. 4624, H.A. Frost.

15 UCA, Methodist Army and Navy Board, box 4, file 95, H.W. Burnett. Burnett spent two months in Montreal meeting troop trains and assisting soldiers on their way home.

16 In the words of one minister: "As I look at it from all angles I am beginning to think that I am going to pay rather dearly for my experience as a chaplain." UCA, Methodist Army and Navy Board, box 5, file 351, J. Reycraft to S.D. Chown, 21 Mar. 1919; also file 108, W.T. Keough file, Keough to Moore, 13 May 1919.

17 See T.A. Moore to G.I. Campbell, 16 Sept. 1919, ibid., box 4, file 96. In one case, however, the board itself refused the application by a Methodist chaplain from the United States to be admitted to the Canadian church. George Plewes had rendered distinguished service to Canadians overseas. The Army and Navy Board in 1918 attempted to have him removed from the Chaplain Service (claiming he was occupying a place that by rights belonged to a "native" Canadian) and, after the war, refused to give him access to the Canadian conferences. Plewes returned to the United States, eventually becoming a social worker with the state of Michigan. NA, Chaplain Service Records, vol. 4639, Plewes file.

18 The first letter decried the sight of chaplains left with the worst pickings of their diocese. The second demanded that they take their chances like every other priest. *Canadian Churchman*, 18 Dec. 1918, 16 Jan. 1919.

19 NA, Chaplain Service Records, vol. 4619, C. Carruthers file.

20 NA, Chaplain Service Records, vol. 4634, C.N.M. McKay file.

21 Ibid., vol. 4535, McCaskill file. On McGreer, see D.C. Masters, *Bishop's University*, 128–34. On Moffit and Graham at Winnipeg, see A.G. Bedford, *University of Winnipeg*, 158, 230–2.

22 Fallis, *Padre's Pilgrimage*, 97.

23 As one chaplain put it, he was eager to get out of the army and back to Canada while there still some "decent" parishes left. NA, Chaplain Service Records, vol. 4640, Rae file, Rae to Beattie, Feb. 1919. Such disillusionments were already too familiar to many veterans from the ranks. See Desmond Morton and Glenn Wright, *Winning the Second Battle*, 117–22.

24 NA, Chaplain Service Records, vol. 4635, McColl file, McColl to Beattie, Feb. 1920. Two who found mission work a relief from the hectic days of the war, however, were George Pringle and Thomas Colwell, who became quite well known up and down the west coast with the Presbyterian and Methodist mission to loggers. After church union, the two missions merged and both ex-chaplains became co-workers with the loggers and their families. See Pringle, *In Great Waters*, 14, 56–62.

25 James White, forced to take up mission work in British Columbia at fifty-four years of age, wrote Beattie, "After the army life the isolation of the peace [time] is like to drive me crazy. I don't think I can stand it much longer ... One cannot but regret that the church in Canada has nothing better to offer its returned men than a position on the outskirts of the wilderness. I am afraid that the tendency is, since the war, to narrow down the opportunity for giving expression of our war experiences. It may be the people want to forget it and its invaluable lessons, and to return again to the beaten track of the prewar days." White proposed leaving the ministry to secure a veteran's land grant for farming but discovered he was considered over-age and too inexperienced by the local allocations board. In the face of these developments, he returned to his mission. See White to Beattie, 3 Nov. 1919, 28 July 1920, NA, Chaplain Service Records, vol. 4645, White file.

26 The most glaring of such post-war diatribes came from Hughes appointees who had been deemed unsuitable by Beattie and Almond and sent home to Canada in 1918. Unable to find a church or militia appointment, they appealed to militia authorities and the Militia Council, as well as their church boards, in vain. One accused Beattie of spreading similar slanders through the home church. By the beginning of 1920 his bitterness had driven him from the ministry. He replied to any correspondence from the Chaplain Service with vituperation and accusations of calumny against the church, the chaplaincy, and the country. See T.A. Patterson to A.S. Grant, 24 July, and to Col. McCordick, 4 Nov. 1918; Beattie to Almond, 5 Dec., and reply, 27 Dec. 1918; also Militia Council Minutes, 6 Jan. 1919; and Patterson to Beattie, 16, 26, 30 Jan. 1920, all in NA, Chaplain Service Records, vol. 4638, Patterson file.

27 NA, Chaplain Service Records, vol. 4631, Lyon file, Lyon to Beattie, 10 Feb. 1920.

28 Here the post-war visit of Geoffrey Studdert-Kennedy, Britain's famous Great War chaplain, to Hamilton gave Renison some encouragement. *One Day at a Time*, 119–24.

29 George Pringle, *In Great Waters*, 58.

30 William Parker, a Baptist chaplain wounded in the hospital air raids of 1918, found his crippled leg made it impossible, among other things, to conduct baptisms. On the basis of his disabilities, Beattie secured him a posting in the post office. NA, Chaplain Service Records, vol. 4638, Parker file, Oct. 1919. John Beattie, one of the original Valcartier chaplains, found his poor health made it impossible to serve in the rural prairie charges available to him. Ibid, vol. 4616, Beattie file, Beattie to William Beattie, May 1920. Australian chaplains encoun-

tered similar difficulties when they tried to resume peacetime work. McKernan, "Clergy in Khaki," 160–1.

31 J.D. Morrow, for example, returned to his Toronto Presbyterian church early in 1918 burned out by his war exertions. Formerly an athlete, he never recovered from the anaemia diagnosed overseas, resigned from the church, and retired to California, where he died soon afterwards. See J.E. Orr, *Always Abounding*, 23, 36–9. See also NA, Chaplain Service Records, vol. 4622, G.A. Edmison file.

32 *New Outlook*, 22 Sept. 1926, 17. Whitaker had suffered from shell shock while overseas and was still affected by painful leg wounds. At least two prominent Anglican chaplains were rumoured to have taken their own lives in the post-war decades, and another poisoned himself while in the United States. By 1939 at least 23 of the 101 Roman Catholic Great War chaplains had died. O'Gorman, "Canadian Catholic Chaplains," *Canadian Catholic History Association Report* (1939–40), 83. Many obituaries of Protestant chaplains emphasize how war service contributed to the early demise of many chaplains. Edward Graham, for example, died of a stroke in 1934. See UCA, Biographical Files of Ministers, Graham file, also Ibid, A.H. Denoon file.

33 Linley Knight to Beattie, 31 Aug. 1920, NA, Chaplain Service Records, vol. 4629, Knight file; also Albert Trench to Beattie, 27 Oct. 1919, ibid., vol. 4644, Trench file.

34 For example, see Georges Coté to Beattie, Sept. 1920, NA, Chaplain Service Records, vol. 4620, Coté file.

35 O.C., M.D. 10 to Militia Council, 10 Dec. 1918, NA, Chaplain Service Records, vol. 4658, M.D. 10 file.

36 Cecil Owen to Beattie, 31 Dec. 1918. The only dissent from the British Columbian churches seemed to be the desire of the local bishop to return Esquimalt naval station to the capitation system. See Gore Barrow to Beattie, 18 Jan. 1919, NA, Chaplain Service Records, vol. 4658, M.D. 10 file.

37 Mewburn to Kemp, Winter 1919, NA, Chaplain Service Records, vol. 4629, A.E. Kemp file.

38 These officers specifically requested a "live wire" battalion padre instead of the old system, on the basis of their own war experience. O.C., R.C.R., to G.O.C., M.D. 6, 6 Nov. 1919; see also G.O.C. to Militia Council, 13 Nov. 1919, NA, Chaplain Service Records, vol. 4657, Permanent Force file.

39 "I do not know how we can keep chaplains on," Mewburn to Adjutant-General, 22 Nov. 1919, NA, Chaplain Service Records, vol. 4657, Permanent Force file; Adjutant-General to Beattie, Jan. 1920; and Beattie to Adjutant-General, 11 Mar. 1920, NA, Chaplain Service Records, vol. 4649, D.C.S., Canada file. See Beattie-G.O.C., M.D. 3 correspondence,

NA, Department of National Defence, Central Headquarters Registry, vol. 6558, HQ 868-15-1. Previously, Beattie had tried to justify retaining permanent force chaplains as educational officers: Beattie to Adjutant-General, 16 Dec. 1919, and Senior Chaplain, M.D. 4, to Beattie, 28 Feb. 1920, NA, Chaplain Service Records, vol. 4649, D.C.S., Canada, file 6; also Adjutant-General to Militia Council, Sept. 1920, NA, Chaplain Service Records, vol. 4674, Chaplains, Permanent Force file.

40 This began with Toronto's Anglican bishop over the care of churchmen in the hospitals of his diocese. See Bishop to Beattie, 17 Feb. 1920; Beattie to Bishop, 24 Feb., and reply, 2 Mar. 1920, NA, Chaplain Service Records, vol. 4657, M.D. 2 file. Soon Sylvestre was making similar arrangements in Quebec: ibid, vol. 4657, M.D. 5 file. See also Beattie to Adjutant-General, 17 June 1920, and his monthly reports between Apr. 1919 and Apr. 1920, NA, Department of National Defence, Central Headquarters Registry, vol. 6420, AHQ 203-1-57-1.

41 Former chaplain James Fortier complained that "soldiers left to themselves became absolutely non-religious and anti-religious. The Halifax Ministerial Association seems to forget that soldiers left to themselves will not go to church." Beattie replied, "For your private information, I can tell you that there are hostile elements to meet. These are definitely opposed to any establishment whatever other than the old capitation basis." Fortier to Beattie, 11 May 1920, NA, Chaplain Service Records, vol. 4623, Fortier file. Cardinal Begin also intervened in vain: Deputy Minister Fiset to Fortier and Cardinal Begin, 21 Jan. 1920, ibid., vol. 4623, Fortier file. Fortier denounced the capitation system: "Having known the appalling moral condition of our Catholic soldiers as it was before the war, I, as a Priest, seconded by His Eminence Cardinal Begin, and Archbishop McCarthy wish to protest against such a system." Fortier to Beattie, 6 Sept. 1920, NA, Department of National Defence, Central Headquarters Registry, vol. 6558, HQ 868-15-1. J.C. Roper, Anglican bishop of Ottawa, added his arguments to the cause. See Beattie to Adjutant-General, 9 Sept. 1920, NA, Department of National Defence, Central Headquarters Registry, vol. 6558, HQ 868-15-1. Beattie also enlisted officer support for this request: see Beattie and Col. Mackie to Militia Minister, 9 Sept. 1920, NA, Chaplain Service Records, vol. 4674, Chaplains, Permanent Force file.

42 The consensus of churchmen and commanding officers, he argued, was that the pre-war system, in the light of their positive war experience, would no longer be satisfactory. They evidently desired chaplains working along the same lines pioneered overseas, especially as new recruits needed the help of a regimental or garrison officer who could act as their guardian, educator, and guide. Such chaplains could smooth garrison relationships with local congregations and prevent

the traditional ostracization of soldiers in garrison towns and ports. Under Beattie and a Catholic deputy, ranked respectively as lieutenant-colonel and major, this force was to consist of seven other padres. Six, with ranks of lieutenant or captain, would be stationed where garrison strengths exceeded three hundred all ranks. Adjutant-General to Minister-in-Council, 24 Sept. 1920, NA, Department of National Defence, Central Headquarters Registry, vol. 6558, HQ 868-15-1.

43 Naval Minister Ballantyne to Beattie, 24 Nov. 1920, NA, Chaplain Service Records, vol. 4650, Canadian Navy Chaplains file.

44 Beattie to Adjutant-General, 26 Nov. 1920, NA, Department of National Defence, vol. 6558, HQ 868-15-1.

45 Beattie to W.T. Gunn, 2 Dec. 1920, and Beattie to Fortier, 9 Dec. 1920, NA, Chaplain Service Records, vol. 4674, Chaplains, Permanent Force file; Beattie, "History," 345.

46 Canada, Department of Militia and Defence, *Militia General Orders* (1921), 19–20, General Order 161, 1 June 1921 (HQ 203-1-98, P.C. 1709 of 25 May 1921).

47 Ibid., G.O. 19, 1 Jan. 1922; G.O. 140, 15 Oct. 1924; G.O. 3, 15 Jan. 1925.

48 Ibid., G.O. 110, 15 Dec. 1927; G.O. 48, 15 Apr. 1929.

49 Ibid., G.O. 80, 15 June 1931, by HQ 203-1-100.

50 UCA, Methodist Army and Navy Board, box 1, file 5, Majors Alan Shatford and George Kilpatrick, n.d., "Circular letter to the Ministers of the Churches in Canada."

51 "The war has clearly shown us the need of consecrated men and women in the realm of education, social service, industrial spheres, politics, civic endeavour. Leaders with high ideals, lofty principles, and dedicated enthusiasm are required in all branches of work. The Church must concern herself with the obligation of awakening a sense of mission in these directions ... Only in this larger sense can we hope to realize the ideal of our Master, Who called into His ministry men and women solemnly pledged in allegiance to Him, and zealously dedicated to the cause of humanity." Beattie "History," 331–44, "A Message from the Chaplains of the Overseas Military Forces of Canada to the Churches at Home."

52 Ibid., 335–7.

53 Ibid., 338.

54 "It is commonplace to urge the essential necessity for the establishment upon earth of the Kingdom of God of a union of all existing Christian forces. Yet the demand comes with such urgency and insistence at this time that its omission from any constructive programme ... would be to take much for granted." Ibid, 339–40.

55 Ibid., 340.

56 While paying tribute to the great success of the association, the padres warned that, in future, "Whatever form the endeavour assumes, one thing we feel most keenly: the work of the YMCA, as of all Christian service, must be related in the closest way to the programme of the Church. As Christian workers we must never lose the true sense of proportion and emphasis. The Church of Christ, which is the Tabernacle of the Master's Spirit, remains the central point from which all Christian activity radiates ... A vision of Christian statesmanship will be realized through the YMCA rededicating its powers of service to an awakened Church, and through the appropriation of these resources by the Church for use in the service of God and our fellowmen." Ibid., 340–1.

57 Ibid., 342–3.

58 Kilpatrick had drafted the introduction and conclusion, as well as sections on church vision and purpose. Mackinnon composed the section on the church's educational responsibility, while McGreer (with Shatford's and Kilpatrick's advice) discussed the church's social program. Warner penned the sections on ministerial training and campaigning for social justice, while Moore covered the need for dogmatic revision and church union. Shatford wrote on the need for worship revisions. NA, Chaplain Service Records, vol. 4675, Chaplains Message file. Compare these with UCA, Kilpatrick Papers, box 1, Correspondence, George to T.B. Kilpatrick, 14 May 1918, and *Canadian Churchman*, 11 Jan. 1917.

59 Robert Renison, *Canadian Churchman*, 16 Jan. 1919; Arthur Emmett, "The Religion of the Soldier," ibid., 13 Mar. 1919; and J.E. Gibson, "Judge Lindsay and the Doughboy's Religion," ibid., 8 May 1919. See also Vipond, ibid., 20 Mar. 1919, 185. "There are other things which might be said, but the Chaplains will say them as they return, and it is to be hoped, for the good of the Church, that they will not all be frowned down. It is, indeed, of the utmost importance that some of the changes the Chaplains ask for be made at once," Moore warned readers of the *Churchman*, 22 May 1919, 233.

60 Ibid., 27 Mar. 1919, 200. Although initially favourable to the chaplains' view of their unique prophetic value, by the spring of 1919 the editor of the *Churchman* had converted to Spectator's pessimistic view (shared with other churchman, such as the bishop of Fredericton) that any "chaplains' gospel" was obviously the product of abnormal conditions and would soon pass away. Padres, he predicted, who tried to spread any well-meaning but naïve theories would be disappointed and eventually proved wrong. Ibid., 21 Feb. 1918; and compare with Spectator's rejoinder, 2 May 1918, 283.

61 Canadian Anglican Church, General Synod Archives, Council for Social Service Papers, box 8, War Service Commission Reports,

1918–22, W.S.C. meeting, 29 Apr. 1919. According to the secretary of the House of Bishops, the Message did come under discussion at a subsequent session of the House, but no word of its conclusions was published at the time. *Canadian Churchman*, 11 Sept. 1919, 585.

62 NA, Chaplain Service Records, vol. 4641, Shatford file, Shatford to Almond, n.d. [1919]. The General Synod did, however, pay its share of the printing expenses.

63 While he had no objection to the revision of church formularies and dated historical proclamations, to him the Creed, with its emphasis on the divinity of Christ, was the one statement of faith that did not need revision. Ibid., 5 June 1919.

64 Ibid., 19 June 1919, 396.

65 For example, see Moore's somewhat chastened lecture to the Trinity College alumni in Toronto, *Canadian Churchman*, 4 Dec. 1919, 778. Here he characterized military religion, with its characteristic stoicism about death, as a kind of fatalism rather than faith in God as Father, while the soldier's view of Jesus was almost entirely untouched by the doctrine of the Incarnation. The army ethic, too, was preoccupied with earthly well-doing and not enough with the crusading for broader social and economic justice. One point Moore asserted with continued vigour was the need to modernize dogma and cut loose from the dictation theory of scripture. Also see Renison to Wycliffe alumni, ibid., 2 Oct. 1919, 634.

66 The commission had been suffering from an unmet budget since Feb. 1919: *Canadian Churchman*, 27 Feb. 1919, 134, and 18 Sept. 1919, 603.

67 NA, Chaplain Service Records, vol. 4663, Publicity file, Shatford to Beattie, 17 Sept. 1920.

68 George Farquhar reported on the situation encountered by Canadians in Siberia, while Kilpatrick reiterated his interpretation of the lessons of the war. John Mothersill, William McNairn, and Clarence Mackinnon also reported on aspects of their work. Only McNairn reported that the soldier did not change overseas, "for he came out of the army generally as he entered it – if a good man, perhaps better and braver, but the inferior man dropping lower." Presbyterian Church in Canada, *Acts and Proceedings* (1919), 45. Regarding the chaplains, the National Service Commission praised them, thanked them, and hoped that "out of their trying experiences, as they return, they may bring a message that will stir the Church to new endeavour." Finally, the commission recommended that vacant congregations seeking a minister give first consideration to ministers in khaki. Ibid., 266–7.

69 Ibid., 61, 262–3. See *Presbyterian and Westminster*, 23 June, 3 July 1919.

70 *Christian Guardian*, 11 June 1919, 29–30.

71 Ibid., 12 Mar. 1919, 2.

72 *Canadian Baptist*, 10, 17 July 1919.

73 Presbyterian Church in Canada, *Acts and Proceedings* (1919), 264–5, Report of the National Service Commission.

74 Grant also remarked that the YMCA was undergoing similar difficulties. NA, Chaplain Service Records, vol. 4625, A.S. Grant to Beattie, 23 May 1919. When the Presbyterian commission set out to learn from its own chaplains what it could do to assist them and the veterans, the chaplains responded with plenty of suggestions. Only a few of them, however, were carried out, owing to shortfalls.

75 Grant reported to Presbyterians the federation's success in allaying public concerns, aided by the Government Repatriation Department, the Great War Veterans' Association, and the Y. The federal commission had also planned for laymen and returned padres to present the "lessons" of the war to the people. This was seen as especially urgent in light of the social unrest that seemed to be threatening the country in early 1919, but owing to lack of funds, the campaign was dropped. *Acts and Proceedings* (1919), 265.

76 UCA, Methodist Army and Navy Board, box 2, Minutes, 30 Sept.–1 Oct. 1919; also *Canadian Baptist*, 1 Oct. 1919.

77 Presbyterian Church in Canada, *Acts and Proceedings* (1920), 41–2.

78 David Bercuson and Kenneth McNaught, *Winnipeg Strike*, 50–1, 68–75, 72. On Ketchen's close relationship with anti-strike leaders, see Bercuson and McNaught, 55, 70. See also D.C. Masters, *Winnipeg General Strike*, 91, 98, and N. Penner, ed., *Winnipeg, 1919: The Strikers's Own History of the Winnipeg General Strike*, 20, 122–6, 131, 135–6. NA, Chaplain Service Records, vol. 4641, Scott file, G.O.C. M.D. 10 to Minister of Militia, 12 June, and reply, 13 June 1919. See also *Toronto Daily Star*, 16 June 1919, 5, quoted in Allen, *The Social Passion*, 114, 122. On Murray's pre-war opposition to Social Christianity, see Pulker, "The Role of Anglicans," 75–6. Unlike Scott, Charles Gordon was unsympathetic to the strike, convinced that its excesses would be prevented from recurring by the creation of a "Council of Industry for Manitoba," with himself as chairman-arbitrator. Gordon, *Postscript to Adventure*, 359–61.

79 A.D.C.S., East, to Beattie, 23 May 1919, in NA, Chaplain Service Records, vol. 4656, A.D.C.S., Reports file.

80 NA, Chaplain Service Records, vol. 4618, Bushfield file, *The Threshold*, vol. 1 (1919). Bushfield, like his Methodist colleague Wellington Bridgeman, played heavily on the nativist fears of Manitoba's Ontario-born population. See also W. Bridgeman, *Breaking Prairie Sod.*

81 "Scores of men have been reached in this way": Gore Barrow, A.D.C.S., West, to Beattie, 30 June, 31 July 1919 reports, NA, Chaplain Service Records, vol. 4656, A.D.C.S., West files. Archibald Graham complained that strikers' shutting down the transit system impeded

their work in hospital visiting. He and his Roman Catholic colleague were forced to purchase bicycles. See Graham to A.D.C.S., West, 30 June 1919, in vol. 4634, Ewen MacDonald file. Also, at the request of militia officers, chaplains were sent out to comb the mob for Canon Scott!

82 After speaking at Wayne, Alberta, he reported, "I found a very enthusiastic and happy community of returned men … it may be of interest to mention that at Wayne the Returned men ran all the O.B.U. agitators out of town as they were perfectly contented with conditions as they are … I feel that a great deal can be done by the chaplain visiting such places from time to time." Sr Chaplain, M.D. 13 to Beattie, Oct.–Nov. report, 1919, ibid., vol. 4658, M.D. 13 file.

83 "It would be difficult to over-estimate the importance of his work in private as well as public G.W.V.A. meetings," wrote Barrow. Ibid., vol. 4656, A.D.C.S., West file. In July 1919 Whitaker's district senior chaplain reported, "He has surprised us all – has had a big influence and held things together well at a most serious time." In light of his performance Barrow, his senior chaplain, stopped criticizing Whitaker for spending too much time with veterans and released him from regular duty. See also Sr Chaplain, M.D. 11, 31 July 1919, ibid.; also Barrow to Beattie, 31 Jan., 30 Apr. 1919, vol. 4646, Whitaker file; *New Outlook*, 22 Sept. 1926, 17.

84 NA, Chaplain Service Records, vol. 4623, Farquhar file, Farquhar to Beattie, 12 May 1919.

85 The DCS attached the letters of appreciation and commendation sent him from such institutions as the Guelph military hospital and Toronto chapters of the GWVA to his report of Farquhar's tour submitted to his superiors. They are cited in Beattie, "History," 306–7, while the originals are in Farquhar's personal file, Chaplain Service Records, vol. 4623.

86 Even when the outcome of both the strike and the bonus agitation led to the denunciation of the GWVA by radical veterans as reactionary, officer-dominated, and pro-government in perspective, the chaplains stood with the executive. In the association's lead were chaplains such as Whitaker and Charles Jeakins (head of the Ontario GWVA) who continued their opposition to the bonus faction. *Canadian Churchman*, 22 May 1919. On this dispute, which broke out in Calgary in early 1919 and virtually broke the back of the GWVA by the end of the year, see Morton and Wright, "The Bonus Campaign," *CHR* (June 1983): 152–63. On the conservative and elitist reputation of the GWVA among disillusioned veterans by 1921, see Eayrs, *In Defence of Canada*, 1:44–8. During this controversy R.H. Steacy reappeared in the public eye, identifying himself with the bonus advocate Henry Flynn and

taking his revenge on the Conservatives for his 1917 dismissal by leading local party hacks in an open rejection of the candidacy of Henry Drayton (who as Finance minister opposed the bonus campaign) in Ottawa's Carleton riding for the forthcoming federal election. See Walker, *Carleton Saga*, 366–8; *Ottawa Citizen*, 14 Nov. 1921. Steacy's one other public action that year had been officiating at the burial of Sam Hughes. Capon, *His Faults Lie Gently*, 15.

87 Sydney Lambert, a Methodist chaplain and head of the Amputations Association of the Great War (later War Amputations of Canada), and Richard Steacy, as head of the ultra-loyalist Grand Army of United Veterans, both contributed to the formation of the Canadian Legion, although Lambert's association eventually chose to maintain its own separate identity. Other ex-chaplains who contributed to the formation of the legion were Father Francis Lockhary and John MacDonald. See Bowering, *Service*, 16–18, 26, 36–7, 55, 62, 125, 189. On the moderate and largely apolitical philosophy of the British Legion between the wars, see Ward, "Great Britain: Land Fit for Heroes Lost," in *The War Generation*, 22–4, 28–31, 34–5.

88 Here contrast Charles Gordon's idealistic novel on industrial justice, *To Him That Hath*, with Douglas Durkin's bitter *The Magpie*. In Gordon's novel the returned officer learns and implements the tactics of industrial arbitration that characterized his work with the Manitoba Council for Industry, thus defeating foreign and labour radicals who threaten industrial peace. In Durkin's novel the veteran officer, while waiting for the fulfilment of his wartime idealism, is ostracized, bankrupted, betrayed by his wife, and suffers a nervous breakdown as the result of his sympathy for Winnipeg's working-class veterans and friendship with labour organizers. Many Australian ex-chaplains, too, found their wartime call for general social and economic reforms at home rejected when they returned. See McKernan, "Clergy in Khaki," 159–60.

89 USA, Oliver Papers, *Saskatoon Daily Star*, 5 July 1919.

90 Gordon, "The Canadian Home – Its Environment," sermon dated 8 Feb. 1920, in the possession of Ruth Gordon. I thank Barry Mack for making this sermon available to me. At the same time Gordon rushed into print his latest novel, based on his overseas chaplaincy days, which had ended on the Somme. Barry Dunbar, chaplain hero of *The Sky-Pilot in No-Man's-Land*, after shedding his priggishness and pre-war self-centredness, earns the love and loyalty of his men in Flanders. He dies a martyr's death on the Somme, but not before influencing his soldiers and friends to dedicate themselves personally to bringing in the Kingdom of God. Gordon's frank depiction of moral conditions in English camps, which he attributed to the existence of wet canteens, outraged Canadian military authorities overseas. As a

result Press Bureau censors in Britain held up its publication there in the spring. NA, Chaplain Service Records, vol. 4625, C.W. Gordon file, Overseas Military Forces of Canada memo, 5 Mar. 1919.

91 *Canadian Churchman*, 27 Feb. 1919. See also "A Tale of Five Cities," Hopkins, *Canada at War*, 361–441, espec. 398–402, 433.

92 *Canadian Churchman*, 6 Mar. 1919, 155. See also University of Toronto, *Jubilee Volume of Wycliffe College*, 215–29.

93 This was not without criticism for his theological liberalism and continued call for credal revision. See his controversy with the bishop of the Kootenays, *Canadian Churchman*, 20, 27 Nov. 1919. On Shatford's preaching, see *New Outlook*, 17 Feb. 1926, 7, and 14 Apr. 1926, 22. Shatford continued to agitate for social and economic regeneration after the war, taking a leading role in the YMCA during the 1920s and helping to establish the Fellowship for a Christian Social Order in Montreal during the 1930s. Allen, *Social Gospel in Canada*, 252–54.

94 Deftly woven into its anecdotal nature and witty diction were hints and outright declarations of the war's meaning and how Canadians ought to respond to the victory. Although undertones of anger often colour the book, it was anger against the selfishness, materialism, and pettiness of pre-war and civilian life. *The Great War As I Saw it*, 28–9; see also 19, 64, 70, 162, 243, 266.

95 Beattie, "History," 14, 15, 19, 25, 214–18, 230, 231–49, 340–2. Such motifs also characterized his addresses to Canadian congregations while DCS, Canada. NA, Chaplain Service Records, vol. 4625, A.S. Grant file, Grant to Beattie, 9 Sept. 1918. When asked by another chaplain to select an inspiring verse for inclusion in his devotional booklet, Beattie chose a verse from J.R. Lowell: "I with uncovered head / Salute the sacred dead. / Who went, and who return, say not so; / 'Tis not the grapes of Canaan that repay, / But the high faith that failed not by the way." Ketterson, *On Active Service*, 18.

96 Beattie, "History," 28, 33–4, 51, 85, 116.

97 Not only the padres but some of the generals found the post-war climate of indifference frustrating. Arthur Currie, inspector-general of the Canadian Militia in 1919, commented in a letter: "It is not the Canada I expected it to be. I came back from the war feeling that all the suffering and sacrifice must have meant something. But I found, as others have done, that there was little change – that there was at any rate no change of heart. Men were fighting for the dollar in the same persistent way. There seemed to be little difference in the viewpoint towards life, little indication of any growth of national spirit and very little appreciation of the world situation and its attendant problems." See Urquhart, *Arthur Currie*, 284.

98 Only two Anglican ex-chaplains seem to have been elevated to the rank of bishop in the post-war years. Arthur Carlisle succeeded J.C.

Farthing of Montreal in 1939, continuing that diocese's sympathy for Social Christianity, while William Moorehead became bishop of Fredericton in 1938. See Erwin, *Political and Ecclesiastical History of the Anglican Church*, 79, 173.

99 *Toronto Mail and Empire*, 30 Jan. 1923, in Walsh, *Christian Church in Canada*, 299.

100 Clifford, *Resistance to Church Union in Canada*, 71–2.

101 Ibid., 99.

102 Farris, "The Fathers of 1925," in Moir, ed., *The Tide of Time*, 99. On Fraser's role, see Clifford, *Resistance*, 106.

103 NA, Chaplain Service Records, vol. 5633, Questionnaire file.

104 On Drummond's (chaplain to the Ninety-first Regiment) proposal, see Morrow, *Church Union in Canada*, 434–5, and Clifford, *Resistance*, 137–9.

105 McLaren remarked to Gordon, "The situation we have been dreading ever since 1916 has arisen ... I do hope it may be possible to call a halt – otherwise disaster! In 1910 I ventured to say to Principal Patrick that the danger to the Union cause would come thenceforward from its friends." QUA, D.M. Gordon Papers, box 2, 1920–23 Correspondence, McLaren to D.M. Gordon, 13 Apr. 1923. On McLaren's role in framing the 1911 vote and his appreciation of the anti-union strength, see Clifford, *Resistance*, 23, 57–8, 61. By the next year McLaren had become a warrior for the preservation of his old church. See *ibid.*, McLaren to D.M. Gordon, Feb. 1924, and McLaren to D.J. Fraser, 21 Jan. 1924, quoted in Farris, "Fathers of 1925," in Moir, ed., *Tide of Time*, 114.

106 *Goderich Signal*, 18 Dec. 1924, in UCA, D.C. Macgregor biographical file. On McConnell and the McCaskill's work for the PCA, see Clifford, *Resistance*, 131–3, 143–54, 170–3.

107 Clifford has charged that, in his crusade to persuade governments that union was the correct course to follow, Oliver exaggerated the support for union in the most western provinces, Clifford, "Church Union and Western Canada," in D. Butcher, et al., *Prairie Spirit*, 282–92. See also Clifford, *Resistance*, 151–7, 189–90.

108 Clarence Mackinnon drew on the poetry of Rupert Brooke as well as the historiography of Harnack in his portrayal of the United Church as the elect body leading an elect nation towards the Kingdom of God: *New Outlook*, 17 June 1925. Oliver tended to use the metaphor and ideology of frontierism in his challenges to convert new Canadians and alert the west to its central place in the new church and young dominion: ibid., 25 June 1925, 2 Nov. 1927.

109 Allen, *Social Passion*, 250, 263.

110 Ex-chaplains George Kilpatrick, J. Bruce Hunter, W.G. Martin, and A.C. Farrell sat on the United Church of Canada's national committee investigating the military training question. See *New Outlook*, 22 Sept.

1926, 14. On the Anglican reluctance to denounce cadet training, see Allen, *Social Passion*, 334.

111 Fallis claimed to have visited 164 American cities on the 1925 speaking circuit. See *Padre's Pilgrimage*, 136–40, 145.

112 H.F. Leach, "The Christian and War: An Appeal," *New Outlook*, 22 Dec. 1926, 4; Allen, *Social Passion*, 328–9. Nevertheless, the authors of *The Christian and War* betrayed an ambivalence towards collective security and defensive wars that diluted their idealistic message. They denounced war as entirely un-Christian and incapable of being waged Christianly, but could not bring themselves, even after the recent carnage, to renounce absolutely the use of force on behalf of right or to condemn the role of Great Britain and her allies. To them, it might still be necessary to police defaulting nations with armies of defence. Socknat, *Witness against War*, 102–3.

113 Gordon, *Postscript to Adventure*, 379–81. On the climate encountered by League of Nations Society promoters in Canada, see Thompson and Seager, *Canada: 1922–1939, Decades of Discontent*, 56, and Eayrs, *In Defence of Canada*, 1:10–25, 112.

114 On Fairbairn, see Socknat, *Witness against War*, 98–9, and Allen, *Social Passion*, 318–19, 326. See also Ahlstrom, *Religious History of the American People*, 776, 906. On Macintosh's refusal to bear arms in future American wars, see Abrams, *Preachers, Present Arms*, 237.

115 Frederick Poole to B.J. Bengough, 9 Dec. 1939, McMaster University Divinity School Archives, Fred Gifford Poole file.

116 In the midst of a study of the Christianization of Canadian life promised by church union, Edmund Oliver dedicated himself to keeping Canada "at peace and free." He died in 1939, before the nation realized that it could not enjoy both at the same time. Oliver, *His Dominion of Canada*, 21. During these years Oliver came to a warmer appreciation of the sectarian pacifists who had come to the Canadian west because of the influence they might have on promoting peace. *Winning of the Frontier*, 239.

117 C.W. Gordon Papers, Peace sermon manuscript, dated 1931, in the possession of Ruth Gordon. By the mid-1930s Gordon was prepared to accept economic sanctions, but still hoped in the good will spread by the churches of League nations. Gordon, *Postscript*, 401–11, 386–9.

118 *United Church Observer*, 6 Feb. 1939, 138–9.

119 Fallis, *Padre's Pilgrimage*, 165. While William Beattie denounced "merchants of Death," Harry Kent attacked such rhetoric as irresponsible. Eayrs, *In Defence of Canada*, 1:114. On Kent, see *Toronto Globe and Mail*, 21 Sept. 1937; on press coverage sparked by Kent's attacks, *Witness against War*, 174.

120 *Canada in the Great World War*, 1:100; also 5:70. "Passchendaele Preparations" and "Battle of Passchendaele Ridge," ibid., 6:209, 226, 232, 245;

Livesay, *Canada's Hundred Days,* 77–9, also 128, 140, 166, 270. See also Foster and Smith-Duthie, *Letters from the Front,* 1:43, 123.

121 *The Story of the 65th* F.C.A., 114, 123; Grafton, *Canadian "Emma Gees,"* 117, 212; Corrigall, *History of the Twentieth Battalion,* xi, 150, 291, 298–300. Typical of this type were the series compiled by R.C. Fetherstonhaugh: *The Royal Montreal Regiment,* 23, 20, 69, 153, 275–7; *Thirteenth Battalion,* 12, 22, 120, 201, 254, 284, 301; and *The 24th Battalion.* See also Fetherstonhaugh with G.R. Steven, *Royal Canadian Regiment,* 1:352, 364, 431, and Fetherstonhaugh, *#3 Canadian General Hospital,* 11, 20, 85–6, also 190, 67, 273, 53, 210, 234. Ralph Hodder-Williams, *Princess Patricia's Canadian Light Infantry,* 2:271 and 378, 405; also Weatherbe, *From the Rideau to the Rhine and Back*; and Ken Cameron, *#1 Canadian General Hospital,* 83–4, 113, 187, 233, 235. See also Singer and Peebles, *History of Thirty-First Battalion,* 213, 282, 458.

122 MacDonald, *Gunfire,* 54, 61, 99, 117, 170, 188, 208. A particularly striking example is Topp's *42nd Battalion.* Topp, who served as deputy commander of the battalion, continually alludes to the prominent role played by Presbyterian chaplain G.G.D. Kilpatrick on the battlefield and behind the lines. Kilpatrick presides at significant events in the unit's history, not all religious. He is athletic, brave on battlefield, and devoted to his regiment from the day he joined it in the summer of 1916 to his investiture with the DSO after the unit had reached Mons. Ibid., 69, 84, 91, 130–1, 169, 176, 282. Topp used Kilpatrick's personal diary to supplement the war diary of the battalion, and much of his account of the human side of the war comes through Kilpatrick's eyes as a result. Ibid., vii.

123 *From* B.C. *to Basieux,* 34, 62–3, 88, 109.

124 "One must, however, mention one chaplain who frequented the front lines, underwent all manner of danger, helped the men to the best of his ability, associated with them and not the officers; the only man wearing an officer's uniform for whom the Corps would have given a cheer; the only one around whose name a legend sprang up; Canon Scott. But few chaplains were like him." Kerr, *Shrieks and Crashes,* 146–7. Another memoir appearing at the time that echoes Kerr is J.H. Pedley's *Only This.* Pedley's account rarely directly criticizes chaplains, but compares them with Canon Scott. In such comparisons few, indeed only the brave and broad-minded, come off well: see 99–100, 118, 367.

125 "I admit that the chaplains were frequently in difficult situations, surrounded by officers who had scant sympathy for them and the things which they stood for; but they ought to have made up for this by an appeal to the rank and file, which, I am sure, would not have gone unanswered if made in the right way." Ibid., 71, 156, 162, 200–1.

126 *Generals Die in Bed,* 3. 6–7, 26, 41, 58, 82, 85, 99–105, 131, 138–9, 194–6. Not all Canadian war writers were as bitter. In a battlefield

dream of the protagonist's, Philip Child's figure of a general (who seems to speak for God) is quite the opposite. Significantly, Child does not include a chaplain in his novel. *God's Sparrows*, 176–82.

127 Bird, *And We Go On*, 3–6. See also *Ghosts*, 119. Bird's most significant religious experiences of the war are his occasional spiritual encounters with the ghost of his brother, killed in action in 1915, which become more real than his hereditary Methodism. *Ghosts*, 23, 41, 75–94, 100–1, 139, 162–3, 186–7ff.

128 Ibid., 192–3.

129 Bird had little good to say for Topp's official history of the battalion. To him, it was written "For Officers Only." "Hundreds of important incidents along the trenches at nights, patrols ... in which the non-coms or other ranks did outstanding things are never mentioned – Veterans serving two or three years, men of the highest standard, conspicuous in every action, only have their names in the Nominal Roll." *Communication Trench*, 132.

130 Of the many references to religion in the trenches and opinions on the subject that have been published, the two that have the most to offer Canadian students are from Australian and British writers. Along with McKernan, Bill Gammage has surveyed the letters of hundreds of AIF members from the Great War. Pointing to the almost complete dearth of religious references, Gammage has argued that the typical Australian soldier was not religious – in fact, he was highly biased against revealing any religious interest or sympathy overseas. He admits that there were devout churchmen among the Australians but concludes that the majority of the troops shunned religion and, consequently, padres, except for those who proved themselves courageous and sympathetic. See his *The Broken Years*, xiv–xv, 108–9, 150–6, 187, 210–11. McKernan agrees that his chaplains found their men largely anti-religious and quotes the pessimistic assertion of one chaplain that barely one in a hundred soldiers found or held to faith in wartime. Most soldiers were prejudiced against the padre from the start, which could only be overcome by physical bravery and by his in some sense disassociating himself from his officer role and status. See "Clergy in Khaki," 150–1, 158–9; see also his *Australian Churches at War*, 129–36. John Baynes' study of British regimental morale in the Great War suggests that, of the officers, half were sympathetic to religion, 15 per cent unsympathetic, and the remainder indifferent or occasionally religious. Of the men in the ranks, however, he suggests that only one-tenth were sympathetic to religion, half probably were hostile, and the remaining 40 per cent would occasionally be influenced by faith. When Baynes refers to chaplains and their influence, however, he falls back on the traditional stereotypes immortalized by Graves and Chapman. *Morale*,

203–8, 217. Baynes' appreciation of religiosity in a BEF unit (Second Scottish Rifles) may, however, not be directly comparable to those of the CEF. Nevertheless, the potential fruitfulness of further comparative scholarship in exploring this question remains quite promising.

131 One recent veterans' narrative that is particularly frank about the careening emotional and spiritual life of the soldier is Victor Wheeler's *The 50th Battalion in No-Man's-Land.*

132 University of Western Ontario Archives, Ross Malcolm Taylor Papers, 1915–17, Taylor to his father, 18 July, 18 Aug., 23 Nov. 1915. See also letters of condolence from fellow soldiers to Taylor's family when he was killed. Taylor was a Methodist student at Victoria College when he enlisted. See also UCA, Nathanael Burwash Papers, box 6, file 84, Private Timura (another Victoria student) to Burwash, 28 May, 22 June 1915. While with the Canadian Corps, Donald MacPhail encountered such soldiers in a discussion of the justifiability of killing in war, "in view of the commandment 'Thou shalt not kill.' A Corporal whose father is a Prussian, who himself is a Canadian clergyman, placed his defence of the Allied aims and work upon high moral grounds ably supporting his view by quotations from Scripture. Out of a dozen or so taking part in the discussion only one stated that he had taken service under the Red Cross because his conscience wouldn't give assent to active participation in offensive war. The delightful thing was that so many men were found to deal with the matter on high moral grounds." NA, Chaplain Service Records, vol. 4667, Chaplain Reports, file 14, MacPhail to McGreer, 16 July 1917.

133 For example, see *Christian Guardian,* 23 Aug. 1916, 23–4; 17 July 1918, 8–9; and *Canada,* 16 Sept. 1916, 341. See also *Presbyterian and Westminster,* 18 Oct. 1917, 374; 29 Aug. 1918, 191; 19 Dec. 1918, 441–2. For a Baptist soldier's denunciation of both padre pomposity and unrealistically optimistic preaching, see McMaster Baptist Divinity College Archives, F.W. Field, "Soldiers and Religion," letter d. "France, March, 1917," 4 pp. See also Marshall, *Secularizing the Faith,* chap. 6. Again, Victor Wheeler is brutally frank about the varied spiritual state of soldiers under fire: *50th Battalion in No-Man's-Land,* 33, 45, 62, 89, 95, 99, 102, 105, 127, 133–43, 179, 337, 353, 355, 358–9, 408.

134 Gauvreau, *Evangelical Century,* 271–8. Gauvreau assumes, however, that William James was not well known among chaplains and student soldiers overseas. Cf Airhart, *Serving the Present Age,* 88–93, 138–141. While both Endicott and Mutchmor found their convictions stripped of crusading overtones and made less dogmatic and more pragmatic, both testified that their faith had been hardened, not blasted, by the war. See Stephen Endicott, *James G. Endicott: Rebel out of China,* 19–31, and J.R. Mutchmor, *Mutchmor,* 21–5, 48, 156. See also Marshall, *Secularizing,* chap. 6.

135 Gauvreau, *Evangelical Creed*, 222–54.

136 Rawlyk and Quinn, *The Redeemed of the Lord Say So*, 25, 36–8. Among the Australians, approximately one-quarter of the Anglican and Methodist seminarians overseas did not complete their program of studies. See McKernan, *Australian Churches at War*, 95–8. The best-known example of this was Pierre Van Paasen. See his *Days of Our Years*, 91–2; see also Marshall, "Methodism Embattled," *CHR*, 58–9.

137 Thomas Dinesen, VC, *Merry Hell! – A Dane with the Canadians*, 70, 74–5, 216.

138 Roy, *Journal of Private Fraser*, 44, 70, 177, 191, 202.

139 For example, see Rogers, *Gunner Ferguson's Diary*, 18–23, 109, 118–19, 122, 146. See also Eric Rosen interview, in Read, *Great War and Canadian Society*, 146; see also the anonymous *Unknown Soldiers*, 28, 77, 170.

140 Dinesen, *Merry Hell!* 190–2.

141 Keith Fallis and Robert Swan interviews, in Read, *The Great War and Canadian Society*, 132, 140.

142 For example, McWilliams and Steel, *Suicide Battalion*, 114, 169; and Bird, *And We Go On*, 255. See also Rosen interview in Read, *Great War and Canadian Society*, 146.

143 Lapointe, *Soldier of Quebec*, trans. R.C. Fetherstonhaugh, 10, 50, 85. H.M. Urquhart, however, in relating the history of the Sixteenth Battalion, claimed that the YMCA officers contributed more than did the chaplains of the brigade to battalion life. The padres remained brigade officers in sympathy and identity, except for Canon Scott. *History of the 16th Battalion*, 222–6. Nevertheless, the commemorative tone did not entirely die out but was augmented by a general contempt for conventional religion, as Kim Beattie's chronicle of the Forty-eighth Battalion indicates: "The stress of life was such that religion had little chance to enter the round of their days. The war wise padre had realized long ago that care of the men's bodies was the greatest work he and their officers could do, and their souls would take care of themselves. The spirit of the front-line was the spirit of sacrifice ... all of them unconsciously felt that daily about them were instances of sheer unselfishness and a purer, more honest Christianity than that of civil life. There was a greatness about the spirit of the front-line such as they had never sensed before and were never, perhaps, to feel again. It was the spirit of sacrifice and comradeship, never spoken of, yet always there and most surely found when Death and Dread strode over the world." *48th Highlanders of Canada, 1891–1921*, 154–5.

144 Mary Clint, *Our Bit*, 47, 98. Chaplain Service bigotry at high levels also drew fire with the publication of the letters of a medical officer stationed in the Mediterranean who rated the Protestant chaplains sent there by the Hughes-Steacy administration as particularly useless,

owing to their bigoted Orange outlook. Mackenzie, *#4 Canadian General Hospital*, 46, 99–100, 124, 216, 228. In 1937 the writings of F. Noyes on the life of a Canadian field ambulance unit advanced the critique in the same direction. Chaplains were appreciated when brave and helpful in spreading comfort and social welfare in the unit, but were also the targets of humour and ribaldry. *Stretcher-Bearers ... At the Double!* 89–90, 115, 168, 198. At the same time, to Noyes, the padre who "pharisaically prays for victory over [sic] our side and disaster for the enemy" must be the object of angry contempt: "We remember only too well how often we were compelled to chase this type of chaplain from our advanced dressing dugouts, to make room for the wounded. We never could understand why this sort of bible-thumper was reluctant to face Death if he really believed all the stuff he poured in our ears." Ibid., 16, 168–9.

145 W.W. Murray, for example, emphasized the humour and ironies of service on the Western Front. To him the padres were good for a laugh, even at their own expense, and Canon Scott again leads among the padres in popularity. *Five Nines and Whiz Bangs*, 132–4, 140–1, 145–6, 212.

146 Moore, by then a Toronto cleric, contributed many articles and statements promoting Christian Socialism. See *Canadian Churchman*, 14 May, 16 July, 20 Aug., 10 Sept., 5 Nov. 1931, and Pulker, *We Stand on Their Shoulders*, 102–3. H.R. Nobles, a Baptist ex-chaplain, after cutting across a Regina common on the eve of 11 Nov. 1929, confronted the bleak prospects ahead. In a poem written that night he portrayed the ghosts of the fallen asking, "Have we failed? Have we failed? Did we die in vain?" Poem in the possession of the author, provided by Mrs Anita Nobles, his daughter-in-law, in 1983.

147 *Canadian Churchman*, 6 June 1935, 357; also 5 Aug. 1943, 440, and 19 Aug. 1943, 456, quoted in Pulker, *We Stand*, 115, 142.

148 "Veterans Appeal to Padres," *New Outlook*, 14 June 1933.

149 Scott's message was widely circulated in the souvenir booklet compiled afterwards, *Canadian Corps, 1914–1934: A Record in Word and Picture*, 5.

150 D.E. MacIntyre, *Canada at Vimy*, 190; of the nearly eight thousand Canadian veterans who went on the pilgrimage, thirteen had been CEF chaplains. See Murray, *Epic of Vimy*, 183–217.

151 *New Outlook*, 29 July 1936, 711.

152 C.C. Owen, 26 July 1936, quoted in MacIntyre, *Canada at Vimy*, 189.

153 Malcolm Omond, a United Church minister who had served in the CEF as chaplain during the war, endorsed the "Witness against War": *United Church Observer*, 15 Oct. 1939. See David R. Rothwell, "United Church Pacifism, October 1939," in *Bulletin of the United Church of Canada Archives* (1973), 37; and Socknat, *Witness*, chap. 7. Other veteran padres

countered the pacifist protest with justifications of the use of force against patent unrighteousness and the need to uphold the soldier in defence of Christendom. See James Faulds, *Observer,* 1 Oct. 1939, 21; also Frank Bushfield, ibid., 15 Nov. 1940.

154 Canada, Department of National Defence, *Canadian Active Service Force Routine Orders,* R.O. 69, 18 Oct. 1939, 5. On 22 November the first War Establishments Lists were published by the Department of Militia and Defence: see *Militia General Orders,* G.O. 221, 22 Nov. 1939. Wells became the Protestant principal chaplain in 1939, Gordon senior chaplain of the Quebec military district; Kilpatrick and Fallis joined their church's chaplaincy committee and served again. Kent became senior chaplain of the First Canadian Division, and Hunter of the Montreal and Fallis of the Toronto garrisons. *United Church Observer,* 1 Oct. 1939, 15 Dec. 1939, 3. On the role played by Wells and other veteran padres in resurrecting the chaplaincy, see Tom Sinclair-Faulkner, "For Christian Civilization," PhD, University of Chicago 1975, 83–9, 156–9.

Bibliography

ARCHIVAL AND MANUSCRIPT COLLECTIONS

ANGLICAN CHURCH OF CANADA, GENERAL SYNOD ARCHIVES (GSA)

Council for Social Service Collection
George Exton Lloyd Papers

ANGLICAN CHURCH OF CANADA, OTTAWA DIOCESE ARCHIVES

Channel G. Hepburn Papers
Bishop John Charles Roper Papers

NATIONAL ARCHIVES OF CANADA (NA)

Record Group 9, Department of Militia and Defence
  Series II A – Deputy Minister's Office, 1867–1920
    1 Correspondence, 1867–1903
    2 Reports and Memoranda, Militia Council Minutes, 1867–1920
    3 Records of Active Service, 1869–1903
  Series II B – Adjutant-General's Correspondence and Headquarters, 1867–1922.
    1 Correspondence, 1867–1922
    2 Returns, Reports, and Memoranda, 1868–1914
    3 Militia General Orders, 1867–1922

Series III A – Overseas Military Forces of Canada/Canadian Expeditionary Force Records
1 Overseas Minister's Records, 1915–19
Series III B – Canadian Expeditionary Force Administration, 1914–20
1 Subject Files, 1914–20
Series III C – Canadian Corps, Units, 1914–22
15 Canadian Chaplain Service Records, 1915–21
Series III D 1 – Canadian Records Office, 1914–20
Record Group 24, Department of National Defence
Series C
1 Central Headquarters Registry files
Manuscript Group 27
Series II D
9 A.E. Kemp Papers
12 George Perley Papers
Manuscript Group 30, Manuscripts and Personal Papers
Series D
20 John J. O'Gorman Papers
Series E
4 William Beattie Papers
25 Edmund H. Oliver Papers
46 Richard E.W. Turner Papers
47 William Fishbourne McConnell Papers
153 H.I. Horsey Papers
158 George Gordon Dinwiddie Kilpatrick Papers
242 William Dillon Otter Papers
300 Albert Hilder Papers

CANADIAN BAPTIST ARCHIVES, MCMASTER DIVINITY SCHOOL:
Biographical files

PUBLIC ARCHIVES OF NOVA SCOTIA (PANS):
MG 2. Sir Frederick Borden Papers

PROVINCIAL ARCHIVES OF ALBERTA
Kenneth C. McLeod Papers

QUEEN'S UNIVERSITY ARCHIVES (QUA)
Lord Dundonald Papers, 1901–03
Alexander MacLennan Gordon Papers
Daniel Miner Gordon Papers
John McDougall Papers

UNIVERSITY OF ALBERTA ARCHIVES
St Stephen's College Papers

UNITED CHURCH OF CANADA ARCHIVES (UCA)
Biographical files of ministers
Methodist Church, General Conference Papers
Methodist Church, Missionary Society Collection
Methodist Church, Army and Navy Board Collection
Methodist Church, Minutes of Conferences, 1896–1901, 1914–19
Nathanael Burwash Papers
Albert Carman Papers
Samuel Dwight Chown Papers
George Gordon Dinwiddie Kilpatrick Papers
John Pringle Papers
Egerton Ryerson Papers

UNIVERSITY OF SASKATCHEWAN ARCHIVES (USA)
E.H. Oliver Papers

UNIVERSITY OF WESTERN ONTARIO ARCHIVES
Private G.C. Markham Papers
Letters of Bombardier Ross Malcolm Taylor, 1916–17

ROYAL CANADIAN REGIMENT ARCHIVES, WOLSELEY BARRACKS, LONDON, ONTARIO
Regimental Records and Orders

PERIODICALS AND NEWSPAPERS

Canada: An Illustrated Weekly Journal for all Interested in the Dominion, 1914–19
Canada Gazette, 1870, 1885, 1918
Canadian Baptist, 1914–19
Canadian Churchman, 1884–1919
Catholic Register and Canadian Extension, 1913–19
Christian Guardian, 1870, 1885–1919
Methodist Magazine and Review, 1900
Montreal Gazette, 1918
New Outlook, 1925–33
Presbyterian, 1914–16
Presbyterian and Westminster, 1916–19
Presbyterian Record, 1885
Presbyterian Witness, 1870, 1885, 1899–1900, 1914

Toronto Globe, 1870–1939
United Church Observer, 1939–41
Vancouver Sun, 1917

GOVERNMENT AND CHURCH OFFICIAL PUBLICATIONS

Canada. Department of Militia and Defence. *Canadian Sessional Paper* no. 35, 1871; no. 35a, 1900; no. 6, 1886; no. 9, 1887; no. 130, 1905.
– Department of Militia and Defence. *European War, Memo #5, Work of the Department of Militia and Defence, from January 1, 1918 to October 31, 1918.*
– Department of Militia and Defence. *Militia General Orders*, 1879–1939; *Regulations and Orders of the Canadian Militia*, 1879; *King's Regulations and Orders for the Canadian Militia*, 1910.
– Department of Militia and Defence. *The Return of the Troops.* Ottawa 1920.
– Department of National Defence. *Canadian Active Service Force Routine Orders*, 1939–40; *Militia General Orders*, 1939.
– *Fifth Census of Canada* (1911). Ottawa 1913.
– House of Commons. *Debates.* 1871, 1900, 1917–18.
Church of England in Canada. *General Synod of the Church of England in Canada, 7th Session.* Toronto: Briggs 1916.
– *The Proceedings of the 8th General Synod of the Church of England in Canada.* Toronto: Briggs 1919.
Presbyterian Church in Canada. *Acts and Proceedings of the General Assembly of the Presbyterian Church in Canada.* 1914–19.

SECONDARY SOURCES

Abercrombie, Clarence. *The Military Chaplain.* Beverly Hills, Calif.: Sage Publications 1977.
Abrams, Ray. *Preachers Present Arms.* Scottdale, Penn.: Herald Press 1933, 1966.
Ahlstrom, Sydney. *A Religious History of the American People.* New Haven: Yale University Press 1972.
Airhart, Phyllis D. *Serving the Present Age: Revivalism, Progressivism, and the Methodist Tradition in Canada.* Montreal: McGill-Queen's University Press 1992.
Aitken, C.D.E. "Background and Details of the Royal Canadian Army Chaplains' Corps (Protestant)." B Litt thesis, Halifax, Pine Hill Divinity Hall 1965.
Allen, A.R. *The Social Passion.* Toronto: University of Toronto Press 1971.
– *The Social Gospel in Canada.* Ottawa: National Museum of Man 1975.
– "Providence to Progress: The Migration of an Idea in English-Canadian Thought." In William Westfall and Louis Rousseau, ed., *Canadian Issues: Religion/Culture.* Comparative Canadian Studies, vol. 7. Ottawa: Association for Canadian Studies 1985.

Anon. (J.J. Callan). "The Canadian Chaplain Services." In *Canada at War.* Vol. 6. Toronto: United Publishers 1921.

Aston, William H., comp. *History of the 21st Regiment, Essex Fusiliers of Windsor, Ontario, Canadian Militia.* Windsor, Ont.: Record Print Co. 1902.

Barber, Marilyn. "The Ontario Bilingual Schools Issue, 1910–1916." MA Queen's University 1964.

Barnard, W.T. *The Queen's Own Rifles of Canada, 1860–1960.* Don Mills, Ont.: Ontario Publishing Co. 1960.

Barnhart, Gordon Leslie. "E.H. Oliver: A Study of Protestant Progressivism in Saskatchewan, 1909–1945." MA, University of Regina 1977.

Baynes, John. *Morale.* London: Cassell 1967.

Beahen, William. "A Citizens' Army: The Growth and Development of the Canadian Militia, 1904–1914." PhD, University of Ottawa 1979.

Beattie, Kim. *48th Highlanders of Canada, 1891–1928.* Toronto: privately printed 1932.

Beauregard, George. *Le 9me bataillon au Nord-Ouest (Journal d'un militaire).* Quebec: J.G. Gingras 1886.

Bedford, A.G. *The University of Winnipeg: A History of the Founding Colleges.* Toronto: University of Toronto Press 1976.

Bennett, S.G. *The 4th Canadian Mounted Rifles, 1914–1919.* Toronto: privately printed 1926.

Bercuson, David, and Kenneth McNaught. *The Winnipeg Strike: 1919.* Toronto: Longman 1974.

Berger, Carl. *The Sense of Power.* Toronto: University of Toronto Press 1970.

Berton, Pierre. *Vimy.* Toronto: McClelland and Stewart 1986.

Bird, C.W., and J.B. Davies. *Canadian Forestry Corps.* London: HM Stationary Office 1919.

Bird, Will R. *And We Go On.* Toronto: Hunter-Rose 1930.

– *The Communication Trench.* Toronto: Briggs 1933.

– *Ghosts Have Warm Hands.* Toronto: Clarke, Irwin 1968.

Birmingham, George (J.O. Hannay). *A Padre in France.* London: Hodder and Stoughton 1918.

Bishop, C.W. *The Canadian Y.M.C.A. in the Great War.* (n.p.: National Council of Young Men's Christian Associations of Canada 1924.

Black, E.G. *I Want One Volunteer.* Toronto: Ryerson 1965.

Bliss, Michael. "The Methodist Church in World War I." *Canadian Historical Review* 49, no. 3 (1968): 213–27.

Borden, Henry. *Robert L. Borden: Letters to Limbo.* Toronto: University of Toronto Press 1971.

Borden, Henry, ed. *Robert Laird Borden: His Memoirs.* Vol. 1. Toronto: Macmillan 1938.

Boss, W. *The Stormont, Dundas and Glengarry Highlanders,* 1783–1951. Ottawa: Runge Press 1952.

Boulton, Charles Arkoll. *Reminiscences of the North-West Rebellions.* Toronto: Grip 1886.

Bowering, Clifford. *Service: The Story of the Canadian Legion.* Ottawa: Canadian Legion 1960.

Bridgeman, Wellington. *Breaking Prairie Sod.* Toronto: Musson 1920.

Brown, R. Craig, and Ramsay Cook. *Canada, 1896–1921: A Nation Transformed.* Toronto: McClelland and Stewart 1974.

Brown, S.M. *With the Royal Canadians.* Toronto: Publishers' Syndicate 1900.

Brown, Tom. "Shell Shock in the Canadian Expeditionary Force, 1914–1918: Canadian Psychiatry in the Great War." In Charles G. Rowland, ed., *Health, Disease and Medicine: Essays in Canadian History.* Toronto: Clarke Irwin 1983.

Brumwell, P. Middleton. *The Army Chaplain.* London: A.C. Black 1943.

Bull, W. Perkins. *From Brock to Currie: the Military Development and Exploits of Canadians in General and of the Men of Peel in Particular, 1791–1930.* Toronto: G.J. McLeod 1935.

Burns, Robin B. "The Montreal Irish and the Great War." *Canadian Catholic Historical Studies* 52 (1985): 67–81.

Burwash, E.M. *The New Theology: A Lecture.* Toronto: Briggs 1910.

Butcher, D., et al. *Prairie Spirit: Perspectives on the Heritage of the United Church of Canada in the West.* Winnipeg: University of Manitoba Press 1985.

Cameron, Alexander. "Padre in Siberia: The Edited Diary of Reverend Captain George Farquhar's Experiences with the Canadian Siberian Expeditionary Force in Vladivostock, and with the 1/9th Battalion of the British Hampshire Regiment in Omsk, 1918–1919." BA Honours, Mount Allison University 1982.

Cameron, Kenneth. *History of No. 1 General Hospital, Canadian Expeditionary Force.* Sackville: Tribune Press 1938.

Cameron, William Bleasdale. *The War Trail of Big Bear.* London: Duckworth 1926.

Canada in the Great World War: An Authentic Account of the Military History of Canada from the Earliest Days to the Close of the War of the Nations, by Various Authorities. Toronto: United Publishers 1917–21.

Canadian Almanac and Directory. Toronto: Copp Clarke 1897–1915.

The Canadian Corps, 1914–1934: A Record in Word and Picture. Toronto: Canadian Veteran Associates 1934.

Capon, Alan R. *His Faults Lie Gently: The Incredible Sam Hughes.* Lindsay, Ont.: F.W. Hall 1969.

Carrel, Frank. *Impressions of War.* Quebec: Telegraph 1919.

Casselman, Ian. "The Secret Plague: Venereal Disease in Early 20th Century Canada." MA, Queen's University 1981.

Cassels, Jay. *The Secret Plague.* Toronto: University of Toronto Press 1987.

Castonguay, Jacques. *Unsung Mission: History of the Chaplaincy Service (RC) of the R.C.A.F..* Montreal: Institute de Pastorale 1968.

Chabballe, J. *Histoire Du 22e Bataillon Canadien-Francais, 1914–1919.* Montreal: Les Editions Chantecler 1952.

Chadwick, Owen. *The Victorian Church, Part II: 1860–1901.* London: Adam and Charles Black 1970.

Chambers, Ernest J. *Queen's Own Rifles of Canada.* Toronto: E.L. Ruddy 1901.

– *The Royal Grenadiers: A Regimental History of the 10th Infantry Regiment of the Active Militia of Canada.* Toronto: E.L. Ruddy 1904.

– *Histoire du 65me Régiment Carabiniers Mont-Royal.* Montréal: La Cie. d'Imprimerie Guertin 1906.

– *The 90th Regiment: Regimental History of the 90th Regiment Winnipeg Rifles.* n.p. (1906).

Chapman, Guy. *A Passionate Prodigality.* 1933; London: Macmillan 1965.

Child, Philip. *God's Sparrows.* 1937; Toronto: McClelland and Stewart 1978.

Christie, Edward Alexander. "The Attitudes and Opinions of the Presbyterian Churches in Canada with Respect to Public Affairs and Social Problems, 1875–1925." MA, University of Toronto 1956.

Clark, Gregory. *A Bar'l of Apples: A Gregory Clark Omnibus.* Toronto: McGraw-Hill Ryerson 1971.

Clayton, P.B. *Tales of Talbot House in Poperinghe and Ypres.* London: 1925.

Clifford, N. Keith. "His Dominion: A Vision in Crisis." *Studies in Religion/ Sciences Religieuse* 2, no. 4 (1973): 315–26.

– *The Resistance to Church Union in Canada, 1904–1939.* Vancouver: University of British Columbia Press 1985.

Clint, Mary. *Our Bit: Memories of War Service, by a Canadian Nursing Sister.* Montreal: Barwick 1934.

Corrigall, D.J. *The History of the Twentieth Battalion, Central Ontario Regiment, C.E.F. in the Great War, 1914–1918.* Toronto: Stone and Company 1935.

Creet, Mario. "H.M. Tory and the Secularization of the Canadian Universities." *Queen's Quarterly* 88, no. 4 (1981): 718–36.

Creighton, Owen. *With the 29th Division in Gallipoli: A Chaplain's Experiences.* London: Longman's, Green 1916.

Currie, J.A. *"The Red Watch": With the First Canadian Division in Flanders.* Toronto: McClelland, Goodchild and Stewart 1916.

Curry, F.C. *From the St. Lawrence to the Yser with the 1st Canadian Brigade.* London: Smith Elder 1916.

Daniel, I.J.E., and D.A. Casey. *For God and Country: War Work of the Canadian Knights of Columbus Catholic Army Huts.* Ottawa: Knights of Columbus 1922.

Daoust, Charles R. *Cent-vingt jours de service actif; recit historique tres complet de la campagne du 65me au Nord-Ouest.* Montreal: E. Sènècal 1886.

Denison, George T. *Soldiering in Canada: Recollections and Experiences.* Toronto: G.N. Morang 1900.

Diary of the Eleventh Field Ambulance.

Dinesen, Thomas. *Merry Hell! – A Dane With the Canadians.* London: Jarrolds 1929.

Disher, A.L. "The March of the Yukon Field Force." *The Beaver* (Fall 1962).

Dow, A.C. *Ministers to the Soldiers of Scotland.* London: Oliver and Boyd 1962.

Doyon, Pierre. "Aumôniers Catholiques dans la marine royale du Canada de 1939 à nos jours." MA, University of Ottawa 1968.

Duguid, A. F. *Official History of the Canadian Forces in the Great War, 1914–1919.* Vol. 1. Ottawa: King's Printer 1938. 1 vol. in 2.

Durkin, Douglas. *The Magpie.* 1924; Toronto: University of Toronto Press 1973.

Durocher, Rene. "Henri Bourassa, Les Évêques et la Guerre de 1914–1918." *Canadian Historical Association Papers* 1971.

Eayrs, James. *In Defence of Canada.* Vol. I. Toronto: University of Toronto Press 1964.

Edmonds, J. *History of the Great War Based on Official Documents: Military Operations, France and Belgium, 1916.* London: Macmillan 1932.

Ellis, John. *Eye-Deep in Hell.* London: Croom Helm 1976.

Endicott, Stephen. *James G. Endicott: Rebel Out of China.* Toronto: University of Toronto Press 1980.

English, John. *The Decline of Politics.* Toronto: University of Toronto Press 1977.

Erwin, S. *A Political and Ecclesiastical History of the Anglican Church in Canada.* Toronto: privately printed 1967.

Evans, W. Sanford. *The Canadian Contingents and Canadian Imperialism: A Story and a Study.* Toronto: Publishers' Syndicate 1901.

Fallis, George. *A Padre's Pilgrimage.* Toronto: Ryerson 1953.

Farrell, J. "Michael Francis Fallon, Bishop of London, Ontario, Canada, 1909–1931: The Man and His Controversies." *Canadian Catholic Historical Association Report* (1968): 73–90.

Farris, Alan. "The Fathers of 1925." In J.S. Moir, ed., *The Tide of Time.* Toronto: Knox College 1978.

Faulkner, Charles Thompson Sinclair. "For Christian Civilization: The Churches and Canada's War Effort, 1939–1942." PhD, University of Chicago 1975.

Faust, Drew Gilpin. "Christian Soldiers: The Meaning of Revivalism in the Confederate Army." *Journal of Southern History* 8, no. 1 (1987): 63–90.

Fetherstonhaugh, R.C. *The 13th Battalion, Royal Highlanders of Canada, 1914–1919.* Montreal: privately printed 1925.

– *The Royal Montreal Regiment, 14th Battalion, C.E.F., 1914–1925.* Montreal: privately printed 1927.

– *#3 Canadian General Hospital (McGill), 1914–1919.* Montreal: Gazette 1928.

– *The 24th Battalion, C.E.F., Victoria Rifles of Canada, 1914–1919.* Montreal: Gazette 1930.

– and G.R. Stevens. *The Royal Canadian Regiment.* Vol. 1. Montreal: Gazette Print Co. 1936.

Flick, C.L. *"Just What Happened": A Diary of the Mobilization of the Canadian Militia, 1914.* London: privately printed 1917.

Fosdick, Harry Emmerson. *The Manhood of the Master.* 1913; London: YMCA Press 1917.

Foster, C.L., and William Smith-Duthie. *Letters from the Front – Being a Record of the Part Played by Officers of the Bank of Commerce in the Great War.* 2 Vol. Toronto: Southam Press 1920.

Fowler, Major Albert. "The Adaptation of the Ecclesiastical Hierarchy to Military Bureaucracy, 1945–1968: The Pursuit of Assumed Status." MA, Carleton 1991.

Fraser, Alexander. *The 48th Highlanders of Toronto: Canadian Militia.* Toronto: E.L. Ruddy 1900.

Fraser, Brian G. "The Christianization of Our Civilization: Presbyterian Reformers and Their Defence of a Protestant Canada, 1875–1914." PhD, York University 1982.

– *The Social Uplifters: Presbyterian Progressives and the Social Gospel in Canada, 1875–1915.* Waterloo: Wilfrid Laurier Press 1988.

Gagnon, Jean-Pierre. *Le 22e Bataillon (Canadien-français), 1914–1919.* Ottawa: Laval University Press and Department of National Defence 1986.

Gammage, Bill. *The Broken Years.* Canberra: Australian National University Press 1974.

Gauvreau, Michael. "The Taming of History: Reflections on the Canadian Methodist Encounter with Biblical Criticism, 1830–1890." *Canadian Historical Review* 65, no. 3 (1984): 315–46.

– "War, Culture and the Problem of Religious Certainty: Methodist and Presbyterian Church Colleges, 1914–1939." *Journal of the Canadian Church Historical Society* 29, no. 1 (1987): 12–31.

– *The Evangelical Century: College and Creed in English Canada from the Great Revival to the Great Depression.* Montreal: McGill-Queen's University Press 1991.

Goodspeed, D.J. *Battle Royal: A History of the Royal Regiment of Canada, 1862–1962.* Toronto: privately printed 1947.

Gordon, A.M. "A Chaplain at the Front." *Queen's Quarterly* 27 (1919): 169–79.

Gordon, C.W. *The Sky-Pilot in No-Man's-Land.* Toronto: McClelland and Stewart 1919.

– *To Him That Hath.* New York: George Doran 1921.

– *Postscript to Adventure.* New York: Farrar and Rinehart 1938.

Gordon, D.M. "Reminiscences of the Northwest Campaign of 1885." *Queen's Quarterly* 11, no. 1 (1903): 3–20.

Gordon, W.D. *Daniel Miner Gordon: A Life.* Toronto: Ryerson 1941.

Gould, L.M. *B.C. to Basieux; being the Narrative History of the 102nd Canadian Infantry Battalion.* Victoria, BC: privately printed 1919.

Grafton, C.S. *The Canadian "Emma Gees."* London: Hunter 1938.

Granatstein, J.L. *Canada's War: The Politics of the Mackenzie King Government, 1939–1945*. Toronto: Oxford University Press 1975.

Grant, J.W. *The Church in the Canadian Era*. Toronto: McGraw Hill-Ryerson 1972.

Gravel, Jean-Yves. *L'Armée au Quebec: un portrait social, 1868–1900*. Montreal: Boreal Express 1974.

Graves, Robert. *Goodbye to All That*. 1929; London: Penguin 1960.

Greenhous, Brereton. *Dragoon: The Centennial History of the Royal Canadian Dragoons, 1883–1983*. Ottawa: Guild of the Royal Canadian Dragoons 1983.

Griesbach, W.A. *I Remember*. Toronto: Ryerson 1946.

Guiou, N. *Transfusion: A Canadian Surgeon's Story in War and in Peace*. Yarmouth, Nova Scotia: Sentinel 1985.

Hankey, Donald. *A Student in Arms: Second Series*. Toronto: McClelland, Goodchild and Stewart 1917.

– *A Student in Arms*. London: Melrose 1918.

Harrison, Charles Yale. *Generals Die in Bed*. 1928; Hamilton: Potlatch 1975.

Hart-McHarg, William. *From Quebec to Pretoria with the Royal Canadian Regiment*. Toronto: W. Briggs 1902.

Haycock, Ronald. "The Public Career of Sam Hughes." PhD, University of Western Ontario 1976.

– *Sam Hughes*. Canadian War Museum Historical Publication 21. Waterloo: Wilfrid Laurier Press 1986.

Hayes, Joseph. *The Eighty-fifth in France and Flanders*. Halifax: privately printed 1920.

Hodder-Williams, Ralph. *The Princess Patricia's Canadian Light Infantry, 1914–1919*. London: Hodder-Stoughton 1923.

Honeywell, Roy J. *Chaplains of the United States Army*. Washington: Office of the Chief of Chaplains, Department of the Army 1958.

Hopkins, J.C. *Canadian Annual Review*. Toronto: Canadian Annual Review 1907, 1912–1919.

– *Canada at War*. Toronto 1919.

Hubly, Russell C. *"G" Company, or Every-day Life of the R.C.R.; being a Descriptive Account of Typical Events in the Life of the First Canadian Contingent in South Africa*. St John, NB: J. & A. McMillan 1901.

Hunter, A.T. *History of the 12th Regiment, York Rangers; with Some Account of the Different Raisings of Militia in the County of York, Ontario*. Toronto: Murray Print Co. 1912.

Hutchison, Paul P. *Canada's Black Watch: The First Hundred Years, 1862–1962*. Montreal: privately printed 1962.

Inglis, *David. Righteousness Exalteth a Nation: A Thanksgiving Sermon*. Hamilton: Spectator Press 1866.

Jackson, H.M. *The Princess Louise Dragoon Guards*. n.p.: privately printed 1952.

James, William. *Varieties of Religious Experience*. London: Longman's 1903.

Jocelyn, Arthur. *Awards of Honour: the Orders, Decorations, Medals and Awards of Great Britain and the Commonwealth from Edward III to Elizabeth II.* London: Adam and Charles Black 1956.

Johnston, C.M. *McMaster University.* Vol. 1, *The Toronto Years.* Toronto: University of Toronto Press 1976.

Jones, W.R. *Fighting the Hun From Saddle and Trench.* Albany: Aiken 1918.

Keegan, Jon. *The Face of Battle.* Harmondsworth: Penguin 1978.

Kelman, John. *The War and Preaching.* New Haven: Yale University Press 1919.

Kerr, W.B. *Shrieks and Crashes: Being Memories of Canada's Corps, 1917.* Toronto: Hunter-Rose 1929.

Ketterson, A.L. *On Active Service: Ideals of Canada's Fighting Men.* Toronto: McClelland, Stewart and Goodchild 1918.

Kierstead, Robin G. "The Canadian Military Medical Experience during the Great War, 1914–1918." MA, Queen's University 1982.

Kiesekamp, Burckhardt. "Presbyterian and Methodist Divines: The Case for a National Church, 1975–1900." *Studies in Religion/Sciences Religieuses* 2, no. 4 (1973): 289–302.

– "Community and Faith: The Intellectual and Ideological Bases of Church Union in Victorian Canada." PhD, University of Toronto 1974.

Labat, Gaston P. *Le Livre d'or (The Golden Book) of the Canadian Contingents in South Africa; with an Appendix on Canadian Loyalty, Containing Letters, Documents, Photographs.* Montreal: n.p. 1901.

Laidlaw, Alexander. *The Campus and the Community: The Global Impact of the Antigonish Movement.* Montreal: Harvest House 1961.

Lapointe, A.J. *Soldier of Quebec, 1916–1919.* Trans. R.C. Fetherstonhaugh. 1919; Montreal: Garand 1931.

Leonard, Jane. "The Catholic Chaplaincy." In David Fitzpatrick, ed., *Ireland and the First World War.* Dublin: Trinity History Workshop 1986: 1–16.

Livesay, J.F.B. *Canada's Hundred Days.* Toronto: Allen 1919.

Loyd, Alan. *The War in the Trenches.* London: Granada 1976.

McCallum, F.H. "Experiences of a Queen's Own Rifleman at Ridgeway." *Third Annual Report of the Waterloo Historical Society.* Berlin, Ont., 1915.

McCormack, Ross. "Cloth Caps and Jobs: the Ethnicity of English Immigrants in Canada, 1900–1914." In J.M. Bumsted, ed., *Interpreting Canada's Past.* Vol. 2. Toronto: Oxford University Press 1986.

MacDonald, J.A. *Gunfire. An Historical Narrative of the 4th Brigade C.F.A. in the Great War, 1914–1918.* Toronto: Greenway Press 1929.

Macdonald, John A. *Troublous Times in Canada: A History of the Fenian Raids of 1866 and 1870.* Toronto: Johnston 1910.

McGowan, Mark. "We are all Canadians: A Social, Religious and Cultural Portrait of Toronto's English-speaking Roman Catholics, 1890–1920." PhD, University of Toronto 1988.

– "The De-greening of the Irish: Toronto's Irish-Catholic Press, Imperialism, and the Forging of a New Identity, 1887–1914." *Canadian Historical Association Papers* (1989): 118–45.

MacIntyre, D.E. *Canada at Vimy.* Toronto: Peter Martin 1967.

Mackenzie, J.J. *#4 Canadian General Hospital: The Letters of Professor J.J. Mackenzie from the Salonika Front.* Ed. Kathleen Mackenzie. Toronto: Macmillan 1933.

McKernan, Michael. "Clergy in Khaki: The Chaplain in the Australian Imperial Force, 1914–1918." *Journal of the Royal Australian Historical Society* 64, no. 3 (1978): 145–66.

– *Australian Churches at War: Attitudes and Activities of the Major Churches, 1914–1918.* Sydney: Catholic Theological Faculty and Australian War Memorial 1980.

McKillop, A.B. *A Disciplined Intelligence.* Montreal: McGill-Queen's University Press 1979.

Mackinnon, Clarence. *A Life of Principal Oliver.* Toronto: Ryerson 1936.

– *Reminiscences.* Toronto: Ryerson 1938.

Macnutt, F.B. *The Church in the Furnace.* London: Macmillan 1917.

MacPhail, Sir Andrew. *The Medical Services: Official History of the Canadian Forces in the Great War, 1914–1919.* Ottawa, King's Printer 1925.

McWilliams, J.L., and R. James Steele. *The Suicide Battalion.* Edmonton: Hurtig 1978.

Magney, William. "The Methodist Church and the National Gospel, 1884–1914." United Church of Canada Archives, *Bulletin* 20 (1968).

Marquis, T.G. *Canada's Sons on Kopje and Veldt: A Historical Account of the Canadian Contingents Based on the Official Despatches of Lieutenant-Colonel W.D. Otter and the Other Commanding Officers at the Front.* Toronto: The Canada's Sons Publishing Co. 1900.

Marrin, Albert. *The Last Crusade: The Church of England in the First World War.* Durham: Duke University Press 1974.

Marshall, David. "The Clerical Response to Secularization: Canadian Methodists and Presbyterians, 1860–1940." Ph.D. University of Toronto 1986.

– "Methodism Embattled: A Reconsideration of the Methodist Church and World War I" *Canadian Historical Review* 66, no. 1 (1986): 48–64.

– *Secularizing the Faith: Canadian Protestant Clergy and the Crisis of Belief, 1850–1940.* Toronto: University of Toronto Press 1992.

Masters, C.K. Memoir in the possession of his son, D.C. Masters, Guelph, Ontario.

Masters, D.C. *The Winnipeg General Strike.* Toronto: University of Toronto Press 1950.

– *Protestant Church Colleges in Canada.* Toronto: University of Toronto Press 1966.

Mathieson, William D. *My Grandfather's War: Canadians Remember the First World War, 1914–1919.* Toronto: Macmillan 1981.

Mellish, Annie Elizabeth. *Our Boys under Fire; or Maritime Volunteers in South Africa.* Charlottetown: privately printed 1900.

Middleton, Sir Frederick. *Suppression of the Rebellion in the North West Territories of Canada, 1885.* Ed. G.H. Needler. Toronto: University of Toronto Press 1948.

Miller, Carman. "The Public Life of Sir Frederick Borden, 1847–1917." MA, Dalhousie University 1964.

– "English Canadian Opposition to the South African War as Seen through the Press." *Canadian Historical Review* 55, no. 4 (1974): 422–35.

– "A Preliminary Analysis of the Socio-Economic Composition of Canada's South African War Contingents." *Histoire Sociale/Social History* 6 (1975): 219–37.

– "Chums in Arms: Comradeship among Canada's South African War Soldiers." *Histoire Sociale/Social History* 13, no. 36 (1985): 359–373.

Miller, J.R. "Anti-Catholic Thought in Victorian Canada." *Canadian Historical Review* 66, no. 4 (1985): 474–94.

Moir, John S. *Church and State in Canada West.* Toronto: University of Toronto Press 1959.

– *Church and State in the Canadas: Basic Documents, 1627–1867.* Toronto: McClelland and Stewart 1967.

– *Enduring Witness.* Toronto: Bryant Press for Presbyterian Publications 1974.

– *The Tide of Time.* Toronto: Knox College 1978.

– "A Vision Shared? The *Catholic Register* and Canadian Identity before World War I." In *Canadian Issues* 7 (1985): 356–66.

Montague, C.E. *Disenchantment.* London: Chatto and Windus 1922.

Morgan, J.H. *Canadian Men and Women of the Time, 1912.* Toronto: Briggs 1912.

Morrison, E.W.B. *With the Guns in South Africa.* Hamilton: Spectator Print Co. 1901.

Morrow, E. Lloyd. *Church Union in Canada.* Toronto: Allen 1923.

Morton, Desmond. "French Canadians and the Canadian Militia, 1868–1914." *Histoire Sociale/Social History* 1, no. 3 (1969).

– "Des Canadiens errant: French Canadian Troops in the Northwest Campaign of 1885." *Journal of Canadian Studies* 6 (1970): 28–39.

– "The Supreme Penalty: Canadian Deaths by Firing Squad in the First World War." *Queen's Quarterly* 79, no. 3 (1972): 345–52.

– *The Canadian General, Sir William Otter.* Canadian War Museum Historical Publications 9. Toronto: Hakkert 1974.

– "The Short, Unhappy Life of the 41st Battalion, C.E.F." *Queen's Quarterly* 81, no. 1 (1974): 70–80.

– "Polling the Soldier Vote: The Overseas Campaign in the Canadian General Election of 1917." *Journal of Canadian Studies* 10, no. 4 (1975): 39–58.

– *Canada and War.* Toronto: Butterworths 1981.

– *A Peculiar Kind of Politics: Canada's Overseas Ministry in the First World War.* Toronto: University of Toronto Press 1982.
– and R.H. Roy, eds. *Telegrams of the North-West Campaign.* Publications of the Champlain Society 47. Toronto: Champlain Society 1972.
– and Glenn Wright. "The Bonus Campaign, 1919–1921: Veterans and the Campaign for Re-establishment." *Canadian Historical Review* 64, no. 2 (1983): 152–63.
– and Glenn Wright. *Winning the Second Battle: Canadian Veterans and the Return to Civilian Life, 1915–1939.* Toronto: University of Toronto Press 1987.
Murdoch, B.J. *The Red Vineyard.* Cedar Rapids, Iowa: Torch Press 1923. 2nd ed., Wexford, Ireland: John English and Co. 1949.
Murray, W.W. *The Epic of Vimy.* Ottawa: Canadian Legion Press 1936.
– *Five Nines and Whiz Bangs.* Ottawa: Legionary Library 1937.
– *The History of the 2nd Canadian Battalion (East. Ontario Regiment), Canadian Expeditionary Force in the Great War, 1914–1918.* Ottawa: n.p. 1947.
Mutchmor, J. *Mutchmor.* Toronto: Ryerson 1965.
Nasmith, George Gallie. *On the Fringe of the Great Fight.* New York: Doran n.d.
Nicholson, G.W.L. *Canadian Expeditionary Force, 1914–1919.* Ottawa: Queen's Printer 1962.
Nobles, H.R. *The New Canadian.* London: Parry 1918.
Noyes, Fredrick. *Stretcher-Bearers … At the Double!* Toronto: Hunter-Rose 1937.
Ogle, R.J. *The Faculties of Canadian Military Chaplains: A Commentary on the Faculty Sheet of December, 1955, and the Directives for Holy Week, Promulgated March 14, 1956.* Ottawa: LeClerc 1956.
O'Gorman, J.R. *Soldiers of Christ: Canadian Catholic Chaplains, 1914–1919.* Toronto 1936.
– "Canadian Catholic Chaplains in the Great War." *Canadian Catholic Historical Association Report, 1939–1940* (1941): 71–84.
Oliver, E.H. *The Winning of the Frontier.* Toronto: Ryerson 1930.
– *His Dominion of Canada.* Toronto: United Church Publishing House 1932.
Orr, J. Edwin. *Always Abounding: A Pen Study of Oswald J. Smith.* London: Marshall, Morgan and Scott 1940.
Otter, W.D., comp. *The Guide: A Manual for the Canadian Militia (Infantry).* Toronto: Willing & Williamson 1880.
Pedley, J.H. *Only This: A War Retrospect.* Ottawa: Graphic 1927.
Penner, N., ed. *Winnipeg, 1919: The Strikers' Own History of the Winnipeg General Strike.* Toronto: J. Lorimer and Co. 1972.
Perley, George, ed., *Canada in Khaki.* Vol. 1. London: Pictorial Newspaper Co. 1917.
Pringle, George. *Tillicums of the Trail.* Toronto: McClelland and Stewart 1922.
– *In Great Waters.* Toronto: Ryerson 1928.
Pulker, E.A. *We Stand on Their Shoulders: The Growth of Social Concern in Canadian Anglicanism.* Toronto: Anglican Book Centre 1986.

Quigley, John Gordon. *A Century of Rifles, 1860–1960: The Halifax Rifles (RCAC) (M); ("cede nullis").* Halifax: privately printed 1960.

Ramlochan, S.R. "The Baptists of Ontario and World War I." Unpublished student paper, McMaster University Baptist Divinity College 1973.

Rauschenbusch, Walter. *The Social Principles of Jesus.* London: International YMCA 1916.

Rawlyk, G.A., ed., *Canadian Baptists and Christian Higher Education.* Kingston-Montreal: McGill-Queen's University Press 1988.

– and Kevin Quinn, *The Redeemed of the Lord Say So: A History of Queen's Theological College, 1912–1978.* Kingston: Brown and Martin 1980.

Read, Daphne, ed. *The Great War and Canadian Society: An Oral History.* Toronto: New Hogtown Press 1978.

Renison, R.J. "A Tale of Five Cities: A Canadian Epic of One Hundred Days." In J.C. Hopkins, *Canada at War.* Toronto: Canadian Annual Review 1919.

– *One Day at a Time.* Toronto: Kingswood 1957.

Rogers, Peter G. *Gunner Ferguson's Diary.* Hantsport, NS: Lancelot Press 1985.

Rose, G.M. *A Cyclopedia of Canadian Biography.* Toronto: Rose 1888.

Ross, M. *The Y.M.C.A. in Canada: The Chronicle of a Century.* Toronto: Ryerson 1951.

Rothwell, David R. "United Church Pacifism, October, 1939." United Church of Canada Archives, *Bulletin* 22 (1973).

Roy, Reginald, ed. *The Journal of Private Fraser.* Victoria: Sono Nis Press 1985.

Ryan, William F. *The Clergy and Economic Growth in Quebec.* Quebec: Laval University Press 1966.

Ryerson, George Sterling. *Looking Backward.* Toronto: Ryerson 1924.

Santor, Donald. *Canadians at War, 1914–1919.* Scarborough: Prentice-Hall 1978.

Schübel, Albrecht. *300 Jahre Evangelische Soldatenseelsorge.* Munich: Bavarian Lutheran Press 1964.

Scott, Brian. "The Western Outlook and Western Baptist and Baptist Social Christianity, 1908–1922." Canadian Society of Church History, Papers (1983): 1–18.

Scott, F.G. *In the Battle Silences.* Toronto: Musson 1916.

– *The Great War as I Saw It.* Toronto: McClelland and Goodchild 1922.

Silcox, Claris. *Church Union in Canada.* New York: Institute for Social and Religious Research 1933.

Silver. A.I. *The French Canadian Idea of Confederation, 1864–1900.* Toronto: University of Toronto Press 1982.

– "Ontario's Alleged Fanaticism in the Riel Affair." *Canadian Historical Review* 69, no. 1 (1988): 21–50.

Sinclair, J.D., comp. *The Queen's Own Cameron Highlanders of Canada: Twenty-Fifth Anniversary Souvenir.* Winnipeg: privately printed 1935.

Sinclair-Faulkner, Tom. "God's Flower of Hope: The Religious Matrix of Quebec's Indépendantisme." *Canadian Issues* 7 (1985).

Singer, H.C., and A.A. Peebles. *History of the Thirty-First Battalion*, C.E.F.. Calgary: privately printed 1939.

Sissons, C.B. *Egerton Ryerson*. Toronto: Clarke, Irwin Co. 1947.

Smith, W.E.L. *The Naval Chaplain in the Days of Sail*. Toronto: Ryerson 1961.

– *The Naval Chaplain and His Parish*. Ottawa: Queen's Printer 1967.

Smyth, Sir John. *In This Sign Conquer*. London: A.R. Mowbray 1968.

Socknat, Thomas P. *Witness against War*. Toronto: University of Toronto Press 1987.

Steele, Harwood. *The Long Ride: A Short History of the 17th Duke of York's Royal Canadian Hussars*. Montreal: Gazette 1934.

Steele, (Sir) Samuel Benfield. *Forty Years in Canada: Reminiscences of the Great Northwest with Some Account of his Service in South Africa*. Ed. Mollie Glen Niblett. Toronto: McClelland, Goodchild and Stewart 1915.

Steven, W.T. *In This Sign*. Toronto: Ryerson 1948.

Stevens, G.R. *A City Goes to War*. Brampton: Charters 1964.

The Story of the Sixty-Six C.F.A.. Edinburgh: Turnbull and Spears 1919.

Stover, Earl F. *Up from Handymen: The United States Army Chaplaincy*. Vol. 3, 1865–1920. Washington: Office of the Chief of Chaplains, Department of the Army 1977.

Strange, Thomas Bland. *Gunner Jingo's Jubilee*. London: Remington 1893.

Thompson, John Herd. "The Beginning of Our Regeneration: The Great War and Western Canadian Reform Movements." *Canadian Historical Association Papers and Reports* (1972): 227–45.

– *The Harvests of War*. Toronto: McClelland and Stewart 1978.

– and Alan Seager. *Canada, 1922–1939: Decades of Discord*. Toronto: McClelland and Stewart 1987.

Tobias, John. "Canada's Subjugation of the Plains Cree, 1879–1885." *Canadian Historical Review* 64, no. 4 (1983): 519–48.

Topp, C.B. *The 42nd Battalion*, C.E.F., *Royal Highlanders of Canada in the Great War*. Montreal: private 1931.

Tucker, A.B. *The Battle Glory of Canada; being the Story of the Canadians at the Front, Including the Battle of Ypres*. London: Cassel 1915.

Unknown Soldiers, by One of Them. New York: Vantage Press 1959.

Urquhart, Hugh. *The History of the 16th Battalion, the Canadian Scottish* C.E.F. *in the Great War, 1914–1919*. Toronto: Macmillan 1932.

– *Arthur Currie: The Biography of a Great Canadian*. Toronto: Dent 1950.

Van Die, Marguerite. *An Evangelical Mind: Nathanael Burwash and the Methodist Tradition in Canada, 1839–1918*. Montreal: McGill-Queen's University Press 1989.

Van Paasen, P. *Days of Our Years*. New York: Houghton Mifflin 1946.

Walker, F.A. *Catholic Education and Politics in Ontario.* Toronto: Thomas Nelson and Sons 1964.

Walker, Harry and Olive. *Carleton Saga.* Ottawa: Runge Press 1968.

Walsh, H.H. *The Christian Church in Canada.* Toronto: Ryerson 1956.

Ward, Stephen, ed., *The War Generation: Veterans of the First World War.* New York: National University Publications 1975.

Warner, D.V. *The Church and Modern Socialism: An Essay.* Truro, NS: News Press 1909.

Weatherbe, K. *From the Rideau to the Rhine: The 6th Field Co. and Battalion Canadian Engineers in the Great War.* Toronto: Hunter-Rose 1928.

Wells, G.A. *The Fighting Bishop; as Recounted in the Eighty-Seventh Year of his Life to his Daughter Jeanne Carden Wells.* Toronto: Cardwell House 1971.

Wheeler, Victor W. *The 50th Battalion in No Man's Land.* Calgary: Comprint 1980.

Wilkinson, Alan. *The Church of England and the First World War.* London: SPCK 1978.

Williams, E.F. "Soldiers of God: The Chaplains of the Revolutionary War." PhD, Texas Christian University 1972.

Wilson-Simmie, K. *Lights Out! A Canadian Nursing Sister's Tale.* Belleville, Ont.: Mika 1981.

Winter, Charles F. *Lieutenant-General the Hon. Sir Sam Hughes,* K.C.B., M.P.; *Canada's War Minister, 1911–1916; Recollections of Service as Military Secretary at Headquarters, Canadian Militia, prior to and during the Early Stages of the Great War.* Toronto: Macmillan 1931.

Winter, Dennis. *Death's Men: Soldiers of the Great War.* London: Allen Lane 1978.

Wood, H.F. *Vimy!* Toronto: Macmillan 1967.

– and John Swettenham. *Silent Witnesses.* Toronto: Hakkert 1974.

Worthington, Larry. *Amid the Guns Below.* Toronto: McClelland and Stewart 1965.

Wright, Robert. *A World Mission: Canadian Protestantism and the Quest for a New International Order, 1918–1939.* Montreal: McGill-Queen's 1991.

Zahn, Gordon. *The Military Chaplaincy: A Study of Role Tension in the Royal Air Force.* Toronto: University of Toronto Press 1969.

Index